CHARLES STEWART PARNELL

Francis Stewart Leland Lyons was born in 1923. He was the first Professor of Modern History at the University of Kent, a position he held for ten years before becoming a Fellow (and later Provost) of Trinity College, Dublin. He was Ford's Lecturer in English History at the University of Oxford, 1977–8. From 1981 until his death, on 21 September 1983, he was Professor of History in the University of Dublin.

His field of expertise was the history of Ireland in the nineteenth and twentieth centuries, and his books include *The Irish Parliamentary Party*; *The Fall of Parnell*; *Internationalism in Europe, 1815–1914*; *John Dillon: a Biography*; *Ireland Since the Famine*; and *Culture and Anarchy in Ireland, 1890–1939*.

Charles Stewart Parnell

F S L LYONS

FontanaPress
An Imprint of HarperCollinsPublishers

First published in Great Britain in 1977
by William Collins Sons & Co. Ltd

First issued in 1978 by Fontana,
an imprint of HarperCollins Publishers,
77/85 Fulham Palace Road,
Hammersmith, London W6 8JB

This Fontana Press edition first issued in 1991

9 8 7 6 5 4 3 2 1

Printed and bound in Great Britain by
HarperCollins Manufacturing, Glasgow

I dedicate this book to
Theodore William Moody
my friend and teacher for many years

Contents

List of Illustrations

Avondale
Aughavanagh
Parnell in 1880
Katharine O'Shea in 1880
The Arrest of Parnell, October 1881
Parnell – the Private Man

Captain O'Shea in the Witness Box
    (NATIONAL GALLERY OF IRELAND)
Parnell in the Witness Box
    (NATIONAL GALLERY OF IRELAND)
8, Medina Terrace, Hove
The House where Parnell Died
The Pigott Incident
Nearing the End

ACKNOWLEDGEMENTS

Having lived, intermittently but persistently, in the strange and fascinating world of Parnell for over thirty years, I have received far more help in finding my way about it than I can hope to acknowledge in this prefatory note. But, while apologizing to any whose names I may have omitted inadvertently, I am glad to record my indebtedness to the following: Dr Philip Bull, Dr A. B. Cooke, Professor L. P. Curtis, jr., Dr R. P. Davis, the late Professor Myles Dillon, Mr James Dillon, Dr John Dillon, Professor R. Dudley Edwards, Mr Owen Dudley Edwards, Father Denis Egan, Dr Roy Foster, Professor R. D. D. Gibson, Professor Walter Hagenbuch, Colonel N. Harrington, Mr Richard Hawkins, Mr C. H. D. Howard, Mr Michael Hurst, Dr John Kelly, Reverend Professor Kevin Kennedy, Mr Richard Langhorne, Professor Emmet Larkin, Mrs M. Lewin, Professor James McCormick, Dr J. F. A. Mason, Dr G. W. Martin, Dr Conor Cruise O'Brien, Dr L. Ó Broin, Mr Ulick O'Connor, Mr G. Phillips, Mr James Shillington, Mr Walter Mahon Smith, Mr W. K. Stead, Dr David Thornley, Dom Mark Tierney, Professor J. R. Vincent, Professor T. Desmond Williams, Dr C. J. Woods.

For permission to make use of and to quote from various collections of papers, I am grateful to the following: the Director and Trustees of the National Library, Dublin; the Director of the State Paper Office, Dublin; the Trustees of the British Museum; the Public Record Office, London; Mr D. F. Porter and the Bodleian Library, Oxford; the Marquess of Salisbury; Earl Spencer; Viscount Harcourt; Sir William Gladstone; the Editor of *The Times*; Messrs W. H. Smith and Co.; Colonel N. Harrington; the Most Reverend Dr Dermot Ryan, Archbishop of Dublin; Mr W. K. Stead; the Library of Birmingham University.

I acknowledge with pleasure the permission received from Senator Michael Yeats and from Messrs Macmillan to quote from W. B. Yeats's poems, 'Parnell's Funeral', and 'Come gather round me, Parnellites'.

I have received much generous assistance from many libraries and particularly from the following: the British Library, London; the Public

Acknowledgements

Record Office, London; the Public Record Office, Northern Ireland; the National Library, Dublin; the Royal Irish Academy, Dublin; the Library of Trinity College, Dublin; the State Paper Office, Dublin; the Bodleian Library, Oxford; Christchurch Library, Oxford; Churchill College, Cambridge; the Library of the University of Kent at Canterbury; the archives of *The Times* newspaper; the archives of W. H. Smith and Co.; the Library of Birmingham University.

For assistance in finding and selecting illustrations I am particularly indebted to Dr Eugene O'Connor, Dr Hubert O'Connor and Dr James White. I acknowledge with thanks permission from Dr Vincent O'Sullivan to use lithographs in his possession relating to the Parnell Special Commission and from the Director (Dr James White) and Trustees of the National Gallery of Ireland to use the portrait of Parnell which is on the cover of this book and also certain drawings relating to the Parnell Special Commission.

The writing of this book has involved an enormous expenditure of secretarial help and I am grateful to the secretaries of Eliot College in the University of Kent for providing most of it, and especially to Miss Margaret Hawkins for her invaluable help in the early stages of the work. In Dublin I have had the opportunity of extensive re-writing and the burden of this has been carried by Miss Ann Sheil with an imperturbable efficiency which leaves me deeply in her debt. For so organizing my time that Parnell was not entirely supplanted by more recent history I owe much to the combined efforts of Miss Aileen Campbell, Miss Winifred Matthews and Mr David White. Miss Campbell's help in many other directions exhausts my superlatives, but not my gratitude.

Two final debts remain to be recorded. What I owe to my friend and teacher, Professor T. W. Moody, goes too deep for words, but he has added to his innumerable kindnesses by allowing me, in dedicating this work to him, to express something of what I feel. To my wife Jennifer, and to my sons John and Nicholas, I have to say that this book depended upon them far more than they imagined and not least upon their calm assumption that it would actually get written.

F. S. L. LYONS

THE PROVOST'S HOUSE,
TRINITY COLLEGE, DUBLIN

ABBREVIATIONS

BM, Add. MS	British Museum, Additional MS
DNB	*Dictionary of National Biography*
DP	John Dillon Papers
EHR	*English Historical Review*
FJ	*Freeman's Journal*
HP	Sir William Harcourt Papers
IHS	*Irish Historical Studies*
JC	Joseph Chamberlain Papers
NLI	National Library of Ireland
PHSP	Printing House Square Papers
PRO	Public Record Office, London
SP	Earl Spencer Papers
SPO	State Paper Office, Dublin
SPONI	State Paper Office, Northern Ireland
UI	*United Ireland*
D. W. R. Bahlman	*The diary of Sir Edward Walter Hamilton*, ed. D. W. R. Bahlman, 2 vols, Oxford, 1972.
J. L. Garvin	*The life of Joseph Chamberlain*, by J. L. Garvin, vols ii and iii, London 1932–4.
R. B. O'Brien	*The Life of Charles Stewart Parnell*, by R. B. O'Brien, 2 vols (2nd ed.), London, 1899.
K. O'Shea	*Charles Stewart Parnell: his love-story and political life*, by Katharine O'Shea, 2 vols, London, 1914.
A. R. Ramm	*The political correspondence of Mr Gladstone and Lord Granville, 1876–1886*, ed. Agatha Ramm, 2 vols, Oxford, 1962.

CHARLES STEWART
PARNELL

CHAPTER I

The Meeting of the Waters

'An Englishman of the strongest type, moulded for an Irish purpose.' (Michael Davitt, *The fall of feudalism in Ireland*, p. 110.)

'. . . above all, Mr Parnell was an Irishman, Irish bred, Irish born, "racy of the soil", knowing its history, devoted to its interests.' (*Drogheda Argus*, 24 April 1875, celebrating Parnell's election to parliament.)

'I have always held that both in appearance and to a large extent in character Parnell was much more American than either English or Irish.' (T. P. O'Connor, *Memoirs of an old parliamentarian*, i, 97.)

I

All the roads that lead from Dublin to the county Wicklow are beautiful. But if there is one more beautiful than the others it is surely the road which rises steeply from Rathfarnham, skirts the head of Glencree where the Sugarloaf mountain floats in the distance, and then, at Sally Gap, follows the route driven through the wilderness by the military after the rising of 1798, until it comes out at Laragh, just above Glendalough. From Laragh it traces the winding course of the little river Avon, through the quiet woods of Clara vale, until it reaches Rathdrum, perched like an Italian hill-town, with its grey and pink and blue houses, on a high ridge looking down on Avoca and 'the meeting of the waters'. There, in the family house of Avondale, Charles Stewart Parnell was born on 27 June 1846.[1]

When Charles was born the Parnells were comparative newcomers to Wicklow, and indeed to Ireland. The family emerged from obscurity only in the seventeenth century. The first of whom any substantial information survives was Thomas Parnell, a mercer and draper in the town of Congleton in Cheshire, of which town he became mayor in the reign of James I. He had four sons of whom one, Richard, was also mayor on several occasions, and the youngest, Tobias, was a gilder and painter. They appear to have been stout parliament men during the Civil War and this may have helped to persuade Tobias's son, Thomas, to move to Ireland soon after the Restoration. He was far from a penniless *émigré*, however, and took with him enough funds to purchase an estate in Queen's county where he settled comfortably into the routine of a prosperous landowner. He was the father of two sons through whom the name of Parnell first began to be known outside the family circle.

The elder of these, also Thomas, was born in 1679, entering Trinity College, Dublin, when only fourteen. Graduating in 1697, he was ordained in 1703 and two years later was appointed Archdeacon of Clogher at the age of twenty-six. Like many eighteenth-century Anglican clergy he was a frequent absentee, preferring literary London to rural Ulster. A quietly persistent poet, not much of his verse has survived the test of time, perhaps because the very qualities a later biographer detected in it reflect equally the limitations of the age, of the genre and of the man. 'His work', says this writer, 'is marked by sweetness, refined sensibility, musical and fluent versification, and high moral tone.'[2] Dr Johnson's verdict is untypically cautious. 'He is sprightly without effort, and always delights, though he never ravishes.' And of the poems he observes: 'It is impossible to say whether they are the productions of nature so excellent as not to want the help of art, or of art so refined as to resemble nature.'[3]

Perhaps, after all, it was the nature that was excellent, for Thomas Parnell had many friends. They included Addison, Steele, Congreve and Gay, but especially Swift and Pope; it says much for him that both these notoriously difficult individuals held him in high affection. Yet his life was short and marked by tragedy. He married Anne Minchin of Tipperary, to whom he was deeply attached, and he never really recovered from her early death in 1711. Oliver Goldsmith, who wrote a life of him, called him 'the most capable man to make the happiness of those whom he conversed with, and the least able to secure his own'.[4] He lost not only his wife, but also his two sons, began to drink heavily and showed marked manic-depressive tendencies – the first known appearance in the family of a strain of mental instability that was to recur more than once thereafter. He died suddenly at Chester on his way to Ireland in 1717 in his thirty-eighth year, leaving behind him a memory which the family at least kept green. Even his remote descendant, Charles, than whom no man who ever lived had less poetic sensibility, could refer knowledgeably to his ancestor and on one occasion went so far as to write a verse which he claimed, wrongly, to be 'as good as any of Tom Parnell's stuff'.*

The death of Thomas Parnell meant that the Queen's county property fell to his brother John, a barrister who sat in the Irish House of Commons, married the sister of a Lord Chief Justice, and became a judge himself. Dying in 1727 he left a son, John, who also sat for an Irish constituency and was created a baronet in 1766. He married the daughter of a judge of the King's Bench, Anne Ward of Castle Ward in county Down. Their son, the second Sir John, born on Christmas Day 1744, was the first of his line to reach the front rank in politics and since his reputation was to open some important doors for Charles a century later, it is worth looking at that reputation a little more closely.

At first glance, it is certainly impressive. Entering the Irish parliament in 1776, when the American Revolution was creating a favourable opportunity for the Anglo-Irish 'patriots' to free themselves from the close control of the British parliament, Sir John commanded a corps in the Volunteers whose mere existence helped to win 'the constitution of 1782' to which Charles was later to look back as his prime model for Home Rule. But that constitution was a defective instrument. It did not really break the English stranglehold on the Dublin government, because that government was appointed by, and responsible to, ministers in London, not to the parliament on College Green. The parliament itself, moreover, remained unrepresentative, consisting essentially of Anglo-Irish Protestants who were imbued not with anything resembling modern nationalism, but with the irritation and frustration of a colonial élite, determined to assert itself against the metropolitan power, yet not daring to go too far lest it should have to admit the Catholic majority to the jobs and pensions and 'connexions' which so faithfully mirrored the grander political world across the Irish Sea.

Some of the 'patriots', it is true, were prepared to move decorously and cautiously towards a progressive emancipation of Catholics.

---

*It was written for Katharine O'Shea, who printed it in her *Charles Stewart Parnell: his love-story and political life* (London, 1914, hereafter cited as 'K. O'Shea'), ii, p. 113. It may be allowed to speak for itself:

> The grass shall cease to grow,
> The river's stream to run,
> The stars shall ponder in their course,
> No more shall shine the sun;
> The moon shall never wane or grow,
> The tide shall cease to ebb and flow,
>   Ere I shall cease to love you.

Gradually most of their legal disabilities were removed, until the Irish parliament found itself facing the biggest questions of all – whether Irish Catholics should be given the vote and whether, once enfranchised, they should themselves be eligible for election to parliament. On these vexed questions (the first of which was decided in favour of the Catholics in 1793, the second of which had not been solved when the Irish parliament ceased to exist in 1800) Sir John Parnell – he had succeeded his father to the baronetcy in 1782 - held distinctly conservative opinions. Although the contemporary view of him as an able and, within the elastic eighteenth-century definition of the term, an honest man, may have been justified, those who knew him well found him mentally lazy and firmly anchored to the status quo.[5] Not surprisingly, since he found life comfortable enough as it was, he came out as an opponent of emancipation, deploying with considerable skill and frequent reiteration the classic conservative argument that he considered 'the moment ill-chosen and the experiment dangerous to do away at once the principle of a century'.[6]

The possession of such views did not, of course, prevent him from climbing the ladder of success. In 1785 he followed his friend John Foster as Chancellor of the Exchequer and in 1786 he became a Privy Councillor. During his fourteen years as Chancellor he did much to reorganize Irish governmental finance on the English model, but the permanence of his work, as of the constitution of 1782 itself, was always in jeopardy because of the impending possibility of a legislative union between Britain and Ireland. This, long contemplated, was hastened on by the threat to established order posed by the '98 rising. After intensive pressure and substantial inducement in the form of grants, pensions and titles, the Irish parliament was persuaded in 1800 to consent to its own extinction. After some initial hesitation, Sir John Parnell came out strongly against the Union and in 1799 was dismissed from office for his pains. But this martyrdom, in which Charles was later to invest considerable political capital, was the gesture of a 'patriot' in much the same sense in which the Irish parliament itself was a 'patriot' parliament. When Sir John told Pitt that a union was 'very dangerous and not necessary', what he was objecting to was the destruction of a system of government which had preserved for him and men like him a Protestant ascendancy with all the fruits and pleasures which flowed from a monopoly of political power.[7] He was dubious also, it must in fairness be said, about the possible effects of a union on Irish trade, on the influx of capital, on land prices and even on the future relations between Protestants and Catholics.[8] In the end, he was outmanoeuvred and out-voted, and although the pangs of defeat were sweetened by a payment of £7500 in compensation for the suppression of the family pocket-borough, he survived the Act of Union by only a few months, dying in 1801.[9]

It was left to his descendants to act on a wider stage a part more distinguished than any he had played in the little arena of Dublin. By his marriage to Letitia Charlotte Brooke of Fermanagh Sir John had six children. One of these, Henry, after education at Eton and Cambridge (where, however, he did not take his degree), had entered the Irish House of Commons in 1797 just in time to share his father's last-ditch stand against the Union. Although not the eldest son, he succeeded to the family estates in 1801; these had been settled on him in anticipation by a private act of parliament of 1789, because the eldest son, John Augustus, was a deaf and dumb imbecile. Henry entered the British parliament briefly in 1802 and on a longer tenure in 1806, when he was returned for Queen's county. From the outset he distinguished himself as a proponent of Catholic emancipation (which had originally been proposed as part of the Union settlement, but which Pitt had failed to carry in face of George III's veto) and, with his lively and incisive mind, interested himself in many other topics. He was not only active in the House of Commons but, a rarity in his family, wrote with authority on questions of the day. He maintained the family interest in Irish affairs, producing in 1808 a well-informed *History of the penal laws*. He also wrote voluminously on the Corn Laws, banking and taxation, and his *Financial reform* (1830) anticipated some of the fiscal innovations later carried out by Peel and Gladstone. Like Charles later, he was a clear but somewhat wooden speaker, with little variety of tone and almost no animation of gesture. He achieved office as Secretary for War in Earl Grey's reform ministry of 1830, but disagreed with his colleagues on several issues and was dismissed in 1832. He came back to power as a Paymaster-General of the Forces under Melbourne in 1835 and kept his post until raised to the peerage as Baron Congleton in 1841. At that point he lost his health, became deranged (that fatal strain again) and in June 1842 hanged himself at the age of sixty-six.[10]

Henry was the second of five brothers. The first, as we saw, was mentally and physically handicapped. Of the fifth, Arthur, little significant is known. The fourth, Thomas, was a saintly eccentric who succumbed to religious mania and for many years spent his share of the family fortune in a so-called 'Protestant Office' in Sackville Street (O'Connell Street) in Dublin.[11] Nor was he the only one of his family to stray from the Anglican *via media*. The second Lord Congleton, possibly under the influence of his uncle Thomas, became much involved with the Plymouth Brethren. After establishing them at Aungier Street in Dublin, he vainly attempted to repeat this success in the more exotic purlieus of Baghdad and also extended his missionary enterprise as far as India. Charles, too, in later life admitted at least twice to a tenderness for the sect, and though one of these occasions need not be taken too seriously – it was an election speech at Plymouth in 1886 – his remark to T. P. O'Connor, when they were travelling to Galway for the famous by-election earlier that year, that he liked their 'quietness', has the ring of truth about it.[12]

It was from the third of Sir John Parnell's sons that Charles himself was descended. This was William, who was born in 1777 and was the first of the family to live at Avondale. The estate of about 4,500 acres (later reduced to under 4,000) passed to Sir John in 1795 on the death of his friend and probable first cousin, Samuel Hayes, as the result of intermarriage between the two families. William Parnell seems to have aspired no higher than the role of country gentleman, which he filled with modest success, preserving his property intact and maintaining good relations with his tenants, both difficult feats in the early years of the nineteenth century when agricultural distress and unrest were almost endemic. He had two further claims to fame. The first was that, like his brother Henry, he gave much thought to the situation created in Ireland by the Union and, like him, was prepared to venture his views in print, publishing a pamphlet in 1805 entitled *An enquiry into the causes of popular discontents in Ireland*, and following this two years later with the more substantial *Historical apology for Irish Catholics*. In his pamphlet he put his finger unerringly on some of the factors which were still to be dominant when his grandson came upon the scene some sixty years later – the race memory of the Irish, the friction between different religious denominations, the degraded condition of the peasantry, the influence of republicanism and, of course, the Union itself.[13] But in analysing these factors he confined himself to theory, and although he represented Wicklow in the House of Commons in 1817 and 1819–20, his impact was virtually nil. His other achievement, if that is the right word, was his friendship with the then fashionable poet, Thomas Moore. It was when staying at Avondale that Moore visited the Vale of Avoca and wrote 'The Meeting of the Waters', though William could never persuade the poet to divulge exactly where it was that he composed what Moore himself complacently described as 'the now memorable song'.[14]

William's life was blameless but it was also brief. He died in 1821 in his early forties, leaving two children, Catherine and John Henry. By his marriage into the Howard family (to which the Earls of Wicklow belonged) he had in his twenty years in the county already put down roots in local society which broadened and deepened in the next generation, so that we hear of the Powerscourts and the Carysforts as being, with the Wicklows, part of the Parnell circle of friends and relations. The name Parnell-Hayes, used by William to commemorate the earlier owner of Avondale, was dropped in the next generation. Of William's two children, Catherine was endowed with £10,000, a portion which was to be a burden on the Avondale estate for a long time to come. John Henry inherited Avondale itself, as well as land at Collure in County Armagh, acquired towards the end of his life by that inveterate collector of property, Sir John Parnell, on long lease from Trinity College, Dublin. John Henry also went in for land speculation, but with much less success, buying from his uncle, Sir Ralph Howard, the estate of Clonmore in Carlow for the very large sum of £69,469. This he did in 1858 and it helps to explain why, when he died only a year later, he left his affairs in considerable disorder.* Like his father, John Henry took naturally to the life of a country gentleman, acting right by his tenants and playing his part as a squire of the manor in the duties, as well as the pleasures, of the countryside.

II

Yet it was this quiet, conventional landowner who introduced into the beautiful but reticent countryside of Wicklow a flaring exotic. At the age of twenty he set out on a trip to America with one of his cousins, the young Powerscourt. Together they met, and together they wooed a young American girl, Delia Tudor Stewart. Tall, vivacious, striking with her oval face, her dark hair and her blue eyes, she was the remarkable daughter of a remarkable man whose family had taken a prominent part in American public life since the Revolution.

Two strands, each unusual, went to the making of the Stewarts. About the middle of the eighteenth century the founder of the family

---

*For this and other valuable information about the Parnell family and their property, I am deeply indebted to Mr Roy Foster whose study, *Charles Stewart Parnell: the man and his family* (Hassocks, Sussex, 1976), was published while this book was in the press.

fortunes, Charles Stewart, emigrated from Belfast to America with his wife (née Sarah Ford). There were eight children of this marriage, the youngest, Charles, having been born in 1778. His father died when he was only two years old and soon afterwards his mother remarried, her second husband being a Captain Britton, commander of Washington's bodyguard. The young Charles had a passion for the sea and, at the age of thirteen, dealt with parental opposition by the simple expedient of running away. Britton, who had shipping interests of his own, accepted the inevitable and gave the boy his earliest opportunities to rise in his profession. By the time he was twenty he was commanding an Indiaman, but soon afterwards transferred to the embryonic American navy. In 1800 the young Charles Stewart received his first independent command and soon gained a reputation as the scourge of privateers. Subsequently, he served in expeditions to Tripoli and Tunis, but fought his most famous engagement in the war with Britain in 1812. In the *Constitution* he defeated and captured two British ships off the coast of Spain. From this time, though he was still under 40, dates his nickname of 'Old Ironsides'. He became a national hero and continued, as Commodore Stewart, to serve ashore and afloat until 1862 when Lincoln conferred on him the title of rear-admiral on his retirement from the navy. He died at his home, Montpelier, more generally known as 'Ironsides', in Bordentown, New Jersey in 1869.[15]

At the height of his fame and just before he took the *Constitution* to sea for his epic fight, Stewart married Delia Tudor. She was descended from a family which claimed kinship with the Tudor dynasty and of which one member, Colonel Tudor, had bought land near Boston in colonial times. After his death his widow and son John moved there and the son amassed a considerable fortune in trade. This he bequeathed to his son William who was born in 1750. Graduating from Harvard in 1769, he was admitted to the bar in 1772, but with the outbreak of the Revolutionary War fought on the American side from Bunker's Hill onwards. Just as the war began he met and fell in love with Delia Jarvis, whom he subsequently married. She was a woman of much character and ability, who lived to be 92. After the war her husband prospered as a lawyer in Boston, became a member of the Massachusetts legislature and held office as United States Secretary of State in 1809 and 1810. He died in 1819, leaving two daughters and two sons. Of the latter, William, the elder, was an intellectual who founded the *North American Review*. In addition, besides helping his brother Frederic (the 'Ice-King') to pioneer the export of ice to hot countries, William was American consul at Lima for several years. Appointed American chargé d'affaires in Brazil in 1827, he died at Rio three years later, aged only 55.[16]

Of his two sisters the elder, Emma, married Robert H. Gardiner of Maine and the younger, Delia, was, as we have seen, swept off her feet by the tempestuous Commodore Stewart. The Commodore had only two children – Charles and Delia the third. Charles Stewart became a civil engineer and made a large fortune in railroads and timber, which he bequeathed eventually to his sister Delia. She, as the daughter of the naval hero, and with her own good looks and monied background, was an extremely eligible young woman who gravitated naturally from Boston to the Washington marriage market. It was there, in 1834, when she was only eighteen, that she met the young Lord Powerscourt and his rather less glittering cousin, John Henry Parnell. A little surprisingly, Delia Stewart preferred the heir of Avondale to his titled cousin.* The two quickly became engaged and were married at Grace Church, New York, on 31 May 1835.[17]

Such varied streams flowed into this marriage as to make it, genealogically speaking, a true meeting of the waters. Even if we discount the royal names of Tudor and Stewart, and Delia Parnell, for one, certainly did not discount them, many different kinds of blood and background came together in the generation immediately preceding Charles's own. And although there was a darker side to his ancestry, it had produced much of distinction before his time. In the paternal line, the law, the arts and, of course, politics, had all been represented, while running through the family history was an attachment to the land going back two centuries. From the time of the Union at least this attachment seems to have been marked by three favourable features not often found together in the landlords of the period. One was the good relationship which, by and large, the Parnells managed to maintain with their tenants. A second was the sympathy which old Sir John's descendants evinced for a cause which had left him perennially cold – the well-being of the Catholic population which surrounded their little islands of Protestantism. And the third was a readiness to perform those duties – Justice of the Peace, High Sheriff, Deputy Lieutenant of the county – which fell naturally to the gentry in England, but which in Ireland were too often neglected. That there was a Parnellite tradition of service to the county may have been a more important influence than is generally supposed

---

*There was a persistent family legend that John Henry's hand was strengthened by his sister Catherine selling him Avondale for £10,000, but, as we saw above (p. 21), this was quite unfounded.

in shaping Charles's resolve to be of service to the country. For the rest, the infusion of the American strain brought some much-needed vigour and vivacity. Men of action, men of business, men of affairs abounded among the Tudors and the Stewarts; some of this incisiveness and practicality were to manifest themselves in Delia Parnell's most famous son.

III

Her own translation from the salons of Washington to the backwoods of Wicklow was a traumatic experience. When John Henry Parnell brought her back there, Avondale was still an isolated place, for the railway did not reach Rathdrum until the early sixties. The house itself, despite its magnificent setting in a park of ancient trees and rolling grassland, is neither large nor particularly impressive. Built by Samuel Hayes in 1779, it has the excellent proportions of its period, but the façade lacks decoration and, like so many Anglo-Irish country houses, conveys an impression of bleakness, even of melancholy, as if the architect has unconsciously symbolized the isolation of the landlord in the austerity of his building. Inside, the dominant feature is the high, rectangular hall reaching up to the roof, with a minstrel's gallery facing the front door; in the nineteenth century tattered Volunteer flags and banners hung from this gallery and a large billiard-table took up much of the floorspace in the hall itself. One of Delia's daughters, Emily, was later to describe this as large enough for a coach and four to be driven round it, but this was a characteristic exaggeration.[18] Shapely and striking it certainly is, but it is not large. On the contrary, it prepares the visitor for the most obvious feature of the house, which is precisely its smallness. On the ground floor there are only three rooms of any pretensions. They are all charming, for they look out upon the woods which slope down to the river and to the Vale of Avoca, but again, they are not large. The drawing-room, with its fireplace of Italian marble and its three bay-windows, is undeniably handsome and so also are the two rooms which balance it on either side. On the right, as you face the house, is, or rather was, the library. In Charles's time it was rich in eighteenth-century works which stirred no echo in his mind. On the left is the elegant Blue Room, now painted green in total disregard of Charles's violent superstition against that unlucky colour. Used in his day as a dining-room, its mirrors and medallions and decorated ceiling still preserve an eighteenth-century grace which is present nowhere else in the house, though one catches a glimpse of it on the staircase, which also has its medallions, leading to the half a dozen bedrooms which constitute the upper floor.

Comfortable but not grand – that was Avondale when Delia Parnell became its mistress. Her husband, naturally, as a working landowner and a magistrate, had his own busy round, but for her, until children began to arrive, time hung heavily. It was not merely that Wicklow was not Washington, it was also that the society, such as it was, in which she had now to move, could scarcely have been more alien. Wicklow, Anglo-Irish Wicklow, had the reputation then of being 'Orange', that is, a county where Protestantism was narrow but ran deep, and where the political expression of that Protestantism took the form of a rigid Unionism. This cannot have been congenial to the young American, brought up to enjoy much greater freedom of expression and of action than English or Anglo-Irish girls of her age would have dreamed of expecting. Moreover, the daughter of a hero of the war of 1812, and the descendant of the William Tudor who had been a friend of John Adams and a soldier in the Revolutionary War, was unlikely to take the British connection so much for granted as did the county families with which her husband was so intimately connected.

It is hardly surprising, then, that she should soon have acquired the reputation of being a rebel, for whom nothing was too bad to say about or against England. Much of this was probably no more than the ordinary anti-British feeling which many Americans shared at that time; and since Delia was accustomed to trade on her wealth and her good looks to say whatever was uppermost in her not very profound mind, she is unlikely to have allowed the complexities of the Irish situation to inhibit her in the slightest. In reality, the desire to shock may have been the main motive-force behind her more blazing indiscretions; and her intellectual *gaminerie* may have sprung, initially at least, less from political conviction than from a craving for attention. At any rate, she made no serious attempt to break the pattern of life into which her children were born and within which they grew up. School in England for the boys and the university (which for a Parnell could only mean Cambridge) afterwards if they wanted it; a more haphazard education for the girls, but directed nevertheless towards presentation at Court (the *real* Court, not your gimcrack Viceregal substitute in Dublin) and the marriage market to which that unappetizing ceremony was the open sesame. Nor did the frequent and loud expression of disloyal sentiments prevent 'society', including officers of the British Army, being invited to Avondale. And when Charles chose to join the Wicklow militia, it is not known that his mother's voice was raised against it.

That her anti-British views may have had some effect upon some of her children – especially the younger girls, who were more in her company – is possible, but it would be quite wrong to assume, as at least one biographer has done, that it was his mother's influence which turned Charles towards Irish nationalism.[19] On the contrary, as he grew to manhood he appears to have been alternately amused and embarrassed by his mother's tirades.[20] The forces that moulded Charles's personality and attitudes were much more complex and to understand them we have to look more closely at his family, his environment and his education.

John and Delia Parnell had twelve children in all, of whom one was stillborn. The others comprised five boys and six girls. The first-born, William, died in 1842 at the age of five. The second, Delia, was born in 1838 and grew up to be a great beauty. In 1859 she married an American millionaire, James Livingston Thomson, who lived in Paris. Her only child, Henry, died there in 1882 when only 21. This event, which impinged upon her brother Charles's career at a critical moment, was fatal in its effects upon herself. She had not only married her husband for his money, but had made the mistake of telling him so. He became extremely jealous, restricted her movements (she tried to commit suicide when he forbade her to ride), and refused to contemplate that they should have any more children. When Henry died of typhoid his mother was overcome with grief, went to America with her husband and died shortly afterwards.

Next, in 1839, came Hayes Parnell, who died aged 15 after a hunting accident. He was followed by Emily, born in 1841. She, in her youth the prototype of 'the wild Irish girl', was the author in later life of the extraordinary memoir entitled, *A patriot's mistake*, ostensibly about her brother Charles, but in reality a fantasy woven round her own love life. At an early age she became infatuated with Captain Arthur Monroe Dickinson, and was disinherited by her father who suspected, with some reason, that she planned to elope. When John Henry Parnell died she at last married Captain Dickinson, by whom she had one daughter, Delia; he turned out a hopeless drunkard and came to a bad end in Brussels. Emily herself died in the South Dublin Union Infirmary in May 1918, apparently in reduced circumstances. After her came John Howard, who was born in 1843 and died in 1923; more will be said of him in due course. Then in 1845 Sophia Katharine was born. She did make a runaway match of the Gretna Green variety with a Dublin solicitor, Alfred McDermott who, because she was a ward in Chancery, later thought it prudent to marry her publicly without informing the Lord Chancellor about the Scottish ceremony. They had four children, but she died in Dublin in 1877 in her thirty-third year. Next to her came Charles, born in 1846 and Fanny, born in 1849. Fanny, who died in 1882, was Charles's favourite sister and reappears more than once in this story, as does their younger sister Anna Catherine, who was born in 1852 and drowned while swimming in 1911. Both of them were unmarried but their brother, Henry Tudor, who came between them, being born in 1850, married the daughter of a Trinity College, Dublin divine, the Reverend Thomas Luby, and had three children; he died at Lausanne in 1915. The youngest was Theodosia, born in 1853 and married in 1880 to Commander Claude Paget of the Royal Navy. They had one son before she, like so many of her family, died young – in London, aged only 38. Seven of the eleven children of John Henry Parnell did not reach the age of 50 and of the remaining four two died before they were 60; only Emily and John lived into old age.

The fact that so many children arrived so regularly meant that each of them experienced the rough and tumble of growing up in a family too large to receive the individual attention of a mother and father who anyway, after the fashion of their age and class, were content to leave the management of young children to a succession of nurses. Charles's nurse, Mrs Twopenny ('Tup'ny') was actually English, but in John Howard's recollection, it was she more than anyone else who instilled into these two brothers the love of the Wicklow countryside which always distinguished them. Their pastimes, in most of which the girls shared, were much as one might expect of children with a demesne as their playground. John Henry expected them to sit a horse almost as soon as they could walk and several of them – Delia, Emily, Charles himself – were passionately fond of riding. There was shooting and coursing and fishing and, for the girls as well as the boys, there was also cricket to which their father was mightily, and fatally, addicted. He had a cricket-pitch prepared in front of the house – it can still be seen to this day – and formed his own Avondale Club, besides going up to Dublin from time to time to play in matches there. On one of these occasions – it was the summer of 1859 – he had been warned not to play, as he was suffering from what was diagnosed as rheumatism of the stomach. Despite a high temperature he insisted on playing, felt ill on returning to the Shelbourne Hotel, sent, too late, for a doctor and died the next day.[21]

The possibilities of schooling at Avondale were almost nil and although a series of tutors passed through the house they had little influence on any of the children and perhaps least of all on Charles, who emerges from the memoirs of both his brother and his sister as excessively self-willed and undisciplined. No doubt this explains why his parents adopted the classical Anglo-Irish solution of transportation to a boarding-school even earlier than was normal in such circles. 'Master Charley is born to rule', said Nurse Twopenny, and since the family was not prepared to be ruled by a six-year-old, it was at that tender age that he was packed off to a girls' school in Yeovil, Somerset, which, many years after, he recalled as being a Plymouth Brethren establishment.[22] This experience apparently cured him of domineering over his sisters, but during his second term he fell ill with typhoid and had to be brought home.[23] He was later to claim that this was the only major illness he had in his life until his health began seriously to break up in the winter of 1886–7, and although this was substantially true, there are indications that typhoid may have left a permanent mark upon his constitution. Even as a young man, despite his good co-ordination and his physical strength, he struck many observers as delicate and fine-drawn, with an unusual pallor in his face, though the latter may well have been inherited from his mother.[24]

There followed a brief and stormy period with his sisters' governesses, as a result of which in 1854 he went on his travels again. This time it was to a school at Kirk Langley in Derbyshire. It was a small private school housed in a Georgian building which still stands and was until recently in the possession of the granddaughter of the owner and founder of the school, the Reverend John Barton, who had opened it in 1845.[25] Not much is known about Parnell's time there, though some legends long survived in the Barton family. It was a place of no great academic distinction, but the food was reputedly good and Mr Barton shared one interest with his pupil – he was an enthusiastic cricketer. Parnell's own behaviour seems to have been as unruly as it had been at home and, though he looked back on his time there as one of the happiest periods of his life, his pugnacity – he is said to have offered to fight the headmaster on one occasion – caused his removal from the school.[26] Back at Avondale, he was rejoined by his brother John Howard, who had been sent to Paris to cure a stammer so remorselessly mimicked by Charles that the latter was in danger of contracting it as a permanent mannerism himself. Charles, seemingly, was soon sent away again – he is believed to have attended the well-known Great Ealing school in London between 1856 and about 1861, though nothing has survived about his time there. During the holidays the two boys ran wild, following the country pursuits of their age and time.

But in 1859 these halcyon days came to an end. John Henry's sudden death found nearly all the family in France and Charles had the traumatic experience of being the only one to follow the coffin to the burial place in Mount Jerome. The children now became wards in Chancery and the family lands were divided between the three surviving boys. John Howard inherited the Armagh estate of Collure; Charles, received Avondale, and with it a considerable burden of debt; the Carlow property went to Henry who, apparently, had sold it all by 1875. Avondale had not been well administered; the recent purchase of Clonmore had seriously diminished the family resources, and stern economies were necessary. While this period of imposed abstinence lasted, the family moved into Dalkey (on the coast about eight miles south of Dublin), where they occupied a house, Khyber Pass, which is still a landmark. A year later they moved to Clarinda Park on a height above Kingstown harbour, where they rented a house belonging to the O'Connor Don, one of those conservatively-minded Catholic landlords whom Charles was later to be largely instrumental in driving out of Irish public life. It was here that Charles's maternal grandmother, Delia Stewart, died suddenly while on a visit to the family during the American Civil War. She died sitting in a chair after luncheon and the shock of this event, following the earlier stress caused by his father's sudden demise, had a deep effect upon Charles. John Howard dates his brother's morbidity about death from this time and it is certainly true that the adult Charles united in his person two formidable obstacles to political success in Ireland – an English accent and an intense dislike of funerals.[27]

It was a relief after this to go down for the summer to the dower-house at Avondale, and to plunge once more into the familiar routine of riding and shooting and cricket. There was a new excitement, too, for the Dublin, Wicklow and Wexford railway was at last reaching Rathdrum and to a boy with an interest in engineering this was pure joy; not only that, but it brought in a much-needed £3000 in compensation for the railway's invasion of the Avondale estate.[28] This onrush of modernity had also a deeper significance. Without that line to Rathdrum, Charles would scarcely have been able to base the early part of his political career upon his Wicklow home in the way he did. For many years a periodic retreat to Avondale was to be an inner necessity for him and that the railway helped to make possible.

IV

This nomadic, suburban existence ended when Delia Parnell took a
house at 14 Upper Temple Street, Dublin, which became the family
headquarters for most of the 1860s. Here further desultory attempts at
education were made – perhaps one should say 'happened', for nothing
seemed to be planned in that casual household. Of Charles there is
little to say except that, if something had not been done about him
quickly, he was in danger of becoming a semi-literate country bumpkin.
Indeed, in later days he himself used to bewail his inadequate schooling
and especially his ignorance of Irish history.[29] This may not actually
have been quite so complete as he liked to make out, for the library at
Avondale was well equipped in this field and political discussion was
often hot and strong at Temple Street, but it is true that systematic
reading was not in Parnell's line and that a good deal of what he eventually learnt about his country's past he picked up as he went along.
Music, the theatre and the arts generally remained closed doors to him
all his life and he had no notion of the historical origins of the western
civilization within which he grew up. His colleague, the novelist Justin
McCarthy, records this revealing anecdote. 'I once told him that I
was about to realize one of the great dreams of my life by spending
some time in Athens. He asked me, with a kindly show of interest,
whether Athens was considered a pleasant place in which to pass a
holiday.' But in the same breath McCarthy notes that 'an error in
spelling was as offensive to him as the sight of a black beetle is to many a
man'. And he once handed back to McCarthy a letter from one of the
latter's constituents. 'Do forgive me', he said, 'and tell me all about it.
I couldn't read through a man's letter who spells agricultural with two
g's.'[30]

However, even his feckless mother was not prepared to let the boy
slide downhill entirely unheeded. A vague notion he expressed of wanting to go to Cambridge suggested the need for urgent coaching, and
Charles was sent forthwith to a highly select cramming academy, run
as a profitable sideline by the Reverend Mr Whishaw in his rectory at
Chipping Norton in Oxfordshire. The instruction given seems to have
been of variable quality, and for Charles, who needed both education
and polish, a special teacher was engaged, between whom and his taci-
turn, wayward pupil there was a total lack of *rapport*. This culminated
in a stand-up quarrel, when Charles was given the ultimatum by Mr
Whishaw of either apologizing or being sent home. For one of the few

times in his life he backed down, but there was no improvement in his attitude and although his unsatisfactory performance may have been connected, as his brother suggests, with a youthful infatuation for a pretty girl of the neighbourhood, it was only the imminent necessity of matriculating at Cambridge that eventually concentrated his mind.[31]

There is no disguising the fact that he was not popular at Whishaw's, making an almost equally bad impression upon the masters and upon his fellow-pupils. He was reserved, nervous, irritable and so prone to sleep-walking that he dreaded being left alone. To the end of his life these traits were liable to reappear under stress and more than once a political colleague had to walk the streets with him into the small hours before Charles would let him go. 'We liked John', one who was at the school with the two brothers later told Charles's Boswellian biographer, Barry O'Brien, 'but we did not like Charles. He was arrogant and aggressive; he tried to sit on us and we tried to sit on him.'[32] It seems to have occurred to nobody that arrogance and aggression were perhaps the way in which an ardent but uncontrolled nature reacted to severance from home and family, and to the substitution of sterile mental labour for the free and easy life of Avondale.

Nevertheless, the university remained the objective and as Charles settled into harness his work and even, apparently, his manners, improved and we learn of village cricket (he was that valuable commodity, a good wicket-keeper-batsman) and of frequent invitations to dances.[33] And at last Cambridge materialized.[34] It was perhaps significant that he was admitted to Magdalene which, being then one of the smallest and poorest colleges, not only had little to offer in the way of teaching, but was also lax in its admission standards. This well suited Charles, whose academic defects were still legion, but produced an undergraduate body consisting largely of 'hearties' of one form or another. The Master was a rigid conservative who liked to think of his college as fashionable, which, with a certain set, it was. It was fashionable with those who had no taste for discipline and it was said to number, at the time Charles joined it, a larger proportion of public school men than any other college save King's, though there was also a considerable number who, like Parnell, were privately educated. But these included the sons of wealthy mid-Victorian parvenus who, said one who overlapped with Charles at Magdalene, 'tried to liken themselves to country gentlemen and succeeded in looking like stable-boys'. With neither of the two main social groups in the college, old rich or new rich, had Charles any natural bonds and it is not impossible that the extreme dislike of 'Englishness' which rapidly became an obsession with him, may have derived originally from his experiences with the limited and untypical range of behaviour and attitudes which was all Magdalene had to offer him. So far as he made friends at all, he made them among the outsiders rather than from the Etonians, Harrovians and Salopians who generally kept their own inviolate worlds to themselves. From this he was to draw in due course a characteristically uncompromising conclusion. 'These English', he once said to his brother John, 'despise us because we are Irish; but we must stand up to them. That's the only way to treat the Englishman – stand up to him.'[35]

As a known sleep-walker, Charles was given rooms on the ground floor beneath the Pepys Library. He seems to have got on reasonably well with his supervisor, G. F. Pattrick, who discerned in him a genuine talent for mathematics, his principal subject; he repaid this sympathetic interest the only way he knew, by offering to protect Pattrick when a fight was in progress outside the college gates. But this was a rare gesture and Parnell at Cambridge, as elsewhere, was withdrawn and moody. Even cricket failed to work its familiar magic and he appears to have played only twice for Magdalene; he got a duck against Peterhouse on 7 June 1867 and nineteen against Trinity Hall on 3 May 1869. But for this there may be a straightforward explanation. With his usual ill-luck he had chosen a rowing, not a cricketing college and one, moreover, where every undergraduate was expected to subscribe to the boat club. Charles did so when he first came up, but never thereafter; this did not endear him to his fellow-students and indeed earned him a disapproving comment in the club records.

Charles spent three and a half largely unproductive years at Cambridge. The circumstances of his departure are notorious, but since they are still frequently misstated it may be desirable to tell the story once more. But first, two of the more obvious errors may be discarded. He did not leave Cambridge because of his political opinions, for the simple reason that while he was there he apparently had none. Things were indeed happening in Ireland which were beginning to force politics upon his attention, but only intermittently and not inspiring in him any desire to participate himself. Equally, he did not leave Cambridge because he had a love affair with a farmer's daughter called Daisy, who drowned herself when the affair ended in the way such infatuations often do. The story is one of his sister Emily's more bizarre fabrications and although it has been accepted in some popular biographies, it has long since been shown that no girl called Daisy was drowned in the Cam during the whole of Charles's time at Magdalene.[36] When Emily published her account in 1905 her brother Henry corresponded with the then Master in an attempt to get at the truth. This elicited letters from two senior Fellows, one of whom was in residence when Charles was up, and another who entered in 1870. Both testified that no such story or report had been current when the incident was alleged to have occurred.

There is in reality no need to postulate a rustic Ophelia to account for the ending of Charles's Cambridge career, though the incident which did terminate it was unsavoury enough.[37] On the evening of Saturday 1 May 1869, he and three companions took a cab to the refreshment rooms at the station. There, for only half an hour but apparently at a great rate, they consumed champagne, sherry and biscuits. They left about ten o'clock and two of them went off to look for transport. Charles was in the condition delicately described in Ireland as 'having drink taken', but was not drunk enough to require the intervention of the law, despite the fact that he elected to await the arrival of a cab by lying full length in the gutter opposite what is now the car park of the Station Hotel. At this point there arrived out of the darkness one Edward Hamilton, manure-dealer, and his servant. 'Hullo', said one of them, 'what's the matter with this 'ere cove?' Charles's companion, Robert Bentley, replied that his friend was drunk and that they were waiting for a cab. Hamilton claimed later that he offered to help, but if he did his offer seems to have been accompanied by some more or less offensive pleasantry, because Bentley replied rather sharply that they wanted none of his damned help and that he could mind his own business. To this the aggrieved Hamilton riposted that gentlemen who sought only to assist did not expect to meet with such bloody impertinence.

Charles scrambled to his feet and joined in the altercation. He aimed a blow at Hamilton and missed – understandable in his condition – but Hamilton, striking back, hit him in the eye. The fight now began in earnest. Charles knocked his man down, may have kicked him, and certainly fell on him and rolled him in the gutter. Having made his point, he then helped his opponent to his feet just as a constable arrived on the scene. Michael Davitt, whose source may well have been Parnell himself, says that the whole matter might have ended there and then but for an unlucky accident. Dimly aware that he would be in trouble with his college if this affray were reported, Charles felt in his pocket for a tip to persuade the constable of his innocence. He intended a sovereign, but in the darkness produced a shilling instead. The canny policeman, verifying it under a lamp-post, reacted predictably and justice took its majestic course.[38] In support of this anecdote it is worth mentioning that the policeman did testify in court that he had been offered money, though it was not of course apparent from his evidence that the damaging circumstance was the amount rather than the fact of the bribe.[39]

The scene then shifted to the police station where Hamilton made a formal complaint. His nose and lip were bleeding, one arm was disabled by a blow on the collar-bone, and his new trousers were torn and stained with blood. He did not, however, require medical attendance and did not call in a doctor until 6 May, the day after he had decided to take legal action so as to teach this undergraduate that he could not 'indulge in such freaks with impunity'.[40] As for Charles, he was so little the worse for his adventure that on the Monday after the fight he made those useful nineteen runs against Trinity Hall mentioned earlier. It seems, though, that on receipt of a letter from Hamilton's solicitor on 5 May, he returned to Ireland, perhaps for a family conclave. If so, it was unproductive, for while it appears that the matter could have been settled if he had agreed to make a donation to Addenbrooke's Hospital, his innate obstinacy asserted itself and he refused to budge an inch.

The case came to the County Court on 21 May. Both judge and jury agreed that Charles had been at fault and Hamilton, who had asked for damages of 30 guineas, was awarded 20. The matter then came before a college meeting. Every college head nowadays, instructed by his Students' Union in the intricacies of double jeopardy, knows how difficult it is to deal with an undergraduate who has already incurred a penalty in the courts. In the Magdalene of 1869, however, a more robust attitude prevailed and Parnell was promptly rusticated for the remainder of the term. Since it only had two weeks to run, this was a mild sentence and there seems to have been no doubt in the minds of the college authorities that Mr Parnell would be among them again in the autumn, though his supervisor and tutor might reasonably have wondered to what purpose. Yet he never reappeared. Injured pride is the usual explanation for his failure to come back and no doubt this played a major part. But his brother Henry, in correspondence with the college in 1906, supplied a more prosaic explanation which may also have been true. This was that Avondale was in such a rundown condition that, so far from frittering away more funds in Cambridge, Charles was anxious to recover his caution-money, which he could only do by not returning for the new academic year.

Nevertheless, the likelihood is that the fight at Cambridge had an influence on him greater than its intrinsic triviality might suggest. The years at the university had been wasted years for him. He was making no mark, he was going nowhere in particular. And even if Emily was wrong in ascribing his restlessness to the urgings of an awakened sexuality, the fact remains that in 1869 he was 23 years old with the normal drives of a healthy young man and no means of releasing them. To be an outsider at Magdalene was not tragic, but it was disagreeable. Added to the frustrations of Chipping Norton and to his underlying homesickness for Avondale, it may have helped to shape his view of English society as something alien to him, and of England as a place where he had experienced coldness and unfairness which contrasted sharply with the warmth and sympathy of his haphazard but affectionate home. To return to Ireland in these circumstances amounted, or could amount in the mind of an obdurate young man given to brooding on any fancied insult, to a kind of rejection. But if so, it could be answered by a counter-rejection which would come easily enough to one whose basic Wicklow granite had stubbornly resisted all those diverse and futile attempts to put an English polish on it.

V

This is not to say that he immediately reacted away from Cambridge and towards Irish nationalism. Cambridge may have been, or become, a symbol of what he most disliked about England, but that did not mean that there were not other things which, almost equally, he disliked about Ireland. Among these were the politics apparently professed by his mother and his sister Fanny. Delia Parnell's propensity to shock her friends by the extremism of her language became, if anything, more unbridled after her husband's death. This would not have mattered greatly if those had not been dangerous days for the unguarded expression of even the most fatuous opinions. That decade of the 1860s was dominated by the rise of the Irish Republican Brotherhood founded in 1858 by James Stephens. The IRB, more generally known at the time as the Fenians from the name of the parallel body which had been simultaneously established in America, was pledged to an independent Irish republic to be won, it was assumed, by an armed rebellion against England. Yet, though secret, the Fenians also needed to influence public opinion and for this purpose launched their own newspaper, the *Irish People*, in 1863, which was suppressed two years later when the government, well apprised by informers, arrested some of the leading Fenians in expectation of an insurrection that did not actually come until 1867.

Within that brief space of two years Fanny Parnell, who was still only sixteen when the paper was suppressed, contributed to the *Irish*

People some of her early, passionate, patriotic verse. She wrote under a *nom de plume*, but whether this was pierced by the police, or whether Mrs Parnell's flamboyant indiscretions were deemed to be in need of checking, the house in Temple Street (not Avondale, as is sometimes stated) was searched by the police one night in 1867 during Charles's absence in Cambridge. They found nothing incriminating, but they took away a sword and some uniforms which were in fact part of the brothers' equipment as officers in the militia.[41] Years later, Charles told the novelist Justin McCarthy that it was this visitation which first drew his attention to Irish politics. 'Parnell's eyes lit up with fire as he told me that if he had been there he would have shot the first man who endeavoured to force his way into Mrs Parnell's room.'[42]

But if the incident caused Charles to think about politics it did not turn him into a nationalist. His furious reaction when he first learnt of the incident was essentially that of his ancestor, Sir John Parnell, when he voted against the Union because it was an attempt by authority to infringe his privileges. No doubt Charles would have shot any policeman who insulted his mother or his sister, but that did not prevent him from going to Dublin Castle to reclaim the treasured uniforms. Nor, if John is to be trusted, did it prevent him either from making fun of Fanny's poetry, or from lying in wait for the raffish hangers-on who haunted Temple Street to profit from Mrs Parnell's gullibility, and, in the belief that they were Fenians, throwing them down the steps.[43]

All the same, an event did occur that year which affected him more deeply than he cared to admit, or perhaps realized at the time. In September 1867 two Fenians were arrested in Manchester and a group of their comrades resolved upon a desperate attempt to rescue them. They attacked a prison van and released the prisoners by blowing off the lock with a pistol. A police sergeant inside was killed by the bullet and for this three men were hanged, protesting to the end that they had neither intended nor committed murder. We shall see presently that when Charles entered the House of Commons his first notable contribution was to repeat this assertion, that the men who were hanged had done no murder. Many years later he was to claim before the Special Commission appointed in 1888 to enquire into possible connections between his movement and Irish crime, that it was Fenianism which had first made him pay attention to Anglo-Irish relations.[44]

So it may have done, especially if, as a probably unreliable tradition has it, his mother subsequently assisted one of the Manchester rescuers to escape to America dressed as a woman.[45] Yet none of this had any effect then or for several years afterwards, either upon his thinking or upon his actions. Not only did he remain at Cambridge for eighteen months after the Manchester episode, but when he finally came home to Ireland, it was to plunge into the affairs of Avondale and become, what had always seemed to be his destiny, a country gentleman *in excelsis*. In the last great struggle of his life, when any mud was good enough to throw at him, it was alleged that he had once taken part in an eviction on his brother Henry's estate in Carlow. This was quite possible – Henry early developed into a Tory absentee landlord of the old school – but Carlow was a far cry from Avondale. There, where the worst that could be dredged up against him was that without his knowledge a lease had been drawn for one of his tenants which compelled the tenant to contract out of the benefits of the Land Act of 1870, it was as a progressive landlord that Charles immediately made his mark.[46] Soon after his return he began to develop the sawmills which afterwards became a feature of the estate and in his efforts (ultimately unavailing) to make Avondale a paying proposition, he later added quarrying and even mining to his timber interests.

For the rest, life settled back into the old easy round of a self-sufficient and highly insulated county society. There were dances and dinner-parties, there was hunting and shooting, and of course there was cricket. As a cricketer Parnell carried what would nowadays be called gamesmanship to positively indecent extremes. When captain of the Wicklow team he indulged in practices which soon became notorious, and although this may simply mean that they were also apocryphal, they have a certain symbolic significance as indicating an attitude of mind which the House of Commons was presently to come to know only too well. For example, it was apparently his habit, when captaining the fielding side, to claim a wicket if, after one batsman was out, his successor delayed in coming to the crease. On another occasion, having taken his team all the way to Dublin to play against the Phoenix Club, he at once fell into dispute with the captain of the opposing side. Failing to get his way, he refused to let the match proceed nd took his angry and frustrated team home. They could not have known it, their captain could not have known it, but they had just experienced a dress rehearsal for the government of an Irish parliamentary party which did not yet exist.[47]

It was, however, the old, simple pleasures of the countryside that attracted him most. They were important because they brought him into contact and companionship with the farmers and labourers who in their own way contributed to his education. He had a shooting-lodge at Aughavanagh, a few miles into the mountains from Avondale. It was a rough, uncomfortable place which he loved dearly all his life and where the few who were allowed to share this pleasure found him more relaxed than he ever was elsewhere. Aughavanagh had originally been a military barracks to house troops engaged in putting down the rising of 1798 and tales about the savagery of the repression which followed it still lingered in the neighbourhood.[48] Such tales Parnell heard often from his old retainers. Apparently they sank home, engendering pride in his native county and perhaps a smouldering hostility towards those who had first crushed the insurrection and then abolished Grattan's parliament which he had grown up to regard, and at bottom would always regard, as the ideal solution to the Irish question.

But meanwhile he was in the spring of life and his fancy turned in the traditional direction. It was not long before his name began to be coupled with that of a certain 'Miss C.', who remains unidentifiable except as a member of a neighbouring county family. Charles, however, could only be got to refer to her as 'an extremely nice girl', hardly the language of high passion. Passion there was though, when he went to Paris in 1871 on a visit to his uncle Charles Stewart. There he met a blonde American beauty, Miss Woods, the heiress to a large fortune. They fell in love at once and were, it seems, actually engaged. In the autumn the Woods family moved to Rome with Charles in attendance. Then arrived a letter from his uncle warning him against 'the Roman fever'. This aroused in Charles his latent hypochondria and, despite his loved one's entreaties, he departed abruptly and ungallantly for Ireland, promising to come to her in Paris when she returned there. It seems he kept his word, found the situation as he thought unchanged, and went home happily to prepare Avondale for his bride. All was in vain. He was followed back to Ireland by a letter from Miss Woods announcing her imminent departure for Newport, Rhode Island and ominously silent about their engagement. Dumbfounded, the suitor, ardent now it was too late, hastened again to Paris only to find the bird had flown. Being Charles, he did not accept this defeat as final and set out at once for America, partly in pursuit of the fair one, partly to look into his coal-mining investments and to visit his brother John who, a year or so earlier, had gone out to Alabama to plant cotton and grow fruit.

Miss Woods revealed a will even more inflexible than her lover's. Arrived in America, Charles went directly to Newport, was graciously but heartlessly received, and in the end beat a retreat to Alabama, where John found him 'sullen and dejected', exhibiting all the typical symptoms of unrequited love. On this occasion he spent three weeks

with his brother and what with the partridge-shooting, the cotton and
the peaches, oblivion did its rapid work. He was not, it seems, greatly
taken with the South, was not at ease with the Negroes, and detested
the cooking. However, he developed an intense interest in the coal-
fields around Birmingham, Alabama, which was very nearly the death
of him. Coming back from a visit to New Orleans, he was met at
Montgomery by his brother John so that they might travel the last leg
of the journey together. When they were nearing Birmingham, the train
jumped the track at high speed and plunged down a steep bank,
finishing upside down. Charles, already perturbed by a Negro's prophecy
in New Orleans that he would shortly be killed, tried to open the door
and jump out as soon as the train began to rock. Had he succeeded, the
carriage would almost certainly have fallen on him and crushed him.
As it was, his coat was caught in the luggage-rack and he was suspended
in mid-air while the carriage turned over. John was not so fortunate.
He was thrown against the roof of the coach and knocked unconscious;
his neck was injured and the fingers of one hand broken. But Charles
too, though able to walk, was severely shaken and for the next month
they had to share the same bed in the scruffy Birmingham hotel which
served them as an impromptu nursing-home. 'Charley', recalled John,
'was the only nurse I had, though he was also suffering from his injuries.
He attended to my wants better and more tenderly than any woman could
have done . . .'[49]

Undaunted, Charles continued to be attracted by the coal-mining
possibilities of Alabama and reached the point of negotiating with the
owners of one concern for a part share in the business in exchange for
a cash investment of £3000. The scheme fell through and he moved
on to inspect the Virginia mines in which he already had sunk some
money. Here also he nearly died horribly, just avoiding decapitation
in the cage going down the mineshaft. According to his brother this
incident, coming on top of the Negro's warning and the railway crash,
'still further increased the superstitions which had grown upon him
during the last few weeks'.[50] This sounds fanciful, but all accounts of
him after he entered public life agree that he was an extremely superstitious man and it is not impossible that this trait in his character dated
from, or was accentuated by, the experiences he underwent in the
unfamiliar and in many ways unsympathetic environment of the southern
United States.

In the end both brothers decided to come home without further delay
and together they sailed for Ireland on New Year's Day, 1872. There
followed some months of assiduous courtship of possible benefactors.

Charles had expectations from his uncle in Paris and visited him there to remind him of his existence. John looked rather to Sir Ralph Howard, their guardian and their father's uncle, who was now old and feeble, dying in London within a few months of their return. John received a substantial legacy, worth about £4000 a year, and also retained the Armagh estate, though this barely brought him anything, since he found it increasingly difficult to collect the rents out of which he had to pay annuities to his sisters and the head rent to Trinity College, Dublin. As for uncle Charles Stewart, he went to Rome and perversely died of 'the Roman fever' against which he had warned his nephew while the latter was pursuing Miss Woods. When the will was read it was found that he had left his large fortune to Delia Parnell who now became a wealthy woman, though over the years unwise speculation reduced her capital to zero. The brothers for their part picked up again the threads of country life in Wicklow and seemed to have no other ambition than to follow the advice Lord Carysfort gave on their return home – to remain on the ancestral estate and play their part in rural society as befitted decent landlords of the old school. But could there any longer be a decent landlord of the old school in an Ireland which, long torpid, now seemed once more in flux? To this question Parnell was soon to return a resounding negative. But to understand why and how he did so we must turn outwards from the family circle towards that wider world of which as yet he knew almost nothing.

CHAPTER 2

Apprenticeship

'My dear boy, we have got a splendid recruit, an historic name, my friend, young Parnell of Wicklow; and unless I am mistaken, the Saxon will find him an ugly customer, though he is a good-looking fellow.' (Isaac Butt on Parnell, 1874, R. Barry O'Brien, *The life of Charles Stewart Parnell*, i, 73.)

I

While Parnell was busy settling down at Avondale the Irish political scene was, as usual, in a state of some confusion. The echoes of the Fenian rising had begun to die away and attention was once more centred upon constitutional agitation. The general election of 1868 had produced a Liberal ministry headed by a Gladstone who was beginning to be conscious of a mission 'to pacify Ireland' and who had already given signs of benevolent intent by disestablishing the Church of Ireland in 1869, by passing in 1870 the first Land Act ever to favour the Irish tenant against his landlord, and by holding out the possibility of creating a university that would be acceptable to Catholic opinion. It is true that none of these reforms struck at the heart of the problem. But they indicated a more flexible attitude on the part of the British government, and though Gladstone himself was partly responsible for spreading abroad the notion that his education about Ireland had been accelerated by the Fenians, it was at least possible to hope that the process might be completed by judicious pressure from the Irish members in the House of Commons.

The same election which had brought Gladstone to power in Britain had produced in Ireland a majority of members – 65 out of 105 – who might loosely be described as Liberal. They were broadly in favour of the policy which Gladstone had set in motion with his legislation of 1869 and 1870, though the Land Act in their view did not go nearly far enough in protecting the interest of the tenant. Some of them, also, were disappointed by the Prime Minister's failure to meet them adequately on the other great Irish issue of the day – to secure an amnesty for the Fenians arrested between 1865 and 1867. Since Irish Conservatives also had grievances – they were alarmed by disestablishment, which they justly regarded as the first major breach in the Union and an ominous precedent – it is clear that a substantial reservoir of discontent was available for exploitation.

The hour produced the man. He was Isaac Butt, a Protestant lawyer who combined political conservatism with a conviction that the land laws should be changed so as to give the tenant farmers real security in their holdings; without this, he thought, the whole structure of property would be endangered. The Young Ireland rising of 1848, which seemed to confirm his worst forebodings, led him to believe that the solution which would best preserve the Union with Britain and at the same time rescue Ireland from misgovernment would be a form of federalism under which the Irish parliament extinguished in 1800 would be revived with power to legislate on internal matters, while for imperial issues Irishmen would still represent their country at Westminster.

The Fenian outbreak in 1867 strengthened Butt's conviction that federalism was the only way to break the dreary cycle of inefficient administration punctuated by incompetent insurrection. In May 1870 he expounded his ideas at a meeting in Dublin from which sprang the Home Government Association, designed to mobilize public opinion behind the demand for an Irish parliament with, as Butt put it, 'full control over our domestic affairs'. This was in no sense a revolutionary organization. On the contrary, its aims were moderate and its members were for the most part men of property.[1] At first, indeed, Protestant Conservatives predominated and though they soon began to melt away as Butt sought to broaden his base among Liberals and Nationalists, he himself remained wedded to methods of impeccable constitutionality.

At the close of 1873 he replaced the Association by a new body, the Home Rule League. This was potentially a more effective force, since membership was open to anyone willing to pay the subscription of one pound per annum (associate members were later admitted at a shilling a year), though Butt regarded the League as essentially a pressure-group, not a political party. And when it was suggested that all Irish members elected on a Home Rule platform should together vote, or abstain from voting, as the majority might decide, Butt sided with the bulk of his League in rejecting the proposal, not only because it affronted the independence of the individual member of parliament, but because the indiscriminate use of an Irish bloc vote 'would destroy every particle of moral influence which any action of his would have in the House of Commons'.[2]

Such was the state of affairs when Parnell first began to consider a career in politics. Fenianism, as we saw earlier, had made it difficult for him to remain entirely ignorant of the Irish situation, but it had not moved him to action. Later, he was to testify that the Ballot Act of 1872, which had introduced secret voting, had turned his thoughts towards the possibility of creating an effective parliamentary party.[3] This smacks of hindsight and at the time, so far from plunging into politics, he devoted much more attention to the duties of his station, representing his diocese in the Synod of the Church of Ireland and in 1874 beginning a term as High Sheriff for county Wicklow.[4]

These modest functions had at least the advantage that they brought some experience and a little discreet advertisement. They were, in fact, as good credentials as most young gentlemen could offer and when in that same year, 1873, his brother John casually suggested that Charles should think of standing for parliament, the family tradition of public service combined with his own increasing status in the county to make this seem not a totally outlandish idea. But when John urged him to help the tenants by joining the Home Rulers, Parnell merely replied, 'I do not see my way. I am in favour of the tenants and of Home Rule, but I do not know any of the men who are working the movement.'[5] Pride as much as ignorance apparently dictated his reaction. 'I could not', he told John, 'because I could not join that set.'[6] It was not an altogether convincing explanation. No member of the squirearchy need have felt himself out of place among Butt's gentlemanly cohorts. If Parnell wished to know the men at the head of the Home Rule League, the obstacles were minimal.

The matter suddenly ceased to be academic when the general election of 1874 gave the Home Rule League the opportunity to consolidate its position in Ireland. When the election came on Parnell was dining one night in Dublin with his sister Emily and her husband, Captain Dickinson. During dinner Dickinson made the same suggestion as John had done the previous year. This time, to everyone's astonishment, Parnell replied at once that he would stand, though it was plain that he had no idea how to go about it. When it was suggested that he should have a word with Edmund Dwyer Gray, the owner of the *Freeman's Journal*, Parnell characteristically rose from the table and went straight to the *Freeman's* office. Gray, probably as sceptical as he was astonished, pointed out that as Parnell was High Sheriff of his county he would have to ask the Lord-Lieutenant to release him from this post.[7] Next morning the brothers waited on Lord Spencer but received a temporizing reply. Taking this as a refusal, Parnell decided to switch roles with John and threw himself forthwith into promoting his brother's candidature as eagerly as he would have done his own.

It was in this context that he made his first public speech. No trace of it survives and, as John warned him that though High Sheriffs supervised elections they did not fight them, it had no immediate successors. John's recollection was that it was 'rather wild', but the manifesto Parnell drew up suggests that his main concern was to draw heavily on the credit presumed to attach to the family name. From this document it is clear that he was not at this stage a federalist in Butt's sense of the term. In essentials, he was already a '1782' man. 'The principles', he wrote, 'for which my ancestor, Sir John Parnell . . . refused the peerage from an English government are still mine and the cause of repeal of the Union under its new name of Home Rule will always find in me a firm and honest supporter.' For the rest, he was for fixity of tenure, for deno-minational education at primary and university levels, and for amnesty for political prisoners. He ended on a note calculated to appeal to what was still a deferential society. 'My grandfather and uncle represented this county for many years, and as you have experienced their trust-worthiness, so I hope you will believe in mine.' Yet all was in vain. John finished comfortably at the bottom of the poll and that could easily have been the last adventure of the two political innocents.[8]

As it happened, however, they were to have a second chance within a matter of weeks. One of the members returned for Dublin county, Colonel T. E. Taylor, joined the government Disraeli had formed after his victory in the general election and this caused a vacancy. The Home Rule League, which Parnell had joined, wanted to fight the seat as a test of strength, though there was little prospect of winning, since the county was a bastion of Conservatism. Parnell promptly offered himself as a candidate and since he bore a famous name and was prepared to pay his election expenses, there was something to be said for running him. On the debit side, few people had heard of him and neither his views nor his capacity to express them had been much exposed outside the family circle. When his name came before the council of the League there was much misgiving, intensified when Parnell attended an adop-tion meeting at the Rotunda on 9 March 1874. For a political neophyte it was an unnerving occasion. The veteran duellist, the O'Gorman Mahon, who had come into politics with O'Connell and was almost to survive Parnell, was in the chair and among those present were Butt, John Martin (of Young Ireland fame), A. M. Sullivan (the owner of the *Nation* newspaper) and Mitchell Henry, MP, a leading authority on tenant-right.[9]

Parnell's speech was a total disaster. He was visibly nervous, his voice did not carry through the hall and he seemed incapable of stringing two sentences together. 'He could not speak at all', recalled one of his later colleagues, who was there. 'He was hardly able to get up and say, "Gentlemen, I am a candidate for the representation of the county of Dublin". We all listened to him with pain while he was on his legs and felt immensely relieved when he sat down.'[10] A. M. Sullivan, who proposed him, tells the same tale. 'To our dismay he broke down utterly. He faltered, he paused, went on, got confused, and pale with intense but subdued nervous anxiety, caused everyone to feel deep sympathy for him. The audience saw it all, and cheered him kindly and heartily; but many on the platform shook their heads, sagely prophesying that if ever he got to Westminster, no matter how long he stayed there, he would either be a "silent member", or be known as "single-speech Parnell".'[11]

Had the seat been a marginal one the League could hardly have gone on with him. Having nothing to lose, Butt, who was captivated by the name of Parnell rather than by the personality of the man who bore it, allowed the candidature to continue with the League's blessing. Parnell made a strenuous, if still amateur, effort to project himself and his views to the electors, while apparently uncertain whether to look for support to his own class, or to rank and file nationalism. Some evidence of the latter was forthcoming from the parish priest of Rathdrum, Father Richard Galvin, who contributed a letter full of goodwill, though a purist might have objected that it said more about Parnell's father and mother than about the candidate. 'I never heard for twenty-seven years', wrote Father Galvin, 'the slightest taint of impropriety alleged against any member of this family or household. I believe your candidate to be in every way a worthy child of such parents. He is a young gentleman of great promise, great shrewdness, and sound judgement. You may rely entirely on his honour and integrity. Such is the decided conviction of his parish priest, who ought to know him well.'[12]

The parish priest of Rathdrum, though his civility was certainly helpful, was unlikely to cut overmuch ice with the squire of Avondale, and it was perhaps more in character for the Parnell of that time that he should have thrown out an anchor towards the aristocracy. It was also in character that his appeal, in a letter to Lord Howth a few days later, should have been of a curtness unrivalled even in his sparse and gritty correspondence. 'Will you', he wrote, 'kindly support me at approaching election for the county? I think there is an important principle at stake.'[13] What the principle was he did not deign to explain in writing to his putative supporter. It is plain, however, from his election address that for him the issue was not merely Home Rule, but independence of all other parties in the House of Commons. For although he also expressed himself in support of the amnesty movement, of tenant-right based upon the Ulster custom, and of denominational education, the core of his statement lay in two paragraphs:[14]

> Upon the great question of Home Rule I will by all means seek the restoration to Ireland of our domestic parliament, upon the basis of the resolutions passed at the National Conference last November, and the principles of the Home Rule League, of which I am a member.
>
> If elected to parliament I will give my cordial adherence to the resolutions adopted at the recent conference of Irish members, and will act independently alike of all English parties.

The electorate was not impressed. Parnell gravitated to the bottom of the poll as surely as his brother John had done earlier, receiving only 1235 votes as against the 2183 cast for Colonel Taylor. Nevertheless, his statement of principles marked an important step towards political maturity, and his commitment to the resolutions of the conference of Irish members (held in Dublin early in March 1874) was to have a significance in the future far beyond anything he could then have contemplated. The explicit intention of these resolutions was that the Irish Home Rule members should form 'a separate and distinct party' in the House of Commons, and that as members of that party 'we should collectively and individually hold ourselves aloof from, and independent of, all party combinations'. But unity and independence were not to be pressed to indecent extremes. The most that members were asked to undertake was to use their 'best endeavours' to achieve unity by taking counsel together, making 'reasonable concessions' to each other's opinions, and avoiding isolated action 'as far as possible'.[15]

Time would tell whether this elegant formula would provide the key to the creation of a truly independent party or whether it would be used merely to paper over the cracks which had begun to appear in the Home Rule ranks almost from the moment the election ended. The portents were not good. For although the results indicated that declared Home Rulers numbered 59, so many of these ostensible enthusiasts were Liberals at heart that the hard core of Home Rule support was probably no more than about 20. Moreover, even if the whole 59 had been thoroughly reliable, they represented only a narrow stratum of society, consisting almost entirely of landowners, businessmen and lawyers. It was true that the landlord element had somewhat declined, and in 1874 there were even two tenant-farmer representatives, but a party which consisted so massively of men of property in one form or another was unlikely to cut a very independent figure in the House of Commons.[16]

II

Yet, it was a party seemingly committed to Home Rule and to some kind of autonomous existence. It was therefore a party to which the young Parnell aspired more than ever to belong. Barely a year after his Dublin fiasco accident gave him a further and decisive opportunity. In February 1875 a vacancy occurred in Tipperary. John Mitchel, the Young Ireland leader who had been deported to Tasmania and had then, after escaping, lived for the past quarter-century in America, decided to contest the seat. His intention, if elected, was not to enter parliament but to use the election to remind Ireland that there still existed an alternative policy to the one for which Butt had been campaigning. Mitchel was returned unopposed in what was widely regarded as a symbolic election, but it was ruled by the House of Commons that because he was an undischarged felon he could not take his seat. A new writ was then issued and it was resolved to run Mitchel a second time. In the interval between the two elections Parnell wrote to the *Freeman's Journal*, enclosing a cheque for £25 towards Mitchel's expenses and warmly endorsing his candidature.[17] But when Mitchel arrived in Ireland it was at once clear that he was too ill to do more than make a token appearance and the campaign was managed by two Fenians – John Daly of Limerick and Charles Doran of Queenstown (Cobh), county Cork – and by an intense, romantic young nationalist, John Dillon, the son of another Young Irelander, John Blake Dillon. Mitchel's re-election was a foregone conclusion, but hardly had it happened when he died at his brother's house in Newry. A few days later his old friend and brother-in-law, John Martin, who had collapsed at Mitchel's funeral, also died, thus creating a further vacancy, since he had sat for Meath.[18]

These events had a decisive influence upon Parnell's whole career. In March 1875 the faithful Father Galvin wrote again on his behalf, this time to a Tipperary nationalist, indicating that Parnell would be willing to contest that constituency against any Conservative. Parnell, wrote the priest, was 'up to the mark on all the great questions', which, for Father Galvin, meant Home Rule, denominational education and fixity of tenure. 'He is of considerable property and he has ever been characterized as an excellent humane landlord . . . He is a young man of great industry, great pluck and great promise. I have no doubt he will prove true to the traditions of his family and that he can be entirely depended on.'[19]

Four days later a feeler went out from a different quarter. William Dillon, brother of John Dillon, wrote to a Tipperary friend, W. H. Madden, explaining that he had met Parnell for the first time the previous week and had had several long talks with him. On first acquaintance, he had not been over-impressed. 'His publishing that letter sending £25 towards the expenses of Mr Mitchel's election looked very like an election dodge. However, the more I see of him the more I like him, and I believe he is a very thorough and sincere Home Ruler, very different indeed from the ordinary Whig type.' Dillon had refused to come with him to the constituency, because 'if the Tipperary electors saw me coming down for Parnell after my brother had been down for Mitchel they would very naturally say that "those young Dillons were setting up to dictate to Tipperary"'. Still, he had promised Parnell that he would write preparing the way for him to travel to Tipperary on his own to meet, among others, Charles Doran, and his letter was the fulfilment of that promise.[20]

In making this tentative approach through William Dillon Parnell was deliberately putting himself in touch with 'advanced' nationalists. This was not quite his first excursion in that direction. In 1873, when the idea of standing for parliament first entered his mind, Parnell had a conversation with John Daly, the Limerick Fenian. According to Daly's account (which should be treated with caution as it was only published 30 years afterwards), Parnell, who was apparently even then critical of Butt, asked if he would get the support of militant nationalists if he went up for election. Daly told him that in his view the people who made the most sacrifices – that is, the Fenians – should have the most control. 'You mean', said Parnell, 'that the parliamentary party to get the support of your people ought to be controlled by them.' 'Or rather', replied Daly, 'that the separatists should not allow themselves to be used by the agitators because separation is the clear issue, the other is only windy.' 'Well', Parnell said, 'do you not think any other arrangement could be come to?' 'I do not know of any', was Daly's dismissive answer.[21]

We need not conclude from this conversation, or from Parnell's eagerness to obtain introductions to men like Doran two years later, that he had already moved far to the left of Butt *before* he had even entered parliament, or that this was a preliminary essay in the art of balancing between extremes of which he was later to become a virtuoso. What it does suggest is that at the very outset of his career he had begun to rub up against the problem which the existence of these two competing nationalist traditions would always pose to any Irishman who thought in House of Commons terms. But he was still so naïve and inexperienced that he had certainly no solutions to offer; indeed, it is doubtful if he was then much more than dimly aware of the nature of the dark and complex relationship between physical force and constitutionalism which was to haunt him all his life. It would be unwise to deduce anything positive about his conduct at this early stage except that he was already revealing in the political sphere something of the aggression he had hitherto confined to the cricket field; just as there any means had served to get the other side out, so here any means would serve to get Parnell in.

The Fenians, as it happened, were not prepared to be used for Parnell's personal ends. Madden did arrange to see him in Clonmel – whether or not they actually met we do not know – and he also forwarded William Dillon's letter to Doran to test his reactions.[22] There, it seems, the matter ended. No doors opened in Tipperary, so Parnell turned instead to Meath. And here, in April 1875, he was for the first time returned to the House of Commons.* Whether his ostentatious subscription to the Mitchel fund helped him in Meath more than in Tipperary it is impossible to say. Electors who lacked the refined susceptibilities of the Dillon brothers may have seen it less as 'an election dodge' than as evidence that the young man, landowning Protestant though he might be, was at least sympathetic towards the emotional residues left by Young Ireland and now jealously guarded by the Fenians. It is probable, though, that he owed his success much more to other considerations.

One was the endorsement of his candidature by the Home Rule League. He had been careful to keep himself in the eye of the Home Rulers by attending a land conference in Dublin in February, where he had observed, and no doubt registered, the critical attitude adopted by the tenant-right representatives towards parliamentarians in general and Butt in particular.[23] The other factor contributing directly to his success was the support of the church. This seems not to have come easily, and his brother later recalled that Charles had told him how 'an animated interview' with the bishop was necessary before the clergy

---

*Parnell received 1771 votes. His nearest competitor, a Conservative, got 912 and an independent Home Ruler J. T. Hinds, who was much criticized for splitting the Nationalist vote, came bottom with 138 (*The Times*, 20 April 1875). The Conservative total is given as 902 in *Dod's Parliamentary Companion* for 1876, p112.

were mobilized on his behalf.[24] What finally convinced the bishop we are not told – probably the candidate's 'soundness' on denominational education helped a good deal – but once the word had been given the clergy rallied round in no uncertain style and two surviving letters of Parnell's express his indebtedness and warm appreciation to individual priests.[25] The decisive moment seems to have come on 12 April when he addressed a great meeting in Navan largely attended by parish priests and curates. In addition to denominational education 'under the proper control of the clergy', Parnell advocated the release of political prisoners and a land policy embracing fixity of tenure and fair rents. As for Home Rule, 'since he first could think he had the principles of that movement firmly fixed in his heart, for he always believed that the day would come when the voice of the people in this country would rule her affairs and make her laws and that was what he meant by Home Rule'. This did not stop him adding a flourish decidedly more congenial to the Fenians than to the bishop. 'England should remember the example set by her American colonies and bear in mind that if she refuse to Ireland what her people demand as a right, the day would come when Ireland would have her opportunity in England's weakness.'[26]

The result was announced on 19 April. On 22 April Parnell took his seat in the House of Commons. He arrived at the moment when the new tactics of obstruction, which he himself was to carry to unheard-of lengths, were first put into practice. The previous year the veteran Young Irelander, Joseph Ronayne, had thrown out the suggestion that since Irish business had so often to give way to English business in the House of Commons, it was time for the Irish members to show that they could play the same game. 'Let us therefore interfere in English legislation', Ronayne said, 'let us show them that if we are not strong enough to get our own work done, we are strong enough to prevent them from getting theirs.'[27] His words seemed to have fallen on deaf ears, for neither Butt nor his gentlemanly Home Rulers were prepared to contemplate a policy which, by enraging British MPs, seemed likely to accentuate rather than to diminish the difficulties of getting Irish legislation through parliament.

One member was prepared to take Ronayne's advice seriously. This was Joseph Gillis Biggar. Biggar was a pork-butcher, born in Belfast in 1828, who spoke with a strong northern accent and had a strong northern partiality for getting his own way regardless of appearances. His own appearance was not attractive – he was short, stout and almost a hunch-back – but he had qualities of courage, of forthrightness and of loyalty which made him a good man to have on one's side. More important still, he was at this time a member of the Supreme Council of the Irish Republican Brotherhood. As such, he symbolized the anxiety of some of the more extreme nationalists to move out of the cul-de-sac of abortive revolution towards a more constructive policy, but he symbolized no less the impatience such men were likely to feel with any failure on the part of Butt to secure positive results by his conciliatory attitude in the House of Commons.

During 1874, his first session in parliament, Biggar had made an exploratory and partially successful probe in the general direction of obstruction. But in 1875, and on the day Parnell took his seat, he began to operate on a larger scale. The occasion was a debate on coercion, during which Biggar spoke unaided for four hours. His voice was inaudible and his accent unintelligible, but this was irrelevant, for he had nothing positive to say. His purpose was to consume time and he did that less by his own observations than by copious reading from a formidable array of blue-books. It was in this setting, and on a subsequent night of the debate, that Parnell made his maiden speech. It was scarcely noticed in the general hubbub and was neither better nor worse than most such efforts, but it closed with a sentiment unmistakably aimed at a public outside the walls of the House. 'Why', he asked, 'should Ireland be treated as a geographical fragment of England . . .? Ireland was not a geographical fragment, but a nation.'[28]

This perhaps is the moment to catch a glimpse of him through the eyes of his contemporaries. Most of their accounts were written some years later and when they looked back to his first entry into the arena they tended to do so nostalgically and also, no doubt, with a keen desire to show how much he had subsequently deteriorated. All those who came to know him well agree that the initial impression he made was of a tall, athletic young man who combined a lithe figure with evident good looks. Here is T. P. O'Connor's portrait of him, overdone as was 'T.P.'s' habit, but also perceptive:[29]

Before ill-health lined and hollowed it, his face was one of the handsomest in the House of Commons. The nose was long, large, straight, well-chiselled; the mouth was small and well-carved, but mobile with pride, passion and scorn; the voice was clear, sure and penetrating, and, when he was excited, could be thrilling, so that sometimes you could imagine that it had a power to control and even terrorize, the House of Commons; his forehead was beautiful – perfectly round, white and lofty. But, after all, in looking at him, as in the case of every remarkable man, the eyes were the most striking feature.

They were the most meaning eyes I have ever seen. They were of the hard dark sort, which you see in the Red Indian – red-brown, like flint; but who can describe their varying lights and impressions? Sometimes you thought they never changed, for they certainly never revealed anything; at others they seemed to flash and burn; and they always had a strange glow in them that arrested your attention.

To this portrait of the hero as romantic symbol, we have to add a few more homely touches to come closer to the real man. Justin McCarthy, who served for a long period as Parnell's deputy after the latter had risen to the leadership of the party, lived near him in London during the early days, and invited him many times to his house in Gower Street. He remembered the young Parnell as handsome, tall and stately, but also with 'a singularly sweet and winning smile'. He was an unassuming guest and particularly popular with children. 'I have never in my life met a better-bred man than Parnell', wrote McCarthy, insisting that, so far as his experience went, the legends of Parnell's aloofness and arrogance towards his colleagues were simply legends and no more. Though in this, as in his physical condition, the years were to bring a change for the worse, the evidence is strong that Parnell in his prime was a gentle, lovable man capable of inspiring the most intense affection even amongst people – like McCarthy himself, or that other novelist-journalist, William O'Brien – whose general culture and gifts of intellect were far above his own.[30]

Both those observers were agreed that he was at bottom an intensely private person who hated public speaking and the ordinary cut and thrust of parliamentary life. This seemed to be borne out by the immediate sequel to his maiden speech, which was a prolonged silence. He was completely ignorant of the rules of procedure and did not even know how to ask a parliamentary question, let alone get up on his legs and badger a minister. Later, indeed, he confessed to McCarthy that while he did not mind jumping up to put a spontaneous question in the heat of the moment, it gave him 'a nervous horror' to sit waiting for his name to be called to put a question printed on the notice paper.[31]

Gradually, of course, he acquired a devastating knowledge both of House of Commons technique and of the shortcomings of his fellow Home Rulers. Unobtrusively, also, he began to attract the attention of nationalists who had always looked askance at Butt's ineffectual moderation. For such men Biggar's unorthodox tactics were preferable because they represented an attempt to keep alive the concept of an Ireland which refused to be merely a province of the United Kingdom. And on this tide, which in 1875 had scarcely begun to rise, Parnell with a sure instinct prepared to float. After his first, largely silent, session was over, he appeared as one of the lesser lights at a great amnesty demonstration in Hyde Park where Biggar was the main centre of attention, and a few weeks later told his own constituents that 'what their representatives had to do was to attend to their own business, to watch by day and night over their national interests, and to fear nothing so long as they had the people of Ireland at their back'.[32]

It was fortunate for Parnell that he arrived on the scene at precisely the moment when the inadequacies of Butt's policies and leadership were being so nakedly exposed by his failure to win substantial concessions on the things that really mattered to most people – amnesty, the land, Home Rule. For him, therefore, it was an obvious manoeuvre to ally himself as closely as he could to Biggar and the handful of Irish members – perhaps not more than four or five – who were prepared to act with him in his obstructive campaign. On the eve of the 1876 session he indicated, in his still inarticulate way, the direction he was likely to take when he told a meeting of the Home Rule League in Dublin that it was important for the people of Ireland and their representatives to be 'in earnest' and that they should consider the winning of Home Rule as 'of paramount importance'.[33]

If this was intended as a warning to that numerous body of Home Rule MPs who did not seem to be in earnest about anything, it was not long before Parnell demonstrated still more plainly where his sympathies lay. During the debate on the address he intervened to protest against the omission of any proposals for Irish legislation from the government programme and it was noticeable that his own speech was centred on the demand for amnesty for political prisoners – an indication to the Fenians, if they needed it, that he was a man to watch.[34] For Butt, on the other hand, the session began badly and developed worse. He lost a land bill (with 45 Home Rulers voting *against* it), he was unable to frame a university bill satisfactory to the Irish bishops, and a petition for amnesty in May produced a major scene, when several Irish members demonstrated their support for the men imprisoned in connection with the Manchester rescue in 1867 and also for a prisoner then confined to Dartmoor in harsh conditions after having been convicted of being implicated in gun-running for the Fenians.[35] This was Michael Davitt. His family had been evicted from their holding in Mayo and had emigrated to Lancashire soon after his birth in 1846. There, Davitt lost an arm while working as a child-labourer in a factory. He was attracted to towards the Fenians as a young man, but, although largely self-educated, his qualities of mind and heart were such that he could never become just 'an organization man'. His destiny and Parnell's were to be closely interwoven.

Worse, from Butt's standpoint, even than these outbursts from his left wing, was the uproar provoked by his own innocuous motion demanding legislative independence for Ireland. By an unfortunate error of judgement, Butt left the House after having made his speech. As soon as he had vanished several Irish members delivered themselves of some extremely heterogeneous definitions of Home Rule. The government spokesman, Sir Michael Hicks Beach, had therefore no difficulty in making play with the internal disunity of the Home Rulers, among whom he singled out Parnell for having said (in a speech during the recess) that Home Rule and repeal meant the same thing. Parnell interjected that 'Home Rule would necessarily entail the repeal of the Union', but Hicks Beach brushed this aside, simply pointing out that Butt, whatever his followers might say, did *not* wish to repeal the Union. He then passed on to ridicule the 'extraordinary delusion' that Home Rule could have the effect of liberating 'the Manchester murderers'. Parnell at once cried out 'No! No!' 'I regret to hear', said Hicks Beach, 'that there is an honourable member in this House who will apologize for murder.' To which Parnell replied: 'The right honourable gentleman looked at me so directly when he said that he regretted that any member of this House should apologize for murder, that I wish to say as publicly and directly as I can that I do not believe, and never shall believe, that any murder was committed at Manchester.'[36]

In thus identifying Parnell Hicks Beach had done him an immense service. Within the ordinary conventions of parliamentary life his solemn rebuke to a young member of little more than a year's standing ought to have had a crushing effect. What Hicks Beach failed to realize was that Parnell was not interested in the ordinary conventions of parliamentary life. That something could be done in the House of Commons by making that life difficult for English members he had already grasped. But he had also begun to understand, though as yet dimly, that the Home Rule party, as it was then composed and as it was led by Butt, would never form a truly effective power base. Before his encounter with Hicks Beach, Parnell, by his persistent demand for amnesty for the political prisoners, had shown that he intended to look for his support to a more active and militant section of nationalist opinion. Now a British minister had given him the opportunity to avow his sympathy for the prisoners, and by implication for what they represented, in the most open and decisive manner. English members – and many Irish members too – might be deeply shocked, but the Fenians drew a different conclusion. 'We did not know very much about Parnell at this time', one of them admitted to Barry O'Brien four years later. 'His defence of the Manchester men in the House of Commons was a revelation to us; but we never lost sight of him afterwards, and I think he never lost sight of us.'[37]

III

Almost at once Parnell began to reap his reward. Just as his declaration of support for 'the Manchester men' drew him to the attention of the Fenians, so his growing involvement in Biggar's obstructive tactics gave him a prominence among the Irish members which was soon reflected in his altered position in the party. Even extreme nationalists did not yet openly attack Butt, whose defence of the Fenian prisoners in 1867 was still remembered in his favour, but it was nevertheless significant that in August 1876 a large meeting in Glasgow, with the 'advanced' nationalist John Ferguson in the chair, when it commended those Irish members who had 'stood up so boldly for the Irish people', should have singled out Biggar and Parnell by name.[38]

This was significant principally because it was in Britain rather than in Ireland that Fenians were beginning to take the Home Rule movement seriously enough to consider infiltrating it for their own ends. In Ireland the official IRB line continued to be that constitutional agitation was a deviation in which no true republican should indulge, but across the Irish Sea a less rigid attitude prevailed. When the English Home Rule Confederation (later the Home Rule Confederation of Great Britain) was founded in 1873 to develop the Irish vote in British constituencies as a political force, although Butt was its first president, the secretary was a Fenian, and in the succeeding years two militants, John Ferguson and John Barry, became vice-president and secretary respectively.

It was this pressure group, more or less avowedly republican, which made the running during the parliamentary recess, and it was on their invitation that Parnell and John O'Connor Power (a Fenian who joined the Home Rule party and was in 1877 expelled from the IRB) undertook to visit the United States in the autumn of 1876 to convey to the President a congratulatory address on the centenary of the American Declaration of Independence; the address itself, despite its grandiloquent attribution to 'the Irish people', had in fact been hastily concocted at an informal meeting of Fenians in Dublin.[39]

Before they left, Parnell's new prominence was further emphasized

at a meeting of the Home Rule Confederation in Dublin in August
1876. Butt only attended under pressure and though he was again
elected to the presidency, he was saddled with five vice-presidents of
whom three – Parnell, Biggar and a newcomer, F. H. O'Donnell –
could be classed as extremists within the parliamentary fold, while one,
Ferguson, was an extremist outside the fold. In addition, Butt had to
accept a resolution 'that before adopting a course of action which may
become necessary – namely, withdrawal – it will be expedient for Irish
members to adopt a much more determined attitude in the House of
Commons upon all questions in which Ireland is concerned . . . .'[40]
For the leader, ageing, burdened with debt and in failing health, the
immediate prospect was bleak.

But for Parnell, it could scarcely have been brighter. The trip to
America, though it involved him in a tiresome controversy, carried
with it the priceless boon of publicity in the 'right' quarters. On arriving
in New York he and O'Connor Power obtained with some difficulty an
interview with President Grant. Grant declined to accept the address
from the Irish people on the ground that the proper formalities had to
be observed. 'Vulgar old dog', Charles remarked angrily to his brother
John, who was then staying in a Fifth Avenue hotel with Mrs Parnell
and Fanny. His characteristic reaction was to go off on a family outing
to Philadelphia where they visited the Centenary Exhibition and
Charles, true to form, took particular note of stone-cutting machinery
that might be useful for the Avondale quarries and also of a new style
of roof over a suspension bridge, eventually adapting this for his sawmills and cattle-sheds at home. He then paid another visit to the Virginia
coal-mines and only after this leisurely circuit returned to Washington
to resume his official business.[41] There, he and O'Connor Power were
confronted by the Acting Secretary of State, who insisted that the address
could not be presented except through the British Ambassador. The
latter maintained stolidly that he could not act without instructions.
By this time, the two delegates' small stock of patience had evaporated
and they announced that since they were speaking for the Irish and not
the British people it was none of the Ambassador's business. But the
Acting Secretary, and behind him the President, remained unimpressed.
The address was not accepted and Parnell and O'Connor Power,
though possibly the unconscious victims of Grant's 'know-nothing'
tendencies, gained some useful sympathy from 'advanced' nationalists
both at home and in the United States, who were only too ready to
assume that Britain had intervened to veto the expression of Irish
sentiments on an historic occasion.[42]

Parnell himself then paid out of his pocket for a new address, this time directed to the people, not the President, of the United States, and sailed for home, leaving O'Connor Power to arrange for its presentation to Congress.[43] On landing at Liverpool he delivered probably the most extreme speech he had yet made in public. He was still a wretched speaker, 'constantly stuck for a word', as one who heard him on this occasion remarked. 'I remember a number of us who were on the platform near him would now and then suggest a word to him in the pauses. But he never once took a word from any of us. There he would stand, with clenched fists, which he shook nervously until the word he wanted came.'[44] Part of what he had to say might be described as normal, progressive Home Rule doctrine. It was necessary, he declared, to educate English opinion, but Irishmen living in England must at the same time be wary of joining English political parties and must hold themselves ready to support their fellow-countrymen at home. Then he addressed himself to the usual Fenian accusation – 'that the Home Rule cause is not the cause of Ireland a nation, and that we will degrade our country into the position of a province'. This he absolutely denied in a passage which revealingly indicated how his recent American experience had mingled in his mind with his ancestral Anglo-Irish memories to produce a still naïve, but potentially explosive, mixture:[45]

I have lately seen in the city of New York a review of the militia in which five or six thousand armed and trained men took part . . . If in Ireland we could ever have under Home Rule such a national militia, they would be able to protect the interests of Ireland as a nation, while they would never wish to trespass upon the integrity of the English Empire . . . It was a foolish want of confidence that prevented Englishmen and the English government from trusting Ireland. They know Ireland is determined to be an armed nation, and they fear to see her so, for they remember how a section of the Irish people in 1782, with arms in their hands, wrung from England legislative independence. Without a full measure of Home Rule for Ireland no Irishman would ever rest content.

IV

It was in this more explicitly intransigent mood that he faced the session of 1877, in which, as has been well said, the policy pursued by him and the small group who acted with him 'effectively shattered the Home Rule movement'.[46] To this policy the name 'obstruction' has been generally applied. Obstruction itself was no new thing, for there were precedents stretching back more than 40 years of English parties in opposition doing their utmost to consume parliamentary time in order to deny to ministers the opportunity for legislation to which they objected.[47] But the damage English parties could do to each other and to parliament had ordinarily been limited by the possibility that a fractious opposition might in due course become a responsible government. The advent of a large if loosely organized Irish party in 1874 complicated what had previously been a relatively simple pattern. Such a party was liable not merely to criticize or oppose measures from an alien stand-point, but also to seek to appropriate an increasing amount of parliamentary time for initiating resolutions on policy or actual legislation of its own. And when it is remembered that parliament at this period usually sat for only about half the year, that much of its business was frequently taken after midnight, and that the passage of routine legislation depended upon the forbearance, or tacit co-operation, of the opposition, it will be obvious that here was an undefended flank at which any determined body of Irish members could strike.

Isaac Butt himself had no objection in principle to Irish members arguing Irish cases at great length, still less to their introducing Irish measures even though these had virtually no hope of passing into law. On the contrary, the more this happened, and the greater the bottleneck that then occurred, the better the chance of driving home to English members that the defects in their method of governing Ireland were beginning to be reflected in the increased difficulty of using the House of Commons to govern Britain. What Butt, who had a lawyer's reverence for what were then called 'the forms of the House', did fear was that too much opposition would be counter-productive, evoking from non-Irish members either outright hostility to Irish measures which might be good in themselves if considered rationally, or, at the very least, in-difference and absenteeism. There had been signs of both these kinds of response in 1876. Worse still, the 'half-past twelve' rule, first introduced in 1871 and dropped in 1874, had been brought back again in 1875 for the express purpose of killing Irish bills. The effect of this was that, except for a money bill, no order of the day or notice of motion was to be taken after half-past twelve at night, if a notice of opposition to it had been printed on the notice paper, or if such notice of motion had only been given on the immediately preceding day. As a direct consequence of this, Irish members between 1875 and 1877 suffered the frustration of seeing their projected bills disappear one by one without so much as the courtesy of discussion.

Naturally, this provoked a reaction from the Irish benches. What made the session of 1877 significantly different from the sessions of 1875 and 1876 was that this time the reaction took the form of a systematic campaign against the government. Battle was joined from the moment, on 13 February, that the '12.30' rule was re-enacted. By an operation without precedent in parliamentary history, Parnell and Biggar at once turned the rule against its framers by entering notice of opposition against every important English or Scottish bill in the ministry's programme. This meant that none of this legislation could be proceeded with after 12.30 a.m. on any day on which it was down for debate, and that an Irish member, if sufficiently thick-skinned, could easily block all such measures by the simple expedient of filibustering, or talking them out, until the hour of 12.30 had arrived. On 26 February Parnell torpedoed several government bills in this way, two days later Biggar wrecked an innocuous measure dealing with threshing machines in the same manner, and on 5 March Parnell moved the adjournment of a debate on the army estimates on the ground that he was not being heard with proper attention.

Some of these motions, though not as frivolous as enraged MPs asserted, were indeed obstructive in a retaliatory sense. But Parnell could argue that in other instances his interventions were constructive and genuinely intended to improve legislation before the House. A case in point was the Prisons Bill, to which on 5 April he moved an amendment to the effect that any prisoners convicted of treason-felony, sedition or seditious libel should be treated as first-class misdemeanants. Clearly, he had in mind the Fenians and an Irish audience outside parliament, but the case he made was sufficiently persuasive for his clause to be added to the bill after he had agreed to withdraw treason-felony from his definition.[48]

A week later, however, he and Biggar were in action on the committee stage of the Mutiny Bill in a manner which much more suggested obstruction for obstruction's sake. Parnell and Captain J. P. Nolan (the member who had introduced him to the House and who was to be a lifelong follower) had proposed several amendments which were either rejected or withdrawn. At 1.15 a.m. Biggar moved to report progress (that is, to adjourn the debate) after clause 55. When the government spokesman replied that, since the bulk of the clauses were unopposed, he proposed to carry on up to clause 93, Parnell and Biggar at once countered by speaking at great length on each clause and solemnly dividing the House whenever occasion offered, while the fury of their opponents, who wanted nothing so much as to get home to bed, grew steadily greater. When this was reported to Butt he entered the House in a state of high indignation and delivered a public rebuke to Parnell. 'He was not responsible for the honourable member for Meath, and could not control him. He, however, had a duty to discharge to the great nation of Ireland, and he thought he should discharge it best when he said he disapproved entirely of the conduct of the honourable member for Meath.'[49]

To preserve the façade of party unity Parnell and Biggar momentarily gave way, but this episode, outwardly trivial, was for Butt a long step down the road to ruin. He had committed the unforgivable sin for an Irish nationalist – to condemn a fellow-countryman in a 'foreign' assembly. Parnell ruthlessly exploited his opportunity. Later that same day (13 April) he wrote to his leader asking him one blunt question: 'Is it true that in your concluding remarks this morning in the House, you expressed your belief or opinion that the amendments, which I had intimated my intention of moving on the Mutiny Bill, had no existence?'[50] To this Butt replied agitatedly. 'I cannot charge my memory', he confessed, 'with any expression I may have used in speaking last night . . . If, however, I may assume that in the question you put to me you mean to ask whether I said that *your intention* to move the amendments had no existence, I can at once assure you that I neither said this or anything that could bear such a meaning . . .'[51]

Unhappily for Butt his tormentors were determined not to let the matter rest there. A leading article in the *Freeman's Journal* on 14 April, charging Parnell with having lost his temper in the debate, provoked him into a direct denial. On the contrary, he said, he had willingly withdrawn a reference to the 'disorderly followers' of the government when cautioned that this was not parliamentary language. He then adroitly changed ground to take up again his dispute with Butt who, he said, sided with the government though he had been absent during the evening. This was a damning enough accusation, but Parnell used it to broaden out his argument, warning his countrymen against undue sensitivity to English censure and reminding his leader that the unity of the party, such as it was, was based on an undertaking to act together on Irish affairs, leaving to each Home Ruler the right to act as he pleased on other matters:[52]

The instinct of snobbery, which seems to compel some Irishmen to worship at the shrine of English prejudice, and to bow down before the voice and censure of the English press, will never gain anything for Ireland, and will only secure for such panderers the secret contempt of Englishmen.

England respects nothing but power, and it is certain that the Irish party, comprising, as it does, so many men of talent and ability, might have that power, which attention to business, method and energy, always give, if it would only exhibit these qualities.

Butt himself now inflamed the quarrel when he published a letter he wrote to Parnell on 21 April, admitting that the latter was generally regarded as inaugurating a new Home Rule policy in the House of Commons, but prophesying that this would arouse so much hostility as to diminish such support for Irish claims as already existed there. 'It must', Butt insisted, 'tend to alienate from us our truest and our best English friends. It must waste in aimless and objectless obstruction the time which we might, in some form or another, obtain for the discussion of Irish grievances. It must expose us to the taunt of being unfit to administer even the forms of representative government, and end in discrediting and damaging every movement we make.' But higher than these prudential arguments he set another – 'the duty of maintaining before the civilized world the dignity of the Irish nation and the Irish cause'. This would only be fulfilled if they respected themselves and their obligations to the House of Commons, 'an assembly to degrade which is to strike a blow at representative institutions all over the world'. And Butt achieved a certain dignity of his own when he recalled how he had brought his fellow-countrymen to the view that the only way to redress Irish wrongs was to persuade intelligent Englishmen that Ireland should be left to manage her own affairs. This might have been right or wrong, but it had twice been unanimously approved by conferences representative of the Irish people. 'Do not let us deceive ourselves', he urged. 'Such a policy, and any attempt at a policy of obstruction are not merely different plans – they are diametrically and irreconcilably opposed. The first principle of the one is to conciliate English opinion; that of the other is to defy and exasperate it.'[53]

This produced from Parnell on 24 May a frigid reply, rejecting utterly Butt's interpretation of the obligations of a Home Rule member. Whenever the party had agreed to act together, said Parnell, he had always cheerfully surrendered to the majority will. But when the party had resolved in February 1874 'to obtain unity by taking counsel together', this was never intended to restrict individual liberty of action on matters where it was *not* deemed necessary to take collective action. 'Were it otherwise', he wrote, in an unconscious prophecy of a state of affairs he would later be charged with bringing about, 'the ties of our association would become a degrading tyranny, and it would be in the power of a majority or a leader at any time, without notice, to check and restrain an individual upon any pretence and without just reason.' Then he went over to the attack. Reminding Butt that the previous autumn the Home Rule Confederation had urged on the party a more vigorous policy, he pointed out that despite this the attendance of Irish members had never been so low – seldom exceeding five or six late at night – as in the 1877 session:[54]

> At no time during the session have you shown that you had any policy at all, much less that you were carrying it out 'boldly or actively'. I should have been only too pleased to follow your lead in anything but inactivity and absence from the House. But I think it is sufficiently evident that no steps have been taken by you to carry out the resolution of the convention in which you took a leading part. I, on the other hand, am denounced because I have not joined the majority in doing nothing, in inactivity, in absenteeism – because I have shown the country that they have a power which they know little of, to use if they desire for the enforcement of their just claims.

As the session proceeded, Parnell and his associates, seldom or never more than half a dozen, continued to move their amendments and adjournments, though in May and June all-night sittings were much fewer, probably because the government had become wary of pressing on with its business if Parnell showed signs of opposing it. In July the pace began to quicken, partly because a new recruit, F. H. O'Donnell, had joined the ranks of the obstructionists. O'Donnell was a product of the Queen's College, Galway and, adept at foreign languages, had become a frequent contributor on European questions to the English press. Quick-witted, pugnacious, dandiacal in appearance, he somewhat despised the rank-and-file Irish members and boasted freely of his superior cultural attainments. He was, in fact, an egomaniac of a particularly virulent kind. Years later, long after he had left politics and after Parnell was dead, he published a so-called *History of the Irish parliamentary party*, intended to prove that he, O'Donnell, had invented obstruction and that Parnell was his grateful and dim-witted accomplice. This was palpably not true, but O'Donnell did bring flair and style, and much greater fluency, to the obstructionist group.

Parnell himself continued to claim that he was not seeking to obstruct simply for the sake of obstruction, though he warned that if the House of Commons persisted in thwarting the demands of Ireland, the Irish people would have to consider whether their representatives 'should not next session enter upon a deliberate course of obstruction of English measures'.[55] Before the time came for that decision, the 1877 session reached its angry climax. It would seem, from Parnell's public statements, that he was spoiling for a fight even before the climactic moment arrived. At the end of June he gave a lecture – in fact a harangue – on the subject of 'Parliamentary Behaviour', ostensibly to raise funds for a Catholic school in Hatton Garden. In this he developed a theme which for the rest of his career was to reappear at intervals in his speeches and writings – the danger of political, and even social, corruption that always threatened an Irish party in the alien atmosphere of London:[56]

> . . . There were [he said] contaminating influences in the House of Commons which required to be guarded against. Had the Irish members done their duty they would have proved that there was a power in them superior to those influences; but they had been allowed to do as they pleased. It pleased some to return to Ireland to attend to their own private affairs; it pleased more to make themselves slaves to English members; while others adopted the tone of the House of Commons, and the constituencies had better not have returned such men to the House of Commons.

This outspoken attack on the majority of the Home Rule party was followed by an undisguised criticism of Butt. Speaking at Liverpool, Parnell claimed that he and his friends could have done far more were it not for the exceptional position in which they stood with regard to the leader of the Irish party. And he then made much the most open bid for Fenian support he had yet permitted himself:[57]

> . . . What did they ever get in the past by trying to conciliate them? Did they get the abolition of tithes by the conciliation of their English taskmasters? No; it was because they adopted different measures. Did O'Connell gain Emancipation for Ireland by conciliation? . . . Catholic Emancipation was gained because an English king and his ministers feared revolution. Why was the English church in Ireland disestablished and disendowed? Why was some measure of protection given to the Irish tenant? It was because there was an explosion at Clerkenwell and because a lock was shot off a prison van in Manchester [*great applause*]. They would never gain anything from England unless they trod upon her toes – they would never gain a single sixpennyworth from her by conciliation.

With Parnell in this mood a crisis could have come at any time and on any subject. In fact it came on 25 July and on an imperial issue, the

South Africa Bill intended to legalize the annexation of the Transvaal. It was a measure which disturbed the conscience of some English members and they joined with Parnell and his group in adopting delaying tactics in committee. Parnell was subjected to constant haranguing and, raising his voice almost to a shriek against the baying of infuriated members, did at last let fall a remark which seemed to indicate a deliberate intention to obstruct. 'As it was with Ireland', he said passionately, 'so it was with the South African Colonies . . . Therefore, as an Irishman, coming from a country that had experienced to its fullest extent the results of English interference in its affairs and the consequences of English cruelty and tyranny, he felt a special satisfaction in preventing and thwarting the intentions of the government in respect of this Bill.'[58]

The Chancellor of the Exchequer, Sir Stafford Northcote, seized on this expression and moved that it be 'taken down', to form the basis for the extremely serious charge of contempt. The member for Meath then withdrew to the gallery and watched with amusement while it was pointed out to the Chancellor and his irate supporters that Parnell had not said that he would thwart the *business of the House*, but only *the intentions of the government*. Since this was a perfectly legitimate function of opposition, he was able to resume his place and to keep the House out of bed until 5.45 a.m. by moving yet more amendments. The natural consequence was a further alteration of the rules of procedure, but although two resolutions were adopted on 27 July with the intention of limiting severely the number of times a member could be heard in any specific debate, the sequel showed that this was quite inadequate. As Butt himself prophetically warned Northcote, Parnell and his allies would be 'quite capable of organizing relays of obstructives within the terms of the resolution'.[59]

This was exactly what occurred. The new rules did not prohibit either the moving of amendments or the making of immensely long speeches and with zest Parnell and six other Irish members applied themselves to obstructing the final stages of the South Africa Bill. The sitting which ensued was without parallel in the history of parliament. From 5.15 p.m. on 31 July until 2.10 in the afternoon of 1 August these seven Irishmen held out against some 300 British members. They were worn down in the end by sheer weight of numbers, but not until the House had sat continuously for no less than 45 hours, 21 of which had been occupied by this single piece of obstruction.[60]

V

That was the last manifestation of the session, for parliament was prorogued a few days later. But it was obvious that the matter could not rest there. Butt had appeared briefly in the middle of the night while the filibuster was in full spate, had remonstrated with the obstructors, and then vanished again, an impotent shadow of his former self. His personal position was seriously weakened, not merely by the fact that his health was failing but because, of the fifteen Irish bills proposed at the beginning of the session, not a single one had passed into law when parliament dispersed for the recess. As against this, the obstructors were a tiny minority and Parnell's contemptuous language and attitude towards the majority of his so-called colleagues had enraged many of them. Already, at a stormy meeting of the party on 27 July, before the main crisis had broken, Butt had threatened to resign if obstruction continued; there were even rumours that he contemplated the expulsion of Parnell, O'Donnell and O'Connor Power.[61] A further meeting to consider the question was arranged for 6 August and when that date came round the obstructionists had demonstrated in the all-night sitting of 31 July–1 August that they intended to go on as before. Only twenty members, including Parnell and Biggar, attended on 6 August and a number of others stayed away with intent. The proceedings began in acrimony and ended in confusion. Two of the conspicuous absentees proposed a resolution, believed to have been inspired by Butt, censuring the conduct of Parnell and Biggar. A moderate, William Shaw, proposed that no decision be taken until after a national conference had been held in the autumn, but no one was in the mood to listen to compromise and he left in disgust. Butt thereupon declared his intention of resigning unless the party agreed to be guided by him, but he had so little control that the two sections almost came to blows in his presence. In the end, the meeting broke up without taking a decision, but with bitter enmity having been so bleakly displayed that the Home Rule party as an entity may be said to have ceased to exist from that moment.[62]

There now began an even more crucial battle – the battle to capture Irish public opinion. In this contest the scales were heavily weighted in Parnell's favour and it was he who led off with a widely publicized letter to *The Times* – which was both a reasoned defence of his parliamentary conduct and a criticism of the majority of his own party. On the first count, he was as concerned as ever to make the point that his obstructionism was intended to be, and frequently was, constructive.

It was true that he had been responsible for late-night sittings, but at least he worked during those sittings, which was more than most of his critics could claim, and by so working, he argued, he had been able to prevent the legislative errors which were liable to occur in measures rushed through late at night without adequate debate. But then he laid aside the tone of sweet reasonableness and struck a more familiar note:[63]

> There seems a disposition to indict me for something. Is it for not being as other members are? I have not been as other members are. I have worked in the House instead of stopping in Ireland or amusing myself in London . . . I have studied the measures submitted to the House and endeavoured to improve them, instead of blindly voting without knowledge or caring anything about the question. But I have done worse than this. There is an unwritten law, hitherto acquiesced in by the Irish members, that no Irish may interfere in English and imperial concerns – at any rate, if they do, their interference must be in homeopathic doses, well covered up with sugar. I have transgressed this law. I have taken a part in those English matters when I have thought it right to do so, and have not troubled myself about the sugar.

This was not just affectation. Parnell did have a genuine interest in his role as the member of an imperial parliament and the time was to come when this would seem to some observers almost to transcend his desire to obtain an Irish parliament, but in 1877 it was not exactly easy to see him as a model legislator. Nor did he do much to encourage the notion. He had not, he admitted, realized just how much his actions would irritate English members, but the realization did not discompose him. 'I did not think myself called on to refrain from acting on English questions for fear of any annoyance the English might feel, any more than the English have ever felt called on to refrain from interfering in our concerns for fear of any annoyance we might feel.'

Declarations on paper were all very well in their way, but votes were what counted most and votes could only be won in Ireland. Thither Parnell repaired without delay and on 21 August received a rapturous welcome in Dublin when he appeared at a large demonstration in the Rotunda. His speech was brief, awkwardly delivered, but burning with conviction. His tumultuous reception, he truly said, was 'because Irishmen always support those who have been surrounded by many enemies'. But enemies within or without would not prevent him from continuing with the policy of obstruction. 'I care nothing', he declared, 'for this English parliament, nor for its outcries. I care nothing for its existence, if that existence is to continue a source of tyranny and destruction to my country.'[64]

This was, or seemed, the language of extremism and once more it riveted the attention of the Fenians upon the member for Meath, this time with important consequences. On 27 and 28 August the Home Rule Confederation of Great Britain held its annual convention at Liverpool. Butt, as president, took the chair on the morning of the first day, but in the afternoon left for London 'on business' after what was described as a 'friendly interchange of opinion' on the active policy. Late that evening at a public meeting his name was received with hisses whereas Parnell's was loudly cheered. Next day, on the motion of John Barry, Parnell was elected to the presidency of the Confederation for the coming year, and Butt thus suffered the humiliation of being publicly deposed. Parnell's biographer, R. B. O'Brien, later obtained an account of this episode from John Barry himself – thinly disguised in the biography as 'X' – but part of this at least was mythical. Barry described with pathos how, having first elevated Butt to the presidency, he had now to steel himself to replace him, and how, when the deed was done, he accompanied the poor old man to the door, expressing his regrets all the while. 'He turned round; his eyes were filled with tears, as he said in the most touching way, "Ah! I never thought the Irish in England would do this to me".'[65] The only thing wrong with this poignant story is that it could not have happened, for the simple reason that Butt was in London at the time.[66] This casts doubt on Barry's general credibility, though when he describes Parnell on the same occasion as 'looking like a bit of granite', and when he recalls him as saying in private, with that effect of suppressed energy he so often gave at this period, that 'something striking must be done', the portrait is at least recognizable. Indeed, it is confirmed to some extent by another contemporary, and less committed, view of Parnell at that critical moment in his fortunes.[67]

This fair well-dressed and well-brushed slender young man is a gentleman every inch of him and the very opposite of an eccentric. He does not need translating. Other [sic] English gentlemen can understand him. At least they can understand everything about him except his pale fanaticism . . . There is no charm in what Mr Parnell says . . . But there is an undoubted power in the clear and grinding sincerity of his manner which is all the more remarkable because this fragile-looking, quiet gentleman is obviously intended by nature for a very modest place in the background.

Having captured the Confederation, Parnell and his allies now turned
their attention to the Home Rule League. Here, however, Butt, though
weakened in health and reputation, was prepared to make some kind
of stand. In September 1877 he published a manifesto defending his
record and attacking obstruction as 'the abandonment of constitutional
action and the adoption of unconstitutional action in its stead'.[68] But
what alternative had he himself to offer? Even those who still regarded
him as an indispensable leader began to urge him to abandon conciliation and adopt a policy of what might be called selective obstruction.
Yet he was as difficult as ever to pin down. At a party meeting in October,
where moderates and militants predictably collided, he did indeed
succeed in winning another twelve months for conciliation, but this
was only because nobody cared to incur the odium of finally splitting
the party. Parnell was not yet ready for an open break and almost
contemptuously agreed to paper over the cracks, while asserting his
right to go on as before. 'Whether you call that a policy of obstruction
or not, I am perfectly satisfied, for I do not think there is a virtue in
a name; but I think it should be a policy of energy, of activity, and
of opposition to the bad measures of every government in detail and
generally until they consent to settle the question we have at heart.'[69]

The child of this compromise was stalemate, as was amply demonstrated by the Home Rule League's national conference early in 1878.
Butt certainly lost ground at that conference – not least through trying
to cancel it altogether because of the eastern crisis caused by the Russo-
Turkish war – and the anodyne motions actually passed had little
meaning. The only moment reality threatened to break in was when
John Dillon moved a resolution calling upon the party to leave the House
of Commons in a body if a division were to be taken on the Balkan
question, and thus to show that Ireland had 'no community of interest'
with England in her dealings with foreign powers. Butt was horrified,
and begged Dillon not to press a motion which, if passed, would be
'the death-knell of the Home Rule party'. How could any responsible
party pledge itself in advance to such action when so much depended
on context? If, for example, 'there was in the Queen's Speech that the
government were prepared to grant Home Rule for Ireland . . . do you
mean to say, if you were able by a party vote to keep them in power
you would not do it?' It was a valid point and Parnell shrewdly intervened
with an anodyne solution recommending that, should the eastern
question be raised, members should 'consult together and carry out as a
party a united line of policy and action'. He himself was not prepared
to force the pace, as he made clear with his usual stony objectivity.

'If', he said, 'I refrain from asking the country today by the voice of this conference to adopt any particular line of action or any particular policy, I do so solely because I am young and can wait.'[70]

This did not mean that he had changed his mind, only that a conference organized by the Home Rule League was not the arena in which he wished to fight. As for the views he really held, he had already expressed them in a visit to Mayo before Christmas, when he strikingly anticipated a phrase he was to make famous in the years ahead. 'Let no man', he said, 'assign a *ne plus ultra* to the march of our nation.' And he added: 'You know that I am pledged to obtain for Ireland the right of national self-government; that I have promised to use every endeavour to secure for the tiller of the soil the fruits of his industry; and that I believe in the right of every Irish parent to educate his children according to his conscience and his religious convictions; and I am at present engaged in helping to direct the attention of the English House of Commons to these questions. How can we best secure that attention? I think by compelling it.'[71] So thought others also. And as Parnell moved forward into 1878, no longer a political tyro, but manifestly the only alternative leader to Isaac Butt, certain significant movements in the shadows suggested that those who believed the whole constitutional movement to be a sham or a farce when divorced from the roots of power, were about to reach out and claim him for their own.

CHAPTER 3

Rising High

'He has many of the qualities of leadership – and time will give him more. He is cool – extremely so and resolute.' (J. J. O'Kelly to John Devoy, 5 August 1877. *Devoy's post bag*, i, 267–8.)

I

The deadlock between Butt and Parnell which the Home Rule conference had confirmed meant inevitably that the two wings of the Irish party would drift further apart during 1878. What was less clear was how much support Parnell would have in Ireland if a general election came while he was still struggling to achieve an ascendancy within that party, or if the policy of obstruction were to be thwarted either by government action or by the physical inability of himself and his colleagues to stand the strain indefinitely. He needed, in short, to broaden his base and, in the Irish context at that time, this could only be by looking towards the more 'advanced' nationalists who, for the most part, remained sceptical of the value of parliamentary action.

But this carried with it the obvious danger that the effect of broadening the base might be less to attract Fenians towards constitutionalism than to distract Parnell from the House of Commons. Much therefore depended upon the kind of relationship he established with these militants in the crucial years of 1878 and 1879. The Fenians had already brought him to the presidency of the Home Rule Confederation, but nobody knew better than Parnell that the issue would really be decided in Ireland. His first instinct was to try to strengthen the extremist element within the parliamentary party. As early as 1877 he sought to enlist the Fenian, Charles Doran of Queenstown. 'I think', he wrote to William Dillon, 'with twenty such men here we can have things at our mercy.'[1] Doran was not to be had, but a few months later Parnell turned to John Dillon, William's brother, for help in finding a suitable candidate for Clare.[2] Significantly, John Dillon gave his full co-operation, since, as he put it in his diary, the question now was 'how to make Parnell's policy the national platform without giving any room for a split'.[3]

The outcome was the election of the old adventurer, the O'Gorman Mahon, who had entered politics in O'Connell's time and in a short while was to be the indirect and uncomprehending instrument that was to change Parnell's whole life.

Just at the moment Parnell was concentrating his attention on these constituency matters, he met for the first time a man who was to become one of his most devoted friends and who did more perhaps than anyone else to introduce him to the inner circle of Fenianism. This was James J. O'Kelly, a Dubliner by birth (he was a year older than Parnell) and by profession a soldier of fortune turned journalist. He had joined the IRB in 1860 and became a member of the Supreme Council in 1867, working closely with Michael Davitt in the business of procuring arms until the latter's arrest in 1870. O'Kelly was bi-lingual in French and English and a close friend of the French politician, Henri Rochefort. He was an altogether formidable man, of bristling appearance and incisive utterance; his loyalty to Parnell, once given, was absolute.

O'Kelly's first meeting with his future chief seems to have been in Paris. He had gone there at the end of July or early in August 1877 on newspaper business and also to visit the exiled Fenian, John O'Leary. At the latter's hotel, O'Kelly bumped into Biggar and Parnell who, it appeared, were anxious to confer with O'Leary. O'Kelly was not much taken with Biggar, but was immediately impressed by Parnell. Writing to his friend, John Devoy, in New York, he singled out Parnell as a natural leader. 'He has the idea I held at the starting of the Home Rule organization – that is the creation of a political link between the conservative and radical nationalists . . . The effect of Parnell's attitude has been simply tremendous and if he were supported by twenty or thirty instead of seven he could render really important services.' Then followed the phrases about Parnell's coolness and resolution quoted at the head of this chapter. 'With the right kind of support behind him', O'Kelly insisted, 'and a band of real nationalists in the House of Commons he would so remould Irish public opinion as to clear away many of the stumbling blocks in the way of progressive action.'[4]

A few days later they met again, this time in London, and O'Kelly found Parnell, as before, 'a good fellow', though 'I am not sure he knows exactly where he is going'. However, he was 'the best of the parliamentary lot' and if he went to America he should be seen and spoken to. 'I have always tried to convince you', he told Devoy, 'of the great moral effect of having Ireland represented by men like Parnell, O'Donnell and Biggar even if they were not prepared to advance one step further and I hope recent events [the obstruction of the South Africa Bill] have convinced you of the correctness of my views. There are many advantages to be gained even at Westminster by a really bold and independent Irish representation and I hope the American-Irish will extend help and encouragement to Parnell and his co-workers.'[5]

Apart from the light these letters throw upon the way in which Parnell's tactics and attitudes combined to influence a strong Fenian in his favour, their main importance lies in their timing and in the fact that they were addressed to a man whose background to some extent resembled O'Kelly's, but whose authority among Irish-American Fenians stood much higher. Devoy was born near Dublin in 1842 and in 1861 had joined both the IRB and the French Foreign Legion, deserting from the latter when the prospects of revolution at home seemed to grow brighter. He then involved himself in the dangerous business of trying to swear into the IRB Irish soldiers from British regiments stationed in Dublin. He was also an active member of the group which produced the Fenian paper, the *Irish People*, and he was largely instrumental in rescuing the Fenian chief, James Stephens, from Richmond jail in November 1865. A few months later Devoy himself was arrested and imprisoned for his part in these events. Released after five years, he went to America and became, like O'Kelly, a journalist in the empire of James Gordon Bennett, the owner of the New York *Herald*. Devoy at once plunged into revolutionary politics and though his bitter tongue brought him many enemies, his dour fanatical tenacity, combined with considerable organizing ability, gave him immense prestige.

The timing of O'Kelly's letters to Devoy was significant because they coincided with a critical phase in the evolution of Irish-American nationalism. After the fiasco of 1867 the Fenians in America regrouped into a new and more effective secret organization, the Clan na Gael, which rapidly came to be dominated by Devoy and another Irish-American, William Carroll, a doctor in Philadelphia. By 1877 the Clan numbered about 10,000 and was sufficiently important for a joint revolutionary directory to be established in that year consisting of three representatives of the home organization, the IRB, three representatives of the Clan, and a seventh chosen by the other six members. At that time, the Clan's policy was still the traditional one of planning another insurrection in Ireland, preferably at a moment when – as during the crisis precipitated by the Russo-Turkish war of 1877 – Britain was preoccupied with foreign difficulties.

The Clan, though the most prominent of Irish-American organizations, did not monopolize the scene. On the one hand there was the preponderant mass of Irish-Americans, who were either non-political and wholly absorbed in making good in their adopted country, or, if political, were obedient to their church and careful to steer clear of revolutionary conspiracies. On the other was that small but desperate minority – of whom another old Fenian, O'Donovan Rossa, was the archetypal figure – who thought the Clan too gradualist and pinned their hopes on terrorism, financed from 1875 by the so-called 'Skirmishing Fund'. This Fund was later virtually taken over by Devoy and his friends, but that did not eliminate terrorism and within the Clan itself the proponents of an active 'dynamite' policy were far from negligible.[6]

O'Kelly's report of his conversation with Parnell thus came at a moment when the leaders of 'active' Irish-American nationalism were assessing a situation which seemed to hold out promise of positive achievement, provided they could devise a policy that would enlist substantial support from Irishmen at home and in the United States. But it was by no means evident that any policy the Clan was likely to embrace, and which would have as its *sine qua non* the complete independence of Ireland, would necessarily lead to an accommodation with Parnell. William Carroll, for example, while conceding that if Parnell came to America he should be got into 'regular work', did not regard parliamentary obstruction as coming within that definition.[7] Yet, ironically enough, it was Carroll who took an important step towards narrowing the gap between Parnell and the Clan. In December 1877 he arrived in France, mainly for the purpose of conferring with representatives of the IRB. And from France he travelled to Ireland, where he had an interview with Parnell under strangely dramatic circumstances.

Towards the end of December a few Fenian prisoners had been released by the government, and it was decided to hold a modest reception for them on their return to Ireland in mid-January 1878. The arrangements were carried out jointly by the Fenians and by Parnell and his friends. After the party had been met at Kingstown they were escorted to Morrison's Hotel in Dawson Street, where Parnell always stayed when in Dublin. There, one of the group, former Colour Sergeant Charles McCarthy, overcome by the occasion and weakened by the rigours of prison life, collapsed and died in Parnell's presence.[8] Another of the ex-prisoners there was Michael Davitt, released from Dartmoor on ticket-of-leave. For the first time the Fenian man of the people came face to face with the Home Rule aristocrat. Davitt was deeply impressed by what, much later, he called 'the power and directness' of Parnell's personality. 'An Englishman of the strongest type, moulded for an Irish purpose' was his inward verdict, as he listened to

Parnell speaking about obstruction and also, with great compassion, about the ordeal of imprisonment. 'I would not face it', Davitt remembered him saying. 'It would drive me mad. Solitude and silence are too horrible to think of. I would kill a warder and get hanged rather than have to endure years of such agony and possible insanity.'[9]

Parnell's plan had been to give the released Fenians breakfast and, learning that Carroll was only a few doors away in the Hibernian Hotel, he invited him to join them. But Carroll, with the ingrained secrecy of the professional revolutionary, preferred to remain unnoticed. After breakfast, and McCarthy's tragic death, Parnell went round to the Hibernian and talked with the American emissary. We have only Carroll's account of what passed, and as that was written 30 years later, it must be regarded as suspect; moreover, Parnell himself had been deeply affected by the scene he had just witnessed and may, momentarily, have been off balance. At any rate, when Carroll asked him if he was in favour of absolute independence for Ireland, he replied – or so Carroll recollected – that he was. But he added a characteristic proviso to this uncharacteristic frankness when he said that 'so soon as the people so declared he would go with them'. Since 'the people' then showed no inclination whatever to declare for independence through armed revolt, this was a considerable reservation. Carroll, however, ignored it, and merely told what he presumed to be a new recruit that they (the Clan) would be Parnell's friends and would ask their friends 'to support him in all he did towards that end'. 'I met him several times afterwards in London', Carroll recorded, 'always on the most friendly terms and with the same understanding.'[10]

Of one of these meetings, held in March 1878, we have three different accounts – one a report from Carroll to Devoy written at the time, one given some years later to Barry O'Brien by J. J. O'Kelly, and one printed by F. H. O'Donnell in his *History of the Irish parliamentary party*, published in 1910. The meeting seems to have been a quite formal conference between Parnell, O'Kelly and O'Donnell on the one side, and on the other, Carroll, John O'Leary and the secretary of the Supreme Council of the IRB, John O'Connor. Carroll's judgement, as he sent it to Devoy in their unsophisticated code, was that 'Emerson' (Parnell), 'Jamison' (O'Donnell) and two other MPs (almost certainly including Biggar) 'express themselves at the firm's [i.e. the Clan's] service for anything they can do in their line'. Devoy himself later recorded in his memoirs the belief that Parnell would have been prepared to come to some definite understanding with Carroll, but that this was prevented by a violent quarrel between O'Leary and O'Kelly on the subject of O'Connor Power (who, with Biggar, had been expelled from the Supreme Council the previous August).[11] On the face of it this is unlikely, and Devoy's memoirs are notoriously unreliable. From the other two accounts it appears that Parnell for the most part preserved an impressive silence, as did Carroll, and that much of the talking was done by O'Donnell, whose flamboyant personality predictably grated on the nerves of John O'Leary. As for Parnell's own view, if O'Donnell is to be trusted, he merely remarked after the conference, 'The Fenians want to catch us but they are not going to.'[12] This corresponds closely enough to the cautious attitude one would have expected him to adopt, but it also incidentally demonstrates how far on occasion he was prepared to stray from the truth, when he testified eleven years later before the Special Commission that it was not until his own visit to America in 1880 that he learned that Carroll, whom he admitted to knowing well, was connected with the Clan na Gael.[13] Had Parnell been so preternaturally innocent as this, even at the outset of his career, the Fenians would not have considered it worthwhile to take the close interest in him which in those years they unquestionably did.

II

His own interest remained firmly centred on the House of Commons. The uneasy compromise of January 1878 began to break down once the parliamentary session got under way and the fact that the ailing Butt was absent more often than ever only emphasized the contrast between his ineffectual leadership and the energy of the young men who were ready to supplant him. In April he offered to resign, but was persuaded to hold out for the remainder of the session, chiefly because it was impossible for the party as a whole to agree upon a successor. Parliamentary absenteeism grew steadily grosser and it was left to the Parnellite group to make what running they could.

But they remained relatively quiet and there were no major crises like those of the previous session. For this there were good enough reasons. Anxious as he was to broaden the base of his movement, Parnell was reluctant to incur the odium of obstruction unless it would contribute to that purpose. The eve-of-session conference had shown that he could not carry the majority of the party with him in an active policy and there was little point in wasting effort on such a policy until a general election had swept the old-style nominal Home Rulers out of their seats. Furthermore, since he was also coquetting with the Fenians, it was inadvisable to play his parliamentary role too vigorously, lest he attract the criticism of those for whom the House of Commons was still the supreme source of contamination.

Yet the Fenians represented only one strand in the complex web of Irish nationalism and it is remarkable evidence of how early in his career Parnell began to evolve the policy of balance which he later personified, that when in 1878 he did make up his mind to attack the government he should have done so in an area – the Irish educational estimates in general and the vote for the Queen's Colleges in particular – which was best designed to attract the sympathy of that section of Irish opinion at the furthest remove from the Fenians, that is to say the Catholic hierarchy. It seems indeed that the mere indication that he was considering an all-out campaign on the education estimates was an important factor in prompting the government to introduce in 1878 the first piece of constructive Irish legislation it had vouchsafed after four years of office. The main purpose of the measure was to establish an Irish Intermediate Board, financed by an endowment, not to exceed one million pounds, taken from the Church Temporalities Fund, and empowered to make grants to affiliated schools on the basis of a standard intermediate examination. In effect, this amounted to an indirect subsidy to church schools, and although it inflicted on future generations of Irish children the grisly regime of 'payment by results', its educational deficiences were held to be balanced by the fact that it was at least evidence that the government was willing to make a concession in a sphere where concessions counted for much.[14]

Unfortunately, though this was substantially an agreed measure, it became a bone of contention between the two wings of the Irish party. Isaac Butt, in a pathetic attempt to claim credit for a reform which had been engineered almost entirely without reference to him, not only corresponded agitatedly with the Chief Secretary, but boasted in the House of Commons of having done so. Now this, as he had apparently forgotten, was a clear breach of the resolution of the party conference of February 1874 that 'we should collectively and individually hold ourselves aloof from, and independent of, all party combinations, whether of ministerialists or of the opposition'.[15] Very soon it was to be made a principal charge against him in the final onslaught which effectually ended his career, but at the time its chief result was to thwart Parnell's scheme to use obstruction so as to keep the government up to the mark. Explaining to Dillon his intention to delay the Queen's Colleges' estimates until after the bill was safely through, he warned him that 'Butt, of course, as usual will want to surrender everything'.[16] And two weeks later a bitter letter confirmed that Butt's arrival at the last minute had wrecked his plans. 'He, I have reason to believe, has persuaded the Chancellor to take these estimates on Monday and has promised him there shall be no opposition.' 'It is madness', he wrote angrily, 'to throw away our weapons before we have won our battle.'[17]

This was but a dress rehearsal for the storm which arose over 'Beaconsfieldism' in foreign policy. Here was a matter on which Irish opinion was deeply moved, partly because the natural 'Christian' line was to oppose the pro-Turkish policy of the government and also, no doubt, because in some quarters what seemed likely to be the actual embroilment of Britain in the Balkan crisis resurrected once more the familiar if fugitive hope that England's difficulty might be Ireland's opportunity. When in July the Liberal leader, Lord Hartington, brought in a motion of censure on the government, Butt caused the utmost offence by speaking according to his conscience and praising ministers for resisting Russian pressures in the eastern Mediterranean. To add insult to injury, one of the principal 'obstructives', F. H. O'Donnell, also took a high imperial line in the debate. Both men instantly became the target for abuse. 'Were they drunk or mad?' asked one angry correspondent, writing to the *Nation*. 'Then, with one accord, and with bitter indignation, we exclaimed "No! not drunk nor mad, but the veriest pair of renegades".'[18]

It was clear then that from the beginning of the 1878 session to the end, there was little to be hoped for from the Irish parliamentary party. But it was no less clear that although the Home Rule League in Ireland was practically defunct, and had virtually to disband its organization before the year was out, the Parnellites were still unable to dominate it. It was hardly surprising, therefore, that Parnell, speaking at St Helen's in Lancashire in May, should have admitted to his audience that those who felt a lack of confidence in constitutional action were 'fully justified'. Typically, his own response to what he himself agreed was a totally unsatisfactory situation, was ambivalent. One of two things, he thought, must happen. Either the Irish members would be expelled in a body from the House, 'which would be equivalent to sending them all back to Ireland, and holding their own parliament in Ireland, and thus they would be themselves repealing the Union', or else the government would feel compelled to make it in the interest of the Irish members to facilitate parliamentary business by passing beneficial Irish measures.[19]

The ambiguity of this passage may partly have been due to the fact that the Intermediate Education Bill had still to be introduced at the time he spoke, but there was an inner meaning to Parnell's words which only one man in his audience was in a position to appreciate. That man was Michael Davitt, who had travelled with him to the meeting. After his release Davitt had taken up the threads of his IRB connection where he had been obliged to drop them in 1870 and on the journey to St Helen's he apparently asked Parnell to join the revolutionary organization, but not, he quickly made clear, to take any 'silly oath of secrecy'. It must be stressed that we have only Davitt's retrospective account of what took place between them and that Davitt had a strong tendency to interpret his own attitudes and ideas at this crucial moment in his history in the light of subsequent events. There is no solid reason for supposing that, though prison had undoubtedly matured and deepened him, it had dramatically changed his thinking. He was still in essence a straightforward Fenian with his gaze set on an ultimate insurrection in arms towards which he would do his bit, as hitherto, by helping the IRB to accumulate the weapons it needed. But the account he published nearly 30 years later in *The fall of feudalism in Ireland* reads quite differently. According to this, he wanted to recreate the organization on a smaller, more selective basis. 'Conspiracy and arms' should not be the sole work of such an organization. 'The first line of defence ought to be an open movement on constitutional lines.' 'This', so he claims to have told Parnell, 'should be made to unite all men of separatist principles, and not to exclude honest, moral-force advocates.' And then he went on to adumbrate a policy about which much more was to be heard before the year was out. 'There must', he allegedly said, 'be more immediate issues put before the people', for example a war against landlordism, better housing for the labourers, above all penetration of all elected bodies from parliament to munici-palities, by men of separatist convictions not openly identified with the Fenians. An Irish party of this calibre would, at the right moment, be able to demand the repeal of the Union, and, in case of refusal, to 'leave the House of Commons in a body and return to Ireland, summon a national convention and let the members of the party go into session as an informal legislative assembly'.

To all of this Parnell listened, says Davitt, in dead silence, which he then broke with a single deflating question: 'And what next?' Davitt does not tell us how he replied to that, recording merely that Parnell 'slowly but clearly' said that he would never join any political society and that he still believed good work could be done in parliament provided the right kind of men were sent there. As for the 'stronger programme', with this, seemingly, he agreed, especially in regard to the land question. But Davitt's suggestion of a secession from parliament he shrugged aside with the kindly remark that perhaps their present policy of obstruction would cause them to be suspended anyway. 'In which event', he added indulgently, 'we could then give your informal Irish parliament a chance.'[20]

It is impossible to tell how much, if any, of this conversation followed the pattern Davitt describes. Almost certainly, his specific proposals represent a projection backwards from a position he actually reached somewhat later. On the other hand, it is not inherently improbable that the Fenian and the parliamentarian should have discussed their different modes of operation and the feasibility of some kind of collaboration between them – this, after all, seems to have been at least intermittently in Parnell's mind since his conversation with John Daly in 1873. If their talk did turn in that direction, then what Parnell is made to say is not out of character. Quite the reverse, it is consistent with the line he was to follow repeatedly in the months and years ahead – that he would not readily acknowledge the failure of constitutional action until it had been thoroughly tested, but if it was then found wanting he would consult with the Irish people about what should take its place.

Meanwhile, Davitt went to America where he speedily fell under the influence of John Devoy. Devoy, though still wedded to the ideal of independence, was coming round to the view, which he aired publicly in September 1878, that the abolition of landlordism was the indispensable preliminary to that objective.[21] In private also he obtained the agreement of the Clan na Gael leaders to this widening-out of their traditional aim.[22] Davitt, despite his later claims that he had anticipated this trend while still in prison, seems actually to have been more 'orthodox' than Devoy at the outset. However, by October, speaking at Brooklyn in the presence of a formidable Irish-American journalist, Patrick Ford, whose *Irish World* was then pursuing a virulent anti-landlord line, Davitt came out in favour of the secret ballot (i.e. that Irishmen should participate in electioneering) and of security of tenure for farmers as the first stage in the evolution of a peasant proprietary. Yet even this was so far behind current American thinking that Devoy hurriedly stepped in with a demand for the root and branch abolition of the landlord system. To that he tied a demand that 'advanced' nationalists should take part in the 'open' movement. In this way, he argued, public opinion would be aroused, authentic nationalists and not limp Home Rulers would represent Ireland, and the way would be prepared for a successful revolution when the moment was ripe.[23]

Shortly after the Brooklyn meeting Parnell was re-elected president of the Home Rule Confederation of Great Britain. He used the occasion to warn his audience against the demoralizing influence of Westminster. 'We should all try', he said, 'to make our stay in the House of Commons as short as we possibly can.'[24] This was language that Irish-American Fenians could understand and approve. And when Butt curtly declined to attend on the second day of the convention, it was easy in New York to jump to the premature conclusion that the long-threatened break between him and Parnell had at last arrived. Believing this, Devoy took an important initiative. After hasty consultation with other members of the Clan (Davitt was away on a lecture tour), on 25 October he sent the following cable to the president of the Supreme Council of the IRB, Charles Kickham, for presentation to Parnell if Kickham approved:[25]

Nationalists here will support you on the following conditions:

1. abandonment of the federal demand and substitution of a general declaration in favour of self-government;

2. vigorous agitation of the land question on the basis of a peasant proprietary, while accepting concessions tending to abolish arbitrary eviction;

3. exclusion of all sectarian issues from the platform;

4. Irish members to vote together on all imperial and home questions, adopt an aggressive policy and energetically resist coercive legislation;

5. advocacy of all struggling nationalities in the British Empire or elsewhere.

To send this telegram to Kickham was a courtesy arguably due to the head of the Fenian organization in Ireland, but it was a gesture somewhat blunted by the fact that Devoy published his message the same day in the New York *Herald*. It seems that Kickham, confronted with a policy which went so totally against his own doctrine of non-collaboration with parliamentarians, did not pass the cable on to Parnell.[26] But it was only the first shot in what rapidly developed into a major engagement. Two days later, on 27 October, Devoy published an article in the New York *Herald*, based ostensibly upon interviews with four prominent nationalists. The interviews, like the article, were concocted by Devoy himself and constituted the basis of what he called 'an Irish new departure'. The essence of this new departure was defined thus:[27]

The change, it is said by those competent to speak on the subject, will take the shape of a combination between the advocates of physical force and those who believe in constitutional agitation, such as will leave the former free to prepare for active work while, in the meantime, giving a reasonable support to a dignified and manly demand for self-government on the part of the constitutionalists.

The phrase, 'new departure', like the policy it enshrined, was a source of controversy from the moment Devoy gave it to the world. Historically speaking, the concept was not original, since those Fenians who had reached a rough and ready working arrangement with Butt some five years earlier to support him for a limited period may be said to have launched the first 'new departure'.* But this second 'new departure' was of far greater significance, both because of the weight Devoy himself could carry and because of the emphasis placed upon the land question. It did not entail any abandonment of the traditional Fenian objective of an Irish republic to be won by armed insurrection, but it did open up an interim policy of collaboration with the parliamentarians who, besides pursuing an uncompromising line in parliament, would, it was hoped, when the right moment arrived, make their contribution by seceding from Westminster in a body and constituting themselves an Irish legislature in Dublin. The general intent of the 'new departure' was, then, to galvanize – or, as Devoy would have said, to 'nationalize' – public opinion and thus prepare the way for the Irish state of the future.

Davitt, on tour in the far west when Devoy launched his bombshell, was at first alarmed – by the publicity accompanying the *démarche* rather than by its content – but on his return to the east coast was speedily reassured by Devoy. So much so, indeed, that he determined to return home at once to propagate the new doctrine and succeeded in persuading Devoy to come with him to help in the complex negotiations with the IRB and with Parnell that were certain to lie ahead.[28]

On 11 and 12 December Devoy and Davitt left for Europe by different routes, having agreed to meet in Paris early in January. To ease the way for their coming, Devoy brought with him a long letter which on

---

*I adopt here the terminology of Professor T. W. Moody, whose forthcoming study of Michael Davitt and the land war deals in detail with the history of the new departure in its various phases. I am deeply indebted to him for allowing me to see in typescript that part of his book which deals with the events of 1878–9. In his view three 'new departures' are to be distinguished – the Fenian *rapprochement* with Butt in or about 1873; Devoy's initiative of October 1878; and Davitt's transformation of that initiative through the medium of the Land League in 1879.

arrival he sent to the *Freeman's Journal*. In this, while reiterating the
essence of the 'new departure', he insisted that it was not an *alliance*
between Fenians and constitutionalists, and that, on the contrary, no
abandonment of the orthodox separatist standpoint was intended.[29]
None of this, however, cut any ice with the Fenian old guard. When,
between 19 and 26 January 1879, Devoy and Davitt conferred with the
IRB leaders they found themselves confronted, in the person of the
deaf and ageing Kickham, with revolutionary conservatism in its
purest form. Nothing could move him or his associates from the simple,
rigid position that to mix with a constitutional party was to risk the
deadliest kind of contamination. Accordingly, while individual Fenians
were left free to vote at parliamentary elections (though not to become
MPs), the Supreme Council firmly condemned any participation in
such elections, or support of a parliamentary party, by the IRB. Equally,
it refused to commit the IRB to becoming involved in an agrarian
agitation. In effect, it decisively rejected the 'new departure'.

It remained to be seen what Parnell's reaction would be. Davitt
arranged a meeting for him with Devoy at Boulogne on 7 March.
Davitt himself was not present, but Devoy was accompanied by
John O'Leary and Parnell by Biggar. The discussion – of which the only
record is Devoy's – lasted for two days and the atmosphere was cordial.
In 'new departure' terms the meeting was inconclusive, though Devoy,
like Carroll before him, was so impressed by Parnell's demeanour as
to believe that he was prepared 'to go more than half way to meet
us . . .' His account continues:[30]

> He did not say definitely, and we did not ask him to say, whether he
> would prefer total separation, repeal of the union, or some form of
> legislative independence involving some connection with England,
> but the impression he left on me was very distinct, that he had not
> his mind made up as to which was the best, or the one most likely
> to be realized, but that he would go with the Irish people to the fullest
> limit in breaking up the existing form of connection with England.

Although there may be an element of wishful thinking in this analysis,
its general drift accords well enough with the line Parnell was likely to
have taken at such a meeting, where his habit was to leave others to do
the talking and to reveal as little as possible of his inmost thoughts.
Clearly, there was no question here of an 'alliance', such as Devoy, his
'Freeman' letter of 11 December notwithstanding, would probably
have liked to conclude. Nor was there any question, as Devoy himself
confirmed, of starting a purely agrarian movement. 'Events in Ireland

which were the result of the terribly wet season, changed all that in a few weeks, but Biggar and Parnell were as ignorant of what was in store for the country when they left Boulogne as was the rest of the world.'[31]

III

Here indeed was the crux. As the politicians jostled for position, and as the revolutionaries defined their 'new departure', Ireland, all unknown to any of them, was entering a fresh phase of her history. The slow and painful recovery of agriculture in the generation after the Famine had made little impact upon the west, which still depended for its main food-crop upon potatoes that were as vulnerable to disease in the 1870s as they had been in the 1840s. It remained, too, a region so over-populated in relation to its resources that seasonal migration to England and Scotland continued to be an essential element in the economy of many hard-pressed families. Further, although it has recently been suggested that rents were not unduly high over much of Ireland, and although the statistics indicate that eviction was for most landlords a weapon of last resort, they still did possess the power to evict for non-payment of rent. There were enough examples of such eviction on the smaller, uneconomic estates for the mere threat of being turned out of their holdings to have an immense psychological effect on the tenant-farmers when times grew hard again.[32]

By the late 1870s times were unmistakably growing hard. After several years of uncertain harvests came the disastrous weather of 1879, which damaged every part of agriculture, but confronted the western districts, where blight struck the potato crop, with imminent famine. Ominously, scarcity was not accompanied, as of old, by high prices, for the disruption of Irish agriculture coincided with the appearance in the European market of American grain on an increasing scale. The direct impact of this on Ireland was, admittedly, somewhat cushioned by the fact that farmers had been tending to move out of wheat and into oats and barley, where competition was less intense, but indirectly the effect was severe. The combination of adverse weather and American grain hit British agriculture hard; consequently, the demand for migrant labour diminished and the Irishman of the western seaboard was thrown back on his own resources at the moment when those resources were being drastically curtailed. In the whole of Ireland the value of the principal crops produced fell by nearly £14 million between 1876 and 1879. And whereas in 1876 the country had produced four million tons of potatoes worth nearly £12.5 million, in 1879 the quantity had fallen to just over one million tons and the value to less than £3.5 million. Furthermore, in Connaught – easily the poorest of the four provinces – the loss of earnings from England during that time amounted to £250,000. The desperate tenants and labourers were driven to seek credit where they could find it – the banks for the more substantial, the village money-lender or 'gombeen man' for the impoverished majority. But these meagre loans were soon used up in the purchase of food and when they were gone starvation loomed. In such circumstances even moderate rents could not be paid. Evictions followed inexorably. Whereas in 1876 the total number of families turned off the land was 553, in 1879 it was 1238.[33] True, in a number of cases tenants were readmitted either *as* tenants, or as caretakers (the latter in the hope that they would redeem their previous arrears), but to the starving farmer the fact that eviction hung over him in one form or another was a powerful impetus to the surge of fear and anxiety which now began to mount in the countryside.*

This disaster was all the more terrible because it took nearly everyone by surprise. So unexpected was it that only gradually did the idea sink in that a major crisis was at hand. Parnell too was caught off balance. In the autumn of 1878 he spoke twice in the west of Ireland at meetings organized by local Tenants Defence Associations and both times confined himself to generalities which suggested that he had not yet seriously given his mind to the long-term solution of the land question, still less to the immediate problem of the agricultural down-turn which was already in progress. Thus, at Ballinasloe, he remarked vaguely that he was in favour of land purchase as it had been carried out in France and Prussia, a reference which the tenant-farmers of the west of Ireland might have been forgiven for finding a little *recherché*. 'In the meantime', he told them, 'they must stop eviction, they must keep the people in the country by keeping the landlords from raising rents.'[34] Again, to people whose problem was the payment of existing rents, and many of whom were only too eager to get out of the country, this was a somewhat esoteric doctrine.

At Tralee a couple of weeks later it was much the same story, though, after haranguing his audience about the need for 'energy and activity'

---

*The official eviction figures for the 1870s are unsatisfactory, as they give only readmissions as tenants and omit the caretakers. In 1880, however, it is known that of 2110 families evicted, 217 were readmitted as tenants and 947 as caretakers. If this is a typical figure, it would suggest both that *permanent* evictions for non-payment of rent were less numerous than has been thought and that they were quite small in relation to the total number of tenants. (B. Solow. *The land question and the Irish economy 1870–1903* (Cambridge, Mass.), pp. 55–7.)

in parliament, he was honest enough to tell them that they need not look to him for 'a learned discourse' on the land question. This did not prevent him from taking his stand on Butt's abortive Land Bill of 1876, which had been intended to strengthen the provisions of the Land Act of 1870 regarding fixity of tenure. As for the landlord system, it was, he said, not calculated for the good of the country as a whole, but since they had it they ought to make the best of it. 'Aren't you a landlord yourself?' asked a voice from the crowd. To which another replied, 'He is, and a good one too.' Parnell was unperturbed. 'Unless they went in for revolution he confessed he did not see how they were going to bring about a radical reform of the system of land tenure in this country.' He did make a perfunctory genuflection towards peasant ownership as an ultimate goal, but for this and for the more immediate objective of keeping down rents, he advised them to trust to 'energetic' MPs. For him, clearly, the land question was still incidental to the political struggle.[35]

If Parnell in these forays was still so evidently obsessed with the internecine war among the Home Rulers, this was because that war was just then reaching its climax. His call for 'energetic' members had provoked an immediate counter-blast from Butt, already alarmed by the publication of Devoy's 'new departure' telegram, in which he denounced Parnell's proposals as a virtual ultimatum that at the next election either various sitting members must be discarded or there would be conflict between the two sections. This, he said, was 'a policy of dissension'. Parnell met this complaint ingeniously, but firmly. 'The time has now gone by', he wrote, 'when vague accusations of dissension and disruption will gain credence in this country. The Irish people, I believe, want sustained action and union and will take steps to secure both. There is no personal question; there is no question of leadership involved . . . but those who think with me, believing in our work, ask the constituencies to increase our numbers, not at the expense of Mr Butt and his friends, but as an exchange for all that is dishonest and bad in the Irish representation.'[36]

Parnell's distinction between Isaac Butt and the 'dishonest and bad' element in the party was a transparent fiction which deceived no one. When parliament was suddenly recalled in December for a winter session occasioned by the Afghan war even this diaphanous veil was rent in twain. Butt publicly warned the party not to obstruct in any way the business of a session which was to be concerned with matters of vital concern to the United Kingdom. This evoked from John Dillon a letter to the press containing the most bitter denunciation the old leader had yet had to face. 'No honest Irish nationalist can any longer continue to recognize Mr Butt as leader', he wrote. 'The only hope that now remains for the country is that Mr Parnell and the active party will take an independent line of action and openly denounce the monstrous piece of traitorism which is about to be enacted.'[37] Parnell, typically, adopted a much cooler tone and in a letter written from Avondale at the end of November referred to the possibility of obstruction during the session in almost dismissive terms. He was reluctant to undertake it with less than twenty members, he said; anything else would be imprudent and might be injurious.[38] He could well afford to stand aloof, because Butt this time had gone too far. Feeling as he did about the paramount necessity of loyalty to the empire, he regarded as tantamount to treason any attempt to make Irish capital out of British difficulties. But to most Irish nationalists, constitutional as well as revolutionary, not to do so was to commit treason to Ireland. 'Traitor to the cause' was the phrase O'Connor Power actually applied to Butt in a letter published on 6 December and although this was still felt in some quarters to be too extreme, the volume of criticism continued to mount.[39]

At last the issue came to a head at a meeting of the Home Rule League in February 1879, where Butt had to face a motion proposed by T. D. Sullivan urging the Irish members to hold themselves apart from English parties, to attend regularly and to show increased activity. In the course of a long and acrimonious debate Dillon, sorrowfully declaring that for a long period he had 'loved and trusted' Butt, now accused him of turning his back on the principles he himself had enumerated in 1874. 'I don't want to call Mr Butt a traitor', he said, 'and I tell you so for this reason – he is getting no *quid pro quo*.'[40] But the effect was much the same as if he *had* called him a traitor and Parnell, with such allies, had no need to make the running. Instead, he was almost conciliatory, demanding only that the Home Rulers should take 'a practical and daily interest in the business of the House of Commons'. Butt, who defended himself as always with dignity, chose to regard the motion as a vote of censure and he was still able to muster enough backwoods support to have a more harmless resolution substituted in its stead.[41] But this was the merest pretence and everybody knew it. The League and the party had been shattered beyond repair and Butt himself was finished. That winter he had suffered much from bronchitis. At the beginning of May he had a stroke and within a week he died, leaving the way apparently open for the man who only eighteen months earlier had said, with his serene arrogance, that he was young and could wait.

IV

Yet the way was by no means so open as it seemed. Within a few weeks of Butt's death the party met to choose his successor and they chose, not Parnell, but a known moderate, William Shaw. Admittedly, he was only elected as 'provisional leader' for that session, but that the choice fell upon him showed plainly that so long as the party retained its existing character, Parnell could never hope to be more than a *frondeur* at the head of a small group of parliamentary guerrillas. This situation would not change unless the party itself could be changed at the next election and *that* would not happen unless he could establish his personal ascendance in the country on a broader basis than any the Home Rule movement could offer. It is easy, with hindsight, to see that the land question and the general crisis of rural Ireland in 1879 gave him the opportunity he needed, but to assume that *he* saw this clearly from the start would be as wrong as to assume that Michael Davitt emerged from Dartmoor 'with the Land League in his brain'. For some months yet Parnell would grope his way forward with little real understanding of the developing situation.

True, his speeches at the close of 1878 had shown that he was at least beginning, albeit amateurishly, to become aware of the land problem. It was perhaps a significant pointer for the future that within a few days of the deadlocked Home Rule meeting of February 1879 he was to be found at a land conference in Dublin attended by tenants' representatives from various parts of the country. Even so, the resolutions passed at the conference were of a distinctly old-fashioned kind – they called for further protection from eviction, for fixity of tenure on the lines of Butt's bill of 1876, for extension of the purchase clauses of the act of 1870, and for improved housing for labourers. From Parnell's standpoint, they were probably less important than the final motion which was to the effect that no candidate should be returned at the new general election who had not pledged himself to these various, and far from extreme, demands.[42]

Whether Parnell himself would have based his campaign on these resolutions we shall never know, for at this point the initiative was firmly seized by Michael Davitt. On his return from America, and after his negotiations with the IRB, he had revisited his native Mayo, to be immediately struck by the plight of the tenants, burdened by rents which, because of the depression, they could not pay. Responding in part to what he learned from local Fenians, he organized a public meeting

at Irishtown. This was held on 20 April, but before it took place he
and Devoy had a further meeting with Parnell in Dublin on either
6 or 13 April. Parnell straightway found himself under pressure from
two directions – Davitt urging him to lead a mass movement of tenants
against landlords, Devoy dangling before him once again the more
sophisticated allurements of the 'new departure'. He responded positively
to neither of these invitations. Sympathetic towards the tenants he no
doubt was, but an agrarian agitation which might easily get out of hand
was another matter. As for that positive understanding with the Fenians,
after which Devoy hankered, he remained as politely non-committal as
before.[43]

They agreed to meet again before long, but by the time they did
– on 1 June – the situation had drastically changed. To this change the
Irishtown meeting directly contributed. Davitt, as a ticket-of-leave
man whose presence might alert the authorities for trouble, was not
present, but he was the driving force behind it. Designed originally to
protest against the pressures exerted by a priest, Canon Geoffrey Burke,
to secure the payment of arrears by tenants on his brother's estate, of
which he was executor, the resolutions (drafted by Davitt) which were
passed at the meeting went far beyond this particular issue. In fact, they
mapped out the programme of the land agitation as it was soon to
develop – the halting of evictions, the reduction of 'unjust' rents, and
the ultimate abolition of landlordism.[44] The meeting was large and
enthusiastic, but it was significant that there was only one MP present
– John O'Connor Power, who held a Mayo seat – and he was by then
regarded with fairly widespread distrust.

A great deal therefore depended upon whether Davitt could now
prevail upon Parnell to involve himself in a way he had refused to do
when they met in April. It is not clear whether or not the two men had
direct contact between that April meeting and their further conference
with Devoy on 1 June. In his book, *The fall of feudalism in Ireland*,
Davitt says that 'Mr Parnell soon learned all the facts relating to the
Irishtown meeting' and Parnell himself testified before the Special
Commission, though with his usual vagueness, that he and Davitt had
had several meetings in the spring and early summer of 1879. From
these two accounts it would appear that Parnell was distinctly chary
of committing himself, as a Protestant landlord, to an agitation whose
first victim had been a priest (after Irishtown, Canon Burke had hastily
granted an abatement of rent), and that he had much in his mind a
warning Butt had once given him against any kind of movement which
involved proliferation of country branches over which an ostensible

leader could have no sort of control. 'But ultimately', Parnell recalled, 'I saw that it was necessary for us to take the risk.'[45] That he was pre- qared to take the risk in response to Davitt's persuasions is evidenced py the fact that he agreed *before* the tripartite conference of 1 June to speak at a further meeting which the latter was organizing at West- port.[46] To what extent he was influenced by Davitt's tactical success in winning from the Supreme Council of the IRB permission for indivi- dual Fenians to take part in the agitation we cannot tell, but it clearly represented an accretion of force he could not ignore.[47]

No formal record was kept of the meeting on 1 June and once again we are dependent upon Devoy's much later and highly subjective account. According to him, agreement was reached, verbally, but none the less 'clear, definite and precise' as to future collaboration. Davitt and Devoy assured Parnell that his leadership would have support from large numbers of Fenians in Ireland and America if he would accept four conditions – that in the conduct of the public movement nothing should be done to impair or discredit the Fenian ideal of complete independence to be won by physical force; that the demand for self- government should not be publicly defined but should never be less than a national parliament with an executive responsible to it and with full power over all vital national interests; that the land question should be settled on the basis of tenant ownership to be achieved by compulsory purchase; that the Irish members at Westminster should form a party completely independent of all others, and seeking no place under an English government. To all of this, so Devoy maintained, Parnell after long discussion agreed, and undertook to commit himself formally to the agrarian agitation by attending the Westport meeting the following Sunday.[48] Having entered into the agreement, Parnell remained faithful to it all his life – so, at any rate, Devoy was still insisting long after Parnell himself had vanished from the scene.[49]

For Devoy, to stress the existence of such an alliance was a political, perhaps also a psychological, necessity. Without this to show for his labours he could scarcely have faced his colleagues in the Clan na Gael and without believing that on 1 June Parnell had in effect accepted the 'new departure' Devoy could never have given him the support he consistently did give him during the remainder of his career, even after Parnell appeared to have turned his back on the alliance and all it stood for.

Yet, though Devoy's sincerity is unimpeachable, his account remains suspect for several reasons. First, it leaves out of the reckoning the fact that by 1 June all three men were well aware that something startling was happening in the west of Ireland and that to define their attitudes to this was a more immediate preoccupation for two of them (Davitt and Parnell) than to make a treaty of adherence to the 'new departure'. Second, it is not true that Parnell used the Westport meeting to commit himself formally to the land agitation – he did not do this for a further three months and when he did it he certainly did not go into the movement on the basis of compulsory purchase. Finally, both Davitt and Parnell subsequently denied that anything like an alliance had ever been concluded. Davitt always maintained that Parnell's part in their conferences was mainly passive; welcoming the infusion of some element of 'advanced' nationalism into the forces he hoped to lead, he entered into no compact and agreed to nothing that would lay him open to a charge of treason. 'Mr Parnell's attitude might be called that of friendly neutrality towards the revolutionary movement and nothing more.'[50] It is true that Davitt wrote this near the end of his life, when he had long broken with his revolutionary past and had quarrelled with Devoy, but such a firm and explicit statement is not easily to be set aside.

If it suited Davitt to disavow the 'treaty' in later years, it was absolutely essential for Parnell to do so. And it is not surprising that his most emphatic repudiation of Devoy should have been made before the Special Commission in 1889, when he was fighting for his political life and seeking to demonstrate that he had never been involved in conspiracies with Irish-American extremists. Questioned by the Attorney-General about Devoy's letter on the 'new departure', written in December 1878 and published in the *Nation* on 4 January 1879, Parnell merely said that he had not read it then, nor even read it since. Whereupon, the Attorney-General asked him incredulously, 'Do you mean to represent . . . that you had no knowledge in 1879 of what "new departure" meant?' To this Parnell made the extraordinary reply: '"New Departure" I understand to mean, if I ever heard the meaning – I understand the term "new departure" to mean the formation of the Land League movement, combining the agrarian and the political question.' This was precisely what it did *not* mean, but when the Attorney-General, not much more accurate himself, tried to suggest that it was really a combination of the physical force men with those advocating the land agitation, Parnell reacted sharply. 'Certainly not. My definition of the "new departure", as far as I ever heard the expression used in Ireland, if at all, is that it was a combination of the political with the agrarian movement.'

This was disingenuous, to say the least, but it was candour personified compared with his reaction to the Attorney-General's attempt to get him to admit that he had met John Devoy in Ireland in 1879. Pressed on the subject of Devoy's presence in the country at that time he replied simply that he had heard of it 'shortly afterwards', though probably not until Devoy had left for America. But when the Attorney-General asked him if he had seen a 'prominent American nationalist' in Davitt's company before going to the Westport meeting, Parnell equivocated: 'I do not recollect', he said. 'You would not forget a meeting at the beginning of 1879 at which Mr Davitt discussed the Land League in the presence of an American nationalist?' asked the Attorney-General in evident astonishment. 'I might or I might not', replied Parnell coolly, 'I have no recollection of such a meeting.' 'Are you quite sure it was not with Devoy?' probed the Attorney-General. 'I am quite sure that to my recollection no such meeting took place.'[51]

This, plainly, was a brazen untruth, uttered at a moment of political crisis when Parnell had his back to the wall. But the fact that Parnell told the court a lie about Devoy does not necessarily mean that he was equally untrustworthy when, recalling his relations with Davitt, he said that they had discussed 'a combined social and political movement' to help the tenants and to work for the restitution of an Irish parliament. It, he insisted, was to be an open and not a secret movement, a combination between the home rule and the land agitations, not a conspiracy between constitutional and revolutionary nationalists to bring about separation between Britain and Ireland.[52] This accords closely with Davitt's recollections and with another passage in Parnell's own testimony to the Special Commission when he pointed out, with that dispassionate common sense which was his *forte*, what his attitude towards extremism had really been in those distant days when the way ahead had been so difficult to discern:[53]

Before we leave this subject, with regard to the question of whether I ought to have forbidden these men to enter our movement, my Lord, I have always thought that in the history of Ireland there has been much justification for the view as regards [sic] the inutility of parliamentary action, and I should have considered it an unreasonable course upon my part to pursue at the threshold of our new movement, when we were yet untried . . . to ask these men to abandon their views and accept unhesitatingly mine, and to shut the door of the constitutional movement in their face at the very commencement of this movement, unless they agreed to forego definitely, and to make public declarations definitely against contingent recourse to physical action thereafter.

This corresponds with his behaviour at the time. A week after the conference at Morrison's Hotel he went down to Westport with Davitt despite a public warning from the veteran Archbishop of Tuam, John MacHale, not to do so and there, on Sunday 8 June, he made his début as a land agitator. That he appeared at all was a guarantee of full coverage from the press and it was from this moment onwards that the movement began to attract widespread attention. The essence of his speech can be summed up in a few sentences which soon became famous. Joining, but more circumspectly, in the general assault upon landlordism which Davitt and other speakers had launched from the platform, he again recommended land purchase on the Continental model to his audience, though with the saving grace that it would be better if this could be done 'without injuring the landlord'. But this was for the long term. In the meantime, the tenant must not be asked to pay more than a 'fair rent' which he defined as 'a rent the tenant can reasonably pay according to the times'. If, in the existing bad times, the rents of three or four years previously were now insisted upon, there would be a repetition of the scenes of 1847 and 1848. 'Now', he said, 'what must we do in order to induce the landlords to see the position? You must show the landlords that you intend to keep a firm grip of your homesteads and lands. You must not allow yourselves to be dispossessed as you were dispossessed in 1847.' As for the political agitation with which he himself had hitherto been chiefly associated, there need be no contradiction between that and the land movement. The best way to get concessions – for example, a good land act – was to replace the existing Irish members by 'men of determination, of some sort of courage and energy'. 'If we had the farmers the owners of the soil tomorrow, we would not be long without getting an Irish parliament.'[54]

V

The Westport meeting was important partly because Parnell had associated himself with men more extreme than himself in defiance of ecclesiastical authority – Davitt was later to call this 'the most courageously wise act of his whole political career'[55] – but yet more because he had lent the already considerable prestige of his name to what was still a struggling agitation confined to the poorest and most backward part of Ireland. However, in June there was no immediate reason to suppose that a national movement was about to burst into flame and, while Davitt and his friends continued their labours in the west, Parnell's own preoccupations remained parliamentary. Indeed, that same month of June witnessed a recrudescence of obstruction, though of an essentially benevolent kind. Its purpose was to achieve Parnell's long-standing ambition to abolish flogging in the army. F. H. O'Donnell may have been correct in asserting that the impetus towards reform came from himself, Alexander Macdonald (the miners' MP) and the well-known Radical, Joseph Cowen, but it was Parnell who took the responsibility for using obstructive tactics.[56] In the end, though flogging was retained for cases where the alternative would have been death, it was abolished in all other cases and even that exception disappeared two years later. This brief and largely successful campaign had an importance beyond its immediate subject, for it was the first real demonstration of how powerful a combination of English and Irish members could be if they chose to act together: coincidentally, it was also the occasion for an early essay in collaboration between the two coming men of the House, Parnell and that rising hope of the stern, unbending Radicals, Joseph Chamberlain.

Within a few days of this episode Parnell was locked in a quite different kind of controversy which, though something of a storm in a teacup, also served as a demonstration – this time of the perils that lay in wait for a Protestant seeking to lead a predominantly Catholic party. The trouble arose over the University Education (Ireland) Act of 1879. Its effect was to abolish the old Queen's University and to substitute instead the Royal University which was, in effect, a mere examining body. This was far short of the hierarchy's demand for a truly Catholic university and Parnell, who identified himself strongly with that demand, fell foul of the moderate Catholic MPs who were prepared to accept any crumbs that fell from the government's table. These moderates included E. D. Gray, the owner of the *Freeman's Journal*. On 1 August that paper attributed to Parnell some extremely rude remarks about his colleagues, made apparently on the station platform at Limerick – that William Shaw was an old woman unfit to lead any party, that Gray should be turned out of his seat at the next election, and that another member was 'a very good dancer, but politically an ass'. Worse still, at a party meeting, when the Irish members had rejected his motion to adopt a more 'Catholic' line on the university question, Parnell was reported to have called those who voted against him 'a cowardly set of papist rats'.

The moment these allegations were published Parnell telegraphed to say they were false. The *Freeman* reporter was unrepentant and backed up the Limerick part of the story with letters sent from there to various Home Rulers in London. But they were at once challenged by

other Limerick letters denying emphatically that Parnell had said anything in the least derogatory. On the whole these tipped the balance in
his favour, as Parnell himself recognized when he wrote to the editor of
the *Limerick Reporter* to thank him for his 'manly and common sense
appreciation' of the situation. 'You have placed the true value on these
statements', he wrote, 'and, as has since been amply proved, I never
made use of any language reflecting on the honesty or usefulness of the
members for Limerick.'[57] This was probably true, if only because
Parnell was never one to make trouble for himself gratuitously. The most
likely explanation is that the Limerick accusations reflected Whig
chagrin that at a by-election in Ennis – whence Parnell was returning
on the occasion in question – he had succeeded in ousting a moderate
by an 'active' nationalist, Lysaght Finegan. The Ennis election was an
early trial of strength for Parnell which was so important to him that he
was later recorded as saying that he would have left public life had he
not won it.[58] If it was important to him, it was scarcely less important
to his opponents and their disappointment, building perhaps upon some
light-hearted banter on the station platform, may have been the basis
for the *canard*.

The 'papist rats' charge was more serious, for although on 3 August
an impressive list of MPs (including Finegan) wrote to the press categorically denying that Parnell had used the language attributed to him,
Gray insisted that he actually had heard the opprobrious words. Parnell
replied abrasively that 'this reiterated attempt to steal away my character
amongst my Catholic fellow-countrymen' was merely an incident in the
struggle for power between old-style Home Rulers and the new-style
activists. Gray in his turn produced a list of MPs (of impeccable Whig
antecedents) who testified that, though the exact phrase 'papist rats'
might not have been used, Parnell had been very angry at the meeting
and had certainly declared that his opponents were a set of cowards
who did not deserve to get a university bill. This is perhaps as near the
truth as we can hope to get. Parnell himself told a young journalist,
T. M. Healy (of whom more presently) that he had called Gray 'a
damned coward', but to Healy and to another friend he was emphatic
that he had not used the words 'papist rats'. 'Why', he reasonably
asked, 'should I offend the Catholics of Ireland by speaking insultingly
of them? Certainly it would be very foolish, to put the matter on no
other ground. An Irish Protestant can least of all afford to offend the
Catholic priests or laity.' In the end, Archbishop Croke of Cashel
mediated between Gray and Parnell, who published a joint letter declaring that 'the temporary misunderstanding between them was at an end'.

So it was, and Gray later became a loyal – though never, perhaps, an ardent – follower of Parnell's. Nevertheless the affair had indicated all too clearly how thin was the ice over which Parnell had to skate.[59]

Part of the quarrel with Gray and the *Freeman* may have gone deeper even than this. Conservative nationalists were watching the development of the agrarian movement in the west with alarm, and Parnell's decision to align himself with it, coming on top of his obstructionism in the House of Commons, made him an obvious target for attack. Certainly, he took no pains to disarm his critics, for although he stayed away at the last moment from a land meeting at Balla (near Claremorris) on 15 August, a month later he appeared on an agrarian platform at Tipperary. Speaking to an audience estimated at 20,000, he came out strongly for peasant proprietorship as the long-term solution, while exhorting the tenants not to rely upon parliament or the Irish party but upon their own resolution. 'Therefore, it is for you to stand together, to be determined, to insist upon a reasonable reduction where a reasonable reduction is necessary and where you don't get a reasonable reduction, then I say that it is your duty to pay no rent at all.'[60]

A week later he was at Tullow, warning that American competition was only just beginning and that the rent situation would become impossible. In Cork the week after that, dwelling on the bad season, the crop failure and the prospect of hardship ahead, he repeated that tenants must take it into their own hands not to pay unjust rents: time had run out and parliament, even if it wished to do so, could not help them.[61] Speaking at Navan, on 12 October, he was more precise and practical. 'Go to your landlord and if he disagrees with your estimate of what the fair rent should be, ask him to appoint one man and say that you will appoint another, and they will settle it between them. If he refuses this arrangement, offer him what you consider you can fairly be called on to pay in these times and ask him for a clear receipt. If he refuses to give you a clear receipt put the money in your pocket and hold it until he comes to his senses [cheers and laughter]. If the tenants on each property join together and do this the cause of the tenant-farmer in Ireland is won. No landlord can prevail against you.'[62] This particular meeting happened to be more fully reported than any he had spoken at hitherto and two contemporary newspaper accounts admirably convey how at this stage in the agitation these weekly occasions had still for ordinary country folk the character of a holiday outing. Here first is a description of how Parnell and his party were received:[63]

A waggonette decorated with evergreens was in waiting and into this the honourable gentlemen were put, Mr Parnell occupying the seat of honour on the box. A procession was then formed, headed by the Emmet's Guard Band of Navan and the visitors were played into the town. At several points along the route from the railway station to the town, triumphal arches were erected, and pendent to them were mottoes, such as 'Farmers who pay rents they cannot afford to, encourage rack-rents', 'Welcome to our faithful representatives', 'Ireland for Parnell', 'Parnell and Home Rule', 'Let Erin remember the days of old', 'Ireland for the Irish', 'Live and let live', 'Down with the land robbers', 'Irish land in Irish hands', 'All hail to the choice of our country'.

The second account then takes up the tale:[64]

Thousands showed bay leaves in their hats or green ribbons in their buttonholes. Hundreds wore handsome green scarves [an abomination to Parnell, but they could not be expected to know that]. Many bands (there were nearly thirty in all) displayed handsome uniforms and all heralded their approach to the appointed place by martial strains and national airs, including 'O'Donnell Aboo' and 'God save Ireland'.

What the effect of all this clamour was upon the hero himself we are not told, though to someone who hated crowds and platform speeches as he did, and who was so totally unmusical as he was, the occasion must have been a kind of nightmare. But that did not prevent him from turning it to account. Addressing the crowd of about 30,000 which was crammed into the market-place, he remarked that nothing like this assembly had been seen since O'Connell had spoken 'on the royal hill of Tara'. O'Connell, he said, had sought civil and religious liberty, but the former remained to be won. 'You can never have civil liberty', he proclaimed, 'so long as strangers and Englishmen make your laws and so long as the occupiers of the soil own not an inch of it.'[65]

What gave this speech special significance was that he was at that very moment moving towards the most decisive step he had taken since he entered politics. In mid-August Michael Davitt had launched 'the National Land League of Mayo' to canalize and direct the energies of the tenants who had been flocking to the summer meetings. Its aim was to abolish the existing land system and substitute for it a peasant proprietorship, but this was obviously for the future. On the short term it was intended to protect the tenants from rack-renting and eviction, to defend them at law when necessary, to help them if driven from the land, to form further defence associations and hold more public meetings, and to act as a 'vigilance committee' to note the conduct of public representatives in regard to the interests of League members.[66] According to Davitt, Parnell had no part in framing the programme or summoning the convention which established the League. He was made aware of the fact that the step was to be taken 'but he had neither expressed approval nor offered objection to what was proposed'.[67] Meeting Davitt quite frequently as he did at this time, it would have been hard for him to remain ignorant of what was in the wind, though how far he knew that the original organizers of the Mayo League were predominantly Fenian is uncertain. He was already adept at not knowing more than he wanted to know, and the opinion he offered to the Special Commission in 1889 is probably close, not only to his own contemporary attitude, but to the situation prevailing when the League was launched, 'that the organization in Ireland [the IRB] constantly and consistently opposed the Land League from first to last and that many of the followers and of the rank and file probably came into our movement, and that that increased the antagonism of the remainder to us, because they blamed us for taking their men from them'.[68]

As the momentum of the agitation grew week by week Davitt began to think of transforming the Land League of Mayo into something much more ambitious and much more difficult to control, a Land League for the whole of Ireland. For this purpose it was essential to harness the prestige of Parnell and in September this was at last achieved. Parnell agreed to take the initiative in forming such a League under his own presidency, but on the condition that its programme should be such as could be freely advocated in the House of Commons. In return, he consented to the merging of the old Tenants Defence organizations in the new body and himself undertook to send out a circular to various representative persons to meet in Dublin for the purpose of creating the League and appealing to America for aid. This he did on 29 September and three weeks later the conference assembled at the Imperial Hotel in Dublin. The chair was taken by Andrew J. Kettle, a 'strong farmer' from Kildare who had been secretary of the Tenants Defence Association and who was to become one of Parnell's most loyal, if also most outspoken, supporters. Apart from Parnell, there were no MPs present and the gathering was composed of tenant representatives, of known Fenians or ex-Fenians, and of a few priests, most of whom were later to take a prominent part in the movement. It was there and then decided to establish the 'Irish National Land League' with but two objects. 'First, to bring about a reduction of rack-rents; second, to facilitate the obtaining of the ownership of the soil by the occupiers.' Parnell was elected president, and Kettle, Davitt and a Fenian already prominent in the western movement, Thomas Brennan, were named as secretaries. The three treasurers were to be Biggar, another 'active' MP, W. H. O'Sullivan, and Patrick Egan. Egan, a dedicated Fenian, was a prosperous Dublin baker of exceptional ability and business acumen. He was to become in many ways the lynch pin of the League during almost the whole of its existence.[69]

With the creation of this new national body Davitt moved, in the terms of Professor Moody's analysis, from the second 'new departure' – that initiated by Devoy and himself in the winter of 1878–9 – to the third, for which he personally bore the chief responsibility. This transition was important because, although both these 'new departures' involved collaboration between constitutionalists and revolutionists, the essence of the third was agrarian, whereas the essence of the second, as indeed also of the much more shadowy first 'new departure', had been political. Events were soon to show how important the change of emphasis would be.

The most immediately practical step taken at the conference was the decision to ask Parnell to go to America to raise funds for the League, but, because it was assumed that it would be the more extreme section of Irish-American opinion which would be most likely to come to the assistance of the tenants, a further resolution was passed 'that none of the funds of this League shall be used for the purchase of any landlord's interest in the land or for furthering the interests of any parliamentary candidate'. This resolution, according to Davitt, was only accepted by Parnell 'with some reluctance' and one can readily see why.[70] In coming into the League he had specifically stipulated that its programme should be capable of being defended in parliament and he himself had never abandoned his fixed idea that the next general election must be used to purge the Irish representation at Westminster of all Whiggish and sluggish elements. This would require money and it was asking a lot of him to engage in an American tour from which his own political interests would draw no material benefit. Had the rule been adhered to strictly it might well have introduced an unbearable tension into his relationship with the League. But in fact, and when the time came, it was relaxed by a grant of £2000 from League funds towards the election expenses of 1880. 'Which', he told the Special Commission, 'was about all we had.'[71]

Once committed to the League, Parnell threw himself vigorously into the campaign. Week after week that autumn he spoke at meetings at Enniscorthy, at Galway, and, in rapid succession, at Manchester, Bolton and Leeds. The essence of his position was contained in the resolution he moved at Enniscorthy, five days after setting up the Land League. Here, where between 15,000 and 20,000 people crowded to hear him in the rain, he was careful to link the ultimate aim of the League with the existing crisis:[72]

> Considering the necessary deterioration of the soil under our present fatal system of land tenure which has been tried, condemned and rejected by every civilized nation; and taking into serious account the increasing competition of free countries, especially America . . . Resolved – that we regard the rejection of our abnormal system, and the establishment in its place of a tenant proprietary, to be the only effectual remedy for the agricultural and trade depression which are fast sinking this oppressed land into cureless ruin.

It was not, unfortunately, clear just how a 'tenant proprietary' might withstand American competition. What was clear was that a tenant proprietary was nowhere in sight, and Parnell himself, introducing this motion, dwelt mainly upon the double problem which clamoured for an urgent solution, how to help tenants with their rents and labourers to find jobs. In subsequent speeches, though he continued to speak about 'the land for the people', it was usually in general terms, and in a tone which suggests that Davitt may not have been far wide of the mark when he wrote later that Parnell's views at this time were in process of formation and that while advocating peasant ownership he was never heartily in favour of it. It is certainly true that with critics already beginning to allege that the Land League stood for communism, he went to considerable lengths to indicate that the value of a farm should be set high for sale purposes – 35 years' rental – and also that landlords should be either compensated or partially paid out of government funds.[73]

But much of this was academic, since, as winter approached, it was nothing less than destitution and starvation that stared the western peasants in the face. For them, eviction for non-payment of a rent for which they had no money was the reality with which they had to reckon. Increasingly, therefore, a more vehement tone began to be heard from the platforms of the League, where rhetorical denunciations of rent and of evictions walked nearer and nearer to the edge of the law. It was only a matter of time before someone stepped over the edge and laid himself open to a charge of sedition. Eventually this happened at Gurteen in county Sligo where on 2 November, three speakers –

Davitt, James Daly of Castlebar and a Belfast barrister, J. B. Killen (or Killeen) – all advised the tenants to look to their own needs first and only then, if they felt charitable, to let their landlords have whatever they could spare. Davitt was arrested on 19 November and taken to Sligo to be charged with sedition – a serious matter for him, since his ticket-of-leave could be cancelled at any time and himself sent back to penal servitude. In Sligo, together with Daly and Killen who were similarly charged, he was remanded until the following Monday when it was intended that all three should stand trial.[74]

Parnell reacted to this situation dynamically, as he always tended to react to anything which called for positive measures. A protest meeting was hurriedly called at the Antient Concert Rooms in Dublin and he used this to contrast the law-abiding nature of the agitation with the counter-measures of the government. In a tone which smacked more than a little of the ascendancy gentleman accustomed to regard the police as his servants he dwelt, a captious critic might have thought, rather less on Davitt's plight than upon the inconvenience he, Parnell, had experienced:[75]

> This morning I considered myself a respectable citizen of this country. I live six months of the year in Ireland and the remaining six months I live in London, attending to my parliamentary duties and the interests of my constituency. I spend a considerable portion of my income on weekly wages amongst my own people. I have some little permanent stake in this country and yet at one o'clock this morning, just as I had got into a sound sleep, I was awakened by a gentleman rushing into my bedroom and informing me that Mr Davitt and I were going to be arrested.

No doubt his anger was genuine, no doubt it was not just a rhetorical question when he asked how much longer Irishmen were going to stand this kind of arbitrary action by the government, but the fact remains that the note he struck on this occasion was primarily that of the man of property offended by a bureaucratic intrusion upon his privacy. There was certainly no sign that he felt any inclination to imitate the intemperate language of the men he was defending. He leaped instinctively to their defence because they had suffered for the Land League and he was their president, but only the previous day, at a meeting in Dublin, he had expounded views on the land question which were the reverse of revolutionary. Much of that speech was devoted to showing that his old policy – fair rents, fixity of tenure and free sale – was compatible with the new policy of peasant proprietorship. To this last, however, he gave a distinctly conservative interpretation, pointing out that if the tenants utilized the purchase clauses of the existing Land Act of 1870, they could become the owners of their holdings; he had to admit, though, that if the idea gathered momentum it would be necessary for the government to supplement from other sources the million pounds it had provided for purchase loans. Significantly, he did not advocate, either then or later, that landlords in general should be compelled to sell. Compulsion was a weapon to be used perhaps against absentees (he seems to have had chiefly in mind the great London companies), but not against gentlemen residing – like Mr Parnell, for instance – on their estates.[76] True, a few weeks later he said that it might not always be possible to draw the line so sharply and that if existing pressures and hard times continued he could not guarantee that 'the whole institution of landlordism will not come down altogether', but this was a warning, not a statement of intent.[77]

It is necessary to insist on the moderation of these proposals because of the contrast they provide with his actions during the exciting days which followed when, for the first time, he fully exhibited his capacity to dominate the forces of violence, or potential violence, while not himself being carried away by them. It so happened that a critical case was pending near Balla in County Mayo, where a tenant farmer, one Anthony Dempsey, with his wife and six children, faced eviction for non-payment of rent. Before his arrest Davitt had arranged to go to Balla on Saturday, 22 November, to hold a protest meeting whether this was banned by the authorities or not. On 21 November, at a meeting in the Rotunda rooms in Dublin, so crowded that he had difficulty in reaching the platform, Parnell announced his intention of taking Davitt's place:[78]

Tomorrow at Balla [he said] we propose to test the rights of Irishmen to assemble in public meeting. I believe that tomorrow will be the turning point of this great land movement. *If the people will contain themselves, if they refuse to be driven by the government into illegal courses, I say that the victory is ours* [my italics] . . . Let them proceed with their action, let them bring forward their false and suborned witnesses, and let them arrest, if they will, all those other men who have made themselves prominent in the agitation and for every one that is lost to you the fresh hopes and aspirations and spirit which tyranny always produces among a people will abundantly compensate.

Few if any in that excited audience were likely to mark the important qualification contained in the sentence italicized above. All they knew was that their hero was going to Balla to vindicate their rights as Irishmen. And to Balla, by night-train directly after the Rotunda meeting, he went. There he faced a test of leadership different, but possibly more congenial, than any he had yet encountered in his public life. Early in the morning bands of men carrying sticks began to converge upon the little town until perhaps eight thousand had assembled in procession. With Parnell at their head they marched towards the hill where Dempsey had his cabin and the police were already awaiting them in force. The danger that any incident, however trivial, might provoke a serious riot was plain to all. As they breasted the hill, news came that Dempsey had been granted a reprieve, but the procession still flowed on inexorably. On approaching the summit it divided into two columns which began to encircle not merely the cabin but the police grouped round it. Hurriedly, their officers withdrew them from the trap and Parnell, focusing the attention of the marchers on himself, led them to a mound some 50 yards away, and there conducted what was, to all appearances, a lawful meeting. But then came an explosive speech from Thomas Brennan, which caused a sensation. It did so, not merely by appealing to the policemen present – they were themselves Irishmen, of course – not to become 'destroyers of your own people', but also because it explicitly recommended a course of action – foreshadowed by John Dillon a few weeks earlier – which was to become the League's principal weapon, though the incident which was to make that weapon, the boycott, a household name was still in the future. Warning his hearers to have nothing to do with any man who took a farm from which another had been evicted, Brennan declared: 'Should such a mean wretch be found in Mayo to snatch such a farm, then, I say, go mark him well – cast him out of the society as an unclean thing [a voice – 'yes, as a mad dog']. Let none of you be found to buy with him or sell with him and watch how the modern Iscariot will prosper.'[79]

This was highly emotive language to use in such a tense situation, but Parnell was more than equal to the occasion. In his usual imperturbable, staccato fashion, he complimented Brennan on his 'magnificent' speech, but dispassionately observed that it would certainly land him in jail – which in due course it did. He then warned the audience not to follow the government in adopting unconstitutional methods. 'You have shown', he said, 'that in keeping a firm grip on your homesteads and in refusing to pay an unjust rent that you know well that in that advice is your only safety. Don't allow provocation to draw you from your duty. Let the leaders go; others will take their places.' That day they had achieved their immediate aim, to prevent an eviction, and no blood had been spilled. They must continue on those lines. 'Our country is a great country, worth fighting for. We have opportunities denied to our forefathers. Remain within the law and the constitution. Let us stand, even though we have to stand on the last plank of the constitution; let us stand until that plank is taken from under our feet.'[80]

VI

This marked the high point of what might be called the first phase of the agitation. The government, after scenes of legalistic farce, dropped the Sligo prosecutions and Parnell, who had gone straight from Balla to attend the trial, reached a new pinnacle of popularity, as yet without himself having fallen foul of the law. Perhaps for that very reason, he felt it necessary to compete with his colleagues in intransigence. But it was a different kind of intransigence which was still much more in the vein of the earlier 'new departure' than of the Land League 'new departure'. At Belfast in October, for example, he was already taking pains to keep his options open in such a way that Fenians and land reformers might each take comfort from what he said. Refusing to define what sort of self-government they should aim at, he recommended his hearers to let that wait until the right time came, which might be sooner than they expected. 'Whether they were to have the restoration of the Irish parliament of 1782, or whether they were to have a plan of federalism such as that which was formulated by the great Isaac Butt [being safely dead, Butt was already 'great'], or whether in the course of the year and in the march of events the Irish nation should achieve for itself a complete separation from England, was a matter which must be left to the course of events for solution.' He himself, he said, believed England and Ireland should live together in amity, connected only by the link of the crown. 'That was Grattan's idea and his dream.'

Leaving aside the fact that it was a dream which went far beyond Grattan's idea and which was only to find expression by Sinn Fein long after Parnell was dead, this formulation had the great advantages of simplicity and vagueness, thus making it possible for Home Rulers and separatists to work for the time being on a common platform. In the circumstances of the time that common platform had to be the land question, though this he still saw as subordinate to the political question, as he pointed out in a peroration which, most unusually for him, even incorporated a brief foray into Shakespeare. 'If they could all unite in Ireland in this way and pluck from the nettle danger the flower safety, he believed they would take one step towards obtaining for their country the inestimable blessing of self-government by fixing upon the soil of Ireland those who cultivated the soil.'[81]

This speech, though its reference to separation evoked loud cheers, stopped well short of sedition. But at the end of November, with the Sligo prosecutions still pending and his own visit to America only a few weeks away, he quite deliberately took up the theme of the Balla speech for which Brennan had been prosecuted and made it his own. It was noticeable, though, that he also quite deliberately chose to take it up in Liverpool because, as he said, he could there make the kind of seditious remarks he could not make in Ireland. Part of the speech was a diatribe against the arrest of Land League spokesmen, part a repetition of the standard advice to the tenants to husband their meagre resources so as to feed their families in the coming winter, and part a reminder to the Irish people not to allow themselves to be stampeded into violence and thus expose themselves to counter-violence by governmental coercion. But he went on to argue that the solution of the land question had to be a preliminary to the solution of the political question because it was only after the landlords had been stripped of the privileges which marked them out as an English garrison in Ireland that they would realize that their best future lay in aligning themselves with their fellow-countrymen. This reveals how much his thinking was still dominated by eighteenth-century precedents, when the gentlemen of Ireland took the lead in opposing English rule. 'Let us see, as in 1782, one hundred thousand swords, both Catholic and Protestant, leaping from their scabbards, and believe me, my fellow-countrymen, it will not be a question of chicanery or of acts of parliament or of anything that can possibly interfere with the right of our own people to make their own laws on the soil of Ireland.' And next night at Birkenhead, he defined the separateness of Ireland as a nation in a way that Grattan would have thoroughly understood. 'The principle they insisted upon', he said, 'was that the people of Ireland were entitled to be governed according to the wishes of a majority of the people of Ireland. It was said – "You have no right to be a separate nation". He replied that the Creator of nations made Ireland a nation [applause]. The Irish people were separate and distinct from the English, and though there was no scientific frontier [laughter], there was a natural boundary between them and nothing but mischief had ever resulted from the attempt of England to rule the Irish.'[82]

Speeches such as these, coming on top of his record of parliamentary obstruction and his appearance at the head of the Land League, naturally earned for the Parnell of this period the reputation of a firebrand who seemed hell-bent on revolution, a view held by conservative Irishmen as well as by most kinds of Englishmen. Yet the man himself remained an enigma, not only because of the obvious paradox of a Protestant landlord leading an organization of Catholic farmers, but because, to those who saw him at close quarters, there was such a contrast between the cold, implacable public man and the unassuming and slightly eccentric individual he appeared to be in private life. A contemporary account by a London journalist catches this duality well. Noting that Parnell had few associates in the Irish party and that, though a landlord, his property, on which he had recently made a twenty-per-cent reduction in the rents, brought him in no more than £1500 a year, the writer detected in this isolated and apparently vulnerable figure two different kinds of person. 'Under a slim and almost effeminate exterior, he has an iron will.' 'Calm, cool and bloodless, he is a man whom nothing can move.' 'Though a man of unbending stamp, he has in personal intercourse, the mildest and most gentle manner conceivable.' Among his eccentricities the same observer noted that Parnell, in an attempt to arrest incipient baldness, had had the upper part of his head shaved; also, that he was 'an inveterate water-drinker'. This was not strictly true. He usually drank a dry, white wine with his frugal meal, but it was certainly the case that he was, and always remained, extremely abstemious by Irish standards, a fact which may well have contributed to the legend of his aloofness and unsociability.[83]

The same opposition between private grace and public rigour was observed by Davitt, who despite the gulf that later opened between them, preserved to the end of his own life a fond memory of the young patrician who was his exact contemporary, but, so different was he, seemed to belong almost to another planet. 'No man', he recalled nostalgically in 1904, 'enjoying such growing popularity and political prospects could be more modest in his talk and manner, or more agreeable to those he met. He had a peculiar personal charm where all formality was suspended. He was in complete health at the time, and looked the very picture of manly strength, being strikingly handsome in general appearance and in facial expression. His laugh was most infectious, the whole countenance lighting up with merriment, and the eyes expressing a keen enjoyment of the fun or point of the story or incident.' But when the talk turned to parliament his whole aspect changed. Davitt, who thought that Parnell's dislike of England and Englishmen had been exaggerated by legend, was quite sure that he had a special detestation of the House of Commons and took a particular pleasure in thwarting its procedures. 'An ounce of parliamentary fear', he would say, 'is worth a ton of parliamentary love.'[84]

Such was the man who on 21 December sailed for America to raise funds, initially for the Land League but increasingly, as news followed him of famine and disease in Ireland, for the relief of the starving people of the west. He took with him John Dillon who, from having been his enthusiastic supporter against Butt, had graduated to the platforms of the League. He was not yet as radical as he soon would be – or rather, Parnell was still able to control his radicalism – but the choice of Dillon as a companion was a discreet signal to the Clan na Gael that Parnell could still be considered a 'new departure' man, for Dillon's contacts with Irish Fenianism were well known. Another similar signal went out while Parnell was still on board ship. Interviewed by a reporter, he was asked directly if the Fenians were sympathetic to the Land League. The reply he gave was at once revealing and adroit, indicating as it did his awareness that a real gap existed between orthodox Fenianism and the agrarian agitation, but also that Fenianism and constitutionalism were the two extremes of a spectrum which was much more subtle and varied than a simple comparison between the two would suggest:[85]

As far as I have been able to gather [he said] the Fenian organization and its leaders are opposed, though not hostile, to our movement, the reason being that it is constitutional. A true revolutionary movement in Ireland should, in my opinion, partake of both a constitutional and an illegal character. It should be both an open and a secret organization, using the constitution for its own purposes, but also taking advantage of its secret organization . . .

These were, from a Clan na Gael standpoint, impeccable sentiments, but for a while it seemed doubtful if the emissaries would survive to act upon them. They encountered the Atlantic in its worst midwinter mood. Even before they left Queenstown on the *Scythia* the rain came down in torrents and the ship rocked at anchor under the buffeting of a south-westerly gale. Parnell, with his habitual indifference to the elements, took the storm in his stride. But Dillon, whose health was always precarious and who suffered especially from gastric trouble and dyspepsia, lay inert in his cabin throughout the voyage. The resulting contrast between the two travellers was painfully obvious and it provided Parnell with a story that he always loved to tell. At one of their meetings in the American West, after both had spoken and the hat had gone round, the Governor of the State remarked that it was Dillon who had made him reach into his pocket. 'Parnell didn't impress me a bit', he said. 'When I saw this sleek young dude, as well fed as you or I and a damn sight better groomed, I said to myself: "The idea of sending out a man like that to tell us they are all starving!" But when the other man, poor Dillon, came along, with hunger written on every line of his face, I said, "Ah! that's a different thing. There's the Irish famine right enough." '[86]

Almost from the moment they landed the emissaries found themselves in difficulties. The critical situation at home had led to the launching of two private funds for the relief of the stricken tenants, one by the Duchess of Marlborough (wife of the Lord-Lieutenant), the other by the Lord Mayor of Dublin, the so-called Mansion House Fund. Since the Lord Mayor was E. D. Gray, with whom Parnell had so recently crossed swords, it was not surprising that the coverage of the American tour in Gray's paper, the *Freeman's Journal*, left much to be desired. In addition to this competition, Parnell had to face the rivalry of yet a third fund sponsored, ironically enough, by James Gordon Bennett's New York *Herald*. Despite Devoy's and O'Kelly's connection with that paper, its general line was hostile towards the mission (largely because Parnell declined to fuse his efforts with those of the *Herald*) and it was noticeable that the further Dillon and he got from the east coast, the fuller and more favourable the newspaper reporting became.

The first man aboard to welcome them at six o'clock in the morning on 2 January 1880 was Devoy himself, and this immediate contact between the envoys and the Clan na Gael was later made the basis for an accusation that the entire trip had been organized by the Clan. When this was put to him at the Special Commission Parnell strenuously denied it, while admitting that in a few cities some leaders of the extreme section might have had a hand in the arrangements.[87] The best reason for believing him is that no tour organized by Devoy and his friends would ever have got into the nearly inextricable tangle in which Parnell and Dillon were enmeshed within days of landing at New York. This was due, not to any malevolent influence, but simply to the fact that neither Parnell nor Dillon was much use at the practicalities of ordinary, everyday existence. Before long they had to send for help, which duly arrived in the shape of a young man who was to have a profound influence upon Parnell's fortunes at two of the decisive moments of his life. This was Timothy Michael Healy. Born in Bantry in 1857, Tim Healy was the son of a Poor Law Union clerk. After some schooling with the Christian Brothers in Fermoy, he moved to Dublin in 1869 to lodge with his uncle, T. D. Sullivan, whose brother, A. M. Sullivan, owned the *Nation* and occasionally published verses submitted anonymously by the schoolboy Healy. In 1872 Healy emigrated to Manchester and came under the influence of John Barry, the Fenian who five years later was to engineer the replacement of Butt by Parnell as president of the Home Rule Confederation of Great Britain. From Manchester he went to Newcastle as a shorthand writer with North Eastern railway; here he began to involve himself in the local politics of the immigrant Irish. In 1878 he got his first real opportunity when T. D. Sullivan brought him to London to write parliamentary sketches for the *Nation*. He speedily identified himself strongly with the 'active' group and his London letters did much to increase Parnell's reputation at home. Healy could have made a fortune from journalism, but he later qualified for the bar and became one of the outstanding Irish advocates of the age. In these early years his admiration for Parnell as a public figure was unbounded, though as early as December 1879 he had begun, characteristically, to discern 'feet of clay' in his hero on the personal and private plane.[88] Healy's virtues – intelligence, quickness, wit – were obvious. His vices – envy, malice, vanity and ruthless ambition – only later became apparent.

When he arrived on 24 February and began at once to take things vigorously in hand, the tour was two-thirds over. By the time it had ended and they sailed for home on 11 March, Parnell had travelled 16,000 miles in the United States and Canada, had spoken in over 60 cities and had raised about £60,000 for famine relief and perhaps another £12,000 for the general purposes of the League.[89] His speeches had three main themes. The first was to rouse the pity of his audiences for the plight of the starving peasants faced with eviction. The fact that such evictions had begun increasingly to happen after he had left Ireland, and had in one instance led to an ugly episode at Claremorris in which women, banding together to resist a process-server, had received bayonet wounds from the police, stirred him to passion.[90] 'Ladies and gentlemen', he said at a meeting just after this news had reached him, 'five or six hundred human beings turned out of their little houses – was not that enough to stir the blood of every man to see his wife and his daughters bayoneted before his eyes ... I say that the British government which does these things, which brings on these conflicts between the people and the police, which sends the police to assist the landlord in collecting rack-rents which are not there and cannot be paid, I charge this government with deliberately conspiring to murder the people of Ireland.'[91]

As time went on this became his most frequent *motif* and there is reason to believe that the effect of these tragic stories from home was to give the relief of famine the dominant place in his thoughts and in his speeches at the expense of his other objective, the winning of financial support for the League. Even Davitt, as sensitive to distress as any man alive, felt that Parnell and Dillon, by emphasizing hunger rather than organization, were departing from their brief. As he wrote to Devoy in the curious commercial phraseology of their amateur code: 'Some of his own and his partner's pronouncements have been somewhat contradictory to the rules laid down for the management of the New Firm [the Land League]. Every effort is made now to turn the flank of the New Firm by those who are dispensing charity and the greatest possible exertion and vigilance is required to prevent the work of the past year being undone through the demoralizing influences of meal and money.'[92]

But Parnell was not just concerned with 'meal and money'. His second theme accorded more closely with the ultimate objective of the League – the necessity to strike at the root of the agrarian problem by abolishing the landlord system. Even here, however, his attack was not so much directed towards securing the funds to enable the League to do the job itself as towards establishing his own credibility as a man capable of approaching the question in a statesmanlike way. This was evident, for example, in the article published under his name in the *North American Review* after he had left for home. Although apparently written by his sister Fanny, it certainly embodied his ideas, some of which he had himself expressed at the climactic moment of his tour, when on 2 February he addressed the House of Representatives in Washington.[93] If the crowded audience who came to hear him came expecting anti-British heroics they were sadly disappointed. What they got was a rather pedestrian history of the land question, followed by a sober analysis of how it might be solved by parliamentary means. For this Parnell borrowed from John Bright, who had recently suggested the creation of a land commission to organize the sale of holdings on a voluntary basis to tenants willing to purchase on the basis of a loan of three-quarters of the price, to be repaid with interest over 35 years. Parnell's own contribution was two-fold. One, which reflected his economic naïvety at this time, and which he later withdrew, was that there should be government-sponsored migration within Ireland from the poverty-stricken west to the grasslands of Meath, Kildare, Limerick and Tipperary. The other was his old panacea of state-aided purchase, revised now to involve the government in the liability to advance five-sixths, or even the whole, of the purchase price to the tenant, who would repay it in annual instalments over 25 years. In America he laid more stress upon the principle of compulsion than he had done at home, but his speech to Congress was, no doubt purposely, vague about how it should be applied, and in his article in the *North American Review* he did not move beyond his declared intention to use this weapon only against absentees.[94]

Fund-raising and careful arguments about land purchase were hardly the stuff of which Devoy's 'new departure' had been intended to be made. It is clear from a circular which Dr Carroll sent out to members of the Clan at the time of Parnell's arrival that American Fenians regarded the agrarian aspect of the mission as subordinate to the main issue. 'It is very important', wrote Carroll, 'that they shall receive prompt and substantial support for the *political* purposes of the Land League they represent.' Parnell and Dillon were therefore to be invited to speak whenever possible with the promise that the receipts from such meetings should be handed over to them 'for the political objects of the League'.[95] This partly explains why Carroll and others were irritated by Parnell's public quarrel with the sponsors of the other relief funds. From the Clan standpoint it was preferable that others should look after famine relief while Parnell left himself free for long-term organization and planning. 'My own views from the first', Carroll complained to Devoy, 'were that charity should have been kept separate from politics . . .'[96] True, the deteriorating situation in Ireland inevitably forced relief into greater prominence and for most of the tour Carroll acquiesced in this. But towards the end his patience snapped. This was mainly because he was incensed by Parnell's decision, on the eve of his departure, to launch an American Land League to keep up the flow of funds. Although Devoy consented to this, the new body was heavily backed by Irish-American moderates and Carroll was probably correct in seeing it as a means whereby Parnell could ultimately assure his movement of funds from the United States without being dependent on the Clan na Gael.[97]

This, however, was for the future. In America Parnell had still to develop the third of his three themes and in doing so to make essentially political speeches in a language Irish-American Fenians would understand. Reaching out towards them as he was obliged to do, his remarks on several occasions were much more extreme than anything that had so far been heard from him in Ireland. Thus, at Cleveland he commented with evident pleasure on the Irish regiments that had frequently provided escorts for him. 'And when I saw some of these gallant men today . . . I thought that each one of them must wish, with Sarsfield of old, when dying upon a foreign battlefield, "Oh, that I could carry these arms for Ireland". Well, it may come to that some day or other.' And at Rochester he said: 'I am bound to admit that it is the duty of every Irishman to shed the last drop of his blood in order to obtain his rights, if there was a probable chance of success, yet at the same time we all recognize the great responsibility of hurling our unarmed people on the points of British bayonets. We must act with prudence when the contest would be hopeless, and not rush upon destruction.' The qualification here was certainly important, but it was not one an excited audience might have been expected to grasp. And there seemed no qualification at all in the words he reportedly used at Cincinnati:[98]

> I feel confident that we shall kill the Irish landlord system, and when we have given Ireland to the people of Ireland we shall have laid the foundation upon which to build up our Irish nation. The feudal tenure and the rule of the minority have been the cornerstone of English misrule. Pull out that cornerstone, break it up, destroy it, and you undermine English misgovernment. When we have undermined English misgovernment we have paved the way for Ireland to take her place among the nations of the earth. And let us not forget that that is the ultimate goal at which all we Irishmen aim. None of us, whether we be in America or in Ireland, or wherever we may be, will be satisfied until we have destroyed the last link which keeps Ireland bound to England.

This speech was to haunt him for many years and when in 1889 the Special Commission was investigating *The Times*'s charges that Parnell had ties with the Irish-American revolutionaries, he was pressed particularly hard about what he was alleged to have said at Cincinnati. One says 'alleged' because recent research indicates that the Cincinnati newspapers did not carry the offending phrase about destroying 'the last link' in their reports of the speech.* It has been suggested that this may have been a later interpolation by the extreme organ, Patrick Ford's *Irish World* which, being an east coast paper, was far from the scene of action. Certainly it seems not to have been so reported in the *Cincinnati Daily Gazette* of 21 February 1880 (the day after the speech was given), even though the account in that paper of the paragraph preceding the disputed passage was very nearly identical with the one given in the *Irish World* of 6 March 1880. Later, the Attorney-General pointed out in re-examination that another local paper, the *Cincinnati Commercial Gazette* for 21 February 1880, did carry a report identical with that in the *Irish World*, but, naturally enough, he did not choose to explore the possibility – a very real one – that the same correspondent

---

*I must acknowledge my indebtedness to Professor Emmet Larkin and Mr Owen Dudley Edwards for assistance on this point.

had written both accounts. In the *Cincinnati Journal* for the same date, the climax of the speech was interestingly different. 'We have a great work before us. With your assistance we can pass the winter in Ireland, can kill the Irish land system, and when that corner-stone has been ground to powder the way is paved for Ireland to take her proper place among the nations of the world.' When the Attorney-General professed not to be able to see much difference between saying this and saying 'break the last link of the Crown', he evoked a characteristic reply from Parnell. 'Well, I see a good deal of difference in it and Mr Henry Grattan also saw a good deal of difference.'

The truth of the matter probably is that Parnell did make an extreme speech at Cincinnati, but that the exact terms of it were garbled, perhaps through the sheer difficulty of hearing what he said against the background of a noisy and emotional crowd. It *sounded* separatist, it may well have *been* separatist, but whether 'the last link' was entirely a journalistic invention or a true report of his actual words it is not possible to determine in the light of the widely differing newspaper accounts. Parnell's evidence at the Special Commission did little to help his case. Asked point-blank whether he did or did not use any such expression, this was what he said: 'I think it is exceedingly improbable, but I cannot at this distance of time undertake to say that I did not use it. I do not believe I did use it. It was very unlike anything else that I said in America.' 'That sentence', he added a moment later, 'is entirely opposed to anything I have ever uttered in any speech during my life, as far as I know, or to anything which I have ever thought, and if I did use those words, or anything like those words, I should say they must have been largely qualified with other matter.' This rather lame explanation was the best he could manage in response to his own counsel and it is no surprise to find that when the Attorney-General cross-questioned him sharply, he became, if anything, even more defensive. 'I believe I did not use them', he said, 'but I cannot be sure about them.'[99]

In 1889 Parnell was intent upon demonstrating the peaceful character of his movement and no less intent upon insisting that Home Rule did not mean separation. His hesitancy in disowning the 'last link' speech is therefore all the more remarkable, so remarkable as to awaken a suspicion that he was deliberately vague in case hard evidence had survived to authenticate the famous phrase or something sufficiently like it to be equally embarrassing. And that in turn suggests something else which is too often overlooked when his career is assessed, as it so often is, in terms of his ultimate, or penultimate, position. This is the simple but cardinal fact that in 1880 he was a young man caught up in what looked like becoming a full-scale revolution. Even before the revolution had begun to loom, he had, as we have seen, maintained close contact with those Fenians who were prepared to work with him on Devoy's 'new departure' lines, even though he had been careful never to commit himself to an absolute alliance. But his disgust with the degenerating remnants of Butt's Home Rule party combined with the social and economic convulsion in Ireland to make the more extreme element in his own nature respond instinctively to the excitements of the American tour. It would be difficult to overestimate the atmosphere of triumph and elation which surrounded him once he got away from New York. Senators, Governors of States, important and influential people of every kind, vied with each other to do him honour, as did the vast crowds which attended his meetings. Those seas of upturned faces, those thunders of applause, those manifestations that the Irish really did count for something in this great country, could not but have their effect upon one whose calm exterior at all times masked an essentially passionate temperament. Barry O'Brien may thus have been nearer the mark than most of Parnell's biographers when he insisted that these speeches were not simply aimed at conciliating the Clan na Gael. 'Far from it. In what he said he spoke the faith that was in him. Other speeches he made to Irishmen who were not Fenians, and then he dealt with the land question alone. But he did not take off his coat to reform the land laws of Ireland. He took off his coat to loosen the English grip on the island. Therefore at Brooklyn, Cleveland and Cincinnati he spoke from his heart.'[100]

In assessing his mood at this critical time one further point has to be borne in mind. This American expedition was as near to a family reunion as the Parnells ever allowed themselves to come. His mother, three sisters – Anna, Fanny and Theodosia – and his brother John were all in the United States while he was there. Mrs Parnell, with Anna and Fanny, were in regular attendance and it was noticed how often, when stressing his American blood, he glanced towards them. 'He almost always refers to it', wrote one reporter, 'with more animation than anything else, boasts his Americanism with great satisfaction, as he gives a pleased look to his mother and sisters, who . . . seem to hang with delight upon his words and to enjoy the applause given twenty times more than he does himself.'[101] The influence of the American side of Parnell's family was generally towards extreme politics and this was likely to have been more rather than less marked on native ground. Fanny once told Tim Healy that she did not think that a dissolution of parliament would bring Charles back again to the grind of House of Commons work. All the sisters seemed perfectly reckless and since they were apparently even capable of ordering the dreaded Devoy to steal a black cat for them from the New York *Herald* office – his response is not known though it can easily be guessed – Healy concluded there were no limits to what they might say or do. 'They are the most extraordinary family I ever came across', he confided to his brother Maurice. 'The mother, I think, is a little "off her nut" in some ways and, for that matter, so are all the rest of them.' But he conceded that Anna and Fanny worked hard for the movement, though he was astonished that Parnell seemed 'sublimely indifferent' to them. In this Healy, accustomed to the womb-like envelopment of the Sullivan clan, was profoundly mistaken. What he took for indifference was no more than the habitual Parnell style, each having been used to go his or her way unchecked from childhood. Charles was very far from ignoring his mother or his sisters and Fanny in particular was close to him – so close that her influence upon him at this period was almost certainly much greater than Healy, baffled by a family which rigorously suppressed all the usual signs of affection, could readily have guessed.[102]

All the same, it was Healy who at this moment gave Parnell the title which was to cling to his name long after he was dead and gone. Early in March they extended their tour to Canada and, after a fairly routine meeting at Toronto, arrived in Montreal. 'I doubt', said Healy, who was not given to exaggerating his tributes to his colleagues, 'whether in the forty-eight years which have since elapsed such a reception was accorded there to any other man.' And it was there, in one of the first speeches he ever made before a large audience, that he transferred to Parnell a phrase that had previously been used of Daniel O'Connell, hailing him as 'the uncrowned king of Ireland'.

That same night came a telegram from Biggar which altered all their plans at a stroke. 'Parliament dissolved', it said. 'Return at once.'[103] This was the opportunity Parnell had been awaiting for more than two years and he dared not linger in America. He went quickly to New York, where he held a somewhat confused conference at which friction between moderates and extremists was ill-concealed. He had no time, even had he possessed the art, to conciliate these rival interests and in the brief interval before his departure he set up a committee to form the American Land League. It was shunned by some of the most 'advanced' men, but though a few moderates found a place on it, four of the seven members belonged to the Clan. Dr Carroll would have nothing to do with it, but since Devoy agreed to be treasurer, it seems that he at least believed that *his* 'new departure' was still in operation. John Dillon was left behind to continue the work, but Parnell and Healy departed in regal style. They were escorted to the ship through a blinding snowstorm by the famous 69th (Irish) Regiment. 'Parnell', recalled Healy, 'stood on the bridge the whole time until the tender left, with head uncovered; and it was a fine sight to see the 69th salute as we sailed off, and Parnell wave his hand in response, looking like a king.'[104]

CHAPTER 4

Crisis

'We are no longer in the region of reform, we are in the very crisis of revolution.' (T. E. Webb, *Confiscation or contract*, 1880.)

'I did not know, no one knew, the severity of the crisis that was already swelling upon the horizon and that shortly after rushed upon us like a flood.' (Gladstone at Edinburgh, 1884.)

I

For a triumphant patriot an Irish homecoming can be a deflating experience, as Parnell quickly discovered. When he arrived at Queenstown at dawn on Sunday, 21 March, the regal honours which had marked his departure from New York were conspicuously absent. Indeed, no welcome of any kind awaited him and Healy, lynx-eyed as always, noted the chagrin with which his hero, or anti-hero, scanned the empty sea. After a few hours a tender belatedly came alongside, bearing, among others, Biggar, Davitt, T. D. Sullivan and Lysaght Finegan. Parnell at once resumed the mask and received them with his usual impassivity. Later that evening, however, speaking in Cork city, he drew a sharp contrast between his arrival in America, where a committee met him three miles out at sea at 6 a.m., and his return to Ireland. 'Our reception committee this morning', he observed acidly, 'was not able to get up to come out until eight o'clock.'[1]

But there was no time for recriminations even if this had been his style. He had come home to fight the election and now flung himself headlong into the campaign with one of those sustained bursts of demonic energy that were typical of his prime. He was scarcely off the boat before he addressed a mass meeting in Cork from the windows of the Victoria Hotel. This was followed by a banquet where he reported in detail on his American tour. From the banquet he went straight to the night train for Dublin which obligingly paused for him to make brief speeches at Mallow (2 a.m.), Maryborough (3 a.m.) and Kildare (4 a.m.). Later in the day he spoke at Newbridge, county Kildare, and was back in

Dublin that same night. On Tuesday he was at Thurles in county Tipperary, in Dublin on Tuesday night and in Athlone the next day. 'He seems never to tire out in Ireland's service', commented the exhausted reporter who toiled in his wake.[2]

Throughout the election, which lasted for most of April, Parnell continued at the same pace, selecting candidates, speaking in their favour, defending his House of Commons record, propagating the doctrines of the League, and circulating dizzily between three constituencies – Cork city, Meath and Mayo – each of which eventually elected him. His victory in Cork, which seat he was to hold for the rest of his career, was achieved almost by accident. Originally, three candidates were nominated – an old-style Whig, a Tory and a moderate Home Ruler. Parnell's name was then put forward by an anonymous nationalist who persuaded others to sign the nomination papers in the belief that Parnell had not only given his consent but had contributed £250 towards expenses. After his papers were in he was summoned to begin his campaign. He duly arrived at two in the morning on 3 April and astonished his friends by asking how they came to nominate him. It was his turn to be taken aback when they replied that they had been told by his emissary that £250 was available if his name was put forward. 'I did not send him a farthing', said Parnell, 'and I know nothing whatever about him; never heard of him. There is something that wants looking into here.' The emissary – he figures in the story simply as 'Y' – was called in and told to explain himself. He then confessed that the Tory camp had paid him £250 to put up an 'extreme' candidate, with the object of splitting the nationalist vote and letting the Tory in – hence his brilliant idea of nominating Parnell. When he had finished, Parnell asked him where the balance of the money was. For a long time Y refused to tell. Finally, Parnell said to him, 'If you do not tell me at once where the money is I will raise that window and denounce you to the citizens of Cork.' As an immense crowd had gathered to hear Parnell speak, Y, after one look at them, disgorged £200 which he still had in his pocket. The money was used for Parnell's expenses and in the result he and the moderate nationalist were elected.[3]

This was one of the rare moments of humour in an election which was often bitter and sometimes violent. Parnell had a difficult and complex struggle to wage. Not only were he and his friends desperately short of money, but they were opposed by three different interests. Only the fact that these interests were divided saved the Parnellites from annihilation, and the sequel was to show that on one critical occasion, when they were not divided, danger immediately threatened. The three interests antagonistic to Parnell were the moderate Home Rulers, the Fenians – in 1880 the IRB withdrew the permission it had given only a short time before for its members to assist at elections – and the church. As the campaign developed it became clear that the church was the most formidable of Parnell's opponents and if its influence had been deployed with anything like unanimity this might well have decided the outcome. That it was not so deployed was partly because the bishops could not always be sure of their own clergy, and partly because even within the hierarchy there were differences of opinion which made united action difficult.

A key figure in this situation was the Archbishop of Dublin, Edward McCabe, who was highly suspicious of the Land League and at the beginning of 1880 had placed himself firmly behind a papal circular warning Irish Catholics against associating themselves with extreme men or wild doctrines.[4] On the other hand, Archbishop McCabe did not see the League as connected either with the Fenians in particular or with the secret societies in general, and he was not anxious to defend the land system, especially since heart-rending accounts were reaching him from western bishops shocked by the sufferings of their people in what had developed into full-scale famine in certain districts.[5] But this did not mean that he could bring himself to approve of a movement directed against property, which inflamed the people by arousing expectations it could not fulfil. As he put it to an English correspondent early in 1880: 'Mr Parnell when travelling through Ireland on his tour of agitation did an enormous amount of mischief. He raised hopes in the minds of his hearers that could never be realized. We cannot tell what his motives were, but certainly his whole course was calculated to create a spirit of discontent. And I believe that the latent Fenianism of the country was called into life and energy by his action . . . I fear Mr Parnell and the League would cure the disease by killing the patient.'[6]

It was hardly surprising therefore that Parnell and his friends should have clashed on several occasions with either bishops or clergy, especially since the friends included men like J. J. O'Kelly and Lysaght Finegan who openly acknowledged their close contacts with the French anti-clerical, Henri Rochefort. Parnell himself must bear some responsibility for the friction that resulted, since in this election he behaved with much less caution than he was later to display when he had become the official leader of the party. It is a measure of his relative immaturity that in three different constituencies he contrived to come into direct conflict with clerical opposition.

The first and most serious of these was in county Wexford, where the Parnellite candidates were John Barry and a Wicklow man, Garret Byrne. It was the decision to run the latter against the sitting member, the Chevalier Keyes O'Clery, which precipitated at a meeting in Enniscorthy on Easter Sunday a scene unique in Parnell's experience until the last year of his life. The local bishop anticipated trouble from the first, but was unsure how best to meet it. 'The great majority of the people wish O'Clery to be returned', he assured Archbishop McCabe, 'but on the other hand our great politician, Fr T. Doyle, P.P., has denounced O'Clery in his strongest form as "a traitor", "a pledge-breaker" etc.' As a result Parnell was coming into the constituency with the express purpose of defeating O'Clery, a prospect which the bishop regarded with impotent terror. 'If I move on this matter publicly I am denounced beforehand and pretty sure of being ignominiously defeated. I thought the only thing I ought to do in the matter was to keep quiet.'[7]

The confrontation was far worse than even the bishop's gloomiest forebodings. On that sunny Easter Day (28 March) a large crowd swarmed into Abbey Square where a platform had been erected for the speakers. O'Clery, flanked by various priests, had taken his place and the proceedings were about to be opened by the chairman, another priest, when down the hill came Parnell with his two candidates and a contingent from the Wexford Independent Club, a local organization apparently catering for 'active' nationalists who were prepared to work with Parnell's parliamentary group. But Enniscorthy, which had a revolutionary tradition going back to 1798, also contained a number of orthodox Fenians who rejected constitutionalism *in toto*. Some of these were undoubtedly present in the crowd and this led several commentators to suppose that the violence which suddenly broke loose was some kind of Fenian backlash against Parnell or against his candidate, Barry, the ex-Fenian now seeking a seat in parliament.[8] The truth was not so simple. The Chevalier O'Clery, though a 'Whig' in the sense that he had not acted with Parnell and his group in the House of Commons, had actually succeeded in 1879 in getting a bill through the House to authorize the raising of a volunteer force in Ireland. It went no further but it gave O'Clery an excellent rallying-cry for the election and it helps to explain why he, a devout Catholic and certainly no extremist, should have received, as it seems he did, Fenian support on this occasion.[9] What this could mean was immediately demonstrated when Parnell, after a preliminary scuffle at the rear of the meeting, pushed his way to the front of the platform, while some of his followers were simultaneously ejected from it. A contemporary account vividly describes the ensuing pandemonium:[10]

> In front the crowd surged to and fro and shouted in a frenzied manner, 'No dictator', 'Down with Byrne' and 'Cheers for O'Clery'. Mr Parnell worked his way to the front and an orange, thrown for him, squashed in his neighbour's eyes. Mr Parnell was at the same time hit with an egg which ran down his face. Shouting, striking and struggling followed, all order was lost, cries of 'It's a shame' and 'Down with him' sounded high. The chairman, whose face was bathed with perspiration, brandished a small blackthorn trying to restore peace. Then a stone or two and some mud were contributed by the crowd . . . but this was directly stopped, and not afterwards repeated. When anything like a pause came, the disturbances were renewed with vigour, apparently caused by the O'Clery party selecting those who should be allowed to remain.

There followed cheers and counter-cheers for Barry and for O'Clery, in the course of which Parnell was pulled to and fro by the crowd, remaining perfectly impassive the while, 'like a man of bronze', as Healy said afterwards.[11] Meanwhile, a member of the Wexford Independent Club was savagely beaten and toppled from the platform, the blood flowing down his face. Next, and not a moment too soon, a detachment of the RIC, complete with rifles, marched into the square and took up station near the platform. 'After some consultation with the clergy', the report continues, 'Mr Parnell, very pale, but determined-looking, with his arms crossed, his neck tie awry, and a button torn off his coat, stood at the barrier of the platform waiting for silence.' Then came a further scene:

> Mr Parnell endeavoured to speak amid constant interruptions.
>
> Father [J] Murphy – You will not insult the priests of Wexford [great excitement].
>
> A rush was made for the platform, attempts were made to catch Mr Parnell by the legs [his trousers were ripped from the ankle to the knee] and efforts were made to push away the assailants.
>
> Mr Parnell – I said nothing.
>
> Father Murphy – You did sir [cries of 'Apologize' and uproar].

Hereupon one priest seized Parnell to drag him back while others (not priests) tried to pull him forward. Eventually, the same Father Murphy who had just clashed with him, intervened to protect him from being torn in two. All this time Parnell made no move either to defend himself or to retaliate. In the brief intervals of calm he continued his speech as if nothing had happened and when he had finished what he had come to say he politely lifted his hat and retired amid the continuing uproar. He had demonstrated his courage, but also, though he later tried to minimize the episode by ascribing the violence to a minority of Fenian extremists, he had demonstrated how far he had still to go before creating a broad-based national movement. Yet he had the last laugh, for the county Wexford gave its own verdict on the Enniscorthy tumult by returning both Barry and Byrne.[12]

If the other two episodes further illustrated the nature of the opposition he faced, they illustrated no less the power he was beginning to wield. In Wicklow he proposed to run two candidates of his own choosing – a local farmer, W. J. Corbet, and T. M'Coan, one of the 'carpet-baggers' whom Parnell had to press into service at this time because they could pay their election expenses and maintain themselves while parliament was in session. A local priest, Father D. Kane of Baltinglass, was prepared to swallow Corbet, but wanted another Wicklow man in place of M'Coan. He was deeply outraged when M'Coan and Corbet descended on the town after nightfall and presented themselves unabashed at his house, accompanied by a train of children and village misfits. 'I resented this very strongly and said what I think', Kane wrote to his archbishop, 'that it was indecent to canvass before the clergy had decided, and that we were not, here at all events, yet prepared to submit even to Mr Parnell when he sent strangers to represent us, and when they set aside every authority except a mob.' 'There is a very strong feeling indeed', he added, 'that it is better to assert the independence of the electors and challenge the intrusion of M'Coan than return two Home Rulers.'[13] But this feeling was not proof against Parnell's impetuous energy. A day or so later he paid a lightning visit to Arklow and Wicklow as a result of which his candidates were not only adopted but returned.[14]

The third incident, which occurred at Mohill in county Leitrim, did not produce for Parnell the same successful result, but it indicated even more strikingly how far he was prepared to go at this period in dealing with clergy who crossed his path. Leitrim was a difficult case, because he was promoting a most unusual candidate, the Reverend Isaac Nelson, a Presbyterian minister from Belfast, well known as a warm supporter of the land agitation. The Catholic clergy of the constituency were firmly behind a local candidate and they did not take kindly to the idea of a stranger being foisted on them, and a Presbyterian cleric at that. Their leader was a certain Father Langan, to whom belongs the melancholy distinction of being the only priest, so far as is known, whom Parnell ever ordered out of his presence. The clash between them was accentuated by the fact that Parnell was accompanied by a notorious Fenian-cum-Land Leaguer, James Daly of Castlebar, and by the knowledge, common to all, that Langan's supporters were at large in the town, blackthorns in hand. In an attempt to avoid a clash the priest sought an interview with Parnell, in the course of which the following extraordinary exchange took place:

> Father Langan said they all honoured and respected Mr Parnell, but they did not honour the man who came to them against their wishes.
>
> *Mr Parnell* – In the Orange city of Montreal I was not molested; in the Orange city of Toronto I was allowed to speak; and it remains for the county of Leitrim to disgrace itself.
>
> *Father Langan* – I will ask you to listen to me. As long as you speak for Ireland we honour you, but in the interests of peace I ask you not to speak for Mr Nelson.
>
> *Mr Daly* (excitedly) – You would not bring bludgeon men here if you honoured him.
>
> [Father Langan here indignantly denied that he had done any such thing and again advised Parnell not to speak.]
>
> *Mr Parnell* – Do you suppose I will be dictated to?
>
> *Father Langan* – I don't dictate to you, but you are dictating to the priests.
>
> *Mr Parnell* – Freedom of speech is one of the few liberties we have in this country and I will not allow my freedom of speech to be taken away.

When Langan again asked him to desist, Parnell replied that he would do his duty and they had better close the interview. There was some further altercation until Parnell went to the door, opened it and said, 'Will you be good enough to retire.' Father Langan went out, baffled, into the crowd, but while there was some stone-throwing, the 'bludgeon-men' were kept at bay behind a line of police. The Reverend Isaac Nelson, however, was not returned for Leitrim, though Parnell, with his habitual tenacity, inserted him later into the Mayo seat he left vacant when he chose to sit for Cork city.[15]

II

The outcome of the election was a personal, if limited, triumph for Parnell. The total number of Home Rulers elected was reckoned to be 63, but two of these sat as Liberals, so the new party really numbered 61. Of these, 24 were definite Parnellites, 21 were definite Whigs, and the remainder were at first undecided, though inclining towards Parnell as time went on. In socio-economic terms landlords were less numerous than before, but this was only to be expected and did not portend any radical shift to the left. The Home Rule representation became, no doubt, more middle-class in its composition, but in income and status it belonged to the upper rather than the lower levels of that middle class in the proportion of 48 to 13.[16] What was significantly novel about it was that it contained the nucleus of the group round which Parnell was to build a much more powerful party in the next five years. Among the newly elected Parnellites were John Dillon (chosen for a Tipperary seat while still absent on Land League business in America), J. J. O'Kelly, Arthur O'Connor (a London Irishman who became the party's acknowledged expert on parliamentary procedure), Thomas Sexton and T. P. O'Connor; to these were soon to be added Tim Healy and John Redmond.

Perhaps the most notable of these newcomers were Sexton and T. P. O'Connor. Sexton was only 32 years of age but moved rapidly into the front rank of the party's spokesmen in the House of Commons, especially on matters of finance. The son of a policeman, he was largely self-educated and began life as a railway clerk. From this he was rescued by the *Nation* for which newspaper he became a leader-writer in 1867. At the time of his election to parliament in 1880 he was strongly identified with the Land League and was a loyal follower of Parnell. In personality he was withdrawn and introspective, a man who almost ceased to exist when he stepped down from the public platform; lacking charisma, he seemed cut out for the role of eternal lieutenant.

T. P. O'Connor, the bustling extrovert of the party, was at the opposite pole. A graduate of Queen's College, Galway, he went to London in 1870 at the age of 22 to try his fortune as a journalist. He quickly made his mark as one of the pioneers of a cheap and popular press. He became, and remained, a 'London Irishman', relatively little known at home, but a great power with the Irish in Great Britain and the driving force in their organization. He had extensive contacts on the left of the Liberal party and in this way was useful to his leader, though his boisterous, almost stage-Irish temperament was of the kind most likely to grate on Parnell's nerves.[17] There is, however, some evidence that at this early stage of their relationship Parnell may have been temporarily influenced by O'Connor to adopt attitudes in the House of Commons more acceptable to English Radicals than to Irish nationalists.

The outstanding instance of this is usually held to have been the great dispute which periodically convulsed the House of Commons in the early eighties as to whether or not Charles Bradlaugh should be allowed to take his seat in the House of Commons. Bradlaugh was a non-believer – or, as the *Freeman's Journal* put it, 'a blatant, brazen, howling Atheist' – and he was, in addition, an advocate of birth control.[18] In both these roles he was anathema to most sections of Irish opinion and it is therefore all the more remarkable that in May and June 1880, when the question first of Bradlaugh's admission, and then of his possible imprisonment for disobeying the orders of the House aroused passionate debate, Parnell should have voted on the atheist's side. F. H. O'Donnell and T. M. Healy both thought this decision wrong and blamed O'Connor for it.[19] O'Connor's version is that he had tried to dissuade his leader, but that Parnell had replied that he was so disgusted by the bigotry of Bradlaugh's opponents that he must speak in his defence, even though Bradlaugh's views, especially on birth control, were abhorrent to him.[20] But not only did he speak for Bradlaugh on both occasions, he went out of his way – so O'Donnell alleged – to shake hands with the 'infidel' when the Sergeant-at-Arms had arrested him.[21] In all of this, though, it is not necessary to discern the unholy influence of the genial 'T.P.'. Two other explanations of Parnell's conduct are probably nearer the mark. One is that he, who did not take his opinions from other people on any matter and in religion was probably also an unbeliever at this period, spoke out of conviction when he supported Bradlaugh, especially since Bradlaugh, like himself, was fighting against the brute vote of the majority. The other is that Bradlaugh had a reputation for friendliness to Irish nationalism. He had helped to draft a Fenian declaration in 1867, had spoken (like Parnell) in defence of the 'Manchester martyrs' and was (again like Parnell) a vice-president of the Democratic League of Great Britain and Ireland. In short, an Irish leader who wanted to demonstrate to his left wing that parliamentary respectability had not seduced him, had something to gain from a demonstration in support of this forlorn cause.[22] How much he might stand to lose, and how far he might have to adjust his conscience, the sequel would presently show.

Although the group of 24 Parnellites returned at the general election was not a majority of the Home Rule representation, it was large enough, and determined enough, to secure Parnell's election as chairman of the parliamentary party. This came about partly because the new party sufficiently resembled the old for only 41 out of 61 members to turn up for the eve-of-session meeting, but it was partly the product of chance. The meeting was due to be held in the City Hall, Dublin, on 17 May. On the previous night several of the newly-elected members gathered at the Imperial Hotel in Sackville Street – the group included T. P. O'Connor, J. J. O'Kelly, Biggar and Timothy Healy, though he was not yet an MP. Healy it was who argued most vehemently for the leadership of Parnell and carried the others with him. Next day they gained the adherence of Justin McCarthy, but the man essential to their plan, Parnell himself, was only to be found when actually on his way from Morrison's Hotel to the City Hall. He merely smiled at the proposition, neither assenting nor dissenting, though that he had thought about the problem was evident from the fact that he showed O'Connor a list of 'doubtful' members, so large as to make it impossible to deduce how a vote would go. For this reason, and also because he seems genuinely to have feared the trammelling effects of office, Parnell's own idea was to put forward McCarthy as a compromise candidate. This was brushed to one side by his friends and his name was formally proposed by the O'Gorman Mahon as chairman for the coming session; the seconder was Joseph Biggar. The alternative candidate was the previous chairman, William Shaw. Quietly, but with the sense strong upon them of making some decisive choice, men gave their votes – 23 for Parnell, 18 for Shaw. After a brief adjournment, E. D. Gray, who had presided, gave place to the new leader. 'With some hesitation', says O'Connor 'and with a certain deprecatory look on his face, Parnell went into the chair.'[23]

One feature of that vote had a significance no one present could then have predicted. T. P. O'Connor, glancing round the room, had noticed among the new members a man he had never seen before and whom nobody seemed to know except the O'Gorman Mahon. 'Slightly overdressed', as O'Connor described him, 'laughing, with the indescribable air of the man whom life had made somewhat cynical, he was in sharp contrast with the rugged, plainly dressed, serious figures round him. If appearances were not deceptive, he bore the unmistakable marks of the Whig.'[24] Yet, when he had cast his vote, that vote was for Parnell. The name of this mysterious newcomer and improbable supporter was William Henry O'Shea.

At this point in his career O'Shea was just 40 years of age. He had been born in Dublin in 1840, the only son of a well-to-do solicitor,

Henry O'Shea, and had received the education typical of a certain kind
of Catholic middle-class youth of the period – school at St Mary's
College, Oscott, and a brief spell in Trinity College, Dublin. At Oscott
O'Shea showed considerable ability, especially in languages, frequently
earning the *feria* or monthly holiday for proficiency.* He was also
something of a bully and the poet, Wilfrid Scawen Blunt, a few years
his junior, long remembered being painfully pursued by him with a
fives bat.[25] His university career was almost non-existent and in 1858
O'Shea took up the more congenial career of a cornet in the 18th
Hussars. A contemporary photograph shows him as the very model of
a young cavalry officer, handsome, debonair, untroubled by the
pressures of thought. But the army did not last long either and within
a few years O'Shea sold out as a captain. He had relations in Spain who
had extensive banking and mining interests and to the extent that he
had a regular income thereafter, it came partly from what his father
allowed him and partly from the intermittent and insufficient commissions he picked up on his Spanish expeditions.[26]

He was still in the army when he first met the girl who was to become
his wife. She was Katharine, the youngest of the thirteen children of
Sir John Page Wood, a former chaplain to Queen Caroline and for
many years rector of the country parish of Rivenhall in Essex. The
Woods were gentlefolk and though far from rich themselves they had
wealthy and influential connections. One of Katharine's uncles, Lord
Hatherley, had been for a time Lord Chancellor in Gladstone's first
ministry and a brother, Sir Evelyn (later Field-Marshal) Wood, VC,
was a distinguished soldier. It was only after a long courtship that
Katharine married her 'Willie', in January 1867 when she was a week
short of her twenty-second birthday, and though O'Shea's superficial
charm made him initially popular with the Wood family, by no stretch
of the imagination could the match – a mixed marriage with an impecunious Irishman – have been regarded as a brilliant one for the bride.
When children began to arrive, Willie soon proved spectacularly
inadequate to provide for them. Having run through his father's money,
he was thrown increasingly on his Spanish resources, for although he
owned some land in Ireland he was the complete absentee and never
seems to have regarded his modest estate there as a source of income.
In the ten years after marriage, though a son (Gerard) and two daughters
(Norah and Carmen) were born to the couple, Willie took to spending

*I am deeply indebted to Father Dennis Egan, of Oscott College, for making
available to me the evidence of O'Shea's performance as recorded in the Mark-
book for the period (1850–5) of his attendance at the College.

longer and longer periods abroad, and it would have gone hard with Katharine had not a rich aunt, Mrs Benjamin Wood, come to her rescue. 'Aunt Ben', the unconscious pivot upon whom momentous events were presently to turn, was a very old lady when she took her niece in hand. It was she who provided Katharine with a house, Wonersh Lodge, across the park from her own grand residence at Eltham, and who set Willie up in an apartment in town.[27]

O'Shea's irruption into politics in 1880 was due to his friendship with the O'Gorman Mahon who, though now at an advanced age, still had more than a trace of the raffish bonhomie which was O'Shea's own hall-mark. The old man suggested to Parnell that he and O'Shea should be run for the two Clare seats and when both were returned it was O'Shea – or rather, Katharine's Aunt Ben – who footed the bill for their expenses. Katharine herself had encouraged her husband's new-found enthusiasm, if only to give him something to do and to keep him away from Eltham. They had not quarrelled catastrophically, but had simply drifted so far apart over the years that they now preferred to lead their own separate existences, she living quietly with her aunt at Eltham, he keeping up a certain style (on Aunt Ben's money) at Albert Mansions, near Victoria, and still travelling frequently to Spain. They preserved appearances in the conventional manner. He descended upon Eltham now and then to take the children to Mass, she went up to London occasionally to be his hostess at dinner-parties for business associates. But in after years she always insisted that by 1880 they had long been effectively parted. Whether this meant that physical relations between them had entirely ceased is open to doubt, but it is clear that to all intents and purposes their marriage had become a façade by the time O'Shea entered politics.[28]

His vote for Parnell as chairman seems to have been a calculated risk, though one he apparently took with some trepidation, telegraphing to his wife his fear that Parnell might be too 'advanced'.[29] On the other hand, the new leader's star could well be in the ascendant and an impoverished retired captain might do worse than rise with it. Consequently, O'Shea began to change the composition of the little dinner-parties at Thomas's Hotel in Berkeley Square to give them a distinctively political character. To these parties Parnell was regularly invited. Some of the invitations he did not answer, some he declined, and some he accepted. But whether he declined, ignored or accepted the invitations, he never actually appeared. Eventually it became a point of pride for Katharine to fill the vacant chair and one fine summer day in 1880 – she does not tell us the exact date, but it was probably early in July

– she drove with her sister Mrs Anna Steele to Palace Yard at Westminster and sent in her card to Parnell. Many years later she described what happened next:[30]

> He came out, a tall, gaunt figure, thin and deadly pale. He looked straight at me smiling and his curiously burning eyes looked into mine with a wondering intentness that threw into my brain the sudden thought: 'This man is wonderful – and different.'
>
> I asked him why he had not answered my last invitation to dinner, and if nothing would induce him to come. He answered that he had not opened his letters for days, but if I would let him, he would come to dinner directly he returned from Paris, where he had to go for his sister's wedding.
>
> In leaning forward in the cab to say good-bye a rose I was wearing in my bodice fell out on to my skirt. He picked it up and, touching it lightly with his lips, placed it in his button-hole.

This account, written in old age, is no doubt romanticized. The encounter was probably seen at the time by Katharine merely as registering a success which had long eluded her, and by Parnell as a tiresome obligation he could no longer avoid. All the same, the letter he wrote her shortly afterwards, on 17 July, renewed his promise to dine after he got back from Paris. Katharine, therefore, went ahead with her plans, booking a box at the Gaiety Theatre and inviting for dinner beforehand Justin McCarthy, Anna Steele, and one or two others. On the appointed day Parnell arrived late – his normal practice – and during the meal addressed most of his remarks to Mrs Steele. Afterwards at the play, he, who never ordinarily dreamed of entering a theatre, settled in a corner of the darkened box and in low tones talked to Katharine about his American experiences including, not very tactfully, how on his last visit he had briefly seen the girl, Miss Woods, with whom, years earlier, he had had that curious on-and-off engagement. The implication – which bore no relation to the facts – was that he had had to choose between the maiden and the cause, and he made it clear that the cause was paramount. She, watching him talk, thought how pale and delicate he seemed, which was doubtless no more than the truth.[31] He was living an irregular bachelor existence, briefly at Avondale, more often in his London lodgings at 16 Keppel Street, and carrying the double burden of the parliamentary leadership and the land agitation. But he was also young and ardent, and she, though a little older and the mother of three children, was still darkly handsome and possessed a quality of maternal solicitude which attracted him from the outset.

Acquaintance ripened into friendship and friendship rapidly into something more. When exactly they became lovers is not clear and his early letters to her, mostly written in September 1880, are cautiously addressed to 'My dear Mrs O'Shea'. We do know, though, that they went for drives in the country together and that there was at least one luncheon party before he left for Ireland that same month. And even these early formal letters contained not very mysterious references to the cause of his discontent at being in Wicklow rather than in London ('perhaps you will help me to find it, or her, on my return') and to the absence of 'a certain kind and fair face'.[32] On 23 September he came all the way from Ireland to visit her, but she was tending her old nurse through her last illness and could not see him, so he returned forlornly to Dublin next day. 'How I wish', he wrote on 25 September, 'it might have been possible for me to have seen you even for a few minutes to tell you how very much I feel any trouble which comes to you.'[33] Some time that autumn he stayed at Eltham, apparently at O'Shea's invitation and in order to restore his health. That seems to have been the decisive moment. By 17 October he was writing to Katharine as 'My dearest love'.[34]

III

We shall soon have to follow the intricacies of their affair further and deeper, but it is time to return to the principal reason why the star-crossed lovers were also so often sea-divided. The inescapable fact was that from the moment the election ended, Irish politics were dominated by the worsening economic situation and by the spreading agitation of the Land League. At the end of April, *before* Parnell became chairman of the parliamentary party, a conference of the League was held in Dublin to formulate a policy which the party should then put forward in parliament. On the eve of the conference, the committee met in all-night session at Morrison's Hotel to prepare the programme for the following day's work. Though Davitt later asserted that Parnell contributed little to the discussion, his speech to the conference followed an impeccable Land League line. Part of the business of the conference was to lay down long-term plans for the future, based upon the proposition which was now almost taken for granted, that 'the establishment of a peasant proprietary is the only solution of the question which will be accepted as final by the country'. But more immediately relevant was the proposition introduced by Parnell himself which called, as an interim measure, for the suspension for two years of all ejectments for non-payment of rent in holdings valued at £10, later increased to £20 a year and under, and similarly suspending for two years in the case of any holding whatever the right of recovery of any rent higher than the poor law valuation.[35]

It was indicative of the complex situation in which Parnell now found himself that while Davitt refused to sign the programme on the ground that the terms to be offered to the landlord were too generous (twenty years' purchase on the basis of the poor law valuation of his estate), a public meeting at the Rotunda on 30 April to ratify the work of the conference was attacked and nearly broken up by Fenians, demanding the right to move a resolution protesting against extreme men taking part in a moral force agitation. Amid pandemonium Parnell permitted them to read their resolution, but as this only provoked more uproar they went away without pressing it to a vote. Whether he felt obliged to compete with them, or because he was momentarily swept off balance by the tumult, Parnell then allowed himself to repeat, to immense applause, the story of a man who at one of his American meetings had come forward to offer 'five dollars for bread, twenty dollars for lead'. This was later brought up against him at the Special Commission, when the Attorney-General tried to prove that this was in effect a subscription to physical force. Parnell smilingly riposted, to the exasperation of the Attorney-General, that it was only 'your side' – by which he meant Tories and landlords – who believed this, but he was hard put to it to answer the Attorney-General's pertinent query as to why, if he was the devotee of non-violence he said he was, he chose to tell this particular story to an already inflamed audience. All he could reply was that 'it was certainly a very stupid recitation to give and I certainly had no particular object in my head'. And he repeated, 'stupid, because there was no object'.[36]

Perhaps there was no object. Or perhaps it was an object which in 1889 Parnell had no wish to disclose to the Special Commission. For the more closely we scrutinize his actions and his words in the summer and autumn of 1880 the clearer it becomes that he was beginning, though in a still crude fashion, to pursue that tactic of balance between extremes which he was to develop and maintain with extraordinary skill and good fortune for the next two years. It has been pointed out by Dr Cruise O'Brien that both left and right in Irish politics were becoming more sharply differentiated at this period. On the left, support had come from the architects of the 'new departure', from the American-Irish with their money and their enthusiasm, from Patrick Ford's *Irish World*, and from the involvement of individual Fenians in the work of the Land

League despite the official ostracism of the League by the IRB. But all this support, without which Parnell could not have risen to the head of a mass movement in Ireland, had to be paid for, and the price was the public expression of intransigence whenever a suitable moment presented itself.

On the other hand, Parnell was beginning to gain ground not only within the parliamentary party, but in the country at large, and also to win the approval of the *Freeman's Journal*, which played a key role in the formation of 'respectable' public opinion. If he was to consolidate these gains he would have to demonstrate that bold speeches at excited meetings did not exhaust his armoury and that as chairman of a revitalized party he could produce positive results in parliament. In assessing his oscillations between right and left it is important to be clear that, although some of the new 'Parnellites' returned in 1880 were of a kind to startle conservative nationalists, the group, and still more the party of which it formed a section, remained essentially moderate. This was partly because it was elected on a restricted franchise which, in the counties and the boroughs, but especially the latter, confined the vote to a more prosperous class, relatively speaking, than in Britain. But partly also it was a consequence of the fact that to get elected to a party which had hardly any money of its own, and when elected to spend long months unremuneratively in London, was something which only men of means could contemplate. And in the Irish context men of means were seldom men of revolutionary opinions. Even if they had been, the fact that the church – in the shape of the local bishop and the parish clergy – frequently had a decisive influence in the choice of a member meant that conservative views would generally be preferred over extreme ones. It is true that in 1880 Parnell was still an object of suspicion to some bishops but it only needed his party to establish itself as a constructive political force, for this important concentration of power to move over to his side. That time was not yet, and Parnell would gravitate, or be pushed, further to the left before he began to swing back towards the right, but when he did so the political dividends to be harvested would be considerable.[37]

The particular situation which the Home Rulers faced at the opening of the new parliament in May 1880 reinforced the arguments for caution and constraint. The election having brought Gladstone and the Liberal party back to power, there was a reasonable expectation that this might result in a more compassionate approach to Irish problems. Events, indeed, were soon to show that 'the Liberal party' was a much fragmented and highly disputatious body, and that Afghanistan was more on Gladstone's mind than Ireland, but it was at least possible to hope that he would prove educable, and might then himself turn to and educate his colleagues. Thus, when Parnell told the Special Commission nine years later that on his return from America he had not concerned himself with the organizational problems of the Land League, he was not just covering his tracks, or exposing his inherent distaste for administrative detail, he was also making a plain statement about his priorities at that time. For him, so long as the parliamentary situation remained fluid, the House of Commons had to be his main theatre of operations.

Everything depended, then, on the response which the new government would make to the two related features of the Irish agrarian crisis which impressed all observers – the impending, in some districts the actual, famine in the west and the tendency of evictions to increase in precisely those areas where hardship was making the payment of even moderate rents impossible. There was no difference between the rival sections of the Home Rule party about the desirability of moving the government to act, but there was a world of difference between them as to how this should be achieved. It was symbolized by the fact that whereas Shaw and those who thought like him sat on the Liberal side of the House, Parnell and his group sat with the Tories, thus stressing their conviction that the duty of an Irish party was to function as an independent opposition. Predictably, it was the Parnellites who took the initiative when O'Connor Power introduced a bill whose purpose was to halt evictions by enacting that compensation should be paid to the tenant in any case of disturbance. This bill had actually passed its second reading in June when the government decided to intervene. On 18 June the Chief Secretary, W. E. Forster, introduced the Compensation for Disturbance Bill which provided that an evicted tenant should be entitled to compensation when he could prove to the satisfaction of the courts that he could not pay his rent for good cause (for example, bad harvests), that he was willing to continue his tenancy on just and reasonable terms, and that these terms had been refused by his landlord.

This replacement of a private member's bill by a government measure was a major triumph for Parnell and the first indication since he had entered parliament that constitutional pressure might produce valuable results. Yet the immediate sequel seemed to demonstrate only the futility of such pressure. By the end of July the bill had gone successfully through the Commons; on 3 August it was rejected by the Lords by a massive majority. At once the news from Ireland reflected an upsurge of violence. Evictions began to be accompanied more frequently by riots, 'land-grabbers' (men who dared to take farms from which the original tenants had been evicted) were assaulted, and on 11 August there was an extraordinary episode when a party of Fenians raided a ship in Queenstown Harbour and carried off a quantity of arms. Even more ominous was the fact that when the local branch of the Land League sought to dissociate itself from the deed, it received a sharp reprimand from the central executive, meeting in Dublin.[38]

It so happened that the chairman of the Dublin meeting was John Dillon, who had returned from America eager to play a central role in the land war. He took his seat in parliament for the first time just as the Compensation for Disturbance Bill was at crisis point. On 10 August, after its rejection, he warned the House that there might be 'bloodshed and massacre to come'.[39] He then returned to Ireland, where he made at Kildare easily the most inflammatory speech which any responsible Irish politician had yet delivered during the Land League agitation. It was an appeal to farmers to organize, parish by parish, in preparation for a general strike against rent. Organizing, it appeared, also meant drilling. 'They had a right to march to their meetings and obey the commands of their leaders', he said. 'They would see that every man in Ireland had a right to have a rifle if he liked.'[40]

This speech threw into sharp relief the kind of problem which Parnell was going to have to face inside and outside the House during the months ahead. It was at bottom the problem of how to control excitable young men who responded emotionally to what was certainly an explosive situation in Ireland but who, in so responding, made difficult, if not impossible, the kind of tactical battle he was intent on waging in parliament. From this standpoint Dillon's outburst could hardly have been worse timed, for it came just when his leader was contemplating a concerted attack on the Irish estimates, as a signal to the country that he was not sinking into a Butt-like stupor of acquiescence. This, indeed, was so well known that one of the surviving 'Whig' members, George Errington, warned Archbishop McCabe that, in the circumstances, the polite debate on teacher's training colleges which he, Errington, had hoped to initiate on the Irish education estimates might have to be postponed, for 'several persons much interested in the training [colleges] think it neither prudent nor useful to bring it on in such company, nor at a moment when the House will be either very weary or very irritated against Irish questions'.[41] In the event, Dillon, by provoking the Chief Secretary into an attack upon him for what Forster called the 'cowardice' of his Kildare speech, precipitated a general debate on 23 August which overflowed into the discussion of the Irish police estimates the following day and led to the only piece of obstruction practised by the new party since parliament had reassembled. But this was very far from the probing debate on the estimates which Parnell had intended and it appears that he did not relish having the initiative taken away from him in this way. He seems, in fact, to have viewed it almost as a sham fight, necessitated perhaps by the Dillon case, yet not to be pushed to extremes while there was still a chance that the government might do something to retrieve the worsening situation created by the rejection of the Compensation for Disturbance Bill.[42]

But the days passed without any sign from Gladstone and on 7 September parliament was prorogued. Parnell went home to Avondale where he seemed more interested in partridges than in agitation. It was not until 19 September that he at last broke silence and launched what quickly developed into a formidable threat to the government's control of the country. This was the celebrated occasion at Ennis, county Clare, where he defined the technique of non-violent intimidation which was shortly to become famous as 'boycotting':

> Now [he said to the excited crowd] what are you to do with a tenant who bids for a farm from which his neighbour has been evicted [Various shouts, among which 'Kill him' and 'Shoot him']. Now I think I heard somebody say, 'Shoot him' ['Shoot him']. But I wish to point out to you a very much better way, a more Christian and more charitable way which will give the lost sinner an opportunity of repenting. When a man takes a farm from which another has been evicted, you must show him on the roadside when you meet him, you must show him in the streets of the town, you must show him at the shop-counter, you must show him in the fair and at the market-place, and even in the house of worship, by leaving him severely alone, by putting him into a sort of moral Coventry, by isolating him from the rest of his kind as if he were a leper of old, you must show him your detestation of the crime he has committed, and you may depend upon it if the population of a county in Ireland carry out this doctrine, that there will be no man so full of avarice, so lost to shame, as to dare the public opinion of all right-thinking men within the county and to transgress your unwritten code of laws.*

It is not strictly true to say that Parnell invented the boycott. On the contrary, in mid-August an American newspaper correspondent,

*There are many sources for this well-known declaration; I cite here the one used by the authorities in keeping track of the agitation with a view to future

James Redpath, who had become personally involved in the agitation, anticipated some of the actual phrases Parnell used three weeks later. Dillon outlined a similar policy in Dublin early in September and a Land League organizer, J. W. Walsh, did likewise in Leitrim about the same time.[43] But obviously this forbidding doctrine gained greatly in impact when enunciated by the man who combined the presidency of the League with the chairmanship of the parliamentary party. It was indeed a doctrine well calculated to impress a tenantry who were intensely dependent upon the close ties of kinship and comradeship that held together their isolated rural communities. In such a context 'social excommunication' was potentially a weapon of tremendous moral force. It had, moreover, the advantage that it not only steered angry men away from violence, but, if skilfully carried out, was difficult to bring within the sanctions of the law. Of course, it carried with it the risk that simple, hungry men might pass easily from peaceful to forcible persuasion. No doubt this did happen in some instances, but mainly at a later phase in the campaign, when, as we shall see, the leaders most closely identified with non-violence had been themselves imprisoned.

For Parnell the new policy offered several advantages. Because it was positive it allowed him to resume his place at the head of the agitation at a moment when his preoccupation with parliament might easily have weakened his influence in the country. Again, because it was ostensibly non-violent, it still left open for him the possibility of increasing his leverage in the House of Commons through his command of a controlled agrarian protest in Ireland. And finally it offered a means of demonstrating how the 'new departure' might work in practice. A land agitation pure and simple, or a parliamentary campaign pure and simple, would not have appealed to Devoy and his friends. But a land agitation combined with a parliamentary campaign, and both pointing, however vaguely, towards the future 'independence' or 'freedom' of Ireland, was something they could understand and appreciate. Indeed, Devoy had already said as much earlier in the summer. In a widely publicized letter to the press he had dealt authoritatively with the attitude of 'nationalists' (he meant separatists) towards the land agitation or towards any 'broad and comprehensive' movement that might grow out of it. 'There can be no question', he wrote, 'that individually

---

prosecutions. Police note-takers attended the more important meetings in the latter part of 1880 and their notes were subsequently printed and bound, though not published. I am grateful to Professor R. Dudley Edwards for making available to me the volume of these printed reports in his possession; they are cited hereafter as *Police Reports*.

the majority of the nationalists give an active and earnest support to the Land League, without relinquishing their own principles, and they would give a similar support to any really sound and well-managed national movement, acting by constitutional methods . . .' In this he may well have been exaggerating and in any case he held no brief for Irish Fenians, but he spoke with some weight when he added: 'This is true to even a much greater extent of Irish-American nationalists.'[44]

Provided Parnell could control the League – and this was the all-important condition – it offered him in the autumn of 1880 the best possible means for strengthening his authority in the country and therefore for increasing his effectiveness at Westminster. The leader of a mass-movement apparently on the brink of revolution was more likely to receive a hearing than the chairman of the fraction of a party. There remained, obviously, the danger that as the agrarian crisis intensified and the language of some of the League Leaders grew more reckless, the effect would be to frighten off conservative nationalists, and especially the church, whose support he needed if his movement was ever to achieve the breadth and solidity he was seeking. Yet even here there was a factor working in his favour – the simple but devastating factor of hunger and distress to which most Irishmen, and especially bishops and priests who felt a direct responsibility for their flocks, would instinctively respond. True, it took time for the full implications of this social disaster to sink in and there is evidence to suggest that during that summer and autumn the bishops felt themselves divided about the attitude they should adopt towards the League.[45] But for those who were nearest to the suffering, it was becoming increasingly difficult to condemn the agitation. A case in point is the report Bishop Duggan sent from Clonfert, one of the worst-hit areas, to Archbishop McCabe:[46]

Here we are, this moment, at a deadlock – no employment worthy the name for the labouring poor, at the commencement of a winter that looks more gloomy than the last.

Worse or better, as people read it, there is a spirit of unrest in the air, and of a recklessness I never observed before. Every member of the Land League is endeavouring to stop outrages. So the military will have nothing to shoot down. The League is striking at the roots of the evils of the land system which was the *insane* competition for land. This once rooted out, the question *must* be settled. The whole force of England is powerless to cope with this resolve of the people.

There was obviously a strong middle ground here for Parnell to occupy and in the closing months of the year he succeeded brilliantly – though admittedly with some unwitting, or witless, help from the government. He followed his keynote speech at Ennis with regular weekly appearances on Land League platforms up and down the country. But, though he frequently reiterated the doctrine of the boycott, he combined this with repeated warnings against the use of physical force and with an exposition of his own solution for the land question which was the reverse of revolutionary. It amounted to no more than a demand for land purchase on the basis of 35 annual payments of the rent. 'Let arbitration be now', he said at New Ross a week after the Ennis speech, 'and you would find that the magic of property, which turns sand into gold, would enable the then owner and the now miserable tenant of the most barren and unprofitable holding in Ireland to bring it into such a state of civilization as to put him beyond the reach of two or even three bad seasons.' In economic terms this may have been, almost certainly was, rank utopianism, but it did at least help to justify the claim he was to make so often in later years that the general trend of his speeches at this stage of the agitation was constructive and non-violent. Indeed, at New Ross he went out of his way to condemn a recent shooting as 'entirely unnecessary and absolutely prejudicial, where there is a suitable organization among the tenants themselves'.[47] And only two days later he spoke very firmly to a meeting in Dublin about the growing tendency to exclude government note-takers from Land League platforms, which, he said reasonably enough, would only increase the risk of a serious incident, since if the note-takers were not admitted voluntarily they would come accompanied by the police.[48]

That his warnings against violence were urgently needed, he had direct personal experience when he visited Cork early in October. In the city itself he was given the most impressive reception he had ever yet been accorded anywhere, but as he passed through the cheering throng – 'it looked as if every brick in the walls of the city was a human face', said T. P. O'Connor, who was with him – there lay behind him an incident which vividly demonstrated the deep currents eddying below the glittering surface. He had left the train at Blarney, a few miles from Cork, so as to make his entry by carriage. In the carriage with him were two converts from extremism to constitutionalism. Before the cortège set off a group of men with revolvers rode up to the carriage and compelled the 'renegades' at gun-point to get out. It was a sobering reminder that there were still some who were impressed neither by the Land League nor by the 'new departure' and that Parnell would do well to remember them.[49]

It may have been with this in mind that at Galway three weeks later he warned his hearers that the land agitation, though significant in itself, was still but a means to an end. 'I wish to see the tenant-farmers prosperous', he said. 'But large and important as is the class of tenant-farmers, constituting as they do, with their wives and families, the majority of the people of this country, I would not have taken off my coat and gone to this work, if I had not known that we were laying the foundations by this movement for the recovery of our legislative independence.'[50]

Yet this statement, famous though it afterwards became, should not be over-emphasized. To use the word 'independence' at all was to make sweet music for the ears of those who did not listen very carefully, and this may have been Parnell's deliberate intention. But for those who *did* listen carefully the key lay in the qualifying word 'legislative'; for legislative independence was precisely what Grattan believed he had achieved in 1782 and Parnell was still obsessed by the precedent or analogy of Grattan's parliament. Moreover, this gesture towards what might, to the superficial observer, have seemed fairly 'advanced' politics, was only a temporary aberration. In subsequent speeches Parnell quickly returned to the comparatively safe anchorage of the standard Land League demands. 'The two chief planks in our programme', he said in Tipperary, 'are, firstly, that tenants shall not pay rack-rents and secondly, that no man shall take a farm from which a tenant has been evicted under such circumstances.' And at Athlone he was still more specific. 'We seek first of all to reduce the rents and afterwards to abolish them altogether. We do not wish either to fix or to maintain them.'[51]

But if Parnell thus tried to point the League towards winning its battle with the landlords by non-violent methods, not all Land Leaguers were prepared to imitate his restraint, and as the doctrine of 'social excommunication' grew more powerful, so the government began to contemplate counter-measures. This tendency can only have been reinforced by the evidence from Mayo where, after prolonged friction between Lord Erne's agent, Captain Charles Boycott, and the tenants, the technique of ostracism – henceforth to be called the boycott – was applied so rigorously that a posse of Orange labourers from Ulster had to be brought in under armed guard to harvest his crops. Even more to the point was the fact that Boycott, having ridden out the immediate crisis with considerable courage, soon afterwards went to live in England.[52] Nor did it pass unnoticed that as the League took hold so too did the evictions diminish. Out of 2110 families evicted in 1880, only 198 were evicted in the last three months of the year and for the year as a whole just over 1000 of these families were readmitted either as tenants or as caretakers. On the reverse side of the picture, it was also to be observed that agrarian crime, despite the denunciations of both Parnell and Davitt, showed an alarming tendency to rise; of the 2590 offences ('outrages' in the official description) committed during 1880, 1696 were committed in that same final quarter.[53]

It was against this background that the authorities made their first serious blunder. The Lord-Lieutenant, Earl Cowper, and the Chief Secretary, Forster, worried by the spread of the agitation, had begun to press in October for the suspension of *habeas corpus*. Gladstone argued strongly against them and although the cabinet was divided he managed to hold the line against this kind of wholesale coercion on the ground that the resources of the ordinary law should first be fully tested. It seems that a decision in principle had been made as early as September to prosecute Parnell, Dillon, Biggar, Sexton, Sullivan, Egan and Brennan, together with some lesser officials of the League, for conspiring to prevent the payment of rents and the taking of farms from which tenants had been evicted, for resisting the process of ejectment and, generally, for creating ill will among Her Majesty's subjects. However valid the charges, and their legal basis was doubtful, to press them in this way was psychologically inept, as Forster was well aware. Writing to Gladstone on 8 October, he pointed out that while the government could no doubt claim that by seeking to punish the leading agitators, it was upholding law and order, the result of taking such action would be to generate enormous enthusiasm for Parnell, to stimulate the flow of funds from America, to heal the quarrel between Land Leaguers and nationalists (separatists), to drive moderates into Parnell's camp, and, after all this, to secure no conviction.[54]

These gloomy predictions were fulfilled almost to the letter. On 23 October it was announced that the prosecutions would be instituted. On 2 November the necessary machinery was set in motion. On 28 December the proceedings opened amid massive demonstrations in favour of the 'traversers'. And on 23 January, following the entirely predictable disagreement of the jury, the government case collapsed. Simultaneously, a subscription – the Parnell Defence Fund – was launched to cover the legal expenses of the state trials and £21,000 was quickly raised. Significantly, although some of this came from League funds, about two-thirds was received through the agency of the *Freeman's Journal*, which now began to give consistent support to Parnell and the League; among those whose subscriptions were registered in its columns were the Archbishops of Cashel and Tuam, and the Bishops of Limerick,

Cloyne and Ross, and Clonfert, together with large numbers of the lower clergy.[55] For the first time and under the combined pressure of the government and of the hard times, it seemed as if a genuinely broad-based national movement was about to come into being.

Obviously, the emergence of such a movement while representing a great accession of strength for Parnell, was liable also to increase his difficulties, since to hold this heterogeneous coalition together would require not only nerve and skill, which he possessed, but also favourable external circumstances which, by definition, were outside his control. Much would depend upon the government's reaction to the failure of the prosecutions. Both Forster in Ireland, and Gladstone and Chamberlain in London, were emphatic that if the next step had to be coercion, then it must be accompanied by a reform which would strike at some of the evils which had brought the Land League into existence. But this required anxious cogitation and until the results of that cogitation were unveiled to parliament at the beginning of the new session in January 1881, an uneasy lull fell upon Irish politics.

CHAPTER 5

In the Eye of the Storm

'There can be no doubt that the country is getting worse and
worse every day. Men of all parties agree that Parnell is king of
Ireland.' (D. P. Barton to W. H. Smith, 2 October 1881, Hambleden Papers.)

I

While the lull lasted many eyes were turned speculatively towards the
Irish leader who, after just five years in public life, now occupied the
centre of the stage. The impression Parnell left upon contemporaries
was that of a young man of vibrant energy but also of incalculable reserve.
Although he could relax in private with a few of his colleagues, this
necessarily happened less often after he fell in love with Katharine
O'Shea and even in his 'bachelor' days his political friends had seldom
been allowed more than a fleeting glimpse behind the façade. T. P.
O'Connor had one such glimpse when he visited Parnell at Avondale
in October 1880. He was immediately struck by how easily Parnell
fitted into the country life which had always been his natural environment. 'He was', recalled O'Connor, 'in splendid physical condition . . .
He had fined himself down to a fine point. He walked, too, splendidly;
with the light and brisk air of a man that had gone through the training
for a prize-fight, or a long-distance match.' His very clothes, which
were usually rough tweed, were cut so as not to impede free movement.
Curiously, so it seemed to T.P., the fact that he was beginning to go
bald accentuated the thinness of his face and contributed to the general
picture of superb fitness. He was sensitive about his baldness – perhaps
at this moment it was the sensitiveness of a lover – and was prepared to
adopt any drastic remedy to arrest it. When O'Connor visited him he had
just shaved his head – to make the hair grow thicker. This changed his
appearance so radically that at one of his country meetings that autumn
there had been an embarrassing contretemps when the reception party
failed to recognize him at the station. And when the state trials were in
progress he caused considerable amusement by wearing a small skull

cap. It looked incongruous on one so youthful, but it was typical of the *grand seigneur* side of his nature that the sensation in court left him totally unaffected.[1]

To those who only saw the public man, his inscrutability and silence were his most imposing qualities. A character-sketch which appeared in the *Spectator* in the summer of 1880 described him as hard and fanatical. 'Keen, capable, in one sense scrupulous, in another the reverse of scrupulous, with more hatred for the English government of Ireland than love for the Irish themselves, possessed of no small power for terse taunts and no small jealousy of rivalry, with a good deal of the lawyer's pleasure in technicalities and the lawyer's satisfaction in so handling them as to make them serve larger purposes.' And again: '"Incorruptible", sitting apart, jealous, solitary, with great intensity of purpose and very narrow sympathies, his mind reminds us of some of those who were most potent in the making of the great French revolution, and in Ireland there is undoubtedly enough combustible element for a small, if not a great revolution.'[2]

In an effort to humanize this enigmatic figure busy correspondents made their way to the silences of Avondale to see if the key could be found in the great man's ancestral home. But the results were disappointing. One, who wandered about the estate in the autumn of 1880, found it distressingly ordinary. There were about 30 tenants, of whom two owned three years' rent and another two were one year in arrears. Leases were long and most rents were below the poor law valuation. Rents had been progressively lowered since the death of Parnell's father and it was not long since Parnell had initiated his own twenty-per-cent reduction. The famous saw-mill was functioning well and expensive, though as yet unremunerative, experiments in lead-mining had been begun. As for the tenants themselves, they were the usual job lot, some prosperous, some poor, and a few almost professionally cantankerous.[3]

Another correspondent, who actually penetrated the house and achieved an interview with its master, clearly found the experience intimidating. Parnell claimed (exaggeratedly) that since he entered politics he had not slept six nights at Avondale, and the reporter noted that it had 'a rather barren and neglectful look, with its whitewashed exterior harmonizing but ill with the tints of the meadowland stretching in a semi-circle, bordered by lofty trees, in front of the house'. Nor was the interior much more cheerful. 'One could fancy that the coverings had just been drawn off the furniture at the expiration of a Chancery suit.' The library impressed the visitor rather more and he admired not only the Volunteer banners of the eighteenth century, but also the shelves of books in bindings of the same period. Apart from new novels and some histories of Ireland, there was little that was modern. A book on a table by the fire in the drawing-room – it was a volume of Carlyle's *Miscellanies* – turned out to be his sister Anna's, and her brother made no bones about the fact that he never opened a book if he could help it. 'When I have any leisure', he said, 'I employ my time in working out new mechanical contrivances', adding, in his best throw-away style, that he had nearly lost a finger while helping to install a water-wheel in the saw-mill. It all seemed very strange to the London journalist, whose curious Pooteresque prose helps us to measure the gulf between the Anglo-Irish gentleman and the English newspaper readers before whom he was obliged to act out so much of his career. 'Mr Parnell is very abstemious', wrote the cockney, 'drinking little but water or tea. He smokes a great deal and is never in want of a good "weed" which he proffers very liberally to his friends. At the same time he keeps a neat little cellar, and can, when the occasion arises, regale his guests with a choice vintage. In other respects his style of living is very homely . . . In the intervals of agitation he is a great rider, a moderately keen sportsman, something of a farmer and often speaks of himself as a Cincinnatus who has been regretfully compelled to relinquish his cabbages.'[4]

II

The year 1881 was to be a bad year for the Avondale cabbages. But it was to be a crucial year for Parnell's own destiny, a year in which he, and his country, were to come to the brink of revolution before turning away towards another and stranger 'new departure'. The scene was an Ireland where the power of the League seemed to be spreading but where, despite the League's leaders, outrages appeared to be increasing in response to the mounting total of evictions. Whereas evictions, as we saw earlier, had fallen under Land League pressure during 1880, during 1881 the number of families evicted rose to 3415. Although 194 families were readmitted as tenants and a further 1691 as caretakers, it is obvious that the mere issuing of notices of ejectment was itself a major factor in contributing to the fear and unrest which swept the country in 1881. The direct product of this fear and unrest was a growth in violent crime. From a total of eight murders, no manslaughters and 25 cases of firing at the person in 1880, the corresponding figures rose in 1881 to seventeen murders, five manslaughters and 66 cases of firing at the person. Agrarian crime, which in 1879 had amounted to just under

25 per cent of general crime, in 1881 reached the extraordinary figure of 58 per cent.[5]

It is against this sombre background that Parnell's policy in the early months of 1881 has to be viewed. To a large extent, initially, he was confined to a waiting game until the government revealed their hand. But in the interval he began to move cautiously towards the creation of that unified and disciplined parliamentary party which was to be his most striking political achievement. At a party meeting in the City Hall, Dublin, on 27 December, attended by 38 members, it was unanimously decided that *all* Home Rule members should thenceforth sit on the opposition side of the House. This was designed to present the 'Whig' members with a brutal dilemma. They must either join the activists or publicly separate themselves from them; in the event William Shaw and eleven other Home Rulers formally seceded in January 1881. The rest, ostensibly at least, aligned themselves behind Parnell.

At this same meeting two other resolutions were passed also tending towards stricter control. One was to the effect that members pledged themselves to 'consult on all questions of importance and to abide by the decisions of the majority, based on the principles upon which we were elected, as to the action to be taken'. This was too vague to be effective, but it showed that they were already groping their way towards the water-tight parliamentary 'pledge' which was soon to be one of the party's most characteristic hall-marks. The other resolution provided for a more elaborate executive structure. In addition to the chairman there was to be a vice-chairman and also two honorary secretaries, two whips, one treasurer and nine other members of committee. That the party was still quick to resent too much overt control from the centre was evident from the hostile reaction to a proposal of Dillon's to vest full powers in the committee in the intervals between party meetings. The comments were so angry that Parnell persuaded his fiery young lieutenant to withdraw his motion. The committee was then chosen, but even though it was heavily packed with Parnell's supporters he virtually ignored it and continued, as always, to consult the handful of members whose views he thought worth gathering and then to make his own decisions; not surprisingly, the committee lapsed in 1883.[6]

The new session had hardly opened before it became plain that the party were going to need all the unity and discipline they could muster. The Queen's Speech, as expected, contained the promise of both coercion and land reform. Parnell's tactic was to argue that redress should precede punishment. As agreed at the party's eve-of-session meeting, he began by moving a moderate amendment to this effect.

When this was rejected by a large majority, he and his colleagues reverted immediately to the old device of obstruction. Though not subtle, it was more effective than ever because it now had the stamina of over twenty members to sustain it. The outcome was that after innumerable interruptions and the generation of much ill feeling, the debate on the address did not end until 20 January.

Four days later Forster brought in his long-threatened coercive legislation, the Protection of Person and Property (Ireland) Bill, which would give the government power to suspend the ordinary law in selected ('proclaimed') districts of Ireland whenever that was deemed necessary. This at once provoked fresh paroxysms of obstruction, for the Land League leaders were under no illusions about what might happen if coercion were to be resolutely applied. 'I am necessitated to take a conservative stand in order to stave off coercion', Davitt had explained to Devoy only a few weeks before, 'for if the habeas corpus is suspended the whole movement would be crushed in a month and universal confusion would reign.'[7] The rearguard action which now ensued was the most tenacious yet. The sitting of 25 January lasted for 22 hours and on 31 January the House was obliged to continue for 41 hours without a break, the second longest sitting recorded for the House of Commons and said to have been the longest for any other legislature, up to that time.

Such behaviour brought its own retribution. On 2 February the Speaker intervened to bring the 41-hour sitting to a close by refusing to call any more members and putting the question from the Chair, whereupon the House divided and the first reading of the Protection of Person and Property Bill was passed. The following day Gladstone moved a resolution to the effect that if, upon notice given by a minister that the state of public business was urgent, 40 members rose to support such a motion, the Speaker should forthwith put the question without further debate. This, somewhat amended, provided the basis for a new set of resolutions presented to the House by the Speaker on 9 February, but it was plain from the moment of his original intervention a week earlier that obstructionism, at least in its 'traditional' form, was dead and that the Irish party would have to revise their tactics. Before they had time to do so, however, they were drawn, or provoked, into a more spectacular clash than any that had yet occurred. It was set off by the announcement on the evening of 3 February by the Home Secretary, Sir William Harcourt, that he had cancelled Davitt's ticket-of-leave and ordered his re-arrest.[8] Dillon, burning with indignation, decided to protest by deliberately interrupting the Prime Minister after the Speaker had called upon the latter. Refusing to give way, Dillon was 'named' by the Speaker amid frantic uproar. His suspension was then voted by 395 votes to 33, and, since he refused to leave voluntarily, he was removed by the Sergeant-at-Arms. Parnell could not afford to be outvied by his lieutenant in this kind of competition and when Gladstone again tried to speak, the Irish leader at once moved that the Prime Minister 'be no longer heard'. Thereupon, Parnell was named, suspended and ejected as Dillon had been. 'From this incident forward', the shorthand writers recorded, 'the business of the House proceeded under indescribable confusion.' In fact, for a long time it could not proceed at all, as member after member rose from the Irish benches until in all 36 had been suspended and removed.[9]

The true inwardness of this episode was hidden from those who witnessed it, as most English members did, with anger and contempt. The incident on the floor of the House was not just a protest against coercion (though it certainly was that), it was part of a major tactical battle then raging within the Land League and the parliamentary party. Parnell had publicly stated on 17 January 1881 that the first arrest under the Protection of Person and Property Act would be the signal for a general strike against rent, with the implication that in such a crisis the Irish members would return to their own country to organize the demonstration.[10] Although Davitt, it is true, was not being arrested under the Act, which had not yet become law, the seizure of such a key figure in the land agitation was certainly sufficient ground for action – if Parnell wished to act in that particular way. But he had already indicated to the Land League executive that he did not wish so to act. Just before Davitt's arrest – the dating is uncertain, but the day was almost certainly 1 February – the executive was summoned to an emergency meeting in London. There, Davitt expounded what Andrew Kettle (at that time one of the League secretaries) later described as his policy of 'dispersion'. This was that Parnell and three or four colleagues should go to America to collect funds, that others should stay in England to work upon public opinion there, and that the remainder – Dillon, Davitt and the League officials – should return to Ireland and fight a rearguard action against coercion. Kettle himself had a different proposal – that it was preferable to follow a policy of 'concentration', by bringing the whole party back to Ireland to face coercion and to launch a no-rent campaign in earnest. According to Kettle's memoirs – written in old age and therefore to be treated with caution – Parnell took hardly any part in this discussion except to protect Kettle from too rigorous cross-questioning.

No decision was taken then and the meeting was adjourned until the following day. Members were still divided between the two policies of 'dispersion' and 'concentration' when Parnell, arriving late as usual, took the chair and proceeded to read a paper containing his own solution. The party would continue to fight the coercion bill fiercely in parliament, but not to the point of getting expelled. When the last stage of the debate had been reached, Parnell would make a final speech of protest and lead his followers out of the House and back to Ireland. There, each member would immediately proceed to his constituency and Parnell would publicly announce that the first arrest under the new law would be the signal for a general withholding of rent until the legislature dealt with the land question in the way demanded by the League. This was enthusiastically accepted, according to Kettle's account, and E. D. Gray, though not a member of the executive, was called in to see if he would give the *Freeman's Journal*'s support to Parnell's plan. He not only promised this, but prophesied that if the plan could be enforced it would settle the business in six months.[11]

On the face of it Parnell seemed to have committed himself irrevocably to the policy of 'concentration', and it might reasonably have been expected that when Davitt's re-arrest was announced on 3 February, and when this was followed by the great suspension scene in the Commons, the plan to withdraw to Ireland would have been put into effect. But this did not happen. Quite the contrary, after a party meeting held that same day a statement was issued which was intended to reduce tension, not to maximize it. 'Fellow-countrymen, we adjure you . . . to maintain the noble attitude that has already assured your ultimate victory. Reject every temptation to conflict, disorder or crime . . . We ask you, by your self-restraint, your unbroken organization, your determined perseverance, to strengthen our hands in the struggle we maintain.'[12] Dillon was sent at once to Dublin, where on 4 February he urged the League to remain calm and not to be stampeded into violence. True, he advised the tenants that if in their own localities the League's organizers were arrested, they should pay nothing until the organizers were released, but he specifically disclaimed any general strike against rent.[13] Since the Protection of Person and Property Bill had not yet passed into law this was no more than common sense. Parnell himself, though he uncovered his inmost thoughts to no one, offered a glimpse of the way his mind was moving when, in reply to a question put to him on 4 February as to whether the party would reappear in parliament after the suspension, he said: 'If we consulted our own feelings we should retire, but we must do our duty.'[14]

In thus pronouncing what was in effect the epitaph on the policy of concentration to which he had apparently committed himself only two days earlier Parnell was probably influenced by several factors. A crucial one was uncertainty as to how many members he would be able to take with him if he did decide to withdraw. Dr Cruise O'Brien has reckoned that not more than twenty could have been relied on to obey an order to secede and that not more than five would actively have advocated such a course.[15] If this calculation is correct, Parnell's Dublin 'parliament', had it ever materialized, would have been little more than a caucus which might quickly have been either dominated or ignored by the more extreme elements in the Land League.

Here a further consideration entered in. To go to Dublin would be to make something approximating to a revolutionary gesture. For Parnell it would be to turn his back decisively, perhaps for ever, upon constitutional action. Although that might be interpreted in America as in the logic of Devoy's 'new departure', even this was open to doubt, for the corollary of abandoning parliament was to become immersed in the Land League, in other words to subordinate the struggle for independence to a social convulsion aimed at the destruction of land-lordism. Conceivably, a war of independence might emerge out of an agrarian *jacquerie*, but this was by no means certain. It was still less certain, given the strength of the government forces and the weakness of the League, that an outbreak of violence would end any differently from the way such outbreaks had ended with monotonous regularity in the past. And Parnell, who greatly admired Washington, and once remarked that Ireland, unlike America, was not good terrain for a revolutionary war because it was not big enough to run away in, was firmly opposed to committing ill-armed Irishmen against either the police or the military.[16]

But there was another and more compelling reason for declining to secede from parliament. The government programme, after all, contained the promise of a land bill as well as the reality of coercion. It was only natural that a parliamentary leader should want to see how and when this promise would be made good before taking his party back to Ireland. Yet, however strong these accumulated reasons for remaining at Westminster, the fact remained that in that turbulent first week of February, a Fabian policy of delay would have been difficult, if not impossible to impose outright either upon the League executive or upon the more restive members of his party. It was essential for Parnell to proceed cautiously if he was to hold his fragile coalition together and for this reason a final decision was deferred until the next meeting of the executive, which, for safety's sake, it was decided to hold in Paris, whither Patrick Egan had already transferred the League's funds. Even before that meeting could be held, signs of division were already apparent. Thus, on 4 February, while Parnell cabled to the American Land League a message of deliberate vagueness, in Dublin Dillon was being briefed by his Land League associates to convey to Parnell their view that he should adopt Davitt's plan of dispersion and himself go to the United States to collect money for the imminent struggle.[17] It was therefore vital that a common policy be hammered out at Paris with the least possible delay.

III

Delay there was, however, delay which was to have important consequences for Parnell's future. The executive assembled in Paris within a couple of days of Davitt's arrest, expecting to meet their leader at the appointed rendezvous. Time passed, days passed, a whole week passed, and there was no sign of him. In desperation they resolved to ask Tim Healy, who was not a member of the executive but was acting as Parnell's secretary, to produce some private correspondence which had arrived for the absent chief and which, perhaps, might provide a clue to his whereabouts. Reluctantly, Healy surrendered a letter in a woman's hand and Dillon and Patrick Egan were deputed to open it. Having done so, they found an address which Healy's account places in Holloway but which, in the folk-memory of the Dillon family, is assigned to Birmingham.[18] According to Healy, whose recollections are frequently unreliable, the letter was from a barmaid who had had a child by Parnell and was in need of money. It was decided that Healy and Biggar should leave next day for this address, but just as they were starting they passed Parnell coming from the station in a cab. Parnell went at once to his room in the hotel where they were all staying, shut the door in Healy's face when he attempted to accost him, and appeared later in the day with no explanation for his mysterious absence. Healy resigned his post as secretary when they got back to London, and although he says that he and Parnell ended this connection quite cordially, it is not improbable that Parnell's deteriorating relations not only with Healy, but with Dillon as well, date from this episode of the compromising letter.[19]

Whether or not the barmaid ever existed remains an enigma. If we remember that Parnell only met Katharine O'Shea about the beginning of July 1880, and that before then he had led a solitary, bachelor life while he was in London, some sort of casual liaison could easily have happened with the natural consequences allegdely stated in the letter. Others saw no need for a barmaid, real or imaginary. T. P. O'Connor, who was not at the Paris meeting, later called this 'the first warning the Irish party had of the opening of the tragedy that finally engulfed Parnell and went near to engulf Ireland'.[20] Davitt, who was also absent (in prison), but who knew the various participants intimately, took it for granted that the letter was from Mrs O'Shea.[21] So, too, did Katharine herself, who not only recorded in her own memoir of Parnell that their affair had first become known to members of his party when they opened one of her letters to him, but also printed a number of letters he wrote to her about two weeks after the episode, letters which bore the address of the hotel in Paris – Hotel Brighton, 218 rue de Rivoli – at which Parnell habitually stayed and where the rendezvous had been fixed.[22] It is much more credible that Katharine should have written to this address than a barmaid who, even if she was not just a figment of Healy's imagination, was unlikely to have had the same knowledge of Parnell's extremely secretive movements. This, admittedly, does not explain Dillon's lingering recollection of a Birmingham address. But that recollection was undocumented and only passed on by him to his family many years afterwards. It is not unreasonable to suppose that he retrospectively confused the gossip of the time with the actual contents of the letter.

If, then, the letter most probably was from Katharine, the question arises – how far had their relationship progressed since October 1880, when he had already begun to write to her as 'my own love'? That autumn, despite his heavy involvement in the land agitation, he apparently seized every opportunity to visit her and she later published three letters – two certainly belonging to November 1880 – which, for purposes of concealment, were headed as if from Dublin, but were actually written in London and sent over to Ireland to be posted. When the state trial began to cast its shadow over Parnell in that same month he evidently feared it might hinder his movements, for on 11 November he wrote to tell her how much she had changed his life. 'What a small interest I take in what is going on about me and how I detest everything which has happened during the last few days to keep me away from you . . .' He even told her that when the trial came on he had 'willed' the jury not so much to disagree (they were bound to do that anyway), but to do it quickly, so that he could catch the night-mail to England and be with her at Eltham the next morning.[23] She claims in her book that towards the end of 1880 she had him to stay at Eltham for a fortnight while he recovered his strength and kept out of the way of government spies. Her placing of events is notoriously inaccurate, but it is quite possible that this may have happened. Equally, she may be correct in stating that he spent some time with her when parliament opened (though she dates that wrongly) and it is not improbable that this was where he was in early February 1881 when his friends were anxiously awaiting him in Paris. At all events, matters had progressed so far that by the end of 1880 he was writing to her as 'My dearest wife' or, in the diminutive form to which he was incurably addicted, 'My dearest wifie'.[24]

This in turn leads to another question far more difficult to answer – how much was known to Captain O'Shea? Years later, when he was seeking a divorce from his wife in 1890, he was naturally concerned to make the best case he could for his ignorance of the whole affair. But even he did not attempt to deny that in 1881 he had had to take notice of Parnell's visits to his wife and had indeed been provoked into challenging him to a duel. That some challenge was issued was (rare occurrence) agreed by both the O'Sheas, though there were (by no means rare occurrence) discrepancies between them as to date. According to her account, published in 1914 but tallying in essentials with what she told the young Parnellite MP, Henry Harrison, in 1891, O'Shea suddenly arrived at Eltham in a state of high indignation under the mistaken belief that she was having his rooms watched at Albert Mansions. Parnell was not at Eltham, but his portmanteau was, and Willie, discovering it, departed in a great rage, declaring in his best Spanish manner that he would obtain satisfaction from Parnell. This apparently occurred at the beginning of the year, since Katharine prints a plaintive letter from Parnell, dated 7 January 1881, in which he asks her to find out what O'Shea had done with his luggage.[25] What in fact seems to have happened, as she herself told Harrison in 1891, was that soon after she first met Parnell, O'Shea had encouraged her to 'take him [Parnell] back to Eltham and make him all happy and comfortable for the night', the idea being to get his support for an unnamed project of O'Shea's. But when O'Shea subsequently discovered that Katharine had fallen in love with Parnell, and was no longer just acting as a decoy for her lord and master, he was furious and resolved upon a duel. We need not believe every word of her story to Harrison (for example her romantic tale of Parnell carrying her off to his bedroom under O'Shea's very nose) to find in it a rational explanation of the way in which the affair may well have developed – a political convenience for the husband turning rapidly, for the wife and her lover, into a grand passion.[26]

If O'Shea marched off in a rage in January 1881, his famous challenge was a long time coming. For this, however, there may have been a simple, if not wholly creditable, explanation. Captain O'Shea was an ambitious politician who aspired to mediate between Parnell and the government. He was to attempt such mediation several times in the years ahead, but his first essay in this delicate art actually occurred in June 1881, which suggests that at that particular juncture, he was either unconcerned about Parnell's relationship with his wife, or had already begun to calculate what the relationship might be made to yield in terms of political advancement.* In the divorce court he himself placed the crisis as late as July when, after a long, angry talk with his wife, he left Eltham on foot and walked all the way to London, arriving at the house of her sister, Anna Steele, at four o'clock in the morning. From there he wrote to Parnell, issuing his challenge. Parnell's answer was prompt and decisive – he would fight. But, so Captain O'Shea testified, Mrs Steele saw Parnell during the day and later went down to Eltham where apparently the two sisters patched the matter up. In court O'Shea swore he had received assurances for the future, but even he had not the gall to say that he had received them from Parnell. The most the latter had apparently contributed to the face-saving operation was to allow it to be conveyed to the Captain that, as Mrs O'Shea had undertaken to act as a political intermediary for him, he trusted O'Shea would not object to him seeing her after the duel. Willie then apparently shifted his ground and merely stipulated that Parnell should not stay at Eltham; no more was heard of the duel. We shall see presently that O'Shea himself soon had reason to doubt that this proviso was being observed and Katharine records in her book what was without doubt the true outcome of the episode: 'From the date of this bitter quarrel Parnell and I were one, without further scruple, without fear and without remorse.'[27] Their first child was born in February 1882.

Of these seething undercurrents the members of the Land League executive were almost certainly ignorant when they agreed to the opening of Parnell's mail. They were so thoroughly abashed by their boldness that when Parnell eventually came downstairs to begin the long-delayed meeting nobody dared to say anything. He sat in his chair with averted gaze and did nothing to help them. It was clear that he was still deeply angry. At last Kettle plucked up the courage to speak. He resumed where he had left off at the previous meeting and urged again the policy of concentration, of returning to Ireland and leading the fight against rent and against coercion. Almost at once he clashed with

*See below p. 161.

Sexton who took a strong 'parliamentary' line. Parnell, with no ceremony, cut them short and proceeded to read out his own proposals. Rejecting the advice which Dillon had conveyed to him from the Land League in Dublin, that he should go to America, he made it crystal clear that he would continue his work in the House of Commons. He directed further that Dillon should take charge of the agitation in Ireland and that Egan should remain in Paris to safeguard the funds and also to keep contact with Irish-American friends.[28] He himself then wrote from Paris an open letter to the Land League, reiterating his intention not to go to the United States and repudiating the notion that 'for the present very little is to be expected from parliamentary action'. After listing the alternatives of 'on the one hand, concentration in Ireland [leading possibly to an appeal to force] and, on the other, widening the area of agitation' in order to include the English masses, he opted firmly for the latter. It is possible that Parnell put forward this tactic, which he seems not to have taken seriously and was later to deride, partly as a diversionary manoeuvre and partly because it would be likely to appeal to Davitt, who was already beginning to be identified with the cause of labour on both sides of the Irish Sea. True, Davitt was at that moment in prison, but a political realist, or cynic, might argue convincingly that that was the best possible opportunity for the parliamentarian to take over one of the supposed revolutionist's more striking ideas. 'This was a sagacious policy at the time', wrote Davitt in after years. So it was, though perhaps not quite in the sense he intended.[29]

This gesture towards Davitt's ideal of a democratic alliance between the working-classes of the two countries was the first of several thrusts Parnell made towards the left during the next few months. The more tenaciously he held to his House of Commons role, the more necessary it was for him to demonstrate in other ways that he was not being corrupted by parliament. One of the oddest of these demonstrations was his return to Paris a few days after the League meeting to visit various notabilities. These included the Cardinal Archbishop of Paris and Ferdinand de Lesseps, but Irish opinion fastened eagerly upon the main event of his trip, which was a dinner-party with Victor Hugo and the 'communard', Henri Rochefort. Parnell did not speak French fluently and he relied mainly upon J. J. O'Kelly to interpret for him. That he should have frequented the company of these men was a red rag to Archbishop McCabe. 'Allies for our country', wrote the Archbishop in his Lenten instructions, 'in her struggle for justice, are being sought from the ranks of impious infidels, who have plunged their own unhappy country into misery and who are sworn to destroy the foundations of all religions.' Parnell was obliged to issue a denial shortly afterwards that he was planning some nefarious combination of international revolutionary movements, but for him to have taken such a risk is inexplicable unless upon the supposition that he felt the need to burnish his extremist image at the very moment when it had become more mask than image.[30]

More secret, and more important, was the interview Parnell had in Paris about 18 February with the fanatical Irish-American William Lomasney who in 1884 was to blow himself up while attempting to dynamite London Bridge. Like other messengers from the Clan na Gael, Lomasney carried away the impression that Parnell was much more committed to their way of thinking than he really was. 'I feel that he is eminently deserving of our support', Lomasney wrote to Devoy, 'and that he means to go as far as we do in pushing the business.'[31] Yet this did not mean that Parnell was going to have his pace dictated from across the Atlantic, as no one had better reason to know than Devoy. In mid-January Devoy had been reported as speaking violently in New York against the impending coercion of Ireland:

> For every Irishman murdered we will take in reprisal the life of a British minister. For every hundred Irishmen murdered we will sacrifice the lives of the entire British ministry. For every two hundred Irishmen murdered we will reduce to ashes the principal city of England. For every wholesale massacre of the Irish people we will make England a smouldering ruin of ashes and blood.

He later complained that he had been misreported, but not before Sir William Harcourt had used his alleged remarks to illustrate the kind of conspiracy the government was engaged in 'stamping out'. Harcourt's language, in its own way also extreme, provoked two reactions – a passionate defence of Devoy by Dillon in the House of Commons, and a telegram from Devoy to Harcourt. 'Two can play at stamping; the greatest sufferers are those who have most to lose. The day when you can stamp with impunity has passed forever.' Such an intrusion of the physical force side of the movement into 'constitutional' territory Parnell was bound to resist to the uttermost and he reacted immediately. Not only did he disavow Dillon's speech, but he sent to Devoy himself one of the sharpest reprimands that intrepid revolutionary can ever have received. 'You are reported to have sent threatening telegram to Home Secretary. If true your action most censurable. If untrue should cable contradiction.' To this Devoy could only reply lamely that his cable to Harcourt was not a threat but a warning, a metaphysical distinction with which neither Parnell nor the choleric Home Secretary had much patience.[32]

Incidents like these were vexatious to Parnell not merely because they complicated his task as a parliamentary leader, but because they threatened his control over the mass movement at home. That movement could hardly sustain its momentum without the support of the Fenians who had come into it in disregard of the official disapproval of the IRB, but if Irish-American pressure were to be so crudely exerted as Devoy's telegram and speech seemed to portend, then Parnell would have to make the *public* choice between extremism and constitutionalism which he had hitherto managed to avoid. To emerge as an overt and total constitutionalist would certainly lose him extremist support – and, more important, Irish-American money – at a time when the agrarian agitation in Ireland was entering its most critical phase. He urgently needed therefore to compensate for the harshness of his rebuke to Devoy by some gesture to show that his heart was still in what his 'new departure' friends would have called the 'right' place. Within a few weeks he made this gesture, but in circumstances so extraordinary that in after years he was at pains to deny all knowledge of it.

On or about 23 May he met in London a man whom he and others regarded as a trusted emissary of the Clan na Gael. This was the spy who went under the name of Henri Le Caron. Born Thomas Miller Beach, at Colchester in 1841, he ran away from home in early youth. After a short period in France, he went to America, fought in the Union army throughout the Civil War under his adopted name of Le Caron, and in 1865 first made contact with Fenianism, at a moment when an attack on Canada was being planned. In letters home he described the plans of the garrulous conspirators who talked freely in his presence. His father showed these letters to the British government and soon afterwards Le Caron became their paid agent with the special task of infiltrating the Fenian organization in America and reporting regularly on its activities. After he had established himself as a medical doctor – this was both a genuine career and a useful 'front' – Le Caron joined the Clan, became intimate with its leaders and for over twenty years betrayed their secrets with a nerveless efficiency. Until he was called to give evidence at the Special Commission in 1889 no one suspected his real identity.

It was J. J. O'Kelly who introduced him to his leader. Parnell walked his guest up and down the corridor outside the Library of the House of Commons, speaking in low tones to avoid being overheard. According to Le Caron, who was known for his accurate reporting,

Parnell complained about the obstructive attitude of the IRB towards the land agitation and wanted Devoy to come to Europe to exert pressure upon them. He then, so Le Caron alleged, exploded 'a veritable bombshell'. 'He started off by stating that he had long ceased to believe that anything but the force of arms would accomplish the final redemption of Ireland. He saw no reason why, when we were fully prepared, an open insurrectionary movement could not be brought about.' All this, of course, would require money, 'which he looked for from the American organization'. From the House of Commons Le Caron went straight to his superior, Robert Anderson, then adviser to the Home Office on Irish political crime, and reported in detail what he had just heard. Le Caron and Parnell, it seems, met once more before the spy returned to the United States, when Parnell was 'as cordial as ever', presenting his new acquaintance with a signed photograph of himself.[33]

When Le Caron's cover was 'blown' at the Special Commission so that he could help to substantiate *The Times*'s allegations about the connection between 'Parnellism and crime', Parnell was naturally examined minutely about these transactions, which Le Caron had revealed in his own evidence to the Commission. Parnell admitted to having met Le Caron, though he also claimed he had made so little impression upon him that it was not until the double-agent was in the witness-box that he even recalled what he looked like. But when asked if he had told Le Caron that he had long ceased to believe that anything but the force of arms would ever redeem Ireland, Parnell denied it categorically. 'I never said that and I never even thought it at the worst period of coercion. I never for one single instant doubted that the constitutional movement and our parliamentary action would succeed in that.'[34] He was scarcely less emphatic in denying that he had ever given Le Caron a photograph, but when confronted with the signed picture, had hurriedly to modify this. 'I am nearly certain I did not give it to him', he said.[35] And likewise, when pressed hard by the Attorney-General to say if he really had no recollection of walking with Le Caron in the lobby parallel with the House of Commons Library, he retreated to a more defensible position. 'I will not undertake to say that, but I should think it most improbable and unlikely.'[36]

Obviously, we have here yet one more of those conflicts of testimony with which Parnell's career is littered, but although certainty cannot be achieved where the two accounts contradict each other so directly, it would be naïve to deny that the balance of the evidence favours Le Caron. Yet, even if Parnell said what he was alleged to have said (or something approximating thereto), it does not follow that that expressed his inmost views. What he might declare to an emissary of the Clan for Irish-American consumption and what he actually believed could be two entirely different things. If he needed at this time to reassure his transatlantic allies – and perhaps also to use them as a counterpoise to the IRB at home – then to employ the *language* of insurrection, without intending the *reality* of insurrection, may well have seemed to him a necessary tactic whereby to hold together the coalition of forces he needed to carry on the land agitation. To discover the true direction of his mind at this vital moment we have to turn from *sotto voce* conversation with supposed revolutionaries to the cut and thrust of parliamentary debate, from hypothetical rebellion to positive reform. Which is another way of saying that for Parnell the land bill which Gladstone had introduced on 7 April was the real pivot on which the future would turn.

IV

The long-awaited bill was immensely complex and only Gladstone and a handful of experts thoroughly understood it. Framed in great haste to pass into law the principal recommendations of the Bessborough Commission, which had reported as recently as January 1881, the bill was intended to concede to the tenants the 'three Fs' – fixity of tenure, free sale and fair rents. The debates occupied 58 sittings, nearly 15,000 speeches were delivered, over 6000 of them by Irish members, and when the bill went to the Lords it provoked 93 amendments.[37] Yet the essence of the act as it was finally passed was quite simple – it was an act to control rent. The principal device for achieving this fundamental aim was the creation of a land court to fix a fair rent between landlord and tenant, or to register such a rent if it had been privately agreed beforehand.

Modern scholarship has been highly critical of this legislation as having missed the heart of the matter. An obsessive concern with tenure and rents, it has been argued, was out of place in a country where rents were not normally so high, nor tenure so insecure, as popular belief held them to be. This is not to say that economic depression and bad weather had not created an abnormal situation, for this they manifestly had. Too many cases of hardship lay nakedly exposed for anyone to doubt the existence of a crisis. But it is to suggest both that the act was insufficient for its declared purposes and that those purposes were not themselves of the highest relevance to an agriculture where the real obstacles to progress were backward farming and inadequate investment. These obstacles the act did not effectively overcome, partly because a large and poverty-stricken class, the leaseholders, were excluded from its operation, and still more because no amount of rent-fixing, or even rent-reduction, would help the miserable farmers of the west, whose holdings were so small and wretched that they could barely live on them if they paid no rent at all. But the Land Act of 1881 was not solely, nor perhaps primarily, concerned with long-term agricultural goals. It was an attempt to cut the ground from beneath the Land League by granting a concession of such magnitude that Othello's occupation would be gone. It was put forward, as has been well said, 'less as an economic policy than as a political stroke'.[38]

For precisely this reason the measure held both dangers and attractions for Parnell. His instinct was to temporize and when the bill was introduced on 7 April he formally reserved judgement until he could see it in print. On 10 April, speaking in Cork, he was, while cautious, not overtly hostile.[39] At Manchester, three days later, he went so far as to admit that 'it would not do' for Gladstone to wreck his party to pass an Irish land bill. The Irish party, he said, did not regard it as a final solution and would strive to amend it in committee. 'When the legislature found that the attempt by legal machinery to apportion the profits between landlord and tenant as this bill attempted to do, was useless and impossible, they would have Mr Gladstone or some other English minister coming to Ireland and saying that the landlords must be expropriated and the land must be handed over to those who cultivate it.'[40]

This prophecy was indeed to be fulfilled in the long run, but in the short run Parnell had still to reckon with his own left wing, of which John Dillon was the most articulate and intransigent spokesman. At a meeting in April to arrange for a Land League convention to consider what policy should be adopted, Dillon declared that he would not vote for the act under any circumstances. 'I very much fear', he said with some reason, 'that this act was drawn by a man . . . who was told to draw an act that would kill the Land League.'[41] However, when the convention met nearer the end of the month Parnell was able to impose a more constructive policy. Briefly, it was decided that the parliamentary party should be asked to press various amendments at the committee stage and, if these were not accepted, to strain every nerve to secure the defeat of the measure. Dillon, while observing that it was 'perfectly hopeless and silly' to expect adequate amendment in committee, acquiesced in the decision, though only after securing a pledge – later *not* redeemed – that a second convention should be summoned before the third reading to judge if the amendments obtained in committee were satisfactory.[42]

The effect of Dillon's grand gesture was, it is true, somewhat diminished when he went straight off to a meeting at Grangemockler in Tipperary and delivered a speech so extreme that the government had little option but to arrest him and lodge him in Kilmainham prison on 2 May. This faced Parnell with a difficult choice. Since Dillon was the first MP to be seized under the Protection of Person and Property Act, his arrest would certainly be regarded by the left wing as providing the occasion for putting into effect the policy discussed earlier in the year – withdrawal from parliament and a general strike against rent. Yet to yield to that pressure was to risk losing the support of the right, or constitutional, wing of the movement, which had begun to rally to his side. Typically, Parnell opted in the end for a course which probably pleased neither wing, but was not sufficiently biased in any particular direction to cost him a substantial body of support. At a meeting of the 'active', or Parnellite, section on 5 May he carried a motion that the party, in order to mark their disapproval of Dillon's arrest, should leave the House in a body when the time came for a division on the second reading. This had the double advantage of being simultaneously dramatic and innocuous – it *looked* fierce, but would not hamper the progress of the bill in the slightest.

This decision produced something like a crisis among his followers. What he proposed was passed by only eighteen votes to twelve and it was strongly rumoured that he had made his resolution a vote of confidence, threatening to resign if it was not accepted. Then, having gained his objective, he nearly lost it again by letting it be known after the party meeting that he was going to move an amendment hostile to the bill in committee, thus infuriating those who wanted to make the best of the measure. O'Connor Power, who had voted against Parnell at the party meeting, announced openly that he would not be bound by the resolution and several members, it seems, wrote to Parnell cancelling their votes in favour of it. Confusion was still worse confounded when Archbishop Croke proffered his advice that the real fight against the bill should be postponed to the committee stage. Parnell's reply to this was interesting, especially in view of the line he had taken at the League convention. To vote for the second reading would, he said, be to assume responsibility for the measure, without any real assurance that it could be effectively reformed in committee. The point of a demonstration on the second reading would not be numerical, but moral – it would mark a protest against the bill's deficiencies without going so far as to destroy it irresponsibly. He left the archbishop and all who anxiously scanned their published correspondence in no doubt of the gravity of the crisis. 'Union was never more necessary than it is at present. The decision of the convention, the magnitude of the interests at stake, the importance of preserving the independence and integrity of the Irish party – all combine to teach us that individual convictions, or even the directions of particular constituencies, should give place to the opinion of the representatives of the majority.' Croke thereupon abandoned his criticism and although the *Nation* newspaper, normally friendly to the party, complained bitterly about Parnell's policy, it too responded to his appeal to accept the will of the majority.[43] But a letter written by its proprietor, A. M. Sullivan, at the end of the year, when he had retired from parliament after a severe heart attack, indicates the strain Parnell was imposing on his moderate supporters at this time. Writing to a northern friend, Sullivan explained that while he had been as fierce as anyone in opposing coercion, the Land Bill was an entirely different matter:[44]

> When, however, the *Land Bill* was introduced, my view was to forget that hateful coercion affair . . . and set ourselves heartily and honestly to make the best of the Land Bill . . . a great and noble monument of justice. But I soon saw that my Land League friends did not want to give it fair play . . . Instead of the language and action of generous appreciation we had that of bitter hate and personal offensiveness . . . At home in Ireland the Coercion Act threw the whole force of the popular feeling to the side of Parnell – delivered Ireland into his hands. Between Russian despotism in Dublin Castle on the one hand and a gospel of mere hatred and passion on the other, I sorrowfully saw that there was now no place for a man like me . . .

For some members the strain was in fact too great. After the failure of a desperate attempt in the party committee to secure an adjournment of the second reading debate so as to allow time for reconsideration, Parnellite solidarity seemed to disintegrate when the actual moment of voting arrived. Out of the 24 members upon whom Parnell could normally rely, no less than fourteen voted for the bill, despite the party resolution to the contrary. This produced characteristic thunders from the left, exemplified in a diatribe from Patrick Egan in Paris against those who ignored the party line. 'I consider', he wrote to Thomas Brennan, 'that they stand exactly in the position of a blackleg on a racecourse who if he wins will pocket your money but if he loses will refuse to pay.'[45] What Egan and the left in general seemed unable to grasp was that this demonstration in favour of the bill was the clearest justification of Parnell's earlier refusal to accept the policy of withdrawal from parliament and 'concentration' in Ireland. Nothing could have shown more pointedly the folly of supposing that a party which could be thrown into such a paroxysm by the mere suggestion that its members refrain from voting on a single division, would have embraced at any time the far more drastic step of mass secession.

Once the bill went into committee, where it stayed between 26 May and 27 July, these tensions largely disappeared, since Home Rulers of all shades could disport themselves happily, proposing their own amendments and countering those of the landlords' representatives, in the comfortable knowledge that they were acting within the lines laid down by the Land League convention. But in all this there was no suggestion of any intent to destroy the bill. On the contrary, in early June an approach made to Gladstone by Captain O'Shea, who claimed to be speaking for Parnell, held out the prospect of a bargain whereby the land agitation would be ended in return for certain Liberal amendments to the bill. These came to nothing for Gladstone, having consulted his colleagues, returned a politely firm *non possumus*, but that the approach should have been made at all was significant.[46] Thereafter the debate continued undisturbed by such subterranean currents. It went so smoothly in fact that although Parnell had left them free to do as they wished, nearly his whole following voted for the third reading.

He himself, on the other hand, with the bill virtually safe, concentrated his attention on reasserting his control over the movement at home. The first step towards doing this was to refurbish his reputation, latterly somewhat obscured, as a parliamentary extremist. On 1 August he deliberately picked a quarrel with the Speaker, by repeatedly demanding a day for the discussion of arrests in Ireland under the coercion act. When the Speaker called him to order Parnell responded with an outburst of almost certainly synthetic rage. 'The minister of the day', he declared, 'of course always gains the sympathies of the powers that be, in this House, and if we may not bring the cause of our imprisoned countrymen before the House, I may say that all liberty and regard of private right is lost in this assembly, and that the minister of the day has transformed himself from a constitutional minister into a tyrant.' The Speaker promptly 'named' him for this outburst, but Parnell contemptuously brushed him aside. 'I will not await the farce of a division', he said. 'I will leave you and your House, and the public will see that there is no longer freedom of discussion left to the Irish members.'[47] He was at once suspended for the remainder of the session and returned to Ireland with this useful bonus in his pocket.

V

At home he set himself to achieve two main objectives. The first was to remedy a weakness which had more than once threatened his entire position. This was the lack of a newspaper which he could control absolutely. Although it was true that the *Nation* and to a lesser extent the *Freeman's Journal*, backed him in most things, they still retained an independent, and occasionally critical, attitude. Parnell needed an organ which would be so much his mouthpiece that he could use it to inflate or deflate the agitation as he chose, without having to explain himself to third parties. Even while the Land Bill was still in committee he had taken the preliminary steps towards buying a paper and choosing an editor. The newspaper, or group of newspapers, which he acquired, nominally on behalf of the Land League, and largely with funds subscribed from America for the general purposes of the League, belonged to Richard Pigott, a down-at-heel journalist who combined the propagation of pseudo-extreme nationalist opinions with sidelines in blackmail and pornography. At none of these enterprises had he prospered and in 1881 was glad to part with his papers – *Shamrock*, *Flag of Ireland* and the *Irishman* – for £3000.[48] The transaction was mainly carried out by Patrick Egan, though Parnell had also to write or sign a few business letters. We shall see presently to what ingenious use Pigott was to put this commonplace correspondence.

For his editor Parnell turned to a young man of real, if erratic, genius. This was William O'Brien. O'Brien was still only 28 years old when in July 1881 Parnell asked him to take on this new and hazardous assignment, but he was already an experienced reporter who, after an apprenticeship in his native county of Cork, had spent several years with the *Freeman's Journal*, where he speedily became an expert on the land agitation. O'Brien had first met Parnell in 1878 when he reported one of the latter's meetings at Tralee. On the long train journey back to Dublin the youthful idealist capitulated completely to a leader who for once seems to have dropped his habitual aloofness. 'He has captured me heart and soul and is bound to go on capturing', wrote O'Brien ecstatically. 'A sweet seriousness *au fond*, any amount of nervous courage, a delicate reserve, without the smallest suspicion of hauteur; strangest of all, humour; above everything else, simplicity . . . As romantic as Lord Edward [Fitzgerald], but not to be shaken from the prosier methods. In any case a man one could suffer with proudly.'[49]

O'Brien never really changed this opinion of his hero, though Parnell was to try his loyalty high on more than one occasion. The leader on his side appears to have responded to the follower's ingenuous enthusiasm with more affection than he showed towards any of his colleagues, with the possible exception of that *beau sabreur*, James O'Kelly. O'Brien's excitability and tendency to fly to extremes, whether of speech or action, sometimes needed to be sharply checked, but most of the time Parnell seems to have regarded them with amusement, tinged with a shrewd realization that O'Brien could now and then be used to say things, in his exaggerated way, which his master might want said without having to take the responsibility himself.

O'Brien having accepted the editorship, Parnell left the running of the concern entirely to him. Indeed, eight years later, when questioned on the subject at the Special Commission, he showed himself almost preternaturally ignorant of what went on in the offices of *United Ireland*.[50] By then, of course, he was intent upon putting as wide a gulf as possible between him and the violence of 1881, but the contemporary evidence concerning the origins of *United Ireland*, and the paper's own files, make it clear that it was intended to be the Land League organ and as such a major instrument in achieving Parnell's second main objective of that summer, to keep the more extreme elements of the League under his direct control. But the business of setting up the new paper quickly showed how difficult this was going to be. Parnell's original aim had been to include John Dillon in the management of *United Ireland* and a letter inviting him to participate was smuggled into Kilmainham, where Dillon was languishing in a state of seriously declining health. The reply the prisoner sent to O'Brien on 12 July, though friendly to him personally, was an ominously uncompromising negative. This did not mean that Dillon would actively oppose the new venture, but it did mean that he would refuse to be associated with a paper which would necessarily be committed to endorsing Parnell's line on the Land Bill. 'I will not do anything', he said, 'which might be interpreted as consent to the policy which has been pursued either in London or Dublin for the past month . . . It is not unlikely that I shall retire from politics.'[51]

Quite suddenly, all the elements for a determination of future policy came together. On 2 August Parnell returned to Ireland after his suspension from the House. On 6 August Dillon was released from prison. On 13 August appeared the first issue of *United Ireland*, striking at once the intransigent note that was to be the hall-mark of O'Brien's editorship for the rest of the decade. And on 22 August, the Land Act, though mutilated by the Lords, passed into law. Now at last the League came face to face with a challenge even more formidable than coercion. The die-hard Leaguers – most of whose leaders either were, or had been, in prison and so were christened 'the Kilmainham party' – were eager to reactivate the agitation and, by a general withholding of rent, to nullify the Land Act as far as it could be nullified. In this they were supported by militant Irish-American opinion which clamoured for a 'no rent' campaign. On the other hand, the right wing of the movement – the church, the *Freeman's Journal*, many of Parnell's more moderate parliamentary followers – welcomed the Act as a major concession anticipating, rightly, that once its attractions were realized, nothing would stop the tenants from flocking into the land court to have their rents judicially reduced.[52]

To resolve these differences was essential and Parnell, while excusing the failure to call the promised Land League convention before the vote on the third reading of the Land Bill – the timetable had made it impossible, he pleaded – announced that it would be held in mid-September. Speaking in Dublin immediately after his return from London, he foreshadowed the line he would take when the convention met. 'Of course', he said, 'it will be the duty of the Land League to select test cases in different parts of Ireland to see what these commissioners will do – how much they are going to lower the rents, that will be the crucial test . . . I should strongly advise the tenant-farmers not to go indiscriminately into court until they have seen the results of the decisions upon the test cases . . .'[53]

Before the convention met, Dillon, who on his release had speedily resumed his attacks on the Land Act, announced his retirement from politics, coupling this with a solemn warning to the country that any parliamentary party the people sent to Westminster must be closely watched.[54] For Parnell, Dillon's withdrawal was an uncovenanted mercy, but when the convention met in Dublin, from 15 September to 17 September, the forces of right and left were still very delicately balanced. True, there was no difficulty about passing three standard resolutions demanding self-government, condemning coercion, and reaffirming the ultimate aim of the League to be the abolition of landlordism, but there was long and hard debate before the policy of testing the act, as Parnell had outlined it the previous month, was finally adopted.[55]

Yet, however reluctantly arrived at, this decision was of fundamental importance. For Parnell it had the great advantage that it cleared the way for the land court to begin to operate while at the same time leaving open the admittedly faint possibility that the tenants might be prevented from abandoning the League *en masse*. But acceptance of the act, even when qualified by the policy of testing it, brought two dangers. One was that extremists at the grass roots might so resent this approach that they would take the law into their own hands and either instigate or authorize further violence. Worse still, such violence might be perpetrated either by secret societies which had never been connected with the League or by wayward individuals who refused to acknowledge any external control. This was all the more likely because the League itself was in serious difficulties during the summer of 1881. After Dillon's arrest Sexton had been appointed to supervise operations, but when he fell ill soon afterwards there was no adequate central direction and before long complaints began to be heard – especially from the western districts – that the executive was incompetent, apathetic, even corrupt, and that it was failing in its primary tasks of protecting the tenants and safeguarding the families of those who had been swept into prison as suspects.[56] The level of efficiency was to some extent dependent upon the flow of funds and here loomed the second danger inherent in the Fabian policy which Parnell had succeeded in imposing upon the League. As always, the main source of supply was America, but Irish-Americans, and particularly Patrick Ford in the columns of the *Irish World*, clamoured for a more dynamic policy which, across the comfortable divide of the Atlantic ocean, they summed up in two simple, pregnant words, 'no rent'.

It was still necessary therefore for Parnell to take uncompromising attitudes on public platforms while endeavouring to secure time for the policy of 'testing' to begin when the land court opened for business in the autumn. Immediately after the convention he made a series of deliberately provocative speeches, starting in Dublin on 25 September, when he was welcomed with a torch-light procession said to have been the greatest demonstration since the days of O'Connell. It was on this occasion that he stopped the cortège outside the Bank of Ireland, where Grattan's parliament had sat a hundred years before, and pointed silently at it – a symbolic gesture which the crowd received with rapturous applause.[57] It was a gesture he was to repeat nine years later in circumstances that were to translate it into a cruel parody of his own past.* Elsewhere, he continued to speak with savage contempt of the 'hollowness' of the act and to the anxious eyes of ministers seemed either bent on intimidation or, alternatively, to be losing control of the

*See below, p. 548.

situation – 'moved by his tail', as Forster put it to Gladstone when commenting on the Dublin speech.[58]

If Parnell really was being moved by his tail, caution might have dictated a policy aimed at separating him from that tail. But Forster, writing again to Gladstone a few days later, also urged the desirability of arresting the Irish leader, which suggests that so far from distinguishing between Parnell and his followers, he saw the whole movement as a conspiracy which must be shattered from the top. He was obsessed, understandably, by the power of the boycott and he was convinced that this power was controlled by Parnell and his immediate lieutenants. 'Unless we can strike down the boycotting weapon', he wrote, 'Parnell will beat us; for men, rather than let themselves be ruined, will obey him and disobey the law.' 'It would be useless and weak', he continued, 'merely to arrest local Land Leaguers and to let off the Dublin leaders, especially Sexton and Parnell. If we strike a blow at all it must be a sufficiently hard blow to paralyse the action of the League, and for this purpose I think we must make a simultaneous arrest of the central leaders who conduct the boycott . . . I think the leaders would cease to boycott if they found out it meant imprisonment.'[59]

The arrest of Parnell and the other League leaders was a grave step, not to be undertaken except by a decision of the cabinet. Before it made that decision Gladstone in a speech at Leeds on 7 October launched an attack upon Parnell remarkable as much for its obtuseness as for its vehemence. Admittedly, he had considerable provocation. Five days earlier, on 2 October, Parnell, speaking at Cork, had made two statements calculated to raise the Prime Minister's hackles. To a mass-meeting during the day, he said: 'Those who want to preserve even the golden link of the Crown must see to it that that shall be the only link connecting the two countries.' In the evening, at a banquet and possibly off guard, he threw out casually the extraordinary observation that 'there is plenty of room for a land reformer of the future in the task of reducing the Irish rack-rental of today from seventeen millions a year to the two or three millions a year which I define as a fair rent'.[60] Both these remarks went far beyond Parnell's normal position at that time and William O'Brien may well be right in attributing them to 'the contagious heat of the revolution surging around him'. 'Even the most expert riders of the whirlwind', he sententiously observes, 'cannot always mark out its path.'[61] To Gladstone, already conditioned to view Parnell as essentially a destructive force, not only was the path of the whirlwind all too plain, but Parnell's progress along it seemed an act of conscious and defiant volition.

How different, he proclaimed at Leeds, was this rake's progress from the virtuous agitation conducted by Daniel O'Connell. 'O'Connell professed unconditional and unanswering loyalty to the crown of England. Mr Parnell says that if the crown of England is to be the link between the two countries it is to be the only link; but whether it is to be the link at all . . . is a matter on which he has not, I believe, given any opinion whatsoever.' It might have been truer to say that Parnell had given varying opinions, but Gladstone passed on, in the plenitude of his wrath, to castigate the policy of test cases which, he assumed, would be carefully chosen as cases of moderate rents which the court would refuse to touch, a refusal which the League leaders would pounce upon to justify their argument that the Land Act was hollow. But then, as if to illustrate his own deep, inner confusion, Gladstone, having condemned Parnell for opposing the Act, attacked him for not voting against it 'like a man' for fear that the League would rise up against him. This seemed to him symptomatic of a wider malaise. 'A general cowardice', he said, 'seems to prevail among all the classes who possess property and the government is expected to preserve the peace with no moral force behind it.' Although Gladstone believed that the Irish people were anxious to take advantage of the Land Act, it seemed that they would not be permitted to do so until Parnell gave the word. 'He says that until he has submitted his test cases any farmer who pays his rent is a fool. It is a dangerous thing for a man to be denounced as a fool by the head of the most violent party in the country . . . It is no small matter if he desires to arrest the operation of the Act, to stand, as Moses stood, between the living and the dead; but he stands there, not as Moses stood, to arrest, but to spread the plague.'[62]

It was obvious from this that action was imminent.[63] In fact, before he went to Leeds Gladstone had warned Forster to be ready to move if, as expected, the cabinet so decided at its next meeting on 12 October. Meanwhile, on 9 October, and as if to remove any lingering doubts which ministers might have, Parnell at Wexford delivered his riposte to Leeds. It was a speech of calculated insolence. Warning his hearers not to throw away their arms and place themselves in the power of 'the perfidious and cruel and relentless English enemy', he turned his attention to Gladstone himself:[64]

It is a good sign that this masquerading knight-errant, this pretending champion of the rights of every other nation except those of the Irish nation, should be obliged to throw off the mask today, and stand revealed as the man who, by his own utterances, is prepared to carry

fire and sword into your homesteads, unless you humbly abase
yourselves before him and before the landlords of the country.

Then, seizing upon Gladstone's fatal admission that the government
was obliged to preserve the peace with no moral force behind it, he
continued:

> He admits the contention that Grattan and the volunteers of 1782
> fought for; he admits the contention that the men of '98 died for;
> he admits the contention that O'Connell argued for . . . he admits
> the contention that the men of '67 . . . cheerfully faced the dungeons
> and horrors of penal servitude for; and he admits the contention that
> today you, in your overpowering multitudes, have established, and,
> please God, will bring to a successful issue – namely, that England's
> mission in Ireland has been a failure, and that Irishmen have estab-
> lished their right to govern Ireland by laws made by themselves on
> Irish soil. I say it is not in Mr Gladstone's power to trample on the
> aspirations and rights of the Irish nation with no moral force behind
> him.

At dinner after this speech two of his colleagues suggested to Parnell
that it would probably land him in jail. Indifferently, he replied that a
speech was not a necessary passport to prison – they could all be sent
there any time. Had he, they asked nervously, any instructions in the
event of his arrest? Who, for instance, would take his place? 'Ah!'
he said consideringly, looking through a glass of champagne which he
had just raised to his lips. 'Ah, if I am arrested Captain Moonlight will
take my place.'[65] 'Captain Moonlight' was of course a synonym for
the agrarian secret societies and since Parnell's remark accurately
forecast what speedily happened, it entered so quickly into the Parnellite
myth as to make it impossible to determine whether he actually said it
or whether it was simply *ben trovato*.

But whether he used those particular words or not, that he and others
anticipated his arrest is beyond doubt.[66] On 12 October the cabinet took
its expected decision and Forster immediately returned to Dublin,
arriving there early on the morning of Thursday, 13 October.[67] At
that moment the police were closing in on Parnell. He had come up
from Avondale to Morrison's Hotel on Wednesday evening as he had
to address a meeting in Kildare next day. He had asked to be called at
8.30 in the morning, but when the porter came to waken him he told
Parnell there were two men waiting for him downstairs. Learning that
they were a superintendent of the Dublin Metropolitan Police – in fact,

the celebrated detective, John Mallon – and a constable, he sent word that he would dress in half an hour and see them then. The porter urged him to escape through the back door, but Parnell declined this for the firmly pragmatic reason that every exit would certainly be guarded. The two policemen were then shown up to Parnell's room where, as the *Freeman's Journal* quaintly put it, 'the documents were presented to him with manly courtesy' by Mallon.[68] According to the warrant, Parnell was 'to be reasonably suspected of having, since the 30th day of September 1880 been guilty as principal in a crime punishable by law, that is to say:– inciting other persons wrongfully and without legal authority to intimidate divers persons with a view to compel them to abstain from doing what they had a legal right to do, namely to apply to the land court under the provision of the Land Law (Ireland) Act 1881 [to pay rents lawfully due by them]* to have a fair rent fixed for their holdings committed in the aforesaid Prescribed District (City of Dublin) and being the inciting to an act of intimidation and tending to interfere with the maintenance of Law and Order.'[69]

Mallon, having served his documents, then expressed some anxiety as to what might happen if a crowd collected. Parnell willingly agreed to a quiet departure by cab. This was unostentatiously joined by other vehicles which attracted only slight attention, and the little procession moved peacefully but swiftly through the city. By 9.30 that morning the doors of Kilmainham had closed behind the old prison's latest and most illustrious inmate.[70]

*The words in brackets appeared in the manuscript draft, evidently in error, and were deleted in the printed warrant which was actually handed to Parnell.

CHAPTER 6

Kilmainham

'Of course the Opposition will now ridicule the Government for having at last to resort to force, which Bright declared was no remedy a year ago. Those words, however, of Bright are greatly distorted. What, of course, he meant was that force could be no *permanent* remedy, nor more can it be – in short any more than a diet on blue pills could cure a patient with a bad liver. The occasional use of them does good and may be resorted to in chronic disorders, but their perpetual use must in the long run impair the constitution, which has been Ireland's fate.' (Diary of Sir Edward Hamilton, 19 October 1881.)

I

The arrest of Parnell caused a major political sensation, but it was a very different sensation on each side of the Irish Sea. In Britain, apart from some Radical dissent, it was hailed with delight, almost as if it were a great victory in the field. On the evening of the day on which Parnell was taken to Kilmainham Gladstone was speaking at the Guildhall. As he neared the end of his speech a telegram was handed to him by a pre-arranged plan. The audience at once grasped its purport and, after one startled and breathless moment, burst into cheer upon cheer. When order had been restored the Prime Minister announced in his most solemn tones the seizure of the man 'who . . . has made himself beyond all others prominent in the attempt to destroy the authority of the law and to substitute what would end in nothing more nor less than anarchical oppression exercised upon the people of Ireland'.[1]

Yet if the oppression which the people of Ireland felt at that moment was anarchical, it was the anarchy of lost leadership, not of imposed tyranny. In Dublin, the blow, though expected, had fallen in the end so swiftly that men felt suddenly bereft. Crowds gathered quickly and swirled through the streets seeking an aim, an inspiration, even perhaps a target. It was an explosive situation and it confronted the League executive with the grave problem of keeping riots in check while at the same time trying to decide whether or not to launch that strike against rent which had for so long been thought of as the ultimate weapon to be used against both government and landlords. It was fortunate in these circumstances that Gladstone, in the same Leeds speech in which he had turned his batteries on Parnell, had drawn, with almost unearthly ineptitude, what he fondly thought was a damaging contrast between the Irish leader and his lieutenant, John Dillon. Dillon, Gladstone had said, was an opponent whom he delighted to honour, because, while not giving up 'his extreme national views', he had stood aside from the policy of testing, and therefore disrupting, the Land Act. This total misreading of his position provoked Dillon to leave his retirement, take the chair at a Land League meeting in Dublin two days before Parnell's arrest, and repudiate with all his force the praise lavished on him by the Prime Minister – the only reason he had not opposed Gladstone's act as it passed through parliament, he said, was because Gladstone's government had shut him up in Kilmainham.[2]

The importance of this exchange was that it brought Dillon back into circulation just when Parnell needed him most. On the very day of his arrest Parnell wrote asking him to resume his place at the head of the movement and this appeal Dillon, with his austere sense of duty, felt it impossible to refuse. Typically, Parnell, in blandly assuming that Dillon would rally to the cause, assumed also that he would now swallow the policy which only a few weeks earlier he had resigned rather than accept. 'I am very strongly of opinion', he wrote, 'that no change should be made, at all events until we can see whether we can keep the tenants out of the court. I would recommend that the test cases be proceeded with . . . If we can do this, and if the government do not suppress the organization, we can I am sure maintain and strengthen the movement.'[3] Reluctantly, Dillon did his best to carry out his leader's instructions and at a crowded and excitable meeting in Dublin that same night urged calm and restraint upon the League.

This policy was immediately shattered when the next day (14 October) Thomas Sexton and the acting secretary of the League, P. J. Quinn, were arrested and taken to Kilmainham. That evening a vast protest meeting was held at the Rotunda and the question of whether or not to launch a general strike against rent was long and vehemently debated. Once again Dillon subordinated his own feelings to the general good, insisting that an all-out 'No Rent' campaign was too dangerous, though he could not refrain from adding that if any individual county cared to initiate such a policy it was free to do so. 'We wish it to be distinctly understood', he said sardonically, 'that the executive of the Land League have no intention of coercing or intimidating people into paying rent.'[4]

On the day that Dillon gave this advice Parnell wrote a second time from Kilmainham cancelling his previous instructions. The new spate of arrests, he said, had made it impossible to carry out the policy of testing the act adopted at the League convention. 'I am therefore with great reluctance driven to admit that there is no resource save the adoption of a strike against all rent, and suggest that you should announce the adoption of this policy at the meeting tonight and the withdrawal of test cases.'[5]

There is a strange mystery here. As William O'Brien later recalled the incident, Parnell had had the letter smuggled out from prison expressly so that it should be read at the meeting, where, if it had been read, it would undoubtedly have precipitated a rent strike. Dillon did not read it, O'Brien suggests, because he thought it wiser for the executive to discuss it further. After the meeting, therefore, the League leaders met at the Imperial Hotel. They separated at midnight without having decided whether to go for 'No Rent' or not. But before they could reassemble next day the government swooped and in a matter of hours Dillon, O'Brien and J. J. O'Kelly had all joined Parnell in Kilmainham.[6]

The strange circumstance about this letter is that Dillon did not receive it on 14 October. In fact, he did not receive it for another 40 years when he had retired from politics and Parnell was long dead. It had been given to a warder who had had no chance to transmit it before Dillon's arrest the next day. He had then apparently put it in a drawer at home and forgotten all about it. It was only when his house was being cleared out after his death that the letter came to light. We have to remember that O'Brien's account was written a quarter of a century after the events it describes. By then he had quarrelled with Dillon and may have succumbed to the temptation to blacken his former friend by suggesting that at a critical moment Dillon, by withholding the letter, had disobeyed explicit instructions from his chief. Alternatively, O'Brien's inaccuracy may have been the product not of malice, but simply of genuine confusion arising from the hectic pace at which the situation developed. Since both Dillon and O'Brien were face to face with Parnell the day after the letter was written, nothing would have been more natural than that its contents would then have been discussed and nothing easier than for O'Brien, looking back in after years, to transfer to the meeting of 14 October knowledge which he and Dillon could only have gained in prison on or after 15 October.

Once they were all thrown together in Kilmainham the crucial decision facing them was still whether or not to proclaim a strike against rent. Everything depended on Parnell's attitude, but about that there is,

as so often, a conflict of evidence. William O'Brien maintained in his
memoirs that his leader was 'most resolute' for extreme measures –
that is, for 'No Rent'.[7] But Katharine O'Shea, than whom no one was
better placed to read Parnell's mind, believed that he was 'really opposed
to it' and Dillon 'openly so', but that a majority in Kilmainham was
firmly for it.[8] Barry O'Brien, who came to know Parnell well a few years
after these events, used exactly the same phrase as Katharine. 'Parnell',
he wrote, 'was really opposed to the manifesto', but was reluctant to
stand out against his left wing, since both Patrick Ford from America
and Patrick Egan from Paris were pressing for a 'No Rent' campaign.[9]
Parnell himself, when examined on the subject at the Special Commission in 1889, defended the 'No Rent' policy on the ground that it was
the only form of pressure left to the League leaders after the virtual
collapse of their organization and he claimed that 'indirectly' it helped
to bring about settlements between large numbers of tenants and their
landlords.[10] There is no evidence that it did anything of the kind, but
his own letter to Dillon of 14 October supports the first part of his
argument at the Commission, that it was a policy of last resort which he
adopted with reluctance. In the end, it was agreed that O'Brien should
draw up a manifesto calling upon the tenants 'to pay *no rents* under any
circumstances to their landlords until the government relinquishes the
existing system of terrorism and restores the constitutional rights of
the people'.[11] This was signed on 18 October by all the League leaders
actually in Kilmainham at the time – Parnell, Dillon, Sexton, Thomas
Brennan and A. J. Kettle; the names of Patrick Egan and Michael
Davitt were also added.

It is in a sense ironic that two of the sternest critics of the manifesto
– Dillon at the time, and Davitt later – should have been the men
who, earlier in the year, had been most urgent for the adoption of a
'No Rent' campaign. Davitt's name was attached to the document without his permission (he was in Portland jail) and Dillon only signed
apparently at William O'Brien's insistence. His objection was partly
that a strike against rent could not succeed because it would not be
supported by the priests. But it was based much more on his growing
realization that a campaign of this kind might easily lead to violence and
that neither the League nor the tenants were so organized as to be
able to resist determined action by the government.[12] Davitt in after
years made essentially the same point, that whatever hope of success
the policy had had in February, it had virtually none in October, with
both the Protection of Person and Property Act and the Land Act on
the statute-book and the leaders in prison. To launch it when it was

launched was, as Davitt truly said, 'an act of desperation'. 'The no-rent shell fired from Kilmainham would only demoralize and could not explode. Its fuse had fallen off.'[13]

A. J. Kettle, who earlier in 1881 had envisaged a no-rent drive as no more than a six-months campaign, took a similar view which he expressed with characteristic bluntness to Parnell as the latter was about to sign the manifesto. 'I shall never taunt you, Mr Parnell', he said, 'even in private, but I must ask you not to blame the people if they fail to carry out this policy now to the extent that was feasible for the six months effort.' And he remembered all his life that when Parnell had attached his signature he straightened up and looked hard at him. Kettle for his part signed in silence, 'the most disappointed man in Ireland', as he said.[14]

Well might Parnell look at his old friend without speaking. It is impossible that he should not have guessed what was about to happen, impossible that he should not have known that O'Brien's flaming prose was no more than a false prospectus. The day before his arrest Parnell had received from Timothy Harrington, one of the ablest of the League's organizers, a report on the demoralization that prevailed nearly everywhere. Some active branches were not recorded on the League's books at all, and others which were seemed to exist only for the purposes of demanding money from people in their locality. Moreover, there was a growing tendency for tenants to regard the League as a milch-cow and only to go to law with their landlords if their expenses were paid for them. Anything less like the 'magnificent organization' of O'Brien's manifesto it would be difficult to imagine.[15]

It is against this background that the letter Parnell wrote to Katharine O'Shea on the morning of his arrest has to be considered. He scribbled it in Morrison's Hotel, with the policemen waiting for him below. It was posted en route for Kilmainham, by Parnell himself, when Superintendent Mallon, still exercising that 'manly courtesy' so much admired by the *Freeman's Journal*, stopped the cab to allow the prisoner to get out and drop the letter in a post-box.[16] This is what it said:[17]

My own Queenie, – I have just been arrested by two fine-looking detectives, and write these words to wifie to tell her that she must be a brave little woman and not fret after her husband.

The only thing that makes me worried and unhappy is that it may hurt you or our child.

You know, darling, that on this account it will be wicked of you to grieve, as I can never have any other wife but you, and if anything happens to you I must die childless. Be good and brave, dear little wifie, then. Your own husband.

Politically it is a fortunate thing for me that I have been arrested, as the movement is breaking fast, and all will be quiet in a few months, when I shall be released.

This letter tells us two important things about Parnell at this crisis in his fortunes. The first is that *before* he reversed his policy on 'No Rent', he had made up his mind that the agrarian movement was 'breaking fast' and had already grasped that there was more political capital to be made from imprisonment in Kilmainham than from leading a forlorn hope outside. There was no doubt a certain cynicism about his action in authorizing the manifesto when he was already convinced that it could not work, but there was an even greater realism. Knowing as he did from Harrington's report that the League was virtually non-operative, he could afford to use the 'No Rent' appeal as a necessary safety-valve for his left wing in the reasonable certainty that no serious damage would result.

The second thing the letter tells us is that his relations with Katharine O'Shea were by this time virtually those of man and wife. Parnell's fumbling endearments are pathetic to the point of embarrassment, but not even the cloying sentimentality of his language can hide his torment that at this climactic moment, when Katharine was carrying his child, he should have been shut away from her in Kilmainham. That it *was* his child she was carrying there seems little reason to doubt, though her own narrative preserves a degree of ambiguity, almost certainly due to the fact that it was written in old age under the eye of O'Shea's son Gerard. When the strange triangular relationship that first developed in 1880-1 was finally exposed to public view a decade later, it was essential for Captain O'Shea to show that he had been a deceived husband over many years, and that he could therefore have had no knowledge that his wife had borne Parnell any children.[18] When Katharine O'Shea's book appeared in 1914, O'Shea had been dead nine years, but as the preface to that book makes plain, the son of their marriage was highly sensitive to imputations against his father.[19] This had curious implications for the book, and still more curious ones for Katharine herself. Thus, in telling of her anxiety about the possible effect of imprisonment upon Parnell's health, she says, or is made to say, that in addition to that anxiety 'the deception I had to practise towards Captain O'Shea, seldom as I saw him, told upon my nerves just now'. The egregious Captain himself arrived at Eltham on the evening of

Parnell's arrest, 'fiercely and openly joyful' at the event and watching Katharine closely as he criticized the leader and expressed his pleasure that he was 'laid by the heels'.[20]

Katharine survived this ordeal somehow – mainly by thinking of her lover while Willie rattled on – but an ugly question remains. Did O'Shea really know whose child it was that was born in February 1882 and died in April of the same year? In her book she implies – or again is made to imply – that he believed it to be his. 'Willie', she says, 'was very good. I told him my baby was dying and I must be left alone. He had no suspicion of the truth, and only stipulated that the child should be baptized at once . . .'[21] Some apparent confirmation of this can be found in two letters, one printed by Katharine herself, the other hitherto unpublished. The unpublished one was written by O'Shea to Joseph Chamberlain on 25 April 1882. Most of it deals with political matters to which we must return presently, but its opening sentences are directly relevant to the question of fatherhood. 'My child is to be buried at Chislehurst this afternoon. Afterwards I shall return to Eltham and I do not intend to come to town unless you want me.'[22] The second, published letter, was written to Katharine a few weeks later by O'Shea's sister Mary. It was a normal, affectionate letter, mostly about Katharine's children, especially the dead baby, Claude Sophie. Referring to the news of the child's death, conveyed by a friend of the family, Mary O'Shea wrote: 'She loved your little Claude, and shared your grief at losing her, but happy child, how glorious is her existence! What a contrast to ours, we who must struggle on, working out our salvation in fear and trembling.' Katharine's own comment on this was that it proved, 'I think very conclusively, that my little one's paternity was utterly unsuspected by the O'Sheas'.[23]

We are left then with two possibilities, neither of which can be proved or disproved. One is that Captain O'Shea, who in general was not an expert conspirator, developed in this matter such a genius for concealment that he was able to deceive, not only the astute Chamberlain, but also his own family; on this assumption the letter he wrote to Chamberlain was intended merely as a blind, a 'show letter' which served to maintain the façade of his innocence. Alternatively, the Captain really did believe that the child was his. But if he believed that, he can only have believed it because Katharine had given him cause to do so. Which in turn involves the supposition, unpleasant but not inherently impossible, that while she was Parnell's mistress, her husband was concurrently, if erratically, asserting his conjugal rights. Even if, as one must presume from the duel episode onwards, Parnell was not aware of this – his reaction would have been murderous if any whisper of it had reached him – the slightest indication of O'Shea's presence at Eltham was enough to bring on acute spasms of jealousy. Thus, when O'Shea actually stayed there for some days in November 1881 the immediate result was a passionate outburst from Kilmainham – 'it is frightful that you should be exposed to such daily torture'.[24] But that it *was* torture, and that Katharine was his alone, he never seems to have doubted for an instant.

II

A man racked by these private anxieties was unlikely to attach to the 'No Rent' manifesto the same importance as did his more committed colleagues and it is improbable that Parnell was much surprised by the immediate sequel. The manifesto was made public on 18 October. It was at once roundly condemned by both the *Freeman's Journal* and the *Nation*, and unkindest cut of all, was denounced by Archbishop Croke of Cashel, generally assumed to be the most sympathetic towards the agitation of all the members of the hierarchy.[25] But this was merely the prelude to the inevitable counter-stroke from the government, which on 20 October suppressed the Land League as an illegal organization. There followed in succeeding weeks the easily predictable result that the tenants, left without leadership (for local organizers were swept into the net as well as national figures), began to 'test' the Land Act in the way that most appealed to them, by taking advantage of its terms.

Yet this did not mean that the country subsided peacefully into the paths of law and order. On the contrary, the winter of 1881–2 was one of the most violent in living memory and the dark nights covered darker deeds than any which the League executive would have sanctioned had its members been at liberty and in control. Thus, whereas in the first quarter of 1881 cases of homicide and firing at the person had together numbered seven, in the corresponding quarter of 1882 the figure was 33.[26] To a large extent these crimes seem to have been the work of secret societies or groups, operating in particular districts along lines familiar since the eighteenth century. Gradually, but only gradually, it became apparent that this ancient agrarian turmoil had been contained and even repressed by the League in its heyday, though this is not to deny that violent men sometimes did violent deeds in its name. When the League discipline, such as it was, broke down or was removed, the centrifugal drives of agrarian anarchy were allowed to operate almost unchecked.

Not totally unchecked, however. There did still remain a skeleton of organization, but of a type scarcely less objectionable to the League leaders than the agrarian anarchy itself. This was the Ladies Land League, and it was ironic, to say the least, that the driving force behind it should have been Parnell's masterful sister, Anna. The idea of creating such a body had originally been Fanny Parnell's. In 1880 she had started a Ladies Land League in the United States to assist the American Land League in raising funds for the land war in Ireland. In January 1881 Davitt proposed the formation of a similar organization in Ireland, with the wider object of providing a means of continuing the agitation should the Land League leaders themselves be arrested. This suggestion was backed by Patrick Egan, but, at first, Davitt later recalled, 'vehemently opposed' by Thomas Brennan, John Dillon and Parnell, who thought the movement would be covered with ridicule if it put women into posts of danger. According to Davitt, Anna Parnell was consulted from the first about the plan; though she later denied this, she was certainly in favour of the idea and this may have influenced Parnell, with his long experience of the difficulty of resisting a sister who had his own imperiousness and tenacity, plus a tincture of revolutionary fanaticism. In the end all objections were overcome and the Ladies Land League was established on 31 January 1881. Anna Parnell was one of the secretaries and it was she who on 13 February addressed the first public meeting of the Ladies Land League at Claremorris.[27]

The original functions assigned to the ladies were the relief of evicted tenants and the supervision of League boycotts against land-grabbers, but to these, once the Coercion Act began to function, was added the important business of supplying food to the 'suspects' shut up in government prisons. Predictably, given the zeal with which the ladies threw themselves into their work, they fell foul of the law and some even ended in jail themselves. This participation in the traditionally male preserve of politics brought down upon them the strictures of Archbishop McCabe, who in March 1881 addressed a public warning to his diocesan clergy: 'Do not tolerate in your sodalities the woman who so far disavows her birthright of modesty as to parade herself before the public gaze in a character so unworthy a child of Mary. This attempt at degrading the women of Ireland comes very appropriately from men who have drawn the country into her present terribly deplorable condition.'[28] Archbishop McCabe, it is true, was hardly typical either of the hierarchy or of moderate Catholic opinion and he received a scorching public reply from no less a moderate than A. M. Sullivan, whose eminently respectable wife had joined the organization. The fact that Archbishop Croke chose this moment to express his delight that someone had come forward from the party 'to vindicate the character of the good Irish ladies who have become Land Leaguers and to challenge publicly the monstrous imputations cast upon them by the Archbishop of Dublin', was a significant indication that on the land question the Irish bishops were still sharply divided, even if Croke did subsequently have to withdraw his criticisms 'unequivocally'.[29]

Yet, despite their energy and devotion, some of the ladies found their experience profoundly disillusioning. Anna Parnell herself wrote a book on the subject twenty years later which never found a publisher. Entitled *The tale of a great sham*, it consisted of a sustained attack on the way the Land League had operated, or rather failed to operate.* The burden of her allegations was that, despite a great deal of speech-making and some genuine cases of stubborn resistance, many tenants were instructed by the League to pay their rents when confronted with superior force. Worse still, it was apparently League policy to give grants to evicted tenants which they could use to pay their rents and thus win reinstatement to their holdings provided this was done within the legal limit of six months; the effect of this was to transfer a large part of the League's funds straight into the pockets of the landlords. Again, when the ladies came to examine applications for relief, they found that the applicants were, almost without exception, people who had been evicted, not for unwillingness to pay, but because of inability to pay. According to strict League doctrine, on estates where this had happened solvent tenants should have withheld their rents in sympathy and thus figured among the evicted seeking relief. But such cases were mysteriously absent and when asked why this was, members of the executive told Anna Parnell – so she says, doubtless with exaggeration – that there was 'not a single tenant in Ireland who would not pay the rent if he could'. Since the ladies' reaction to this was to try to stimulate real resistance to rent, it was not surprising that they incurred considerable hostility from League organizers who deeply resented such an intrusion of feminine logic and tactless energy.

Against this background, which temperament, prejudice and policy probably led Anna to oversimplify, it is easy to understand why the character of the formal agitation changed so much after the imprisonment of the leaders and the suppression of the League in October 1881. What the ladies tried to do between then and the following May

*The manuscript is now in the National Library of Ireland (NLI MS 12144). For an account of its genesis see T. W. Moody, 'Anna Parnell and the Land League', in *Hermathena*, cxvii (summer 1974), pp. 5–17.

was not only to continue to care for evicted tenants, but also to try to make a reality of the 'No Rent' manifesto. In addition, and seemingly with remarkable success, they took a major part in keeping *United Ireland* in print after William O'Brien's arrest. Yet their effort came too late. The results of two years of maladministration could not be cancelled in six months, especially in a climate so much changed by coercion and by the Land Act. And though the ladies fought valiantly, and suffered much, they were to find, when Parnell emerged from prison to give the kaleidoscope a further shake, that in his eyes they were peripheral, expendable and a greater nuisance to him than to the government.

III

But this was for the future. So long as he remained in jail, Parnell, however much he might disapprove of the Ladies Land League, could only watch its activities from the side-lines. As for the agitation itself, there was little for him to do but to follow its course with philosophic resignation. There is reason to believe, not only that he saw the Land Act as working towards the ruin of the landlords, but also that he himself was in a position, as a landlord, to contemplate this possibility with some detachment. William O'Brien in after years told the story, often since repeated, of how Parnell, when asked about the behaviour of his own tenants, would humorously reply, 'they are standing by the "No Rent" manifesto splendidly'.[30] The government had different information. On 24 October an anonymous letter to Dublin Castle alleged that the writer had met Parnell's agent in Hastings and that the latter had told him that Parnell had arranged for the collection of his rents '*before* entering upon the more serious part of the present agitation'. It was thought worthwhile to set a local investigation on foot and on 1 November, an RIC officer reported, correctly, that there was no agent as such, but a land steward, Mr William Kerr, who lived at Avondale. The constable had made careful enquiries and elicited the information that nearly all the current rents had been collected. 'Mr Kerr commenced to collect the rents due this half-year about three weeks ago, and up to this has received all rents due. I believe Mr Parnell's rents are secure.'[31]*

Parnell's views on the working of the Land Act while he was in prison

---

*The accuracy of this information could only be tested against Parnell's rent-books, which have not survived. But the government were less likely to have been interested in accuracy than in the evidence which the report seemingly provided that there was a significant difference between Parnell's public speeches and his private conduct.

are rather more difficult to assess. On 7 November the *Freeman's Journal* published a detailed account of a visit paid to him by two prominent members of the old Home Rule League. According to this report, Parnell expressed the opinion that the decisions already made by the land court in the north of Ireland accorded roughly with the League's doctrine that rents ought to be based on Griffith's valuation and that presumably the Ulster tenants would resort to the court in large numbers, though this would not necessarily happen elsewhere since the judgements would probably be less favourable. Asked what might be the effect of a general application of Griffith's valuation, he was reported to have replied that it would drive many landlords into actual bankruptcy because they needed the existing rents to service mortgages and other charges on their estates. When the rental was reduced, he is alleged to have said, 'a state of things would ensue which would compel the government to adopt the plan of buying out the landlords or else they would be confronted with a claim for the landlords whose living in fact depends upon their exaction of rack-rents above the government [Griffith] valuation'. If Parnell really did speak in this unguarded way, it would have been clear to all who read the report that, while remaining true to the Land League ideal of expropriating the landlords, he was looking for the achievement of this aim not to the 'No Rent' manifesto, but to an intelligent use of the Land Act. Nothing could have been more likely to embroil him with his own left wing and it is scarcely surprising that immediately the account of this interview appeared Parnell sent a strong repudiation of it to the *Freeman's Journal*.

This was no more than might have been expected, for he was always a master of strategic withdrawal. But in fact the official minute of the interview, at which the deputy governor of the prison was present, indicates that the land question was very little discussed, since political conversation was forbidden on these occasions.[32] Nevertheless, and although the newspaper report was no doubt much garbled, it did represent a strand in his thinking. Even William O'Brien, despite his anxiety to claim him as a willing signatory of the 'No Rent' manifesto, never regarded him as opposed to the operation of the land court. 'He did not believe', O'Brien wrote in after years, 'that the advice to the Irish tenants to endure evictions rather than pay their rents would be generally obeyed; but he anticipated that it would be on a sufficient scale to exercise upon the new land courts [sic] the same wholesome influence as the test cases, and to make the government of the country by Forster's ruthless coercive methods impossible.'[33] This may overstate the extent to which Parnell actually believed that rents would be withheld, but it is probably as fair a statement as we are likely to get of how he saw the situation while in prison.

Whether tenants did or did not pay their rents and whether they crowded into the land court, left it severely alone, or concluded private bargains with their landlords, were questions which would have to be answered without Parnell. 'I shall take it as evidence that the people of the country did not do their duty if I am speedily released', he told a reporter who visited him just after his arrest.[34] But this gnomic utterance – which left it unclear whether he was referring to the use of the land court or the non-payment of rent – belonged to rhetoric rather than reality and no one knew better than himself that 'the people of the country' would make their choice as self-interest seemed best to dictate. All that remained for him to do was to acclimatize himself as well as he could to an experience which for him was unique in two distinct ways. It was the only period of his life that he ever spent in prison; and it was the only period of his life that he ever spent in prolonged and close contact with his followers.

He was in most respects a model prisoner. In general, he was amenable to prison rules, though when admitted to Kilmainham, he reacted so violently against the proposal to weigh, measure and search him – Healy says it was because he had a revolver in his pocket, but there is no other evidence of this, which seems improbable – that this routine procedure was hastily abandoned. His presence, of course, presented serious problems for the authorities, and though William O'Brien may have been indulging his novelist's imagination in asserting that Parnell was speedily supplied with a set of keys that could have gained him his freedom at any time, his contacts with the outside world were so numerous that he never had the least difficulty in obtaining whatever publicity he needed.[35] There was a constant flow of visitors – reporters, politicians, his solicitor (whom he saw 42 times between October and April), well-wishers of every kind. Since many, possibly most, of these visits took place without an official being present, it was hardly surprising that there were frequent breaches of security, and one can sympathize with the governor when he minuted angrily: 'It is absolutely impossible for me to hold myself responsible for these irregularities, so long as prisoners hold interviews with visitors and friends, without any guard over their words or actions.'[36] But even with such precautions it is doubtful if leakages could have been prevented since there were always some warders who, for patriotic or commercial reasons, could be persuaded to pass out messages or letters.

The real danger was not that Parnell would disappear, but that he might fall seriously ill. Kilmainham was at best a cold, dark, damp institution and in winter it was at its worst. The leading 'suspects' were suspect in health as in much else – Sexton was sick when he was arrested and had soon to be released, Dillon was threatened with tuberculosis and also had a troublesome digestive ailment, O'Brien was frail, even Kettle fell into something like a decline, and only the iron O'Kelly seemed unaffected. Parnell, like other inmates who were used to country life, showed the effects of prison life rather more than townsmen habituated to a sedentary existence. He was never in actual danger, but there are frequent references, official and unofficial, to a whole series of vexatious ailments. He was fortunate to have at hand the medical help of Dr Kenny – also under arrest – and through Kenny's insistence all the 'suspects' whose health gave grounds for anxiety were removed to the hospital wing where conditions were less rigorous. Not that they were unduly rigorous for Parnell once a routine was established. He was given a room fourteen feet by eight and twelve feet high – 'the best room in the place', according to a reporter who visited him on 17 October – and this rapidly came to be the focal point for his colleagues, where they assembled for their interminable discussions. It was not indeed a very bright room, though there was some sunlight and the Ladies Land League did their best with curtains, furniture and books. Its heavily barred windows were set high in the massive walls and looked out on to a small dark courtyard. This served as the exercise ground for the 'suspects' and Parnell used it for handball and also – surely another breach of the regulations – for target-practice with an airgun. They could only spend six hours there out of the 24 and the rest of the time were under stricter confinement. Lights were officially turned out at nine o'clock, but Parnell frequently read until midnight, going to bed and getting up pretty well when he liked.[37]

He had not been very long in prison before the irksomeness of this regime began to have both physical and psychological effects. His fellow-inmates noticed particularly his nervousness about contagious diseases and his rampant superstition. William O'Brien records how on one occasion he told Parnell that he had had a letter from one of his *United Ireland* sub-editors, telling him that two of the latter's children were down with scarlatina. 'My God, O'Brien', said Parnell, 'what did you do with the letter?' O'Brien said he still had it in his pocket and was told to throw it in the fire instantly. Having done so, he was then commanded to wash his hands, and when he dallied, thinking Parnell was joking, his leader fetched a basin of water and stood over him until he had 'disinfected' himself.[38] As for superstition, what he seems to have found hardest to bear was the flood of green scarves, green cardigans, green smoking-caps, green counterpanes with which benevolent ladies inundated the prison. Parnell would not touch one of them. O'Brien suspected that at the root of this particular fetish was a fear of arsenic poisoning. It sounds fantastic, but it is important to remember that there was one part of Parnell's mind where fantasy had its own reality.[39] No doubt it was in that strange region that his dread of the number thirteen was also located. This too was evident in Kilmainham, to such a degree, it is said, that after striking out a clause in a draft bill to amend the Land Act of 1881 brought to him by Tim Healy's brother Maurice, he reinstated it the moment he realized that its deletion would reduce the number of clauses to the detested thirteen.[40]

His physical deterioration was not so great as anxious sympathizers supposed, but it was real and it began quite soon after his arrest. Partly it was the effect of idleness upon a naturally active man, partly also it was connected, initially at least, with prison diet. It may have been a combination of the two which caused the 'violent spasms' and 'severe abdominal pain' which Dr Kenny reported as having attacked him on the night of 30 October. But these, which the doctor was able to relieve without too much difficulty, were worrying less in themselves than because of what might lie behind them. 'The attack from which he suffered today', wrote Kenny, 'alarmed me not so much on account of the local affection [sic] as on account of the symptoms which accompanied it in other directions. It was accompanied by an alarming tendency towards syncope which however did not last long but which was subsequently followed by very violent central irritation. I have already warned the authorities that Mr Parnell suffers from an affection of the heart, but from facts which have recently come to my knowledge concerning him, I have to warn them very strongly that effects of a still more serious nature to his nervous system may and are very likely to follow prolonged confinement in his case.'[41]

What these recently discovered facts were Dr Kenny never disclosed, but his assertion that he – or his distinguished patient – feared further damage to the 'nervous system', suggests that we may have here a reference to the family mental history and an early example of Parnell's tendency, of which more was to be heard later, to brood upon the possibilities of madness. The prison doctor, Dr Carte, took, it must be said, a more robust view of the situation. On the day of the attack he had observed Parnell playing handball with other suspects and at seven o'clock that evening had been summoned to visit him. He found the patient lying on a bed in one of the other prisoners' rooms. 'Stated that he had been ill, but was then better.' He appeared apologetic that Carte had been sent for at all and although Kenny imparted to the prison doctor 'a circumstance connected with Mr Parnell's family' – presumably the 'facts' Kenny had mentioned in his report – Dr Carte's attitude was dismissive. 'I regard such statements as of little import.'[42]

That particular incident ended there, but only a couple of weeks later Kenny's journal reflected renewed anxiety. 'I am becoming more seriously alarmed concerning the condition of Mr Parnell's health. He has lost his appetite almost completely, sleeps very badly and suffers much from sciatica. He is rapidly losing flesh and appearance, the confinement is evidently telling on him very heavily. If I do not find a change for the better within the next day or so I shall consider it my duty to ask for further professional assistance.' Two days later, after sulphur baths and 'Faradization', the pain was considerably reduced, though Kenny was still dissatisfied. 'His liver also has latterly become very torpid and inactive and is beginning to be very troublesome.'[43] It has to be remembered, however, that Kenny's journal was kept with an eye to the prison authorities and that he was concerned to make the most of any ailments the 'suspects' might suffer so as to buttress their case for special treatment. Apparently he did not succeed in this instance, for whereas his reports were followed by visits from independent physicians for Dillon, Kettle and one or two others, that was not deemed necessary for Parnell.

Parnell himself, in the letters to Katharine O'Shea which he smuggled out with ease and frequency, naturally made light of his ill-health in an effort to minimize the anxiety which she, midway through her pregnancy, was clearly feeling. At the outset, after only a week in prison, he wrote that he was 'obliged to invent little maladies for myself from day to day in order to give Dr Kenny an excuse for keeping me in the infirmary'. The latest, he said, was 'heart affection', 'but I have never felt better in my life'.[44] By early November, though, he was admitting to the first signs of indisposition, which he ascribed to indigestion, or else to the '*mal du prison*' that everyone experienced after the first few weeks.[45] A month later he wrote that he had caught cold but tried to reassure her that the gloomy account of his health which was about to appear in the *Freeman's Journal* would be deliberately exaggerated to prevent his room being changed.[46] This took the form of an interview with F. H. O'Donnell, who visited him on 8 December, and reported that Parnell had had a 'smart, febrile seizure' the previous day and was evidently suffering from the effects of insufficient air and exercise.[47]

Although Parnell repeated his warning to Katharine that this report was 'carefully got up', he did admit to having had a feverish cold, probably brought on by getting chilled after having become overheated at handball.[48] But so far was he from suffering any permanent ill-effects that by mid-February he was actually complaining of growing fat.[49] His weight apparently increased from 170 pounds when he was arrested to about 175 pounds at the end of March.[50]

This increase of weight helps to explode one of the myths which the leading 'suspects' in Kilmainham deliberately fostered – that rather than be a burden on their friends they would content themselves with prison food. The normal prison diet was no doubt repulsive enough and Parnell probably spoke no more than the truth when he told O'Donnell that the porridge was uneatable and that he could not distinguish between the tea and the coffee.[51] There is a tremor of genuine horror in William O'Brien's account of the stew which Parnell and Kenny concocted out of lumps of inferior beef and watery vegetable soup.[52] But it is clear from Parnell's letters to Katharine that the public fuss which was made about the prison diet was artificially created partly to move the government to action, partly to launch a fund for the proper mainten-ance of the 'suspects', and partly to relieve the League resources of a burden which in November 1881 was calculated at £400 a week and may have been considerably more.[53] 'We hope by the row we are making', he wrote, 'to compel government to make the food sufficiently good to satisfy the men and take expense of their keep off our resources.'[54] The immediate consequence of this, however, was that a special sus-tentation fund was established by Anna Parnell, to which by Christmas time about £9000 had been contributed. From this, it was reckoned it would be possible to provide every suspect in all the prisons (not just Kilmainham) with one good meal a day for another seventeen weeks, provided there was no serious increase in their numbers. Whether by chance or by design that period of seventeen weeks terminated at the end of April, which, as we shall see, was precisely the moment when Parnell negotiated the Kilmainham 'treaty' that brought their ordeal to an end.[55]

The leaders themselves do not seem to have made more than a token genuflection to the idea of restricting their nourishment to prison fare and even when the public protest was in full cry Parnell was able to reassure Katharine that 'whatever happens we will take good care of ourselves – at present we are living upon all the good things of the world, game etc'.[56] On 3 December he reported that he was not really on prison diet at all and a few days later wrote to say that he was getting all his food from the governor's kitchen.[57] On the whole, it is not surprising that Parnell suffered more from indigestion than from malnutrition.

It is deeply significant that this evidence of what the grand gesture towards prison fare really meant, and also the evidence of so many other aspects of the Kilmainham imprisonment, should be derived primarily from Parnell's letters to Katharine O'Shea. For they indicate more clearly than any other documents of the period that Parnell was living simultaneously at two levels of existence. On the surface, he was the adored chief of a small circle of intimates – joining in their games, undergoing the same privations (such as they were) and enduring amiably what he may well have felt to be their altogether excessive powers of conversation. But privately, in that strange correspondence he carried on with Katharine, with all its cloak-and-dagger paraphernalia of invisible ink and misleading cover letters, he was manifestly turning away from a movement which had served its purpose, had begun to dissolve, and in dissolving had fundamentally changed its character. It has always to be remembered that Katharine was unwell and worried, making heavy weather of a pregnancy which had come upon her after a long interval. Parnell, in his desperate anxiety about her well-being, was only too likely to tell her what she most wanted to hear, that compared with their love politics was a tiresome irrelevance. Yet it is impossible not to read his letters (hers, unhappily, have not survived) without realizing that whether partly under Katharine's influence, or wholly from a cold, matter-of-fact assessment of the situation, he was adopting, deliberately, an attitude of cynical aloofness towards the agitation of which he was still, at least in name, the leader.

We saw earlier that at the moment of his arrest he wrote to her that 'the movement is breaking fast'. It seems that he expected then to be released within a few weeks, when all was quiet.[58] But as the weeks passed and this did not happen he began to dwell increasingly upon how Katharine and he could come together again. More than once, in his infatuation, he toyed with the idea that she (O'Shea being conveniently absent in Spain), might come over to visit him, posing as one of his married sisters or as a cousin, but even he came to realize that this escapade – which he proposed both before *and* after Katharine's child was born – was totally impractical.[59] Failing this, he tried to reassure her by telling her that the authorities had twice approached him to say he could be released any time if he would promise to go abroad. He had merely replied that he was in no hurry to leave. 'In fact, I much prefer to wait here till the meeting of parliament.'[60] But this may not have gone down too well at Eltham, for a month later he promised her that rather than suffer 'my beautiful wifie' to run any risk, he would resign his seat, quit politics and go wherever she wished.[61]

To what extent he really meant this we cannot say and she was far too perceptive to hold him to any such pledge, but the letter shows how far he was prepared to commit himself for her sake, and apparently it did evoke from her a suggestion that he might instead come to terms with the government. That, however, touched his pride. 'I could not well make any arrangement or enter into any undertaking with the government unless I retired altogether from politics.'[62] Instead, he looked forward to being released just before parliament met and in January wrote promising that he would go to her the moment he was set free. She need not fear, he added, that he would be quickly re-arrested, for he had made up his mind not to speak again in Ireland so long as coercion was in force.[63] As the time for the opening of parliament drew closer even this hope faded. Word reached him that the government were contemplating new rules of procedure to curb obstruction and he needed no telling that he would probably be kept where he was until those were safely through.[64]

As the weeks dragged on he became more obviously impatient, bitterly regretting, as he wrote, that he had not returned to England after the Wexford speech, thus avoiding arrest and sparing her 'such a long, long separation'. But this was fantasy and he knew it. Instead, he worked off his spleen in a diatribe directed about equally at the League and at the government's efforts to suppress it:[65]

> At least I am very glad that the days of platform speeches are gone by and are not likely to return. I cannot describe to you the disgust I always felt with those meetings, knowing as I did how hollow and wanting in solidity everything connected with the movement was. When I was arrested I did not think the movement would have survived a month, but this wretched government have such a fashion of doing things by halves that it [sic] has managed to keep things going in several of the counties up to now. However, next month, when the seeding time comes, will probably see the end of all things and our speedy release.

During that next month Parnell himself gave the first sign that he was prepared to consider release, if only for a short time and a specific purpose. Towards the end of March he, Dillon and O'Kelly, asked to be allowed out on parole to enable them to vote on an amendment to the new regulations concerning parliamentary procedure. Not unnaturally, this was politely but firmly refused by Forster and Parnell relapsed into silence.[66] Yet little more than a week later he mentioned to Katharine that he thought it likely the government would shortly 'do something' about the arrears question – that is, to help tenants who were in arrears with their rents so that they could come within the scope of the Land Act. 'If this be so, things will undoubtedly quiet down a great deal, and it will give us an opportunity of coming to some arrangement.'[67] But at this point misfortunes seemed to come upon him suddenly from all quarters. Katharine had to break to him that their daughter, Claude Sophie, born on 16 February, had not long to live and Parnell, naturally, longed to be with her and to set eyes on the child who had come into the world with such difficulty and was leaving it so quickly. In addition, so he told Katharine, his mother was reputed to be ill and he might have to apply for permission to go to her. Finally, his sister Delia's son Henry died suddenly in Paris.[68]

IV

Curiously enough, it was this last event which turned the key in the lock. As soon as he heard of Henry's death, Parnell telegraphed to Forster for permission to attend the funeral. This was immediately granted and he left Kilmainham at six in the morning on 10 April. Arriving in London that evening, he did not go through to Euston in the ordinary way, but got off at Willesden junction, where he was met by Justin McCarthy, F. H. O'Donnell, P. J. Quinn and Frank Byrne, the last-named being secretary of the Land League organization in Great Britain and at that time deeply involved with a secret society, soon to be notorious as 'the Invincibles', which was plotting political assassination in Dublin. However, as Parnell insisted in after years, there was no talk about assassination at Willesden. Indeed, there was little talk of any kind, for he was pledged, as a condition of his parole, not to engage, at least overtly, in political activity. Instead, the group went by train to Camden Town and thence to McCarthy's house in Jermyn Street. Asked later at the Special Commission if that meant that he spent the night in London, Parnell replied 'Yes', 'Where?' 'I spent it at some friends', he evasively replied. 'Was it at the house of Mr Justin McCarthy?' 'No, it was not', said Parnell. He went on to explain that he had a long talk with McCarthy about the failure of the 'No Rent' manifesto – it had been 'practically withdrawn', he said – and about the necessity of urging a legislative solution to the problem of the 100,000 tenants who were in arrears with their rents and so debarred from the benefit of the Land Act. But he was not pressed to say, and certainly did not volunteer, where he went when that conversation was finished.[69]

He went of course to Eltham, where his 'wife' placed their dying child in his arms. He spent that night and, apparently, most of the next day with Katharine, but came up in the evening to have dinner and political talk with Captain O'Shea before going on to Paris. Years after, at the Special Commission, the Attorney-General came perilously close to uncovering the real nature of the O'Shea-Parnell triangle when questioning O'Shea about this episode, and though he forbore to press his examination of the Captain to its logical conclusion, what O'Shea let fall was revealing enough. Having established that O'Shea was in his London apartment and that Parnell visited him there, the Attorney-General in his ham-fisted way, asked, 'Were you not well then, or why were you at 1 Albert Mansions?' To this O'Shea replied: 'I had had an attack of gout from which I was recovering. Mr Parnell went first to Eltham, I was unable to go there and he came up to me.' 'You mean', persisted the Attorney-General with all the delicacy of a bull in a china-shop, 'you knew from Mr Parnell himself that he had been to Eltham?' 'Yes', said Captain O'Shea.[70]

This convenient attack of gout did not, however, prevent the Captain from engaging in frenetic political manoeuvres during the next few days. Even before Parnell's release on parole, he had approached Gladstone with a reminder of the proposals he had made to him on the land question the previous June.* That particular overture, O'Shea later admitted, had been made without Parnell's knowledge, but since it elicited a reply from Gladstone on 11 April, the day on which Parnell came up from Eltham to see O'Shea, it opened possibilities which the Irish leader was quite ready to explore.[71] As a result of his conversation with Parnell, before the latter caught the night train to Paris, O'Shea wrote again to Gladstone in his most self-important style. 'At the eleventh hour and even under the aggravated circumstances I believe that the pacification of Ireland is by no means so difficult as it appears to be. But you must pay for it and you must cease to ignore an important Irishman.' Then followed a trumpet solo by Captain O'Shea entirely on his own behalf. 'The person to whom Mr Parnell addresses himself in many cases (much as I differ from him in serious matters of politics and policy) is myself. He considers, I believe, that I am not without insight into Irish affairs, necessities and possibilities and he knows that

*See above, p. 161.

no other member of parliament has nearly so much influence with the clergy . . . Eighteen months ago he used every effort to induce me to take over the leadership of the party.* I mention these things . . . as an explanation of what would otherwise appear to be fatuous officiousness.' Whether fatuous or not, O'Shea was certainly officious. The rest of his long letter was devoted to instructing Gladstone that *if* he amended the Land Act to include leaseholders and tenants in arrears, *if* he extended the purchase clauses, and *if* he set up a commission to look into the wretched condition of the agricultural labourers, *then* outrage would decline, the act would work its expected magic, and even the contemplated changes in parliamentary procedure to end obstruction 'might henceforth not be virulently or persistently opposed'.[72]

This was merely the beginning of O'Shea's activities. Nor was he the only Irish member to concern himself with the question of improving the Land Act by extending its operation to tenants in arrears. On the day that O'Shea wrote to Gladstone, F. H. O'Donnell published in *The Times* a letter on the same problem, and although communications from O'Donnell, like those from O'Shea, were generally works of self-glorification, this letter had a significance beyond its outward seeming. For several days previously he had been in correspondence with Gladstone's son Herbert, who, since the previous August, had been assigned to the Irish Office, mainly to help Forster with House of Commons business. It is clear from Herbert's journal, and from his other papers, not only that O'Donnell was in the field before O'Shea, but that Herbert believed he had something positive to offer.[73]

O'Shea, on the other hand, was playing for larger stakes and had access to bigger fish. On 15 April he wrote to Joseph Chamberlain, 'as you appear to be a minister without political pedantry', enclosing a copy of his letter of 13 April to Gladstone. Like that epistle, the letter to Chamberlain fell not far short of being an impertinent lecture on how the government should conduct their business, but it did at least hold out the prospect that all was not yet lost if the Liberal leaders could bring themselves to make an honourable compromise. Such an effort, O'Shea intimated, 'might be met by the most influential Irishman of the day in a candid and moderate spirit'.[74]

This was the beginning of a collaboration which was to take both men far along then undreamt-of paths. Chamberlain, though conscious of being in a minority in the cabinet and totally unable to speak for his

---

*There is not a scrap of evidence to support this extraordinary statement which O'Shea presumably invented to inflate his own reputation.

colleagues, responded with unusual warmth. It seemed to offer a point of departure, a means of retrieving a situation which had been bedevilled first by the Lords' rejection of the Compensation for Disturbance Bill in 1880, and subsequently by the introduction of coercion before the land grievance had been dealt with.[75] All the same, there was a hint of menace in his reply. Agreeing that the government had a duty to consult representative Irish opinion, he observed tartly that hitherto Irish members had acted 'as if their object were to disgust, embitter and prejudice all English opinion . . .' 'The result is that nothing would be easier than to get up in every large town an anti-Irish agitation almost as formidable as the anti-Jewish agitation in Russia.'[76] O'Shea countered next day with a letter admitting the justice of Chamberlain's complaint, but stressing that 'what the French call the psychological moment' ought not to be lost. He asked permission to forward Chamberlain's letter to Parnell in Paris and this was graciously conceded.[77] Chamberlain himself thought sufficiently well of O'Shea's initiative to write to Gladstone on 18 April, suggesting that negotiations might be opened and offering to see O'Shea, Healy and others to find out 'in what humour they are – that is to say, whether they are still anxious to make all government in Ireland impossible, or whether they are now ready to unite with us to secure the good government of their country'. Might not Forster, he added, offer Parnell an extension of his parole?[78]

Gladstone, confronted with this gathering momentum, reacted circumspectly, referring the O'Shea-Chamberlain correspondence to Forster. But the position was complicated by two factors. The first was the growing realization in Gladstone's mind that the Irish Lord-Lieutenant, Lord Cowper, ought soon to be replaced. Cowper's relations with the masterful Chief Secretary had not been happy and Gladstone was groping his way towards substituting Earl Spencer, a manoeuvre not only difficult in itself, but bound to raise awkward problems with Forster, especially if, as was intended, Spencer were to be given a seat in the cabinet. The other and graver factor was that Forster himself was tired and disillusioned and unhappy with an Irish situation where, although boycotting appeared to be diminishing, open resistance to the law had virtually ceased and rents, generally speaking, were being paid, serious crimes – murder, manslaughter and firing at the person – were actually on the increase. As he pointed out in an important letter to Gladstone on 7 April, these serious crimes were worse in the last quarter of 1881 and the first quarter of 1882 than in the combined three first quarters of 1881.[79] Yet Forster entirely missed the significance of the fact that the sharp rise occurred *after* Parnell and the other Land

Leaguers had been imprisoned. To Forster, the increase was partly a consequence of criminals so often escaping punishment (which was certainly true), but partly also due to the influence of the 'No Rent' manifesto, even though, on his own showing, rents were actually being paid. Such muddled thinking was a sad commentary on the state of mind into which he had got himself. His own remedy was bleakly predictable – the forces of law and order must be strengthened by special legislation. It was hardly surprising that his colleagues, most of whose views on Ireland amounted to little more than a confused impression that Forster was losing his grip, should have begun to think in terms of his retirement also, though any immediate move in that direction was checked by a savage attack on him by John Morley in the *Pall Mall Gazette* just at this time, and also, no doubt, by the extreme difficulty of finding someone to replace him.[80]

In the circumstances, Forster's response to O'Shea's initiative could only have been discouraging. He saw through the Captain without much difficulty – 'I do not believe he has the influence either with Parnell or the priests that he claims' – and devoted himself to the two more pressing problems of arrears and the 'suspects' (including Parnell) still held by the government. As to the former, he told Gladstone, he would limit arrears to rent owing for the year preceding the rents now falling due on tenancies below a valuation to be specified. On the other question of whether or not to detain the suspects, his view was clear. 'I adhere to our statement that we detain these suspects, and all suspects, solely for prevention, not punishment. We will release them as soon as we think it safe to do so.' But he then defined this in a way that was soon to become crucially important:[81]

There are three events which, in my opinion, would imply safety:–
(1) the country so quiet that Parnell and Co. can do little harm;
(2) the acquisition of fresh powers by a fresh Act which might warrant the attempt to govern Ireland with the suspects released;
(3) an assurance upon which we could depend, that Parnell and his friends, if released, would not attempt in any manner to intimidate men into obedience to their unwritten law.

These conditions have to be seen in relation to the running battle Forster had been conducting with his colleagues for over a year. In the early part of 1881 he had carried the Protection of Person and Property Act, empowering the arrest and detention of anyone reasonably suspected of treasonable offences, or of committing or inciting to acts of violence and intimidation, or of 'tending to interfere with or disturb the maintenance of law and order'; he had done this because he had been able to convince a reluctant cabinet that only thus could life and property be protected and strong government restored in Ireland. Reasonable suspicion of complicity, not punishment for crimes actually committed, seems to have been the principle originally underlying the act, but from that principle there followed the important corollary, as Forster had expressed it in anticipation to Gladstone as far back as 1880, that it must give power to the executive 'to shut up any person they consider dangerous'.[82] By the beginning of October 1881, alarmed by the prevalence of boycotting and intimidation, Forster had moved on from this position to the point where he felt that the act should be given a wider interpretation than hitherto, by which he meant that its chief use should now be to arrest the leaders of the agitation to 'prevent a collison'.[83] In other words, it was no longer enough to arrest a man under the act as a substitute for an indictment under the ordinary law which, given the state of Ireland, was extremely unlikely to issue in a conviction. It had become necessary to seize 'suspects' for prevention – that is, for fear of what they might do rather than on suspicion of what they might have done.

Even this still seemed insufficient to Forster when he left Dublin on 19 April for an important cabinet meeting on 22 April. He was lucky to get to London at all, for assassins were waiting for him to board the boat-train at Westland Row station and were foiled, not by the police, but by the sheer accident that he had elected to leave by an earlier train.[84] Forster came to the cabinet having made clear his view that not only should the Protection Act be retained for use as a reserve weapon, but it should be reinforced by additional legislation.[85] Almost certainly he failed to realize the gulf that was opening between him and his colleagues about how to deal with Ireland. Gladstone's secretary, in his private journal, expressed irreverently what others were more decorously thinking. 'Old Forster', wrote Edward Hamilton, '. . . never seems to know his own mind from day to day. One day he thinks it best to carry on as he is; three days later he says he must have this and that at a moment's notice.'[86]

It was in this unpromising climate that Forster had his first shock. The cabinet of 22 April agreed to empower Chamberlain to communicate on his own responsibility with Captain O'Shea and other Irish members to ascertain their views, though *not* to negotiate with them. It may have been influenced in this direction by a further piece of evidence that the ice was beginning to break. On that same day, 22 April, Herbert Gladstone at last met F. H. O'Donnell and hurriedly reported on his interview in a memorandum which he managed to get to the cabinet while it was still sitting. O'Donnell told him that the Irish 'extremists' were ready for a compromise. They wanted the suspects to be released, the arrears question to be settled, and the purchase clauses of the land legislation to be extended. In return, the suggestion was that the League leaders might declare in favour of law and order when the suspects were set free. The leaders of the agitation, O'Donnell apparently added, were anxious to withdraw the 'No Rent' manifesto and to co-operate with the Liberals. As for Home Rule, 'the Irish detest and repudiate the notion of separation, as their interests are identified with those of England'. 'All they want is to manage their own affairs and to get as much as possible out of England.' Although Herbert Gladstone had enough sense to record in his journal that 'the Irish party are supposed to distrust O'Donnell', what the Irish MP had to say tallied sufficiently with rumours already current not to be dismissed out of hand. Chamberlain, for one, took it sufficiently seriously to ask Herbert for more particulars and to mention the matter to O'Shea afterwards. O'Shea, his jealousy clearly aroused by this unwelcome competition, reported the incident to Parnell on 24 April, remarking censoriously that it had taken place 'without your knowledge or authority'.[87]

On the evening of 22 April, after the cabinet had met, Chamberlain summoned O'Shea to his London house. O'Shea announced that Parnell was staying with him and proceeded to give a résumé of his leader's views. Chamberlain thereupon recorded these, in O'Shea's presence and as O'Shea had retailed them, in writing:[88]

Memorandum

72, Prince's Gate, S.W.

If the Government announce a satisfactory plan of dealing with arrears, Mr Parnell will advise all tenants to pay rents and will denounce outrages, resistance to law and all processes of intimidation whether by Boycotting or in any other way.

No plan of dealing with arrears will be satisfactory which does not wipe them off compulsorily by a composition – one-third payable by tenant, one-third by the State – from the Church Fund or some other source – and one-third remitted by the landlord, but so that the contribution by the tenant and the State shall not exceed one year's rent each – the balance, if any, to be remitted by the landlord.

Arrears to be defined as arrears accruing up to 1 May 1881.

V

Matters had now reached the stage where some more decisive intervention was required from the key figure who still lurked in the shadows. Parnell's stay in Paris had not been a happy one. Writing to Katharine about the typhoid which had carried off his nephew, Henry, he displayed his usual fear of infection, but comforted her, and himself, with the reflection that since he had had the disease in his youth, he would probably not get it a second time.[89] He had hoped to leave Paris on 15 April, but on that date wrote to say that he had caught cold and that the doctor had warned him against travelling. Next day he reported that he had applied his sovereign remedy – not one, but *two* Turkish baths – though whether this alleviated or intensified the cold is not clear.[90] At any rate, he was still in Paris on 17 April, when he wrote to his sister, Emily Dickinson, describing the stricken household. 'Delia is much cut up by her dreadful loss', he wrote, 'but is somewhat better now; my being here has done her a great deal of good. It appears Henry used to live in an apartment of his own, and it was quite by accident that they discovered he was ill . . . He used to devote himself entirely to music, composing etc., and it is thought that his brain was injured or weakened by dwelling too much upon this one subject, and so was unable to stand disease.'[91]

According to O'Shea, Parnell returned from Paris on 19 April. It seems, if the same source is to be trusted, that he went at once to Eltham and telegraphed O'Shea that he had arrived.[92] O'Shea went down to join him and it was there, in the same house where the woman who was wife to one and mistress to the other nursed the dying child which each apparently believed to be his, that the conversation took place which O'Shea reported to Chamberlain on 22 April.[93] Parnell, with that cat-like instinct of his for danger, had no intention of trusting his political reputation solely to the hands of Katharine's husband. That same day – 22 April – he wrote to Justin McCarthy to arrange a meeting for the afternoon of the next day, Sunday. On that occasion they discussed the situation at length and on 24 April Parnell made his way unobtrusively back to Dublin, re-entering Kilmainham at about seven o'clock that evening. The faithful O'Kelly had aired his bed carefully and they were all, he wrote ironically next day to Katharine, very glad to see him again, with the exception of his jailers.[94] On Tuesday, 25 April (the day Katharine's child was buried), Parnell wrote to McCarthy, enclosing a letter embodying the gist of their conversation on Sunday and authorizing him to take the earliest opportunity of showing it to Chamberlain without letting the original leave his own hands. It is clear from the letter to Katharine already mentioned that Parnell took this step deliberately so that negotiations, if they resulted at all, should go on independently of whether or not O'Shea participated in them. What Parnell wanted McCarthy to convey to Chamberlain was that no time should be lost in settling the arrears question along the lines of an Irish bill just then due for its second reading, that the Land Act should be improved in its operation, and that leaseholders should be admitted to a share in its benefits. If the arrears question in particular were satisfactorily solved, then Parnell undertook to have the 'No Rent' manifesto withdrawn and to advise the tenants to settle with their landlords. Were the solution of the arrears question to be combined with the other suggested reforms, this should bring the country back to normal; in which case, he concluded, 'we should hope that the government would allow the Coercion Act to lapse, and govern the country by the same laws as in England'.[95]

If Parnell's intention was thus to cut O'Shea out of the negotiations he reckoned without his host. The Captain, once embarked on his intrigue, prosecuted it vigorously. On Sunday, 23 April, he called on Chamberlain again, having in the meantime acquainted Parnell with the details of the Chamberlain-O'Shea interview of 22 April. To the Sunday meeting he brought two letters, both dated 23 April and signed by himself. One was in general terms and declared Parnell's readiness to exert himself to stop outrages and intimidation on condition that the arrears question was dealt with by a grant, not a loan. The other referred specifically to the position of the suspects. 'While Mr Parnell does not wish to urge the question of his own release, he mentions that any doubt whatever of *immediate* pacification would be removed were Davitt and he at liberty . . .' O'Shea added that if the country did *not* settle down as quickly as Parnell expected, 'I have reason to believe that he would *ipso facto* be brought to see the necessity of not offering an embittered opposition to the passage of temporary provisions aimed at individuals and localities tainted with crime'. Chamberlain thought sufficiently well of these initiatives to communicate them to Forster. Forster found them not unhopeful, but reserved his opinion on the arrears question, writing later in the day to Chamberlain in a way which suggested that he would be even more difficult to move in the matter of the 'suspects'. 'What we want', he said, 'is not their promise to try to prevent outrages, but an assurance by which they will be bound in honour before the public – that is an undertaking that they will not themselves renew an agitation to replace the law of the land by their law . . . If we release them without getting the country quiet – or a fresh [Coercion] Act – or such assurance, I believe we should make matters worse in Ireland, and be probably turned out ourselves by an indignant House and country, as would be our desert.'⁹⁶

At this point Chamberlain belatedly became aware that O'Shea was not Parnell's sole channel of communication. On the evening of 24 April Justin McCarthy accosted him in the House of Commons and gave him the essence of his, McCarthy's, interview with Parnell the previous day. Chamberlain made a non-committal reply, but as a result of this conversation he was better placed to deal with O'Shea when on the morning of 25 April he received from the Captain (who, that day, was at Chislehurst for the funeral of Claude Sophie) a letter setting out an ambitious six-point programme relating not only to arrears, but to land purchase, the condition of the labourers and the future of coercion. Meeting O'Shea next day, Chamberlain remarked sharply that he seemed to be raising his terms. O'Shea at once retreated in some confusion. 'I am not sure', he confessed, 'that I have any authority at present to go beyond the subjects in the Land Act.'⁹⁷

Meanwhile, on 25 April the cabinet had met to consider the Irish situation, both in the light of what Chamberlain had to report on his interviews – he had spoken (on 24 April) to Tim Healy, as well as to O'Shea and McCarthy – and in the knowledge that on the day following (26 April) John Redmond would be moving the second reading of the bill amending the Land Act which had been drafted by Maurice Healy in conjunction with Parnell. Conscious that the Irish members would put every word under the microscope, the cabinet settled the line Gladstone should take in the debate – it was that the bill should be rejected as a whole, but that a pledge should be made to deal promptly with the question of arrears. This task Gladstone duly performed and the Irish reaction was so favourable that, in Herbert Gladstone's words, 'people began to say what does it all mean?'⁹⁸

The sense of movement towards some as yet undetermined goal was heightened by the announcement on 28 April of Earl Cowper's resignation as Lord-Lieutenant. This, as we know, had been imminent for several weeks, but as Cowper himself pointed out, a connection would undoubtedly be made between his resignation and the decision as to whether or not the 'suspects' should be released. It was a decision which was rapidly being still further complicated by indications from both sides of the House that the operation of the Coercion Act was about to come under attack and that there might even be a Radical motion calling for the release of the 'three members' – Parnell,

Dillon and O'Kelly.[99]

At this critical moment both O'Shea and McCarthy reappeared upon the scene. On the day that Cowper's resignation was announced, O'Shea came to Chamberlain and urged that the favourable Irish debate of Wednesday, 26 April, offered an opportunity for Parnell to give some public expression to the views he had already revealed in conversation, but that 'he could not say or do anything which might seem to be with a view to his own release'. That same day Chamberlain had a further talk with McCarthy, who immediately afterwards sent him the relevant part of the letter Parnell had written McCarthy from Kilmainham – the letter which contained the essence of the bargain he was prepared to strike.* McCarthy's covering note insisted that the letter must not be published and on 30 April Chamberlain replied regretting this, but promising that he would try to make good use of the contents.[100] Had matters continued along this orthodox channel it might have been better for everybody, but in the meantime Captain O'Shea had been galvanized into action. On the evening of Friday, 28 April, Forster told Chamberlain that O'Shea had asked permission to visit Parnell in prison. Forster had given it, since he attached great importance to getting a declaration from the Irish leader – if there was to be one – before the debate on a motion against the renewal of coercion which was to come before the House the following Tuesday. This initiative of O'Shea's can scarcely have come as an overpowering shock to Chamberlain, since it seems likely that he himself had suggested it.[101]

O'Shea, armed with his permission, hurried off to Kilmainham where he spent most of Saturday, 29 April, closeted with Parnell. Subsequently, he gave different accounts as to whether or not Parnell had consulted his colleagues in Kilmainham before taking the decisive action he was now about to take. To Forster on 30 April he said that Parnell had told him he had had much talk with Dillon, 'and had brought him round to be in full agreement with himself upon the general questions'.[102] To Gladstone on 5 May he asserted that Parnell's colleagues were aware of what was afoot.[103] Later, before the Special Commission, he swore that the negotiations were *not* known to them.[104] Davitt, who of course was still in prison at the time but who was soon to be in the closest contact with the Kilmainham 'suspects', wrote afterwards that Parnell 'had not imparted a word' to his fellow-prisoners, and Dillon, in the House of Commons, declared on 6 May that he personally had had no communication, direct or indirect, with ministers or with the Irish

---

*See above, p. 197.

government.[105] This, obviously, did not preclude his having had the kind of private conversation with Parnell which O'Shea described to Forster. Parnell himself testified at the Special Commission that when he had talked with O'Shea at Eltham on his return from Paris he had stipulated that he wanted to confer with all the League leaders who were available as he did not wish to seem to be acting behind their backs.[106] The most probable explanation, where no certainty is possible, is that Parnell made his initial moves – the letter to McCarthy and the letter to O'Shea described below – on his own initiative, but that when the situation began to develop he told his colleagues what it had become necessary for them to know before they emerged again into the outside world.

At all events, after his discussions with O'Shea, Parnell wrote him a letter which he dated 28 April, presumably to convey the impression that it predated O'Shea's visit. It ran as follows:[107]

Private and Confidential

> Kilmainham
> 28 April 1882.

My dear O'Shea,

I was very sorry that you left Albert Mansions before I reached London from Eltham as I had wished to tell you that after our conversation I had made up my mind that it would be proper for me to put Mr McCarthy in possession of the views which I had previously communicated to you.

I desire to impress upon you the absolute necessity of a settlement of the arrears which shall leave no recurring sore connected with them behind, and which shall enable us to show the smaller tenantry that they have been treated with justice and some generosity.

The proposal you have described to me as suggested to me in some quarters, of making a loan (over however many years the repayment might be spread) should be absolutely rejected for reasons which I have fully explained to you. If the arrears question be settled upon the lines indicated by us, I have every confidence – a confidence shared by my colleagues – that the exertions which we should be able to make strenuously and unremittingly would be effective in stopping outrages and intimidation of all kinds.

As regards permanent legislation of an ameliorative character I may say that the views which you have always shared with me as to the admission of leaseholders to the fair rent clauses of the Act are more confirmed than ever. So long as the flower of the Irish peasantry are kept outside the Act there cannot be the permanent settlement of the Land Question which we all so much desire.

I should also strongly hope that some compromise might be arrived at this Session with regard to the amendment of the tenure clauses.

It is unnecessary for me to dwell upon the enormous advantages to be derived from the full extension of the purchase clauses, which now seems practically to have been adopted by all parties.

The accomplishment of the programme I have sketched out to you would in my judgement be regarded by the country as a practical settlement of the Land Question and would enable us to co-operate cordially for the future with the Liberal Party in forwarding Liberal principles and measures of general reform. And I believe that the Government at the end of this Session would from the state of the country find themselves thoroughly justified in dispensing with further coercive measures.

Yours very truly,

C. S. PARNELL

This letter, less explicit and more cautious in some ways than the one Parnell had written to McCarthy four days earlier, was apparently intended mainly to save the Captain's face. Indeed, Parnell had tried hard to prevent O'Shea from coming to see him at all, writing on 27 April to suggest that he should not do so.[108] However, when he turned up in spite of this plea there was nothing for it but to humour him. 'He came over to see me', Parnell explained to Katharine, 'so I thought it best to give him a letter, as he would have been dreadfully mortified if he had nothing to show.'[109] To save O'Shea's face was no doubt conducive to preserving Parnell's privacy at Eltham, but if he thought that his letter to McCarthy had made the letter to O'Shea superfluous, he was seriously mistaken.

Back in London with his prize O'Shea presented himself at Forster's house on 30 April. He found the Chief Secretary in an unaccommodating mood. Only the previous day Forster had written to Gladstone doubting that O'Shea would bring back anything that could be published. 'I think, unless we get such a declaration, or get the country much more quiet . . . or get an Act with fresh powers we cannot release these men without weakening government to an extent which I do not believe to be safe or right.'[110] Perhaps then, it was not so surprising that after he had read the letter carefully he should have said to O'Shea: 'Is that all, do you think, that Parnell would be inclined to say?' To which O'Shea, clearly somewhat taken aback, replied naturally enough, 'What more do you want? adding, 'Doubtless I could supplement it.' Forster refused to comment further beyond saying he would show the letter to Gladstone and one or two others, but O'Shea, with that fatal tendency of his to elaborate verbally on other people's documents, then used a remarkable phrase that at once caught Forster's attention. 'If these words will not do I must get others; but what is obtained is . . . that the conspiracy [later in the House of Commons O'Shea claimed that the word he actually used was 'combination'] which has been used to set up boycotting and outrages will now be used to put them down, and that there will be a union with the Liberal party.' Even more remarkably, O'Shea gave a specific illustration, when he said that Parnell hoped to make use of P. J. Sheridan (an agitator for whom a warrant was out, but who had long eluded the police) to help quieten the west, which he knew intimately.[111]

In forwarding this letter to Gladstone, Forster made it clear that it did not meet his conditions. It said nothing, for example, about a public declaration by Parnell, while the mention of the sinister Sheridan had only strengthened the Chief Secretary in his conviction that there was, and remained, a connection between the Irish leader and the 'conspiracy'. Gladstone took a different view. He pointed out that Parnell had equated the settlement of the arrears question with the cessation of outrage and intimidation. 'With great sagacity, Parnell goes on to state his other aims under the Land Act. But he carefully abstains from importing any of them as conditions of the former remarkable statement.' 'He then proceeds to throw in his indication or promise of future co-operation with the Liberal party', continued Gladstone. 'This is a *hors d'oeuvre* which we had no right to expect and, I rather think, have at present no right to accept . . . Upon the whole, Parnell's letter is, I think, the most extraordinary I have ever read.' And the Prime Minister ended with a tribute upon which one would give a great deal to have had Parnell's comment. 'I cannot help feeling indebted to O'Shea.'[112]

Gladstone could not guess at Parnell's eagerness to end the agitation, but what he had read convinced him, as he wrote to Granville, that about the release of the three MPs 'I see no remaining room for doubt'.[113] Next day, 1 May, the cabinet met to consider this point. It could not reach a decision that day, though it was clear enough that Forster was becoming isolated and that the drift was towards release.[114] Even Forster was not totally opposed to this, but he coupled it with a condition that new coercive legislation (he had himself previously drafted a bill) should at once be introduced. This was politically unacceptable to his colleagues and when they met again on 2 May there was nothing for him to do but to leave them. 'However much we may try to hide the fact, release is a new departure, and if so, let it be made with the probability of success. It is in fact a concession to Parnell.'[115] So he believed. So he wrote to a friend on the day of his decision. So he resigned. Subsequently, a determined effort was made, chiefly by Gladstone himself, to propagate the legend that Parnell was released because by April 1882 the suspicion of implication in crime – the original ground for his arrest – no longer attached to him. This being so, Gladstone argued, the law required that his freedom be restored. That interpretation reached its apotheosis in an article he wrote in 1888, when it was almost as important to the Liberals as to Parnell to demonstrate that in 1882 not only was the Irish leader innocent of crime, but the government of the day had made no bargain with him.[116] The opposite view of the transaction, widely canvassed at the moment of Parnell's release, was that, so far from this event being a mere administrative incident, a fully-fledged 'treaty' had been signed between Parnell and his captors.

Both these extremes are equally wide of the mark. The release of the 'suspects' was not due simply to their innocence having been established, but rather to the fact, as Gladstone himself intimated to the Queen, that 'an important part of the evidence, both public and private, is that which shows that the no-rent party are sensible of their being substantially defeated by the Land Act, and have altered essentially their views with regard either to the encouragement or at the very least the toleration of outrage . . .'[117] In the recollections of no fewer than six members of the cabinet which ordered the release – recollections gathered and published in *The Times* by a seventh, the then Lord Chancellor, Lord Selborne – it was later emphasized that it was not the question of guilt or innocence which had preoccupied ministers. If it had been, O'Shea's report to Forster about Parnell wanting to use Sheridan to put down the agitation would certainly have told against the Irish leader. The real issue was whether or not it was *safe* to release him and his colleagues. Once this was established, the road to a decision was open.[118]

Nor can the argument be sustained that Parnell's letter to O'Shea – still less his side-tracked letter to McCarthy – constituted a treaty. On the contrary, as Gladstone had at once pointed out to Forster when the latter forwarded the document O'Shea had brought him, Parnell had *voluntarily* gone far beyond what the Liberals had any right to expect, or even perhaps to accept, when he offered future co-operation.

As to the coupling of a satisfactory settlement of the arrears question and Parnell's undertaking to discourage outrage, the government had already decided to deal with arrears *before* Parnell had written his Kilmainham letter (though it could not have been unaware of pressures emanating from him and others when coming to that decision), so that nothing resembling a formal bargain had been reached. As Gladstone put it to Lord Cowper, still waiting disconsolately to leave his post as Viceroy: 'The information we have had is in the briefest words shortly this. We know authentically that Parnell and his friends are ready to abandon No Rent formally, and to declare against outrages energetically, intimidation included, if and when the government announce a satisfactory plan for dealing with arrears. We had already as good as resolved upon a plan and we do not know any absolute reason why the form of it should not be "satisfactory".'[119]

With the cabinet thus inclined, and Forster so determined to go that keen judges thought he was looking for a way out, there was no longer any obstacle to the release of the three MPs. This was announced in the House of Commons on 2 May at the same time as Forster's resignation and – final stroke of irony at the latter's expense – Gladstone followed it immediately by a statement that the existing Coercion Act would be allowed to expire in the autumn, but that the government were drafting a bill to strengthen the ordinary law in the light of recent experience.[120] Later that day Parnell, Dillon and O'Kelly left Kilmainham, intending to go straight to Wicklow. In fact they got no further than Kingstown where they spent the night. Next morning Dillon went to his home in Dublin, but Parnell and O'Kelly paid a flying visit to Avondale.[121] The latter was deeply moved at the welcome Parnell received from his old retainers, but even more deeply shocked by his leader's frigid response. 'I thought he was the most callous fellow I had ever met', said the warm-hearted O'Kelly afterwards. Parnell made some casual reply – truth to tell, such scenes only embarrassed him – and they passed on into the drawing-room where Emily Dickinson was waiting for her brother. Now it was O'Kelly's turn to witness the family insouciance which had so flabbergasted Healy in America two years before. 'Ah, Charley, is that you?' said Emily. 'I thought they would never let you back again.' 'Well, what did you think they would do to me?' her brother replied. 'I thought they would hang you', she said. 'Well', he smiled, 'it may come to that yet.' And with that, before the astonished O'Kelly's eyes, they fell to discussing family affairs.[122]

That evening O'Kelly and Parnell went back to Dublin, were rejoined by Dillon and crossed by the night-mail in time to appear in parliament at the moment when Forster was making the customary statement to explain his resignation. Parnell's own speech was brief, and though Gladstone was not pleased with it, he thought it would 'pass muster'.[123] In it Parnell was at pains to point out, in the face of raucous Tory disbelief, that 'I have not in conversation with my friends or in any communication to my friends entered into the question of the release of my friends and myself as any condition of our action'. This was no more than the truth and deserved the 'hear, hear' it elicited from Gladstone. And since Parnell followed it with a declaration that a settlement of the arrears question 'would have an enormous effect in the restoration of law and order in Ireland' and would enable him and others 'to take such steps as would have material effect in diminishing those unhappy and lamentable outrages', he could reasonably be said to have honoured his undertaking.[124]

That day was marked also by two further announcements in the House, one of which evoked rage, and the other derision, from the Tory benches. One was Harcourt's decision to order Davitt's release from Portland prison and the other was Gladstone's declaration that the post of Chief Secretary for Ireland vacated by Forster would be filled by Lord Frederick Cavendish. Davitt's release was at once hailed by the government's critics as a further surrender to Parnell, though there is some evidence – dependent, admittedly upon O'Shea – that Parnell asked for Davitt's release to be deferred until he could have an opportunity to explain the changed state of affairs to him.[125] The appointment of Cavendish was a surprise because he was an essentially second-rank figure being put at a critical moment into a vital office; it also had, however unfairly, the air of being a family job, since he was Hartington's brother and was married to Gladstone's niece. Many tipsters, including Chamberlain himself, had imagined the choice might fall on Chamberlain. O'Shea, on 2 May, had even written to his Birmingham hero assuring him that if he accepted, 'it will be a point of honour with Mr Parnell to work as if for himself to secure the success of your administration'.[126] Chamberlain's name was on Gladstone's list, but it seems unlikely that he ever had much chance, or risk, of being chosen and it was Cavendish who set out on his fateful journey to Dublin on the evening of 5 May.

Meanwhile O'Shea was exerting himself, whether maliciously or not is hard to say, to impress upon Gladstone the kind of connection allegedly existing between Parnell and crime, which was probably what the Prime Minister least wanted to hear. On 5 May he called on Gladstone at six in the evening. He said he had been up all night talking to Parnell, whose views he purported now to pass on to Gladstone. According to the memorandum of the conversation which Gladstone sent the new Viceroy, Spencer, Parnell had not objected to the announcement of strong measures for Ireland 'but is most anxious that they should not be precipitate'. The Irish leader had been confident that the state of Ireland would improve shortly, but to hasten this he relied much on Egan and Sheridan, who, it was implied, must be allowed to get to work unimpeded by policemen with warrants. 'It is already made known in Ireland that the No Rent Manifesto is void and Parnell is anxiously considering what further practical steps he can take with regard to getting generally rid of it.' Gladstone's memorandum ended with a significant admission, cutting diametrically across the explanation for Parnell's release which he was to begin to fashion only a few days later. 'As nothing can be clearer', he noted, 'than that he has used lawlessness for his ends, so O'Shea's statements tend to impress the belief that he is now entirely in earnest about putting it down; but that he feels himself in some danger of being supplanted by more violent men.' Among these, apparently, O'Shea was inclined to number Dillon, whose speech in the House of Commons the previous day had been noticeably more intransigent than Parnell's. But, Gladstone recorded: 'He [Parnell] considers that he has now got his hand upon Dillon who is difficult to manage and intensely ambitious.'[127] For this reason, Gladstone mentioned in his covering letter to Spencer that he had promised to send the Lord-Lieutenant a list of suspects 'whose release is desired *in order* that Parnell, who relies upon them, may *actively employ* them in the restoration of obedience to the law'. 'As far as I can judge', he added, 'Parnell is remaining true.'[128]

Nothing now remained, apparently, but to put the new course into operation – to push on with a settlement of the arrears question and to watch Parnell's success in damping down the land agitation. Afterwards there was the '*hors d'oeuvre*' of Liberal-nationalist co-operation to look forward to and beyond that – who could tell? During Saturday the players were moving smoothly into the positions allotted to them and the drama seemed about to begin. But the drama which actually ensued was a stark tragedy that came upon all these anxious, over-burdened men like a thunder-bolt out of a clear sky. That morning Cavendish and Spencer made their entry into Dublin city. At about the same time, Davitt, enjoying the sunshine in the infirmary garden of Portland prison, was handed a letter from Parnell. Addressed simply to 'My dear Sir', which struck Davitt as ominously cool, it informed the prisoner that Dillon and he were coming down to meet him that afternoon on his release and accompany him on his journey back to civilization.

They duly arrived and by mid-afternoon all three were bound for London. While the train rattled through the peaceful heart of England, Parnell did most of the talking, explaining, from his point of view – which was far from being Davitt's – how the changed situation had veered away from agitation and towards constitutional pressure for fresh land legislation and even for Home Rule. Awkward subjects like the 'No Rent' manifesto or the Ladies Land League no sooner came up than they were cavalierly dismissed and for part of the journey they amused themselves allotting cabinet posts to each other in a future Home Rule administration in Dublin. It was not necessary to name a role for Parnell, but Dillon was to be Home Secretary, Sexton Chancellor of the Exchequer, and Davitt – macabre touch – was to be Director of Prisons.[129]

That same evening in Dublin, Lord Frederick Cavendish was walking through the Phoenix Park towards the Viceregal Lodge, with T. H. Burke, the Under-Secretary. They were actually within sight of the Lodge when a group of men – assassins belonging to the Invincibles secret society – sprang upon them and stabbed them to death with long surgical knives. Lord Spencer, who had ridden home by a different route, had barely reached the Lodge when the thing happened. In after years he seldom referred to the supreme horror of the next few minutes, but on at least two occasions he broke silence. The first was at a breakfast party given in his honour in 1889 by Robert Spence Watson, one of the most prominent Liberals in the north-east of England. Quite suddenly, Spencer chose to unburden his mind and later that day Spence Watson dictated an account of what he said. The key passage was as follows: 'I had gone upstairs in the Viceregal Lodge and was looking out of the window over the park talking with a member of my family when I heard a wild cry and saw a man running towards the house waving his hands and shouting out murder.'[130] Some years later, Lord Spencer gave Barry O'Brien a second account which, allowing for some possible dramatization by O'Brien, substantially confirmed his earlier recollections. 'Shortly after reaching the Lodge I heard a shriek which I shall never forget. I seem to hear it now. It is always in my ears. This shriek was repeated again and again. I got up to look out. I saw a man rushing along. He got over the sunk fence and dashed up to the Lodge, shouting: "Mr Burke and Lord Frederick Cavendish are killed".'[131]

With that wild cry, that shriek of agony, seemed to have perished all the brave hopes that were still only four days old.

CHAPTER 7

The New Course

Is it worthwhile – the crime itself apart –
To pull this settled civil state of life
To pieces, for another just the same,
Only with rawer actors for the posts
Of Judges, Landlords, Masters, Capitalists?
  (Samuel Ferguson, 'At the Polo-Ground'.)

I

After their arrival in London on Saturday evening the three colleagues separated, Dillon and Davitt putting up at the Westminster Palace Hotel, Parnell heading for Eltham. Dillon and Davitt had hardly sat down before a newspaper man rushed into the room, brandishing a telegram which announced the double murder. According to Davitt's account, he and Dillon, though shaken, went to bed believing that the telegram was a false alarm – the news seemed too dreadful to be true. But at five o'clock next morning Davitt was woken by his friend, the American writer and social reformer, Henry George, to learn that what had seemed fantasy was horrific reality.[1]

Meanwhile Parnell, having passed the night at Katharine's house, was astir early to rejoin his friends in London. She drove him to Blackheath station and stayed in the carriage while he went to fetch a newspaper. He got the *Observer* and casually opened it as he came towards her, looking for what it said about Davitt's release. 'He had now come to the top of the steps', she remembered afterwards, 'and, as he suddenly stopped, I noticed a curious rigidity about his arms – raised in holding the newspaper open. He stood so absolutely still that I was suddenly frightened, horribly, sickeningly afraid – of I knew not what, and, leaning forward, called out, "King, what is it?". Then he came down the steps to me and, pointing to the headline, said, "Look!" And I read, "Murder of Lord Frederick Cavendish and Mr Burke!"'

Parnell's face, she noticed at once, was ashen, as he stared in front of him, unconsciously crushing her hand in his. The train came in just then and there was no time to talk. 'I shall resign', he said, turning heavily away. 'No', she cried, as she ran beside him to the platform, 'you are not a coward.'[2] But Parnell was in a state of deep shock by the time he arrived in London. He went first to O'Shea's apartment at Albert Mansions and wrote a message to Gladstone which was delivered to the Prime Minister at lunch-time by O'Shea himself. It said in effect that if Gladstone thought it necessary for the maintenance of his, Gladstone's, position and for the carrying out of the policy they had agreed upon that Parnell should resign, he was prepared to do so immediately. To this Gladstone at once replied: 'My duty does not permit me for a moment to entertain Mr Parnell's proposal . . . that he should, if I think it needful, resign his seat; but I am deeply sensible of the honourable motives by which it was prompted.'[3]

From O'Shea, Parnell turned to the Westminster Palace Hotel, where he found Davitt, Dillon and Justin McCarthy. At once they began work on a manifesto 'to the Irish people', denouncing the murders in the strongest possible language. It was mainly the work of Michael Davitt and though O'Shea told the Special Commission in 1889 that later that day Parnell had expressed his distaste for the 'bombast' of the manifesto – an allegation which Parnell denied before the same tribunal – this was no time for refinements of literary criticism and he, Davitt and Dillon all apparently signed it unhesitatingly.[4]

Parnell remained profoundly disturbed and still talked of resignation. From the Westminster Palace Hotel he went with McCarthy to visit Dilke and Chamberlain, either of whom might well be asked to take Cavendish's place. They called first on Dilke who said, as McCarthy recalled, that if Gladstone offered him the post he would take it. Dilke also, it seems, drew McCarthy aside and warned him not to allow Parnell to walk about the streets lest he should be recognized and attacked. Next, they went on to Chamberlain and had a long talk with him. He too was willing to go to Ireland, with the significant qualification that he must have his own way there.[5] Chamberlain's account of this visit – which was not written until 1891 and may well have been influenced by the recollections Captain O'Shea published in *The Times* in August 1888, when the latter's hostility to Parnell was building towards its climax – was that Parnell was 'white as a sheet, agitated and apparently altogether demoralized'. 'At the time', added Chamberlain, 'I thought he was abjectly afraid for his own life which he said was in danger.'[6] Chamberlain urged him not to resign, for the good Chamberlainite reason that this might give rise to a suspicion of complicity. While they were still talking, in came Captain O'Shea.*

It was then, and apparently by O'Shea, that the question of police protection was raised. This was later to give rise to serious disagreement between O'Shea and Parnell at the Special Commission. O'Shea swore that he and Parnell had left Chamberlain's house in a cab and that Parnell had asked him to obtain a guard for him. This was emphatically denied by Parnell when his turn came to give evidence, and although it is clear that O'Shea did at once seek protection from the Home Secretary, Sir William Harcourt, and apparently sought it both for Eltham and for Albert Mansions, the clash of testimony as to whether he did this on his own initiative or at Parnell's request seems impossible to resolve.[7] Justin McCarthy's recollections, however, written down about a year before the Special Commission began to hear evidence, incline the balance in Parnell's favour:[8]

> Captain O'Shea came in while we were talking. When we were leaving, Chamberlain gave us much the same kind of caution that Dilke had given. I suggested to Parnell that we should take a hansom, and I hinted the reason to him. He replied rather sharply that he would do nothing of the kind. He said he had done no wrong to anyone, and that he intended to walk in the streets like anyone else. Some man from the top of an omnibus passing us called out – 'There's Parnell!' but whether in friendship or animosity I don't know; but otherwise we were unnoticed.

This description, with the professional writer's eye for detail clearly evident, has the ring of accuracy about it. It suggests a conclusion which is nearer to the psychological truth about Parnell than the evidence of Chamberlain or O'Shea, or even that of Davitt. This is that though Parnell, from the moment he first opened the *Observer*, had realized that the murders were as great a blow to him as to the government, his realization was based not on fear for his own safety, but on intelligent anticipation of what this terrible event was likely to do to the Kilmainham settlement when, as was virtually inevitable, coercion would once more take precedence over redress. No doubt he *was* profoundly shocked for most of that day – a natural reaction in one of his highly-strung,

---

*Chamberlain's account has the Irish members going on to Dilke from his house, but McCarthy's recollection was exactly the reverse. Davitt, trying to piece the record together some twenty years later, thought Dilke had joined them at Chamberlain's house. Such differences of testimony regarding the events of a tense and crowded day are probably inevitable and the sequence is not important.

nervous temperament – but if McCarthy's recollection means anything it means that by the afternoon of Sunday he had regained his self-control, if not yet his political bearings.

Next day in the House of Commons he repeated his condemnation of the murders in unequivocal terms, while recognizing, almost fatalistically, that the immediate consequence would be a fresh dose of coercion. This indeed proved to be the case. But it is not true, as has often been stated, that the Phoenix Park murders *provoked* the government to coercion, for, as we know, some kind of exceptional legislation had been in prospect long before the Kilmainham agreement, which itself had not changed this aspect of the situation. What the tragedy did was to accelerate the timetable and to impose upon the government the necessity of a new Coercion Act significantly harsher than the one which in ordinary circumstances might have come into operation when the Protection of Person and Property Act expired in the autumn. The bill which was now speedily introduced certainly measured up to this description. Its chief provisions were that trial by jury was to be replaced in certain cases by trial by three judges; the Lord-Lieutenant was to be given authority to forbid public meetings and to suppress newspapers; increased powers were to be conferred on magistrates; incitement to crime was to be summarily punished where necessary; and, in some ways most odious of all, the police were to be given extensive powers of search. It was highly unfortunate that it should have fallen to Harcourt to introduce this punitive measure on 11 May. Harcourt's explosive temper was matched only by his verbal brutality and both were given free rein in a speech which actually fell so low as to include a reference to the necessity of taking 'the surgeon's knife' to 'the poison that courses through the veins of the Irish social system', and this in a House where every member was vividly aware of the precise nature of the weapons which had dispatched Cavendish and Burke.[9]

Even without such an introduction the Prevention of Crime (Ireland) Bill would have encountered fierce resistance from the Irish members. They were bound to oppose it fiercely for the old, familiar reason that if they were to condemn violence in Ireland they must display their own kind of intransigence in England. But, unhappily, coercion could not be argued on its merits, for it had to be debated both in the shadow of the Phoenix Park murders, and also in the context of the Kilmainham releases. That transaction, though unknown in detail to the public, seemed to savour of a bargain and Forster's resignation speech of 4 May, though reticent by his standards, had contained a warning to his ex-colleagues not to submit to blackmail which had aroused immediate suspicion.[10] When the releases were followed so swiftly by the murders the temptation to connect the two was irresistible and was not turned aside even by Parnell's pale and rigid denunciation of the latter on 8 May. That was the moment *The Times* chose to remark: 'Not more than four days have elapsed since the policy of conciliation was thus set in motion and already we have its hollowness exposed by the tragedy in the Phoenix Park.'[11]

In such an atmosphere the opposition demand for the production of documents could not be ignored and two days – 15 and 16 May – were set aside for a discussion of what was already beginning to be miscalled 'the Kilmainham treaty'. Though there was no treaty, there was Parnell's letter to Captain O'Shea which Parnell had probably intended for Chamberlain's eye, but which the Captain, in his busy ineptitude, had handed straight to Forster. Behind the letter were all the other comings and goings in which Chamberlain, McCarthy, O'Shea and Parnell had been involved and of which the cabinet had been in part apprised. It was therefore fatally easy to represent the government as having negotiated with their principal prisoner and to point to the releases as the product of some corrupt and shameful bargain. The fact that this was a total misrepresentation of what had really happened in no way diminished the fury of the Tory onslaught.

It was difficult for Gladstone, and still more difficult for Parnell, to decide how best to meet this onslaught, especially with the vengeful eye of Forster implacably fixed upon them. Parnell's instinct was to take the bull by the horns and read out his letter of 28 April to O'Shea. Yet even here disaster dogged his footsteps. He read from a copy supplied to him by O'Shea, which *omitted* the crucial sentence near the end where Parnell had said that the accomplishment of the programme he had sketched out 'would in my judgement be regarded by the country as a practical settlement of the land question and would enable us to co-operate cordially for the future with the Liberal party in forwarding Liberal principles and measures of general reform'. Forster at once interjected that Parnell had not given the whole letter and he thrust his own copy into the hands of the unfortunate O'Shea, who had then and there to read it *in extenso* to a House quivering with excitement. When on top of this Forster read out the memorandum of his conversation with O'Shea on 30 April, including the reference to employing known extremists like Sheridan to put down the agitation, the link between Parnellism and crime seemed firmly established in the minds of those who had always wanted to believe it existed.

Whether or not Parnell was aware that the letter he read out lacked the fatal phrase is uncertain. Questioned at the Special Commission, O'Shea predictably said Parnell 'knew, of course, that I had left it out'.[12] But in a press interview immediately after the debate Parnell gave a more convoluted account of the incident. 'I read the letter from a copy supplied me from [sic] Captain O'Shea, in his own handwriting, the only copy I had in my possession since I wrote the letter. Captain O'Shea, on his own responsibility, omitted the paragraph in his copy to me as he was desirous that the portion of the letter should be published which he wished to have submitted to the cabinet.'[13] This ambiguous statement may reflect no more than the fact that a weary reporter was taking it down from an overstrained MP at two o'clock in the morning, yet, though confused, it seems to go some way towards confirming O'Shea's statement.[14] True, it attempts to put the onus on the Captain, yet it does not avow ignorance that the crucial passage was missing; on the contrary, it appears to imply, damningly, that the passage was omitted because it would be embarrassing if it were made public. Certainly, when it was made public the effect was far worse than embarrassing and it is difficult not to agree with the view Herbert Gladstone expressed in his diary: 'Why Parnell should have read a garbled letter when he must have known direct questions, which could not be evaded, would be asked by someone, is a question I cannot answer. He had no right to do it; but it hurts him more than anyone else. I know that it was father's wish that the facts should be known.'[15]

The *gaffe* may, of course, have been a genuine mistake, appearances notwithstanding, though the chief ground for believing this is the negative one that to omit the passage deliberately was so risky, so potentially damaging, that no one in his senses would knowingly have done it. Parnell's own view, as expressed in the interview he gave after the debate, militates against the theory that this was simply a slip, and indeed it is hard to believe that Parnell himself could, either by a lapse of memory or some other oversight, have read out so vitally important a letter without realizing that a major point had been left out. But if we reject, or doubt, that this blunder was merely a mistake, we are driven to consider other possibilities, not all of them creditable. It may be that he hoped to conceal from watchful eyes in Ireland the extent of his surrender – the passage omitted, after all, was precisely that *hors d'oeuvre* which Gladstone had neither sought nor expected. It may be that he wished to make it easier for the Liberal government to implement the bargain by minimizing its content. It may simply be that his judgement failed him under stress.

Whatever the reason it was an unnecessary and costly error, especially since it was committed on the day chosen by the government to bring in the Arrears Bill which was their main contribution to the fulfilment of the so-called 'treaty'. It followed closely the lines of Parnell's own proposal. Applying only to holdings valued (on Griffith's valuation) at £30 or under, it proposed that if the tenant paid one year's arrears and satisfied the Land Commissioners that he could not pay his antecedent arrears, the state would pay half the sum due to the landlord and cancel the remainder. The money for this transaction was to be taken from the Irish church surplus, to be supplemented, if need be, from the Exchequer. Most remarkable of all, compulsion was to be applied to both landlord and tenant.

With this major concession dangling before him it was certainly not in Parnell's interest to make the parliamentary existence of the government any more difficult than it already was. To do him justice he did his best to retrieve the situation by attempting to moderate the passions of those of his followers who were inflamed by the rigours of the proposed new coercion bill. We need not trace the details of the battle that now developed – both over coercion and over the Arrears Bill – during the rest of the session, but in assessing Parnell's role it is important to realize that two struggles were going on simultaneously. One was the struggle within the cabinet, broadly between those who wanted to conciliate Ireland and those who wanted to punish her; in its simplest terms it was a struggle between Gladstone and Chamberlain on the one hand and Sir William Harcourt on the other. Ordinarily this would have been a foregone conclusion, with Harcourt hopelessly out-classed, but on this occasion he had considerable, though not unqualified, support from Spencer, whose calm and resolute handling of the aftermath of the Phoenix Park murders aroused general admiration and gave exceptional authority to his pressure for firm measures.

The other struggle, the one in which Parnell himself was deeply implicated, was both baffling and dangerous. It took two forms. One of these was well described by the Radical, Henry Labouchere, in a letter he wrote to Chamberlain in mid-May, after having had a talk with Parnell about the Prevention of Crime Bill. 'He says that he is in a very difficult position between the government and the secret societies. The latter, he says, are more numerous than are [sic] supposed; that most of those connected with them only wish to be let alone, but that he greatly fears that if they are disgusted [sic] they will commit outrages.'[16] Of course, for Parnell, anxious to limit the impact of coercion so far as possible, it was an obvious ploy to use the secret societies for leverage against the government, but the Phoenix Park murders were only ten days old when he talked to Labouchere, and neither he nor anyone else could be sure that Ireland was not on the edge of some great convulsion.

The difficulty about secret societies was that they *were* secret and hovered in the background as a mainly unseen threat. But the more immediate, and potentially more formidable, threat with which Parnell had to deal was also a more open one. The whole concept of co-operation with the Liberals, with its corollary of slowing down the land agitation, was certain to bring on a confrontation with those who were still deeply involved in the fight against the landlords, especially Dillon and Davitt. This was well known to English ministers, who watched with the closest attention to see whether Parnell would withstand this pressure from the left and whether he could fulfil his part of the bargain in the teeth of his intransigent colleagues.

It was to be a long, dour struggle, but what the watching ministers could scarcely have known was that it had begun even before the Kilmainham 'treaty' had been mooted. While the 'suspects' were locked up in Kilmainham it became apparent to the authorities that they fell broadly into two categories – Parnellite or Dillonite. The distinction between them hinged largely on the attitude to be taken towards the wilder spirits on the fringes of the League who, it was alleged, had committed outrages either for a stipulated sum of money or for a guarantee that their interests would be protected if they fell foul of the law. A case in point was that of one Patrick Duffy, who had been arrested in June 1881, on suspicion of burning a house at Mulrany, county Mayo, the property of a local JP. Duffy was known in the neighbourhood to be a violent man and his prison file contains agitated demands from the JP that he should on no account be released. This, it seems, was also the view of the moderate, or Parnellite, party in Kilmainham, who feared that if set free Duffy would so discredit the League by renewing his unsavoury activities that it would be gravely damaged. From the police point of view this was perhaps a strong argument for releasing him, but the piteous pleas of the JP so far prevailed that despite questions being asked in the House, Duffy was held in custody until August 1882.

What interested the authorities most about the case was that it typified the problem with which, after the suppression of the Land League itself, the Ladies Land League was confronted – whether or not to pay some form of subsistence or compensation to extremists who had been plying their usual trade under cover of the land agitation. The Dillonite view was that where conditions or promises had been made, these should be honoured. But in practice, Anna Parnell, however

militant her language, was not inclined to give the blank cheque to
extremism which this view implied. Superintendent Mallon noticed
with interest that 'on every occasion when she was appealed against
Mr Parnell supported her'. This touching family solidarity is not to be
taken as evidence that Charles by any means agreed with Anna's
conduct of affairs. Yet it does indicate that brother and sister both
realized that the subvention of violence could only lead to intensified
anarchy. 'The spirit of dissatisfaction had reached such a pitch',
commented Mallon shrewdly, 'that Duffy and men of his advanced
views were determined to openly oppose the more moderate promoters
of the League.' The fact that this particular episode ended with the
claims of all the 'suspects' being settled by the Ladies Land League,
though it helps to explain Parnell's subsequent hostility towards that
body, does not affect the main conclusion to be drawn from the saga
of Patrick Duffy – that extremism and moderation faced each other
with unconcealed enmity during those final months in Kilmainham.[17]

II

Particular importance attached therefore to how Parnell handled
Dillon in the weeks after their release. His first real test came towards
the end of May, when Dillon delivered a full-blooded defence of
boycotting, which Gladstone denounced as 'heart-breaking' for those
who were working to improve relations between the two countries.[18]
Writing that night to Spencer, he said that Dillon 'in I think the worst
Irish speech I have ever heard, lifted the banner at once of illegality and
of revolt from Parnell'. The effect of it, he thought, had been to rally
opinion behind the government, but how it would influence the Irish
situation he dared not forecast. 'Parnell has thus far run quite true, but
it seems very doubtful whether he can hold his ground.'[19] Others
evidently felt likewise, for that same evening O'Shea went down to
Eltham with Parnell and, so he reported next day to Chamberlain,
extracted from him a promise to repudiate Dillon and all his works.[20]
A promise to O'Shea probably meant little enough to Parnell – in
political terms at least – and he was perfectly capable of recognizing
and meeting a challenge on his own account. At any rate, on 25 May
he rose in his place and made one of the most brilliant of his 'balancing'
speeches, so brilliant that it earned applause in nearly every quarter
save among his own left wing.

He began by observing cautiously that the impression made on
members by Dillon's speech, and the deductions made from it by

Gladstone, were equally unwarranted. It was not correct, he said, to suppose that Dillon meant that while they would use their influence to put down outrages, intimidation would continue. Dillon's words, he insisted, conformed to what he, Parnell, had said in the past, that boycotting was defensible only when used where *unjust* evictions had occurred. So far from stirring up violence, he and Dillon and others, while they were in Kilmainham, had anxiously debated how best to tranquillize the country. For Parnell himself the best means of achieving this end would be a satisfactory Arrears Act and so he had always told his friends. It was urgently necessary, however, that the Arrears Act be given a chance to operate before coercion was applied. 'The government', he declared, 'ought not to shut the door in the face of the vast majority of the Irish people, who desired to see Her Majesty's Government return to constitutional courses, and who desired to see any determination to the much vexed Irish question.' Arrears, he repeated, were the key to the situation, and he ended with a grave warning that this must not be lost sight of in the general surge towards vengeance for the Phoenix Park murders. 'Between the secret societies on the one hand and the government on the other, it would be practically impossible for moderate politicians to act.'[21]

Not the least important consequence of this speech was that it helped to intensify the argument inside the cabinet as to whether the policy to be pursued towards Ireland should be predominantly conciliatory or predominantly punitive. Chamberlain, who had defended the Kilmainham 'treaty' on 16 May, four days later circulated a minute to the cabinet about the coercion bill, urging that because 'Parnell and his friends behaved very well over second reading', some concessions should be made to them in committee, otherwise there would be ill-will and endless obstruction. The amendments to which he thought the Irish members attached most importance were those to limit the duration of the new law and to define more precisely what constituted offences under it.[22] Harcourt, who was prepared to fight for every clause of his bill like a tigress for her young, could see what Parnell was trying to do, but was apparently not capable of drawing the right conclusion from it. Complaining to Spencer on 17 May that Gladstone was 'very much disposed' to meet the Irish on the points in dispute 'for the sake of peace', he said he had already made it clear that he thought the amendments bad in themselves and that to yield to them would be taken as a sign of weakness.[23] Yet five days later, acknowledging that Parnell had made 'a very moderate speech', he quite failed to see why. 'He is I believe n a state of great alarm as to his own personal safety and he let fall a hint that very likely he and his immediate friends might retire from political life; a thing which I think it not unlikely that he and Dillon may carry out and leave the thing in the hands of the more desperate men like Healy who take every occasion to declare their hatred to [sic] English rule in every form.'[24]

It would be difficult to decide which of Harcourt's theses was the more comic – the idea of Dillon and Parnell resigning in unison or the vision of the opportunist Healy as a desperado – but although his mis-reading of the alignment of forces inside the Irish party was at one level ludicrous, at another level it was dangerous, for as Home Secretary he was in a position to do a great deal of damage to Anglo-Irish relations. In justification of his deep scepticism regarding Parnell, it has to be remembered that the reports he was receiving from the police who were shadowing the Irish leader at this time threw a lurid, if not altogether reliable, light upon the O'Shea connection. According to a note in Sir Charles Dilke's diary, Harcourt was said to have told the cabinet on 17 May that the Kilmainham 'treaty' would not be popular 'when the public discovered that it had been negotiated by Captain O'Shea, the husband of Parnell's mistress'. Dilke's record then continued: 'He [Harcourt] informed the cabinet that he knew that in the previous year O'Shea had threatened Parnell with divorce proceedings and that it was only Mrs O'Shea's discovery of adulterous relations of her husband which had put him in her power; and that O'Shea had shut his eyes and made the best of it.'[25]

This account is suspect on other grounds beside its garbled version of O'Shea's relations with his wife. It cannot be regarded as first-hand information because Dilke was not then in the cabinet, which in any case did not meet on 17 May. As against this, it is known that Chamberlain regularly informed Dilke about cabinet proceedings and also that when he saw Dilke's memoir of these events (based upon his diary) several years later he did not dispute its accuracy. The fact that the cabinet did not meet on 17 May weakens but does not necessarily destroy Dilke's story. He may have been misled by the fact that there was a Privy Council meeting on that date.[26] Alternatively, and more probably, he may simply have got the date wrong and have been refer-ring to a cabinet either side of 17 May. This probability is increased by the fact that Earl Granville, who, as Foreign Secretary, would normally attend all cabinets, was also aware of the rumour. Writing to Gladstone a few days later, Granville remarked of Mrs O'Shea, 'She is said to be his [Parnell's] mistress'.[27] On the other hand, when Granville's nephew, George Leveson Gower, referred to the matter about this time, Glad-

stone severely snubbed him. 'You do not ask me to believe', Leveson
Gower later recalled him saying, 'that it is possible a man should be so
lost to all sense of what is due to his public position, at a moment like
the present, in the very crisis of his country's fortunes, as to indulge
in an illicit connection with the wife of one of his very own political
supporters, and to make use of that connection in the way you suggest.'[28]

This perhaps tells us more about Gladstone than about Parnell, but
whether the Prime Minister did or did not accept the existence of the
liaison at that particular point in time is not important. What is important
is that the rumour was current, or the fact was known, precisely when
Parnell's difficulties in controlling the more extreme members of his
party were attracting general attention. It was not surprising, therefore,
that Harcourt should have had his doubts about the Irish leader or
that in a counter-minute of 22 May to Chamberlain's minute of two
days earlier he should have maintained his unyielding position:[29]

> The cabinet stands on the ground that the principal provisions of
> this bill were deliberately debated and arranged before and indepen-
> dently of the assassinations in the Phoenix Park . . . If after that we
> are to confess that we have propounded so serious a measure as this
> without due reflection and that we are now disposed to recall our
> discussions everyone will say, and justly say, that we are extremely
> unfit to govern Ireland or indeed anybody anywhere. As to buying
> off Irish opposition, that cannot be done. There is not one of them to
> be trusted.

Nevertheless, even Harcourt was impressed by Parnell's performance
on 25 May. 'I have just been listening to Parnell's very remarkable
speech', he wrote that night to Spencer. 'He very boldly and completely
threw over Dillon and said all that O'Shea ever gave us reason to believe
he would say against outrage, intimidation and boycotting . . . His
speech was listened to with marked attention and created a great and
I think a favourable impression.'[30] If this was the view of the minister
perhaps most hostile to the Irish, it was *a fortiori* that of the minister
most favourable. Chamberlain was favourable, admittedly, for reasons
not entirely altruistic. 'If we do not make some concessions to the Irish
party', he had told Spencer when sending him a copy of his minute, 'we
shall fall back to the position we occupied last season. All business will
be blocked. The House of Lords will be able to force a dissolution and
the General Election will turn out the Government. Then you will
see that the Tories will at once come to terms with the Irish . . .'[31]
No doubt this grisly scenario was mainly designed to make Spencer's

flesh creep and thus render him more amenable, but it was touched by prescience. And it did indicate that Chamberlain was in earnest about concessions to Parnell.

Spencer, naturally, was unconvinced. Though less of a diehard than Harcourt, he had the task of governing an Ireland still seething with rumours and alarms and he had no doubt that coercion was needed.[32] But Chamberlain, who was so incensed by the support given in the cabinet to Harcourt's 'Draconian laws' that he was seriously thinking (or allowed it to be known that he was seriously thinking) of resignation, was moved by Parnell's speech on 25 May to impress upon the Lord-Lieutenant that the Irish leader's standing must not be put at risk by governmental rigidity on coercion. Parnell's statement, he wrote, was 'very remarkable'. 'I think it was most creditable to him, and fully justified the view we took of his release.' And he continued:[33]

> His influence with his party is unimpaired by what has happened and he is still the most powerful popular leader in Ireland. I do not think that anyone else will try to undermine his authority. I am assured that instructions have been given to the tenants to settle with their landlords and not to act on the 'No Rent' manifesto. Dillon's speech represents Dillon only and is universally condemned.

Chamberlain could write with some confidence about Parnell's intentions because he was receiving, through Labouchere, frequent bulletins about the Irish leader's state of mind. Admittedly, Labouchere was, next to O'Shea, about the most untrustworthy source that Chamberlain could have chosen, but at this particular juncture he was in almost daily touch with several of the Irish members, including Parnell, and what he reported corresponded closely to Parnell's views as expressed in his speech of 25 May. Thus, in that letter of 16 May already quoted,* in which Labouchere conveyed Parnell's anxieties about the secret societies, he was also able to say that Parnell had assured him that if the Irish amendments to the coercion bill were conceded, or if the government at least met them in a conciliatory spirit, their opposition would be conducted on 'honest parliamentary lines'. 'He fully admits', added Labouchere, 'that a bill is necessary on account of English opinion, but he does not wish to have it applied to himself and he doubts whether it will be really effectual against the outrage mongers.'[34]

A few days later Labouchere again reported to Chamberlain. The Irish, he said, were on the whole pleased with the Arrears Bill, but they

*See above, p. 214.

were worried about coercion. Parnell had told him that while he himself was 'most anxious' for a *modus vivendi*, if the moment were allowed to pass, it might not return. 'He and his friends, he says, are incurring the serious risk of assassination in their efforts to bring it about, and he thinks that his suggestions ought to be judged on their merits, but that, with the Coercion Act [sic] as it is, there will be so much anger and ill-feeling in Ireland, that an alliance with the Liberal party will be impossible.'[35]

The amendments which the Irish sought were not, on the face of it, such as to destroy the efficacy of the new law. They wanted its duration reduced from three years to, at most, two; they wanted the exclusion of treason and treason-felony from its scope; they wanted 'incitement' not to be embraced in the definition of 'intimidation'; they wanted the right of search to be limited by imposing a necessity to include a precise description of the house to be searched in the warrant authorizing the police to enter; most of all, perhaps, they wanted to substitute county court judges for the hated resident magistrates on the tribunals of summary jurisdiction. Harcourt, however, remained adamant and relations between Chamberlain and himself steadily deteriorated. In the House of Commons, also, there were signs that Parnell could not go on indefinitely repressing the anger and discontent of his party. To do so would be to risk, not merely his parliamentary leadership, but his authority over the movement in Ireland. The first indication that he was reaching the end of his patience came early in June when a determined, but vain, effort was made to secure the exclusion of treason and treason-felony from the bill. Parnell made it plain to Labouchere, and Labouchere passed it on to Chamberlain, that unless concessions came soon, he would find it difficult to hold his own and he hinted that the alternative to his authority would be that of Egan, operating from Paris. Opposition to coercion apart, Parnell's long-term plans were interesting and constructive. To Labouchere he defined them thus:

> I ask, in order to put an end definitely to the land agitation: that a clause should be introduced into the Arrears Bill, allowing small tenants in the land court to pay on Griffith's valuation until their cases are decided: that there should be an expansion of the Bright clauses next year if not this: and that a Royal Commission be appointed to keep the labourers quiet by taking evidence. Then I propose to ask for a fair and reasonable measure of local self-government such as an English government can grant . . .

Parnell, it seems, was also prepared to vote with the Liberals on all important questions. 'I believe that he is perfectly sincere', wrote Labouchere, 'and that he is thoroughly frightened by threats of assassination; indeed he told me that he never went about without a revolver in his pocket, and even then did not feel safe.'[36]

Harcourt remained unimpressed. He thought the Parnellite resistance to the bill 'rather necessary than severe', he told Spencer at the end of May. On 8 June he reported: 'Parnell is evidently disposed to be as moderate and conciliatory as he dares – the recalcitrants are Healy, Dillon and O'Donnell, but as yet P. seems to hold his own.'[37] But that 'P' should be given some assistance in holding his own appears never to have entered Harcourt's head. On the contrary, his persistence in the delusion that the split in the Irish ranks was essentially amongst parliamentarians rather than between parliamentarians and extremists, actually contributed to his intransigence by leading him to believe that because Parnell was standing firm, there was only tiresome opposition from a handful of malcontents to be anticipated.

Others saw things differently. On the same day that Harcourt was airily dismissing the Irish opposition to the bill, Labouchere was conveying to Chamberlain Parnell's view that 'it is absolutely necessary that something should be understood, and that if no concession be made on the intimidation clause, he considers that things revert to where they were under the Forster regime'.[38] This letter coincided with the first serious Irish obstruction which produced from Gladstone a characteristic reaction. Although still in principle anxious to meet Irish objections constructively, he bridled at any hint of duress. To Chamberlain, who sent him a copy of Labouchere's letter of 8 June, he replied that any 'covenant' with the Parnellites was inadmissible and that obstruction of the coercion bill 'will react powerfully on the Arrears Bill and upon all other legislation possible for Ireland'. He added tartly: 'It is not for me to take any notice of what some would call the threat that things may revert to what they were under the Forster regime. My duty is only to examine what justice requires us to do towards promoting harmony and forwarding business.'[39]

III

Matters now began to move rapidly towards a kind of crisis. In Ireland a new double murder was a reminder that violence had yet to be brought under control, and Gladstone's secretary noted that Colonel Brackenbury, who had gone to Ireland 'as a sort of head detective' had reported that the secret societies were 'terribly rampant'.[40] It seemed no time for concessions on boycotting and on 10 June there was a violent quarrel in cabinet between Chamberlain and Harcourt on the whole subject of coercion.[41] Chamberlain's later recollection was that some modifications in the bill resulted from this passage of arms, but Harcourt assured Spencer that 'it was resolved to stick staunchly by the bill without negotiation of any kind with the Parnellites, and with no changes except those which you have recommended . . .'[42] The issue went far deeper than the emendation of the Prevention of Crime Bill. It was, in its starkest form, whether Parnell should be regarded as a moderating force, and therefore to be strengthened, or whether he was held to be useless for that purpose, and therefore expendable. Harcourt's success was a triumph for the latter point of view and it meant the virtual end of any hope of an agreed policy on coercion.

The changes which Spencer recommended – he wanted to limit the operation of the exceptional law to 'proclaimed' districts and he did not share Harcourt's enthusiasm for encouraging the police to burst into private houses at dead of night – came nowhere near the modifications the Irish demanded. Consequently, their attitude hardened and as it did so the progress of the bill became perceptibly slower. For although Labouchere continued to pass on Parnell's views to Chamberlain, the failure or refusal of the government to make the concessions he needed rendered it impossible for him, even had he wished it, to restrain his more uninhibited followers. There was a suspicion, shared by Gladstone's secretary, that Labouchere himself was prodding the Irish into greater obstruction than they really wanted to engage in, but if this was true they were apparently not held in check by Parnell.[43] On the contrary, as O'Shea complained to Chamberlain, he was frequently 'in a "moony", drifting state of mind, nowadays, with which it is difficult to keep one's temper'.[44] This soon became Chamberlain's view also and, forgetting how little Parnell's moderation had brought him, he protested vigorously about the Irish leader's inability, or unwillingness, to call off the resistance to the Prevention of Crime Bill, even though O'Shea had twice conveyed to him Parnell's promises to do so:[45]

> These letters fully justify the confidence I have always felt in your good faith and honour. I wish I could say the same of Mr Parnell's conduct which is most disappointing to me and gives colour to the arguments of those who have always opposed any communications with him on the ground that he either would not or could not carry out his engagements.
>
> I consider that he is bound in honour to make a public effort

to bring the debates on the Crime Bill to a close – indeed he ought to have done so at least a week ago.

If he will not do this there is no power to make him, but he has himself destroyed all possibility of a *modus vivendi* such as he so often expressed himself desirous of securing.

If Parnell paid little attention to the Captain as a political negotiator, this was at least in part because he was paying much more attention to the Captain's wife in this, for her, unaccustomed role. On 23 May she wrote to Gladstone asking if he would have a private interview with Parnell. The Prime Minister replied with a courteous but firm negative. He had no prejudice, he said, against seeing him for 'a public object', and he regarded it as a duty 'carefully to avoid any act or word that could injure his position or weaken his hands in doing good'. He believed that a private interview would have this very effect, besides possibly impairing his, Gladstone's, own position.[46] Since Parnell, for obvious reasons, could not seek a public meeting without alarming his followers the proposal lapsed. But Mrs O'Shea was not so easily to be shaken off. She wrote again, asking if Gladstone would see *her*. Rather surprisingly, he agreed. Much more surprisingly, he went to her favourite rendezvous, Thomas's Hotel in Berkeley Square. Her recollections of the strange relationship which now began are extremely unreliable and have been severely criticized on points of fact by Gladstone's son Herbert.[47] Not only does she misdate their first meeting, but she constantly makes other errors of detail, sometimes of a quite crucial kind, as when she conveys the impression that her meetings with the Prime Minister were frequent occurrences. In reality there were only three; besides the initial interview at Thomas's Hotel on 1 June, she called on Gladstone in Downing Street on 29 August and 14 September. After 1882 she did not meet him at all and Parnell, extraordinary as it may seem, did not have any personal contact with Gladstone until 26 February 1886. It is true, however, that Katharine wrote numerous letters both to Gladstone and to Lord Richard Grosvenor (the Liberal Chief Whip) and that Gladstone wrote her some 25 letters in reply.

Yet, although the relationship was not so intense as she subsequently claimed, it had an importance of its own, not least in 1882 when Parnell was doing his utmost to persuade the Liberals to moderate their coercion bill. Just how far he was prepared to go was revealed in a letter she wrote on his behalf on 17 June, barely a week after Harcourt had trounced Chamberlain at the cabinet which had resolved not to modify coercion on essential points. If her letter represented him correctly – and his practice seems to have been to dictate to her what she was to say – he offered to withdraw opposition to the bill if the government excluded treason-felony from its scope, and if they limited its duration to three months after the assembly of a new parliament, provided the existing parliament were dissolved within the next three years.[48] Gladstone took this proposal seriously enough to send it on to Harcourt and Spencer for their comment. Unhappily, it came at an inopportune moment. A large seizure of arms at Clerkenwell, apparently intended for Irish uses, enabled Harcourt to take refuge behind exasperated public opinion, while in Ireland Spencer was preoccupied by police intelligence (ill-founded, as it turned out) that large-scale dynamite operations, or even a series of assassinations, were being planned for 20 June.[49] Neither man was in the mood to yield and neither did yield.

The consequence was that Irish obstructionism intensified. It reached a climax on 30 June–1 July, when the House had to sit continuously for 28 hours discussing clause 17 of the bill, which proposed that districts should be rated for compensation, to be payable for cases of maiming and murder occurring therein. The blockage led inevitably to the use of the closure, but after seventeen members – including Parnell as well as Dillon and the other *enragés* – had been suspended, the remaining clauses passed through so rapidly that the bill became law by mid-July. This left the way open for the Arrears Bill, which had been seriously endangered by the slow progress of the Prevention of Crime Bill. The government's intentions were framed broadly on Parnell's own suggestions and, naturally, they were hailed as a brutal assault on property. As such, they were not only bitterly attacked by the Tories, but roused little enough enthusiasm among the Liberals, including, of course, the die-hard Harcourt. It was Harcourt, while the bill was labouring through committee, who chose to make the most ferocious attack on the policy of conciliation which had yet come from any of Gladstone's colleagues. All the efforts that had been made from 1869 onwards, he told his chief, had absolutely failed. 'They have only been regarded as signs of weakness and inspired fresh demands which will never rest short of absolute confiscation of the property of the landlords and a total separation of Ireland from England. These are the avowed objects of Davitt and Parnell, and their ideas have entirely permeated the Irish people.' As for the Arrears Bill, 'no one in Ireland cares a straw about it' and it would probably perish in the Lords in any event. 'There remains now in my belief only one remedy for Ireland, and that is in the most resolute and stern determination to enforce the law and to exercise to the utmost the powers of repression.' 'I think', he added, 'our language ought to be strong and our action still stronger. It is no use trying to soothe these tigers by stroking their backs. They are avowed rebels and they are covertly assassins. And that I believe is the state of mind of the leaders as well as of the disciples.'[50]

Harcourt admittedly was a special case. As Home Secretary he was under considerable strain and by temperament he found Irish nationalists distasteful and Ireland a country he had no wish to visit. When Gladstone circulated this letter to the cabinet it aroused general dissent. Ministers felt themselves committed to the Arrears Bill and when, as Harcourt had anticipated, the Lords sought to wreck it by destructive amendments, Gladstone was able to rally his colleagues for a stand against the Upper House. But the House of Lords was not so monolithic as it seemed. Irish landlords had considerable weight there and to them the Arrears Bill offered a chance of obtaining at least some of the backrent they would never otherwise have seen. Their pressure was sufficient, the peers recoiled from the brink and by 18 August the bill had received the royal assent. It was an immediate success and out of 135,997 claims submitted under the new law, no fewer than 129,952 were allowed.[51] Thus, at last, a burning question was taken out of the political arena.

IV

This prolonged and intense parliamentary campaign, which Parnell had had to wage incessantly since he came out of Kilmainham, was a necessary consequence of his coming out. But the true complexity of those summer months which were so crucial to his whole career can only be fully understood if we realize that simultaneously he had to regain his hold on the movement at home. The secret societies and the agrarian vendettas were of course outside his grasp, and both constituted as great a danger to him as to the government. So also were the old-style Fenians, but since they too disliked the current lawlessness, he had little either to fear or to expect from them. His main problems were three, all to some extent interlinked. He had first to bring the remnants of the Land League organization under control; effectively, this meant that he had to prevent the League funds in Paris from being used by Patrick Egan for further agitation and that he had also to assert his authority over the Ladies Land League. Second, he had to re-establish the primacy of parliamentary over agrarian action, which meant that he had either to reach a *modus vivendi* with Davitt and Dillon, or else drive them out of the field. Finally, and perhaps most difficult of all, he had so to arrange matters that Irish-American financial support would continue to be available for his constitutional purposes at a time when faction fighting inside and outside the Clan na Gael was exceptionally bitter and when there was a marked trend in some quarters towards a renewal of violence against England.

It was too much to hope that he would be equally successful in achieving all these objectives, but what was in his power to do he did. The most immediate task was to 'freeze' the League funds in Paris and so to prevent Egan and others from dissipating them on policies over which Parnell could exercise no restraint. Just how necessary it was to keep a firm hand on these funds may be judged from the fact that in May 1882, Alexander Sullivan, a dominant figure in the Clan na Gael who had gone to Paris to co-ordinate the activities of the Clan with those of the remnant of the Land League executive, had persuaded Egan to part with £20,000 'for the purpose of retaliating on the English government for the coercion in Ireland'. This was a murky transaction about which the real truth will probably never be known, but Sullivan's assertion that Egan refused to transmit the funds until he had received Parnell's instructions, does not accord with the recollection of an IRB witness, John O'Connor, who was present at the meeting between Egan and Sullivan and believed that Egan had had no contact with his leader.[52] It is indeed unlikely that Parnell, intent as he was upon bringing the Kilmainham understanding to fruition, would have endangered that whole policy by authorizing League funds to be handed over for the dubious purposes of Alexander Sullivan. It is much more in character that the next month, June 1882, he, Biggar and McCarthy instructed the Paris bankers that no bonds should be released in future except upon their signatures, in addition to those of Davitt and Egan, the other trustees.[53] His hold over these resources was further strengthened when in October Egan, announcing his resignation as treasurer, transferred a balance of about £31,000 to his successors. This was not merged with any other monies at Parnell's disposal and was kept in reserve as 'the Paris fund' until it became the subject of acute controversy in the vastly different circumstances of 1890.[54]

Pari passu with Parnell's repossession of the Land League funds went his suppression of the Ladies Land League, which had continued to spend money freely on the care of the evicted tenants even after his release from Kilmainham. It was imperative to end, or at least curb, this expenditure, which Katharine O'Shea had told Gladstone in August had been as high as £7–10,000 a week.[55] Almost certainly, this was a gross exaggeration and Parnell himself, after he returned to Ireland in August – when, admittedly, the demand for financial

help had slackened – reckoned that outgoings then stood at £700 a
week, not £7000. Even so, he was anxious not to press the ladies
too hard, for fear of driving them into premature retirement. 'Should
the ladies resign now', he told Dillon, 'I think they will be acting
very badly, and may do considerable mischief.' 'But', he added in a
burst of candour which, had she read it, would have interested Katharine
greatly, 'as I have never heard that anybody could ever persuade a
woman to do, or not to do, anything which she had made up her mind
to do, no matter what the consequences to herself or others might
be, I cannot help it if they do resign.'⁵⁶

The whole operation took about six weeks, from the latter part of
August to the end of September. It was achieved by the simple expedient
of cutting off their funds and discharging their debts with monies
supplied by Egan from the Paris fund.⁵⁷ As an interim measure, a
winding-up committee was appointed, but Parnell made it plain that
he did not think it should have 'any other functions than to act under
our instructions'.⁵⁸ That, indeed, was how things turned out and with
little or no interference from outsiders Parnell rid himself of the ladies
without further delay.

This made inevitably for bad relations with Anna, the sister who most
resembled him. Unpleasant at any time, the rift was made more painful
because it came directly after the sudden death of Fanny, the sister of
whom he was fondest. On 20 July, she went out walking with her dogs
in the hot sun at Bordentown, New Jersey, where she and her mother
were living. Delia Parnell had been ill with malaria and Fanny, after her
midday meal, retired for a siesta without disturbing her. When Mrs
Parnell looked into her room a little later, she found her daughter
unconscious, having apparently suffered a heart-attack, and by the time
the doctor arrived she was dead, aged only 33.⁵⁹ As for Anna, who was
three years Fanny's junior, after her brother's suppression of the Ladies
Land League she withdrew into embittered spinsterhood and took hardly
any further part in public life, with one notable exception, when, with
a true Parnellite flair for the coming vogue, she vigorously supported
the first Sinn Fein candidate ever to take the field in an Irish election,
C. J. Dolan in North Leitrim in 1908. Three years after that, she was
drowned while swimming at Ilfracombe, in September 1911, at the age
of 59.⁶⁰

V

Less wounding but more serious than the estrangement of Anna was
the estrangement of Dillon and Davitt. Parnell affected to make light

of it, writing to Katharine in August that 'the two D's had quarrelled with him because he would not sanction any further expenditure by the Ladies Land League'.[61] She duly embroidered this when talking to Gladstone a few days later. They were, Gladstone noted, 'in great dudgeon with Parnell by reason of his restricted action on the land and national questions. She speaks of him as thoroughly bent on legality (which I tell her is the whole question), and does not say anything otherwise, but she impeaches Davitt for vanity and Dillon for being a *tête montée*.'[62]

Yet it would be wrong to make too much of the break which undoubtedly did occur at this time. Although in some important ways decisive, it was neither so abrupt nor so angry as legend subsequently painted it. Dillon, especially, though still extreme in debate and virtually disowned by Parnell in his speech of 25 May, not only remained in parliament throughout the fight against coercion, but on his return to Ireland went out of his way to do homage to his leader, than whom, he said, no one was ever 'more tolerant of difference of opinion, less anxious to take credit for himself and to give all possible credit to the men under him'.[63] Two weeks later he and Parnell were together in Dublin to receive the freedom of the city and to attend the opening of the Irish National Exhibition of Industries. Each took as his theme the need for industrial development, but whereas Parnell spoke vaguely of 'voluntary protection' to be accorded by consumers to Irish goods, Dillon looked forward hopefully to a trade dispute with British manufacturers which might lead, on the eighteenth-century American model, to a movement 'to establish the independence of Ireland'.[64] Even this, though it suggested significant differences, did not fully reveal them. In fact, they never were fully revealed, for Dillon continued to co-operate with Parnell into the autumn. He participated in a parliamentary conference on 8 August to lay the foundations of an 'Irish labour and industrial union' and he was also present on 21 August when a larger meeting was held in Dublin to put the new body on its legs and when Parnell proclaimed the need to help the labourers to organize themselves to improve social conditions.[65]

More important than this initiative was the conference held at Avondale in September for the purpose of replacing the defunct Land League by a new, open organization. Davitt was later to say that Parnell only agreed to launch this under pressure from many of his supporters, including Dillon and, we may reasonably assume, Davitt also. This may or may not have been true. Most probably it was true in the sense that Parnell was reluctant to involve himself again in any renewal of the land agitation, but not true in the sense that he was opposed to any and every kind of organization. On the contrary, to create a new base for a popular movement in the country was a paramount necessity for him, provided he could control it and guide it in the direction he wanted to go. It was interesting, all the same, that the group which went to Avondale to plan this newest of new departures should have included not only Davitt and Dillon, but also Thomas Brennan, the one-time firebrand of the Land League. This certainly suggests that Parnell was still prepared to work with old colleagues of the land war, but if he was, he was careful to balance them with members of the parliamentary party, and the signatures to the invitation to a full conference which resulted from this Avondale meeting included also those of Sexton, Tim Healy and Arthur O'Connor.[66]

Yet, if Parnell in the autumn of 1882 appeared to be aiming at some sort of equilibrium between right and left, the scales were about to be weighted heavily in favour of the former, for the left quickly suffered two crippling blows in the loss of Dillon and the virtual loss of Davitt. Immediately after the Avondale conference Dillon announced that he was leaving politics 'for the next few years'. Since he was threatened with tuberculosis, there can be no doubt that his public reason for resigning – the state of his health – was genuine enough. But his friends were almost certainly right in concluding that he went because he could not stomach Parnell's change of course after Kilmainham. Even so he went apparently without rancour and certainly without intention to disrupt. Dropping out of public life in October, he departed to Colorado in the spring of 1883, and for two years almost nothing was heard from or about him.[67]

Davitt's case was more complicated. For him, as for Parnell, imprisonment in the winter of 1881–2 had led to a profound rethinking of his position. But whereas Parnell had emerged from Kilmainham intent upon parliamentary manoeuvre, Davitt came out of Portland in the grip of an enthusiasm which was still essentially agrarian, though in a strikingly novel way. Under the not too arduous terms of his sentence he had been able to read and to absorb Henry George's book, *Progress and poverty*, which had been published in 1880. One strand in the American's thinking coincided closely with his own inmost conviction. Henry George laid great stress upon the land as the prime source of wealth. From this it followed that the monopolization of land in the hands of 'owners' was a great evil which could only be cured by the abolition of *all* ownership of land – that is, by land nationalization. Davitt had actually met Henry George at the home of Patrick Ford during one of his trips to America, and had even then become convinced that land nationalization was the gospel of the future. But would it work in Ireland? During his sojourn in Portland he apparently convinced himself that it would.

The shock of the Phoenix Park murders seemed to make such speculations vain. Davitt reacted to the assassinations much as Parnell had done. Just as Parnell had offered his resignation to Gladstone, so on 11 May Davitt sought an interview with the then Chief Commissioner of Police, Howard Vincent, during which he said some remarkable things. They were so remarkable that Vincent sat down at once and wrote this report to Sir William Harcourt:[68]

Dear Sir William,

I have just had a long interview with Davitt and he has undertaken to assist the authorities by every means in his power and if earnestness of manner is any guarantee he will do so.

He says he was a Fenian but is no longer so; he held the British government in contempt and plotted against it but will not do so in the future.

He says that his life is in the greatest peril, that prior to his re-committal his assassination had been resolved upon, and that his life was prolonged by the revocation of his licence [that is, his ticket-of-leave].

He is convinced that the murders of Saturday will stamp out assassination and exterminate Fenianism.

He is convinced that they were the result of a long existing plot to assassinate Mr Burke and Mr Forster, and that the death of Lord Frederick Cavendish was in no way intended. He does not believe that Rossa* – 'arch-scoundrel' he termed him, 'one whom he would himself shoot' – had the courage to organize it, but that it had rather been undertaken by a few desperate ruffians who are, he thinks, still in Dublin.

Davitt will do anything I want, and give every assistance that is possible. At the end of the week he will ask leave to go to Ireland to have an interview with Brennan.

If I may venture to express an opinion it is, that by negotiation with the Land League, both it and Fenianism may be put down.

Yours truly,
C. E. H. Vincent.

---

*For Rossa's connection with Irish-American extremism, see p. 73 above.

Vincent, deeply impressed by Davitt, probably over-estimated the latter's power to calm the situation. Yet there was no mistaking Davitt's eagerness to turn his back on violence. Soon it became apparent that this was not just a panic reaction to the murders, but also a response to a far deeper stimulus. The stimulus was his passionate ambition to overthrow landlordism in Ireland, but this now took a form which Davitt's absorption of Henry George's ideas had dictated to him. On 21 May, apparently against Parnell's wishes, he took the chair at a meeting addressed by George in Manchester and himself announced his conversion from peasant ownership to land nationalization. Not content with this, he went on to outline what was to be the *Leitmotiv* of much of his subsequent career – that Irishmen should work for a democratic alliance with Englishmen and that this could best be accomplished if outrage in Ireland were to cease and the way thus be cleared for the outpouring of English sympathy which the exposure of Irish social evils would, he was sure, evoke.[69] He followed this a couple of weeks later with a much more explicit statement at Liverpool defining what he meant by the nationalization of the land. He meant primarily that the state should assume – or resume – the ownership of the soil, thus re-establishing that communal property which he claimed (quite wrongly) had been the norm before the imposition of a landowning class upon Irish society. That class, having demonstrated its inadequacy, must now be replaced, *not* by another property-owning class, but by the community as a whole.[70] This was crude even by Henry George's standards, but those who read his speech in Ireland and America were little concerned about whether or not Davitt had got George's doctrines right. The question they asked was whether or not Davitt had parted from Parnell and from the original programme of the Land League. Davitt in all sincerity claimed he had not. The almost universal consensus was that he had.

Two days later Davitt was at Cork en route for the steamer that would carry him to America, where he had a deal of explaining to do but where he hoped nevertheless to win financial support for his campaign. To the reporters who crowded round him he commented that he could make no speech because he had promised Parnell not to speak in Ireland 'and I would be the last man to do or say anything to embarrass Mr Parnell's work or action in the House of Commons'.[71] Yet this was precisely what he appeared to be doing. The Kilmainham 'treaty' was barely a month old and the whole policy which it embodied was still in the balance, threatened equally by Irish suspicion of what was clearly a new direction, and by English inclination to use the Phoenix Park murders as an excuse to intensify coercion. For Davitt to launch his programme of land nationalization at such a critical juncture looked like a challenge not only to the 'treaty', since nationalization could only be promoted by the kind of agitation which Parnell had forsworn, but also to the Land League itself, because the new doctrine was so obviously at variance with what the tenant-farmers themselves understood by the sacred slogan of 'the land for the people'.

Yet in reality Davitt's conversion was for Parnell less a threat then a blessing in disguise, as he was quick to realize. After reading the Liverpool speech, he remarked to William O'Brien: 'If I were Davitt I should never define. The moment he becomes intelligible he is lost.'[72] How lost, he now proceeded to demonstrate. While Davitt was crossing the Atlantic Parnell gave an interview to the New York *Herald* which, with devastatingly accurate timing, was published on 18 June, the day of Davitt's arrival in the United States. Asked what he thought of the new campaign, the Irish leader blandly replied that he could not see it ever becoming practical politics in Ireland. Recalling that the original programme of the Land League – rent-reduction in the short term, the conversion of tenants to owners in the long term – had been adopted at a meeting attended by both Davitt and himself, he added pointedly that 'so far as I am aware', it had never been departed from since.

This was hard-hitting enough, but Parnell continued to score points with almost contemptuous ease when the interviewer asked him what he thought about the issue being raised at that particular moment. Condescendingly, Parnell observed that it was merely a temporary aberration and that Davitt would return to their former joint policy when he found he was getting little support for the new doctrine. 'We should', he remarked, 'incur the imputation of not knowing our own minds if, after two years of successful agitation towards an occupying proprietary, we start an entirely different theory . . . I recognize to the fullest extent the right of any person to formulate his own opinions, and influence the people to follow him in the direction of these opinions, but having regard to all the circumstances of the case, the great risk of division in America, and the serious evils which have always attended division in the ranks of our people, I cannot view the steps lately taken in formulating this new plan as likely to be justified by successful results.'[73]

Davitt was thus thrown on the defensive from the start of his tour and he never fully recovered the initiative. It was in vain that on 19 June he told reporters that there was no breach between Parnell and himself. 'Mr Parnell is the head of the movement, inside and outside parliament. There can be no rivalry, no jealousy between us.'[74] It was in vain that at his first public meeting in New York he embarked on a vigorous defence of his policy. It was in vain that he pleaded absolute innocence of any wish to take over the leadership, on the ground – itself revealing as to a major source of Parnell's power – that the Irish would never accept him 'because I belong to the ranks of the people'.[75] As he moved across America the current of feeling was such that, while by no means abandoning his doctrine of land nationalization, he was forced to see that the chances of raising money for a substantial campaign to promote it were virtually nil.[76] On 27 July, therefore, he returned to Ireland, for the time being at least a diminished political force.

In reality, though he could scarcely have been expected to appreciate this himself, Davitt had acted as a lightning-conductor for Parnell. The Kilmainham 'treaty' had marked a perceptible turning away from the 'new departure' so eagerly mooted three years earlier. Even amongst Parnell's own followers acceptance of the change of direction was not free from the kind of misgiving which one of the most loyal of them, Richard Power, expressed to Dillon at the time of the latter's resignation. 'You know how I have always feared and hated private treaties and government negotiations and I would much prefer to follow your example and resign at once than remain a member of a party which was not thoroughly independent and perfectly indifferent to English interests.'[77]

Checked first by the horror of the Phoenix Park murders and then by the necessity to present a common front against the Prevention of Crime Act in the House of Commons, this feeling was nevertheless far from negligible. That it did not lead to some critical questioning of Parnell's leadership may partly, and paradoxically, have been due to the brutal insensitivity of Sir William Harcourt's presentation of the case for coercion, but it was due still more to Davitt's inspired ineptitude in choosing this of all moments to launch his grand diversion. In America, where the parliamentary situation was of minimal importance, and where even the murders could be viewed less emotionally, what attracted attention was that Davitt's initiative appeared, his own declarations notwithstanding, to be *both* a revolt against Parnell's leadership *and* a repudiation of the basic tenets of the Land League. This was perhaps unfair, but when Parnell stepped in so adroitly to reaffirm his own commitment to the Land League objectives he contrived at one and the same time to dish Davitt and to make a clear signal to Irish-Americans who might otherwise have been expected to suffer serious qualms about the Kilmainham 'treaty', that he was still what they would have regarded as fundamentally sound at heart.

VI

Whether or not he really was fundamentally sound in that somewhat specialized sense the sequel would reveal. But the Davitt episode was a warning as well as a reprieve. Although firmly in control of the parliamentary party, he could not count upon retaining that control if he allowed the leadership of the popular movement at home to fall into other hands. Although his own desire was to turn away from an open confrontation with the government on the land question, it remained essential to create a substitute for the defunct Land League, which would help in the future not merely to define aims and mobilize opinion, but even perhaps to deliver votes at elections. Hence the hurried summons to Avondale of the old guard of the Land League to plan for a conference to bring the League's successor into being. If we are to believe Davitt – and William O'Brien said the same – Parnell's instinct was to lie low and let the first impact of coercion spend itself. 'I see nothing for it', he said, 'except to "duck" for these three years, and then – ah – resume.' To the chorus of disapproval which this evoked, he merely replied, in his blandest manner, 'I don't intend to go to jail again myself, but I have not the least objection that anybody else should go'.[78]

The conference to establish the new body – to which was given the name, Irish National League – was held in Dublin on 17 October 1882. Delegates to the conference were presented with a draft constitution which was largely the work of Timothy Harrington and T. M. Healy. October was Parnell's 'black month', which he always dreaded, and, sure enough, he fell ill at Morrison's Hotel on the eve of the meeting.* Healy visited him to go through the constitution before it was presented to the conference and lit four candles to work by. Presently, according to Healy's account, one of them guttered and went out, whereupon Parnell sat up in bed and blew out another. 'Why lessen my light?' asked Healy. 'Don't you know', muttered Parnell, 'that nothing is more unlucky than three candles burning? Your constitution of the new League would not have had much success if I allowed you to work with three candles.' He then lay down again and turned his face to the wall.[79]

Weird though this superstition was, and deeply as it impressed Healy, it did nothing to hinder Parnell's effectiveness when the day of the conference dawned. The constitution, as he introduced it, listed five major objectives for the new organization to pursue: national self-

*He was arrested in October 1881 and died in October 1891.

government; land-law reform; local self-government; extension of the parliamentary and municipal franchises; the development and encouragement of the labour and industrial interests of Ireland. Of these, the first was subsumed in the demand for 'the restitution to the Irish people of the right to manage their own affairs in a parliament elected by the people of Ireland'. As for the land, he reiterated the old Land League position that the ultimate goal was that the farmers should own the holdings they cultivated. The party would press also for the transfer to county boards by compulsory purchase of land not cultivated by the owners and not in the occupation of tenants, for resale or reletting to labourers and small farmers in plots or grazing commonage. Tenants' improvements must be protected from attracting heavier rents and this would involve a revision of the 'Healy clause' of the Act of 1881, its effectiveness having been reduced by legal decisions since it was passed. In addition, leaseholders and others excluded from that Act must be brought within its scope.

In political terms, Parnell looked forward to the creation of representative county boards to which would be transferred the fiscal and administrative powers of the grand juries as well as various functions hitherto exercised by other bodies. On the parliamentary level he and his friends would press for the extension of the franchise (as also the municipal franchise) and the adoption of the English system of registration. At that moment, he pointed out, the party numbered only 40, but to be able to press effectively for Home Rule 'we need to return 80 or 90 members . . . and we cannot hope for this until the franchise has been lowered at least as far as the basis of household suffrage'. Aiming next at the working classes, he promised the agricultural labourers legislation for the provision of houses, the abolition of poor rates in respect of such dwellings, and the removal of the old quarter-acre clause from the poor law, so as to entitle them to outdoor relief during illness. For industry he envisaged the appointment of an industrial committee, on which manufacturers, shopkeepers, artisans and farmers should have proportional representation, and whose function it would be to encourage the use and sale of Irish products, especially the development of local and cottage industries.

The structure of the League itself was to be relatively simple. It was to consist of branches and a central council. The council was to consist of 48 members, 32 to be elected by county conventions and 16 by the Irish parliamentary party; the county conventions were themselves to consist of delegates from the branches. The composition of the council represented a compromise between those, for whom

Davitt was the chief spokesman, who wanted a body free from domination by the parliamentarians, and the party representatives, notably T. P. O'Connor, who did not take kindly to the idea of policy being determined by a group from which they were excluded. The sequel was ironic. The council never came into existence, but the organizing committee which had planned the conference instead became the permanent executive organ of the League. From the outset this committee was effectively controlled by the parliamentary party and the stranglehold over the League thus established was never to be broken while Parnell remained in power.[80]

The decisions taken at this conference, as Davitt observed years later, amounted themselves to a veritable 'new departure', marking as they did the transition from the Land League of proto-revolutionary character to a quite different kind of organization which from the beginning was dominated by parliamentarians, preoccupied with parliamentary objectives, and committed to constitutional rather than agrarian agitation. It had indeed a social philosophy, but it was a philosophy which was to be realized by legislation, not by mass-pressure. It would not be unfair to describe October 1882 as the Thermidor of the land war, but it was Davitt who saw most clearly beyond the Thermidorian reaction to the Brumaire that loomed ahead. And he, who perhaps suffered most from this newest 'new departure', may be allowed the last word about it. 'It was, in a sense, the overthrow of a movement and the enthronement of a man; the replacing of nationalism by Parnellism; the investing of the fortunes and guidance of the agitation, both for national self-government and land reform, in a leader's nominal dictatorship.'[81]

CHAPTER 8

Gathering Pace

'It is impossible to hear or read this man without the magnetic feeling that we have here no meteor of a moment, but a man who knows where to lead . . . If it be hero worship to follow such a man as trustfully as a Pillar of Fire, the Irish people are not likely to shrink from the imputation . . .' (*United Ireland*, 24 December 1882.)

I

Although Parnell may have been only half serious when he outraged his young bloods in the autumn of 1882 by suggesting that they should 'duck' for the next three years before resuming their agitation, the period which elapsed between the excitements of 1882 and his own re-emergence at the centre of the political stage in 1885 was almost exactly the three years he had prophesied. Most studies of the man and his times leap from the earlier date to the later and there seems to be a general assumption that the intervening space was filled by 'lost years' during which nothing happened of any great importance. This is far from being true. On the contrary, they were highly significant years in the main task of his life, which was to build a united and disciplined parliamentary party and to use it as the means of enunciating Ireland's claim to Home Rule.

By its very nature this task seemed humdrum compared with the drama of the land war and its sequel. Moreover, although Parnell was much more deeply engaged in it than has often been supposed, there were undoubtedly times when he withdrew from the battle and this is the period when the legend of his inaccessibility first became firmly rooted. It was a legend founded on two kinds of reality. One was his physical condition. Although commentators seldom ventured on a diagnosis of what was wrong with him, and although his frequent indispositions seem to have been much less serious than the grave illness which struck him in the autumn and winter of 1886–7, references to his poor or uncertain health abound. He himself recorded just before the conference that launched the Irish National League in October 1882 that he had had an attack of what the doctor called 'dysenterical diarrhoea', and almost immediately afterwards had to confess to Katharine that the very first time he left his room after this illness he caught a cold.[1] Such ailments, to which he had been liable since childhood, were to recur more and more often in the years ahead.

When they did recur it was Katharine's business to nurse him back to health, which she did repeatedly with a blend of tenderness, competence and anxiety. But here we meet the second reality behind the legend of his aloofness. The frenzied love affair of the previous two years settled, from the end of 1882 onwards, into a routine of domesticity which was to suffer no major interruption for the rest of Parnell's life. The outward sign of this was the birth in 1883 and 1884 of his two daughters, Clare and Katharine (Katie). It is true that when Captain O'Shea divorced his wife in 1890 he claimed that the girls were his, but there is ample evidence to disprove this assertion, which of course he had to make in court to support his case that he had not connived at the relationship between Parnell and Katharine. Even O'Shea's own counsel, Sir Edward Clarke, noted in his memoirs that while his client had 'mistakenly' believed the child who died in 1882 to have been his, the two later daughters were unquestionably Parnell's.[2] Henry Harrison, who became a member of the Irish party in 1890 while still an undergraduate at Balliol, and devoted himself to Katharine's service immediately after Parnell's death, found the two children accepted in the household as Parnell's. And Katharine's eldest daughter, Norah, herself indubitably an O'Shea, wrote in later life of their resemblance to their dead father.[3]

Given these facts and given that Parnell not only passed an increasing amount of time at Eltham but also began the practice of renting houses elsewhere for joint use with Katharine, the question inevitably arises – how did Captain O'Shea react to this developing intimacy between his wife and his leader? To answer this we have to distinguish sharply between the story he told and the evidence he offered in the divorce court, and the situation as it actually existed during these twilight years.

In court, where the case was not contested, it was easy to exhibit him as having acted like a man of honour and Parnell as having behaved with squalid perfidy. The outstanding instance of this, which needs to be examined in some detail because of the damage it did to Parnell's reputation when the affair became public, was the so-called 'fire-escape episode'. Just before Christmas, 1883, Katharine arranged to rent a house in Brighton. Willie, learning of this, came down to examine it and persuaded her to cancel the lease and take a better one close to the sea, No. 8 Medina Terrace. According to Katharine, he and Parnell stayed there together discussing questions of local government, but whereas Willie stayed on over Christmas to be with the children, she went back to Eltham where Parnell joined her. Immediately afterwards she returned to Brighton and Willie went to Ireland, calling again briefly at Medina Terrace on his way to Portugal on business. He later testified in court that while he was at Medina Terrace, Parnell visited there frequently. 'It was never within my knowledge', added the Captain, 'that he slept in the house or visited there in my absence.'[4]

Now, part of the evidence produced in 1890 to show that O'Shea was a grossly deceived husband was given by one Caroline Pethers, hired with the Brighton house to act as cook while Mrs O'Shea was in residence. She identified a photograph of Parnell as someone she knew as Mr Charles Stewart, who nearly always called at the house when Captain O'Shea was away, drove out with Mrs O'Shea in the dark but never in daylight, spent much time with her behind locked doors, and was observed at night by Caroline Pethers and her husband going into the same bedroom with Mrs O'Shea. Asked by counsel if she remembered a particular occasion when O'Shea called while 'Mr Stewart' was in the drawing-room, she replied that she did. She had gone upstairs to light the gas and found the door locked. She heard talk in the room and Mrs O'Shea called to her not to bother about the lamps. At that moment Captain O'Shea rang the front-door bell and Mrs Pethers went to answer it. The Captain went first into the dining-room and then upstairs. Ten minutes later 'Mr Stewart' rang the door-bell and asked to see O'Shea. 'Could he [Parnell] have gone down by the stairs?' asked counsel. 'No', replied the witness, 'there was a balcony outside the drawing-room. There were two fire-escapes hanging from the window.' The unmistakable inference was that this was how Parnell had got out of his awkward predicament; indeed, Mrs Pethers indicated that he had used this device not once but three or four times.[5]

This uncorroborated story by a single witness, based apparently on half-heard conversation and on inference rather than observation, was later severely criticized by Henry Harrison. In his book, *Parnell vindicated*, he pointed out that the cook's story was not open to cross-examination or rebuttal, since Parnell's determination to have a divorce and marry Katharine, *côute que côute*, meant that neither of them was actively represented in court (he not at all, she only by an observer). Had the story been closely investigated its inherent improbability would have been exposed. Parnell, as Harrison points out, would have been much better placed to deal with O'Shea by simply awaiting him in an armchair in the drawing-room, than by clambering down a rope-ladder, which would have been both an athletic and a time-consuming performance. Moreover, both the time of day and the exposed situation of the house made it extremely unlikely that Parnell could have achieved this feat 'three or four times' without discovery. As Harrison puts it succinctly: 'The spectacle of a bearded Romeo hurriedly descending by a rope ladder, during afternoon calling-hours, in the presence of a Junoesque Juliet standing by to remove the apparatus of flight, could scarcely be counted upon to escape all eyes at the moment or to be spared the picturesque repetition of the eye-witnesses' accounts thereafter. There can be but one answer to the question. On the given assumptions, no sane man would have considered the fire-escape a practical resort. Least of all a man, proud and practical, like Parnell.'[6]

The episode then, though not necessarily and absolutely the 'large lie' which Harrison calls it – it could have happened once in twilight and escaped notice, and it was, *pace* Harrison, by no means incompatible with Parnell's penchant for vigorous action in a crisis – seems retrospectively to have been either inflated or invented. What is not in question is that the course of triangular true love did not run smooth thereafter and in 1884 – to go no further, for the present – certain rumours apparently reached the Captain's reluctant ears. Accordingly, on 4 August he wrote to Parnell as follows:[7]

> You have behaved very badly to me. While I have often told you that you were welcome to stay at Eltham whenever I was there, I begged of you not to do so during my absence, since it would be sure at the least, sooner or later, to cause a scandal. I am making arrangements with a view to taking my family abroad for a long time, and I hope that they will be sufficiently advanced to allow of my asking for the Chiltern Hundreds before the end of the session.

To this Parnell replied three days later in his most unyielding manner, 'I do not know of any scandal, or any ground for one, and can only suppose that you have misunderstood the drift of some statements that may have been made about me.' Nor did he attempt to dissuade the Captain from resigning, merely observing that the most convenient time would be just before the end of the session, so that the election could be held in the recess. It so happened that on that same day Katharine, who was then six months pregnant, wrote to her Willie referring to an evidently disagreeable conversation they had had a few days earlier and telling him that she did not feel strong enough to travel up to town in the heat for a further meeting.[8] Apart from the coldness of its tone, this letter is interesting because it helps to establish that

O'Shea met his wife at a time when, to the eye of one who knew her well enough to penetrate even the reticences of late Victorian clothing, she was plainly carrying a child. From this fact only one of two conclusions can be drawn. Either, O'Shea was still on such terms of intimacy with his wife that he could believe this child to be his, as he had perhaps believed Claude Sophie to be his in 1882 – a supposition which, given the closeness of the relationship between Parnell and Katharine, is so inherently improbable as to be unacceptable. Or else O'Shea was well aware of what was in progress, in which case his protest of August 1884 was made not against the fact of the liaison, but against the risk of public discovery that the lovers were running. For public discovery could only mean that the injured husband would have to take public action, and this action once taken he must bid farewell to the two inducements which made silence seem golden – the political advancement he still hoped for from Parnell and a share in the fortune he expected Katharine to inherit from her aged aunt.

Public discovery was to be avoided for several years yet, but the incidents of 1883 and 1884 ominously indicate the extent to which Parnell was having to devote time and energy to burying his private life from the eyes of the curious. Even more than that they indicate that his obsession with Katharine was beginning to interfere with the performance of his duty as leader. A few years later, T. P. O'Connor recalled the extreme difficulty he and his friends had to get Parnell to go down from Dublin to a banquet given by his own constituents in Cork just at this time.[9] They could only guess at what magnet was pulling him back to England, but it is clear from one of Parnell's letters to Katharine that the reason why he almost threw over the Cork engagement was that he was in a fever of anxiety because on one of the few occasions in their whole time together she had recently expressed doubts about his conduct.[10] In the end, having with an ill grace agreed to go, he spent barely two hours in Cork before returning by the night-mail to Dublin and thence to Eltham.

II

It would be quite wrong, though, to assume that because these domestic preoccupations were becoming more insistent, they had displaced politics from their central position in his life. A few years later this was arguably to be the case, but between 1883 and 1885 Parnell had three main tasks, each of which required stamina, tenacity and detailed attention. First, he had to restore his position in the country, but to do this in such a way that the loss of the irreconcilable left would be balanced by the accretion of compensating power on the right. Next, he had to strengthen his existing parliamentary group to prepare the way for the creation of a much larger and more efficient force at the next election. And finally, given his commitment to constitutional action, he had to try to manipulate the political situation at Westminster to carve out a special role for his own 'third party' in a system where most of the rules and conventions assumed that the parliamentary norm was a polarity between Liberals and Conservatives.

The creation of the Irish National League had been a vital preliminary to the first of these objectives, but two other, almost fortuitous, events helped him further towards the same goal. One was that, at the beginning of the 1883 session of parliament, Forster used the fact that the Phoenix Park murderers had recently been brought to trial to accuse Parnell of what was in effect complicity in Irish crime. It was Parnell, charged Forster, who 'more than any other derived advantage and power' from the 'systematic boycotting' out of which had come terrorism and violence. 'I will repeat again', he said, 'what the charge is which I make against him . . . It is not that he himself directly planned or perpetrated outrages or murders; but that he either connived at them or when warned – '. Here Parnell called out 'It is a lie'. The cry was at once taken up by James O'Kelly, who created such an uproar that he had to be suspended. Only then was Forster able to deliver his final thrust. 'Those miserable wretches who planned the murders in Dublin, they took not, indeed, the letter of the Hon. Member's advice, but what seemed to them its spirit.'[11]

When Forster had ended there were loud demands that Parnell should reply, but he sat silent and impassive. That night, however, back at Eltham with Katharine, he showed, she says, 'a fierce joy' at what he at once recognized to be a fatal *faux pas* by the ex-Chief Secretary. Forster, by attacking Parnell for criminality, was in effect writing him the testimonial best calculated to regain the esteem and confidence of the restive left wing in Ireland and America.[12] Yet he was at first reluctant to take advantage of the opening – perhaps, as more than once in his career, because pride inhibited self-defence – until urged to do so by his party. When he did speak the following day he made one of the most effective interventions of his whole parliamentary career. As always with him, the best weapon was counter-attack and seldom, if ever, did he use it so effectively. With the cold scorn that the House had already come to know so well, he swept aside the notion that he had to justify himself before an English public opinion from which, he said, he had nothing to hope. 'I have been accustomed during my political life to rely upon the public opinion of those whom I have desired to help . . . and the utmost I desire to do in the very few words I shall address to the House is to make my position clear to the Irish people at home and abroad.' The way he chose to do this was to meet contempt with contempt, invective with invective, brutality with brutality. Forster's revelation of cabinet secrets relating to Kilmainham he compared with the treachery of James Carey, the informer who had sprung the trap on the Invincibles. The suggestion of any link between him and the assassins he rejected with frigid finality. He condemned the 'torrent of prejudice' which the murder trials had released in England. He asked sarcastically why Forster 'who, according to his own account knew everything, although he was invariably wrong' had been deposed. Ought he not to be sent back forthwith to help Spencer 'in the congenial work of the gallows'? 'The time will come', he warned, 'when this House and the people of this country will admit once again that they have been mistaken . . . that they have been led astray as to the right method of governing a noble, a generous, a brave, an impulsive people; and they will reject their present leaders . . . with just as much determination as they rejected the services of the Rt. Hon. gentleman the Member for Bradford.'[13]

From Parnell's own viewpoint this episode could not have happened at a better time. In the middle of the previous December the Irish newspapers had carried a laconic but shattering announcement – that the Irish leader had filed a petition in the Landed Estates Court for the sale of all his Wicklow property. The petition had been filed the previous November but it was not until February 1883 that an order for sale was made, when the charges on the property had mounted to £18,000 in mortgages and an annuity of £100 p.a. payable to Parnell's sister, Emily Dickinson.[14] This was to be the signal for an extraordinary outburst of emotion. The way for it was prepared, characteristically, by William O'Brien in *United Ireland*. Seizing upon a remark Parnell had made in Cork, to the effect that he regarded his time in parliament as 'seven years' hard labour', O'Brien burst into the paean of praise part of which has been quoted at the head of this chapter. 'High above the tumult and doubts of the moment rises that serene figure', he wrote. 'If he can look back upon seven years of anxious trial with complacency, the Irish people can look back with triumph and gratitude. If his keen eyes can discern no difficulty in the future that prudence and pluck and tenacity cannot overcome, into that future the Irish nation plunges with all the fervour of its soul at its command.'[15]

It was not immediately clear that this plunge would extend to the actual disbursement of hard cash, or that the country as a whole would take the hint dropped by a friendly priest at the October conference which had launched the Irish National League, that those who had served the country well were entitled to some reward.[16] In the neighbourhood of Avondale, however, the immediate effect of Forster's attack was to give point and substance to the idea of a national testimonial. Within a few days of the scene in the House of Commons, the Avoca branch of the Irish National League formally resolved that 'in order to manifest our undying admiration of Mr Parnell, we propose to open a subscription list for the purpose of clearing off the inherited mortgage on his estate'.[17] Even so, it was by no means a foregone conclusion that what Avoca thought today, the rest of Ireland would think tomorrow, and Parnell himself was apparently anxious to scotch the notion as quickly as possible. Writing to the American Land League, where the same idea had been mooted, he rejected their offer of help quite categorically, adding: 'I could not on any account, even if the circumstances were otherwise, consent to accept the kind proposals which have been made by friends in Ireland of a similar nature to your own; much less could I permit a collection to be made in America.'[18]

Vowing he would ne'er consent, he nevertheless consented. The chief agent in this remarkable transformation seems to have been the Archbishop of Cashel, Dr Croke, whose intervention, though doubtless benevolent, owed something to a human, if unarchiepiscopal, desire to score points off his brother of Dublin. Archbishop McCabe, or Cardinal McCabe as he became in March 1882, was bent upon steering the Irish clergy away from political involvement, a course of action warmly endorsed by Pope Leo XIII.[19] Dr Croke, so far from feeling himself bound by this prohibition, gave his active and influential support to William O'Brien when he successfully contested a by-election at Mallow in 1883. This earned him a reprimand from the Pope, and although the archbishop apologized effusively to His Holiness, he compounded his offence by supporting a firm Parnellite for the Tipperary seat vacated by John Dillon and followed this by a letter to the press on St Patrick's Day, 1883, enthusiastically approving the Parnell testimonial and, final flourish, enclosing his cheque for £50.[20]

From that moment the testimonial rolled forward irresistibly. A committee was formed, the *Freeman's Journal* guaranteed publicity, other bishops rallied round and the money began to flow in from Irishmen at home, in Britain and in America. If further stimulus were needed, it was provided in May by an inept circular from Rome condemning the testimonial outright. 'It cannot be tolerated that any ecclesiastic, much less a bishop, should take any part whatever in recommending or promoting it.' The circular was the work of Cardinal Simeoni, prompted by the Irish 'Whig' MP, George Errington, who at this period acted as a more or less unofficial agent for the Foreign Office at the Vatican. The Irish reaction was entirely predictable. On all sides there was an upsurge of bitter resentment against what was seen as a blundering and insensitive interference by Rome in a purely Irish matter and the testimonial fund benefited accordingly.[21]

By the end of 1883, with nearly £40,000 collected, the moment was ripe to celebrate the occasion at a banquet in Dublin, though it was not until January 1885 that Parnell's solicitor moved for an order dismissing the original petition and returning the title-deeds to their owner.[22] Beforehand, the Lord Mayor and a group of distinguished citizens called on Parnell at Morrison's Hotel to present him with a cheque. There followed a most curious incident. The Lord Mayor had come prepared with the hyperbolical speech usual on such occasions, but had scarcely opened his mouth when Parnell said abruptly: 'I believe you have got a cheque for me.' The Lord Mayor, somewhat taken aback, said that he had and addressed himself once more to his oration, only to be interrupted a second time. 'Is it made payable to order and crossed?' asked Parnell. Again the Lord Mayor said yes, but before he could launch into his encomium Parnell took the cheque from him, folded it and put it in his waistcoat pocket. The interview ended there and then and the Lord Mayor never was delivered of his speech.[23] Nor did the banquet go any better. Parnell chose to confine his remarks almost entirely to the political situation. All that he said to the expectant audience, and to the expectant nation outside, in return for this great outpouring of trust and affection were two cold sentences: 'I don't know how adequately to express my feelings with regard not only to your lordship's address, not only to the address to the Parnell National Tribute, but also with regard to the magnificent demonstration. I prefer to leave to the historian the description of tonight and the expression of opinion as regards the result which tonight must produce.'[24] As Sexton whispered to Tim Healy, 'a labourer would acknowledge the loan of a pen-knife more gratefully'.[25]

It would be wrong, however, to assume that the apparent boorishness which Parnell exhibited on both occasions was due simply to ingratitude or to bad manners. Normally, as nearly all accounts agree, he was a man of almost ostentatious courtesy, most sensitive to kindnesses done to him by others. What he seems to have been exhibiting at this critical moment were two other characteristics, each fundamental to him and together an important part of the magic he so often worked with his fellow-countrymen. He was exhibiting his pride and his dedication to politics. Reticent about his private affairs to an extreme degree, the mere business of receiving a gift of money to set right his financial position can only have been deeply humiliating to him, and his clipped remarks to the Lord Mayor and to the Rotunda audience were almost certainly the reaction of a highly embarrassed man. At the same time, his instinct was to make the maximum political capital out of the event, and this was why he laid bare, with his usual dispassionate clarity, the political significance, not merely of the tribute itself, but of the fact that it had been collected in the face of papal censure. It represented, in short, less a form of outdoor relief for the landlord than a massive vote of confidence to the politician in the way he was going; for him this was of greater importance than personal considerations of any kind whatever.

III

But what way was he going? Several events of that same year, 1883, indicated the direction clearly enough. Perhaps the most significant of these was the clarification of his attitude towards Irish-American support. In 1883, and scarcely less so in 1884, it was the more imperative for him to make his position unequivocally plain because of the wave of dynamite outrages which hit England, mainly London, during those years. That these were the work of a minority group of terrorists, who were repudiated by many Irish-Americans, was a refinement which British opinion could scarcely be expected to grasp, and it was therefore essential for Parnell to dissociate himself as emphatically as he could from such acts of violence. The fact that at this time he became the target for extremist Irish-American vituperation, especially the brand purveyed by Patrick Ford's *Irish World*, indicates the extent of his success. On the other hand, his task was complicated by the fact that some of those with whom he had worked in the past – notably in the Clan na Gael – were by no means as detached from dynamitism as he was. The further difficulty, that the Irish-Americans were fiercely divided by personal feuds – especially the quarrel between Devoy on the one hand, and Alexander Sullivan and his two Clan associates (known collectively as The Triangle) on the other – and by differing loyalties in the wider arena of American politics, made it very hard to build a firm alliance with any section.

The main objective was a reorganization of Irish-American resources, to be achieved by the winding up of the American Land League and the creation of a new body, analogous to the Irish National League, which could attract the loyalty and the subscriptions of a wide spectrum of supporters. At first it seems to have been Parnell's idea to go to America and see to things himself.[26] However, he soon abandoned this, probably because it was impossible to foretell what might happen at the convention summoned to launch the proposed Irish National League of America. Instead he sent an anodyne cable. 'I would advise that a platform be so framed as to enable us to continue to accept help from America, and to avoid offering any pretext to British government for entirely suppressing the national movement in Ireland . . .'[27]

This, though vague, was aimed unmistakably at the moderate Irish-Americans who were heavily represented at the Philadelphia convention that met on 26 April to set up the new League. Yet, from Parnell's standpoint, the result was disappointing. Clan na Gael influence proved so decisive that not only was Alexander Sullivan elected president, but he and his friends dominated the executive committee. A report drawn up for the cabinet early in 1885, almost certainly based on information supplied by the spy, Le Caron, claimed that secret discussions at the convention had endorsed the dynamite policy, though care was to be taken that the Clan should not be *publicly* identified with it. Members of the Clan were also to be encouraged to infiltrate the Irish National League of America.[28] Perhaps because of this ambiguity in its origins the League contributed relatively little, either in influence or in money, to the Parnellite cause. Irish-American subscriptions to the home organization amounted only to £2000 in 1883 and just over £3000 in 1884.[29] And for the purely parliamentary purposes of the Irish party, the American League had subscribed by August 1884 a mere five thousand dollars.[30] No doubt this was partly due to the slowing of the political tempo after Kilmainham, but the fact remains that when in 1885 subscriptions began to flow in again more freely in response to a changed situation, they came mainly from Irish-Americans – for example, the so-called Hoffman House Committee – who dissociated themselves from the turbulence of the League. These funds, besides being vital to the maintenance and enlargement of Parnell's party at Westminster (the Hoffman House Committee alone contributed 150,000 dollars between November 1885 and August 1886), demonstrated conclusively the wisdom of his decision to stand apart from the faction-fighting of the Clan na Gael.[31]

IV

This was the more necessary because of the consolidation of forces he was simultaneously aiming at in Ireland. Here there were two main problems – to increase the size and stature of the parliamentary party and to convince the more conservative elements of Irish nationalism that Kilmainham really did mark a turning away from the violence of the land war, and still more from the excesses of the secret societies, towards an open and effective constitutional movement. As for the first of these problems, it was almost a case of *solvitur ambulando* – that is, of taking advantage of each successive by-election to tighten his grip upon the constituencies. The most spectacular example of this process was at Monaghan where the party put up one of their ablest members, Tim Healy, as a candidate. Parnell came in person to fight for Healy. This was already a rare thing for him to do, and it was rarer still for him to speak in Ulster, though Monaghan hardly deserved his description of it as 'the remote north'. The contest mainly revolved round the Land Act of 1881, since, regardless of religion or politics, the Ulster tenants stood to gain as much as anyone else from an extension of the purchase clauses and the inclusion of leaseholders within the terms of the Act. Healy won narrowly and Parnell was moved from his usual impassiveness to something near jubilation, though it is difficult to be sure whether this was because the result would, as he told a reporter, 'teach the Ulster Orangemen a lesson', or because it represented a triumph over the unlucky number thirteen. Both the reporter and the successful candidate recorded later in their memoirs the scene that Parnell created in the country hotel at Castleblayney on being assigned the best bedroom which happened to be numbered thirteen. To placate him Healy moved into it instead, disregarding his chief's warning that this would lose him the election. He did in fact suffer two minor injuries – the window sash fell on his hand and a cork from a soda-water bottle hit him in the eye – but although Parnell observed these mishaps with a Cassandra-like complacency, Healy's 300 votes margin gave him the last laugh. To the end of his days he remembered how they drove together round the constituency after the result had been declared and how at every cross-roads Parnell shouted to the onlookers 'Healy, Healy, Healy'.[32]

Monaghan was exceptional because at that time it was still *terra incognita* for the Parnellites, but elsewhere their successes were more predictable. By the end of 1883, Parnellite candidates had won, in addition to Monaghan, Mallow, Westmeath, Wexford county, Tipperary, Wexford city and Sligo. 'Next to Mr Gladstone', wrote a perceptive commentator, 'he [Parnell] is the man whom everybody wants to see . . . He is recognized as the depository of an enormous present power, and of an indefinitely enlarged one after a general election.'[33] An important element in that power was the growing co-operation of the bishops and clergy. A striking example of this occurred in Meath early in February 1884, when the bishop, the redoubtable Dr Thomas Nulty, wrote to his priests and curates informing them that the Lord Mayor of Dublin had consented to stand 'at the special request of Mr Parnell and with my humble but cordial approval'. True, Dr Nulty was careful to add that 'in *suggesting* a member for Meath, Mr Parnell fully recognizes the privilege of choosing its own representative as belonging of *right* to the electors . . .', but he would have been a bold elector who would have ignored both the bishop *and* Parnell.[34] Victory in Meath resulted as a matter of course and when that in turn was followed by the election of a staunch supporter, John Deasy, to be Parnell's partner in Cork city, there seemed to be no resisting the new wave.[35]

Not every constituency, admittedly, was disposed to accept this degree of dictation from the centre, with or without ecclesiastical connivance. But Parnell was beginning to feel strong enough to dispense with kid gloves when dealing with political nonconformists. Belfast was a striking case in point. In the summer of 1884 he was invited to attend a convention there, to which various INL branches in Ulster were to send delegates. Among the resolutions to be moved, two struck him immediately as objectionable – one because it seemed to raise the old spectre of land nationalization, the other because, by calling on the organizing committee of the League to summon conventions in every county, it appeared to arrogate to the Belfast meeting the work of the central authority and thus to be in effect a criticism of that authority. He demanded their withdrawal, but the local committee, while agreeing to drop the land resolution, clung to their demand for county conventions. This produced a rebuke of magisterial severity:

I regret [wrote Parnell] that I can only regard that portion of the resolution to which I drew your attention as an indirect censure upon the organizing committee, and I believe it would be regarded by the country generally as such. I also think that it might be a matter for consideration by your committee whether it quite becomes them, living in a city where neither the present Coercion Act nor previous ones have ever been enforced, to appear to prescribe to the rest of Ireland the pace at which the movement is to proceed, and to stimulate others to action, the peril of which they will not be in a position to share.

Not unnaturally this evoked a resentful reply – to which Parnell paid no attention whatever. Instead, he simply wrote to the other Ulster branches asking them not to send delegates to the convention. The convention then collapsed.[36]

There was a double moral to be drawn from this obscure episode. The obvious one was that Parnell, being leader, intended to lead. The other was that the skeleton created in October 1882 was badly in need of flesh and blood. The constituencies could not be left to their own devices, yet Parnell, on his own admission at the end of 1884, had not addressed any county meetings since the suppression of the Land League three years previously.[37] Consequently, from early in 1883 onwards he began to receive increasingly emphatic signals that in the absence of proper guidance the constituencies, without necessarily intending disloyalty, would stray in diverse directions. Thus in February there came from Mayo the hair-raising suggestion that the constituency should elect a member pledged not to take his seat at Westminster. Galvanized by this resurrection of the 'secession' plan he had defeated in 1881, Parnell wrote a stern letter reprobating a policy which would merely be tantamount to the loss of a seat and reminding the local enthusiasts that such grave matters fell to be decided by the party as a whole, not by individual constituencies. But he used the occasion to suggest an alternative solution, which was to return a man pledged to work with the party, the county undertaking to pay his expenses while on duty in London. At this stage he had not thought the problem through and was still against the creation of some central parliamentary fund for the payment of members' salaries. He preferred, he said, the experiment of local subventions then being tried in Queen's county and elsewhere. These need not be extravagantly high, but some support there would have to be, otherwise, 'I certainly should not continue to ask members to place themselves in a false position by undertaking duties which they are not financially able to carry out, and I should be obliged to consider on my own part whether I could persevere with the thankless task of endeavouring to keep together an independent Irish party'.[38]

The sequel was not encouraging. Queen's county, which had aspired to raise £1000 to be divided between its two members, was only able to find half that amount and it was clear that something more reliable and systematic would be needed if the party were to grow as Parnell wanted it.[39] If this was true of finance, it was no less true of discipline.

A few months after his brush with Mayo, Parnell's old friends of the Wexford Independent Club gave him a piece of advice which was to have a notable future. It was, they said, 'absolutely indispensable' that candidates in the various constituencies should not only declare their support for Parnell's leadership, but should pledge themselves to vote with the Irish party on all occasions when the majority decided that the party should act in unison.[40] This idea, which was to be crucial to the emergence of Parnell's followers as a disciplined force in the House of Commons, was slow to develop but by the beginning of 1885 three instances had been reported. Richard Power in Waterford, J. J. Clancy in Dublin and John O'Connor in Tipperary – all had pledged themselves to sit, act and vote with the parliamentary party.[41]

The last of these cases, that of O'Connor, illustrated that all was not yet plain sailing and that some constituencies could still bridle at what seemed to them undue pressure from outside. When the vacancy in Tipperary fell due Parnell wrote to Archbishop Croke to ask if he had a candidate in mind.[42] The question itself is an interesting indication of how closely Parnell was prepared to work with a 'sympathetic' cleric, and when he and Croke agreed on O'Connor, it would have been natural to assume that the job was done. But when a convention met at Thurles, supposedly to ratify their choice, it 'bolted' and refused to accept him. Parnell, however, made short work of this mutiny. Summoning a second convention, he went down in person to preside and not only carried his man, but persuaded the previously selected candidate to make a public withdrawal. Since the selection proceedings were in private, we do not know the kind of pressure he brought to bear, though he was reported as saying that he had only put up O'Connor in the absence of a suitable local man. 'He did not claim the right to dictate to any constituency; but they [he and his colleagues] claimed . . . that they were entitled to the trust and confidence of the people.' This was indeed the safest line for him to take, that a vote for his candidate was a vote of confidence in him as leader, but the gloss put upon his words by the friendly *Nation* – 'Mr Parnell, of course, easily showed that he had in no way dictated to the constituency' – may have seemed to some readers, and not only in Tipperary, singularly unconvincing.[43]

V

The Tipperary incident was revealing, not only of the dangers of neglecting grass-roots opinion in the way that Parnell had been doing, but also because it illustrated the distance he had already come in his realization of the necessity of working closely with the church. The strong national reaction against the papal letter condemning the Parnell Testimonial had marked an important advance for him, but there was still a lot of ground to make up and from that moment onwards he made strenuous efforts to achieve the 'respectability' he needed if he was to win support, not just from the bishops, but from the parish clergy whose influence in the constituencies could be decisive. Two things in particular were involved here.

The first was that the Irish party should be seen to steer rigorously clear of those English Radicals whose views, especially on religion and education, did not commend them to Irish piety. This policy of decontamination was presently to claim some eminent victims, but its most immediate manifestation was a sharp reversal of Parnell's own conduct towards the 'atheist', Charles Bradlaugh. The support he had given Bradlaugh in 1880, in the teeth of Irish opinion, was abruptly withdrawn in 1883 when Gladstone's Affirmation Bill, to enable Bradlaugh to occupy his seat by 'affirming' rather than taking the oath, had provoked anti-Bradlaugh petitions, signed by every Catholic bishop in England and Ireland. Since there is no reason to suppose that Parnell himself had undergone any spiritual crisis in the interval, we may assume that his action was entirely tactical. To vote against the Affirmation Bill was probably repugnant to him as an independent-minded, free-thinking individual, but as a politician seeking to consolidate the forces of the right in his own country he could scarcely avoid it.[44]

The second stage on his journey towards respectability was that Parnell, as a Protestant, would have to identify himself positively with those causes which were most relevant to the needs and desires of Irish Catholicism. Yet, precisely because he was a Protestant, any unilateral steps he might take in this direction were liable to be interpreted as the impertinent interventions of an outsider. To some extent, no doubt, this is exactly what they were and it is difficult not to sympathize with the disgruntlement of that keen ecclesiastical politician, Dr W. J. Walsh, then President of Maynooth, when he contrasted the opportunism of Parnell with the slackness of the old-style Home Rulers. The occasion was the annual vote for the Queen's Colleges in August 1883. The Colleges, being ostensibly interdenominational, were a perennial bugbear to the hierarchy and it was normally expected that the Irish party would bestir itself in criticism whenever the estimates came round. Yet, despite a resolution by the bishops and the dispatch of letters to individual members, the Catholic representatives were conspicuously absent when the moment of debate arrived. 'So far as I know', wrote Walsh to Cardinal McCabe, 'Parnell was not spoken to or communicated with, at all. I carefully avoided meeting him . . . Yet, with his usual skill, he seized the opportunity and in the absence of everyone else (except Colonel Colthurst) made a Parnellite stand against the Queen's Colleges. This is the sort of thing that is throwing the whole country into the hands of him and his followers.'[45]

It was significant that such a letter could still be written in February 1884, nearly a year after the papal letter on the Parnell Testimonial had created a revulsion of feeling in his favour. That movement of opinion was something of which the bishops clearly had to take account, but the new situation which was emerging left them, naturally enough, hesitant and confused. They found it difficult to believe that the leopard really had changed his spots. So did others. In May 1884 the Irish 'Whig', Henry Bellingham, a Catholic gentleman of the old school, wrote to Cardinal McCabe in a state of shock that 'at a regular meeting of the Parnellite party attended only by the extreme members', Parnell had been deputed to ask the Prime Minister a parliamentary question about the 'spoliation' of papal property by the Italian government. 'For my part I regret to see any question so purely Catholic brought before the House of Commons by Parnell who is both a Protestant and very much disliked by the majority of members which will invariably prejudice them.'[46] This particular peril seems to have been averted by that devout Catholic, F. H. O'Donnell, asking the question himself, but that did not dispose of the central problem, which was that if Parnell really was well on the way to becoming a responsible leader with wide support at home, ought not the bishops to reconsider their attitude towards him?[47] Dr Higgins, Bishop of Kerry, was admittedly no politician, but he may stand as the very embodiment of the perplexity of the hierarchy when confronted by an Irish party which was apparently undergoing some mysterious transformation. Like most bishops, he was much exercised over the problem of education. Dimly, he was groping his way towards the notion that the Liberal government, which seemed to him 'very much in the hands of the Irish party', might be brought by that fact to recognize 'the intrinsic merits' of the Catholic case, even though it remained difficult for the bishops to interfere directly. In March 1884 he put his naïve views on paper in a letter whose erratic punctuation and syntax reflect his agitation:[48]

Once we take a position, it seems to me, we must bring our influence to bear thro' the government or thro' the representatives. If the former; first: such a position towards a government in actual incessant conflict with the Irish party, will be likely to embroil us with, or at least to make us a neutral party towards, the Nat. Party: and to be neutral in the circumstances, will be easily read, *to be hostile*, in the eyes of the people. Then, if the government deal with us, they will have their *quid pro quo*: they will have pronouncements on the agitation: or the public will be led to suspect secret relations in that sense. No one would like to run such a risk.

It was all very difficult. The more so because, as Dr Higgins pointed out, there was an equal risk in the episcopate committing itself to any Irish party that was likely to be returned to parliament 'before the present excitement has cooled down to the temperate degree'. At this point he became more disjointed than ever, but what he seemed to be saying was that if the bishops 'let well alone' until the temperature did drop, they would be rewarded by the emergence of a moderate, by implication non-Parnellite, party. The reason he gave for this wishful thinking is particularly interesting in the light of subsequent events:

Mr Parnell has by promises [? won] himself a more perfect dictatorship, because he can calculate on a larger number of MPs ostensibly pledged to his programme. It strikes me, that power of contradiction and self-assertion, as well as capacity of corruption, will increase in more proportion to the increase of the numbers of his party. In the sense that I have no desire to see the landlord and Protestant tyranny merely giving place to another tyranny, as complete, as galling, and, *in the long run*, as injurious to the country, I am glad to be able to look to such a result as the only chance for freedom in Ireland.

Other bishops, however, were more tough-minded and during 1884 the hierarchy moved towards a highly important decision. By March of that year, Dr Woodlock was instructed to circularize the Parnellite MPs asking them to do battle, this time officially, on the estimates for the Queen's Colleges. Once this gnat had been swallowed, the hierarchy did not strain at the gigantic camel of entrusting the care of Irish educational interests as a whole to the Irish party. That was done by resolution of the bishops at a meeting on 1 October and it produced from Parnell a letter which, despite its carefully deferential tone, revealed clearly enough the importance he attached to this prize. 'I need scarcely say', he wrote, 'how highly my colleagues and I value the mark of confidence in us which the resolutions of the hierarchy convey.'[49] No one, indeed, needed to be told the significance of what had happened.

The hierarchy had committed itself to definite, if limited, approval of the party and the *Nation* quickly drew the appropriate conclusion. 'This much is a triumph for the national leaders the greatness of which can hardly be exaggerated.'[50]

Before long the party began to reap practical benefits from this turn of events, a process greatly helped by the death of Cardinal McCabe in February 1885.[51] His successor, William J. Walsh, was a man of very different stamp. He came to the archbishopric from the Presidency of Maynooth, where he had been an outstanding success. An intellectual of the most diverse talents and a natural leader, he early established an ascendancy over his fellow-bishops, most of whom responded by making him the repository for all their confidences and worries. He was a firm nationalist, not in the flamboyant manner of the Archbishop of Cashel – Walsh would never be loved as Croke was – but with a level-headed appreciation of tactical possibilities that at times brought him close to Parnell. At other times, as we shall see, clashes of personality between these two inflexible characters were liable to produce severe tensions between the hierarchy and the party. But at the moment of his accession Walsh was welcomed with open arms by the Parnellites, not least because of their well-founded suspicions that the British government had made representations at Rome to prevent his appointment.[52]

Archbishop Walsh's elevation could not have occurred at a more critical juncture. With a general election on a wider franchise imminent, it was urgently necessary for Parnell to organize the constituencies much more comprehensively than before. In practice this meant that he would have to accede to the growing pressure for some system of county conventions to help to select candidates and to ensure that the nationalist vote would be mobilized when needed. The original constitution of the League had provided for county conventions to elect delegates to the central council. Since that body had never met it was decided by the organizing committee of the League to use the conventions for the selection of parliamentary candidates. They were to consist of four delegates from each branch of the INL in the county, along with any of the Catholic clergy of the county who wished to attend, and two or three representatives of the parliamentary party. The model, on which numerous other county conventions were to be based, was the meeting held at Wicklow in October 1885. Parnell took the chair, Timothy Harrington (the League secretary) read out the 'Rules for the guidance of county conventions' and the clergy were present in considerable numbers. They too had rules for their guidance, not made public but provided for them by Archbishop Walsh himself. No closer identification of the church with the party had yet been made.[53]

The 32 conventions which were held in connection with the 1885 election averaged some 150 laymen and 50 priests each. They met generally at a hotel in the county town and went into private session under the chairmanship of an MP. Assuming all went well and a candidate was selected without difficulty, a public meeting was then held, usually with a priest in the chair; city conventions operated in the same way and with much the same membership, reinforced by nationalists from the local corporations. But in reality, in 1885 at least, the essential part of the selection process – the preliminary sifting of candidates – was done by an inner caucus consisting of ten or a dozen MPs meeting at Morrison's Hotel and dominated by Parnell himself. It is fairly clear from the results of the conventions that the MPs duly instructed by the caucus, and often themselves members of it, kept tight control over the constituencies. Here and there signs of revolt did occasionally surface, but it was usually enough for Parnell to appear in person for opposition to collapse. Undoubtedly the most important commitment entered into by a successful candidate, and to which he had to give his written assent before nomination – was the party pledge. In and after 1885 it was required in principle of all candidates – though there was to be one notorious exception in 1886 – and the essence of the undertaking was that the candidate pledged himself, if elected, to 'sit, act and vote with the Irish parliamentary party'. In addition, the candidate promised to resign his seat if at a specially convened meeting a majority of the whole party decided that he had not fulfilled the pledge.[54] So far had the party travelled from the gentlemanly anarchy of Butt's day, so quickly had it arrived at the discipline and unity which made it, for a few brief years, the wonder of the political world.

VI

Machinery, though important, was only the means to an end which had yet to be defined. But here we meet a paradox. Between the Kilmainham 'treaty' and the downfall of the Liberal government in the summer of 1885, Parnell's authority over his party and in the House of Commons undeniably increased, yet this increase was not reflected, with one major exception, in the Irish legislation of those years. Indeed, it would be difficult to identify anything of real significance relating solely to Ireland which had been won by the parliamentary efforts of himself and his colleagues. His status, his influence, his mastery depended on something quite different, something that was still in the future but was felt on all sides to be approaching inexorably – the assumption that at the next general election, whether the franchise was widened or not, he would come back at the head of a much larger and more homogeneous party, and would thus be poised to threaten the flank of whatever government came to power.

British politicians reacted to this gathering cloud in different ways, but whether Whig or Radical, orthodox Tory or 'fourth party' Tory, all had to pay close attention to what Parnell was actually saying and where he might conceivably be going. Since this was a period during which he said little, the task of divining his intentions was difficult, producing exasperation in some quarters, bewilderment in others, and frequently both together. Nevertheless, his infrequent but carefully phrased speeches do yield unmistakable evidence of the direction in which he was cautiously moving. Several themes recur, though only one is dominant. But first there is an important negative point to be made. This is that his utterances were marked by a decisive turning away from the land agitation. As early as December 1882 he almost casually threw overboard the 'No Rent' manifesto, in which, he now admitted, he had never been a believer. 'I never supposed that the policy of "no rent" would do more than effect good indirectly in enabling tenants to obtain large abatements from the landlords under pressure of the threat to pay no rent.'[55] Thereafter, he spoke at no county meetings in Ireland for more than two years and, although he did continue to press at Westminster for changes in the law, it was clear that he had little now to say to his fellow-countrymen on the subject.

His one major contribution to the debate was essentially destructive, when in Drogheda, in April 1884, he hit out vigorously at Davitt's twin panaceas of land nationalization and of a wonder-working alliance between the 'democracy' of Britain and Ireland. For the latter concept he had only pity tinged with derision. 'We are told', he said, 'of some great wave of English democracy which is now to come over here to Ireland and assist the Irish democracy. Well, I do not believe in the English democracy. The poor Irish democracy will have, I fear, to rely upon themselves in the future, as they have had to do up to this moment.' As for land nationalization, he disliked it just as much in 1884 as he had done in 1882, both for itself and as a source of disunion. For him, he proclaimed, the original objectives of the Land League remained paramount. 'The desire to acquire land', he pointed out, 'is everywhere one of the strongest instincts of human nature and that instinct is never stronger and never more developed than in a country such as Ireland, where land is limited and those who desire to acquire it are numerous . . .' The answer was still the old answer – the abolition of landlordism – but it was characteristic of his shift away from agrarianism *per se* that he now tended to speak of this familiar goal in essentially political terms. Condemning both the Repeal movement of O'Connell's time, and the earlier Home Rule agitation under Butt on the ground that they had engaged in 'the perfectly futile attempt' to conciliate the landlords, he insisted that they must be got rid of if a determined drive for self-government was to be made by orderly, parliamentary means. 'My proposition is this', he said, 'that the Irish land question must be settled before the nation question, if constitutional measures are to be adopted.'[56]

Yet if the land question was henceforth to be regarded as only the prelude to 'the nation question', how was the latter to be defined? Between 1882 and 1885 Parnell offered several clues but no precise explanation. Precision was beyond him, one may suspect, partly because he was an improviser, not a theorist, and partly because he was a pragmatist, not an idealist, who knew that vagueness was the path of wisdom when it was impossible to tell how the British political situation would develop and whether it would affect the Irish demand for good or ill. It was noticeable, though, that his public statements, though confusing in their variety, were more often moderate than extreme. At Cork in December 1882, for example, he spoke very much in his 'Kilmainham' vein, advancing for the first time a doctrine of reciprocal rights, of which a good deal was to be heard in the future:[57]

> I think [he said] that if our rights to self-government were recognized by the parliament of Great Britain . . . the strife of centuries might be terminated . . . and that there is no reason why the Irish nation . . . should not acknowledge and respect equally the rights of the larger nation so close to our shores. I trust that the solution will be in that direction. I believe it will be in that direction, that it will be a peaceful and constitutional one . . .

This still did not state explicitly what Irish rights might be, but the reports of an interview he gave in Paris a few months later would hardly have reassured any English politicians who saw them. Speaking to the editor of a Catholic newspaper he said that Irishmen were 'tired of the position of pariah', and wanted for themselves the rights enjoyed by other United Kingdom citizens. What did this mean? 'A parliament of our own, with a natural result, liberty. You had better understand me when I say that we shall be assimilated to a state of things that exists in Canada or the Isle of Man.' The quaintness of the phraseology was probably due to the fact that his remarks had to be translated into French by J. J. O'Kelly, and then back again into English for British and Irish readers, but the bizarre comparison between Canada and the Isle of Man suggests what was almost certainly the case, that the whole concept of dominion status was still a sealed book to him. Certainly, contemporary political scientists would have been hard pressed to understand the gloss he put on these remarks, a gloss which went much closer to anticipating the Statute of Westminster (nearly half a century in the future) than to expressing the realities of his own time. 'We would not cease to be subjects of the Queen', he explained. 'The Queen would be our Queen. She would be the link that would attach Ireland to Great Britain. We would consent even to be governed by a Viceroy, provided there were no exceptional laws [he meant coercion] and the Viceroy had no more rights, no more arbitrary powers, over us than Queen Victoria has over her English subjects.'[58]

It was not until the beginning of 1885 that he began to be any more explicit and then, significantly, the model he chose was exactly the model he had chosen when he first went into politics – Grattan's parliament. In two speeches in January, at Clonmel and Cork, he held this up as the minimum demand with which Ireland would be satisfied. These declarations, though they sounded conventional, almost traditional, had a two-fold importance – one obvious, one hidden. The obvious one was that a general election was approaching and that he was certain to monopolize about four-fifths of the Irish seats at that election; consequently, when he spoke, it behoved others to listen. The hidden importance was that when he made these speeches he was, as we shall see presently, under heavy pressure to accept a form of elective local government as a substitute for Home Rule and had therefore to make clear, as he said at Clonmel, that any interim concessions could not be 'taken by our enemies as an admission that we had given up our national rights'.[59] It was at Cork that he elaborated on this theme in words which became so famous that they were later engraved on his statue in Dublin:[60]

We cannot ask for less than the restitution of Grattan's parliament . . . We cannot under the British constitution ask for more than the restitution of Grattan's parliament, but no man has the right to fix the boundary to the march of a nation. No man has a right to say to his country, 'Thus far shalt thou go and no further', and we have never attempted to fix the *ne plus ultra* to the progress of Ireland's nationhood, and we never shall.

The calculated ambiguity of these sentences needs no stressing. To some of those who heard or read him he seemed to have left the road to full independence wide open. To others, although their knowledge of Grattan's parliament might be rusty, the phrases in which he described it sounded agreeably constitutional and that could not be bad. For Parnell himself there can be little doubt it was the commitment to the re-creation of the parliament of 1782 which mattered more than the commitment to some more perfect form of freedom laid up in an indefinite future. While he was still in Cork he took advantage of a strange opportunity to say so in no uncertain terms. Under pressure from the local Young Ireland Society he agreed to give a lecture on 'Ireland and her parliaments'. A more unlikely exponent of Irish constitutional law it would be difficult to imagine and his host, M. J. Hogan, later recorded how appalled he was by Parnell's casual preparations for this taxing occasion. The lecture was due to start at eight in the evening. At a quarter to eight Parnell got up from dinner, professed his ignorance of Irish history, asked for some books and set to work. At a quarter to nine his host found him ready to start for the lecture, clutching several sheets of writing-paper with about three notes in large script on each sheet. They arrived at the crowded hall an hour and a quarter late, but the reception he got was magnificent. 'What a king he looked standing on the platform that night', Hogan recalled, 'so handsome, so quiet, so self-possessed, so dignified. People thought of looking at no one but him. He dwarfed all around him. There was a majesty about the man which fascinated and awed you. I felt horribly nervous for him. I knew how he had got up the lecture, and I feared he would break down. I felt so anxious that I really did not follow the lecture at all. But I heard the cheers and they cheered from beginning to end.'

Coming home he was as pleased and proud as a child. 'I think', he said, 'I got through very well.'[61] So no doubt he did, for he concentrated almost entirely on Grattan's parliament and although in fact he got it quite wrong – 'It had a constitution which would have enabled it to remedy all its own defects . . . it had power over itself, over its own formation and future, as well as the future of Ireland' – his audience, mesmerized, as Irishmen *were* mesmerized at this time, by the power of his personality, was in no condition to judge his words by the touchstone of historical pedantry. What they wanted to hear, and what they were given, was the message that legislative independence had once meant genuine independence and that this must be the basis of comparison for whatever the future might bring forth. 'We stand on unapproachable ground', as Parnell said in his peroration. 'We are entitled to ask that that which has been stolen from us by means which nobody now seeks to defend for a moment shall be restored to us.'[62]

VII

The question was – how? Parnell's answer to this question was curiously ambivalent. On the one hand, he appealed to the country for support in the confident expectation that, even without a widening of the franchise, he would be returned at the next election at the head of a party of between 70 and 80 members, to say nothing of the influence which the Irish vote might be expected to have in a substantial number of English constituencies.[63] On the other hand, and as if to check the mounting anticipation in Ireland that the emergence of such a party would in itself bring about some miraculous change in the situation, he continued at intervals to hammer away at the theme which he had never ceased to stress since he first experienced the frustrations and humiliations of being an Irish member in the days of Isaac Butt. The party was vulnerable to English pressures, he admitted in 1882, but the way to deal with that was not to withdraw from parliament altogether – that would merely create a vacuum which would quickly be filled by old-style Whigs and Tories.[64] What was really needed was a party which would stick to the job at Westminster, while remaining entirely independent of all other parties and external sources of aid. 'I have always', he said in 1884, 'endeavoured to teach my fellow-countrymen whether at home or abroad the lesson of self-reliance . . . I do not depend upon any English political party. I should advise you not to depend upon any English political party.' 'Some people', he added, clearly with Davitt in mind, 'desire to rely upon the English democracy – they look for a great future movement amongst the English democracy; but I have never known any important section of any country which has assumed the governing of another country awaken to the real necessities of the position until they have been compelled to do so.'[65]

The lean parliamentary sessions of 1883 and 1884 seemed to bear him out. With a maximum of 40 members – in practice, generally rather less – he was in no position to compel anyone to do anything. Nor was the climate encouraging. The situation in 1883 was clouded by the revelations of Irish criminality made during the Phoenix Park murder trials and by the reluctance of Gladstone's colleagues to launch into a major measure of Irish local government reform. Harcourt, as usual, was the most emphatic advocate of letting sleeping dogs lie. Anything else, he told Spencer, would be 'little short of madness'. To grant local government there and then would be 'like handing revolvers to the Dublin assassins, thinking that by "placing confidence" in them you will induce them to behave well'. 'Gladstone', he added, 'still cherishes the illusion that the *feeling* of the people is changed, that Parnell is really converted. But the leopard has not changed his spots . . .'[66]

Much more was to be heard of local government, though not in 1883. Nor was it the only casualty. Persistent attempts by Parnell and others to move in a 'Kilmainham' direction by amending the Land Act of 1881 roused no sympathetic echoes from the government and the Irish party carried away from that barren session only three minor measures. One provided for a subvention from the Irish church surplus to encourage sea fisheries in Ireland. A second, close to Parnell's heart, was the Labourers (Ireland) Act. This authorized Boards of Guardians to build cottages for labourers and to let them with a plot of land attached, at a rent that would pay the interest on the money borrowed for this purpose. Modest though it was, it broke new ground and was the harbinger of other, more generous, legislation in later years.

The third measure had the dubious distinction of tempting Parnell into a business partnership with Captain O'Shea. This was the Tramways and Public Companies (Ireland) Act which, among a variety of functions, was intended to help in the opening up of agricultural areas beyond the railheads, by giving grants for emigration and lending money on easy terms to companies to enable them to purchase estates and resell these to the tenants. Parnell's interest in the scheme was to utilize it for migration rather than emigration and soon after the act was passed he began to solicit investments from the most unlikely sources, including that upstanding Tory, W. H. Smith, to whom he wrote 'as one of those who are known to be most liberally and favourably disposed towards any scheme for ameliorating the condition of the people of Ireland'.[67] Smith, understandably at a loss to recognize himself in this role, merely replied that he had no means of forming an opinion about the scheme, but would watch Parnell's efforts 'with great interest and great sympathy'.[68] It does not appear, though Parnell, nothing daunted, sent him a prospectus a month later, that Smith was ever actually moved from passive to active philanthropy.[69]

Parnell's own investment was £2000, which he could ill afford. At the end of May 1884 he visited Tuam with O'Shea and Colonel Nolan, to inspect an estate for possible purchase.[70] Unhappily, no record of this strange interlude survives, but it must have taxed Colonel Nolan's diplomatic and conversational powers to the utmost. The career of their enterprise, the Irish Land Purchase and Settlement Company, as it was grandiloquently called, was brief, obscure and inglorious. The laudable intention of the directors was to buy land in the west of Ireland in order to settle on it families from the over-populated or 'congested' districts. But, as anyone could have told them in advance, the landlords raised their prices as soon as they saw them coming, since the word had gone round that they had access to £50,000 of government money. In the event, having apparently failed to fill in their application form correctly, they did not qualify for the grant on which they had counted so heavily. They purchased one estate, Kilcloony in county Galway, but since hardly anyone agreed to take shares in the company they had to wind it up soon afterwards.[71]

If 1883 was a thin year for Irish legislation, 1884 was even thinner. Part of the explanation, no doubt, was that English ministers had had their fill of Ireland. Gladstone was too weary to struggle against colleagues, some of the ablest of whom thought much less about redress than about order, while even those who were disposed to be more constructive had other and more urgent matters on their minds. Specifically, they, like most politicians, had the Third Reform Bill on their minds.* Yet, if this distracted attention from the Irish situation, it was by no means irrelevant to it as Parnell was well aware. About his own attitude towards parliamentary reform there is, however, a singular dearth of information.

But a few things are clear, and at least one other may be surmised. It is obvious, for example, that Ireland loomed large in the debates and that while there was a school of thought which felt that so destructive a force as the Irish 'democracy' was assumed to be, ought at all costs to remain outside the pale of the constitution, there were others on both sides of the House who realized, as Lord Randolph Churchill put it with his usual brutal candour, that the Irish vote was 'in the market'.[72] And it is no less obvious that the attitudes of English politicians were conditioned, not only by the prospect of Parnell returning at the head of an enlarged phalanx of disciplined and dedicated nationalists, but also by the realization that the extension of the franchise in Britain would give the vote to many thousands of Irishmen dwelling in the big

---

*For an admirable recent study, see A. Jones, *The politics of reform, 1884* (Cambridge, 1972).

cities and that this might have consequences for party groupings at the next election which were, literally, incalculable. Further, it was only to be expected that the widening of the Irish franchise (it increased the number of voters by about half a million*) would intensify the demand for Home Rule, especially since Parnell himself had more than once gone on record that the broader franchise was a necessary prelude to winning legislative independence. 'To get such a representation as would secure, for instance, the creation of a national self-government for Ireland', he had told his audience at the founding of the Irish National League in 1882, 'we require to return 80 or 90 members to the House of Commons; and we cannot hope for this until the franchise has been lowered at least as far as the basis of household suffrage.'[73] In January 1885, after the Reform Act had been passed, he still seemed prepared to strike the same note. Only when the new franchise had begun to operate, he said in Cork in that hastily concocted lecture of his, would there be a true expression of Irish opinion. 'When Whigs and Tories are stamped out', he cried, 'when we have a united representation from Ireland amounting to 85 members, it will be impossible for any people, for any parliament – even so intolerant and haughty an assembly as the English parliament – long to withstand our claims.'[74]

Yet there was a different way of regarding his position and a different set of utterances defining it. Between 1882 and 1885 the Irish by-elections told steadily in his favour. By the end of 1883 he was professing himself indifferent as to whether Ireland was or was not included in the projected reform, for even without it he reckoned that his party would win between 70 and 80 seats at the next election.[75] In the following March, when interviewed about the prospect of an election if the Franchise Bill came to grief, he repeated his previous estimate, claiming that on the old register and with the old franchise he would still win 75 seats.[76] It was at this time also, when asked about the possibility of holding county conventions, that he replied with extreme caution that 'after a time' they might make satisfactory choices of candidates, but that at that moment too many constituencies were in want of organization and should consult with the party before coming to any decision.[77] In the end, of course, he only did adopt the county convention system after a clerical – in effect, a conservative – element had been built into it.

*In 1884 (excluding the two university seats) there were 225,999 voters returning 101 members. In 1885 there were 737,965 voters returning the same number of members (B. Walker, 'The Irish electorate, 1868–1915', in *IHS*, xviii, no. 71 (March 1973), pp. 359–406, especially Table 8, pp. 386–91).

If one puts this caution towards county conventions alongside Parnell's confidence about the way his party would perform at an election held under the existing conditions, the suspicion dawns that perhaps, after all, the extension of the franchise was not his highest priority. Already by January 1884 that shrewd observer, Gladstone's secretary, noted that the same suspicion was beginning to strike at least some politicians. Recording that Lord Richard Grosvenor had heard from Labouchere that the Irish would support the bill if ministers undertook to stand or fall by it in its entirety, Edward Hamilton added: 'At the same time it is believed that Parnell in his heart of hearts is not very keen about a Reform Bill in Ireland. He would have preferred a Registration Act with the present franchise, as more likely to secure for him a greater number of electoral votes than an electoral system on an assimilated basis.' A week later, while recognizing that the Irish would certainly not accept any bill which excluded Ireland, he still believed that 'Parnell is not much pleased with the idea of a Reform Bill'. 'But he will not dare to resist the measure so long as it includes Ireland . . .'[78]

Nor was this merely idle gossip. Gladstone himself advanced as a serious argument for extending reform to Ireland that the admission of the labourers, enfranchised on the basis of household suffrage, would be '*quite* as likely to establish a dual current in the constituencies as to increase the volume of that single force which now carries all before it'.[79] In the light of after events this may seem naïve in the extreme, but contemporary judgement was not so far wrong in taking note – as Parnell had warned his fellow-countrymen more than once – [80] that there was a deep gulf fixed between the tenant-farmers who had done well out of the land war and the agricultural labourers whose situation, never good, was largely unchanged.* To Englishmen, whether Liberal or Tory, the prospect of sowing dissension in the Irish ranks and splitting Parnell's monolith down the middle was obviously attractive. And there were, of course, other, non-Irish, reasons for including Ireland in the reform. Tories and Whigs might welcome it as a means of goading the Lords into outright rejection of a Bill they disliked on

---

*This was the distinction Parnell himself habitually made. A more accurate division, at least so far as voting was concerned, would have been between the 'middling farmers', who had the vote, and the 'small farmers' and labourers who were both disfranchised. Indeed, in many Irish counties, it has been estimated, 'the small farmer was the chief new addition to the electorate'. (B. Walker, 'The Irish electorate, 1868–1915', in IHS, xviii, no. 71 (March 1973), pp. 364–6.)

diverse grounds, while Radicals might look forward to the crisis which that action would precipitate as a means of purging the Liberal party and democratizing it after their fashion.[81]

Such motives and suppositions belong to British history. What is relevant to the biography of Parnell is that this belief in the possibility of using the labouring and small farmer vote to diminish his influence at home provides yet another striking example of the inability of English politicians to understand either the man or his movement. If the creation of a labouring vote worried him, it was surely because such a vote, being unpropertied and raw, was *more* rather than *less* open to subversive influences. One of the last recorded comments of that inveterate old Fenian, Charles Kickham, bears directly on this point. Writing in May 1882 to refuse an invitation to a demonstration in county Tipperary, he observed tartly that 'the land agitators seem to have done their best to demoralize the people'. 'I hope you will have no Land League balderdash', he added. 'I'm sure there will be a fine lot of Tipperary boys there, and I hope many of them will have something higher and better in their minds than the utterances of parliamentary agitators.'[82] 'Higher and better'? Or 'lower and more violent'? It depends upon the point of view. But it seems not to have occurred to Gladstone that in providing this supposed alternative to Parnell, he might himself be acting the part of Frankenstein, recklessly creating a monster far more difficult to handle than the parliamentarian who, since Kilmainham, had given substantial evidence that constructive politics was now his chosen line. It is idle to argue that because in fact Parnell controlled the new vote for the next five years as easily as he had controlled the old vote in the previous five, there was no cause for alarm in extending the franchise. The point rather is that in 1884 no one could have foreseen that this would happen, any more than they could have foreseen that in 1890–1 it would be Parnell himself who would take a sledge-hammer to the electoral machine so carefully constructed in and after 1885.

However, if Parnell regarded the Liberals with some justice as Greeks bearing dubious gifts, there was one concession in Gladstone's cornucopia which might go some way towards compensating for the hazards of the wider franchise. This was the magical calculation by which Ireland, despite her declining population, emerged with the same number of seats as before. Even this concession would be valuable only to the extent that Parnell could count upon incorporating the nationalist share of those seats – generally computed to be 85 within his own disciplined party. But again, this could not be guaranteed in 1884. What was certain was that to capture those 85 seats, whether under the old franchise or the new, would entail more strenuous organization and much heavier expenditure of funds than at any previous election. The final irony was that this accession of strength was likely to make the Parnellites more rather than less dependent on the Irish-American money for which it was common in British political circles to revile them. In this sense, no less than in the problems of control with which an enlarged party was bound to confront him, reform could scarcely be other than an embarrassment to Parnell; so much so, indeed, that such support as he gave it was probably less a tribute to the merits of the Franchise Bill than a signal that a *quid pro quo* was expected.[83] As if on cue that *quid pro quo* appeared at the end of 1884. It was the offer of a limited instalment of local government, which Gladstone had vainly tried to press upon his colleagues in 1883, but which was now sponsored by the energetic Chamberlain, once more aided and abetted by the irrepressible O'Shea.

VIII

Parnell's attitude towards the Liberals in general, and the Radicals in particular, in the three years after Kilmainham had seemed at times ambiguous. His slighting remarks about 'the English democracy' and his throwing-over of Bradlaugh may have been dictated by the exigencies of Irish rather than of British politics, but on important issues in the House of Commons, where a free vote was possible, it was remarkable how often he and his party cast that vote against the government.[84]

On the other hand, there is some evidence in Chamberlain's papers that in matters affecting his own department, the Board of Trade, he was able to count, intermittently at least, on Parnellite support. In August 1883, for example, we find him, in a letter to O'Shea, 'glad to recognize Parnell's perfect loyalty', in the matter of a Bankruptcy Bill, and a fortnight later he wrote again to express his appreciation. 'It was in accordance with the assurances you were able to give me and justifies the reliance I have always placed both in the influence that Mr Parnell is able to exert, and in the honourable way in which he has always fulfilled any engagements he has made.'[85] Next year it was Parnell himself who wrote to reassure Chamberlain, then anxiously recruiting aid for the Merchant Shipping Bill, that 'the great majority of my friends will support the second reading and the motion for a reference to a Grand Committee'.[86] It is not, therefore, wholly correct to suggest, as Dr Cruise O'Brien has suggested, that 'the general climate of Irish politics' had become 'distinctly hostile to Radicalism', when at the end of 1884

Chamberlain resurrected the idea of local government for Ireland.[87] There was occasional Parnellite rudeness towards the English left, no doubt, but this was partly a function of Parnellite wooing of Irish Catholicism and partly a warning shot across the bows of Michael Davitt. It left entirely open to Parnell the decision as to whether or not it would be desirable for him, as leader, to deal with Chamberlain or any other Radical – for that matter, any other Englishman – who had something to offer him.

It was unfortunate all the same that what began as a serious transaction should so nearly have toppled over into farce and should actually have ended in fiasco. The story has been told before in lavish detail which need not be repeated here, but it must be touched on briefly for the light it throws on the three principals involved – Chamberlain, Parnell and O'Shea – and also because of its lingering consequences for Home Rule and its effect upon the controversies arising out of Home Rule.[88]

Towards the end of 1884, when ministers were beginning to become conscious again that there were other things in the world besides franchise reform and the Sudan, Chamberlain discussed with O'Shea the possibility of establishing some kind of *modus vivendi* between the government and the Irish party. There were two obvious bases for such an arrangement – local government and a change of attitude on coercion. Chamberlain had been interested in the possibility of Irish local government reform since 1879 and although the whole subject had been firmly set aside by Gladstone's colleagues early in 1883, times had changed since then in two important ways. First, the enlargement of the franchise had ensured that at the next election not only Parnell's Irish members, but the new Irish votes in British constituencies, would have an important part to play. Secondly, the Prevention of Crime Act was due to expire at the end of the 1884–5 parliamentary session and if it, or any part of it, were to be renewed, this would provoke such opposition from the Parnellites as would jeopardize all other legislation. Since an election must come in 1886 at latest, if not before, a government which went to the country with nothing to its credit in the session preceding the dissolution of parliament except a bitterly contested coercion act would not be in a strong position. On the other hand, if coercive legislation had to be persisted with, its chances of success, or at least of a calmer passage, might be considerably increased if a remedial measure of local government were also to be passed.

On 27 November conversation began to be supplemented by documentation. On that date O'Shea left with Chamberlain an *aide-mémoire* which purported to represent Parnell's view that any partial renewal of the Prevention of Crime Act should be balanced either by the introduction into the same bill of a considerable instalment of 'county government', or else by limiting the duration of the re-enactment to one year from September 1885. At the same time, it seems, O'Shea also handed to Chamberlain a copy of the act from which certain sections had been cut out and others deleted with strokes of a pen. What remained was said by O'Shea to be what Parnell would accept by way of re-enactment.[89]

Both O'Shea and Chamberlain then proceeded independently to put on paper their ideas of what kind of local government might be appropriate for Ireland. Chamberlain was first in the field with a letter, written on 17 December, to a Walsall solicitor, W. H. Duignan, who had travelled extensively in Ireland in 1881 and 1883-4 and whom Chamberlain authorized to show the letter 'to any leading politicians of the Irish party whose opinion on the subject might be valuable'.[90] O'Shea's scheme was embodied in a memorandum entitled 'Local self-goverment in Ireland', and dated 14 January 1885.[91]

There were some similarities between the schemes, but also two important differences. First, while both envisaged the creation of an elective 'Irish board', or 'central board', O'Shea saw it as endowed with merely administrative functions, whereas Chamberlain was prepared to concede legislative powers over such major topics as land, education and communications. The other difference was that O'Shea envisaged his scheme as being bound up with the partial renewal of the coercion act in the 1884-5 session, whereas Chamberlain's more ambitious proposals were to be the work of a new parliament.

In concocting his proposals O'Shea had taken counsel with Parnell and the latter certainly encouraged him to put forward his scheme for local government, even describing it to O'Shea himself as 'the central local government body which I propose'.[92] *But*, he made it very plain to O'Shea from the outset that this was a limited operation:[93]

> In talking to our friend [he wrote] you must give him clearly to understand that we do *not* propose this local self-government plank as a substitute for the restitution of our Irish parliament . . . The claim for restitution of parliament would remain. Some people think it would be weakened, others strengthened, by the concession. I myself think that this improvement of local government in Ireland if carried out would have very little effect one way or another upon the larger question.

And when O'Shea protested in reply that this unfairly narrowed his room for manoeuvre, Parnell again insisted that 'the two questions of the reform of local government and the restitution of an Irish parliament must, as I explained to you from the first, be left absolutely separate . . . I have not gone into the latter question at all in the communications with you.'[94]

Parnell's insistence on this crucial distinction may have been partly due to his knowledge of the Captain's slap-dash way of doing business, but it was also prompted, as he explicitly stated in his letter to O'Shea of 13 January, by the fact that word had reached him of Chamberlain's letter to Duignan with its proposals of legislative powers for the 'central board'. Parnell, rightly, read this at once as a substitute for, rather than a complement of, an Irish parliament. 'This', he said, 'is a power I have not claimed as it would cross the border-line between legislative and administrative functions which I have endeavoured to follow in all important particulars.'[95] To this day it is impossible to say with certainty how far O'Shea misled Chamberlain about Parnell's real views, or even whether he did so consciously or unconsciously. Chamberlain himself, in his memoir composed in 1890–1, claimed that O'Shea did not tell him at the time of Parnell's letters and that he only learned of them several years later. That may or may not be true, but Chamberlain was scarcely correct in adding: 'I further understood that Mr Parnell proposed the scheme as a final settlement.'[96] If he read the newspapers at all – and few front-rank politicians paid more assiduous attention to the press – he must have realized from Parnell's speech at Cork on 21 January that, so far from accepting *local* government as a substitute for Home Rule, he was not even prepared to say that Home Rule was a final settlement.* And, as the leading authority on these transactions has pointed out, it may be a significant pointer to the true extent of Chamberlain's realization of Parnell's attitude that in subsequent versions of his proposals the Radical leader substantially reduced the legislative element.[97]

However much or little he knew of Parnell's mind, Chamberlain was at any rate prepared to continue in consultation with O'Shea and indeed learnt from him in mid-January that if a central board were to be created, 'Parnell would be most probably willing to accept the chairmanship'.[98] This, which sounds unlikely, may well have been one of those instances of O'Shea's tendency to embroider the facts, which from time to time he found irresistible. If so, it was the merest *petit point* compared with the letter in which he reported to Parnell on the interview with Chamberlain. Written in his brashest style, it represented

*See above, pp. 260–1.

Chamberlain as being ready to snatch the reins of leadership when they fell from Gladstone's fingers and also as proposing what appeared to be a full-scale alliance with the Irish party.[99] It was a vulgar, tasteless letter and Chamberlain, who received a copy of it from Katharine O'Shea (acting on her husband's instructions), refused to accept it as an adequate rendering of the conversation.[100] It was indeed not a letter that he would wish to be made public and, as we shall see later, the realization that the original of it was probably still in Parnell's hands halted him in his tracks when in 1888 he was locked in deadly conflict with the Irish leader.*

At this point, with Chamberlain's confidence in his go-between understandably shaken, and Parnell refusing to make any move towards a Radical alliance, the negotiation hung fire, only to burst fitfully into life again when it became clear towards the end of March that Lord Spencer was going to require the re-enactment of a substantial and controversial portion of the expiring Prevention of Crime Act. But even Spencer did not contemplate coercion without redress and he circulated to the cabinet his view of what was needed. This included representative county councils; a further instalment of land purchase; the replacement of the vice-royalty by a secretary of state; and the establishment of a royal residence in Ireland. Chamberlain was stimulated by this, to him inadequate, programme to circulate to the cabinet a revised version of his central board scheme.[101] But before his colleagues had had time to digest this, the situation took a new turn with the intervention of Cardinal Manning. Manning was opposed to an Irish parliament but he was in favour of local government, the more so when in April 1885 he learned from a group of Irish bishops that they were of much the same opinion. One of them, the redoubtable Dr Croke no less, had even professed himself frightened of 'the extreme nationalists' and in favour of the maintenance of the Union. Dilke, who had this from Manning, whom he visited on 23 April, recorded the essence of that interview as follows: 'The cardinal declared that the Roman Catholic clergy were ready to pacify Ireland if we would pass Chamberlain's local government Ireland scheme, with a central board such as Chamberlain proposed. The bishops and clergy would be prepared to denounce, not only separation, but also an Irish parliament.'[102]

After seeing Chamberlain to cross-question him about his scheme, Manning undertook to make contact with Parnell. But before he did so he received from Chamberlain a document, dated 25 April, entitled

*See below, pp. 396-402.

'Local government in Ireland'. It was yet another version of the central board scheme, but this time much more 'administrative' than 'parliamentary'.[103] On 30 April Manning saw Parnell and had an hour's conversation with him. 'It was satisfactory', he told Chamberlain a few days later, 'and as the Irish bishops are of the same mind two conditions of acceptance for the scheme appear to be secure.'[104] Manning was here overstating the case. He himself told Dilke on 1 May that he had had 'a more completely satisfactory interview' with Sexton, and the following year, when the whole episode was already enveloped in controversy, he described the Irish leader's attitude in terms which accord much more closely with the line Parnell had consistently taken with O'Shea. 'I understood him to accept the scheme, but not as sufficient or final. His acceptance was very guarded, and I did not take it as more than not opposing it.'[105]

Meanwhile opinion in the cabinet was hardening against Chamberlain's scheme, even in its modified form. The arch-enemy was Spencer, who wanted a strong coercion act, renewable for *three* years, and who was not prepared to offer what Chamberlain considered a sufficient *quid pro quo*. Once again Chamberlain resorted to Captain O'Shea. On 28 April the latter recorded that Chamberlain had told him that he and Dilke were prepared to make this a resignation matter (and that two other ministers, Shaw Lefevre and Trevelyan, would probably be influenced in the same direction) 'on condition of my obtaining Parnell's full support for Irish local government scheme proposed by myself to Chamberlain in January last, and Parnell's engagement to prevent obstruction to renewal of crimes act for one year'.[106] Two days later Parnell called at Albert Mansions and, recorded O'Shea, 'after much conversation', accepted the proposal.[107] O'Shea, promptly conveying this gratifying news to Dilke and Chamberlain, wrote out, apparently in his own hand, two versions (though the authorship of one of them is dubious) of the undertaking he alleged Parnell to have given. The gist was that Parnell, while still strongly opposing coercion, would endeavour to prevent obstruction on the understanding that the Irish local government bill would be introduced before the coercion bill.[108] This document did not actually commit Parnell, who had signed nothing and written nothing, to any more than a promise to take a sensible parliamentary line in return for a specific gain. It did not change his fundamental position, which was that all such proposals were incidental to, and not destructive of, his continuing demand for Home Rule.

In the last resort the decision rested with the cabinet. There, on 9 May, the scheme provoked a long and bitter debate. Broadly, according

to Dilke's record, it was supported by all the commoners except
Hartington and opposed by all the peers save Granville.[109] The verdict
was for rejection, Gladstone prophesying of his colleagues in a phrase
variously reported that within five (or six) years, 'if it pleases God to
spare their lives, they will be repenting in ashes'.[110] Discussion in the
next few days veered to consideration of the coercion bill and again
there was prolonged debate – this time over the duration of the measure.
In the end Gladstone was reduced to announcing to the House on
15 May that the bill would be renewed, but was unable to define
either what it would contain or how long it would last. Worse, he made
it clear that time would permit of no remedial legislation. Five days later
he changed his mind on the latter point and gave notice of a land purchase bill, apparently failing to understand, or perhaps simply ignoring,
that Dilke and his friends regarded this as a wrong order of priorities.
Dilke and Chamberlain thereupon resigned and Shaw Lefevre followed
suit a day later. Matters remained in this state, the resignations having
been neither accepted nor withdrawn, when on 9 June the government
fell, in circumstances to be explained in the next chapter.

Whether these resignations were genuine expressions of frustration
at the government's inability or reluctance to grapple with Ireland, or
whether, as the most recent interpretation suggests, they – and especially
Chamberlain's – had much more to do with the future balance of power
within the Liberal party, are questions irrelevant to the biography of
Parnell.[111] But there is a brief coda to the affair which deserves to be
noticed. After the government had fallen, Chamberlain communicated
once more with Parnell through O'Shea, asking if the Irish leader still
adhered to 'his' (i.e. Parnell's) proposals and offering, on behalf of
Dilke and himself, a pledge that they would not join any cabinet which
did not make them a part of its programme. 'We were also ready to
speak in the country in favour of these proposals and to go to Ireland
on a visit to study the question there with a view to further discussion.'[112]
Parnell might reasonably have replied that the proposals were Chamberlain's, not his. In fact, he seems not to have bothered to reply at all.
Nor need a reply have been seriously expected. The change of government had opened up to the Irish leader a whole new vista and with it
the opportunity to move closer to that point of balance which might
enable him to gain the maximum advantage from whatever party
proved least able to resist the temptation to bargain with him. In such
circumstances Radical blandishments lost even the limited allure they
might previously have held.

CHAPTER 9

Towards the Fulcrum

'No one I think can doubt that, according to all present appearances, the greatest incident of the coming elections is to be the
Parnell or Nationalist majority. And such a majority is a very
great fact indeed. It will at once shift the centre of gravity in the
relations between the two countries.' (Gladstone to Earl Spencer,
30 June 1885.)

I

Although there is a strong case for arguing that 1885 marked the climax
of Parnell's political career, much of what he thought and did in the
first half of that year is shrouded in mystery to this day. That it remains
a mystery, despite the intensive researches of many historians, is a
remarkable tribute to that talent which he could always deploy at need,
of retiring into the shadows and leaving scarcely a trace behind him.
Thus although the hectic events leading up to and following the collapse
of the Liberal government on 8 June have been minutely investigated,
and although the English sources for those events are almost embar-
rassingly rich, the contribution of Parnell to the gathering crisis is still
difficult to assess. This is partly because he never committed himself
revealingly or intimately to paper at this time; we have only public
statements or formal letters to go upon and these have always to be
interpreted in the light of the often very precise purposes they were
intended to serve. But it is also because a waiting game was quite
evidently the game for him to play. The semi-subterranean negotiations
about the 'central board' scheme, though they came to nothing, had
been at least an indication that the Irish vote was thought to be worth
bidding for. It was only common sense to see who else besides Chamberlain might bid and how far they might go.

We do know, however, both from the 'central board' negotiations
and from his occasional interventions in debate, that he was fairly
constantly in or near London during the first six months of 1885 and
that he did not speak in Ireland between his famous outburst at Cork

in January and the beginning of May. We know also that from the beginning of the session it was widely suspected that he and the Tories were beginning to draw closer together. On 24 February, for example, Gladstone's secretary was puzzled by a curious incident when, after a bout of Irish obstruction, the Speaker's move to apply the closure was almost defeated by a number of the Tories voting with the Parnellites against it; to Edward Hamilton, as to Gladstone also, this seemed a sinister portent of a new political alignment.[1] Three days later Hamilton noted that 'constant communications' were in progress between the two parties. 'Some sort of compact is evidently being made between the Tories and the Irish Nationalists.'[2]

Hamilton was not far wrong, but also not quite right. That same day, 27 February, Parnell did have an interview with the Conservative Chief Whip, Rowland Winn, which the latter duly reported to Salisbury. One immediate result seemed to follow that evening, when a combined Tory-nationalist vote reduced the government majority on the vote of censure following the fall of Khartoum to fourteen, thereby causing the cabinet seriously to contemplate resignation.[3] It was rumoured subsequently that Parnell himself had been reluctant to go against the government, but that a pledge had been obtained from Salisbury that, if the Liberals were defeated and the Tories came in, the Irish members would not, under the impending redistribution of seats to accompany the recent extension of the franchise, be reduced in numbers. It was true that Parnell had sought, and received, satisfactory assurances from Winn that if there was a change of government the Irish representation at Westminster would remain unchanged and that the work already done by the Boundary Commission in redrawing the Irish constituencies would not be affected, but these assurances were not part of some package deal. 'No arrangement, compact or agreement was come to between us', Winn assured Salisbury, 'nor was anything of such a nature either asked for or alluded to by either of us.'[4] Nevertheless, the gossip about an 'alliance' continued merrily. It was said, apparently without foundation, that Winn had promised Parnell Tory support in challenging the conduct of the Speaker in imposing the closure the previous week. And it was even suggested, admittedly by the unreliable Labouchere, that unless the Liberals gave him satisfaction over coercion, Parnell would promise the Tories to shelve Home Rule for three years while they, the Tories, dealt with the land question and provided money for public works in Ireland.[5]

Behind all this rumour lay little solid substance other than the Winn-Parnell interview of which few people can have known much, if anything, while the general thesis upon which so much of the rumour depended – that the Tory leadership was panting to succeed the Liberals in office – is not borne out by the behaviour of Salisbury and his senior colleagues in the early months of 1885. On the other hand, that the Parnellites were playing some deep game did seem to be evidenced by the fact that just at this moment they risked recommending to their fellow-countrymen that they should receive the potentially embarrassing visit of the Prince and Princess of Wales to Ireland with dignified reserve, avoiding all acts of discourtesy.[6] Parnell's authority was sufficient to ensure that this attitude was adopted in most parts of the country, though there were rowdy scenes in Cork and in some districts black flags were hung along the route, together with placards proclaiming 'We will have no prince but Charlie'.[7] The anonymous scribe who seized upon this slogan to adapt an old Jacobite song to contemporary purposes may not have risen far above bathos, but his little poem was a timely reminder that political manoeuvre at Westminster, all-absorbing to the Irish politicians involved in it, could easily seem an esoteric irrelevance to the unsophisticated electorate upon whom those politicians ultimately depended. A few lines will illustrate the point:[8]

Our Own Beloved Charlie

I

When famine o'er our suffering land
Her wings of woe extended,
And hardly once the royal hand
Our hungry poor befriended.
What hero brave stood forth to save
And keep us late and early?
Ah! need I tell it was Parnell –
Our own belovèd Charlie!

Chorus

May blessings bright
Upon him light!
God guard him late and early!
For there is none
Our hearts has won
Like our own belovèd Charlie!

II

And when the tyrants of our race
With bayonets stood surrounded
To ruin many a happy place
Where plenty once abounded,
Who bid us then *at last* be men,
And hold no peace or parley
With villain foes? The world well knows,
'Twas our belovèd Charlie!

Chorus

O heaven save
A chief so brave
And guard him late and early,
For there is none
Such good has done
As our own belovèd Charlie!

These naïve verses, with their note of adoration, tell us a good deal about Parnell's hold upon the hearts of simple people. But, until he came among them in the summer, they could only worship from afar. All they had to feed on in the interval was the speech he made at a St Patrick's Day banquet in London. And there, although he eccentrically chose to devote part of his time to a disquisition on the state of the piers in the two principal harbours of his constituency, Arklow and Wicklow, the main burden of his message was a muted version of what he had said in Cork in January:[9]

I do not pretend to predict in what way the rights of Ireland will be ultimately gained . . . but a man in my position ought to consider that in anything that he does, or in anything that he says, he ought not to hamper the people in their march for their liberties . . . although our programme may be limited and small, it should be such a one as shall not prevent hereafter the fullest realization of the hopes of Ireland.

This was characteristically, no doubt intentionally, vague, but it was 'independent' enough to allow the hat to be passed round in America with some hope of success. And success was essential if the approaching election were to be exploited to the full. Soon Parnell had his reward, for it was certainly no accident that the League funds, responding to the rapidly developing situation which seemed to prove his mastery, rose from £11,686 for the year 1884–5 to £47,275 for 1885–6: the accounts do not specify how much of this was American money, but it is likely that it accounted for a large proportion.[10]

Perhaps, also, Parnell's speech was intended as another warning to Chamberlain that his scheme of local government was in no sense a final solution. If so, it went unregarded and Chamberlain pressed ahead with the 'central board' negotiations until checked by the cabinet veto of 9 May. Parnell, meanwhile, drew quietly closer to the Tories. About the middle of May he called at Lord Randolph Churchill's house in Connaught Place and had the first of at least two meetings with him at this time. It appears that Churchill pledged himself that if the Tories came in and he were a member of the government, he would oppose the renewal of coercion. To which Parnell allegedly replied: 'In that case you will have the Irish vote at the elections.'[11] This account, which is Churchill's own version (Parnell, as usual, said nothing afterwards), is to some extent borne out by the fact that Churchill spoke in the same sense, though rather more guardedly, at a public meeting in London on 20 May.[12] From this tremor of the veil, from the previous suspicions about Tory-Parnellite co-operation, and from the fact that the government fell at 1.45 on the morning of 9 June to an amendment on the budget for which these strange allies voted in apparent collusion, Liberals soon began to manufacture the theory that they were the victims of a conspiracy. 'The defeat of the Gladstone government', as John Morley wrote later, 'was the first success of a combination between the Tories and the Irish, that proved of cardinal importance to politics and parties for several critical months to come.'[13]

Yet although clearly there had been coquetting between the opposition and the Parnellites, not only is the evidence for a firm alliance impossible to come by, but there are at least two alternative explanations as to why the government fell when and how it did. One relates to its internal divisions and to its lax discipline. During the day (8 June) preceding the fatal vote in the House of Commons the cabinet had had another inconclusive wrangle about coercion and ministers left it apparently expecting to be put out of office by a combination of the opposition and the Irish. Yet the debate itself suggested suicide rather than murder. For while Sir Charles Dilke was insisting that the clause then at issue – the imposition of an increased duty on beer rather than wine – would be treated as a matter of life and death, enough of the government's supporters were either absent unpaired or abstained from voting to give the Tory-Parnellite combination their twelve-vote majority.[14]

The alternative explanation is that the Radical wing of the Liberal party may have engineered the collapse in order to end a well-nigh intolerable situation, not necessarily by bringing in the Tories – there was a wide-spread view that Salisbury would be too wily even to attempt to form a minority government – but rather by reconstructing the Liberal government so as to exclude the older Whigs. Perhaps the strongest pointer in this direction was the letter Lord Acton, who had Joseph Chamberlain for his London tenant, wrote to Gladstone's daughter Mary, indicating 'on the best Birmingham authority' that the defeat was manufactured in that thriving city to avoid the impending collision between the two wings of the government.[15] But hypothesis is not proof and there is no conclusive evidence that the Liberal government perished by parricide any more than by suicide or murder. Indeed, since, in the view of the most recent investigators of this strange episode, 'neither party was behaving very competently', it may well be that they blundered jointly into a situation which ended in a happy release for the Liberals, but brought only vexation of spirit to Lord Salisbury.[16] In that case the appropriate verdict must surely be 'death by misadventure'.

Parnell's only interest was to see what the new turn of the kaleidoscope might produce for Ireland. By 11 June the Queen had accepted the resignations of Gladstone and his colleagues and Salisbury had reluctantly begun to form a new government. This was a lengthy business, for Salisbury had to tread carefully among Tory jealousies, which were almost as intense as those exhibited by the lately departed Liberals. It was noticeable, however, that amid the anxious confabulations about jobs and personalities there was a general feeling that Irish coercion could be done without for the present, which indicated that Churchill's declaration the previous month was not just a personal eccentricity, but a negotiable asset for the Conservative party as a whole. Among the discussions of that unsettled time was one which attracted little attention, but was pregnant with possibilities. In conversation with Rowland Winn, the Parnellite Chief Whip, Richard Power, held out the prospect of Irish support in the coming elections, calculating that this would yield for the Tories fifty seats in England and five in Ulster. In return, he intimated, Parnell wanted the Labourers Act of 1883 amended, and a measure to be passed eliminating sheriffs' expenses in uncontested elections. It seems also that the Irish were simultaneously consulted about who should be Chief Secretary and although the candidate finally appointed, Sir William Hart Dyke, was not their ideal choice, he was not unacceptable to them; more important perhaps than his acceptability was the fact that they had been asked for their opinion.[17]

The oddest thing about this odd conversation was the seeming triviality of the price the Irish were at that time prepared to exact for their great reversal of alliances. But it was not long before Parnell began to tighten the screw. The way was opened for him to do so by the continuing confusion in the Conservative ranks. While the cabinet was being formed there was little sign of any coherent Irish policy. When this did begin to emerge in July, it seems to have been worked out at two different levels – that of the cabinet (where Lord Randolph Churchill was of course included) and that of Lord Randolph Churchill and his friends outside the cabinet. The symptoms of this incipient schizophrenia were to be much aggravated by the events of the next few weeks. Something of what might be in store was revealed as early as 24 June, the day on which the new government formally came into being, when Parnell gave notice in the House of Commons of his intention to raise the question of the administration of the Prevention of Crime Act in Ireland by the late government and to call for an independent enquiry into the conduct of crown officials during certain trials. The implications of this manoeuvre were unpleasantly plain. The new government was to be asked not only to declare itself on the general issue of coercion, but also to establish the dangerous precedent of calling into question executive action and judicial decisions made under the previous regime. This was serious enough, but what made Parnell's motion so potentially damaging was that he included in the list of proceedings to be reviewed the notorious Maamtrasna case which already had a dark and stormy history behind it.

On the night of 8 August 1882, a band of armed men entered a peasant cabin at Maamtrasna, in the wilds of Mayo, and attacked the family who lived there. The father, mother and three children were killed – only one son survived his wounds. The mainspring of this appalling crime may have been a rural vendetta, or it may have been committed by one of the secret societies flourishing at that time. To English, and initially, to Irish opinion, profoundly shocked by this fresh horror so soon after the Phoenix Park tragedy, it was the crime, not the motive, which mattered. In due course the men alleged to be responsible were arrested and tried. Three were hanged and five sentenced to penal servitude for life, largely on the evidence of two brothers, and of the son of one of the brothers, who swore that they had seen the accused and followed them on the night of the murders. One of those hanged, Miles Joyce, died protesting his innocence, and it gradually came out that the other two, before their execution, had declared him not guilty. Other circumstances then combined to cast further doubt on the verdict. In response to public outcry Spencer held an enquiry, but it was not searching enough to satisfy the Irish party which, led by Parnell and Tim Harrington, had held up parliamentary business for four days in October 1884 while they raked over the case in detail. The Liberal majority was sufficient to withstand their censure, but it was noticeable that Randolph Churchill and two other prominent Conservatives had supported the abortive Irish demand for a Select Committee. When, therefore, Parnell raised the matter afresh in June 1885, it was understandable that the spectre of Maamtrasna should arouse a tremor of excitement and apprehension in more than one quarter of the House.

II

Parnell's motion did not come on until 17 July, by which time the situation had developed still further. To some of this development there had been a considerable pre-history, antedating even the fall of the Liberal government. During the autumn of 1884 the former Young Irelander, Sir Charles Gavan Duffy, who since leaving Ireland in 1856 had had a distinguished political career in Australia, was deep in discussion of Irish politics with the Earl of Carnarvon. Carnarvon had twice been Colonial Secretary in previous Conservative administrations and within the year was to become Lord-Lieutenant of Ireland. Gavan Duffy suggested to him that the Conservatives should seriously consider the idea of granting an Irish parliament, promising to use whatever influence he possessed in Ireland to secure the support of the bishops and of moderates in general. By agreement with Carnarvon, Gavan Duffy put these ideas into an article in the *National Review*. Carnarvon then drew Salisbury's attention to the article, making it plain that he agreed with it in principle.[18] Salisbury replied pessimistically, though this did not inhibit him from persuading Carnarvon to accept the Lord-Lieutenancy when the time came to construct his government. Choosing Carnarvon, however, did not mean that Salisbury had in any way adopted the Carnarvon doctrine. True, in the interval between the Liberal defeat and his own assumption of office he had discussed with a friend the possibility of giving Ireland provincial councils for private legislation only, but this, it seems, was merely to test the temperature and was in any case far from what any Home Ruler would have considered adequate. In short, the probability is that the new Lord-Lieutenant was chosen not because of, but in spite of, his Irish views, these perhaps being outweighed in Salisbury's opinion by the realization that in Carnarvon he had a Tory magnate of the old school, reliable and – more important still – amenable.[19]

Carnarvon was sworn in on 30 June and went at once to Ireland, whence he returned on 4 July with evidence that Dublin Castle was prepared to acquiesce in the abandonment of coercion. That same day the cabinet unanimously decided not to renew the expiring Prevention of Crime Act. They also resolved to introduce a further instalment of land purchase and a Labourers Act; to these valuable concessions was added subsequently, and as an afterthought, what was to become the Educational Endowments Act, a measure which gratified the Irish hierarchy by bringing about a redeployment of endowment funds worth £140,000 in such a way as to benefit Catholic schools and colleges considerably.[20] But at the cabinet meeting of 4 July ministers also agreed to refuse Parnell's motion to reopen the Maamtrasna case.[21]

It is against this background of quite deliberate Conservative effort to meet the more constructive Irish demands while standing firm on Maamtrasna that Carnarvon's next initiative must be seen. For some time he had been under pressure from Howard Vincent, the former Director of the CID, to meet Parnell. Carnarvon was willing, but Parnell was not so easily reached. Vincent therefore approached the vice-chairman, Justin McCarthy. He and Carnarvon met at Vincent's house in Grosvenor Square in early July. They had a friendly talk about the possibility of a conciliatory policy towards Ireland being adopted by the government. 'Lord Carnarvon', McCarthy later wrote, 'distinctly told me that for his own part he was prepared to go as far in the direction of Home Rule as either Parnell or I could desire. But he did not convey to me, and I am sure did not intend to convey, that he was speaking on behalf of Lord Salisbury's government.'[22] Writing to his literary collaborator, Mrs Praed, soon after the interview, McCarthy admitted that he did not believe much would come of the business, or that 'our mutual friend' (Carnarvon) would be able to carry his party with him.[23] Carnarvon was apparently more sanguine and on the afternoon of 6 July made an important speech in the House of Lords outlining the constructive policy for Ireland previously agreed by the cabinet.

McCarthy, despite his own misgivings, tried hard to persuade his leader to see Carnarvon. Parnell was not enthusiastic and refused emphatically to use the same rendezvous as McCarthy had done. To hob-nob with a senior member of the government in the house of one who had recently been head of Scotland Yard was not Parnell's idea of how to do business. However, he agreed eventually to a meeting which took place on 1 August. Salisbury, though informed that the interview was in train, was apparently somewhat uneasy, still more so when he learned that the original intention of having the Irish Lord Chancellor, Lord Ashbourne, present as a witness had been dropped. Still, in conversation with Carnarvon early in July Salisbury had impressed upon him that 'my objection to Home Rule was so strong that even if the Conservative party – which I believed to be impossible – were to adopt it, I never would, under any circumstances, be a member of the government that proposed it'.[24] He might therefore reasonably have supposed that whatever happened at the interview would be no more than exploratory.

But first came the Maamtrasna debate. Parnell raised the subject, as he had promised, on 17 July. Two days previously there had been ominous signs that some members of the government, including Sir Michael Hicks Beach, were preparing, in the teeth of Salisbury's disapproval, to go back on the cabinet decision not to reopen the case. In the event, although Parnell offered to withdraw his motion, he only did so after the debate had run its course. During it, both Hicks Beach and Churchill were severely critical of Lord Spencer's regime in Ireland; and to make matters worse, there were no balancing statements from other ministers.[25] Not surprisingly, the rumours of an unprincipled entente between the Tories and the Irish were intensified. The effect was not only to embarrass Carnarvon, whose conciliation policy certainly did not include criticizing his predecessor and thus sawing off the bough on which he himself was sitting, but also to alarm Tory opinion in general that a disreputable deal was in the offing and so to make more difficult the conclusion of a reputable deal, if such were found to be possible.

This division of opinion among the Conservatives may or may not have been known to Parnell, but the growing tension after the Maamtrasna debate obviously increased the difficulty of his meeting Carnarvon. Consequently, on 31 July, the day before they finally did meet, he chose to publish a firm denial of the charge, recently made by Herbert Gladstone in a speech at Leeds, that there had been a 'treaty' between the Conservative party and the Irish. Churchill and Rowland Winn issued similar denials at the same time, but Parnell's, made when he already knew he was about to meet Carnarvon, is an interesting example of how he could remain just within the borders of the literal truth, while at the same time being completely misleading:[26]

> I can only say that there is not the slightest foundation for any of these statements of Mr Herbert Gladstone. I have no knowledge of any such alliance, nor have any of my colleagues. I have held no communication upon any of the public matters referred to with any member of the present government – or any of their officials, directly or indirectly, except across the floor of the House of Commons.

Hard on the heels of this *démenti* came the celebrated interview. It was held in an unoccupied house in Hill Street and no one was present save Carnarvon and Parnell. This in itself was a recipe for trouble and trouble was soon to come, stemming from discordant recollections which led, almost inevitably, to charges of misrepresentation. The main source for what was said remains Carnarvon, who went straight from the meeting to Salisbury's house, Hatfield, and there drew up a memorandum of the conversation This memorandum was later printed by Carnarvon's biographer, but the original has since disappeared.[27] It is important, in assessing Carnarvon's own role, to be clear that at least two cabinet ministers, Salisbury and Ashbourne, knew that the interview was to take place and that one of these, Salisbury, had urged his colleague, as Carnarvon subsequently acknowledged, to be 'extremely cautious'.[28]

No doubt it was with this caution in mind that when he met the Irish leader the Lord-Lieutenant made three stipulations – that their conversation was to be strictly private; that there was to be 'no sort of bond or engagement', merely an exchange of opinions; and that Carnarvon would not entertain any proposals that excluded the Union. To all of this Parnell apparently agreed without demur, but it seems, despite Carnarvon's later statement to the contrary, that he was *not* told that the cabinet as a whole had not been informed of the meeting. Nor, probably, was Parnell aware of how far Carnarvon's conciliatory views had already diverged from the party line, though, to be fair, in this his ignorance was fully shared by Carnarvon himself. Part of their talk was concerned with landlord-tenant relations, but both regarded that as peripheral compared to the question of Home Rule. On this, Parnell was emphatic that any permanent settlement must be based on the concession to Ireland of a central legislative body with jurisdiction over purely Irish affairs. Among these, he appeared to include the power to encourage Irish industries by means of a protective tariff. In regard to local government, Carnarvon gathered that he was prepared to look at a scheme of elective councils, *provided* these did not take away from the authority of the central parliament. On the wider issue of whether or not the Irish members should be retained at Westminster, his preference was that they should stay, but he would accept exclusion if that was necessary to the final bargain. Parnell's attitude, Carnarvon recorded, was 'singularly moderate throughout the whole discussion, and not so absolutely cold as I had expected'.[29]

Parnell, for the time being, kept his opinion to himself and told even McCarthy so little that when in later years Barry O'Brien asked him about it, McCarthy said that his leader 'never gave me an account of the interview'. This was not strictly true, for in his *Reminiscences* the vice-chairman noted that Parnell had told him in general terms that there seemed some hope of a satisfactory understanding with the government, though no pledge had been given on either side.[30] The episode did, of course, become public knowledge eventually, under the worst possible circumstances for elucidating the truth. On 7 June 1886, two hours before the crucial vote was to be taken on the second reading of Gladstone's Home Rule Bill, Parnell rose and asserted that had the Tories won a majority at the 1885 election (which, at the time of the Carnarvon interview was still some months in the future) they would have granted to Ireland a statutory legislature with power to protect Irish industries. For the Conservatives, Sir Michael Hicks Beach at once denied this categorically, whereupon Parnell coolly replied that he had got his information at a meeting with one of the then Tory ministers. Assaulted on all sides with cries of 'name', he refused to say anything further until he had the permission of the gentleman in question, but though some newspapers went off on the false trail of Lord Randolph Churchill, the *Pall Mall Gazette* by pointing the finger unequivocally at Carnarvon made it impossible for the ex-Lord-Lieutenant to remain silent.[31] Consequently, on 10 June, and in face of Salisbury's strenuous objections, Carnarvon made a statement in the House of Lords. He was careful not to implicate Salisbury in any way and insisted that 'I was acting for myself by myself'. The conversation, he said, was for purposes of information only. He learnt from Parnell 'his general opinions and views on Irish matters'. 'Both of us left the room as free as when we entered it.' At the same time, Carnarvon made it quite clear that he himself favoured Home Rule of some kind and even went so far as to say that he hoped to see the day when Ireland's 'national aspirations' might be satisfied.[32]

That phrase alone was enough to damn him in the eyes of his party, but Parnell's rejoinder weakened Carnarvon's position still more.

Writing to the press on 12 June, he contradicted absolutely Carnarvon's account, which had stressed the preliminary conditions confining their secret conversation to a mere exchange of opinions. On the contrary, said Parnell, the Lord-Lieutenant had been much more specific and had sought his views on 'a constitution for Ireland'. Carnarvon's own views had in reality occupied the larger part of the conversation, though, Parnell observed, they had found themselves in agreement on the necessity of giving to Ireland a central legislative body which should be 'a parliament in name and in fact'. Carnarvon indicated that he had thought much about colonial precedents for dealing with the Irish problem, and when Parnell intervened to say that protection for certain Irish industries against English and foreign competition would be essential, Carnarvon allegedly replied, 'I entirely agree with you, but what a row there will be about it in England'. At the end of their hour-long discussion, Parnell's account concluded, he had left the room believing that they were in complete accord on the main outlines of a Home Rule settlement. 'In conversing with him I dealt with the Lord-Lieutenant of Ireland, who was responsible for the government of the country. I could not suppose that he would fail to impress the views which he had disclosed to me upon the cabinet, and I have reason to believe that he did so impress upon them, and that they were strongly shared by more than one important member of the body, and strongly opposed by none.'[33]

Much of this was tendentious and some of it no more than exploratory probing in the hope of producing a positive reaction. In the correspondence that followed, Parnell receded from his initial claim that a statutory legislature had been promised and it is indeed most improbable that Carnarvon would have been nearly so explicit as Parnell made him out to be; the Lord-Lieutenant's memorandum, though doubtless shaped so as to show him in the best available light, must remain the most reliable source for this curious episode.[34] Parnell's own disclosures, made as they were at the height of the Home Rule crisis, were almost certainly tactical in motivation. He could scarcely have hoped to influence votes in the division lobbies of the House of Commons, but he could reasonably have expected to sow dissension among his enemies and implant in the public mind a nagging doubt about the extent to which the opponents of Home Rule really meant what they said. In these two aims he may have had considerable success, though it may reasonably be argued that for one who aspired to negotiate with governments, this calculated breach of confidence was a high price to pay for the furore he achieved.

Two questions remain – how far did Parnell take Carnarvon's opinions seriously and to what extent did the interview influence his electoral strategy? Or, was the whole affair for him 'an excellent parody of a historically significant fact', as a recent study has called it?[35] Given his habitual taciturnity, we cannot be sure of the exact weight which he attached to the conversation, or to Carnarvon himself. But Parnell was not exactly naïve and he is unlikely to have believed everything he said he believed in his public statements. What he may well have believed, what it would have been difficult for him not to believe in the light of the conciliatory policy the government had pursued in the weeks they had been in office, was that the situation was opening out in a most promising way. It had certainly begun to seem as if some Conservatives at least were thinking in terms of an Irish settlement, and since the 'central board' negotiations had shown that some Liberals were also thinking in such terms the possibility clearly existed of playing one side off against the other.

III

Yet if this expectation was present in Parnell's mind, and if it helped to shape his approach to the general election, the manoeuvre to achieve a balance between the two British parties was not at first distinguished by any high degree of skill, a fact which suggests that, once the Tory scent was in his nostrils, Parnell became preoccupied with private negotiation at the expense of public attitudes. The most conspicuous example of this was the contemptuous reaction by Irish nationalists to the declared intention of Chamberlain and Dilke to visit Ireland after the fall of the Liberal government. That the men who had to all appearances championed the Irish cause while that government lasted, should immediately become the target of abuse when they sought to reinforce their benevolence by seeing the problem at first hand for themselves, seemed to the two Radicals, and to many others as well, not merely ungrateful but also bewildering.

This sudden frost, which nipped the impending visit in the bud, has been explained in various ways, none of them entirely convincing. The most marginal explanation, that the visit was called off because of Dilke's involvement in the Crawford divorce case, is also the least satisfactory, partly because the nationalist hostility preceded the *cause célèbre*, and still more because the misfortune to Dilke need not have prevented Chamberlain from making the trip. A more compelling reason is that for a Catholic country – and more especially for the Irish bishops – too close a Radical embrace could only be an embarrassment. This was particularly true of matters concerning education. Indeed, it is probable that the readiness of members of the Irish hierarchy to entertain Chamberlain's advances in the spring of 1885 had been due to their realization that under the 'central board' scheme education might have been a transferred subject and therefore protected evermore from Radical impiety. Once that scheme collapsed, and when Carnarvon went out of his way to demonstrate his amenability on educational questions, the bishops turned like sunflowers towards his warming beams. From that it was but a step for first Cardinal Manning and then Archbishop Walsh to find themselves mysteriously indisposed to provide useful introductions for the Radical leaders.[36] Chamberlain would not have been pleased had he known that the day before he declined to help the Radical leaders, Manning had had a confidential talk with Carnarvon in which he pressed upon him an Irish solution which was in part a plagiarism of the ill-fated 'central board' scheme itself.[37]

Ecclesiastical rebuffs were tiresome but not crucial. What was crucial was Parnell's attitude towards the projected visit. As usual, it was difficult to elicit, though Chamberlain did his best. On 17 June he made a slashing public attack on 'the absurd and irritating anachronism known as Dublin Castle' and held out the prospect that in the new parliament after the election reform would take the shape of 'the concession to Ireland of the right to govern itself in the matter of its purely domestic business'.[38] Simultaneously, he tried through O'Shea to ascertain whether Parnell was favourably inclined or not. O'Shea had still not induced the oracle to speak when on 27 June *United Ireland* began the series of articles in which the Radical tour was brutally pilloried. Responsibility for the articles seems to have been shared by William O'Brien and Tim Healy, but Parnell, though pressed by an indignant O'Shea, himself pressed by an even more indignant Chamberlain, would not disavow them, explaining merely that he would not do anything to 'break up his party' on the eve of a general election. O'Shea's report to Chamberlain was a characteristic blend of wounded vanity and wishful thinking. 'Although my temper is not that of an angel, but of an archangel', he wrote at five o'clock in the morning on 29 June, 'I made believe to lose it yesterday afternoon. Mr Parnell sat under a tree for an hour and a half reflecting on all my observations, and although he would not confess everything, I cannot help thinking he must take steps to prevent *United Ireland* . . . continuing the course commenced in the last number.'[39] But no such steps were taken, the attacks continued and Parnell went his own way, which at that particular moment was leading him towards his interview with Carnarvon.

Chamberlain had no option but to cancel his visit. Nursing a resentment which he was to discharge with momentous effect the following year, he ascribed Parnell's unhelpfulness to the fact that the Irish leader 'was trying to negotiate a better bargain with the Tories'.[40] This was partly true, but it was not the whole truth. William O'Brien wrote afterwards that Parnell was faced with 'a choice between Gladstone and Chamberlain', and a contemporary comment, which found its way to Dilke, who made a note of it, points in the same direction. 'He [Parnell] discussed the project with one of his colleagues, Mr John O'Connor, to whom he expressed the view that Mr Chamberlain was aspiring to replace Mr Gladstone in the leadership, and that he would do nothing which could assist him in this purpose because he thought that he "could squeeze more out of Gladstone than he could out of Chamberlain".'[41]

Even this, however, was an over-simplification, for Parnell at this time had not one but two private negotiations in hand which allowed him to be equally cavalier with Carnarvon on the one hand and Chamberlain on the other. The first of these is hidden, no doubt deliberately, in the deepest obscurity, but we have it on Randolph Churchill's own authority (in a conversation which took place in 1890) that Parnell was several times at his house in the summer of 1885 and that together they 'arranged a great many things' in connection with the general election, 'the most perfect confidence existing between us'. So much was this the case that when Churchill finally decided to 'play the Orange card' in 1886 and go against Home Rule he fully expected Parnell to disclose these conversations. In fact, he never did so, either because he had insufficient evidence to make such a revelation convincing, or, more likely, because he saw no point in quarrelling when he might need to do business with the Tories again in the future. That this did not prevent him from making equally damaging disclosures about Carnarvon does not invalidate the argument; it merely shows that with his usual acuteness he had discerned that Churchill mattered more than Carnarvon.[42]

The other negotiation, much more indirect and protracted, but better documented, was with Gladstone. The Liberal leader's attitude remained virtually impenetrable throughout that summer and not even his closest colleagues seem to have been sure whether he would retire, or remain leader for the election only, or go on leading after the election, or even, if he fought the election, on what platform he would fight. But we do know that within three weeks of the fall of his government he wrote to Lord Spencer enquiring about a paper said to contain Parnell's views on local government. This had been sent to Gladstone early in 1885 by Mrs O'Shea and seems to have resembled, or perhaps to have been a copy of, the document presented by Captain O'Shea to Chamberlain on 15 January, which purported to give Parnell's views about the composition and functions of the 'central board' scheme then beginning to take shape as a possible basis for a settlement.[43] Gladstone had paid it little attention at the time, but in the summer, groping for an Irish policy, he thought of it again, and wrote to the former Chief Whip, Lord Richard Grosvenor, asking him to find out if Parnell's views on 'local government' were still represented by that paper.[44] Grosvenor passed on this enquiry to the most likely source of information, Katharine O'Shea.[45] It so happened that on that same day (14 July) Herbert Gladstone made an incautious speech at Leeds in which he came out strongly for a parliament of sorts in Dublin to be fitted into some, as yet ill-defined, federal arrangement.[46] Katharine's reply, therefore, can scarcely have come as a surprise. 'I believe', she wrote, 'that nothing less than a scheme based on the lines of Mr Herbert Gladstone's last speech at Leeds would be acceptable now, or considered calculated to settle the Irish question.'[47]

Although Grosvenor wrote twice more to Katharine in the hope of eliciting something more specific, he might have spared himself the trouble.[48] Parnell was waiting for a bigger fish to rise to his fly and he did not have long to wait. On 6 August Gladstone himself entered the correspondence, writing to Katharine and asking precisely the same question he had already told Grosvenor to put to her. This produced a longer and much more informative letter from Eltham than any that had yet come from that address. Moreover, it carried the *imprimatur* of the man whose views alone counted. 'I have shown this letter to Mr Parnell', Katharine wrote delicately, 'who says it expresses exactly what he means.' No doubt it did, since it is virtually certain that he dictated it to her. It began by dismissing the case for local government reform as 'putting the cart before the horse' and its essence was contained in a single sentence which, though lengthy, was uncompromisingly plain:[49]

In view of recent events, however, and of the present attitude of both the great English political parties towards Ireland, it is now felt that leaders of English public opinion may fairly be asked to consider the question of granting to Ireland a constitution of a similar nature to that of one of the larger colonies with such modifications as may be necessary to secure practically certain guarantees, firstly for the maintenance of the supremacy and authority of the Crown, secondly for the equitable treatment of landowning interests and thirdly for the security of freedom of conscience and the fair treatment of the minority by the majority.

This marked a significant transition from the limited negotiations of the earlier part of the year to the opening of the Home Rule issue in a much grander, if still undefined, sense. It is particularly striking that only four days after the Carnarvon interview Parnell should already have been talking of a constitution similar to that of 'one of the larger colonies'. He had yet to say exactly what he meant by that, but he instructed Katharine to include in her letter an offer to send a draft of more detailed proposals if Gladstone showed any disposition to consider the question further. This, Gladstone, in his reply to Katharine, described as 'too interesting, almost, to be addressed to a person of my age and to weakened sight, since it substitutes for a limited field one almost without bounds'. He diagnosed it, correctly enough, as the outcome of the changed attitude of the Tory party and its 'heightened biddings'. 'It is right I should say', he added sternly, 'that into any counterbidding of any sort against Lord R. Churchill I for one cannot enter.' If actual negotiation were to be involved, he said, he would have to consider whether any project presented by Parnell might not be extinguished like its predecessor two or three months hence on account of altered circumstances. But since there *was* no question of negotiation, it would be an advantage if Parnell were to put his views on paper.[50] In fact, since Gladstone was going to Norway on a cruise and Parnell was about to leave for home to set the stage for the general election, no further exchanges took place at that time. Nor was it to be expected that they should, for nothing effective could be done by either side until the polls had delivered their verdict.

IV

Parnell arrived in Ireland on the evening of 12 August and went at once to Avondale for a rest before beginning the most critical campaign he had yet fought. Some days before leaving London he presided at a dinner given at the Café Royal for General P. A. Collins, one of the more moderate luminaries of the Irish National League of America. Normally, such occasions bored him excruciatingly; perhaps this one did too, but he behaved so well that the impressionable McCarthy was ravished. 'I don't know how it is', he wrote to his literary collaborator, 'but he has in his manners as a host the sweetness of a woman as well as the strength of a curiously cold, self-contained, masculine nature.'[51] If it is not altogether fanciful to regard the 'feminine' side of Parnell's nature as being embodied in his more conciliatory moods and his masculinity as displayed in his bouts of almost demonic energy, then the speech he delivered on this occasion might reasonably be classed as 'feminine'. It was a plea for caution, summed up in a single sentence. 'Our movement this winter should be distinguished by its judgement, its prudence and its moderation.'[52] This was the speech of a man preoccupied with private initiatives which he could not share with his audience. It probably struck some of them as distinctly out of key, for there were signs that agricultural depression was pointing the way to a new crisis in the countryside and there were those, as Parnell himself warned in his speech, who had already begun to advocate the revival of the Land League.

On top of this, a serious enough threat in itself, there were obscure stirrings of discontent within his own party. They were so subterranean that it is difficult to be sure of anything save that they generally seemed to lead back to Tim Healy. Parnell's biographer, Barry O'Brien, records a rumour that about this time Healy was invited by Chamberlain to dine with him to discuss Irish affairs. Healy sought Parnell's advice, or permission, and, so the story runs, was peremptorily told not to go.[53] Whatever the truth of this, it happened that on the day of Parnell's speech at the Café Royal Healy spent three hours with Labouchere, who straightaway sent a long report to Chamberlain. In the course of their talk, the Radical mentioned that Parnell seemed set on Grattan's parliament as his target and that this was 'thoroughly impracticable'. 'Healy said', noted Labouchere, 'that Parnell in his heart cared little for the Irish, particularly since a mob ill-treated him [at Enniscorthy] in 1880.' He also believed that Parnell's attitude towards the Liberals was inspired by resentment at his imprisonment in Kilmainham. This led Labouchere to ask about the possibility of a rebellion in the near future. 'But he [Healy] said that this was altogether impossible because the present policy of all Irishmen was hanging together, for they attributed their troubles to divided counsels. He said that Parnell is very astute. He generally finds out which way the feeling is amongst his followers before he suggests anything, but, in one or two cases, he has put his foot down, when he obtained his way.' Later, however, Healy, perhaps recollecting that tale-bearing was a two-edged weapon when dealing with Labouchere, himself wrote to the latter, declaring

that of course he would be bound by the majority, 'and would steadfastly carry out Parnell's policy, whatever it is declared by the party
to be'.[54] All the same, against this background of barely concealed
restiveness, the comment of the *Nation* (with which paper Healy had
a family connection) on the Café Royal speech sounds distinctly
ominous:[55]

> By the verdict of the nation and by virtue of his extraordinary services
> he occupies the position of leader of the Irish people. This fact alone
> entitles him to be heard. It does not, of course, necessarily entitle
> him to claim exemption from criticism or to be obeyed in all cir-
> cumstances, for even leaders may go astray; but it does impose on
> such of his followers as would attempt the task of criticism the neces-
> sity of approaching it in a grave and cautious spirit.

These were qualified raptures indeed. Much importance clearly
attached to the speech Parnell was to make in Dublin on 24 August and
he himself seems to have realized that the time had come for a little
'extremism' which might, among other things, serve to remind those who
had been negotiating with him in private that the alternative to giving
him what he wanted might be a demand for something much worse.
Accordingly, he came out boldly for 'a platform with one plank only
and that one the plank of national independence'. Everything else, he
said, land, labourers, home industries, educational reform, must wait
until they had won their parliament, which he hoped would be a
unicameral legislature, unencumbered by a House of Lords.[56] Captain
O'Shea, whose relations with Parnell were now, according to himself
'strained', and who had just refused an invitation to shoot at Avondale,
was in Dublin soon afterwards and gathered that this pronouncement
was expected only by 'the faithful and the few' who were let into the
secret a few hours before the speech was given. O'Shea was so much an
outsider by now that his word is not to be trusted, but he was still a
shrewd politician and his analysis of the public meaning of the speech
(as distinct from its private meaning to Carnarvon and Gladstone, of
which he can hardly have known anything) was probably correct. 'It is
too soon', he told Chamberlain, 'to form an opinion as to the effect of
it in the United States, where it was intended to create immediate
sympathy and subscriptions. But it has most certainly dished Davitt.'[57]

This 'one-plank platform' immediately exposed Parnell to such
wide-ranging attack in England that it became urgently necessary for
him to explain further what he meant by it.[58] His first attempt to do
this came at the beginning of September when he attended a banquet

given by the Lord Mayor of Dublin. O'Shea, who was present on this occasion, reported sardonically to Chamberlain. 'Bye the bye, he did his business at the Lord Mayor's dinner excellently. He had had his hair cut and his beard trimmed and he wore a pretty "button-hole". He held himself up and his bow to the Lord Mayor would have been worthy of Louis XIV.'[59] But what he had to say was worthy exclusively of Parnell. While repeating his earlier warnings against violence and about the difficulties and dangers of the coming winter, he again took a strong line on Home Rule:[60]

> They will have to grant to Ireland the complete right to rule herself or they will have to take away from us the share – the sham share – in the English constitutional system which they extended to us at the Union, and govern us as a Crown colony without any parliamentary representation whatever. The government of Ireland as a Crown colony . . . would simply lead to the concession of a constitution similar to that which is enjoyed by each and all of the larger colonies and that is practically what we are asking for.

This seemed to be both a demand for dominion status and a strong hint that it should be conceded now rather than extorted later by an Ireland which had proved itself ungovernable as a crown colony. But it still required further elaboration and this was what Parnell attempted to give it when he spoke in October at the public meeting which followed the Wicklow convention for the selection of the county's parliamentary candidates. Defending the 'one-plank platform', he pointed out that the situation had developed in two important ways since he had first enunciated it in August. First, Gladstone, after much heart-searching, had issued his 'address to the electors of Midlothian' in mid-September. The Irish section of it was long and involved, reflecting the author's rueful reflection that 'I find the whole, in every line and word a trouble'.[61] Essentially, what Gladstone was saying in his most convoluted style was that a limited form of self-government might now safely be conceded to Ireland. 'To maintain the supremacy of the Crown, the unity of the Empire, and all the authority of parliament necessary for the conservation of that unity, is the first duty of every representative of the people. Subject to this governing principle, every grant to portions of the country of enlarged powers for the management of their own affairs is, in my view, not a source of danger, but a means of averting it . . .'[62]

Elaborately vague though this was, and in no sense a capitulation to the idea of Home Rule as Parnell had expressed it, it did nevertheless indicate movement, and movement, however crab-like initially, might in certain circumstances be accelerated. But the second development of that summer seemed at first to point rather towards deceleration and for this Parnell had only himself to blame. Speaking at Arklow at the end of August he had proclaimed that without a freely elected national assembly with the power to protect Irish manufacturers, 'in my opinion, as a practical man, it is impossible for us to revive our native industries'.[63] This quickly brought down upon him the wrath of Chamberlain who denounced at Warrington not merely the notion of tariff autonomy for Ireland, but the whole wider concept of Home Rule towards which Parnell seemed to be tending.[64] Chamberlain's motives need not concern us, but it is certainly true that the protectionist doctrine to which Parnell himself was almost emotionally attached, soon became a serious embarrassment, not merely because it stirred English anxieties, but because it aroused no compensating enthusiasm among his own followers, of whom several of the more intelligent thought it both impracticable and undesirable.[64a]

Parnell's Wicklow speech had therefore to deal both with Gladstone's reservations and Chamberlain's denunciations. On the question of tariff autonomy he drew back a little, though not to the extent of abandoning his demand – he was content merely to postulate some protection for some industries for a few years. But in taking up Gladstone's point that no Irish settlement could be entertained which would endanger the unity of the empire, he made a more sustained and sophisticated analysis of the difficulties inherent in Anglo-Irish relations than any he had yet attempted. It was not possible, he said, to forecast the future. He preferred to point to the fact that under the Union Ireland had become 'intensely disloyal and intensely disaffected':[65]

My advice to English statesmen . . . would be this – trust the Irish people altogether or trust them not at all. Give with a full and open hand – give our people the power to legislate upon all their domestic concerns and you may depend upon one thing, that the desire for separation, the means of winning separation, at least, will not be increased or intensified. Whatever chance the English rulers may have of drawing to themselves the affection of the Irish people lies in destroying the abominable system of legislative union between the two countries by conceding fully and freely the right to manage her own affairs. It is impossible for us to give guarantees, but we can point to the past; we can show that the record of English rule is a constant series of steps from bad to worse, that the condition of

English power is more insecure and more unstable than it has ever been.

We can point to the example of other countries, of Austria and Hungary – to the fact that Hungary, having been conceded self-government, became one of the strongest factors in the Austrian Empire. We can show the powers that have been freely conceded to the colonies – the greater colonies – including this very power to protect their own industries . . . We can show that disaffection has disappeared in all the greater colonies; that while the Irishman who goes to the United States carries with him a burning hatred of English rule . . . the Irishman coming from the same village . . . who goes to one of the colonies of Canada or . . . of Australia, and finds there a different system of English rule to that to which he has become accustomed at home, becomes to a great extent a loyal strength and prop to the community amongst whom his lot has been cast . . .

This was a genuine and statesmanlike attempt to show that Home Rule, properly considered, could be a reconciling rather than a divisive force and Gladstone for one was not unresponsive to it. 'I considered Parnell's last', he wrote to Granville, 'as a *step* not in the wrong direction, perhaps as much as he dared.'[66] This seemed to show that he understood the Irish leader's predicament, the need for him to balance between right and left. But when, in response to that need, Parnell a few days later described the landlords as 'standing on the brink of a precipice' and observed that to him judicial rents (those fixed under the Land Act of 1881) were no more sacrosanct than any others, Gladstone, wounded in his tenderest spot, drew back disapprovingly from what seemed to him 'a new proclamation of war'. 'And how', he asked the long-suffering Granville, 'can we make over the judicial rents to his mercy?'[67]

As the election campaign got under way it became impossible for either British party, deeply divided and uncertain as both were on the Irish question, to pass that question by in total silence. And so, although the election was not fought on Home Rule, which nobody yet had succeeded in defining, Ireland inevitably cast a shadow over the proceedings. What principally emerged from the cloudy rhetoric of the hustings was that Tories and Liberals alike approached the problem with extreme caution and that neither side had any urge to be tarred with a Home Rule brush. Even Randolph Churchill, who had perhaps the most open mind on the matter of any Tory, was careful to reassure his Conservative friends in Ireland that, despite his dealings with the

Irish party, he had never, directly or indirectly, countenanced Home Rule.[68] Only Carnarvon, who was deeply disturbed by the increase of boycotting but believed that the Irish party were doing their best to put it down, seemed prepared to draw from the restlessness of the country the conclusion that what was needed was to concede to the Irish a parliament of their own.[69]

When, therefore, Salisbury made a much-publicized speech at Newport on 7 October he gave an excellent imitation of an elephant walking on egg-shells. About 'the large organic questions' he seemed emphatically negative. 'We look upon the integrity of the Empire as a matter more important than almost any other political consideration that you can imagine, and we could not regard with favour any proposal which directly or indirectly menaced that which is the first condition of England's position among the nations of the world.' Towards Parnell's Wicklow speech he was more equivocal. Taking up the reference to Austria-Hungary, he surmised that Parnell had some notion of imperial federation 'floating in his mind'. That, no doubt, was one of the questions of the future. 'But with respect to Ireland, I am bound to say that I have never seen any plan or suggestion which gives me, at present, the slightest ground for expecting that in that direction we shall find any substantial solution of the problem.'[70] The beauty of this seemingly stern pronouncement was, of course, that it could be interpreted in exactly opposite ways. It was a declaration against Home Rule, if the hearer happened to believe that Home Rule was destructive of the empire; it left the road open for Home Rule if the hearer happened to believe that it was a solvent of ills and therefore a contribution to imperial strength.

From Parnell's viewpoint this was encouraging, at least to the extent that it appeared not absolutely to run counter to his secret exchange of views with Carnarvon, but this did not mean that he therefore relaxed his efforts to make his other secret exchange – with Gladstone – yield appropriate fruit.[71] In the Irish camp it was increasingly assumed, though without adequate justification, that from the moment he published his Midlothian manifesto Gladstone had begun to move towards Home Rule.[72] On the other hand, a Liberal-nationalist alliance presented one major problem which Healy was quick to grasp. The root difficulty, he thought, lay with the House of Lords, which would be certain to veto any Liberal Home Rule bill, even if such were to get through the Commons. From this he drew a clear conclusion which he passed on to Labouchere in mid-October. 'We have to make the best fight we can for a small country, and clearly, if we could put the Tories in and hold them dependent on us, that is our game. With the House of Lords behind them and our help, they could play ducks and drakes with the Union, were they so minded.'[73]

V

This was a cogent argument, but it did not conflict with Parnell's essential strategy, which was to see how far each party would be prepared to go to meet the Irish demand. It remained important for him, therefore, to exploit his existing line to Gladstone to the utmost. He did not, it seems, confide much in his colleagues except about election matters, but he did apparently ask Healy and Sexton to frame some specific suggestions for Home Rule. Whether these were or were not the basis of the 'proposed constitution for Ireland' which Katharine O'Shea sent Gladstone on 30 October we cannot be certain, though it closely resembles the summary of Parnell's ideas which Healy gave Labouchere in the letter just quoted. The 'constitution' was much the most precise formulation to which Parnell had yet committed himself. In it he postulated a unicameral Irish parliament, weighted to secure proportionate representation for the Protestant minority, 'with power to make enactments regarding all the domestic concerns of Ireland, but without power to interfere in any imperial matter'. The domestic concerns included taxes, tariffs, police and judges, though the British government was to retain responsibility for the naval and military establishment. Ireland was to make an imperial contribution of £1 million p.a., which could be counted towards the cost of this establishment. As to the continued presence of Irish members at Westminster this 'might be retained or might be given up', but if retained might only be for imperial purposes to be certified by the Speaker.[74]

Upon these proposals Gladstone commented in a letter to Katharine which was not sent but nevertheless throws light upon his initial reactions. 'I could not enter', he wrote, 'into any competition with others upon the question how much or how little can be done for Ireland in the way of self-government.' On the contrary, his advice was that Parnell would do better to seek a settlement from the party actually in power. 'What I think essential to any hope of a satisfactory issue is that any answer given on behalf of either party should be given on its own ground, and quite independently of the other party.' The reply he did send, through Lord Richard Grosvenor, was rigidly noncommittal, though it included a titillating promise to speak soon in Midlothian about the Irish question and its bearing on British politics.[74a]

He carried out this promise at Edinburgh on 9 November, the day on which Salisbury also made an important speech in London. Both speakers no doubt had present in their minds two significant statements by the Irish leader. The first was an interview which Parnell gave to the New York *Herald* on 30 October. In it Parnell again made a quite deliberate overture to Gladstone. Extracting from the latter's election manifesto far more than Gladstone had ever intended to be read into it, he supplied this gloss: 'Mr Gladstone's declaration that legislative control over her own affairs might be granted to Ireland, reserving to the imperial parliament such powers as would insure the maintenance of the supremacy of the Crown and of the unity of the Empire, is in my judgement the most remarkable declaration upon this question ever uttered by an English statesman.' Why then, asked his interviewer, would Parnell not give guarantees that legislative independence would not be used as a stepping-stone to separation? 'I refuse to give guarantees', said Parnell bluntly, 'because I have none of any value to give. If I were to offer guarantees I should at once be told that they are worthless.' In this he was both correct and prudent. He had, as he truly said, no mandate from the Irish people to bind the future.[75] But in his second utterance he showed that on the main issue he had not receded from the 'one-plank platform' he had constructed in August at the Wicklow convention. Speaking at Wexford on 5 November, he told his audience that there would be no need 'to peddle and trifle with bills for the amendment of the Land Act . . . and bills for this, that and the other amelioration of your condition'. They were going now 'to the root of the matter'.[76]

With Parnell in this mood it was only common sense for both Gladstone and Salisbury to equivocate. Salisbury was the more cautious of the two. He had nothing to add, he declared, to what he had already said about 'the large organic questions'. Once again he stressed his party's commitment to 'the integrity of the Empire' and he acknowledged a degree of responsibility for the future fate of the non-nationalist Irish minority. 'But', he added with vague benevolence, 'within those lines . . . the policy which every English government, and, I am sure, the present, would pursue would be to do all that is possible to give prosperity, contentment and happiness to the Irish people.'[77] Gladstone, as his custom was, spun a wordier cocoon, but he did seem to hold out a more definite promise when he observed that if after the election a 'vast majority' of the elected representatives of Ireland were to make a constitutional demand for 'large local powers of self-government accompanied by the condition that the unity of the Empire is not to be impaired', this would sweep everything else into the shade. 'The satisfactory settlement of that subject, which goes down to the very roots and foundation of our whole system and political constitution, will become the first duty of parliament.'[78]

This was encouraging enough for Parnell, speaking at Liverpool next day, to hail it as 'the most important pronouncement upon the Irish question which has ever been delivered by any English minister'. Even though it fell far short, as he hastened to add, 'of the exigencies of the position', he was certainly ready to agree that until the Home Rule issue was settled it would be impossible for English questions to be dealt with. 'I wish to guard myself', he added ironically amid loud laughter, 'against being supposed to have even the idea of a threat, much less any threat of obstruction.' But he then passed on to criticize Gladstone's refusal to frame proposals until the general election had produced its result. If, he pointed out, they took Gladstone at his word and presented him with his large majority in Britain – apart altogether from any support he might get from the Irish party – and if Gladstone *then* passed a bill through the House of Commons, it would immediately be rejected by the Lords on the ground that the issue had not been submitted to the electorate, and they would be entirely within their rights to do so.[79]

This objection was not only sound, it was highly relevant to what happened next. Parnell ended his speech by inviting Gladstone to frame his proposals *now*. Gladstone replied a week later in a vein of ponderous jocularity, twitting Parnell with wanting to conduct his negotiations through the public press, and this though it was Gladstone himself who had effectually sealed off all private approaches. Until Ireland had spoken at the polls, he said, there was no authoritative voice to speak for her. He himself, not being a minister, could not assume ministerial functions.[80] Four days after that, on 21 November, Parnell delivered his riposte when he authorized the publication of a document that immediately became famous, the manifesto to the Irish in Great Britain, recommending them to vote for the Conservative candidates when these were confronting Liberals or Radicals. This was a big enough shock in itself, but it was accentuated by the tone in which the Liberals were denounced as the exponents of coercion and as the party which, with its 'free schools' programme, had made an insidious attempt to destroy religious education. Nor was this all. The Liberals were further attacked because they were campaigning for the reform of parliamentary procedure and on the need to avoid dependence on the Irish party. The former simply meant 'a new gag' and the application to all non-Radicals of 'the despotic methods and the mean machinery of the Birmingham caucus'. The latter was an appeal for sufficient strength to be able 'to force down a halting measure of self-government upon the Irish people, by the same methods of wholesale imprisonment by which durability was sought for the impracticable Land Act of 1881'. Consequently, the Irish in Great Britain were asked to place no trust in the Liberal party and instead 'to prevent the government of the Empire falling into the hands of a party so perfidious, treacherous and incompetent'. There would be a few exceptions to the rule which would be notified in due course, but that was all. 'In every other instance we earnestly advise our fellow-countrymen to vote against the men who coerced Ireland, deluged Egypt with blood, menaced religious liberty in the school, the freedom of speech in parliament, and promise to the country generally a repetition of the crimes and follies of the last administration.'[81]

This brutal document which, as its real author, T. P. O'Connor, later observed, 'did not err on the side of reserve', caused a sensation at the time and has been for many commentators a stumbling-block ever since. Even to J. L. Hammond, an English Liberal historian with exceptional insight into Irish affairs, the manifesto betrayed 'Parnell's misunderstanding of British politics'.[82] In reality it did nothing of the sort, as may be seen from its context. Several facts are relevant. First, the decision to swing the Irish vote behind the Tories was made very late. On 16 November Parnell wrote to T. P. O'Connor that it was 'almost certain', though not fully settled, 'that we shall have to vote for the Tories at the general election'.[83] Parnell himself said at Liverpool the day after the manifesto was issued that it was 'drawn up in consultation with me on Saturday [21 November]'.[84] Next, it was apparently written and issued with little or no consultation with other nationalists. T. M. Healy, whose name appeared among the signatories, and who prided himself on being very much of the inner circle, claimed later that he only learnt of it when he read it in a Dublin evening paper.[85] Finally, when Parnell came to read over O'Connor's burning phrases, he showed himself, so the vexed author recorded, 'somewhat tepid'.[86] For this, as O'Connor afterwards realized, Parnell had a private reason which we must soon explore, but his indifference sprang also from something of greater moment, the fact that he knew, and his adversaries knew, that the manifesto was no more than a move in the game – a daring move perhaps, but still only an incident in a complex and developing situation.

What then was the motive behind this sudden shift of emphasis?

The key, surely, lies in the timing. The manifesto was not finally decided upon until after Gladstone's public refusal to compete with the Tories. But once that refusal had been made several factors combined to push Parnell along the path he eventually followed. One, probably, was his own estimate, or over-estimate, of the lengths to which very different kinds of Tory – Churchill as well as Carnarvon – were prepared to go to satisfy Ireland. And even if it was true, as Parnell must have been perfectly well aware, that the final decision in that party rested with Salisbury, Salisbury himself had not finally closed the door when the manifesto was published.

A second factor which weighed heavily with some Parnellites, and no doubt with their chief as well, was the one which Healy had earlier pointed out to Labouchere – that the House of Lords, while a very Cerberus to a Liberal Home Rule bill, might well become Salisbury's poodle if he chose to force through an Irish settlement. And to this may be added a third point, also made to Labouchere, though this time by Davitt, that there were 'Tory' nationalists as well as 'Radical' nationalists among the Irish and that the former would much prefer to deal with a Conservative government which had already, in the Ashbourne Act passed during the brief summer session of 1885, shown signs of being prepared to solve the land question in the only lines along which a solution beckoned – the creation of a peasant proprietary based upon a state guarantee of satisfactory prices for landlords.[87]

Moreover, Tory nationalism had an important additional reason for preferring Conservatives – the well-founded assumption that the latter would be more sympathetic than the Liberals to the educational problems of Catholics. Indeed, these problems were as important to the Irish in Great Britain as to the Irish in Ireland. So important were they that it has been plausibly argued that the Irish vote in British constituencies was more influenced by the educational question – and especially by Cardinal Manning's call to vote against the supporters of 'free schools'[88] – than it was by the Parnellite manifesto.[89] This argument, it is true, has been criticized as being based on insufficient evidence and instances have been adduced of some Irish voters ignoring Parnell's instructions to vote for the Liberals in a few special cases, and of other Irish voters ignoring his instructions to vote Tory in a different set of special cases.[90] Not too much, however, need be made of these inconsistencies, for the obvious conclusion is surely the right one – that in most instances the Parnellite manifesto and Cardinal Manning's summons, so far from being in competition, marched together towards the same objective, even if for different reasons.

One further factor which may have had a bearing on the decision to throw the Irish vote behind the Tories ought perhaps to be mentioned, though its significance is difficult to assess. This is what Dr Cruise O'Brien has called 'mimetic snobbery', which he defines as 'the assumption, by middle-class professional people who were often of peasant origin, of the aristocratic contempt for persons "in trade"'.[91] When, as in the case of Chamberlain, 'shop-keeping' was allied to 'anti-Christian' radicalism, then the scorn of men like Tim Healy or William O'Brien, as evidenced in the *United Ireland* attacks on the abortive Irish tour, was apt to be corrosive. Captain O'Shea, no mean connoisseur of the snobbery of power, acutely analysed for Chamberlain's benefit how mimetic snobbery could work in reverse. 'It would be fatuous', he wrote, 'to believe that the Parnellites do not see through the insincerity of Lord R. Churchill . . . I am sure his tactics do not deceive Parnell, but O'Brien is his most powerful rival and the *democrat* in question loves a lord.'[92] Parnell himself was largely immune from such infections. But he was, after all, of the gentry and it may be no accident that, whereas he met Carnarvon and Churchill face to face, he dealt only with Chamberlain through O'Shea; the fact that Chamberlain appeared to repose such confidence in Katharine's husband was no doubt a further reason for Parnell to avoid a personal encounter.

How effective was the manifesto in achieving its object? The answer is clouded by contemporary, and subsequent, misconceptions of the situation prevailing at the time it was issued. The simplest misconception is to assume that by 21 November Gladstone's high-minded devotion to the necessity for an Irish settlement was fully formed and that the manifesto greatly increased his difficulties thereafter in educating his party to the point he had already reached.[93] But even if that were true, and Gladstone had set his course towards Home Rule, it by no means followed that to return him with a large majority would be the best means of ensuring that his supposed conversion would issue in actual legislation. Those who, like Michael Davitt, believed this to be the case were being more than a little naïve.[94] It was not an attitude shared by those closer to political realities. Healy, in that conversation with Labouchere on 22 July mentioned earlier, had forecast that 'according to present arrangements', the Irish in Great Britain would be called on 'to vote solid for the Conservative candidates'.[95] And in October, as we saw, he outlined to Labouchere very precisely the policy of balance which the manifesto a month later was designed to put into effect.[96]

It is difficult therefore to accept the accuracy of Davitt's recollections, when he wrote long afterwards that Parnell confessed to him 'more than once' that his tactics had been mistaken.[97] This is not to deny that there might have been an outcome to the election still more favourable than the one eventually arrived at. It could have happened that, with the aid of the Irish vote in the constituencies, the Tories would have come back with a small majority dependent upon Parnellite support in the House of Commons – a situation which would have tested to the utmost their previous professions of goodwill toward Ireland. But the situation which did emerge was very nearly as apt to Parnell's purpose. Leaving Parnell's own phalanx out of account for the moment, the elections produced a total of 335 Liberal seats and 249 Conservative seats. How many of the Conservative victories were due to the transfer of the Irish vote in British constituencies it is impossible to state exactly. Contemporary estimates, as John Morley recorded, varied from 20 to 40. Chamberlain, a shrewd political arithmetician, reckoned the total at 25.[98] T. P. O'Connor, on the other hand, who as virtual head of the Irish organization in Britain, was well placed to know, asserted that Liberals had been defeated by the Irish vote in 46 seats outside London, and that inside London their influence on the result in 19 contests might have been decisive.[99]

The exact proportion of seats 'controlled' by the Irish vote was less important than the result. And the result was that Parnell with his 86 seats (85 of them in Ireland and one in Liverpool), had at last arrived at the fulcrum, where he could hold the balance, either doubling the Liberal majority or destroying it utterly as circumstances might dictate. This represented a triumph not merely of tactics but of organization. The convention system had worked so well in Ireland, with a few exceptions, that in the whole of Munster, Connaught and Leinster the Parnellites captured every seat except the two belonging to Trinity College, Dublin. More striking even than that was the measure of their success in Ulster. There, a special manifesto was issued on 24 November laying down the most precise instructions how the nationalist vote was to be cast in those constituencies which Parnell could not hope to win. Once again, the policy of balance was much in evidence.[100] As a consequence, in the nine counties of Ulster the nationalists had a majority for the first time. True, it was a bare majority – 17 seats out of 33 – but it produced more delight among the Parnellites than anything else in the election. 'Ulster is Ireland's at last', declared the *Nation* ecstatically. 'Nevermore will a West-British faction or a bitter Orange clique be able to rise in the House of Commons and deny that a united Ireland demands the restoration of a native parliament.'[101] This was a dangerous delusion which coming events and later elections were to expose with cruel clarity. But for the time being it was, after its uncertain fashion, a triumph.

VI

The success in Ireland was in large part the success of the Irish National League and of the MPs who cheerfully went the weary, sometimes stormy, but more often tedious, round of the conventions. Parnell's own contribution to this combined effort was not negligible but it was more fitful than is sometimes realized. This was mainly because, as we shall see presently, his energy was diverted elsewhere at a crucial moment. And even the energy he did spare for Ireland was devoted almost as much to a vendetta, possibly not unconnected with his private life, as it was to the general prosecution of the campaign. This was the campaign he personally conducted against Philip Callan in Louth. Callan aroused Parnell's displeasure for several reasons. One was that though an able speaker he had been observed drunk in the House of Commons. During this election Parnell went to Louth and repeated this charge publicly in Callan's presence. 'And I will leave it to your good sense', he told the audience, 'to judge how many other occasions also.'[102] A second reason for getting rid of Callan was the belief that he had 'leaked' party business to the newspapers. When Healy remonstrated with him for his harshness, Parnell sternly replied: 'Healy, you know better than anyone else that, except for the time Callan was in South America, the secrets of this party were never for a day withheld from the press.'[103]

But there was another and more mysterious dimension to the quarrel. This was that Callan was supposedly in possession of Parnell's own secret and might, if returned, hold it *in terrorem* over him for an indefinite future. According to Healy, whose account is guardedly and partially confirmed by T. P. O'Connor, during the Monaghan by-election of 1883 a then nationalist MP had opened in error a telegram intended for Parnell. Allegedly, it read as follows: 'The Captain is away. Please come. Don't fail. Kate.'[104] The MP, instead of destroying this, handed it to Callan who may have given it some private circulation. To crush him, or at least to draw his teeth, therefore became for Parnell a burning necessity. A. J. Kettle, who saw something of both men during the 1885 election, recorded long afterwards that Callan was offered an alternative seat further north, but refused to leave his native ground.[105] There then ensued a bitter and violent contest, the only occasion up to then, except at Enniscorthy in 1880, when Parnell was ever subjected to ill-treatment by an Irish crowd.[106] The crowd became even more hostile when on 3 December the result was shown to be a victory for the Parnellite candidate, Joseph Nolan, by over a thousand votes. Parnell himself gazing calmly down on the scene, reckoned that there were no more than twenty troublemakers and remained as unperturbed as usual. He must have found it more difficult to keep his impassivity when Callan, shaking his fist at him, launched into an impassioned attack on the unfairness with which he had been treated compared with the efforts made on behalf of Captain O'Shea. The report of what followed is somewhat confused – not unnaturally, since the meeting was so rowdy – but the key passage ran as follows: 'He [Callan] asked Mr Parnell, face to face, what was there in the character or private history – in the public character or private history – of Captain O'Shea, what was there superior in his political character or private history superior to that of Phil Callan and his wife* that Mr Parnell should malign and traduce him (Mr Callan) and support with his best exertions Captain O'Shea (cheers).'[107] After the presiding officials had said a few words, there was an awkward pause, as if everyone was waiting for Parnell to speak. He made no sign to do so and after a few minutes withdrew with his party to Nolan's committee-rooms. Well might he keep silence. This was the first lurid flash from the depths and to notice it at all would probably only serve to concentrate attention on what the public at large did not know then and were not to know for long afterwards. But it was a warning, nevertheless, of the hazards inherent in the O'Shea connection.

Once the outcome of the general election was clear, Parnell's work was for the time being done. What would happen between the declaration of the poll and the meeting of parliament would be decided by the Liberals and the Conservatives and there was little he could do in the interval except continue his policy of probing, probing, probing to find the best point of pressure. Interviewed by an American correspondent before the final results were known, he admitted the future was difficult to forecast, but said he expected a settlement would now be more

---

*I have reproduced above the exact phrasing of the *Irish Times* report. It remains mysterious that Philip Callan should have introduced his own wife – so far as is known a perfectly blameless person – into the discussion and the words 'and his wife', as actually spoken, may have been intended to go directly after the reference to Captain O'Shea. On the other hand it is possible that even Callan may have blenched from mentioning Mrs O'Shea directly, and contented himself with making his point obliquely but still intelligibly, to those who could read between the lines.

likely to come from the Liberals.[108] In fact, throughout December,
by means of Mrs O'Shea, he bombarded Gladstone in an attempt to
get him to disclose his intentions. Five times she importuned the Liberal
leader and five times, with growing emphasis, he repelled her. On 12
December, in what was presumably intended as a dismissive gesture,
he advised that Parnell should make what terms he could with the
Tories. But a few days later Katharine returned to the charge, passing
on to him one of Parnell's elaborate 'political' letters, written ostensibly
to her, but intended for Gladstone. In this letter Parnell, after declaring
that the 'constitution' he had submitted before the election still represented 'the smallest proposal which would be likely to find favour
in Ireland if brought forward by an English minister', stressed that it
had been drawn up 'with a view to propitiate English prejudice',
that it offered various guarantees against hasty or discriminatory
legislation, and that it provided Protestants with proportionate representation. 'These', he said reproachfully, 'are all important concessions and guarantees and some opinion must surely have been
formed by now upon these and other details.' As a final *douceur*, he
added that he had not seen Lord Carnarvon and would not arrange to
do so for another week or so. 'I have always felt that Mr Gladstone is
the only living statesman who has both the power and the will to carry
a settlement it would be possible for me to accept and work with.'
After this veiled flattery came a threat rather less veiled. 'I doubt
Lord C's power to do so, though I know him to be very well disposed.
However, if neither party can offer a solution of the question I should
prefer the Conservatives to remain in office as under them we could at
least work out gradually a solution of the land question.'[109]

The correspondence straggled on, but it led to nothing for the good
reason that Gladstone was at that moment dangling before the Conservatives the possibility that they might take the initiative themselves.
On 14 December, the date of Parnell's letter, Gladstone met Salisbury's
nephew, Arthur Balfour, at Eaton Hall, the Duke of Westminster's
house in Cheshire, and to him expressed the hope that he, Gladstone,
would be able to support the Conservatives in an Irish policy. On 20
December he followed this with a letter in which he used a phrase
which became famous. 'I think it will be a public calamity if this great
subject should fall within the lines of party conflict.' He therefore
repeated his offer to regard the Irish question as a national, not a party,
issue if the government were to attempt a solution. Balfour responded
civilly though with scarcely concealed scepticism. Other letters followed
and finally, as requested, he showed the correspondence to his uncle.[110]

The reaction was entirely predictable. The Conservative instinct, naturally, was to treat Gladstone's overture as hypocritical and to see in it nothing but a Machiavellian device to involve them in the quicksands of Home Rule. The olive branch was therefore politely but firmly rejected.

This may, or may not, have been too cynical a view. Gladstone's son Herbert always maintained that it was and that his father was perfectly sincere. But it was Herbert himself who made it difficult for contemporaries to share that interpretation. On 17 December, mid-way between the Liberal leader's verbal and epistolary approaches to Balfour, there appeared the celebrated 'Hawarden Kite'. This was the statement which appeared in the *Leeds Mercury* and the *London Standard* of that date that Gladstone was about to come out in favour of Home Rule. Herbert Gladstone had made the statement entirely on his own authority – it was in the first instance intended as a private word to three journalists, though he was excessively naïve if he really believed it would remain private. It seems that he took this strange initiative in an attempt to pre-empt what he feared was a Radical conspiracy to oust Gladstone from the leadership on an anti-Home Rule basis, and although Gladstone's prompt repudiation of the allegation appeared in the evening papers that same day, there was a widespread and natural disposition among both Liberals and Tories to believe that Herbert's indiscretion really had been inspired by his father.[111]

Not indeed that the Tories needed the Hawarden Kite to warn them off Home Rule. The cabinet had already decided on 14 December not to 'tamper' with that question, and Carnarvon, the chief protagonist of tampering, had with difficulty been restrained from resigning there and then. But the decision can hardly have taken him by surprise. Meeting Justin McCarthy at dinner on 13 December he had told him he could not carry his colleagues with him and that negotiations were at an end.[112] The other 'ally' of the Parnellites, Randolph Churchill, had already made it plain to McCarthy that things had changed since the election. 'We've done our best for you', he said, 'now we shall do our best against you.'[113] McCarthy noted further that Churchill was taking the line that the Tories 'had no chance about Home Rule after Gladstone had taken it up'. 'Lord Randolph says that his strong wish is that the Conservatives should be turned out at once. They cannot govern, he says, under present conditions. And he wants to have them out of the responsibility.'[114] Ten days later Churchill was in Ireland hob-nobbing with his Unionist friends and arranging with the leader

of the Ulster Unionists, Colonel E. J. Saunderson, the details of a visit
he was to pay early in the New Year.[115] This did not mean that he was
necessarily opposed to a constructive policy for Ireland – on the contrary he continued to act in concert with Carnarvon in these last days
of the Salisbury ministry. But being constructive about Ireland had
never with him amounted to conversion to Home Rule. All he was
doing now was to take advantage of favourable circumstances to make
the fact crystal clear.

Not even Churchill, however, could stop the government's drift
towards coercion, especially since the news from Ireland told of increasing lawlessness. The dangers inherent in this situation were fully
apparent to Parnell and in a letter to Healy of mid-December he suggested that *United Ireland* should denounce the spreading outrages.
'We shall get no settlement of national questions from the Tories, but
it is exceedingly probable that they will try to keep themselves in office
on proposals to renew coercion and on the anti-Irish cry.'[116] Anti-
Irish cry perhaps, but retention of office decidedly not. The surviving
evidence suggests that the Tory cabinet was at least as anxious to be
out of power at the end of December as the Liberal cabinet had been
at the beginning of June. By mid-January 1886, only a few days before
the new parliament was due to get down to serious business, ministers
were discussing how best to put renewed coercion into effect. On 26
January they resolved that two days later they would publicly announce
a return to coercion, but in the interval, at one o'clock on the morning
of 27 January, the government were defeated on the address through an
amendment on agricultural policy, moved by Chamberlain's henchman,
Jesse Collings, but apparently concocted in advance by Chamberlain
himself with Parnell's collaboration.[117] Thereupon, as speedily as he
decently could, Salisbury brought his ministry to an end.

Throughout the period between the end of the election and the end
of the ministry the air had been thick with rumours. That the government could not last was a general assumption, but what might take its
place was anybody's guess. Every kind of combination was mooted in
those hectic days, but Parnell, on whom so much depended, maintained
his usual imperturbable reserve. Pressed by Henry Labouchere on
17 December to declare his views, he merely replied that it would be
best to await events and see what the new parliament produced.[118]
Not all his followers were so patient. Nor were they so uniformly
docile as his great electoral triumph might lead one to expect. Two days
after his leader's non-committal reply to Labouchere, Healy called on
the Radical MP, stayed six hours and, among other things, delivered

himself of a series of extraordinary remarks which Labouchere summarized for Chamberlain thus:[119]

> Parnell is half mad. We always act without him. He accepts this position; if he did not we should overlook him. Do not trouble yourself about him. Dillon, McCarthy, O'Brien, Harrington and I settle everything. When we agree, no one can disagree. We are forming a 'Cabinet'. We shall choose it. We shall pass what we like in this Cabinet . . .

The interest of this strange farrago is not that it described a real situation, which it manifestly did not, but that it indicated with startling clarity the gulf which had opened between Healy and Parnell by the end of 1885. That might not have been of great importance had not the moment simultaneously arrived when Parnell found himself obliged to put the loyalty of his followers to a supreme test. For now at last the nagging friction with Captain O'Shea precipitated the major crisis which had threatened for so long.

CHAPTER 10

The Galway 'Mutiny'

'The question was, in the special circumstances of the moment, whether we should swallow O'Shea or utterly destroy our movement and party at its brightest moment for a personal reason which we could not even explain.' (William O'Brien to John Dillon, Galway, 7 February 1886.)

I

The failure of the 'central board' scheme, and its displacement during 1885 by Parnell's drive for full Home Rule, had left Chamberlain's bedraggled Mercury, Captain O'Shea, resentful and unemployed. With the onset of the general election towards the end of the year his position became increasingly precarious and he himself correspondingly querulous. By that time, though he still dreamt of being returned again for an Irish seat, his ties with the Irish party and with his own constituency had been almost completely severed. Early in February 1884 he had, indeed, appeared at a party meeting after an absence of about two years, but his ex-colleagues seem to have regarded his attendance much as Macbeth regarded Banquo's ghost, an apparition as disagreeable as it was unexpected, and this impression was confirmed when the following day he took his usual seat on the government benches. Such in-and-out running did not go unnoticed. 'From all we can learn', observed the *Nation*, 'the men of Clare will have nothing to do with the confidant of Forster at the next election . . . and we must say that we, for our part, share to the full their dislike of so slippery and piebald a politician'.[1]

This verdict seemed to be confirmed when in June 1884 a branch of the Irish National League in Clare passed a resolution of no confidence in O'Shea.[2] But the Captain had no intention of being shrugged off in this fashion. In October he visited the constituency and boasted to his wife that his supporters, whom he claimed to be the Fenians, had come out so strongly for him that 'there will be murder in the Co. Clare if I am opposed'.[3] Almost certainly he exaggerated the extent of their support, but he had from their standpoint the one substantial advantage that he stood to all intents and purposes outside the parliamentary party they distrusted and detested. It was not necessary that they should agree with his politics or even understand them. To the extent that they did understand them they probably disagreed with them violently. But his function in their scheme of things was scarcely that of a practising or practical politician; it was much more that of a spanner in the works of the official party machine.

Yet, as the election drew near, it became plain that it was the machine which would in the end have most influence on the result – especially the parliamentary pledge binding all members of the Irish parliamentary party to sit, act and vote together and to resign if the party by majority vote held that this pledge had not been properly carried out. Captain O'Shea refused absolutely to take the pledge, but he still expected Parnell to come to his aid in Clare.[4] Mrs O'Shea in her book states that the impulse behind his candidature was hers and that the motive was to keep him out of the way. 'I was very anxious that Willie should remain in parliament. Politics were a great interest to him and gave him little time to come down to Eltham . . . Years of neglect, varied by quarrels, had killed my love for him long before I met Parnell, and since the February of 1882 I could not bear to be near him.'[5]

This may have been true, but it was not the whole truth. Captain O'Shea approached the election of 1885 swelled with a sense of self-importance, derived mainly from the active if dubious role he had played in the 'central board' negotiations, but partly also from his delusion that he had helped to influence Cardinal Manning in backing the candidature of Dr W. J. Walsh for the archbishopric of Dublin in the summer of 1885.[6] He was still, partially at least, in Chamberlain's confidence and looking to him for political advancement. On St Patrick's Day, 1885, he wrote to Katharine, deploring Parnell's reluctance to accept the local government offer, and adding: 'It is too bad, as it is a great chance, especially as it would probably allow of my being Chief Secretary in the next parliament.'[7] In May he was still nourishing this hope and before long his fertile imagination had converted a remote prospect into an imminent reality:[8]

Today C [hamberlain] promised me the Chief Secretaryship on the formation of the government after the election.

He would, while holding his own office (probably Secretary of State for the Home Department), help me in the matter.

This is an enormous thing, giving you and the chicks [their three children] a very great position.

Once again, allowance has to be made for O'Shea's infinite capacity for self-deception. A few years later, when he was treading delicate ground in his testimony to the Special Commission, he first denied that the splendid promise had been made at all, and then reduced its dimensions by saying that 'if the Local Government scheme had been adopted, the thing was talked of'.[9] Perhaps it was. Perhaps it suited Chamberlain to tickle his jackal's vanity without making any firm commitment. We cannot be certain, for we have only O'Shea's version. The point of his story, however, is not whether it was objectively true, but that O'Shea, believing himself to be riding high, continued to cherish political expectations of no common order. Yet, if the collapse of the 'central board' scheme did not warn him that the ground was quaking under his feet, by the summer of 1885 he had belatedly come to realize that the *United Ireland* attack on the Chamberlain-Dilke visit was a clear threat to his own ambitions. We saw earlier how desperately he tried to get Parnell to approve the visit and it is clear from a letter he wrote his wife at this time that it was upon Parnell he laid the chief blame for the *débâcle*. 'No rational beings who have had dealings with Mr Parnell would believe him on oath.' He had, he added, already told 'the scoundrel' what he thought of him, but he felt a fool all the same. 'I am worried, if not out of my wits, out of my hair. The little left came out this morning after a sleepless night and I am balder than a coot is. Such fun.'[10] Nevertheless, so long as there remained a possibility that Chamberlain would emerge strengthened from the complex political manoeuvres of that summer, O'Shea could indulge his daydreams for a little longer.

But those daydreams were not to include the representation of the county Clare. As early as September, at the end of the letter to Chamberlain in which he described his relations with Parnell as being 'very strained',* O'Shea added that he was 'a little uneasy' about his seat and would be grateful if Chamberlain would give him 'a lift' in one of his speeches:[11]

> What I want [he wrote] is somebody to inform my deluded country-men that although a reasonable man, I am intensely Irish in sentiment and political design; that although not inferior in ability to other Irish members, I have been content constantly to efface myself in debate in order otherwise to gain substantial benefits for the Irish people; and that my influence, apart from the Kilmainham treaty, *was a more potent factor throughout the parliament than the speeches*

*See above, pp. 294-5.

and antics of those who now take to themselves the credit of everything that has been attained.

That Chamberlain would oblige in this matter seemed only one degree less improbable than that his support would do anything save alienate Irish opinion. But he replied that he was prepared to write O'Shea a eulogistic letter if approached, though, as O'Shea ruefully admitted, it was unlikely that anyone would approach him, given the way the situation had developed since the fall of the Liberal government and the abandonment of the 'central board' scheme. O'Shea was still obsessed by what he took to be Parnell's responsibility for the 'central board' fiasco and refused to believe that the latter had anything better to offer in its place. 'I have little or no doubt', he wrote sourly, 'that now, as he leads them to the "victory" in which he, at any rate, is no strong believer, he is riding for a fall.'[12]

This discharge of bile may have assuaged O'Shea's self-esteem, but it did nothing to help him towards an Irish seat. When he got to Dublin he was soon left in no doubt that not just Clare, but any nationalist constituency, would be closed to him. As it happened, he and Parnell, who was accompanied by T. P. O'Connor, met on the platform at Euston. They travelled together on the Irish Mail and during O'Shea's momentary absence from the carriage, Parnell, with that deprecating smile he sometimes assumed when he was in a difficulty, asked O'Connor whether the party might not after all accept O'Shea again for Clare. O'Connor, a good deal shocked by the question, answered emphatically that it would not.[13]

Parnell conceded this himself in a letter he wrote to Katharine after his arrival in Dublin, adding the significant detail that James O'Kelly, who called to see him next morning (and upon whose judgement he normally relied) was of the same opinion as O'Connor. While they were talking O'Shea tapped on the door. Invited to join their discussion, he declared openly that he would not take the pledge, to which O'Kelly retorted that it was beyond the power of mortal man, even of Parnell, to get him elected for a nationalist seat. Yet, since O'Shea was adamant that Parnell had promised him a seat 'without trouble or expense' (in return, so he told Katharine, for his vote on one of the close House of Commons divisions on Egyptian policy earlier in the year), it was finally agreed that efforts should be made to put him forward for an Ulster constituency which the Parnellites did not themselves intend to contest.[14]

II

Some such eventuality seems to have been in Parnell's mind even before he left London, for on the same day that he wrote to Katharine, she, presumably on his instructions, made a remarkable proposition to the Liberal Chief Whip, Lord Richard Grosvenor. This was that if O'Shea were adopted as Liberal candidate for Mid Armagh Parnell would get him the whole of the Catholic vote (which he reckoned to be within 600 of the combined Episcopalian and Presbyterian total) and would also throw the nationalist vote in four other Ulster constituencies behind the Liberal candidates; as an additional favour, he would secure the Irish vote in Wolverhampton for the hard-pressed Liberal, Henry Fowler.[15]

It was characteristic of the man to assume that the nationalist voters in Ulster and Wolverhampton would do as he told them, though even for Parnell it was stretching the limits of audacity to suggest a traffic in seats with the Liberals at the precise moment when his strategy was moving towards support for the Tories. But not content with this, he made Katharine combine her appeal for help for O'Shea with an attempt to inveigle Gladstone into public acceptance of Home Rule. No wonder Gladstone, taken aback by this shameless juxtaposition of the general and the particular, commented dryly to Grosvenor that 'the subject matter . . . is very curious'.[16]

It was so curious that caution might well have dictated giving it a wide berth. Yet Grosvenor, apparently with Gladstone's approval (the latter still retained an exaggerated notion of O'Shea's services in 1882), exerted himself to help. Unfortunately, matters at once began to go awry. The Ulster Liberals, finding themselves in demand, raised their price to include another seat, South Tyrone. This had the drawback of being a seat which nationalists might hope to win themselves and for which the redoubtable William O'Brien had just been selected as a candidate. Yet, so urgent was the need to find O'Shea a seat that Parnell was apparently prepared to try to have O'Brien's nomination withdrawn, if the Liberals could be persuaded to accept O'Shea. Meanwhile, 'in order to avoid all appearance of collusion', as O'Shea himself put it, the hopeful candidate was to disappear for a few days and then, when all the necessary strings had been pulled, publicly announce his candidature.[17] This plan fell through when the conspirators realized that O'Shea, never exactly an unconspicuous figure, had been recognized while returning from an exploratory tour in Ulster and it was instead decided that he should do his best to ingratiate himself with the electors and especially with the clergy, of Armagh.[18]

Alas, for these great expectations. The Ulster Liberals showed a tiresome disposition to prefer one of their own sort; worse still, Parnell's estimate of the Catholic vote turned out to be greatly inflated.[19] There was nothing for it, as Grosvenor told a reluctant Gladstone, but to withdraw O'Shea's candidature.[20] Even so, he feared, with some reason, a leakage to the press.[21] It was probably this leakage which produced from one prominent Ulster Liberal, Samuel Walker, dire warnings that any suspicion of a Liberal-nationalist compact would alienate the Presbyterians throughout Ulster 'and put a trump card into the hands of the Tories over the province'.[22] And since this was the general view, O'Shea had no option but to accept with regret, as he put it to Grosvenor, 'not having been able to secure a seat for the advantage of the Liberal party'.[23]

Not surprisingly, the Captain now began to turn nasty. This may partly have been because he had fallen ill in Dublin. Marooned in the Shelbourne Hotel (not exactly the harshest of fates), he was soon awash with self-pity and a stream of querulous letters and telegrams flowed ceaselessly to Eltham. In her book Katharine attempts to explain his attitude on the ground that he was too vain to accept the fact of his unpopularity in Ireland, and so convinced of his own importance that he ascribed Parnell's failure to find him a seat to ingratitude and treachery in not supporting his candidature more strongly. 'That Parnell had', she adds, 'and was pressing it so strongly as to jeopardize his own position he could not understand. His true reason for doing so – my desire – he did not know; nor did he know, what Parnell knew, that ugly rumour had already begun the campaign of brutality . . .'[24]

This passage bears strong traces of having been composed long after the event in order to accord with the story told by Captain O'Shea in the divorce court in 1890, when it was essential for him to demonstrate how late the realization dawned upon him that Parnell had stolen his wife away. But the venom shown by O'Shea in 1885 was so intense as to suggest that something more than the wounded vanity of a disappointed politician was in question. 'All I know', he wrote to Katharine early in November, 'is that I am not going to lie in ditch. I have been treated in blackguard fashion and I mean to hit back a stunner. I have everything ready; no drugs could make me sleep last night, and I packed my shell with dynamite. It cannot hurt my friend, and it will send a blackguard's reputation with his deluded countrymen into smithereens . . . I wonder the little girls have not written to me; no one cares a bit for me except my poor old mother.'[25]

The friend in question was Chamberlain, whom O'Shea had mobilized a few days earlier to the extent of telegraphing Grosvenor to say he would write in the Captain's support, though not to the extent of getting him actually to put pen to paper.[26] And Chamberlain, as so often before, was once again the chief recipient of his henchman's woes. Writing on 8 November to cadge a bed at Highbury on his way back from Ireland, O'Shea gave this lurid glimpse of how far his relations with Parnell had deteriorated:[27]

> Parnell called on me yesterday afternoon and began to mumble something about sorrow that I had not seen my way to contest Mid Armagh and hope that an English seat might yet be found for me. I soon cut matters short by telling him that I did not want any more beating about the bush, that no man had ever behaved more shamefully to another than he had behaved to me, and that I wished to hold no further communication with him. He enquired whether I wished him to leave and I replied, most certainly. He then crossed the room and held out his hand. I informed him that I would not touch it on any account.
>
> I do not suppose he has feeling enough to have felt the blow long, but I never saw a man slink out of a room more like a cur kicked out of a butcher's shop.

Even allowing for O'Shea's habitual peacock strut when retailing his adventures to Chamberlain, this letter has an unpleasant ring about it. O'Shea may not have behaved quite as outrageously as he describes, and he may have spoken in his role of frustrated politician rather than that of cuckolded husband, but the fact remains that even if he had said only half what he claimed to have done, he was still using the kind of language to Parnell which that proud man would have suffered from no one else. If the sordid little scene does not tell us the final truth about the extent of O'Shea's awareness of the real situation, it tells us a great deal about the shifts and humiliations to which Parnell's infatuation with Katharine had already reduced him.

Katharine herself was so frantic to obtain a seat for Willie at all costs that from the moment the Mid Armagh candidature was doomed she bombarded Lord Richard Grosvenor with letters, telegrams and even personal visits to move him to action. Eventually Grosvenor admitted that there might just possibly be an opening at Liverpool in the Exchange Division. To engineer a vacancy when a hard-fought election was actually in progress was practically unheard of, but on this occasion there was the further complication of Parnell's 'vote Tory' manifesto of 21 November. Nevertheless, Katharine persisted. She not only harried Grosvenor into promising to go to Liverpool himself, but got him to extract from Gladstone a letter (harping, as usual, on Kilmainham) which could be used as an endorsement for O'Shea's candidature.[28]

As with the proposed candidature in Ulster, so now with Liverpool – a price had to be paid. The price authorized by Parnell was complex and curious. It was that the Liberals should adopt O'Shea for Liverpool Exchange and withdraw their candidate from one or other of the two Kirkdale seats in Lancashire, so that Parnell himself could stand for the vacancy thus created. In return, the Irish vote would be switched to Liberal candidates elsewhere in Liverpool (except in the mainly Irish Scotland Division which was hall-marked for T. P. O'Connor) and at Bootle. The result would be almost certain victory in three out of four of these divisions. If this were not agreed to, however, Parnell and three other nationalists would contest each of the four seats, with possibly disastrous effects on the Liberal fortunes.[29]

For reasons largely internal to Liverpool Liberalism, this tortuous intrigue had to be abandoned. What actually happened was that while a nationalist, John Redmond, stood for one of the Kirkdale seats (and lost it), Parnell came forward as a candidate for Liverpool Exchange. Speaking there on 22 November, the day after the 'vote Tory' manifesto had appeared, he solemnly announced that after mature consideration he had decided to stand, because Irishmen could be sure of only one seat in Britain (the Scotland Division), whereas the Unionists would secure some sixteen Ulster seats which would in effect be representative of British interests. O'Shea was also nominated for the constituency as a Liberal, and the field was completed by a Conservative and another Liberal. But immediately after the time for handing in the nomination papers had elapsed, Parnell dramatically withdrew from the contest.[30] From then until the poll closed he worked hard – 'harder than he had ever worked before' according to Katharine – to win O'Shea that elusive success. So too did Katharine. Visiting the hard-pressed Grosvenor yet again, she urged him to fulfil his promise and go to Liverpool to bring pressure to bear upon the local Liberals.[31] And down to Liverpool he went, a man without illusions and without much hope. Five years later, when the affair was public knowledge, E. R. Russell of the Liverpool *Daily Post* sent Gladstone a satirical article from another Liverpool journal, *The Porcupine*, referring to the fact that at the time of the Exchange contest in 1885 a member of the former Liberal government had shown himself fully aware of the Parnell-O'Shea triangle. In his letter enclosing the article Russell confirmed the allegation. 'When

Lord Richard Grosvenor came down in the middle of the night in 1885 to support the effort to return O'Shea for the Exchange Division of Liverpool he said in the hearing of several persons, in reply to the question how it was that Mr Parnell made an exception of him, "Oh! he sleeps with O'Shea's wife".[32]

But no efforts, not even the combined efforts of Parnell, Katharine and Grosvenor, could impose O'Shea upon Liverpool as a Liberal member. The fight was fierce but the Conservative beat him by 55 votes and the work was all to do again. Yet, in a curious way, Liverpool cast its shadow over the next phase of the story. T. P. O'Connor, who had been triumphantly elected in the Scotland Division, had also been returned for Galway city, but chose to sit for the former. It was not long before O'Shea's imagination began to work upon this situation. Already, while the Exchange contest was still in the balance, he had thrown out the suggestion that O'Connor might decline the Scotland nomination and leave him to fight it as a Liberal.[33] All his advisers, with rare unanimity, combined to quash this audacious proposal, but the fact remained that O'Connor had two seats and O'Shea had none. Might not Galway city supply the long-sought haven?

III

The preliminary moves to explore this possibility were made within weeks of the Liverpool disaster. On 22 December O'Shea, writing to his wife mainly about other matters, noted that an official of the Irish National League of Great Britain was about to go to Galway. 'This looks like business', he added hopefully.[34] But Parnell moved in the matter with extreme reluctance and caution. According to Katharine's own account, the three of them discussed Galway about this time, Parnell stressing repeatedly his inability to force O'Shea upon the party. 'Presently Parnell said consideringly, "And you will not take the pledge even . . .?" and Willie answered, "No, he would sit where he liked and vote as he pleased", to which Parnell could only reply; "Then the thing is not worth discussing" and left him.'[35] But O'Shea could cling like a limpet where his own interests were at stake, and behind O'Shea stood Chamberlain, prepared to support his claim on the ostensible ground of his value as an intermediary. Thus, on 22 January 1886 he wrote to O'Shea suggesting that one of the seats in Ireland left vacant by double election was the answer to his problem. 'Surely it must be to the interest of the Irish party to keep open channels of communication with the Liberal leaders? Can you not get Mr Parnell's *exequatur* for one of the vacant seats? It is really the least he can do for you, after all you have done for him.'[36]

By the time Chamberlain dropped this hint, Parnell had already begun to take soundings. Writing on Christmas Eve to E. D. Gray, he posed the problem of O'Shea. At the late election, he said, he could not possibly have recommended him to any Irish constituency unless he had taken the pledge without jeopardizing the proceedings at all the county conventions where the pledge had been made an integral part of the proceedings. 'I do not see even now, when the situation is very materially changed . . . how I could undertake the responsibility of recommending his candidature to Galway unpledged in any respect even as regards his vote.' On the other hand, he said, he had to take account of what Gray had just written him in a letter which seems not to have survived – that Chamberlain was known to be hostile to Home Rule (Chamberlain had written to Gray in that sense only a few days earlier) and that there was a possibility that O'Shea's influence upon the Radical leader, if it were exerted, might be helpful, supposing a seat could be provided in Galway. Then Parnell delicately cast his fly:[37]

> Under these circumstances do you think I should be justified in saying to you that if you can induce the leading members of the party to tolerate O'Shea's unpledged candidature for Galway neither would I oppose it? If you think so, it would be well for you to see O'Shea yourself soon, and try to restore his good-humour before his visit to C [hamberlain].

Gray's reply to this exists only in draft, but it leaves no doubt that while he thought O'Shea might be of some use in conciliating Chamberlain and Dilke, to espouse him openly as a candidate for Galway would involve 'a certain amount of risk'. But it was for Parnell to decide whether the risk was worth while. 'No one else can do it – the intervention of no one else could do any good – least of all mine. I may be able to support you. I could not initiate anything. *I could only follow you.*'[38]

With this fairly blunt intimation that the business of a leader was to lead, the ball was thrown back into Parnell's court and he was left to make up his mind alone. During January he continued to brood, but on 1 February the writ for the by-election was moved in the House of Commons. Already by then a local candidate, Michael Lynch, had been started and if Parnell was to act at all he had now to act swiftly. Characteristically, having once come to a decision he carried it out with brutal directness. Accosting T. P. O'Connor outside the House of Commons on the night of Friday, 5 February, he told him of his intention to run

O'Shea. O'Connor, who had his own candidate in mind for the vacancy, was dumbfounded and showed it. 'You should have seen his face, my Queen', Parnell told Katharine when he went home to her afterwards, 'he looked as if I had dropped him into an ice-pit.'[39]

O'Connor protested, but, as he well knew, his chances of changing Parnell's mind by his own unaided efforts were virtually nil. He therefore rushed off to find Biggar, then living at a London hotel. Biggar, that capable but crude man, provided the touch of farce which seems to have been almost obligatory in the crises of the Irish party, by rising out of slumber clad in something resembling a bearskin. But comical though he might appear, Biggar, like Parnell, was a man of decision and he determined at once that the candidature should be opposed.[40] O'Connor, who at this moment of shock felt likewise, telegraphed the dread news to Tim Healy in Dublin, declaring he would resign in protest if Healy would do so too. Healy, much startled, cabled back his agreement, but by then O'Connor and Biggar were en route for Dublin, preceded by another wire from O'Connor asking Healy to solicit an article from Gray in next day's *Freeman* to nip the project in the bud.[41]

Given Gray's previous correspondence with Parnell such an initiative was not to be expected from him; on the contrary, as the situation developed the weight of the *Freeman's Journal* was swung more and more firmly behind the leader. Gray was doubtless influenced by a telegram which Parnell sent him from London on 6 February and which John Deasy, one of the party whips, relayed to Healy. It read: 'Advise friends that I have promised if certain person adopted his Chief's views regarding Irish government, O'Shea should have my strongest support. I consequently feel bound if [O'Shea] not returned to resign my seat. Ask friends if under these circumstances feel desire to see me.'[42]

This was a most misleading statement, but entirely typical of Parnell's ruthlessness when driven to the infighting which, with his innate fastidiousness, he normally avoided. What he was saying to Gray in plain words was that if Chamberlain (the 'certain person') accepted his chief's (i.e. Gladstone's) supposed views on Home Rule, Parnell had promised to support O'Shea. There is no evidence whatever to suggest that, directly or indirectly, Parnell had promised any such thing. Nor is there any contemporary documentation for the statement made four years later by Tim Harrington, admittedly in the heat of the party quarrel after the O'Shea divorce case, that in the Galway election Parnell had only adopted O'Shea 'at the special request of Mr Chamberlain'.[43] Parnell, as we know, was well aware of Chamberlain's restiveness on the subject of Home Rule and it is just conceivable that he thought it worthwhile to run O'Shea for Galway as a conciliatory gesture. But on the face of it this is extremely improbable, for Parnell, having good reason to know just how unreliable O'Shea could be, was not likely to want to use him as a go-between. Moreover, all that had actually come from Chamberlain had been an expression to Gray of his hostility to Home Rule and a suggestion to O'Shea that he explore further the possibility of an Irish seat. It is hard to see in these *obiter dicta*, which were not even addressed directly to him, a sufficient explanation for Parnell's intervention.

Nor did Biggar and Healy accept it as a sufficient explanation. Biggar, with T. P. O'Connor in tow, having crossed by the night steamer, presented himself at Healy's house at dawn on 6 February, just as Healy had got to bed after vainly wrestling with Gray all night to persuade him to publish an attack on O'Shea's candidature. What actually appeared in that morning's *Freeman* was O'Shea's election address which, as both Biggar and Healy immediately realized, meant that there would now be no hope of stopping the candidature behind the scenes. If they wanted to oppose O'Shea they would have to do it *in coram publico* and that in turn meant that they would have to face the wrath of Parnell. This was more than T.P. had bargained for and at this point he withdrew from the hue and cry which he himself had set on foot.[44] He gives his reason for doing so in the memoir of Parnell he wrote just after the latter's death and it was a reason which was to weigh with many people as the crisis developed. By supporting O'Shea Parnell had made the primary issue *his* leadership, not O'Shea's election, 'and as his leadership, and the national and racial as well as the party unity which it symbolized, were then the chief hope of the coming proposal of Home Rule, everything else was to be sacrificed to that, and even the lesser evil of Captain O'Shea's election was to be accepted'.[45]

Arrived in Galway, which they reached late on Saturday, 6 February, and whither O'Shea had preceded them by a few hours, Healy and Biggar found the constituency in an uproar, with local opinion strongly in favour of the local candidate, Lynch. Both MPs wrote to Gray to tell him what they had found and to give him their reaction to the Deasy-Parnell telegram which had followed them to Galway. Biggar was, as usual, abrupt and totally honest. 'I cannot believe Parnell can have wired such rubbish. Surely he's not insane. Nothing can tempt me to support such a wretch as O'Shea.' Healy took the predictable line that Parnell's threat to resign was a form of blackmail – 'it would if Parnell's threat were serious mean that every time he wanted to do wrong he need only make this threat'. And in a postscript he added: 'We believe Parnell's wire instigated by O'Shea and I am well able to judge of O'Shea's supposed influence with the cabinet.'[46]

Why did this formidable pair mount such a desperate opposition to the O'Shea candidature when they must have known the risks that not only they, but the whole party, would incur if a serious split were to develop just when a Home Rule Bill was at last in prospect? Their motives were mixed and what was true of one was not necessarily true of the other. Two things, however, can be said with reasonable certainty. One is that both men had good political grounds for resisting O'Shea. To Biggar he was a detestable 'Whig' who had never run straight with the party. To Healy, besides being an opponent of the pledge, O'Shea was also objectionable as the confidant of Chamberlain whose visit to Ireland the previous year Healy had played a large part in thwarting.[47]

But there was a second reason for the opposition to O'Shea – the fact that it was already well known or suspected in the inner circles of the party that O'Shea's wife was Parnell's mistress. From that the irresistible conclusion had to be drawn that this was the reason why Parnell was supporting O'Shea's candidature, and to those who took parliamentary politics seriously the bartering of a nationalist seat in furtherance of an intrigue of this kind was deeply repugnant. Of all who have written about Parnell only Henry Harrison has disputed the connection between the Galway election and the O'Shea-Parnell liaison. Since Harrison did more than anyone else to uncover what seems to have been the true facts about the liaison, his views naturally command attention. His thesis was that this accusation about the Galway seat was a fabrication by Parnell's enemies. 'The charge was, in some form or another, that Parnell had made Captain O'Shea member for nationalist Galway as the price of Mrs O'Shea's honour. It was wholly false.'[48] But that is not a correct presentation of the case. If Parnell had offered Galway to O'Shea so that he might *thereafter* have undisputed possession of O'Shea's wife, then the charge might indeed have been as Harrison describes it. But, in *Parnell vindicated*, Harrison has himself supplied the best grounds for believing that O'Shea had known about the affair for years and had kept silent to suit his own purposes. In 1886 his most pressing need was to get back into parliament and his demand for support must surely be interpreted as the blackmailer's turn of a long familiar screw. Galway in short, was the price, not of Katharine's dishonour, but of her husband's silence.

Yet, although the two mutineers were in part actuated by unwillingness to accept as an Irish member (unpledged at that) the husband of Parnell's mistress, they seem to have referred to this aspect of the matter almost entirely in private and to have been circumspect in their public utterances. Healy later claimed that it was only his intervention which prevented Biggar's 'scorching allusions' from being published by the *Freeman's Journal*, but since E. D. Gray was already committed to Parnell it was highly unlikely that the paper would have reported such allusions, unless they were so public and so scandalous as to be impossible to ignore. It is doubtful if Biggar really was so outspoken as legend has it and almost certain that he did not tell the electors openly, as Barry O'Brien put it, 'that Parnell had chosen O'Shea because O'Shea's wife was Parnell's mistress'.[49]

In private, though, Biggar was undoubtedly more explicit. For this we do not have to depend solely on Healy, who afterwards claimed that he persuaded Biggar to change an uncoded telegram to Parnell from 'Mrs O'Shea will be your ruin' into 'The O'Sheas will be your ruin'.[50] There has survived a narrative of the events of those tense days made by a Galway student, John Muldoon, who was reporting the election for the *Galway Vindicator* and who later became a barrister and a much respected member of the Irish party. His account, which was published in 1930, was intended to correct errors in the principal memoirs of the period, virtually all of which had appeared before he went into print. Muldoon asserts that from the moment Biggar reached Galway he made no secret of his beliefs. '"The candidate's wife is Parnell's mistress and there is nothing more to be said", were the words frequently on his lips. Mr Healy said nothing, but Lynch [the local candidate] told me on the evening of the day upon which Healy and Biggar arrived that he took Healy into a quiet corner and asked him what in the name of heaven was the cause of the contest? Healy replied: "It has its entire origin in a woman of evil character and is an abominable scandal".' But Muldoon was careful to add that in public Biggar, and by implication Healy as well, never alluded to what both of them clearly regarded as the true source of the crisis.[51]

This account is supported by the evidence of T. P. O'Connor, who, in his *Memoirs*, emphasizes that though rumours were circulating, the 'terrible suspicion which none of us wanted to face' did not emerge into the open.[52] O'Connor's recollections, however, were challenged when they first appeared in print as part of his evidence in a libel case, by another Galway journalist, Thomas Marlowe, also a student of the local Queen's College (as it then was), who had attended the open-air meeting which Biggar and Healy addressed on Sunday afternoon in

Eyre Square the day after they arrived. According to Marlowe, Biggar made his allegation about Mrs O'Shea 'in the plainest language', though he could not recall whether Healy, while in general supporting Biggar, actually repeated Biggar's charges.[53] But Muldoon was also at that meeting and he carried away a different impression. In his memory the nearest the secret came to breaking surface was when Healy looked straight up at O'Shea, sitting in a window of the Railway Hotel behind him, and exclaimed: 'We may yet have to raise other issues in this election and we shall not fear to do so before we allow the honour of Galway to be besmirched.'[54] Where there is such a direct conflict of evidence certainty is not to be achieved. Perhaps the most accurate assessment may be that on the platform and in the press it was the political side of the question that was ventilated, but that in private conversation the liaison was freely referred to, with the natural consequence that rumours circulated furiously in the town.

IV

Ironically, the very fact that Biggar and Healy concentrated on the political issue meant that they were almost certainly doomed to defeat. If the issue was thus presented, it would be comparatively easy for Parnell and for all who were concerned about the future of Home Rule, to insist that his leadership and the success of the cause were inextricably bound together. This was what T. P. O'Connor had immediately sensed when he arrived in Dublin and it rapidly turned out to be the crucial factor in determining attitudes within the parliamentary party. Soon a stream of telegrams began to pour into Galway urging the rebels to draw back – telegrams signed among others by O'Connor, by William O'Brien, by Dr Kenny, by Gray, and by Tim Harrington.[55]

Perhaps the key figure in the developing situation was William O'Brien. He was close to Parnell, he was close to Archbishop Croke, he virtually controlled *United Ireland*, yet at the same time he was on intimate terms with the two men who, for different reasons, most distrusted Parnell – Healy and John Dillon. On 7 February O'Brien wrote one extremely important letter and received another. The letter he wrote was to John Dillon and it may well have done more than any other single factor to keep the party intact. Dillon's role in these events has given rise to some confusion. It has been conjectured, for example, that he was in Galway for part of the time and even that he went there with some thought of supporting O'Shea.[56] Neither of these conjectures is correct. Dillon was at his home in Ballaghaderrin when the crisis broke and was mainly dependent upon William O'Brien for his information. As he later told the story, his first impulse had been to go to Galway and take his place with Biggar and Healy. He had actually been about to leave for the train when there came a telegram from O'Brien urging him not to go.[57] This was followed by the letter of 7 February thanking him for his action, or rather, his inaction. O'Brien's normally breathless style collapsed occasionally into incoherence under the stress of the crisis, but he managed to convey to Dillon, who was well placed to read between the lines, the true extent of the gulf that was opening under their feet:

> Your feelings and ours about O'Shea are, of course, the same – loathing. So is our feeling about the infamous way in which Parnell has put him forward and slighted the party. The question was, in the special circumstances of the moment, whether we should swallow O'Shea or utterly destroy our movement and party at its brightest moment for a personal reason which we could not even explain. It was a most bitter and scandalous alternative, but it seemed to us an alternative between accepting an odious personality and chaos. We were all thoroughly in favour of terrorizing Parnell by every means short of public scandal; but when he had committed himself by the announcement in the *Freeman* [of 6 Feb. 1886] and the letter he gave O'Shea, it became a question as to which [sic] if defeated by members of his own party, it was impossible [*sic*] for him to continue leader.

Interestingly, O'Brien's view was that Healy and Biggar, to whom he had put the same points without effect, went to Galway 'knowing full well Parnell's determination and, I am afraid, determined to pick a quarrel'. They had ignored all requests to desist, including even Parnell's own telegram. 'We pressed Parnell by all possible means short of open revolt, but his answer was emphatic and he is plainly bound by some influence he cannot resist.' If Parnell went to Galway, as he was now threatening to do, Healy would either retire 'or there will be a conflict in which, if Parnell loses, all is up'. 'It is a terrible pass but I think we cannot hesitate. Posterity would execrate us for wrecking this movement at such a moment for so miserable a cause.'[58]

The letter O'Brien received from Healy that same day can have done nothing to reassure him. Healy began by explaining that the local nationalists were not supporting Lynch 'blind-fold'. Healy himself had read them a telegram from Parnell to Lynch, putting the utmost pressure on him not to stand. 'Before you decide, it is my duty to inform you that I leave for Galway tonight to support O'Shea's candidature,

and that the responsibility resting upon you or anybody else who
attempts to weaken my power and influence at present juncture will
be grave.'[59] But this had made no difference. The situation might still
be saved, Healy thought, if even at this late stage O'Shea were not
nominated. On the other hand, if Parnell was determined to continue
the fight, 'it will simply be . . . to meet a deplorable defeat'. And
Healy left his friend in no doubt about his and Biggar's intention to
stand fast. 'Should he [Parnell] come down, we shall reply firmly to
every attack and maintain our position come what may.'[60]

This ominous letter was written after a nationalist meeting that same
day (Sunday) had selected Lynch to go forward against O'Shea. It
was noticeable that the clergy, who would normally have been out in
force, were conspicuously absent when Lynch was nominated. This may
partly have been because Lynch was believed to have Fenian connections or antecedents, but also, apparently, because O'Shea had taken
considerable pains to enlist the support of the local bishop, Dr Thomas
Carr. Five years later, when defending in the press the line he had taken
at the divorce hearing, O'Shea claimed that on the night of 6 February
he had met Dr Carr, together with the Archbishop of Tuam and other
clerics, and had had a sympathetic hearing. Though, being O'Shea,
he could not refrain from adding that next day, when the opposition
of Healy and Biggar manifested itself, 'Dr Carr and his clergy, with
commendable prudence, adopted an attitude of expectation and reserve'.[61] He omitted to mention, being O'Shea, that in face of this
opposition Dr Carr had attempted to persuade him to withdraw. Nor,
for obvious reasons, did he refer to the fact, which seems well authen-
ticated, that he had absolutely denied to his proposer, Father Joseph
O'Shea, OSF (who claimed to be a close relation), that Biggar's accusations about Parnell and Katharine had any truth in them.[62] Healy,
possibly embroidering upon this story, was later to record in his
memoirs that the bishop had told Biggar and himself that 'O'Shea had
gone down on his knees before him and vowed there was no truth in
any allegation which connected his wife's name with Parnell'.[63]

The nomination of Lynch meant that the struggle was irretrievably
out in the open and would have to be fought through to the end.
Healy made this inevitable by fastening on the indisputable fact that
O'Shea could not be an 'official' candidate because he did not intend
to take the pledge. 'Let me say', he declared, 'that if Captain O'Shea
poses here as the choice of the Irish party, I am here to say that the
Irish party was never consulted.'[64] But on 8 February, the day this
challenge was reported in the press, the Parnellite forces began to

mobilize in strength. Every member of the party was asked to declare his support for the leader and to those who could not be reached in person a telegraphic appeal went out, signed, among others, by William O'Brien, Sexton, Harrington and T. P. O'Connor. It minced no words: 'Parnell has intimated to us his leadership is at stake in Galway contest. Healy's speech has created impression that party generally is against Parnell. Will you authorize us to attach your name with ours to public declaration upholding Parnell?'[65] This initiative produced an immediate rally behind 'the Chief'. In a short space 50 signatures had been obtained for a declaration calling on the Galway electors 'to uphold the authority of Mr Parnell as leader of the Irish people'.[66] It received powerful support also from outside the party. Archbishop Walsh stated roundly that 'the question now is of union or disunion', and the *Freeman's Journal* came out with an editorial intended to put the whole question on a more elevated plane:[67]

> The issue is not between Captain O'Shea and Mr Lynch but whether at the very moment of the crisis, when the question of Home Rule hangs in the balance, when Mr Parnell almost holds it in the hollow of his hand, Galway will strike a blow at his prestige and his authority . . . The power of Mr Parnell has consisted, and must consist, in English statesmen recognizing that he is the personal embodiment of the Irish nation, delegated by them to speak and act on their behalf.

There were, admittedly, some ominous abstentions. Dillon replied to Harrington: 'Regret deeply I cannot give my name. I shall say nothing unless Healy is attacked.' And T. D. Sullivan, with others of 'the Bantry band', abstained in solidarity with his kinsman, Healy. Alone of the important papers which normally supported Parnell, the *Nation*, while accepting the necessity of bowing to the authority of the leader, was critical of his behaviour, suggesting that he 'should act up to the advice which he has so often tendered to his countrymen, to the effect that in the conduct of the Irish cause we should be prepared . . . to make sacrifices of personal feelings, personal friendships, preferences and prejudices, and look only to the national good'.[68]

The fact that the *Nation* was in such a minority was itself evidence of what became clearer hour by hour once the bulk of the party had committed themselves to Parnell – that the Galway rebels were backing a losing cause. Although Parnell took the threat to his supremacy seriously enough to answer O'Shea's direct appeals for help and come to Galway in person the worst that Biggar and Healy could do had probably been done by the time he arrived there on 10 February. However, up to 8 February at least, Healy continued to put a bold face on the situation and to insist, in a second letter to O'Brien, that if Parnell appeared in Galway he would 'advance upon his ruin'. 'Whereas, if he stays away from a place where he can do no good all will be right. I hope in God his gift of missing trains will stand to him now.'[69]

On this occasion Parnell missed no train. On 9 February he travelled to Galway accompanied by a formidable entourage which included T. P. O'Connor, Arthur O'Connor, Sexton and J. J. O'Kelly. T. P. O'Connor, who had completely boxed the compass in the course of this episode, looked forward to the journey with understandable apprehension, but, true to his unpredictable form, Parnell chose to spend part of the time discussing religion. His hearers, Catholics to a man, were intrigued to learn that after a period of falling away from his faith, he had come back to it again. 'I believe in the religion I was born in', he said. It did not appear, though, that this meant he could now be expected to be in love and charity with his neighbour, if that neighbour's name happened to be Healy. O'Connor, still hoping to build bridges, asked him to go easy. Parnell replied, smiling, with a parody of the famous phrase Gladstone had used about himself just before committing him to Kilmainham – he would use 'the resources of civilization' to bring about a settlement. But, with a hardening of tone, he added that Healy had been trying to stab him in the back for years and had clearly seized on this as his opportunity.[70]

When they reached Galway they were greeted by a large and hostile crowd. Some shouted 'Hie for Lynch', others 'To hell with O'Shea', and others again 'To hell with Parnell and Whiggery'. Parnell, one reporter noted, looked thunderstruck, but when the crowd began to close in on O'Connor, Parnell's instinct for leadership reasserted itself and taking O'Connor by the arm, and at the same time evading O'Shea's painfully obvious attempt to shake him by the hand and thus advertise their 'solidarity', brought him into the hotel by the entrance which led straight from the platform.[71] Once inside Parnell, who had travelled all the way from England without pause, disappeared to his bedroom, washed, carefully brushed his thinning hair, and came downstairs to confront the mutineers in private session.

Healy began the proceedings by stating the overt case against O'Shea – that he was unpledged and a Whig and altogether unsuitable. He spoke emotionally, his voice thick with tears, conscious no doubt that in the group round Parnell he had few if any friends. Parnell heard him calmly and then demolished him with two sentences in which he contemptuously threw overboard the argument previously used on his behalf, that he would resign if O'Shea were not returned. 'I have no intention of resigning my position. I would not resign it if the people of Galway were to kick me through the streets today.' According to O'Connor, this 'swept Healy off his feet' and he capitulated there and then.[72] Biggar, however, was made of sterner stuff and argued as strongly as ever against O'Shea. Nearly everyone present was on tenterhooks lest his proverbial bluntness should lead him to blurt out a reference to Mrs O'Shea, and Healy at one point sprang to his feet and made as if to catch him by the throat to prevent such a fatal indiscretion. But Biggar, though unrelenting in his opposition, kept his argument impeccably political.[73]

All the same, he was in a minority of one, and Lynch was called in to be told that the opposition to O'Shea had been withdrawn. This unpalatable news had next to be conveyed to his supporters at a hastily summoned meeting. The crowd was noisy, confused and deeply angry. Parnell, so often a halting and uninspiring speaker, rose to the occasion like one possessed. No account of the proceedings was published but John Muldoon, Thomas Marlowe and T. P. O'Connor all produced reports of the leader's key remarks which, while differing in detail, agree in essence. 'I have', he said, according to Marlowe and O'Connor, in a phrase which echoed the *Freeman's Journal*, 'a parliament for Ireland in the hollow of my hand.'[74] Or, as Muldoon recorded it in the form of a question: 'When was it so absolutely essential to uphold my authority as at this moment when I hold in my hand the measure that will secure peace and prosperity to this long neglected country?'[75] 'It was', as even Healy conceded in retrospect, 'an impressive sentence, a revelation. The people learned for the first time how near they were to victory. Every man in the crowd was awed, except Biggar.'[76] But the sentence in which Parnell described the consequences if he were defeated was no less electric. 'There will rise a shout from all the enemies of Ireland, "Parnell is beaten, Ireland no longer has a leader".' 'It is impossible', says O'Connor, 'to describe the effects of these words on the audience. You could almost hear the shudder of emotion which they felt. Enough; Parnell had awed them into silence; into grudging and hateful obedience; it was one of the most complete subjugations of a crowd in history.'[77]

This was an exaggeration. There were to be other speeches and wild fluctuations of mood before the issue was finally decided. Biggar stood out stubbornly against O'Shea and was fiercely applauded. Healy, on the other hand, retreated, covering his withdrawal in the language of Gethsemane. 'It is a bitter cup for you', he told the people. 'God knows it is a cup of poison for me, but even so, let it be taken for the unity of the party we love . . .'[78] But it was not until O'Brien made a tumultuous speech – not so much a speech as a thunderstorm, said Muldoon – that the matter was put beyond doubt and the meeting passed a resolution authorizing Lynch to retire in favour of O'Shea 'in obedience to the advice of our leader and his colleagues of the Irish parliamentary party'.[79]

The 'mutiny', such as it was, was now formally over. Lynch was unable for technical reasons to withdraw his candidature, but he did not campaign and on polling day (10 February) received only 54 votes as against the 942 cast for O'Shea. The size of the majority is an impressive testimony to Parnell's mastery of the situation, though it may have been helped by a totally unfounded rumour which spread through the town at the last minute that Captain O'Shea had finally agreed to take the pledge.[80] The mere suggestion that he might have taken the pledge was most offensive to O'Shea, whose sense of personal honour, though not as other men's, was in some ways acute. Not only did the incident involve him in an angry correspondence with Healy in May, but it worried him so much, he later claimed, that after the result he had consulted the Bishop of Galway as to whether or not he should resign, in case it might be thought that he had won the seat under false pretences. The bishop, somewhat improbably, advised him to consult Chamberlain. Chamberlain, less improbably, advised him to sit tight.[81]

As for Parnell, having stayed to see the election through, he turned his mind to more congenial matters. The afternoon of polling day he spent at the Galway Marble Works where he bought a mantel-shelf and, as befitted a respectable Wicklow quarry-owner, displayed particular interest in a machine for cutting and polishing granite.[82]

If the Galway election had proved anything it was that the granite of his own indomitable personality had never had a sharper edge or a more perdurable quality. The crisis had brought out in Parnell all his salient characteristics – the early lethargy and inaccessibility; the swift action when action was needed; the physical courage which enabled him twice to face down a hostile crowd; the tactical skill which fastened unerringly on the central issue besides which O'Shea's candidature dwindled to insignificance; the ruthlessness with which he imposed his will on all save Biggar; the sense of timing he applied to his *coup de théâtre*, unveiling the imminent prospect of Home Rule at the exact moment when his authority seemed most fallible.

Yet, if contemporaries were right in seeing Galway as victory snatched from the jaws of defeat, there remains an important sense in which that was an illusion. True, Parnell did reassert his supremacy; true also, he led a united party back to Westminster for the critical Home Rule session. But Galway, if it was a triumph, was also the first rumbling of the coming storm. It demonstrated publicly, what had been evident inside the party for some time, though usually veiled from outsiders in decent obscurity, that factions, jealousies and hatreds festered under Parnell's sway. While Home Rule beckoned these internal dissensions were forgotten, but if the promise should fade, if Parnell should fall back into lassitude and indifference, worse still if the land question should reawaken the old quarrel between activists and constitutionalists, then the monolith of 1886 might turn out to be in reality no more than lath and plaster, liable to collapse under pressure. And behind the stresses resulting from clashes of personality within the party was the darkest question of all – whether or not the root cause of the Galway incident, Parnell's infatuation with Katharine, could any longer be kept out of the public eye. So long as it could be, Parnell was safe. But what Galway showed beyond question was that his safety still depended, perhaps more than ever depended, upon the co-operation or connivance of Captain O'Shea. And this in turn depended upon the satisfaction of Captain O'Shea's ambitions.

V

What were those ambitions? Up to 1886 they had seemed to be predominantly political and Galway, if it did not bring the Captain any closer to the mirage of the Chief Secretaryship, at least seemed to hold out the pleasing prospect of a return to his native habitat of surreptitious intrigue and negotiation. Yet the sequel was startlingly otherwise. Within four months of his frantic campaign to get back into parliament, O'Shea walked out of the House of Commons rather than vote on the second reading of the Home Rule Bill and immediately afterwards resigned, to be known no more in the precincts of Westminster.

This abrupt end to his career baffled contemporaries and is still difficult to explain. Adequate evidence on which to make a firm judgement is lamentably lacking. Instead, we have to rely upon fragments, some supplied, usually unwittingly, by O'Shea himself, others from sources of uneven reliability. From all of this it would appear that despite the circumspectness publicly displayed at Galway, the love-affair between his wife and his leader began about this time to obtrude itself upon the Captain in a way he could no longer ignore. It has been suggested already in this biography that long before 1886, if not actually from the beginning of the affair, he had known of the relationship between Katharine and Parnell and had connived at it, both because of the financial rewards for doing so, and because silence seemed most likely to promote his political career. But obviously, such silence could only be purchased up to a point – there was a degree of exposure beyond which O'Shea could not be expected to function as a *mari complaisant*.

The signs are that this degree was passed some time in the spring or summer of 1886. As early as 11 February, the day on which the result of the Galway election was published, the Dublin *Evening Mail* casually mentioned 'a toast of some elderly wags – the family friendships of the O'Sheas and the Parnells . . . It seems simple enough, but there is more in it than politics apparently.'[83] And on 12 February, Wilfrid Scawen Blunt wrote of his astonishment that 'nobody' seemed to know that 'the true reason' for O'Shea's candidature was that the latter's wife 'has been, and I fancy still is, Parnell's mistress'.[84] Yet, rumours were undoubtedly circulating, as they could hardly have failed to do in view of Biggar's blunt statements made in the kind of 'privacy' which almost invites violation. And although F. H. O'Donnell was altogether too naïve when he asserted years later that it was taunts made during the election which first aroused O'Shea's suspicions, we saw earlier that in Galway itself the Captain had been so far unable to ignore the innuendoes that he had had to go out of his way to assure influential ecclesiastics that there was nothing in them.[85]

Despite these indications that the affair was at last beginning to surface, O'Shea did not immediately break with Parnell. When giving evidence before the Special Commission in 1889, he declared that he had been on friendly terms with him 'until June 1886 – May or June 1886'.[86] In the divorce court he merely said, and then only in response to probing by a juror, that his suspicions about his wife and Parnell were first aroused 'in the spring of 1886'.[87] Katharine, for her part, alleged that her husband's connivance in her relations with Parnell lasted from 1880 until 'the spring of 1886'.[88] When asked at the Special Commission what changed his attitude towards Parnell, O'Shea gave this mysterious reply: 'Negotiations took place at that time previously to the division on the second reading of the Home Rule Bill and certain things came to my knowledge at that time which absolutely destroyed the good opinion I had hitherto held of Mr Parnell.'[89] He was not asked what the 'certain things' were, but Parnell himself supplied a possible clue when in a moment of rare expansiveness, he referred publicly to the affair in an interview he gave in December 1889, just after O'Shea had filed his suit. O'Shea, he maintained, had always been aware that he, Parnell, had been constantly at Eltham in his absence from 1880 to 1886, and from 1886 onwards had known that Parnell constantly *resided* there from 1880 to 1886.[90]

It seems, then, that a change of some kind occurred at a point between 'the spring of 1886' and 7 June, the date of the decisive vote on the second reading of the Home Rule Bill. While it is plain from O'Shea's letters to his wife and to Chamberlain that his 'good opinion' of Parnell had disappeared long before 1886, we have still to ask whether anything occurred during that period which might have caused a further deterioration. Something did indeed occur which caused considerable vexation at each point of the triangle. One day in May 1886, Parnell, who was of course living at Eltham, became involved in a minor accident with a market-gardener's cart when returning from London. It seems probable that he was then being regularly shadowed by detectives employed by the *Pall Mall Gazette* (which may, incidentally, explain why, as the editor, W. T. Stead, complained to Wilfrid Scawen Blunt, Parnell regularly refused to meet him)[91] and at once there appeared in that paper a paragraph entitled 'Mr Parnell's suburban retreat', stating that the Irish leader habitually lived at Eltham during the parliamentary sessions.[92]

Given what we know already of the previous history of the affair it can hardly be supposed that this report suddenly awakened the doubts of a hitherto unsuspecting O'Shea. But the paragraph did create exactly that condition of exposure which, if his connivance were not to be exhibited to the world, made it necessary for the Captain to behave like an aggrieved husband. Accordingly, he telegraphed to Katharine to know the meaning of it. She replied dismissing the report cavalierly as an invention by Healy and his friends to get their own back for the Galway election. However, Parnell took the matter seriously enough to write her a formal letter, explaining his presence on the flimsy pretext that he had horses stabled in the neighbourhood (which indeed he had – in her stables!) and regretting that she had been troubled in the matter. This letter was later produced in the divorce court and contemptuously described by O'Shea's counsel, Sir Edward Clarke, as 'invented for the purpose of setting Captain O'Shea's suspicions at rest'. Asked if he had really accepted his wife's assurances in May, O'Shea made a strange reply. 'Well, yes, but I had found out something which had nothing to do with the matter, and I desired her again before I went abroad [in June 1886] to have no communication with Mr Parnell.'[93]

Even stranger than this remark was the fact that no one in court asked

him to explain it. It still remains a mystery. Henry Harrison, in the
detailed analysis of the problem which he published in *Parnell vindicated*,
advanced the hypothesis that the 'something' was an intimation made
to O'Shea in the early part of 1886 by one or other of the members or
ex-members of the previous Liberal cabinet that the existence of the
liaison had been known in high official circles for several years. The
inference O'Shea would have drawn from this, Harrison suggests, is
that the increasing publicity which his affairs had attracted at the Galway
election had made him, politically speaking, a spent force, since no
responsible politician would make use of a man whose career was liable
at any moment to erupt into a spectacular scandal. There is almost no
evidence of substance to support this hypothesis except one passage from
a letter O'Shea wrote his wife in October 1886 when they were in the
midst of an angry correspondence. 'No, I make no attempt to put your
name in the newspapers. Indeed, one of the effects of its having been
there has been to end my public life.'[94] But there is nothing to indicate
either that O'Shea was himself involved in political negotiation in the
critical spring of 1886, or that any influential politician – or, for that
matter, any other person – allowed him to know that his secret was known
in quarters which could prove so damaging to him that it would be
wise for him to quit politics immediately. Nor is the thesis itself inherently
convincing, for everything that could be said about O'Shea's vulnerability in 1886 could equally well have been said – apparently was said
by Sir William Harcourt – in 1882.* Yet this did not prevent Gladstone
from using Katharine extensively as a medium for communication
with Parnell right up to 1886, nor Chamberlain from using O'Shea in
like manner up to the fall of the Liberal government in 1885.

In a rather different sense, it is true, O'Shea did receive fairly
conclusive evidence from a highly authoritative source in 1886 that he
was no longer regarded as indispensable. On 16 April Katharine O'Shea
wrote a remarkable letter to Gladstone of which the following is the
essence:[95]

My husband begs me to write and ask if you can, and will, give him
the promise of some colonial appointment later on – the fact is that
he is in *very great* pecuniary difficulties owing to his not having been
able to get any rent from Ireland for some time, *and* from other
causes.

My aunt, with whom *I* have been living for many years and who,

*See above, pp. 218–9.

although she is in her ninety-eighth [sic] year, is as keen and far-seeing as ever, will, she says, assist my husband out of his present difficulties, for my sake, if she has any hope of his getting any lucrative occupation, but if not, she will not help him, so you will understand how important your answer is to us in every way.

I should not have ventured to trouble you on the subject had you not kindly promised some years ago to remember him in case of a suitable appointment becoming vacant – which I told him at the time – hence his desire that I should write and beg you to give some hope of one [sic] kind. I fear that unless something can be done for him *at once* he will become so hopelessly embarrassed as to render it difficult to do anything later. My husband says he is willing to go *anywhere*. Hoping you will pardon my appeal I shall feel deeply grateful if you will let me hear as soon as possible, as I fear it will be difficult to get him an appointment if he is made a bankrupt, and I am afraid he will be, unless you can give me some hope for him.

Gladstone's reply to this affecting appeal has not survived, but its tenor can be deduced from the barely legible note he scribbled on the back of Katharine's letter. After a perfunctory acknowledgement of Mrs O'Shea's political services and a lukewarm expression of the pleasure it would have caused him to meet her request, he delivered the *coup de grâce*. 'Though on this occ[asion] I mention it with regret', he wrote, it was his 'invariable rule' not to interfere with the departmental perquisites of his colleagues. In saying this, Gladstone was probably only exercising his usual well-known punctilio in such matters, but it is just possible that O'Shea, in his frustration, may have read into it more than was intended and in doing so may have jumped to the conclusion that his marital difficulties were now so notorious that he had become for that reason *persona non grata* to the Liberal leaders.

There is, however, another hypothesis which, though also speculative, comes closer to the probabilities of the case. This is that when O'Shea mentioned 'certain things' at the Special Commission and 'something which had nothing to do with the matter' he was inventing red herrings, designed to distract attention from the real point at issue – that his prime anxiety was to avoid any admission of 'discovery' of his wife's guilt. Against this it may be argued that he was taking a grave risk that he might be asked to explain what this mysterious new dimension actually was. But was the risk so grave? At the Special Commission, counsel for *The Times* was unlikely to wish to embarrass one of the paper's star witnesses and counsel for Parnell was certain not to want to raise the issue. Similarly, in the divorce court, since neither Parnell nor Katharine was actively represented, there was a virtual guarantee that awkward questions would not be put. If Captain O'Shea was not asked to explain himself on either occasion, it may well have been because it was in the interest of too many people that he should not be asked.

One important advantage of this hypothesis is that it need not conflict with the main conclusion towards which all the evidence points – that between the Galway election and the second reading of the Home Rule Bill there was a significant deterioration in the triangular relationship which had persisted, albeit precariously, for so long. Two pieces of generally neglected information are relevant here. One is that when O'Shea was fighting desperately to obtain a seat in 1885 – *before* having to resort to Galway – his correspondence with Katharine was in terms of close familiarity. He frequently complained to her of Parnell, as a man might write who expected a sympathetic hearing from the wife of his bosom, and he continued to use endearments originating in a happier time, addressing her as 'My Dick' and initialling his telegrams 'B', which was short for the nickname 'Boysie' she had given him long previously.* The other piece of information is that, as O'Shea himself testified in the divorce court, on several occasions in 1886 (though not after May) he took Parnell down to dine at Eltham. When we put alongside these evidences of domesticity the *Pall Mall Gazette* paragraph about 'Mr Parnell's suburban retreat' and Parnell's own statement of 1889 that 'since 1886' O'Shea had known that Parnell resided at Eltham constantly from 1880 to 1886, the inference is irresistible that for the Captain the situation had quite suddenly gone very sour indeed. What may in fact have happened may have been that O'Shea, while certainly aware for years past that an affair was in progress between his wife and his leader which had profitable potentialities for him as an ambitious politician, and probably (though not certainly) aware that illegitimate children had resulted from the liaison, did not fully realize until 1886 that matters had progressed far beyond recall and that he had been supplanted so completely that his wife was now – and apparently had been for some years – his rival's wife in all but name.

It is symptomatic of the altered condition of affairs that the letters which Willie and Katharine exchanged in the second half of 1886 are much more acrimonious than those of any earlier period. A letter of his

---

*It is characteristic of the element of farce which was never far from this essentially tragic affair that in her book (K. O'Shea, ii, 88n) this nickname is misprinted 'Bopsie', which takes us straight into the world of Beatrix Potter.

written in August she described as 'one of the most mean and insolent you have ever written' and the general tone of his communications was increasingly that of a much-put-upon but still credulous husband rebuking his erring mate.[96] His acerbity at least was undoubtedly connected with the fact that newspaper comment was linking her name with Parnell's much too often for comfort. In July, August and September 1886 such rumours and reports drove O'Shea to write to her forbidding her to have any further communication with Parnell, to which protests she regularly returned emollient, if somewhat perfunctory, replies. Notwithstanding this, in October the *Sussex Daily News* was able to report, correctly, that Parnell had been staying with Mrs O'Shea at Eastbourne. Again O'Shea protested, again Katharine fobbed him off with a denial, though on that occasion it was later stated in the divorce court, his suspicions 'were not altogether allayed'.[97] Yet, when in December 1886 the *Pall Mall Gazette* published another paragraph, this time stating that Mr Parnell was visiting Captain O'Shea at Eltham, O'Shea, after demanding that the statement should be contradicted, personally assured W. T. Stead that the relationship between his wife and Parnell was one to which he could take no objection.

This interview, which Stead described as 'one of the most curious I have ever had', took place on 20 December 1886 at O'Shea's request. During it O'Shea insisted that the difference between Parnell and himself was purely political and had nothing to do with Mrs O'Shea. Stead then asked about a report he had seen in an American newspaper which had described Parnell as living at Eltham. O'Shea then made an extraordinary reply: 'Believe me, there is not a word of truth in the story. Mr Parnell has never been at Eltham since our difference, and notwithstanding all rumours there has never been the least cause for me to suspect my wife . . .'[98] This was, of course, completely at variance with the facts, with O'Shea's own protests at the time, and with the evidence he gave in the divorce court four years later. Yet Stead could hardly call him a liar to his face. In his account of the episode he says he had 'no option' but to believe Captain O'Shea, though when he published the interview at the time of the divorce, it was perfectly clear to him, or to anyone who cared to think about the matter, that the story O'Shea told in December 1886 was totally incompatible with the story he told in November 1890.

Why all these shifts and evasions? Why were the rumours not investigated and proceedings set in motion in 1886 if enquiry revealed that his wife had presented him with grounds for divorce? Not, evidently, because O'Shea still looked to Parnell for political advancement; the division on the second reading of the Home Rule Bill marked the end of that road. But there remained one powerful incentive for the Captain to preserve the status quo as long as he could. This was the large fortune which Katharine's aged Aunt Ben was expected to leave to her niece and in which that niece's lawful, wedded husband might hope to share so long as he remained lawfully wedded; added to which, and to sweeten the pangs of waiting, was the continuing assistance he received in maintaining his bachelor establishment at Albert Mansions. This gave Katharine a considerable leverage. Thus, when in one of his more petulant letters, O'Shea threatened to remove her and the children from Eltham, she could reply devastatingly:[99]

> My Aunt says she will not give one penny to me either for the support of myself or the children, or of course for yours either. She also says she understood that she was asked to buy the lease and furniture and pay the rent of your rooms at Albert Mansion . . . If you mean to take a house for us away from Eltham let me know . . . Of course in that case you will provide all monies for the children and myself.

As this was precisely what the Captain could not do, no more was heard of that particular project. But since in 1886 Aunt Ben was 93 years old, it did not seem that the difficult triangle would have to be kept in being much longer. None of those involved could have imagined that the indestructible old lady would survive for another three years. The consequence was that each member of the triangle had to continue playing the role assigned to him or her. Parnell and Katharine had to be as discreet as they could and avoid newspaper gossip like the plague. This is the explanation alike for Parnell's numerous aliases (mostly adopted after 1886) and for the nomadic existence they began to lead, flitting from rented house to rented house to avoid detection. But it was not an effort to avoid detection by Captain O'Shea. His part in the far from casual comedy was to assume the role, but not the reality, of a deceived husband – to erupt into righteous indignation whenever his wife's name was mentioned in the press, to relapse into subsidized somnolence when the immediate crisis was past. For all of them it was a perilous existence, which grew more perilous the further it was prolonged.

For Parnell it meant that the danger which had so narrowly been averted at Galway stood ever after by his elbow. For Ireland it meant that the future of Home Rule rested with a man whose own future could be destroyed at any moment.

CHAPTER 11

The View from Pisgah

'And Moses went up from the plains of Moab unto the mountains of Nebo, to the top of Pisgah, that is over against Jericho. And the Lord said unto him, "This is the land which I sware unto Abraham, unto Isaac, and unto Jacob, saying, I will give it unto thy seed: I have caused thee to see it with thine eyes, but thou shalt not go over thither".'

(Deuteronomy, chap. 34, verses 1–4.)

I

When Parnell came back from his Irish adventure to the political realities of London, he may not, as he had proclaimed at Galway, have held a parliament for Ireland 'in the hollow of his hand', but he had certainly reasserted his personal authority in the most resounding fashion. Thereafter, and for as long as the Home Rule crisis lasted, there was an abrupt cessation of the kind of assurances that Healy had been giving to Labouchere the previous year, that the 'leader' counted for nothing and would readily fall in with whatever the 'followers' decided. In the coming weeks it would be Parnell who would be courted by the Liberals, Parnell who would make the key speeches in the House, Parnell who would take the crucial decisions, after only minimal consultation with the inner circle of the party.[1] His position had never seemed stronger, for he had behind him virtually the whole of articulate Irish nationalism at home and abroad. The party had triumphed at the polls. The bishops had finally accepted Home Rule as that which alone could satisfy 'the legitimate aspirations of the Irish people'.[1] Money was pouring in from America. Even that intrepid spokesman of the agrarian left, John Dillon, who had returned from Colorado in time to be elected again to parliament, recognized Parnell as 'the accredited leader and ambassador of the Irish people'.[2]

By contrast, Gladstone's course was one of dizzying complexity. The business of constructing a cabinet was excruciatingly difficult and the business of keeping Chamberlain either inside it, or if outside, effectively muffled, was no less vexatious. But if it was true, as has recently been plausibly argued, that Gladstone's preoccupations were as much about his continued leadership of the Liberal party as about an Irish settlement, for Parnell there was only one issue.* It mattered relatively little who was or was not a member of the government, but it mattered a great deal that that government should commit itself without delay to some specific plan of Home Rule. It was in character, therefore, that on 29 January, the day after Salisbury's cabinet had decided to resign, Parnell should have conveyed to Gladstone his anxiety for closer and more direct contact with him. To this Gladstone immediately replied in soothing terms. His previous embargo, he told Mrs O'Shea, applied only to the period when he was a private member, 'and when also I was deeply anxious on all accounts that the Tory government should take up the question'. 'Full interchange of ideas with Ireland through her members, and with them through their leader, is in my opinion an indispensable condition of any examination of the subject which he has well called "autonomy" undertaken by a responsible minister.'[3]

But it was not until 26 March that Gladstone was in a position to bring before the cabinet the draft of the Home Rule Bill which resulted in the immediate resignations of Chamberlain and G. O. Trevelyan. On the eve of that important meeting, Parnell, who had hitherto been fobbed off with interviews with the new Chief Secretary, John Morley, renewed his pressure for a meeting with Gladstone. 'I hope you will be able to see him [Parnell] at any time', wrote Katharine, 'for I am sure it will do good if you do, and strengthen him. He is unable to consult his party much, as they are nearly all connected with the press in some way.'[4]

Parnell had indeed been holding himself aloof and the fact had already attracted attention. The gentle McCarthy, writing to his friend, the lady novelist, reported in February that a colleague had complained to him that Parnell was growing 'terribly dictatorial'. 'The fact is', McCarthy commented, 'that Parnell is nervously afraid of anything being said or done which might give our enemies the slightest chance or handle against him – and he is quite right.'[5] Perhaps this was true, but it was not the whole truth. If Parnell seemed dictatorial, it may have been partly because after Galway he felt he could afford to be, and partly because he, who had never been exactly effusive at the best of times, was less inclined that way than ever in an enlarged party which

---

*The most recent, and best, account of these events is in A. B. Cooke and John Vincent, *The Governing Passion*. (Brighton, 1974.)

contained men he had not even met. 'Who is that convict-looking fellow?' he asked his secretary when confronted with Alexander Blane, a worthy tailor just elected for South Armagh, and the question tells us as much about Parnell as about the convict-looking fellow.[6]

All the same, though only on the eve of the bill's introduction, when there was no longer any point in concealing its details, Parnell did assemble a handful of his principal colleagues at the Westminster Palace Hotel.[7] The report Parnell gave them was not encouraging. After renewed pressure he had at last succeeded in seeing Gladstone on 5 April. John Morley, who arranged the meeting, recorded the encounter in his diary. 'He [Gladstone] shook hands cordially with Mr Parnell and sat down between him and me. We at once got to work. P. extraordinarily close, tenacious and sharp. It was all finance. At midnight, Mr Gladstone rose in his chair and said: "I fear I must go; I cannot sit as late as I used to." "Very clever, very clever", he muttered to me as I held open the door of his room for him.'[8] As for Parnell himself, on leaving Morley he summoned William O'Brien and remarked, 'I never saw him so closely before. He is such an old, old man! . . . Once, when he yawned, I really thought he was dying, but he flared up again.' Asked how the bill was going, Parnell replied, 'Badly, and going to be worse.'[9] This gloom was confirmed by McCarthy, who found him 'less optimistic than I have seen him yet during this chapter of our history. He is afraid Gladstone may be led to make concessions to English partners which might make it difficult for us to accept his scheme.'[10]

Understandably, therefore, at the meeting with his colleagues he was bleakly discouraging. Much deflated, they began to criticize the measure, especially the niggardliness of its financial proposals. 'Gentlemen', said Parnell, 'I share your regrets. I took up my hat today at one point to leave, and break off the negotiations with Gladstone. If any of you wish to renew them, and think you can do better, take my place.'[11] Nobody did so, of course, and agreeing finally to let others have the onus of rejecting even an imperfect bill, they trooped out disconsolately into the midnight frost and fog. It was of this meeting, incidentally, that Parnell afterwards remarked to John Morley, as proof of the incorruptibility of the new Irish party (and, interestingly, in contradiction of Katharine's warning to Gladstone), that although there were several journalists in the group, all of them poor men, not a word about the bill leaked out to the public.[12]

The root difficulty remained finance, where there were two problems. One concerned customs and excise. Parnell had set his heart on tariff autonomy and now it seemed he was not to get it. The other was the question of the 'imperial contribution', the amount Ireland was annually to contribute to the British Exchequer in return for the services with which she would be provided as a continuing part of the Empire. The government's contention was that the Irish share should be one-fourteenth, or possibly one-fifteenth, of the whole. Parnell argued that it should be a twentieth or even a twenty-first part. This was not just a quibble about figures. When, subsequently, a Royal Commission enquired into Anglo-Irish financial relations, it strongly supported the view that since the Union Ireland had been consistently over-taxed. But Parnell's position went beyond this. Looking to the future and to the possibility of Britain being engaged in a major war, he pointed out that Ireland was in effect being asked to sign a blank cheque for an amount indefinitely expandable by wartime inflation.[13] He felt so deeply on this matter that he tried once more to secure a reduction just an hour or so before the bill was due to be introduced for the first time, only to be refused yet again. Morley, who bore the chief brunt of this importunity, came to believe as a result that if the bill had reached the committee stage the Irish party might well have rejected it on that score alone.'Mr Parnell never concealed this danger ahead.'[14]

When the Government of Ireland Bill was at last introduced on 8 April the effect was in a sense anti-climactic. Everyone knew that the real battles lay ahead, not merely on the bill itself, but on the ambitious measure of land purchase which Gladstone was to bring forward eight days later, deeming this, despite its widespread unpopularity with his own party, to be a necessary concomitant to Home Rule. But what, in precise terms, did Home Rule involve? The bill provided for the establishment of an Irish parliament, with an Irish executive responsible to it for the management of Irish domestic matters. Large imperial issues were to be reserved to the parliament at Westminster – these included the crown, peace and war, the armed forces, foreign relations and certain other items. The Irish parliament was specifically forbidden to endow any religion, restrain educational freedom, or control customs and excise. The Royal Irish Constabulary were to remain for some years under imperial authority but were eventually to be handed over to the local parliament. The imperial contribution was to be fixed at one-fifteenth. The Irish members were to be excluded from the House of Commons. Their own parliament was to consist of two 'orders', the first of these, or 'upper house', was to be partly elective but also weighted in favour of property, while the second was to be wholly representative. These might meet together for certain purposes and each was to have a suspensory veto on legislation introduced by the other.

Immediately after Gladstone's exposition, the Irish party held a fully attended meeting at which general dissatisfaction was expressed about four points – the customs; the imperial contribution; the constabulary; voting by 'orders'. It was agreed that Parnell should voice these criticisms in that evening's debate, but that he should also be empowered to state that if the bill was satisfactorily amended in committee it would be accepted by the Irish people.[15] His speech a few hours later followed this prescription exactly. It was highly critical in detail but it ended with the significant conclusion that, duly amended, the bill would be 'cheerfully accepted by the Irish people and representatives as a solution of the long-standing dispute between the two countries . . .'[16]

If Parnell and his party were careful to give only a guarded welcome to Gladstone's olive-branch, the reaction at home, and in Irish-America, too, was initially much more euphoric. Looking back with hindsight this may seem strange. To us it is the obstacles of 1886 which now seem far more impressive than the opportunities. The split in the Liberal party, the determination of the Tories to pull no chestnuts out of the fire for Gladstone, the intransigence of Ulster Protestantism, the obvious fact that even if the bill did struggle through the House of Commons it would be promptly knocked on the head by the House of Lords – all these pressures seemed to work so uniformly and powerfully against the bill that it is hard to see how on any rational calculation Irish onlookers can have expected success. The answer probably is that such expectation flowered only during April, when the political situation still looked fluid and it was possible to hope against the odds that all might yet turn out well. After the Easter recess, and more specifically from mid-May onwards when it became increasingly obvious that Chamberlain's influence, as well as that of Hartington, would be thrown against the bill, and when Salisbury had firmly bolted all Tory doors in a speech to the National Union of Conservative Associations, the tendency, even in the Irish camp, was to anticipate defeat.

But this was by no means incompatible with the great upsurge of emotion which the bill itself evoked. It evoked this emotion not so much because of what it offered but because it symbolized a mighty change in Ireland's affairs. At last a great statesman and a great party had been brought to embody Irish aspirations in legislative form. Compared with this, from which it was assumed there could be no going back, the immediate fate of the bill was of secondary importance. If it did not come now, it would come soon. What mattered most in the short term was to consolidate the bridgehead which had been won and to do so by constructive criticism combined with convincing assurances to English opinion that the bill, suitably improved, would be accepted by Irish opinion as a satisfactory and permanent settlement.

This was the line followed by the Irish party when the crucial second reading debate opened on 10 May. Parnell, who had his earlier 'separatist' speeches to live down, was asked categorically if he accepted the bill as a final settlement. To this he replied monosyllabically, 'Yes'.[17] He reserved his main effort, however, for the last night of the debate, 7 June. By then, the situation had greatly changed since he had welcomed the bill on its first appearance. For one thing, the ambitious Land Purchase Bill which had worried so many Liberals, had been dropped. Although not compulsory, the measure had marked an advance on previous legislation by proposing that parliament should authorize an advance of £50 million, and more later if required, for the sale of Irish land on the basis of twenty years' purchase of the new rental, less all deductions. Parnell was unreservedly critical of some parts of the scheme. His harshness towards the Land Bill is interesting evidence, as has been pointed out, of the continuing fragility of Liberal-Parnellite relations, but it is no less interesting as an indication of his increasing tendency to regard land as a secondary problem to be dealt with *after* Home Rule had been achieved.[18]

Nor was the Land Bill the only casualty. The cabinet eventually decided that if the Government of Ireland Bill got through its second reading, they would seek to introduce it afresh in the autumn. Further, and in response to severe criticism of the original intention to exclude the Irish members from Westminster, Gladstone let it be known that he was prepared to abandon this point and consider instead any reasonable scheme for retention.

Both these changes were changes in response to English pressures and they carried with them the corresponding danger of arousing Irish opposition. On the question of exclusion, Parnell's views were possibly more fluid than those of some of his followers, but when both Morley and Gladstone tried to pin him down they detected a certain hardening of tone. 'He is much more stiff against the retention than he ever was before', reported Morley after an interview on 8 May. 'His new argument is that their presence would be used as a justification for raising their imperial contribution, and an excuse for varying it, and getting more out of them "in our usual rapacious fashion".'[19] This was not in fact Parnell's only reason for resisting the new tack. He seems genuinely to have feared that a Dublin parliament might be to some extent devalued if Irish MPs still came to Westminster and he also foresaw logistical difficulties in getting them to travel, especially if some happened to be members of both parliaments.[20] But he was never a diehard on this question and later came round to accepting some sort of retention without undue difficulty.

The proposal to withdraw and later to reintroduce the bill was a much more serious matter. When he got word of it just before Gladstone announced it to a meeting of his supporters at the Foreign Office on 27 May, Parnell took the exceptional step of writing to Morley to warn him of the possible consequences of which the worst would be the encouragement given to the enemies of Home Rule and the loss of morale among its supporters.[21] Morley, reporting this to Gladstone, noted that 'for a single instant' his patience broke and the lightning flashed. But he agreed to see Parnell with Morley in the evening after the Foreign Office meeting. Parnell was courteous, but depressed and gloomy, Gladstone was 'worn out and fagged'. On the whole, the meeting was not a success. After the Prime Minister had gone, 'Parnell repeated moodily that he might not be able to vote for the second reading, if the bill was to be withdrawn thereafter'. Morley's reply, as he himself records it, also shows signs of strain. ' "Very well", said I, "that will of course destroy the government and the policy; but be that as it may, the cabinet, I am positive, won't change their line." '[22] Parnell was not impressed and, after this unsatisfactory encounter told O'Brien that the time had arrived to call a meeting of the party 'to decide whether we should not straightly throw out the bill'.[23]

This proved unnecessary, for the situation rapidly developed in such a way as to make it morally certain that the bill would be destroyed anyway without the Irish party having to lift a finger against it, which, if it had to fail, would from their point of view be a much better way for it to go. On 28 May Gladstone announced that the bill, if passed, would be withdrawn and reintroduced with amendments. Among the amendments that the government were believed to be considering was that Irish members would be brought back to Westminster whenever questions of taxation were involved, but this belated concession was far from placating their critics. On 31 May the most formidable of those critics, Chamberlain, held a meeting in the House of Commons of over fifty Liberal 'doubters'. The question was whether they should abstain or whether they should vote against the second reading. Much influenced, apparently, by a letter from the veteran John Bright announcing his intention to vote against the bill, they decided to do likewise. In so deciding they effectively signed the death-warrant of Home Rule in that session and for as far ahead as anyone could dare to look.

II

It is against this background that Parnell's speech on 7 June has to be considered. John Morley judged it 'one of the most masterly speeches that ever fell from him' and thought that his performance made 'even able disputants on either side look little better than amateurs'.[24] In retrospect, it hardly seems to deserve such praise. Parnell's requiem for a bill which was all but dead when he rose to speak, moved at two quite different levels.[25] At one level, the level at which he disclosed his interview with a Tory minister (Carnarvon) the previous summer, it was obviously a debating speech designed to create doubt and dissension and to harvest votes, if not to save the second reading, at least for the general election which would follow the bill's defeat. But at another level it was indeed a statesmanlike, if in some aspects also superficial, attempt to grapple with the future and to establish the Irish party as committed to a constitutional settlement.

His major preoccupation, naturally, was to justify the change, or apparent change, in his own position. How could he, who had so consistently defined Home Rule in terms of Grattan's parliament, accept wholeheartedly something that was in certain key respects less than Grattan's parliament? His answer was frank and probably genuine, though no doubt it failed to convince many who heard him. He would, he said, have preferred the restitution of Grattan's parliament, but he refused to admit that he was on that ground precluded from accepting Gladstone's alternative. He did accept it, because it conferred practical benefits which would make it 'more useful and advantageous to the Irish people than was Grattan's parliament'.

Grattan's parliament, it now conveniently turned out, had laboured under certain disadvantages, two of which were paramount. First, it had perpetuated the Irish House of Lords, which Parnell contrasted unfavourably with Gladstone's 'two orders' meeting from time to time in joint session. Secondly, and more realistically, Parnell had come at last to grasp the all-important fact about the constitution of 1782, which was that the executive had remained under English control, whereas in the bill of 1886 the Irish government would be responsible to the Irish parliament – subject, in the final instance, to the ultimate supremacy of the imperial parliament. 'You will have', he said earnestly, 'the power and supremacy of parliament untouched and unimpaired, just as though this bill had never been brought forward.' And he continued: 'I now repeat what I have already said on the first reading ... that we look upon the provisions of the bill as a final settlement of this question, and that I believe that the Irish people have accepted it as such a settlement [Cheers and counter-cheers]. Of course you may not believe me, but I can say no more.'

In saying this he was really trying to unsay what he had more wisely said the previous year – that he could not give guarantees about the future because the future was not his to command. Nothing could get round the crucial point which Englishmen found so hard to understand, that the offer of self-government had to be an exercise in trust or it was better not to make it at all. That said, opponents of Home Rule could legitimately argue that trust must not be blindfold, that some protection must be afforded to the Protestant minority which would find itself isolated under a Catholic and nationalist-dominated parliament. The deep atavistic fear that Home Rule would mean Rome rule had to be met, but Parnell was not well placed to meet it. True, as the Protestant leader of a Catholic movement, he seemed the embodiment of Irish tolerance, but this was subject to two important qualifications. The first was that, precisely because he *was* a Protestant, he found it difficult to speak out on those issues, particularly educational, which were of such overwhelming importance to the church. Admittedly in 1884 he had eagerly welcomed the bishops' mandate to the Irish party to represent the educational interests of Irish Catholicism in the House of Commons. But this, while a major political advance for him, did not argue well for a more objective approach to educational policy by a Dublin government whether led by him or by another. Nor were his few remarks on the subject in the Home Rule debate exactly reassuring. 'You may depend upon it', he said, 'that in an Irish legislature Ulster, with such representatives as she now has in the imperial parliament, would be able to resist successfully the realization of any idea which the Roman Catholic hierarchy might entertain with regard to obtaining an undue control of Irish education.' As to how this might be done, or as to the stresses which such resistance would certainly introduce into Irish life, he remained silent.

That he did so suggests the second qualification to his own position as the Protestant leader of a Catholic movement. This was that the degree of clerical, still more of episcopal commitment either to the party or to the leader was always limited. From time to time the ineptitude of British attempts to persuade the Vatican to intervene in Irish affairs did no doubt push the party and the church closer together, but the emergence of a parliamentary party with independent ideas of its own was not one which gave the Irish bishops unmixed satisfaction. Parnell himself never made close or permanently friendly contact with any

Irish ecclesiastic of note, and although country curates might show themselves enthusiastically Parnellite whenever occasion offered, this was not necessarily a recommendation to their religious superiors. A recent description of the leader's normal dealings with the bishops as 'shrewd but distant' strikes exactly the right note.[26]

This, however, does not exhaust the criticism of Parnell's attitude to the religious problems of his country, as exemplified by the line he took in the Home Rule debate. More serious than the fact that he kept Irish Catholicism at arm's length was his failure to appreciate fully the fears of Irish Protestantism in general, and of Ulster Protestantism in particular. Not only did he gloss over the crucial issue of Catholic control of education in a self-governing Ireland, but he refused absolutely to admit that either the socio-religious or the economic circumstances of Ulster might entitle it to special treatment. For this there seem to have been two reasons. First, he was anxious to destroy at the outset the notion, which Chamberlain had been mooting, that the province, or part of it, should be granted a separate parliament of its own. In resisting this suggestion Parnell was driven to strange shifts, of which undoubtedly the oddest was his contention, based upon a juggling of the income tax statistics, that despite the fact that in terms of what he called 'relative wealth' the north-east might be better off than the rest of the country, the taxation returns showed that Leinster and Munster were both richer than Ulster. Even if his information had been accurate and his deductions impeccable (both were in fact open to doubt), this dismissive assessment of the potential of the one truly industrial region in Ireland was a strange cul-de-sac for the champion of Irish industry to find himself in.

The second reason for Parnell's attempt to minimize the separateness or difference of Ulster was that he looked at it incorrigibly through the eyes of a southern Protestant, using an argument which would have warmed the hearts of those Wicklow gentry with whom he had long since parted political company. In a sentence, his argument was this – that if Ulster were subtracted from the rest of Ireland, the Protestants who lived outside the nine counties would be 'infinitely less secure'. Of course, as he readily admitted, it could be maintained that the nine counties did not form a homogeneous community and that attention ought properly to be focused on the three counties (he seems to have meant Antrim, Down and Londonderry) where the Protestant majority was clear. But in his comment on this it was still the voice of the quintessential southern Unionist which spoke through the mouth of the renegade landlord:

Here again comes in the difficulty that, instead of protecting the majority of the Protestants of Ireland by constituting a legislature for the north-east corner of Ulster, you would abandon the majority of the Protestants to their fate under a Dublin parliament. Seven-twelfths of the Protestants of Ireland live outside these three counties . . . and the other five-twelfths . . . live inside those counties. So that, whichever way you put it you must give up the idea of protecting the Protestants either as a body or as a majority by the establishment of a separate legislature either in Ulster or in any portion of Ulster. No, Sir; we cannot give up a single Irishman. We want the energy, the patriotism, the talents and work of every Irishman to ensure that this great experiment shall be a successful one.

Seen in retrospect, this seems a sadly inadequate approach to the most difficult and dangerous of all the problems which any attempt to repeal the Union and restore some form of self-government to Ireland would have to solve. But it is too easy, with hindsight, to condemn Parnell for failing to think his way through a riddle which neither he nor anyone else had had to face in its full complexity up to that time. For if it be true that in his confident enunciation of the one-nation theory he entirely disregarded the possibility that the theory itself might be defective – at no point in his career did he define what he thought the Irish nation to be, a dereliction in which he was by no means alone among nationalists – then it has to be said that many others, Gladstone included, fall under the same indictment.

The most fundamental question remains – how genuinely and for what reasons did Parnell accept Gladstone's bill as a final settlement? Since his sincerity was never tested, it is impossible to prove or disprove the argument of finality. But we shall see later that his ideas about Home Rule did not remain frozen at the point Gladstone had reached in 1886 (neither did Gladstone's) and it is reasonable to suppose that had the goal been achieved in that year, the grant of a legislative assembly with an executive responsible to it would have resulted, in Ireland as elsewhere, in a steady constitutional evolution towards dominion status. Whether it would also have resulted, sooner or later, in complete independence and republican status, as the opponents of the bill dreaded, is a possibility which is naturally much more difficult to assess. No man, as Parnell himself said, can fix the boundary to the march of a nation. But we may reasonably suppose that it was more rather than less likely that a regime which started life under his aegis would have been a conservative one and that in the foreseeable future a Parnellite administration would have taken at least as strict a view of its responsibility for law and order as any British government.

There is no reason to doubt that Parnell's motives for accepting the settlement were those he openly avowed – that this was the opportunity for which generations of Irishmen had striven, that it offered a chance of real, if limited, success, and that the best safeguard of its permanence was that the great (though depleted) Liberal party had assumed responsibility for it. Yet there was a reverse side to the coin. If Home Rule had now, by Gladstone's decision, become the responsibility of the Liberal party, then the logical corollary of this was that the *ad hoc* alliance between the Liberals and the nationalists in 1886 must be expected to develop into something more permanent. But if it so developed, what then became of Parnell's own doctrine of independent opposition? Before the year was out he was to give ample evidence of how central that alliance had become to his whole political strategy; before the decade was out he was to demonstrate dramatically how central it had become to his own political existence.

III

No speech of his could arrest the march of events and, after Gladstone had wound up the debate at midnight, the bill was rejected at one o'clock in the morning of 8 June by a margin of thirty votes. On 10 June parliament was dissolved and the ensuing general election followed almost immediately. The result was a decisive rejection of Home Rule, even though a large number of seats was left uncontested and though in those seats which were contested the poll was lower overall than it had been in 1885. In Great Britain only 193 Home Rulers were returned and although the nationalist representation was virtually unchanged (it actually dropped to 85 but was quickly restored at a by-election to 86), the end result was a Unionist majority of 117. Since 77 of those seats belonged to dissentient Liberals, or Liberal Unionists as we may now call them, it was evident that the ministry which Salisbury proceeded to form would be heavily dependent upon the *beaux yeux* of Hartington and his followers and of the much smaller Chamberlainite faction.

Parnell himself chose to fight the election in Britain and for the first time in his life – the last time also, with a few notable exceptions – was to be seen on platforms up and down the country. His task, obviously, was to cancel the 'vote Tory' manifesto of the previous November, but the poor showing of Home Rule candidates in England (they did much better in Scotland and Wales) suggests that in a number of con-

Avondale

Aughavanagh, Parnell's shooting lodge in County Wicklow,
later the home of John Redmond

Parnell in 1880. A photograph taken by his nephew, Henry Thomson, and given by Parnell to Katharine O'Shea

Katharine O'Shea in 1880. Parnell had this photograph with him in Kilmainham and carried it with him until his death

The Arrest of Parnell,
October 1881 (from
Illustrated London News)

Parnell – the Private Man.
From a photograph taken by
Katharine O'Shea in the
sitting-room of her house,
Wonersh Lodge, Eltham

Captain O'Shea in the Witness Box

Parnell in the Witness Box with black bag. One of Sidney Hall's drawings of the Parnell Commision.

8 Medina Terrace, Hove, where the 'fire-escape incident' was alleged to have taken place

10 Walsingham Terrace, Brighton, where Parnell died

The Pigott Incident, February 1889 (from a contemporary
sketch by Harold Wright)

Nearing the End – Parnell at the Kilkenny Election (from *Illustrated London News*)

stituencies the voters had not readily forgiven him for the apparent cynicism of that manœuvre. Perhaps more importantly, it suggests also that the weight and influence of the Irish vote may have been exaggerated even in the bonanza year of 1885. On the other hand, it may simply have been the case that there was in the English urban constituencies a large potential anti-Irish vote, which had been latent in 1885 when Ireland was not strictly an issue, but which emerged unmistakably in 1886 when Home Rule was the dominant question before the electorate.

The line Parnell followed in his speeches may not much have influenced the outcome, but it demonstrated beyond question how completely he had made the Liberal alliance the pivot of his policy. His first foray into an English constituency was at Portsmouth, where he spoke on 25 June. Here he developed an argument to which he was to return increasingly in the years ahead – that if Home Rule were conceded on Gladstone's plan and if, *after that*, a separatist rebellion were attempted in Ireland, Britain would have an unassailable 'moral power' to suppress it, a moral power which was lacking so long as the grant of Home Rule was withheld. Not, he said, that he believed in the feasibility of Irish separation. It was 'the hollowest and most absurd talk that ever was given utterance to'. How could Ireland rebel in face of England's numerical superiority and when, among her own population, two million out of five were 'what they call loyal'? He was, however, no more sympathetic to these 'loyalists' than he had been during the Home Rule debate. To give Ulster separate treatment, he repeated, would be no help to the 400,000 Protestants left outside, and suppose there was to be a separate Ulster parliament, would not the nationalist majority in the province ensure that the first act of that parliament would be to reunite the province to the rest of Ireland?

In saying this he was unwisely assuming the permanence of a majority which was actually so precarious that the 1886 election tilted the scales in the opposite direction, but in prophesying that if the Tories came to power as a result of that election the immediate sequel would be a renewal of coercion, he was on firmer ground. The only thing that could prevent this, he said, with evident malice, would be the return of Lord Carnarvon as Viceroy, in which case, he added sardonically, they would get an even better Home Rule Bill than Gladstone had offered them. 'You will see', he said, lapsing into an untypical vulgarity which he may have thought suited to an English audience, 'we may be wanting to make a little treaty with these gentlemen by and by again, and it does not do to split too much on your old pals.' But mischief-making was not his main concern. For him the keynote of the campaign was as he stated it in his peroration – it was to reassure English opinion that what was proposed by the Liberals was both a moderate concession to Ireland and also one that laid the basis for a lasting settlement. 'But small as it is we cheerfully accept it as a final one ... Untold is the guilt of that man who, for party purposes, does not take advantage of the spirit that is abroad among the English to put together the hand of the Irish nation and that of England, to close the strife of centuries ...'[27]

The danger inherent in such a doctrine was that it tended to convey the impression that Home Rule had only to be conceded for the Irish question to disappear. This was so palpably not the case that Parnell, in another speech only two days later, went to some lengths to identify, but also to minimize, the source of potential future trouble. He had to take into account that Belfast was at that moment being torn by serious sectarian riots and that within Ireland the opposition to Home Rule was not negligible. He had also to reckon with the fact that gathering agricultural depression was renewing the familiar tensions in the Irish countryside. 'Outrage' had never died out, but with the prospect of further evictions coming steadily closer it was certain that agricultural unrest would again flare up. Parnell's tactic was to link these two kinds of malaise together in an analysis which, while grossly over-simplified, identified a recognizable and vulnerable target. Pointing the finger of scorn at the Orangemen of Ulster, he described them as no more than a clique of greedy bigots:[28]

> This battle is being waged against Ireland by a class of landlords. Their loyalty that they boast of is loyalty to their own pockets. Have they not repeatedly threatened, not now for the first time, that if the Queen, Lords and Commons of England pass a certain act they will rebel against the imperial authority? Is that loyalty? Much fight there is in them. I know these gentry well. They talk about the Protestants of Ireland of whom I am proud to be one. The Protestants of Ireland despise this miserable gang who trade upon the name of religion; they despise them and apprise them at their true worth ... All I can say is that 1000 men of the Royal Irish Constabulary will be amply sufficient to cope with all the rowdies that the Orangemen of the north of Ireland can produce.

The interest of this extraordinary outburst is that it exemplifies in almost classical fashion the anti-northern prejudice which caused Parnell, as it also caused Catholic nationalists, grotesquely to mistake both the character and the extent of Ulster resistance to Home Rule.

This was dangerously misleading because, while it directed attention towards an admitted problem, it did so by ignoring a quite different problem which, to most onlookers, was far more immediate and grave. To put the matter another way – Parnell, by dismissing the Orange factor in this fashion, did a double disservice to his cause. He did so on the one hand by wrongly devaluing that factor as soon as he had identified it, and on the other hand by playing down the factor of agrarian unrest which was a universal Irish problem and not merely a north-eastern one, indeed if anything rather less a north-eastern problem than one for the rest of Ireland.

Even the agrarian agitation, important though it certainly was, was only part of a larger question which, put crudely, was the question whether the rejection of Home Rule would stop the Kilmainham policy in its tracks and bring about a reversion to extremism. Inside Ireland itself the question seemed hypothetical, for the time being at least, since political militancy had been beaten out of the field by Parnellism, as the elections of 1885 and 1886 had amply demonstrated. But beyond Ireland lay Irish-America where there was no such unanimity about the superiority of constitutionalism over physical force. The crucial consideration in the aftermath of the crisis of 1886 was not what effect the rejection of Home Rule would have in Ireland, but what effect it might have in the United States. Particular importance attached, therefore, to the convention of the Irish National League of America, due to be held at Chicago in August. As we saw earlier, the League had been overshadowed from its inception by the Clan na Gael, and the Clan itself, under the influence of Alexander Sullivan and his colleagues of the Triangle, had been implicated to some extent in the dynamite campaign of 1883 and 1884. Should the failure of Home Rule to materialize now lead to a resurgence of Irish-American violence, Parnell and his movement would be seriously, perhaps mortally, injured and Gladstone's chances of ever securing a British majority for an Irish settlement might be fatally compromised.

Parnell was perfectly well aware of the danger. In the spring of 1886 he had been visited by an emissary from the United States who conveyed to him the clear impression that the temperature was rising among the Irish-Americans.[29] As soon as the election was over Parnell dispatched a group of parliamentarians – William O'Brien, John Redmond and John Deasy – to represent the Irish party and the National League at the convention in Chicago. They were accompanied by Michael Davitt who, though unpopular in more 'advanced' Irish-American circles because of his own rejection of violence, still maintained close ties with Alexander Sullivan and had therefore a potentially valuable role to play. The political atmosphere in Chicago was sultry when the delegates arrived and they had immediately to face severe pressure from those, especially Sullivan, who advocated a renewal of terrorism, using the seductive argument that 'even from the parliamentarian standpoint . . . worse might happen than extreme measures from an irresponsible left wing'.

To meet this pressure O'Brien took a stand which was consistent with his inmost attitudes, but which was soon to bring him into collision with his leader. He pointed out that, given the agrarian tensions already present in Ireland, further evictions were bound to occur. If and when they did, they would be fiercely resisted and 'at any peril of our own liberties and lives, the government of Ireland by force could and would be made impossible'.[30] This was 'extreme' enough to swing the balance and, reinforced by Davitt's private representations, ensured that the convention next day went on record as approving Parnell's conduct and thanking not only Gladstone but 'the democracy' of England, Scotland and Wales for their support of Home Rule. Irish-America was thus to all appearances ranged firmly behind Parnell. Admittedly, appearances were in one sense deceptive, since the Clan na Gael was deeply split between the Devoy and the Sullivan factions. This split had a paralysing effect upon the extremist element and it may even be as a modern authority has argued, that the American nationalists at this time 'probably felt a greater need for Parnell than he for them'.[31] He, after all, had brought Home Rule to the centre of British politics, a glittering achievement which contrasted starkly with the internecine and sterile feuds of the Clan. Still, it was fortunate for him that while those feuds persisted peace was as necessary for the 'advanced' men as for himself.

But peace in Ireland was always precarious and whether it would be preserved or not would depend neither upon manœuvres at Westminster nor upon secret conclaves in the smoke-filled hotel bedrooms of Chicago. In the last resort it would depend, as so often before, upon the reaction of the Irish farmer to the pressures of his landlord and of his environment.

CHAPTER 12

In the Shadows

Parnell: '. . . I think that if we had a parliament in Ireland it would be wiser to drop the land question.'

Davitt: 'Drop the land question! How on earth could you drop the land question after all we have done during the last seven years?'

Parnell: 'Oh! I don't mean that there shall be no land legislation . . . But there should be no revolutionary changes. No attack upon the land system as a whole.'

Davitt: 'Mr Parnell! how on earth could you resist attacking the land system, as a whole, after your speeches? If you were Irish Secretary in an Irish parliament, how could you defend yourself in the face of these speeches? What would you do?'

Parnell: 'The first thing I should do would be to lock you up.'

(Conversation during the Home Rule crisis of 1886, reported in R. Barry O'Brien, *The Life of Charles Stewart Parnell*, ii, 158–9.)

I

Even while the Home Rule Bill hung in the balance Ireland had begun to exhibit once again all the familiar symptoms of a familiar disease, agrarian discontent. The disease was aggravated by depressed agricultural prices which made it increasingly difficult for tenants to pay even the relatively modest rents fixed under the Land Act of 1881. For two years past the economic return from both crops and livestock had been falling catastrophically, due partly to American competition and partly to soil exhaustion; and now this already dire situation was rapidly being made still worse by the restriction of credit on the part of Irish banks, shops and village moneylenders.[1]

During the winter of 1885–6 there had been sporadic outbursts of disorder, though these had been held more or less in check by Parnell's specific instructions to the Irish National League to keep its branches under tight control and also by the natural preoccupation of most Irishmen with the central issue of Home Rule. Nevertheless, evictions had occurred, especially on the estates of the notoriously unsympathetic Marquess of Clanricarde at Woodford in county Galway, and a ground-swell of resistance had developed despite the efforts of the party leaders to minimize it. Indeed, they dared not minimize it too much for fear of weakening their own influence over the demented farmers and it was noticeable that as early as January 1886 a party meeting, at which Parnell was not present, recorded its disquiet at the developing crisis. True, when the party met again to consider what action it could take, this time with Parnell in the chair, it was decided to maintain the policy of quiescence adopted the previous year and members proposing to attend meetings in Ireland were warned to watch their language and not to become involved in demonstrations.[2] This was, no doubt, the common-sense attitude to take while the future of Home Rule was still un-certain, but once the scales had begun to tilt against Gladstone's bill it was inevitable that agrarian grievances would force their way to the surface. Already in May 1886 Davitt was telling Wilfrid Scawen Blunt that the party's neglect of the land question was causing great dissatisfaction and the following month Dillon assured the same ob-server that if Salisbury came to power after the election 'all were pre-pared for a new land struggle'.[3] The predictable sequel was the passing by the party at their meeting in Dublin on 4 August of a resolution warning the government that payment of the judicial rents (rents fixed by the land court under the act of 1881) had become impossible.[4]

This gathering storm confronted the Irish leader with a difficult and potentially dangerous situation. On 17 August, which happened to be the day that Gladstone and his ex-colleagues were dining together to discuss their future policy for Ireland, Parnell arrived in London from Wicklow, where he had been for the shooting, and went straight from Euston to Justin McCarthy's house. 'He was got up', noted McCarthy, 'in regular moor costume – Irish, that is to say, in light tweeds, and looked very much better than when I saw him last, very strong and very handsome.' The object of his visit was to brief John Morley, who came in at six o'clock, only two hours before Gladstone's dinner. Morley radiated gloom, which was not lightened when Parnell told him straight that the rents would not be paid in Ireland during the coming winter and that unless the government did something there would be trouble. True, Parnell added that trouble was precisely what he did not want and Morley easily divined why. Organized resistance to eviction would inevitably lead to coercion and coercion, if it was ruthless enough, could not be defied indefinitely. Also, a disturbed Ireland was not a good advertisement for Home Rule, would in fact make nonsense of Parnell's conciliatory speeches in the recent election campaign. Accordingly, he made it clear both to Morley and to McCarthy that 'we had better for the present fall back upon an attitude of great caution and reserve'. The talk then turned briefly to what attitude the Liberals might be expected to adopt. McCarthy was worried that Gladstone might be tempted to suppose that the nationalists could be weaned from the Liberal alliance by a Tory offer of local self-government, but Parnell brushed this aside with a fine contempt. There was 'not the slightest chance', he said, expressly for Morley's benefit, that the Irish party would ever accept anything smaller than Gladstone's bill. When Morley departed shortly afterwards, Parnell reiterated to McCarthy his conviction that in the immediate future they must concentrate on land reform to help the tenants through the period of crisis. As to Home Rule, he insisted that it must come soon. 'It is only a question of a very short time. We can afford to take an attitude of reserve for the present.'[5]

He began at once to translate these ideas into action. When parliament reassembled he moved an amendment to the address, calling attention to the hardships of the tenants and especially to the evictions in progress at Woodford. He then uttered a solemn warning. 'Neither the Irish members nor the government', he said, 'had any control over the events which might occur in Ireland during the months of the winter.'[6] A little later he followed this with a Tenants Relief Bill designed to enable the land court to suspend evictions in cases of proved insolvency, to admit leaseholders to the benefits of the Land Act of 1881, and to give the court power to reduce the judicial rents already fixed before 31 December 1884 for tenants who had paid half the rent due in 1886 and half their previous arrears. The government, predictably, were not impressed. In August they had adopted the classic delaying tactic of appointing commissions to study the land question and the possibility of developing Irish industry. This meant that constructive legislation could hardly be introduced before 1887, but in the meantime General Sir Redvers Buller was sent to the south-west of Ireland as a 'special commissioner' charged with suppressing boycotting and outrage. The General, however, though firm enough on law enforcement, proved disconcertingly squeamish when it came to evictions and the maintenance of landlords' rights.[7] Nevertheless, since the evictions did not stop, the Irish members at Westminster responded to the news from home by bouts of prolonged obstruction.

The omens were not therefore propitious for Parnell's Tenants Relief Bill. Admittedly, Gladstone spoke and voted for the second reading, and the Gladstonian Liberals were in general faithful to the alliance, but behind the scenes there were signs of tension. On his first sight of Parnell's proposals, before the bill was introduced, Gladstone wrote to Harcourt that 'I do not see my way to any of them', particularly to the clause which, as it originally stood, granted a stay of ejectment to tenants who paid three-quarters of their rent. This looked to him 'like a permission to the Irish people to deduct 25 per cent from their rent'. He would have preferred Parnell and John Morley to concoct a more acceptable measure between them, but when a few days later he received the details of the actual bill – with the safeguard against ejectment fixed at payment of *half* the rent, not three-quarters – he shied away nervously from such radical interference with the sacred Land Act of 1881, reserving his position until the committee stage.[8] That stage was destined never to be reached. The bill came under heavy attack from the moment it was published. *The Times* dismissed it as 'irrelevant, futile and iniquitous', and many on the Tory benches suspected Parnell of producing a controversial measure either to drive a wedge between Conservatives and Liberal Unionists or, more crudely, to provide a *casus belli* for opening a new phase of the land war.[9] Government speakers queried his statistics, poured scorn on the notion that a crisis was brewing, and ridiculed the proposals for rent reduction as a device to secure 'compulsory credit' for Irish tenants. The outcome was a foregone conclusion and the only doubt concerned the size of the government's majority against the bill; in the event it was a comfortable 95.

As Parnell had foretold, the situation in Ireland at once began to deteriorate. In the middle of October John Dillon, speaking at Woodford which was at the centre of the developing struggle on the Clanricarde estates, advised the tenants to organize themselves, estate by estate, to offer to the landlord a proportion of the rent due and, if this were refused, to lodge it with trustees of good repute who would then use it to pay allowances to those evicted for non-payment of the full rent.[10] A week later his advice was embodied in an article in *United Ireland* written by Timothy Harrington, the secretary of the Irish National League. This article, entitled 'A Plan of Campaign', both set the tone and provided the name for the fresh wave of agitation which now commenced. The basic idea of withholding excess rents and using the money to provide a fund to protect tenants in case of eviction, was elaborated in detail. Estate-funds, the article suggested, should not be dissipated on legal proceedings and the National League itself should not only guarantee the tenants against embezzling trustees, but should also undertake to maintain grants to the evicted tenants after the individual estate funds had been exhausted. Harrington made it clear that boycotting would be brought to bear whenever it was needed. 'That the farms unjustly evicted will be left severely alone, and everyone who aids the victims shunned, is scarcely necessary to say.'[11]

As soon as this article appeared various members of the Irish party, headed by Dillon and William O'Brien, began to spread the gospel it preached in different parts of the country. Then on 19 November the two leaders carried out a much publicized 'collection' of the Clanricarde rents at Portumna. This was a danger-signal to which the government quickly reacted by citing Dillon before the court of Queen's Bench to give bail for 'good behaviour' and by 'proclaiming' a meeting in Sligo. But the agitation continued to grow so fast that although the Plan of Campaign was officially designated 'an unlawful and criminal conspiracy', by the spring of 1887 most of the 116 estates which were ultimately to be involved in the struggle were already affected.

For Parnell no less than for the government this sudden resurgence of large-scale unrest posed a serious problem. As far back as the previous August he had gone out of his way to stress that 'it should not be supposed that . . . he was going again to lead such an agitation as took place in the winter of 1880'.[12] Yet, though the Plan of Campaign was not on the scale of 1880, something of moment was clearly happening in Ireland and it was natural that people should ask where the Irish leader stood in the matter. To this the short answer was that he was in no condition to make his position plain on this or any other issue because of an illness which remains mysterious to this day, but was both genuine and serious. At first, he gave it out that he was suffering from a gastric complaint and was lying ill under his mother's care. This provoked from F. H. O'Donnell a scurrilous parody of a popular Victorian ballad which, to those who could read between the lines, indicated that O'Donnell at least was not taken in:[13]

> Who is the being sent to guard
> My freedom from a prison ward,
> Perhaps my pate from truncheon hard?
> My Mother.
>
> Who fondly nursed my gastric pain,
> While Dillon roamed the Connaught plain,
> And Bill and Timmy bawled in vain?
> My Mother.

Who kept newspapers far away
That might have forced me plain to say
My mind upon the coming fray?
My Mother.

The reality was different, but scarcely more reassuring. On 6 November
1886 Parnell, accompanied by Katharine, paid a visit to the Harley
Street consultant, Sir Henry Thompson. The visitor was announced as
'Mr Charles Stewart' and the specialist did not immediately recognize
him, taking him, as he said afterwards, 'for a quiet, modest, dignified,
English country gentleman'. It was to be the first of several visits
(during which Parnell's real identity emerged), and although on this
particular occasion Sir Henry confined himself to questions of diet, it was
evident that something more fundamental was wrong.[14] The medical
details were never disclosed, but Parnell was extremely ill for most of
the winter of 1886–7 and a number of clues as to his condition gradually
emerged. Those most familiar with him noted anxiously a wasting
away of the flesh on his face and on his body.[15] It became known that he
was subject to intermittent fever and that even in warm weather he felt
intensely cold. He himself supplied the most direct hint when he told
William O'Brien that he had suffered much and for a long time from a
grave kidney ailment.[16] This, combined with the symptoms already
described, suggests that a journalist who was close to him in these years,
Alfred Robbins of the *Birmingham Daily Post*, may well have been
correct in asserting that what was really wrong with him was Bright's
disease.[17]

Such an illness was enough in itself to relax his grip upon the movement. The medical factor, however, was not the only one involved.
Later he was to maintain that he had not been consulted before the
Plan of Campaign was launched, but there is the usual conflict of
evidence among his followers about what his role actually was. Healy
thought he was against the Plan because of the danger it presented to the
fragile alliance with the Liberals, and Davitt's recollection was that he
'severely criticized the tactical wisdom of the whole proceedings'.[18]
Barry O'Brien, when writing his biography, consulted one who was
'behind the scenes' and wished to remain anonymous – almost certainly
Timothy Harrington – and gathered from him that William O'Brien
had tried to see Parnell but had failed because of the latter's illness. It
was only then that O'Brien turned to Dillon, who took up the idea of the
Plan with enthusiasm. Asked whether Parnell had been for or against it,
Barry O'Brien's informant replied that he was 'dead against it'. 'He was

really thinking more of the national question at this time and meant to keep the movement on national as opposed to agrarian lines.' And meeting Parnell's secretary, Henry Campbell, at the end of 1886 or early in 1887, Barry O'Brien elicited from that normally unresponsive individual the decided opinion that the chief had not been consulted by the authors of the Plan. A short time afterwards this view seemed to have been confirmed by an official announcement from the London office of the Irish party, stating that Parnell would not express a view on the Plan until he had been to Ireland and consulted with those responsible for it whom he had not seen since the end of the parliamentary session. 'Mr Parnell', it added, 'was not aware that the Plan of Campaign had been devised or was going to be proposed until he saw it in the newspapers.'[19]

All this cumulative evidence sounds impressive. But against it has to be ranged the evidence of William O'Brien, one of the key figures in this whole new departure. O'Brien stoutly maintained that he had approached Parnell while the fate of the Tenants Relief Bill was still in the balance, suggesting that they should 'put it in force themselves' in Ireland. According to O'Brien, Parnell left him in no doubt that he was 'in absolute agreement' with those who might be prepared to suffer the penalties normally inseparable from an agrarian agitation, provided that criminality or extremism likely to embarrass Gladstone were avoided.[20] This rings true, though allowance has to be made for O'Brien's tendency to assume he had only to state his case to compel acceptance of it. But Parnell was not one to be compelled by anyone, least of all by O'Brien, whose enthusiasms he had so often had to temper in the past. Most probably the two men did meet, and O'Brien talked at large about the prospects for an autumn campaign, while Parnell managed to avoid hearing anything too specific. O'Brien's account goes on to state that the Plan, as published in *United Ireland*, was only composed *after* he had met Parnell. To that extent, therefore, Parnell's public announcement was consistent with the literal truth. Yet it is inconceivable that he had failed to sense that something was in the wind, since after his Tenants Relief Bill had been rejected he had himself written to the president of the Irish National League of America, seeking help for an anti-eviction fund in view of the imminence of 'a trouble and peril which has seldom been equalled in the troubled history of Ireland'.[21]

The most important thing about this same appeal was the strong emphasis on the Home Rule *motif*. In supporting the fund, Parnell told the Irish-Americans, 'you will assist in preserving for our movement that peaceable character which has enabled it to win its most recent and almost crowning triumph, while you will strengthen it to bear oppression and encourage our people until the final goal of legislative independence has been won'. But the moment the movement began to show signs of losing its 'peaceable character' Parnell made it clear where he really stood. On 5 December Dillon delivered a fiery speech at Castlerea in which, unwisely, he indicated that when Ireland had her own government there would be a day of reckoning for police and others who had assisted at the present wave of evictions.[22] The next day Parnell called on John Morley to learn from him what effect he thought the Plan of Campaign would have on English opinion. Morley, who found his visitor looking 'very ill and worn', told him frankly that 'in England the effect is wholly bad' and that the Plan was regarded as being even more offensive than outrages had been in the past. The note he made of Parnell's reply indicates beyond any reasonable doubt the Irish leader's order of priorities. 'He said he had been very ill and had taken no part, so he stands free and uncommitted. He was anxious to have it fully understood that the fixed point in his tactics is to maintain the alliance with the English Liberals. He referred with much bitterness, and very justifiable too, to the fact that when Ireland seemed to be quiet some short time back, the government had at once begun to draw away from all their promises of remedial legislation. If now rents were paid, meetings abandoned, and newspapers moderated, the same thing would happen over again as usual.'[23]

The upshot was that Parnell agreed to send for one of his lieutenants and to press for an immediate end to violent speeches. The lieutenant – it was William O'Brien – came post-haste and somewhere between 7 December and 12 December had with his leader one of the most extraordinary interviews of his career. According to his subsequent account, his first attempt to find Parnell in the wastes of south-east London miscarried owing to faulty directions. Eventually, he found himself at Eltham. 'The name gave me an unpleasant start, resolutely though I had shut out any belief in the tittle-tattle which Parnell's enemies of the more verminous sort had associated with it.' Still, he plucked up his courage and enquired at the local police-station for Captain O'Shea's address. On presenting himself at the door he was told that the Captain was not at home. However, O'Brien was shown into the drawing-room and learned, either from Mrs O'Shea herself or from some intermediary, that she believed Parnell was at a nursing-home on the Kent Road, the address of which she had forgotten! Swallowing this unlikely story as best he might, O'Brien was taken by his disgruntled cabman back to the Westminster Palace Hotel, where he

found a message from his leader, summoning him to a new rendezvous behind the Greenwich Observatory at half past ten the next
morning. What happened then is best described in O'Brien's own
words:[24]

> In Greenwich Park I found myself, accordingly, at the appointed
> hour in a clammy December mist that froze one to the bone . . . I
> suddenly came upon Parnell's figure emerging from the gloom in a
> guise so strange and with a face so ghastly that the effect could
> scarcely have been more startling if it was his ghost I had met wander-
> ing in the eternal shades. He wore a gigantic fur cap, a shooting-
> jacket of rough tweed, a knitted woollen vest of bright scarlet, and a
> pair of shooting or wading boots reaching to the thighs – a costume
> that could not well have looked more bizarre in a dreary London park
> if the object had been to attract, and not to escape, observation. But
> the overpowering fascination lay in the unearthly, half-extinguished
> eyes flickering mournfully out of their deep caverns, the complexion
> of dead clay, the overgrown fair beard, and the locks rolling down
> behind almost to the shoulders. It was the apparition of a poet
> plunged in some divine anguish, or a mad scientist mourning over
> the fate of some forlorn invention.
>
> 'Good God, Parnell, what induced you to trust yourself out in this
> infernal place upon such a morning?' was my first cry of horror.
>
> 'Oh', he replied, with the smile, like a wintry sun, with which he
> was always able to wave off ill-fortune, 'I am all right. But, I have
> been ill – very ill.'
>
> 'My cab is still here. Let us drive to my hotel or anywhere else you
> please out of this murderous fog.'
>
> 'I've seen as bad on the Wicklow hills. Nobody will observe us
> here.'

If this seems strange we have always to remember that O'Brien was a
novelist as well as a politician. Nevertheless, though the *mise en scène* may
have owed a good deal to his imagination, his record of the conversation
into which his leader then plunged, sounds accurate. Referring specifically to Dillon's Castlerea speech, Parnell warned O'Brien that the
Liberal alliance was being imperilled by such extreme statements.
Guessing that the source for such a warning was Morley, not Gladstone,
O'Brien retorted by urging Parnell to inform himself directly of how
Gladstone's mind was really working. 'If you are both genuinely persuaded we are doing mischief, it is not yet too late to pull up.' Dillon,
he explained, had not yet decided whether to obey the court order to

give securities for good behaviour.* 'If he refuses and is locked up, and
if I resign the charge of *United Ireland*, as I shall gladly do, to anyone
you name, the movement will quietly fizzle out.' 'That', Parnell replied,
'would be madness for you and for me and for the country. In our
family we do not use the word madness lightly. All I propose is that you
should set bounds to your operations, or we shall be bankrupt and the
Liberals will shake us off.' O'Brien sought to reassure him that it was
their intention to confine the Plan to selected estates, though he also
made the valid point that if this leaked out the landlords would concentrate all their efforts upon a limited front with disastrous effects upon
the tenants.

Parnell remained unimpressed. His lieutenant, he suggested, expected too much of human nature. When O'Brien retorted that that
might be the way to get the best out of people, Parnell replied curtly
that he never generalized. His concern rather was to make a practical
point – that the Irish farmers and priests, to say nothing of the English
nonconformists, would not stomach a scheme for fighting landlords
with their own rents. And then he put his finger on the real weakness of
the Plan. 'What', he asked, 'will you do for money? You will never
succeed in collecting your rents a second year.' O'Brien had to admit
that this was the crucial difficulty and that the Plan was devised as an
expedient for one winter only. But he argued, not without reason, that
if the landlords reacted to the Plan by a counter-campaign of eviction,
money would flow in from America and the sympathy of English
Liberals would also be engaged. In the end, it was apparently agreed
between them that the Castlerea speech should be explained away (in
effect, disowned), that where the Plan was already in operation it should
be pursued with full vigour, but that no new commitment was to be
undertaken unless special circumstances demanded it.

By this time the fog was being overtaken by darkness and Parnell
asked O'Brien to allow him to share his cab into town. Indeed he did
more. Disregarding, with characteristic insouciance, his own elaborate
precautions for secrecy, he took his friend and follower to dinner in one
of the most conspicuous spots in all London, the French room of the
Criterion. Parnell ate little and drank only his customary pint of white
wine, but he was more relaxed and communicative than O'Brien had
ever known him. O'Brien was deeply shocked by the pallor of his face
and the dark shadows under his eyes, but he could not bring himself to
end the conversation as Parnell, 'speaking in gentle and caressing tones',

*See above, p. 361.

revealed a range of interest and information hitherto unsuspected.

It was on this occasion that he discussed his illness with unusual frankness, giving O'Brien to understand that it was kidney disease, coupled with insomnia. O'Brien blurted out that he should have a woman, some member of his own family, to look after him. Parnell took this monumental indiscretion in his stride, merely remarking that, although as a family they were fond of one another, they did not get on so well when they were too much together. But he surprised his follower with the remark that even the history of the saints showed that 'life is not supportable without the friendship of a woman be she good or bad'. Smiling, he added: 'You would never have got young men to sacrifice themselves for so unlucky a country as Ireland, only that they pictured her as a woman.' Then they spoke a little about Parnell's earlier years and his preference for a military career – 'but not under the British flag'. Next, and surprisingly, the talk turned to religion on which, O'Brien gathered, Parnell had no dogmatic views. To him it was 'that something in life we don't understand and never will'. In his fumbling way he tried to reconcile his own enslavement to superstition with a belief in the supernatural. O'Brien's record of what he said is probably too literary to be exact, but it conveys something of the man's groping intelligence. 'Don't you think', said Parnell, 'that the Apostles had just as lively a horror of the number thirteen the day after the Last Supper? I should never have burned the witches of old. Macbeth's mistake was not in consulting the witches, but in only believing the portion that pleased him in their advice. You never know in what strange quarters knowledge may be hidden. The foolishness of the Cross was the breath of life of Christianity.' From this they veered to astronomy and to the possibilities of space travel. Parnell was quite sure that once the problem of supporting life in a different atmosphere was solved, 'a voyage to the planets or even to the stars won't be much more difficult than that of Columbus when he set out to discover America'. This led him on to abstruse calculations as to how weights and distances might be measured in an interplanetary existence. O'Brien's non-mathematical brain retired from the contest at this point, but he did recall one last significant detail about their strange encounter. 'During our three or four hours' table talk', he noted wonderingly, 'he did not revert, directly or indirectly, to the Plan of Campaign or to the Castlerea speech.'[20]

Nevertheless, the Plan of Campaign had still to be dealt with. When Parnell saw Morley again on 12 December the Liberal attitude towards it had perceptibly hardened. Not only had Morley himself remonstrated with Dillon about the Castlerea speech, but, more important,

Gladstone had made his own position clearer. Writing to Morley on 8 December he described the speech as 'very bad' and expressed his determination to remain in the background. 'Upon the whole I suppose he [Parnell] sees he cannot have countenance from us in the Plan of Campaign. The question rather is how much disavowal?'[26] Parnell for his part reported to Morley that while 'the lieutenant' had defended the Plan, he had persevered in his disapproval, though Morley was almost certainly wrong in interpreting that in his diary as meaning that the meetings already advertised would be dropped.[27] There is no evidence that Parnell went as far as this in his interview with O'Brien, for no one knew better than he that to do so would be to precipitate a crisis with his followers. But upon O'Brien and Dillon, as upon Gladstone and Morley, the most lasting impression left by the Greenwich interview was the true one – that for Parnell the Liberal alliance took precedence over all else and that an agrarian movement which disregarded this cardinal fact would get no help from him.

II

But would he be allowed to dissociate himself so emphatically from the new agitation? The answer to this question did not rest wholly, or even mainly, with him. At the precise moment in the autumn of 1886 when he was explaining to his Liberal allies that a policy of 'reserve' was what he proposed to follow, the first steps were being taken by his enemies to link him, not just with agrarian lawlessness, but with violence of a darker kind – the Phoenix Park murders. The trail towards this objective had begun to be blazed in the latter part of 1885, when the Liberal Chief Whip, Lord Richard Grosvenor, was approached by the seedy Irish journalist, Richard Pigott, whom we last saw disposing of his failing newspapers to the Parnellites to make way for *United Ireland*.* By 1885 Pigott was in low water and needed money badly. He had a young family to whom he was devoted – it was his sole redeeming feature – and to raise the wind he suggested to Grosvenor that the latter should finance the publication of a pamphlet, to be called *Parnellism Unmasked*, which would alert all defenders of the Union to the allegedly violent propensities of the Home Rule movement. Grosvenor referred him to Edward Caulfield Houston, a young man who had been on the staff of *The Times* correspondent in Dublin and had subsequently become secretary of the leading Unionist organization in Ireland, the

*See above, p. 162.

Irish Loyal and Patriotic Union. Houston rapidly concluded that Pigott was a man worth cultivating. He knew everyone in Irish political life, in his shady past he had moved much among the Fenians, and if there were unsavoury secrets to be discovered, his was just the nose to smell them out. Houston therefore agreed with him that he was to receive a retaining fee, plus travel expenses, while he pursued whatever researches were necessary to establish the links, which Houston was convinced really did exist, between Parnellism and crime.

This was manna from heaven to Pigott. He began to travel in some style, turning up in Paris and Lausanne and even making a trip to America. After a while it struck him that it would be much easier to manufacture the required evidence than to seek it in quarters where, it was increasingly clear, nothing of a seriously incriminating nature was likely to be found. Having already in his possession correspondence from various Land League leaders, including Parnell and Patrick Egan, about the sale of his newspapers and other matters, Pigott proceeded to invent documents which would link these leaders to the Phoenix Park murders; first he contented himself with forging their signatures, but, growing bolder and more competent, he went on to create whole letters in a passable imitation of their handwriting. To sell this material to Houston as genuine evidence presented less difficulty than might have been supposed, since Houston, convinced that he was on the verge of a sensational disclosure, proved a gullible young man. Summoned to Paris by Pigott in July 1886, he met his informant at an hotel and was told that two agents, who waited downstairs for payment but whose identities must not be disclosed, had provided crucial letters – said to have been found in a mysterious black bag – linking Parnell with Irish criminality. The letters were duly produced and Houston, who was accompanied by another Unionist stalwart, Dr J. F. Maguire, a Fellow of Trinity College, Dublin, was so eager to be convinced that he gave them only the most cursory inspection. Having accepted them as genuine, he then and there paid over to Pigott the sum of £500 for 'the men downstairs' and a bonus of £105 for Pigott himself. He made no effort to see the mysterious emissaries, but perhaps this was just as well, for they existed only in Pigott's lively imagination. The latter pocketed the whole of the money himself and in due course began to fabricate fresh forgeries; these, too, he had no difficulty in selling to Houston.[28]

These transactions occupied the greater part of 1886. By the time Houston had his 'evidence' firmly in his hands the Tory government was in office, the Plan of Campaign had been launched, and it was becoming plain that before long the two would be in collision. The situation was too explosive for Houston to handle on his own. He decided to ask the advice of Lord Hartington, the *de facto* leader of the great majority of the Liberals who had seceded from Gladstone. Lord Hartington refused to touch either Mr Houston or his letters. Houston therefore resorted yet again to an expedient he had tried twice before without success – he approached George Buckle, editor of *The Times*. On this occasion Buckle referred him to the manager of the paper, J. C. Macdonald, and the latter, without cross-examining Houston about the provenance of the letters, agreed to submit them to the proprietor, John Walter. He in turn consulted his legal adviser, Joseph Soames, and as a result of this consultation took the momentous decision to buy the letters from Houston. At this stage no one in *The Times* office knew where the letters had come from. Houston had refused this vital information on the ground that he was pledged to secrecy; all he would admit – and it was alarming enough – was that they came from a 'tainted' source.[29]

It was now incumbent upon *The Times* to investigate the genuineness of the letters. The first step was to secure some authentic specimens of Parnell's signature, so that they could be compared with those in Houston's documents. This proved more difficult than expected, for Parnell was habitually reluctant to sign anything unless satisfied that he ran no risk in doing so; it had been observed in the lobby of the House of Commons, for example, that he even carried this caution to the pitch of waving cheques in the air to dry his signature rather than leave an imprint upon blotting-paper.[30] Just before Christmas, therefore, *The Times* adopted the device of advertising in the 'agony' column for autographs of various parliamentary figures, including Parnell.[31] This produced a crop of well-attested signatures and the way seemed clear for verification.

At that point things began to go wrong. The letters were only of use to the newspaper if they could be used to discredit the Parnellite movement as a whole by planting in the public mind the conviction that there was a direct connection between Parnellism and crime. It was the more urgent that this connection should be established quickly because the rapid spread of the Plan of Campaign in Ireland was bringing a clash with the government steadily closer. It was the intention of *The Times* to publish its supposedly incriminating letters on the actual day that parliament assembled to hear the Queen's Speech, which was likely to contain a reference to the necessity for a fresh dose of coercion for Ireland. Clearly, if *The Times* were simultaneously to produce material so potentially damaging to Parnell, the passage of a coercion act might be considerably eased.[32]

But on the eve of the meeting of parliament, only a few hours before *The Times* went to press, Macdonald and Soames held a consultation with the distinguished lawyer, Sir Henry James, to discuss how best to deal with any legal proceedings that might result from publication. To their consternation, James expressed serious doubts about the authenticity of the letters and advised against printing them. Most ominously, it emerged that he had seen them before. The indefatigable Houston had tried to interest him in them some months previously and Sir Henry James had then gained the clear impression that Richard Pigott had been in some way or other concerned in procuring them. This was a warning light, indeed. Yet *The Times*'s authorities apparently missed its significance entirely, as the official history of the paper later made clear in a single devastating sentence. 'The name [of Pigott] was unknown to the representatives of *The Times*, nor was it regarded as of sufficient importance to require the consultation of those members of the staff of the paper who were specially conversant with Irish affairs.'[33]

The rulers of *The Times* were now in a dilemma. On the one hand, they so badly wanted to believe the letters genuine that they could not bring themselves to discard them. On the other, James's advice could not lightly be ignored. As Walter wrote to Macdonald, 'the documents would be sadly discredited if the fact came out – as it would be bound to do – that they had been seen and examined by high legal authorities, and had been rejected by them, before being submitted to us'. Walter's main indignation was reserved for Houston, who had concealed this information from them. The original bargain must therefore be considered at an end, and if there was to be further negotiation it must be based upon results, 'i.e. the attainment of the object for which the documents were placed in our hands, i.e. the absolute and undeniable proof of P's complicity'.[34]

This was the heart of the matter. Would the proof be forthcoming or not? Not only *The Times* was vitally interested in this question, and not only *The Times* might help to answer it. Hard on the heels of the James interview Macdonald wrote a letter to W. H. Smith, First Lord of the Treasury and Leader of the House of Commons, which suggests that Smith at least, if not also his cabinet colleagues, might have been expecting to learn something to the government's advantage in *The Times* of 27 January. The letter ran as follows:[35]

My dear First Lord,
    A curious disclosure at a consultation with Sir Henry James yesterday evening compelled us at the last moment to postpone the

announcement intended to be made this morning. It turns out that
the letters had been under the highest legal consideration before being
offered to us, and that the opinion pronounced upon them was that
they were inadequate to sustain the case put forward.

I still feel firmly convinced that they are perfectly genuine documents and that much may be done to strengthen the weak points in
them as evidence available in a Court of Justice. But more time is
indispensable for this and meanwhile we must be silent.

> Ever yours truly,
> J. C. Macdonald.

This letter, striking as it is, does not in itself establish collusion between
The Times and the government, though its phraseology was such that
Smith would have found it impenetrably cryptic if he had not had some
advance notice of what was brewing.* But if the government was not
involved at the outset, it soon showed itself extremely sympathetic to
The Times's efforts to substantiate its case. Little more than two weeks
later the Home Secretary, Henry Matthews, took steps to supply the
paper with information about the personnel of the Land League and
about where the League's accounts had been kept. 'This', he wrote, 'is
all I have gathered as yet in answer to your enquiries. I am expecting
further information, which I will communicate to you.' Two months
after that, in April, he wrote again explaining that the Irish Attorney-
General had promised to prepare the Irish Prison Board for a call from
Soames to inspect the visiting books at Kilmainham prison, whence
Parnell was presumed to have smuggled out one of the most incriminating documents.[36] Soames was to spend much of his time in Ireland during the months ahead collecting evidence to substantiate *The Times*'s
case, and in this he was to be assisted by a wide range of government
officials from resident magistrates to police constables.

Meanwhile *The Times* began its assault. On 7 March appeared the
first of a series of articles, entitled 'Parnellism and Crime', in which the
Parnellite movement was described as 'essentially a foreign conspiracy'.
Its chief authors, thundered the paper, 'have been, and are, in notorious
and continuous relations with avowed murderers'. In striking at
Parnell, *The Times* struck also at his Liberal allies, as a second leader in
the same issue later made perfectly plain. 'Mr Gladstone and his party',

---

*His private archives (the Hambleden Papers) reveal no trace of any written
communication. He could of course have received such a communication and
destroyed it; alternatively, and more probably since he and Walter were old
friends, he could have been informed by word of mouth.

it proclaimed, 'are deliberately allying themselves with the paid agents of an organization whose ultimate aim is plunder and whose ultimate sanction is murder, to paralyse the House of Commons and to hand Ireland over to social and financial ruin.'[37] Neither this article nor its two sequels of 10 and 14 March attracted as much attention as no doubt the editor had hoped. Parnell, their chief target, ignored them completely and, so far as his still fragile health permitted, continued to play the congenial role of a strictly constitutional leader provoked by an unjust government into taking up rather more of the time of the House of Commons than his natural modesty would have dictated. On 7 February he had moved an amendment to the address in reply to the Queen's Speech, wherein he argued that the remedy for the existing crisis 'is not to be found in increased stringency of criminal procedure . . . but in such a reform of the law and the system of government as will satisfy the needs and secure the confidence of the Irish people'. He then proceeded to make one of those 'balancing' speeches which were to become so familiar in the next two or three years. Attacking ministers for embarking on the 'slippery slope' of using coercion against their political opponents – the authors of the Plan of Campaign – he adroitly dissociated himself from the new movement while crediting it with prompting the Irish administration to exert its own pressure upon the landlords. 'I believe . . . had it not been for the Plan of Campaign many poor tenants who now have roofs over their heads would have been cast out on the bare hillside.' His fear was, however, that in combating it the government would be led on into even more extreme positions and he pleaded for a reconsideration of policy before it was too late.[38]

It was ominous that the debate on this amendment, which was negatived by a predictably large majority, should have spread over six nights. And it was no less ominous that Parnell himself should have appeared in the course of it to one observer as thin and careworn and 'far from being strong or well'.[39] These two signs together portended that, if coercion was introduced there would be a long and angry session, but that Parnell's own contribution might be at best intermittent. This was exactly how it turned out. During March the House was much occupied in amending the ordinary rules of procedure so as to clear the way for the introduction of a new coercion bill. At the start of this manœuvre Parnell was endlessly active and no less an authority on obstruction than T. M. Healy provided the readers of the *Nation* with a eulogy of his chief which contrasted oddly with some of his private utterances. 'Never', he wrote rhapsodically, 'since his earlier struggles has Mr Parnell developed more energy or watchfulness than he is showing now, throwing himself into the discussion of every technicality as if he were as friendless and unsupported as in the days when everything depended on his single arm.'[40] Perhaps there was a barb in that last phrase, but if so it was hardly needed, for illness soon again removed the leader from the scene. He was to reappear spasmodically when the long-threatened coercion – the Criminal Law Amendment Bill – was introduced on 28 March by Arthur Balfour, who had just succeeded Hicks Beach as Chief Secretary, but when the real battle developed at the committee stage in the early summer, the Irish members were left so much to their own devices that by the end of May Healy was striking a different note. 'The Irish party', he wrote, 'have suffered very keenly from the enforced absence of Mr Parnell; and though it is hard to say how or why, yet, undoubtedly, a sense of slackness creeps in when the general of the battalion is stricken down.'[41] When he did return shortly afterwards Healy recorded that his friends were shocked by his pale and wasted aspect; he was thought to be recovering, though 'the inartistic silk handkerchief that swathes his neck still gives him the air of a convalescent'.[42]

III

Long before then *The Times* had at last unmasked its batteries. On the morning of 18 April, the day on which the crucial vote on the second reading of the Criminal Law Amendment Bill was to be taken, the paper announced that it possessed documentary evidence 'which has a most serious bearing on the Parnell conspiracy', and, breaking with all precedent, it published in large facsimile on an inner page what purported to be a letter from Parnell to an unnamed correspondent, dated 15 May 1882 and apologizing for having been obliged, as an act of policy, to condemn the Phoenix Park murders. The body of the letter was clearly not in Parnell's hand and all that did seem identifiable as his were the words 'Yours very truly', followed by his signature. To understand the sensation caused by this disclosure it is only necessary to consider the text.[43]

Dear Sir,

I am not surprised at your friend's anger but he and you should know that to denounce the murders was the only course open to us. To do that promptly was plainly our best policy.

But you can tell him and all others concerned that though I regret the accident of Lord F. Cavendish's death I cannot refuse to admit that Burke got no more than his deserts.

You are at liberty to show him this, and others whom you can trust also, but let not my address be known. He can write to House of Commons.

> Yours very truly,
> Chas. S. Parnell.

The natural assumption in the minds of most readers on seeing this damning letter most probably was that *The Times* must have been extremely sure of its ground to have taken the enormous risk of publishing it. In reality, the ground could scarcely have been more shaky. A year or so later, when much murky water had flowed under the bridge, John Walter wrote an undated 'statement' in which he recorded that it was primarily upon the internal evidence of the *facsimile* letter that he and his advisers based their conviction that it was genuine.[44] Long afterwards the official *History of The Times*, while stressing that the letters had been adjudged genuine by a leading handwriting expert, G. S. Inglis, repeated that it was the internal evidence – in effect, the feeling that this was just the kind of letter which Parnell might have been expected to write – that clinched the matter. 'External evidence there was none and from the nature of the case none was to be expected.'[45]

Perhaps to those who did not know Parnell the internal evidence may have seemed conclusive, but to anyone familiar with his style of writing, still more with his habitual caution when committing himself to paper, the facsimile letter can only have appeared a grotesque parody. Nevertheless, with what purported to be his signature staring up from the foot of the letter which, if not at once disowned, could quickly ruin him and his cause, prompt action was urgently necessary. There are conflicting accounts of how he received the news. According to Katharine, she herself propped up *The Times* for him against the teapot at breakfast. He read it silently over his toast and marmalade and only when he had finished and had clipped the end off his cigar did he smile and say: 'Now for that assaying I didn't finish! Wouldn't you hide your head with shame if your King were so stupid as that, my Queen?' Whereupon, for the next two hours he buried himself in his experiments and had eventually almost to be pushed out of the house with instructions from Katharine that he must 'attend to *The Times*'. As she tells the story, he returned in the evening, mentioned briefly that he had consulted the famous advocate, Sir Charles Russell, and then turned with obvious relief to the important business of extracting minute particles of gold from his stock of minerals.[46]

Although it is possible that Parnell did first see *The Times* in this way, it is certain that the day did not end as Katharine says it did. Another version, which Barry O'Brien had from Timothy Harrington, suggests that Parnell only read the facsimile letter when he strolled into the House of Commons that evening and Harrington accosted him with it. Harrington expected an outburst of rage, but was treated instead to an impressive example of Parnell's famous sang-froid – not in this instance difficult to achieve if he had already seen the paper at breakfast and had had time to arrange his thoughts. Together they examined the document carefully in the Library. 'He put his finger on the S of the signature', Harrington recalled, 'and said quite calmly as if it were a matter of the utmost indifference, "I did not make an S like that since 1878." "My God", I thought, "if this is the way he is going to deal with the letter in the House, there is not an Englishman who will not believe that he wrote it." '[47]

It was by just such an impassive front that Parnell maintained his personal ascendancy over his followers. But of course he was as much aware as any of them of the need to repudiate the letter at the earliest possible moment. His first instinct, apparently, was to write out two copies of his usual signature so that they might be reproduced to prove the facsimile a forgery. Almost immediately he changed his mind and decided not to publish on the ground that the reproduction of his real signature would have no effect upon those who wanted to believe in his guilt.[48] When he went into the House, therefore, he had still not decided on his course of action. Sexton was in the middle of a speech and Dillon and Justin McCarthy were sitting nearby. The latter asked him *sotto voce* what he was going to do about *The Times*. McCarthy's account, dictated by him three days later, continues:[49]

> I said: 'Of course it is a forgery?' He looked at me in a wondering way and said: 'Well, I shouldn't think you had much doubt in your mind about that?'
>
> I said: 'Oh no, none whatever', and then asked him what he meant to do.
>
> He said he had come down to the House intending to denounce the forgery immediately after question-time.
>
> I said: 'You can denounce it in your speech later on.' He said: 'Yes, but I should like to have done it at once – to let it go to the world at once.'

In fact, he was unable to intervene until one o'clock in the morning, near the end of the debate on the second reading of the coercion bill. In a hushed House he denounced the letter as 'a villainous and bare-faced forgery'. His first thought, he said, had been that a blank sheet with his signature must have fallen into unauthorized hands, but as soon as he saw the facsimile he realized that it was 'an audacious and unblushing fabrication'. 'My writing, its whole character', he explained, 'is entirely different. I unfortunately write a very cramped hand . . . It is in fact a labour and a toil to me to write anything at all. But the signature in question is written by a ready penman who has evidently covered as many leagues of letter paper in his life as I have yards.'[50]

This was scarcely good enough, and many people at the time thought that Parnell should have followed his formal repudiation by suing *The Times* for libel. He considered doing so more than once – and did actually take an action later on – but was initially persuaded against this course by his Liberal allies, especially John Morley. The ostensible ground for this advice was that a suit tried before a London jury would be a serious risk because an unprejudiced hearing could not be guaranteed. Equally, a trial in Dublin would have been unconvincing in English eyes because the prejudice would then have operated the other way round.[51] The truth was, as the Irish members speedily discovered, that the facsimile letter had thrown the Liberals into a state of considerable confusion. Word reached Justin McCarthy from the Liberal MP, J. Stuart, editor of *The Star*, that Gladstone's first reaction had been that Parnell should ask for a select committee of the House of Commons to investigate the charges, though this, it seems, was opposed by some of his senior colleagues. Stuart's own view was revealing. He thought Parnell should not go to law because of the risk that severe cross-examination might bring to light dubious transactions from past history. Indeed, since the Liberals themselves had entertained suspicions about Parnell between 1880 and 1882 not markedly different from those now trumpeted abroad by *The Times*, it was understandable that in 1887, when they were trying to establish the sweet reasonableness of the Liberal-nationalist alliance, they should have felt strongly inclined to damp the issue down rather than exploit it.[52]

The outcome was that although Gladstone did demand a select committee early in May, his motion was not vigorously pressed and the government had little difficulty in refusing it. But by then there had been a marked reaction in Parnell's favour. Those who wanted to think him guilty no doubt continued to do so, encouraged by the Prime Minister himself. Speaking on 20 April, Salisbury had no compunction in prejudging the whole issue and utilizing it for the purposes of party warfare, taunting the Liberals for their alliance with a man who had 'mixed on terms of intimacy with those whose advocacy of assassination was well known'.[53] On the other hand, the inherent improbability that Parnell had been foolish enough to write a letter giving so many hostages to fortune, inclined those whose prejudices were not already hopelessly engaged, to feel upon reflection that this must be a case of forgery. Thus, by the end of the week Alfred Robbins of the *Birmingham Daily Post* was able to record a striking change of mood. 'On Monday', he wrote, 'the day of its publication and before it could be scrutinized, the opinion was very general that the letter might be genuine: today [Saturday] after ample opportunity had been given for considering it, the opinion is almost equally general that it is a fabrication.'[54]

A further reason why the question dropped from view was that Parnell himself departed to Ireland. The explanation for his absence – that he had again fallen seriously ill – was at first treated with understandable scepticism, but it was only too true. While he was still at Avondale a rumour actually circulated that he was dead and when he appeared again in the House of Commons in mid-May his friends realized with a shock how close to reality the rumour had come. 'Appeared is a fitting word to use', noted McCarthy, 'for no apparition – no ghost from the grave – ever looked more startling among living men. Only one impression was produced among all who saw him – the ghastly face, the wasted form, the glassy eyes gleaming, looking like the terrible corpse-candles of Welsh superstition. If ever death shone in a face it shone in that one. I came on John Morley a moment after. We both cd. say only in one breath, "Good God! have you seen Parnell?" '[55] Nor was this merely the reaction of intimates who might be expected to register minutely every variation in his condition. Alfred Robbins, whose diagnosis that what Parnell was suffering from was Bright's disease dates from this period, wrote on 21 May that 'those who have seen him within the past few days have been astonished at the alarming change in his appearance a few weeks have made'.[56]

Fortunately, Queen Victoria's golden jubilee celebrations intervened to distract attention from Parnell's predicament, but nothing could long keep Irish business off the agenda of the House of Commons. Slowly and inexorably the Criminal Law Amendment Bill ground its way through parliament in the teeth of Parnellite obstruction, becoming law by mid-July. It was a formidable weapon Balfour took with him to Dublin. The act provided for the prosecution of certain offences in courts of summary jurisdiction; these offences included boycotting, intimidation, criminal conspiracies against rent, unlawful assembly, resistance to eviction, or the incitement of others to commit such crimes. The act provided also for the transfer of cases involving trial by jury from one district to another. In addition, it gave power to the Lord-Lieutenant to declare by proclamation that the act was in force in named parts of the country, or that specific associations were 'dangerous' and their members liable to prosecution. Finally, although the clauses relating to proclaimed districts and dangerous associations were subject to parliamentary review, the act itself did not have to be resubmitted periodically for renewal and was therefore deemed to be 'permanent'. The new coercive legislation was used by Balfour, at first hesitantly, then with increasing firmness, during the next three years. While he did not succeed in stamping out the Plan of Campaign, his ruthlessness made it virtually certain that collisions with the Plan would not only occur but would produce violent incidents with equally violent political repercussions.[57]

It was not long before the first of these happened. On 9 September William O'Brien and a local farmer, John Mandeville, came up for trial at Mitchelstown in county Tipperary on a charge of making inflammatory speeches. In protest, the Irish National League called a meeting in the market square, which was attended by several MPs, including John Dillon and the English Radical, Henry Labouchere. When the magistrate in charge ordered a path to be cleared through the dense crowd (many of them carrying blackthorn sticks) so that the official reporter could take down the speeches from the platform, the audience began immediately to obstruct the police. Vastly outnumbered and severely manhandled, the latter retreated to their barracks overlooking the square and, seemingly in a state of panic, opened fire on the crowd outside their windows. As a result, three men were killed and others wounded. The matter was immediately raised in parliament and though Balfour, while privately critical, stood by the police uncompromisingly, Liberals and nationalists united in condemning the incident. As a consequence the alliance between them, which had been threatened by the facsimile letter, was opportunely strengthened. 'Remember Mitchelstown', Gladstone proclaimed and the propagandists of the Plan of Campaign thenceforward made sure that English audiences would have little chance of forgetting it.[58]

Such events only intensified Parnell's difficulties. He had no desire to involve himself again in an agrarian movement and even if he had, his health would not have allowed it. Every act of violence in Ireland, whether perpetrated by the police or the tenant-farmers, imperilled his set objective of navigating towards Home Rule by strictly constitutional means. Worse still, it imperilled his leadership, since his absence from the scene inevitably threw into prominence the men who bore the brunt of the struggle. Although both Dillon and O'Brien remained impeccably loyal, nothing could disguise the fact that in this latest crisis of the land war it was they and not the titular leader who carried the responsibility of command.

It was therefore fortunate that Balfour's two-pronged approach to Ireland, which involved remedial legislation as well as coercive pressure, ensured that parliamentary activity continued to be of central importance. While the Criminal Law Amendment Bill was passing through its various stages, the government had given an earnest of their more benevolent intentions by introducing a land bill which, though little more than a holding operation, did at least take up one of Parnell's constantly reiterated points – that leaseholders should be brought within the scope of the Land Act of 1881. Since the measure also provided machinery whereby the county courts could grant stays of eviction, and since Parnell's own amendment to enable judicial rents to be revised was accepted, it was easy for him to welcome it unaffectedly.[59]

But there was a price to be paid and once again it was physical. Although in July, for the first time for many weeks, he managed to preside over a meeting of the party, McCarthy thought he looked 'ghostly', noting with alarm that though it was hot summer weather Parnell wore a thick outside coat and a soft felt hat – and still shivered.[60] Despite this, he struggled that same month to a banquet at the National Liberal Club attended by 80 Liberals and 50 Irish members. He used the occasion partly to pay his now almost ritual compliments to Gladstone, but also to urge restraint upon his own people. 'They would be fools', he said, 'if by any word or by any acts or by any programme or any policies they were to endanger the position – I won't say endanger the position because that would be impossible – but to retard the progress of the great Liberal party in their path of justice towards Ireland.'[61] But, as Mitchelstown showed in September, the danger of provocation was ever present and he acknowledged the fact when that affair was being debated in parliament. 'You find Ireland peaceful and law-abiding', he told the government. 'You are doing your best to drive them to despair.'[62]

This was to be his last public appearance for several months and already by October McCarthy was lamenting his leader's absence. 'If it were a question of what Ireland would assent to', he explained to his literary collaborator, 'there is no man living but that one who could possibly pretend to give an authoritative answer ... and we can't get to him or within speech and hearing of him.'[63] This *cri de coeur* is interesting, not merely as establishing the fact of Parnell's absenteeism, but because of its emphatic affirmation that he was still the only one 'who could possibly pretend to give an authoritative answer'. Clearly, his powerful personality, which in his prime had dominated the party, continued despite his obvious debility, to overshadow his colleagues. A sketch of him just at this time by an American journalist suggests that this dominance was as strongly marked as ever:[64]

The deference which is paid to him by his followers has no close parallel anywhere within my knowledge . . . Most nearly he rules them as an emotionless archbishop might rule the priests of a province. He is the embodiment of authority, a being to be obeyed, to be salaamed to, to be addressed with ceremonious deference; yet, who must in turn keep up all the dignities of his high post, must have no favourites, must be urbane and polite and considerate, and must be at once approachable and solitary. It is really the Catholic training and instincts of the Irish members, I fancy, which has developed this curious hierarchical relation, and it is not made the less interesting by the fact that their primate is a Protestant.

IV

Parnell passed the recess partly in seclusion with Katharine in England, partly at Avondale. In England his and Katharine's ambition to keep out of the public eye was becoming steadily more difficult to achieve and towards the end of 1887 he was traced by a detective employed by *The Times* to an address at Brockley, No. 112 Tressilian Road. This was a house he had taken about a year previously but, according to Katharine, had never liked because he felt himself under constant observation there. Certainly, the detective had no difficulty in establishing that the 'Mr C. Preston' who had rented the house was in fact Parnell. He was easily identified by his photograph, but was described by a woman who lived opposite as looking very unwell – the local gossip was that he had cancer. He was not often seen there, and used the place mainly for keeping a groom and two horses within easy reach of London.[65] Not surprisingly, in view of these determined attempts to track him down, Parnell crossed to Avondale in the New Year for ten days' respite. But on the journey back he was recognized again and in the train between Holyhead and Chester had to undergo an interview with a special correspondent of the *Freeman's Journal*. To the inevitable question about his health he replied that it had somewhat improved, though this did not prevent him from using it as an excuse for not having visited his constituents in Cork and also, shortly afterwards, for summoning the party to meet him in London, instead of holding the eve-of-session meeting as usual in Dublin. The main theme of his conversation in the train, however, was not his own condition but the political situation. The government, he reckoned, was in serious difficulties (it was little more than a month since Lord Randolph Churchill had caused a sensation by resigning the Chancellorship of the Exchequer over the defence estimates), and the best line for the Irish party to pursue in the coming session would therefore be *not* to obstruct business and so allow the ministry rope to hang itself if that was what it wanted to do.[66] This advice he proceeded to follow himself when the new session opened. His amendment to the Address pointed clearly away from the angry clamour of the previous session and towards a peaceful restatement of the case for Home Rule. Ireland, he maintained, was ripe for self-government because, whereas for every person favouring parliamentary action when he entered public life there were nine or ten who looked to violence, by 1888 these proportions had been completely reversed.[67]

It is in the light of this placatory speech that we have to assess the private interview he had with Gladstone a few weeks later. The purpose was to discuss some of the more fundamental problems likely to arise in the shaping of a new Home Rule bill. Gladstone found him 'extremely moderate and reasonable' and thought his tone 'very conservative'. 'I was not', he added acutely, 'entirely without apprehension that the energies of his political pursuits were somewhat abated by his physical condition.' But what struck Gladstone most was that his visitor was quite open-minded about the form Irish self-government might take in the future,* apparently even to the point of being prepared at least to consider a settlement which might give Ireland a position analogous to that of a state of the Union under the American constitution.[68] That this was not just a gambit for Liberal consumption, but a serious assessment of a real possibility, appears from the similar views Parnell expressed to Justin McCarthy about the same time.[69]

Yet the ugly reality remained that, despite Parnell's assertions to the contrary, Ireland remained in a deeply disturbed condition. While this was so all definitions of Home Rule would remain academic. A winter of coercion had not crushed the Plan of Campaign out of existence, but it had exacerbated feeling and this had led, or was shortly to lead, to the

---

*For a more detailed discussion of the political content of this interview, see below, pp. 440-2.

imprisonment of numerous Irish MPs and of some of their English Liberal sympathizers. In such circumstances, Balfour and Salisbury, like Gladstone before them, turned a speculative eye towards the Vatican. Nor were they alone. Two Irish bishops, Dr John Healy of Clonfert and Dr Edward O'Dwyer of Limerick, complained to Rome early in 1887 that boycotting was on the increase and that too many clergy were becoming deeply involved in the Plan of Campaign. Both complaints were well-founded, but the bishops could also have added that clerical commitment to the agitation did not stop short at parish priests or country curates. On the contrary, the two leading princes of the church, Archbishop Croke of Cashel and Archbishop Walsh of Dublin, had given the Plan their support, the latter after some severe heart-searching, the former with the bluff, stand-no-nonsense enthusiasm for which he was famous.

Prompted partly by this episcopal complaint, but also, it would seem, by the intense diplomatic activity in the winter of 1887–8 of an English mission to Rome headed by the Duke of Norfolk, Pope Leo XIII dispatched an envoy, Monsignor Persico, to report on the Irish situation at first hand.[70] Persico was not unsympathetic to the tenants' cause, but in the nature of the case he could not do other than draw attention to the perfectly obvious fact that in those areas where the Plan operated, the pastors had frequently sided with their flocks.[71]

The outcome of the various pressures converging upon Rome was the issuing on 20 April 1888 of a Papal Rescript condemning the Plan and the practice of boycotting as illegal and forbidding clergy to take any part in either.[72] While this does not seem to have had the desired effect of frightening the priests away from the agitation (though they tended thenceforward to be circumspect in their behaviour), the hierarchy was bound to treat the Pope's letter with becoming seriousness. The reaction of the leaders of the Plan has been analysed elsewhere and need concern us here only to the extent that the episode forced Parnell's hand and opened up a gulf between them and him.[73] Briefly, what happened was this. On 28 April Archbishop Croke discussed the Rescript with Dillon, and on 1 May an article appeared in the press, apparently inspired by Croke and taking a line agreed upon between Dillon and himself. This was that the Plan was indeed to be condemned if it fell within the categories outlined in the Rescript, but as it did not, and since the Rescript was based on a misunderstanding of the true relationship between landlords and tenants, it was not applicable to Irish conditions. Next, it was decided, with Parnell's consent, to hold a meeting of the Catholic members of the party (which meant all save about a dozen) on 17 May. However, before this took place both Dillon and Parnell broke silence, each in a highly characteristic way.

On 7 May Dillon, speaking at Drogheda, asserted that Irish Catholics would not accept the bidding of the cardinals of Rome in the conduct of their national politics and complained bitterly that the influence of English Catholics – 'a miserable crew' – had prevailed at the Vatican over the voice of the bishops of Ireland. His speech was in the truest sense a Home Rule speech, for every word of it breathed contempt for the notion which the Tories had condemned while in opposition but which they were now eager to exploit – that Home Rule meant Rome rule. 'We owe it', he said, 'to our friends in England, we owe it to the ancient traditions of our country, we owe it to our Protestant fellow-countrymen who expect they are about to share with us a free Ireland . . . that it will not be an Ireland that will conduct its affairs at the bidding of any body of cardinals.'[74]

This passionate outburst appeared in the newspapers of 8 May. On that same day Parnell addressed a meeting of English Liberal sym-pathizers with Home Rule at the Eighty Club in London. His speech has been described by a modern authority as masterly and, as a demon-stration of his capacity to combine detachment with insight, it certainly deserves that epithet.[75] Almost casually, he dismissed the Papal Re-script as bound to be a 'disastrous failure' which, as a Protestant, he was content to leave to his Catholic colleagues to deal with. As for the Plan itself, he did not so much repudiate it as go out of his way to stress that he had had nothing to do with its gestation. He had been very ill, he said, when it was started, or he would have advised against it because of its bad effect on English opinion. By the time he was able to pronounce upon it, at the beginning of 1887, both Dillon and O'Brien were under arrest and it was then too late for him to disown it. He had then asked that neither the League nor the party should be identified with it, that it should be restricted to the estates where it was in operation, and that it should be conducted in a moderate manner. He believed these stipulations had been generally observed, though he had come to believe that the Plan would have to be replaced by a different method of agrarian organization which he had been privately maturing for some time. 'But', he remarked ominously, 'we shall now have to wait.' Mean-while, his advice to his fellow-countrymen was to place their reliance upon 'the great Liberal party of England'.[76]

This speech invites several comments. First, if all of it was masterly, some of it was also untrue. Parnell's interview with William O'Brien, as we know, was in December 1886, not early in 1887, and neither Dillon nor O'Brien was in prison when Parnell was called on to give his verdict on the Plan. Secondly, his dismissal of the Rescript as politically irrelevant was a risk, but a calculated risk. He knew that feeling against it was running high in Ireland and by identifying himself with that feeling in advance of the party meeting to which, as a Protestant, he could not go, he was in a sense pre-empting the position which his Catholic colleagues might be expected to take up. To put it more crudely, he was taking the wind out of their sails and quietly underlining the fact that he was still the leader. Thirdly, his emphasis on the importance of the Liberal alliance was not only a deliberate reiteration of what he had been saying repeatedly since 1886, in this particular context it was a plain indication that the political movement must be expected to take precedence over the agrarian one. Finally, and as a logical consequence of this emphasis, by dissociating himself from the Plan of Campaign in the most public manner possible, he effectively succeeded in deflating its importance.

One of the people he met at the reception after his speech was Elizabeth Mathew, a descendant of the great temperance reformer, Father Mathew. Her father, educated at Trinity College, Dublin, was a judge in England and the Mathews were a prime example of an Irish Catholic professional family successfully transplanted to England. They knew many of the leading Liberals and Irish nationalists quite intimately and John Dillon habitually stayed at their house when in London. Elizabeth was already deeply in love with Dillon and they were to be married seven years later. For her, therefore, the Eighty Club speech was a painful experience. But she shared to the full the romantic infatuation with Parnell which was common among young ladies in her circle and even on this occasion, when she so much disapproved of what he had been saying, she still found it impossible to resist his good looks and his 'cold, impassive majesty'; he, 'looking like a king', as she noted in her diary, 'accepting the homage with passive acquiescence'. He was probably bored to distraction, but he exerted himself a little more than usual when introduced to her. She told him how much she loved Ireland. 'Ireland', he replied a trifle bleakly, 'is a delightful country from June to October, but on the whole England is a pleasanter place to live in, at any rate now.' That 'now' sounded uncomfortably like a side-stroke at the Plan of Campaign and perhaps he may have realized this himself, for he went on to speak of her connection with Father Mathew. He greatly wished there was another such apostle of temperance at the present time, he told her, since a campaign against drink, besides being good for the people, 'would put the government in a difficulty . . . by diminishing an enormous source of revenue'. She was then left to digest this original, and typical, view of Father Mathew's life-work as an incident of the fiscal system. Perhaps it is not surprising that she allowed a note of doubt to creep into her record of the conversation. 'I fear Mr Dillon may have a feeling of being deserted', she wrote, adding loyally, 'but that would not be a true feeling.'[77]

Mr Dillon did indeed have a feeling of being deserted and still more did Mr O'Brien. Immediately on learning of the Eighty Club speech, the latter wrote an emotional leader for *United Ireland* which dangerously combined both protest and acquiescence. 'Mr Parnell', he wrote, 'has come to the conclusion that the Plan is a mistake and has taken a solemn occasion to state that as his responsible opinion and advice . . . We cannot honestly endorse Mr Parnell's reasoning: we loyally and finally bow to his authoritative judgement. He is the only man living who has both the right and the power to wound the Plan of Campaign in a fatal spot.' But the article never appeared. Many years later a proof of it was found among the Dillon Papers in an envelope on which Dillon had written as follows: 'Proof of article telegraphed from London to *United Ireland* by William O'Brien on Wednesday, 9 May 1888. This article was stopped by Tim Harrington and me. Had it been published it would utterly have ruined our movement and driven me and others out of public life.'[78]

Since O'Brien acquiesced in the censoring of his article it was possible to weather the crisis without a public controversy. The bishops, it is true, were irritated by Dillon's diatribes against the Vatican interference and Archbishop Croke had hard work to prevent them from passing a vote of censure on the outspoken patriot, but when the hierarchy as a whole pronounced upon the Rescript at the end of May, their resolutions, while profuse in expressions of loyalty to the Pope, and insistent on his overriding authority in matters of faith and morals, nevertheless managed to convey the impression that none of this was exactly germane to the needs of a hard-pressed tenantry fighting for survival. As for the Catholic members of the Irish party, their meeting on 17 May was notably uninhibited. The MPs declared the 'allegations of fact' in the Rescript to be unfounded; drew attention to official perversions of justice ignored by the Vatican; claimed that agrarian reform and political liberty were just and necessary demands put forward in a legal and constitutional way; and ended with this ringing declaration:[79]

While unreservedly acknowledging as Catholics the spiritual jurisdiction of the Holy See, we, as guardians in common with our brother

Irish representatives of other creeds, of those civil liberties which our Catholic forefathers have resolutely defended, feel bound solemnly to reassert that Irish Catholics can recognize no right in the Holy See to interfere with the Irish people in the management of their political affairs.

Effectively, this meant that the Plan of Campaign would go on, as it duly did. It is true that it remained limited in scope (on most of the 116 estates involved peaceful settlements were reached sooner or later), and that the bishops were more cautious in their attitudes than formerly. So much was this the case that it rapidly became the convention to maintain that the Plan as such had ceased with the issuing of the Rescript, or even before it, and that what remained was either a residual agitation or a justifiable reaction by tenants to unjustifiable demands by landlords.[80] In reality, the essence of the agitation continued unchanged and the under-secretary, Ridgeway, while no doubt correct when he wrote to Balfour that Parnell's speech had been 'another blow at the Plan', was quite out in his calculation that it was within sight of being vanquished.[81] It was to persist for another two years as a complicating and exasperating factor in the relations between Britain and Ireland.

More than that, it was to contribute directly to the widening rift between Parnell and his principal lieutenants. Despite the line he had laid down so emphatically at the famous fog-bound interview at Greenwich, both O'Brien and Dillon continued to assume that the moment they got into deep water he would come to their aid. It took time for them to realize that he really meant what he said and that for him the political drive for Home Rule by means of the Liberal alliance took absolute precedence over the agrarian clash with landlords and government. Dillon was the first to sense that all was not as it should be, though even he found it hard to believe that they genuinely were on their own. For him the moment of truth seems to have come about the end of 1887 when the new coercive regime was beginning to bite and when both he and O'Brien had to face the danger of simultaneous arrest. The strain of this burden expressed itself in a bitter protest to Harrington that unless Parnell broke his long and pointed silence the movement might well collapse:[82]

The situation has become very serious indeed. I have utterly failed to get any word of him. He plainly means to boycott us till the opening of parliament at all events. I would have no fault to find with his not appearing publicly to communicate with us. But it is an extraordinary line of policy to go off without a word – and most of all without so far as I know making any arrangement to secure that we shall not be stranded for money . . . it will be simply monstrous if we run short of money in a crisis like this.

When Parnell did at last break silence at the Eighty Club that speech revealed to his two lieutenants as by a lurid lightning-flash that what they were running short of was not just Parnell's funds but Parnell's confidence. And because the speech was made with the utmost publicity in front of a gathering of Liberal notables, it was not surprising either that they should have felt in a measure betrayed or that the loss of confidence should have been mutual. In the long term Dillon, O'Brien and Parnell himself would each be powerfully affected by this dangerous fracture of their former solidarity.

In the short term Parnell's manœuvre seemed to have paid all sorts of dividends. At a single stroke he had reasserted his authority, had checked the influence of Rome, and had once more emphasized that the Liberal alliance was the cardinal point in his policy. Yet, at the very moment when he seemed to be riding as high as he had ever been, incipient disaster fell upon him out of a clear sky. In the previous year his old colleague, F. H. O'Donnell, conceiving himself to have been libelled by one of *The Times* articles on 'Parnellism and Crime', had sued the newspaper. The case only came on early in July 1888 and from the start it was very strangely handled, or mishandled, by O'Donnell's counsel, who decided not to put his client in the witness box. The case failed ignominiously, but before it collapsed counsel for *The Times*, who happened to be the Attorney-General, Sir Richard Webster, was able without contradiction to traverse the whole ground covered by *The Times*'s original attack upon Parnell and to add fresh matter, including what purported to be further incriminating letters by Parnell and other Land League leaders.[83] O'Donnell, in his admittedly unreliable recollections, recorded many years later that when in April 1888 Parnell went with him to inspect the originals of the documents in *TheTimes*'s possession, the Irish leader had displayed intense anxiety as they walked into the solicitor's office – not, as O'Donnell concedes, on his own behalf, but lest one of his erstwhile associates might have exposed a vulnerable flank by writing some thoughtless word in defence of violence. When he saw the documents Parnell's face cleared as if by magic. The letters attributed to him, which contained two spelling mistakes that were later to spring the trap on the forger, were so palpably not his that although he did not then know who the culprit might be, he went away confident that his counterstroke against *The Times* would be devastating when the moment came to deliver it.[84]

What he did not sufficiently realize was that the uncontradicted disclosures at the trial would not allow him to choose that moment to suit himself. All the old suspicions and fears which had died away after Parnell's denials of the previous year woke again to new and teeming life. Since the initial charges were not only repeated but amplified, he was suddenly faced with the brute fact that unless he could clear his name absolutely and unequivocally all his recent labours to establish himself in British eyes as a constructive, even a conservative, force in politics would be in vain. Willy-nilly he was drawn into the most dramatic battle of his career so far, a battle which rapidly became nothing less than a struggle for the survival alike of Parnell and of the whole constitutional movement.

CHAPTER 13

Ireland in the Strand

'Ireland is in the Strand; and behind the light and play of her contemporary life looms, perpetually, a dark background. Lawyers may wrangle and differ, but underneath all their differences lies this fact, which none can dispute – that Ireland is wretched, miserable, demoralized, sick unto death. This is a legal trial. It is also the *viva voce* history of a people – one of the dreariest, saddest histories in the world. And when one listens to it, one feels, with something like despair, how little Englishmen know of this mournful Ireland, which is only twelve hours journey from London.' (J. Macdonald, *Daily News diary of the Parnell Commission*, p. 27.)

I

Parnell lost no time in confronting the new material thrown up by the O'Donnell case. The day after the case had ended, he gave the House – 'in his most frigid manner', as John Morley noted – a detailed analysis of the various letters which had been ascribed to him and others and which the unexpected collapse of O'Donnell's action had prevented him from giving in court.[1] He was careful to distinguish between some trivial and innocent letters which might, he admitted, have been genuine, and the sinister ones, which he denounced as totally false. The latter included one which was presently to play a vital role. Allegedly in the handwriting of his secretary, Henry Campbell, and signed by Parnell himself, it ran as follows:[2]

9/1/82

Dear E,*
What are these people waiting for? This inaction is inexcuseable [sic]. Our best men are in prison and nothing is being done. Let there be an end to this hesitency [sic]. Prompt action is called for. You undertook to make it hot for old Forster and Co. Let us have some evidence of your power to do so. My health is good, thanks.

Yours very truly,
Chas. S. Parnell.

*Supposedly Patrick Egan.

On this damning epistle Parnell's comment could not have been more emphatic. 'Now, Sir, I denounce this letter as an absolute forgery. I never wrote it; I never signed it; I never directed it to be written; I never authorized it to be written and I never saw it.' So also with the others, until after a whole series of explicit repudiations of specific letters, he ended with a blanket rejection of the entire body of the documents so far produced:

> The great majority of them are palpable forgeries – most undoubted forgeries; they bear the look of forgery on their very face . . . In order to attach any credence to them you must suppose that I deliberately put myself in the power of men who had halters round their necks . . . and that I put myself in the position of being accessory before or after the fact.

Mere denial was no longer enough. The charges, if they were to be convincingly dispelled, must be dealt with by some kind of legal or official enquiry. Parnell's instinct was still to take a libel action against *The Times*, but for the time being he was again dissuaded by John Morley on the old ground that cross-examination before an unsympathetic jury might lead to disaster.[3] The case against a libel action was stronger than Parnell was prepared to admit and Harcourt, who had been an acute lawyer before he became an obstreperous politician, put it better than anyone else:[4]

> If [he wrote to Morley] P. brought an action and it extended (as it must) over the whole ground he would be in the same position in point of principle (though of course in a less degree) as O'Donnell. He would lead *The Times* in defending itself to involve a number of other persons . . . indeed the whole of the Land League, who would be attacked and have no means of defending themselves.
>
> Indeed, it is impossible to see how this could be avoided except by making any one implicated by *The Times* plaintiffs in the suit. *Quod est absurdum.*

If, then, a libel suit was ruled out, there remained the possibility of a select committee of the House of Commons. This too was far from ideal, since a majority of the members of such a committee might well be opponents of Home Rule and its findings might therefore be held to be affected by political considerations. Nevertheless, to Parnell, who was rapidly becoming obsessed by the need to clear his name, this seemed a risk worth taking. On Monday, 9 July, he came down to the House in an unusually excited frame of mind, determined to ask for a committee.

Morley, meeting him in the lobby, took his usual negative line. The new batch of letters, he said, contained some obvious forgeries which weakened *The Times*'s case and so diminished the need for an enquiry. Besides, public opinion was no longer excited by the affair and since the government would almost certainly refuse his demand anyway, what was the point in asking for something which he knew in advance would be withheld?[5] But the only effect this had upon Parnell was to stiffen his resolution. Speaking, as Justin McCarthy noted, 'between his set teeth', he told his vice-chairman that 'the whole opposition bench' was against them, but this in no way affected his resolve to press on with his demand for a select committee.[6]

His initial request elicited from the Leader of the House, W. H. Smith, the blunt reply that parliament was 'absolutely incompetent' to deal with the matter.[7] On 12 July Parnell returned to the charge and was met, as before, by an uncompromising negative. This time, however, Smith had also a positive proposal to make – that the government would propose to parliament an act appointing a Commission, to consist wholly or mainly of judges, with full powers 'to enquire into the allegations and charges made against certain Members of Parliament by the defendants in the recent action of "O'Donnell *v* Walter and another"'.[8] Five days later the terms of the enquiry, which already went far beyond the letters of which Parnell complained, were significantly widened by the insertion of the words 'and other persons' after 'certain Members of Parliament'.[9] In thus denying Parnell a select committee, which, apparently, they had been on the verge of granting the year before, the government seems to have been influenced chiefly by the advice of the Solicitor-General, Sir Edward Clarke, who had pointed out on the previous occasion that such a body would be hamstrung if the editor of *The Times* refused, as he was virtually certain to do, to supply the names of his informants and contributors. Since each such refusal would have to be treated, and debated, as a fresh breach of privilege, the work of the entire session would soon be disrupted as effectively as any Irish obstructionist could wish and all this with probably no compensating result.[10]

Nevertheless, though a select committee was avoided, ministers themselves were not happy with the alternative they were offering and the law officers especially were reluctant that judges should be used in what had increasingly the appearance of a political trial.[11] That they offered it at all seems to have been due partly, perhaps mainly, to the importunities of Joseph Chamberlain who pressed the government to set up a Royal Commission. 'I am convinced', he wrote on 10 July to the lady who was shortly to become his third wife, 'that this Commission will elicit some astounding facts and if the result is to show that more than one member of the so-called nationalist party has been dabbling in assassination the effect will be prodigious.'[12] And a week later, on the day when the proposal for a judicial enquiry was brought forward in the House of Commons, Chamberlain was able to inform his fiancée that he had been talking to Salisbury 'and find that the government is inclined to take my view and press for the Commission in any case, and whether Parnell accepts it or not . . .'[13]

Chamberlain's motives for intervening are obvious. It was the Irish question which had separated him from the main bulk of the Liberal party, and the recent failure of the Round Table Conference with his former colleagues had condemned him to an indefinite term in the political wilderness unless he could make himself useful to the Conservatives. Besides, he had still at his elbow the tenacious O'Shea who had by now settled into an implacable hatred of Parnell.[14] Yet, if Chamberlain's pressure was decisive, he was pushing at an almost open door. Evidence of how ministers reached the decision to enlarge the scope of the enquiry (and thus, arguably, to reduce the importance of the letters, should they turn out to be forgeries) is suspiciously lacking, but there was certainly a widespread contemporary view that the government had succumbed to the temptation to use its parliamentary majority to create a Commission which, despite the veneer of legality conferred by the appointment of judges to preside over it, would in effect be what Randolph Churchill called it, 'a revolutionary tribunal for the trial of political opponents'. 'The fate of the Union', he warned, 'may be determined by the abnormal proceedings of an abnormal tribunal. Prudent politicians would hesitate to go out of their way to play such high stakes as these.'[15]

A lecture on prudence from Lord Randolph of all people was unlikely to appeal to his former colleagues. In any event their handling of the debate in the House of Commons suggested that prudence was not a word which figured largely in their vocabulary. On 16 July W. H. Smith moved to introduce the Members of Parliament (Charges and Allegations) Bill, commonly called the Special Commission Bill, before it had even been printed or before those whom it most directly affected had any notion of what it contained.

All he was prepared to say was that the bill accorded with the offer he had previously made to Parnell. 'It is for him to say whether he will accept the proposal of the government.'[16] Parnell, pale with fury, objected with all his force to this mode of procedure. 'A more monstrous proposition was never made', he said, 'by a minister occupying the position of the right honourable gentleman.' If the libels were true, he agreed, then Smith and the Attorney-General ought to have told the House that they were determined to have the investigation whether the Irish liked it or not. But Smith had taken a different line:[17]

> He, as First Lord of the Treasury, the constitutional representative in this House of a great party, of the government and of the nation, comes and says to me, this Bill Sikes – 'It is for the Hon. Member to say whether he will take this Bill or not.' He asks me to accept the Bill before it is printed or even explained. He offers me this as a substitute for a jury. He asks me to accept this tribunal without knowing the names of the judges ... or whether the number is to be three, five or seven ... Well, Sir, why should I trust the right honourable gentleman, I, knowing that he and his party and his Attorney-General have made themselves accomplices in these foul, scandalous and disgraceful libels?

The main clash occurred in the debate on the second reading. Smith, having announced the names of the three judges who would compose the tribunal, began badly with an embarrassing Freudian slip when he referred to 'this great trial', which he had then to alter hurriedly to 'this great enquiry'.[18] Parnell, following him, concentrated his fire on the government's action in extending the scope of the enquiry from MPs to 'other persons', with the result that the Commission would be investigating not merely his conduct, and that of his parliamentary colleagues, but the whole Land League agitation in Ireland, Britain and America. The effect, as he pointed out, was so to enlarge the scope of the allegations as to afford an avenue of escape from the breakdown of the letters, which, he asserted, the government had good reason to anticipate. 'We are now told that these letters are only secondary matters, and even if proved up to the hilt, as it will be proved, that each and every one of the letters mentioned the other night are bare-faced forgeries, it will not affect the case of *The Times*. You seek now to raise this turgid cloud in order to cover your retreat ... which you know well will soon be forced upon you.'[19]

II

It is unnecessary to follow in all its stages a debate which was predictably bitter. Two incidents among many are sufficient to illustrate both the complexity of the issues involved in this tremendous struggle and the depth of the feeling it aroused. Throughout the verbal battle a major aim of the opponents of the government was to establish a connection between ministers and *The Times* in order to demonstrate that the onslaught against Parnell was part of a conspiracy in which the cabinet and the newspaper were jointly engaged. Although there were indeed good grounds for suspecting a substantial amount of collusion, it was hardly to be expected that this would be exposed in the House. Nor was it. But what was brought out was sufficiently damaging. After much harrying of the Attorney-General and the Leader of the House, the latter was at last driven to admit that while the details of the Special Commission Bill were still under discussion by the cabinet he had had a visit from an 'old friend', who turned out to be none other than John Walter, the proprietor of *The Times*. It was in vain for Smith to protest, with perfect truth, that Walter was indeed an old friend, dating back from Smith's business career as a bookseller; in vain also for him to assert, with rather less credibility, that their conversation had avoided the great matter in which they were both so deeply interested. The mere fact of the visit, combined with the other unpalatable fact that the Attorney-General (even though in his private capacity as Queen's Counsel) had acted for *The Times* in the O'Donnell case, left an indelible impression, at least upon the minds of those who were ready to be so impressed, that the conspiracy was both real and sinister.[20]

Much more explosive, and more far-reaching in its consequences, was the clash which occurred between Parnell and Chamberlain. It was largely provoked by the latter, whose intervention in the second reading debate was, he complacently reported to his fiancée, 'one of the best speeches I have ever made in the House' and one which, in his own judgement, had 'settled the bill'.[21] He began ingenuously with an unsolicited testimonial that from his early experience of Parnell he had 'formed a judgement of the Honourable Member for Cork, of his character, of his motives, of his honesty, of his sincerity, of his patriotism, that will not allow me easily to accept the charges which have now been made against him'. Knowing as we do how energetically Chamberlain had pressed the whole idea of a Commission on the government, we are perhaps in a better position than his hearers to assess this testimonial at its true value. But almost at once he changed course significantly. The only thing, he said, which could shake, or had shaken, his confidence in Parnell's ability to disprove the charges 'is his reluctance to face a full enquiry'. He then proceeded to speculate as to why Parnell did not choose trial by jury in Dublin, expressed his own preference for a select committee, and ended with the adroit but un-

scrupulous comment that since the Irish members were apparently prepared to accept the Special Commission, it ought not to be fettered by
the sort of limitations Parnell seemed to want to put upon it. Only by
allowing the whole record of the Land League to be investigated could
Parnell and his colleagues convincingly clear themselves from the
charge of complicity in outrage.[22]

Since it was Parnell's aim to accept the Special Commission, so that it
could get to work with the minimum of delay, he made no immediate
retort to Chamberlain. But after the bill had been allowed its second
reading without a division, he turned on his tormentor with cold and
calculated violence. Late on the night of 30 July, in a passage which does
not appear in the official report, but was reproduced in *The Times*, he
said this:[23]

> I have not, Sir, had an opportunity before this of thanking the right
> honourable gentleman, the member for West Birmingham, for his
> kind references to me and for the unsolicited character which he was
> kind enough to give me . . . He spoke of not long ago, when he said he
> entertained a better opinion of me than he does today. I care very
> little for the opinion of the right honourable gentleman. I have never
> put forward men to do dangerous things which I shrank from doing
> myself, nor have I betrayed the secrets of my colleagues in council. My
> principal recollection of the right honourable gentleman, the member
> for West Birmingham, before he became a minister is that he was
> always most anxious to put me forward and my friends to do work
> which he was afraid to do himself, and after he became a minister my
> principal recollection of him is that he was always most anxious to
> betray to us the secrets and counsels of his colleagues in the cabinet,
> and to endeavour, while sitting beside those colleagues and while in
> consultation with them, to undermine their counsels and plans in our
> favour. If this enquiry is extended into these matters, and I see no
> reason why it should not [be], I shall be able to make good my words
> by documentary evidence which is not forged.

The venom of this attack created an immediate sensation. The Parnellites, for whom Chamberlain was 'the man who killed Home Rule',
followed their leader's every word with glee and when they punctuated
his charges of betrayal with shouts of 'Judas, Judas', even the normally
unruffled Chamberlain was visibly discomposed.[24] Next day, Parnell,
completing his speech, this time reported in Hansard, not only returned
to the assault, but broadened it into a general defiance of all those who
looked to the commission to establish his guilt. 'It is not', he said bitterly,

'the first time that fair play has been denied to Irishmen, and I do not suppose it will be the last. It is not the first time that you have poisoned the bowl and used the dagger against your political opponents in that country, where you could not overcome them in fair fight.'[25]

Chamberlain, recovering his self-possession, mounted an immediate counter-attack. Such political communications as he had had with Parnell – he was referring to Kilmainham and to the 'central board' scheme of 1884–5 – had, he said, been carried on with the full knowledge and approval of the then Prime Minister, Gladstone. But, he claimed, the 'central board' scheme had been Parnell's solution for Ireland until he had dropped it in the hope of getting more elsewhere. When Parnell at once denied this, Chamberlain refused to accept his word, declaring, in pointed reference to *The Times* facsimile letter, that he had documentary proof consisting of letters 'in his own [Parnell's] handwriting and not in that of his secretary'. The controversy rapidly widened out to include the part played by Captain O'Shea in these events, and from parliament the denials and counter-denials spread to the newspapers, becoming more emphatic and far-ranging as they did so.

Yet despite the vehemence of the quarrel, the position of the two antagonists was critically different. For Parnell this was a side issue which offered a welcome opportunity to pay off old scores. But for Chamberlain, whose record of loyalty to his cabinet colleagues was highly vulnerable, to be worsted in this duel with Parnell would be a serious set-back to his campaign for political rehabilitation.[26] A concerted effort was therefore imperative and on 1 August he spent some time with Captain O'Shea planning what form that effort should take.[27] 'The strain of this personal controversy is tremendous', he told his fiancée. However, she could rest assured that all would come right in the end. 'Tomorrow there will be a letter from O'Shea in *The Times* which ought to complete Parnell's discomfiture.'[28]

That letter dealt both with the events of 7 May 1882 and with the 'central board' negotiations of 1884–5. The reference to the aftermath of the Phoenix Park murders need not concern us, except to note how skilfully O'Shea seized the opportunity to imply that Parnell was so terrified by the fear that he would be the next victim that as well as offering his resignation to Gladstone he had gone cap in hand to Chamberlain for advice. 'Full of horror as Mr Parnell was on that day', wrote O'Shea waspishly, 'not only that two lives had been sacrificed but that a third was in danger, it is not astonishing that he should have forgotten that he had asked me to arrange an interview with a minister whom he considered as his benefactor.' As to the more important question of the 'central board' scheme, O'Shea was apparently as specific as anyone could desire:

> The scheme was altogether Mr Parnell's and Mr Chamberlain adopted it with considerable hesitation because of its not being sufficiently consonant with Radical principles. But Mr Chamberlain accepted it with all its blemishes because it was Mr Parnell's very own. Why the latter should repudiate it is a mystery; the original claim to its creation and construction exists not only above his signature, but in his own handwriting.

And, for good measure, O'Shea threw in the gratuitous information that Parnell had also furnished Chamberlain with his own version of a coercion bill to take the place of the expiring Prevention of Crimes Act. 'It is a copy of the original act altered by his own hand into the form in which he proposed it should be passed with just enough show of opposition in the House of Commons to satisfy those concerned.'[29]

This letter seemed to show the Captain at his most ingenious. In half a dozen paragraphs he had contrived to represent Parnell as a physical coward, as a dishonest politician and as a leader who hypocritically made a show of resisting coercion while actually devising a coercion bill himself. Yet appearances were misleading. The innuendo about the events of 7 May 1882 fell completely flat, partly because nobody was interested in such ancient history, but mainly because too many people knew what really happened on that day to be much impressed by O'Shea's 'revelations'. The further allegation about 'Mr Parnell's Coercion Bill' also had a short and undistinguished career when it was subsequently revealed that it was no more than a copy of the existing act with a pen drawn through various clauses, but with nothing to show that the pen or the deletions were Parnell's.[30] In the end, therefore, the controversy narrowed down to the question of whether Parnell was or was not the author of the 'central board' scheme which he ultimately repudiated.

The Irish leader's riposte appeared in *The Times* four days later. He scarcely deigned to notice O'Shea's letter, concentrating mainly on the parliamentary exchanges between Chamberlain and himself about the 'central board' scheme. 'If, as is alleged', he wrote, 'Mr Chamberlain possesses such proofs in my handwriting why does he not publish them? Nay more, I think he is bound to publish these alleged proofs and I call upon him to do so . . . If Mr Chamberlain should still decline to publish these letters and content himself with misleading declarations of their purport, the public will appreciate his conduct, and will understand that it is because the publication will neither substantiate his truthfulness nor vindicate his candour.' Knowing as we do how careful Parnell had been throughout the negotiations to impress upon O'Shea that local government was to be considered on its own merits, and *not* as a substitute for Home Rule, we can appreciate, what Chamberlain had now to learn the hard way, that Parnell's position in this quarrel was virtually impregnable.* Indeed, his confidence rode so high that he extended the same cavalier treatment to 'the astounding statement of his chosen go-between, Mr O'Shea, that Mr Chamberlain was supplied in 1885 with a copy of the Crimes Act [the Prevention of Crimes Act] altered by my own hand'. This, too, ought to be published – if it existed. 'It is not to be supposed for an instant that an astute politician of the Chamberlain-O'Shea type, having got hold of so important a document as "Mr Parnell's own Coercion Bill" would have been so careless as to mislay or lose it.'[31]

Chamberlain rose immediately to the bait, telegraphing to *The Times* that he accepted Parnell's challenge and would forward to the paper 'in the course of a few days' a full statement of the communications which had passed between him and Parnell in 1884 and 1885.[32] It is more than a little surprising that Chamberlain should have dashed into the fray so readily in this matter, since even in 1885 he had had to remonstrate with the Captain about both the tone and the accuracy of the letter O'Shea had written Parnell on 19 January 1885, setting out, in O'Shea's most cynical vein, what purported to be Chamberlain's view of how best to proceed with 'administrative reform' in Ireland.† So perturbed had Chamberlain been about his henchman's indiscretion that he had written two days later to John Morley putting his real views on record and confessing that 'I am beginning to be a little uneasy on the subject of Captain O'Shea's volunteered communications'.[33] At the time O'Shea had been able to gloss over his own performance by blaming the breakdown of the negotiations on Parnell's bad faith. Chamberlain had accepted his version of the transaction then, and since the whole trend of events in the interval had been such as to lead him to think the worst of anything Parnell might say or do, he presumably still thought in these terms when on 8 August 1888 he sent for O'Shea in order that they might prepare a joint statement. If he did so think, he was quickly disillusioned, as he explained that same day to his fiancée:[34]

---

*For Parnell's attitude in 1884–5, see above, pp. 270–4.
†For the context of this letter, see above, pp. 271–2.

In the course of conversation he referred to something I had entirely forgotten, namely, that in 1885 he had written a letter to Parnell purporting to give the result of an interview with me. He showed me this letter at the time and I protested against it as inaccurate and was very angry about it, but it suddenly struck me that Parnell has this letter. From indications in some of the papers it is quite probable that he means to publish it, although, of course, it was confidential in the highest degree. It is an odious letter, cynical, personal and mean . . . but unfortunately O'Shea put his thoughts and interpretations into my words and in writing to Parnell has credited me with his own political morality. What will happen if this letter is produced? In my own defence I must throw over O'Shea, and say what is the truth, that he grossly misrepresented me; but then, if he misrepresented *me*, may he not also have misrepresented Parnell? And he is my chief witness against Parnell. Altogether it is a nice dilemma. Either he is a trustworthy witness, in which case my negotiations with him were of the most selfish and ignoble kind; or else he is untrustworthy, in which case I have no evidence to convict Parnell.

On 9 and 10 August he saw O'Shea again. What passed between them we do not know, but they cannot have been comfortable interviews for the Captain, who that same day sent Chamberlain what amounted to a full confession:[35]

I suppose I ought not to have written as I did, but anyone knowing the terms on which I then was with Parnell would make some allowance for the style.

What, however, I want to say now is that I fully admit that the letter did not contain or pretend to contain a literal account of our interview, but was rather my own version of it, interspersed with my own comments on the political situation suggested by general personal observation.

I cannot at this distance of time separate what was yours from what was mine in the picture I drew, but if Parnell should be capable of the indescribable meanness of using such a letter to damage you, you may rely on my being ready to state the true facts, even though they do not redound very much to my diplomatic reputation. Parnell knows perfectly well that you at once repudiated all responsibility for my description of the interview, for I told him so the next time I saw him and I often spoke to him about it afterwards.

There is a certain irony about this letter of O'Shea's and about Chamberlain's letter to his fiancée, for here were two men who were prepared to use any means to destroy Parnell complaining querulously that he would be guilty of 'indescribable meanness' if in defending himself he were to use the weapon their own carelessness had put into his hands. The carelessness, admittedly, was chiefly O'Shea's and the episode finally shattered whatever faith Chamberlain had still retained in his reliability. The Captain might still have his uses, and Chamberlain had not quite finished with him, but, as his biographer says, 'he never again gave an opening to his diplomatic talents'.[36]

Meanwhile, Chamberlain had still to extricate himself from his predicament. O'Shea's apology was quickly brushed aside with an acid rejoinder that John Morley was prepared to produce the letter Chamberlain had written him in January 1885 which gave a truer account of the matter than O'Shea's travesty.[37] But, though this might indeed represent Chamberlain's views on Irish local government more accurately, it still would not save him from derision and contempt if the O'Shea version were made public.

To prevent that there was only one step to take and on 13 August Chamberlain took it, gall and wormwood though it must have been. On that date he published in *The Times* a long letter which began on a suitably subdued note. 'A great pressure of work has prevented me from replying earlier to Mr Parnell's letter of the 4th of August.' Chamberlain then observed disingenuously that he now had difficulty in ascertaining what was at issue between them. 'Previously to the appearance of his letter I had understood that he denied that Mr O'Shea had any authority to represent his views, and that he repudiated all responsibility for the scheme for a national council or central board submitted to me by that gentleman. Now, however, I gather that what Mr Parnell intended to repudiate was all cognizance or approval of what he calls my plan . . . I am consequently ready to admit Mr Parnell's disclaimer of any assent to it.' As for the scheme which Chamberlain had attributed to Parnell, but which had reached him only in O'Shea's handwriting, he had a further admission to make. 'The correspondence . . . corroborates Mr Parnell's statement that he did not put forward this proposal as a substitute for an Irish parliament.' Finally, after admitting that what had previously figured as 'Mr Parnell's own Coercion Bill' was in reality a revised version of the Prevention of Crimes Act, 1882, Chamberlain conceded that Parnell had been prepared to consent to more stringent provisions if the new act were to last for only *one* year than if it were designed to last for three years or longer. The letter ended with a passage in which discretion triumphed mightily over bile. 'In con-

clusion, I may be allowed to say that neither at this time nor subsequently has it appeared to me that there was anything in these communications of which Mr Parnell had cause to be ashamed.'[38]

III

This represented, as both men knew, a virtually complete capitulation
by Chamberlain. Yet Parnell's triumph was precarious, since Chamberlain had been deeply wounded in his *amour propre* and he was never
more dangerous than when exposed to personal humiliation. But for
Parnell the discomfiture of Chamberlain was of merely secondary
importance. It was the future of the Special Commission, and behind
that the future of the Liberal alliance, which was still the all-engrossing
priority.

As the bill moved through committee there was little to be done but
to register protests which were well understood to be for the record only.
True, the battle was fought by Liberals as well as by nationalists and to
all outward appearances the debates offered an impressive spectacle of
the Home Rule alliance in action. But below the surface there were
ominous signs of a tendency among some of Parnell's new-found friends
to keep their distance until he had proved his innocence. Part of the
difficulty was tactical. The Liberal leaders had wanted a real fight to be
made on the first and second readings, and failed utterly to understand
that since, for Parnell, the Special Commission which was being so
contemptuously offered was better than continued uncertainty, it was
preferable to let the bill pass quickly into law. Harcourt, especially,
refused to be bound by considerations of this kind. He found the
Attorney-General an irresistible target and buried the harpoons of his
invective in Sir Richard Webster's quivering carcase with a ferocity
which astonished even those who were used to his methods of debate.
The Attorney-General, he thundered, had flouted the best traditions of
the Bar in the O'Donnell case when he spent one and a half days making
statements which had no relation to the plaintiff, but were calculated to
injure others 'whom he knew could not come there to justify and defend
themselves'. As for the Special Commission itself, Harcourt rose to an
ecstasy of denunciation:[39]

> You say that this tribunal are not to be bound by technical rules. Is
> it a technical rule that a man should know whether he is charged and
> what he is charged with? Why, that is the fundamental essence, and
> the first conception of justice; to have the right hon. gentleman the

Home Secretary and the Law Officers of the Crown disparaging that which is the first principle of justice, and denouncing it as a technical rule, is one of the most shocking things I have witnessed in this House. Nothing would shock you [turning to the government benches]; for we know very well you are racing for blood. What we protest against is that any man, even an Irish member, should be called upon to plead to a sort of hotchpotch, miscellaneous slander.

That significant phrase, 'even an Irish member', though no doubt ironical, expressed an inner reservation which Harcourt always had about Irish members in general and about Parnell in particular. It was a reservation which coloured his private correspondence at the moment he was making his public protestations. To Morley he wrote with his usual brutal humour that it would save everyone time and trouble if W. H. Smith and Parnell could settle the matter by personal combat; he backed the elderly and portly Smith to win. But he was also at pains to impress upon Gladstone the more serious point that the Liberals must at all costs avoid entering into an arrangement with the government as to the actual appointment of judges. 'It would make us parties and partners in a concern with which we ought to have nothing to do, besides I do not see how we could act in such a matter without the co-operation of Parnell and to do that seems to me open to every possible objection. I see no safe course for us except to stand aloof altogether and to accept no responsibility in the matter.'[40]

Morley took the same line, but *con brio*. His links with the Irish party were closer than those of any of his Liberal colleagues and he was perturbed to discover that Parnell, against the advice of his counsel, Sir Charles Russell, still hankered after a libel action against *The Times*. Morley's reaction was to urge Gladstone to leave the Special Commission severely alone.[41] Gladstone concurred reluctantly, recognizing that his own responsibility to his party counselled caution, but wishing that someone else would put the details of the unsavoury transaction on record – 'so unjust to Parnell and so disgraceful to the government and to parliament'.[42] But John Morley remained unmoved, even advising strenuously against any Liberal contribution to the defence fund which was now being organized to assist Parnell and his colleagues with the expenses of the Special Commission. A subscription, wrote Morley, would not be popular among Liberals 'until they are more completely satisfied that Parnell's hands are clean'. 'Would not a bad impression be likely to be created', he added, 'if we take action which will look like hurrying to assume P's innocence, before the case has been heard? Parnell at present has no sort of claim on us. He has brought on the whole of this evil business, by his steady disregard of our advice.'[43]

Nothing shows more clearly than these exchanges the extent to which *The Times* allegations had driven a wedge between the Liberals and their Irish allies. And the Irish allies themselves had good reason to be on edge and apprehensive. As the Commission was finally constituted, the three judges were empowered to enquire into a wide variety of charges and allegations made against a wide variety of people. The latter fell broadly into two groups. The first consisted of 63 members of the Irish parliamentary party, together with two retired members, and the second of 67 'other persons', Irish and Irish-American, most of them extremists, with whom the accused MPs were alleged to have associated. The list of MPs included the most prominent members of the party (which at this time numbered 86 in all), but, strangely enough, the list of 'other persons' omitted Michael Davitt, whom the judges, and most other people, regarded as standing in a class by himself. Although not one of those accused by *The Times*, Davitt's involvement was total from the moment it became clear that the whole history of the Land League was to be minutely investigated. In effect, Davitt and the 65 named MPs (past and present) were the real respondents in the case.

The charges against the respondents were not formulated until after the Special Commission began to hold its preliminary meetings in September 1888. Then counsel for *The Times* submitted particulars of the charges they intended to substantiate, and these in turn were summarized by the judges under the nine heads which ultimately served as the framework of their report. These nine heads concerned three main issues. It was alleged first that the respondents were members of a conspiracy to bring about the absolute independence of Ireland. Secondly, that it was an immediate aim of the conspiracy to promote, by coercive methods and intimidation, an agrarian campaign against the payment of rents, with the object of bringing down the landlord system. And finally, that in pursuit of these objectives, the respondents either committed crimes themselves or were accomplices in crimes: by failing to prevent such crimes or express *bona fide* disapproval of them, but on the contrary condoning in private what they thought it necessary to denounce in public; by assisting criminals and their dependants; by circulating, or allowing to be circulated, newspapers and other literature which incited to and approved of sedition, crimes, boycotting and other outrages; and by intimately associating with monstrous criminals and inviting and accepting help from advocates of crime and dynamite. In addition, it was charged against Michael Davitt that he assisted in the formation of the Land League with money contributed for the purpose of outrage and crime, and that he was the main instrument whereby an alliance was forged between the Parnellite party in Ireland and the revolutionary wing of the Irish-American nationalists.[44]

Even this brief summary of the charges is enough to show that if what was intended was not the indictment of a nation it was at least a grand inquisition into the history of a movement, thus spreading far beyond the narrow confines of establishing the authorship of *The Times*'s letters which had been Parnell's sole, original concern. For the accused Irish respondents such an enquiry was a heavy burden, not merely because of the nerve-racking possibility that the constant probing of *The Times*'s counsel would uncover some damaging episode from the past, but because a long-drawn-out enquiry – and this one occupied 129 sittings between 17 September 1888 and 22 November 1889 – was certain to be extremely expensive. The latter problem at least was solved by the 'defence fund' of about £40,000 which was raised for the express purpose of paying the costs, but nothing could alter the fact that while the Commission sat and until it reported in February, 1890, the Irish leaders, and Parnell especially, remained under a shadow which held their whole political movement in suspense.

In such circumstances the choice of counsel was for Parnell a matter of crucial importance. Yet even here he was dogged by mischance and ill-feeling. In choosing Sir Charles Russell he certainly selected one of the foremost advocates of the day. But Russell was not an easy man to work with. Parnell would probably not have worked easily with him at the best of times, but under the stress and strain of this momentous enquiry friction was constant from the outset. Russell was an Ulster Catholic from Newry who had risen in his profession by great ability allied to immense industry.[45] As Davitt shrewdly observed, 'His sympathies leaned towards Ireland, his ambitions towards England.'[46] He had taken an early interest in the land question, but he was never a nationalist and adopted Home Rule only when Gladstone did, just in time to become Attorney-General in the latter's 1886 administration. Russell was a man of imposing presence and strong personality, a strange mixture of sensitive perception and overbearing arrogance. He was not only a technical expert, but a forensic orator of outstanding excellence in an age when these abounded. However, he liked to dominate his clients and in Parnell he had a client who did not like to be dominated. They seem never to have taken to each other and although on one occasion during Russell's opening speech Davitt was startled to observe Parnell actually in tears (for the first time in his life, he told

Davitt) when the great advocate was describing the poverty of the west of Ireland, Russell was not placated. 'I'm glad something can move him', he muttered. To the end he was constantly irritated by Parnell's habit of not appearing in court unless it suited him. 'Tell him straight from me', said Russell to Davitt on the eve of one of the more important sessions, 'if he does not turn up in good time tomorrow I shall throw up my brief.' Parnell was wholly unperturbed by the message. 'Oh', he said, 'Russell is a bully, you know, and you have to tame him a little.' All the same, he did come to court the next morning, only to give his entire attention to a small brown-paper package which he laboriously unwrapped for Davitt's benefit. It contained a tiny particle of gold. 'After fourteen years' search at Avondale', he exclaimed in high delight, 'this much has at last been found. I got it out of a parcel of stone sent to me two days ago by my agent.'[47]

Although the two men were temperamentally poles apart and liable to clash on that account alone, Parnell's attitude to Russell may partly have been affected by the O'Donnell trial. Russell had attended that trial expecting to be summoned as a witness.[48] He was not called because of the way in which O'Donnell's counsel had conducted the case, keeping his client and his supporting evidence out of the witness-box until it was too late for them to be called. The barrister in question was admittedly inexperienced, but it did not escape attention that he had been accosted by Russell during the proceedings and it was widely believed that he acted as he did on Russell's advice. If Russell did so advise him, his motives have remained obscure. He may, as a good Gladstonian, have been taking the orthodox Liberal line of 'least said, soonest mended'. Alternatively, he may quite genuinely have feared that cross-examination whether of Parnell or others, would provide *The Times* with fresh ammunition which ought, if possible, to be denied to the newspaper. Or, as he apparently told O'Donnell himself in 1890, he may simply have thought it was not in O'Donnell's best interest to pursue the matter further – an opinion, given O'Donnell's marked eccentricity, which cannot but command respect.[49] But whatever the reason for his intervention, and whether the effect of that intervention was to set O'Donnell's counsel on his ignominious course or not, the end result was the same – Webster was presented with an open door through which he at once proceeded to charge, doing the maximum of damage in the process.

It is possible also that Russell on his side felt some irritation at Parnell's cavalier treatment of the suggestion that T. M. Healy should be briefed as one of the defending counsel. The solicitor for the defence,

Sir George Lewis, actually wrote to Healy in September, 1888, inviting him to hold a brief and Healy accepted the retainer. But a month later, after consultation with Parnell, Lewis had to write to say that his client's view was that Healy should appear as counsel only on his own [Healy's] behalf. Healy, not unnaturally, was mystified. He thought at first that it was because he had taken too prominent a part in the Plan of Campaign, but Davitt may well have been nearer the mark when he commented in after years that this was Parnell's tit for tat for Healy's Galway 'mutiny'. The incident left Healy bitterly resentful. 'In Parnell's career', he wrote to his brother, 'there has been nothing more monstrous than his action in taking this whole business into his hands without consulting anybody. He is the last man I would select to entrust with such a business.'[50] It was one more irritation to be added to the festering suspicion and dislike which had come to mark the two men's relations with each other.

Yet, if Liberals and nationalists thus approached the great ordeal in a disjointed frame of mind, the government was scarcely any happier. The Attorney-General, who had already come under fire for his Jekyll and Hyde performance in the O'Donnell case, had no mind to repeat the experience and begged piteously to be let off.[51] Salisbury, who had already had similar overtures from the second counsel for *The Times*, Sir Henry James, would not hear of such desertion. 'The simultaneous refusal of these men to go on', he wrote to W. H. Smith, 'will have the worst possible effect. There will be no persuading the outside world that they have not run away from the case because on scrutinizing the evidence they satisfied themselves that the case was bad.'[52] Webster protested feebly that the Commission was very different from the O'Donnell case and that if he appeared for *The Times* people would say that 'the government have been conducting the prosecution and no amount of argument will satisfy the country to the contrary'.[53] But the pressure from Salisbury and the cabinet was irresistible and Webster had to yield. 'Every day I curse Chamberlain and the Unionists for their obstinacy', he wrote to his brother law-officer, Sir Edward Clarke, 'but perhaps they are wiser than I am.'[54] Even so, Salisbury kept a close eye on him. 'I suppose you have heard from Smith', he told his nephew, Arthur Balfour, 'of Webster's attempt to get out of his collar. We have kept the harness tight on him – but I am afraid he shows signs of gibbing still.'[55] These exchanges, apart altogether from their testimony to the stresses within the government, throw a double light upon the Special Commission. First, they confirm, from one of the chief actors in the drama, that pressure from Chamberlain was an important factor in the creation of the tribunal. Second, and more important, they demonstrate the extent to which the government were prepared to go to link their fortunes with those of *The Times* to achieve the grand objective of bringing down Parnell.

Nor was the alliance limited to the comparatively simple matter of bullying the Attorney-General into presenting *The Times*'s case before the Commission. There is ample evidence that the resources of Dublin Castle, such as they were, were freely made available to Joseph Soames, who was mainly instrumental in collecting evidence for the newspaper. Arthur Balfour, who as Chief Secretary was closer to Irish realities and therefore more alert to their capacity for potential disaster, put the dilemma to his uncle thus: 'It is clearly legitimate for us to make what investigations we please with a view to coming at the truth: but ought we, or ought we not, to communicate the results of our investigations to *The Times*? If we do not, it may get wasted – if we do shall we not find ourselves in a somewhat embarrassing position?'[56] To this Salisbury replied, predictably, that if evidence which would fix someone's guilt had come 'naturally' into the government's hands, 'then we shall be fulfilling an obvious and elementary duty in facilitating the proof of it before the Commission'.[57]

Much depended on the definition of that term 'naturally'. It had already involved substantial assistance from the Home Secretary, Henry Matthews, which included supplying *The Times* with information about the Land League and also facilitating Soames's visit to Kilmainham.* In addition, it is now known that the second series of the 'Parnellism and Crime' articles was written by R. A. Anderson, who, since 1867, had been adviser to the Home Office in matters relating to political crime and who in 1888 was promoted to be head of the Criminal Investigation Department. Anderson had obtained his materials from the spy, Henri Le Caron, and returned the compliment by helping Le Caron to marshal his evidence when the time came for him to emerge into the open by testifying before the Special Commission. It was Anderson, furthermore, who arranged with *The Times* that Le Caron should receive suitable compensation for the ending of his career in espionage.[58] Although Anderson apparently acted without obtaining permission from his superiors, and was technically not a civil servant when he wrote the articles, they were nevertheless based on knowledge he had previously acquired in his capacity as a public official.

Dublin was no less helpful than London. As early as May 1888, Soames, searching through the official files, made what he called 'a great

*See above, p. 372.

haul' of Land League papers and succeeded in convincing the under-secretary, Ridgeway, that *The Times* would have a watertight case.[59] Soames was inclined to become over-demanding and Webster had to remind him of 'the extreme difficulty of anything being done for one side which if asked could not be done on the other'.[60] No doubt this *was* the strict legal position, but that it never remotely corresponded to reality was evidenced by the stream of Irish testimony which, by the nature of the case, simply could not have been requisitioned by Parnell and his friends. It included the criminal files of the Irish administration; the interrogation of convicted prisoners; the dispatch to London as wit-nesses of numerous police constables, district inspectors and magistrates; and, finally, the full-time employment, with the sanction of Arthur Balfour, of a former police officer and acting resident magistrate, W. H. Joyce, to prepare documents and witnesses on behalf of *The Times*.[61]

IV

From all this accumulated evidence counsel for *The Times* were able to construct a comprehensive picture of Irish agrarian disturbance which did indeed convey an impression, at once horrifying and distressing, of the state of the country during the land war. But this evidence did not touch the issue which had originally brought the Special Commission into being. It bore no relation to what *The Times* had published and it threw no light on the crucial question which agitated contemporaries to the exclusion of almost all other aspects of the enquiry – did Parnell write the letters attributed to him or did he not?

On this crucial question the defence approached the Special Com-mission far more confidently than the prosecution. Right up to the moment when the Commission began its hearings *The Times* had still made no serious effort to establish the provenance of the documents upon which the case against Parnell and his associates so largely de-pended. In his evidence at the Commission, *The Times*'s solicitor, Soames, testified that it was only when the Special Commission Bill was introduced in the House of Commons (July 1888) that Pigott had re-leased Houston from his vow of secrecy as to how the letters were obtained, while of course telling him nothing about how they were written. It was then that Soames himself had his first interview with Pigott, who told him merely that he had found them in the summer of 1886, but not where or through whom. 'And I believe that even now', said Soames during cross-examination in February 1889, 'Mr Mac-donald does not know and that Houston does not know.'[62] It was certainly not until after the Commission had got under way that the rumblings of coming disaster began to make themselves heard. Even then it was not *The Times* but the government which began to realize that something was wrong. Early in November 1888 the under-secretary, Ridgeway, learned for the first time that the letters had originally belonged to Pigott. Since Pigott's reputation was a by-word in Dublin, Ridgeway was at once alarmed and communicated to Balfour his fears that the defence would have little difficulty in proving the letters to be forgeries. '*The Times*', he added, 'has been so extraordinarily reckless that one is naturally inclined to deny it credit for ordinary caution and common sense. They have never made any enquiry here concerning Pigott's character or antecedents before or since they accepted his information.'[63]

The Parnellites, by contrast, had penetrated Pigott's secret even before the Commission began its sittings. Parnell himself had at first been on the wrong track. He thought that O'Shea, if not the actual forger, had been the moving spirit. But Davitt and most of the other leading nationalists thought otherwise – Patrick Egan spoke for all of them when he said of O'Shea that 'the fellow is incapable of playing the role of heavy villain'.[64] During the summer of 1888 they obtained what they regarded as conclusive proof of the identity of the culprit. In August Davitt received from Egan (then in Lincoln, Nebraska) a letter naming Pigott as the forger. Egan's evidence was decisive, because it was he who had negotiated with Pigott for the purchase of the latter's newspapers in 1881 and, comparing letters he had had from Pigott and copies of those he had himself written to Pigott with the letters published by *The Times*, he had at once noticed not merely obvious similarities in the handwriting, but even that *The Times*'s letters contained words and phrases taken from the original correspondence.[65]

Armed with this information, Parnell's solicitor at once served Pigott with a subpoena. Not only that, an agent employed by Henry Labouchere (who acted closely with the Parnellites throughout), ran Pigott to earth in Ireland and induced him to come to London, ostensibly to meet a man from America who wished to see him on important business. A meeting was arranged at Labouchere's house, where on 24 October Pigott duly appeared. He was shown into a sitting-room, only to find himself confronted by Parnell and Labouchere. They charged him point-blank with forgery. He denied it. Then Lewis, the solicitor, entered the room and Parnell and Labouchere withdrew. What passed between Pigott and Lewis is not known, but apparently Pigott collapsed after a show of fight and promised to call on Lewis next day to give him a written confession.[66] According to Labouchere's account, Lewis came back to the dining-room, where Labouchere and Parnell were waiting, and told them that Pigott was going to make a complete statement next day but wanted first to speak to Labouchere. 'Mind, whatever you do', warned Lewis, 'don't give him any money; if you do, he will bolt.' Labouchere returned to Pigott who asserted that *The Times* had promised him £5000 to go into the witness-box. What would Labouchere give him not to do so? 'Nothing', said Labouchere. What he wanted were the originals of Egan's letters to Pigott, since they would prove the forgeries up to the hilt. If these were satisfactory, he would pay for them. Would he pay £5000? asked Pigott. More like £1000, replied Labouchere. But he must first see the documents. And on that note they parted.[67]

Next day, however, Pigott recanted and apparently decided to brazen it out. The official *History of The Times* declares that the paper knew nothing of this interview in Labouchere's house.[68] But Pigott's every move was watched by detectives from both sides and it is clear from a letter read before the Special Commission after Pigott's cross-examination that Soames at least had known of the rendezvous of 24 October.[69] It appears in fact that what Davitt feared when he learnt of the interview came close to happening. As he tells the story, Parnell burst in on him the morning after the interview, exulting over Pigott's confession. He became noticeably subdued, says Davitt, when the latter pointed out that if Pigott chose to report the interview to *The Times*, all they had to do was to pay him a sufficient sum to induce him to absent himself and, after he had vanished, then accuse Parnell, ostensibly the last man to see him, of having bribed him to disappear – the implication being that Pigott had been paid to take the blame which rightly belonged to Parnell.[70] Although Davitt's superior wisdom smacks of hindsight, it does seem that Pigott went some way towards fulfilling his prediction. He did indeed go to *The Times*, loudly proclaiming that he had been offered £1000 by Labouchere and Parnell to admit guilt, but he had virtuously refused.[71] Nevertheless, his self-confidence had been shaken and a couple of weeks later he gave Soames a most explicit warning. 'You must take it', he wrote, '. . . as certain that any proceedings that will rely for success on any testimony of any character whatever from me will fail.'[72] Most remarkably, Soames seems to have paid no attention either to this or to an agitated plea from Pigott for money to enable him to disappear; on the contrary, he subpoenaed him, insisting that he must confirm in the witness-box the statements he had already made under oath as to the authenticity of the letters.[73]

Labouchere meanwhile continued to keep an eye on Pigott and saw him again early in December 1888. This time the Radical was quite specific in his demands. He now wanted from Pigott not only the originals of Egan's letters, but also the signatures of Egan and Parnell from which Pigott had traced his copies, together with a few further forgeries executed by Pigott on the spot. Pigott was not unwilling to exhibit his art, but asserted he had destroyed the Egan letters and that the signatures were no longer in his possession. Labouchere then disclaimed all interest in whatever else he had to offer, but out of curiosity asked him what he was going to do. Pigott admitted that he was in 'a terrible mess', but saw no clear course open to him but to go into the witness-box, swear that he had bought the letters, and that if they were forgeries he had been deceived. Labouchere told him he would be a fool if he did, that it would be better to tell the truth and ask for an indemnity. 'That is all very well', the wretched man replied, 'but on what am I to live?'[74]

Doubts about Pigott may all the same have helped to determine the tactics adopted by Sir Richard Webster and his colleagues. From the outset the Attorney-General made it very clear that, as his main objective was to establish the existence of a 'conspiracy', he would ransack the proceedings of the Land League and explore the relations between the Parnellite party and the Clan na Gael for proof of his thesis. So it was that for week after week the Commission moved at a snail's pace through old newspaper articles, stale speeches and the rambling and sometimes almost unintelligible evidence of numerous witnesses. But this leisurely progress did not appear to be pointing towards any definite conclusion and to one acute observer at least it had begun to occur by December that '*The Times* is bent on playing the simple game of wearing down the other side. If the case is only spun out long enough, the counsel for the Parnellites will throw up their briefs in sheer desperation in order not to be utterly ruined.'[75]

Whether that was the game or not, the Commission remained somnambulistic from the moment of its opening in October 1888 until the dramatic events of February 1889. To this there was only one exception – the appearance, as third witness for *The Times*, of Captain O'Shea. On 31 October, Alfred Robbins of the *Birmingham Daily Post*, taking his seat as usual at the Commission, noted on his pad: 'Parnell very early. Why?'[76] The arrival of O'Shea speedily provided the answer. As he stepped into the witness-box, the journalists eyed him greedily. 'I remembered him as a spruce, dandified man, filled with belief in himself and disbelief in others', wrote Robbins. 'He was the kind of gentleman-

like adventurer, cynically contemptuous under the guise of *bonhomie* . . .
who makes the world his oyster and is disappointed at the size of the
pearls.' Robbins thought he had changed for the worse and now verged
on 'the shabby genteel'.[77] Others, however, saw him differently and the
correspondent of the *Dublin Daily Express* could not withhold his
appreciation from an actor who played his part with a certain style. 'If
possible he was a greater dandy than ever. There was a fresh cluster of
curls about his ears, and his well-oiled poll shone beautifully in the
electric light. We all looked intently for the gold eye-glasses and, to our
joy, they were produced. "He uses them", said an Irishman sitting close
to me, "with an eighteenth-century grace."'[78]

But both these descriptions missed the mark. O'Shea resembled
nothing so much as a time-bomb with an uncertain mechanism, and
counsel on either side circled warily round him as if they were fully
aware of the fact. Most of his evidence concerned the Kilmainham
'treaty' and what took place in London on the day after the Phoenix
Park murders. This has already been considered in its context and only
two things need concern us here about O'Shea's appearance in the
witness-box – how he came to be there and the attitude he displayed
towards Parnell.

It appeared from cross-examination that *The Times* had approached
Joseph Chamberlain in August 1888 with the suggestion that O'Shea
might be an important witness and that Chamberlain had discussed this
when they were planning their abortive counter-stroke to Parnell's
attack upon Chamberlain in the House of Commons on 30 July. A few
days later E. C. Houston called on O'Shea and this was subsequently
followed by a dinner-party to enable the Captain to meet George
Buckle, the editor of *The Times*.[79] At that dinner, as O'Shea reported to
Chamberlain, 'I told him I would have nothing to do with "charges and
allegations", but that I had no objection to talk about the Kilmainham
'treaty', which I as usual minimized to the utmost'.[80] O'Shea was then
subpoenaed by Parnell's solicitors and retaliated by asking *The Times* to
subpoena him also. In the witness-box he made it perfectly clear that he
regarded himself as a *Times* witness, and claimed that his object in
appearing was partly to explain the Kilmainham 'treaty', but partly
also 'to refute the slanders which had been circulated about me by Mr
Parnell and his friends with regard to these letters'. Asked what he
meant by this, he replied that when he came back from abroad at the
end of July Chamberlain had told him he had heard that Parnell believed
that he, O'Shea, had had something to do with procuring the letters, or
at least the facsimile one. But O'Shea added, under pressure from Rus-

sell, that it was Houston who told him of a more specific rumour that he had had dealings with Pigott (or, alternatively, with the disgruntled ex-MP, Philip Callan) to obtain the letters.[81] To Chamberlain himself, however, O'Shea represented the letters as less important than the Kilmainham negotiations. 'Parnell's Plan of Campaign is this', he wrote. 'He puts me in the box, on the ground that he wishes to show that Ministers who had the fullest knowledge of the secret service of Dublin Castle, were so certain of his being clear of all connivance with crime that they were willing to take his support in parliament . . . Such matters have nothing to do with "charges and allegations".'[82]

They had, perhaps, a closer connection than O'Shea was willing to recognize. But still more germane was the venom which crept into his replies when he was asked directly whether or not he really thought Parnell had written the letters published by *The Times*. 'As the witness approached this part of his narrative', Robbins noted, 'he became more and more nervous. He unfolded his arms; leant an elbow on the ledge and his head on his hand; frequently wiped his face; hurriedly stroked his chin; and almost turned his back on the cross-examiner.'[83] He began innocuously enough. 'I believe Mr Parnell to be absolutely free from any connivance with outrage', he said. But he added mysteriously that he still did not think him implicated, 'even after I changed my opinion of Mr Parnell'. Russell, prodded it seems by Parnell, then asked him a dangerous question. 'I wish to know, at the suggestion of my client, what altered your opinion in June or July 1886?' To this O'Shea gave the cryptic reply we noted earlier:* 'Negotiations took place at that time previously to the division of [on] the Second Home Rule Bill, and certain things came to my knowledge at that time which absolutely destroyed the good opinion I had hitherto held of Mr Parnell.'[84]

Russell did not dare to elucidate what the Captain was driving at, or rather insinuating. The time-bomb had suddenly begun to tick loudly and he moved hurriedly away. But not before O'Shea had reaffirmed what he had said earlier to Sir Richard Webster in direct examination – that he believed Parnell's signature to the facsimile letter to be genuine. 'I wish the question had never been put to me', he said. 'I want to tell you that at first when I saw the letter in *The Times* I did not think it genuine. Not', he added in evident confusion, 'that I thought the hand-writing was not genuine, which I did, but I did not think the letter was genuine.'[85]

There, apart from an awkward moment at the very end, when Tim

*See above, p. 334.

Healy intervened for the express purpose of getting O'Shea to admit that Healy and Biggar had opposed his candidature in Galway, the Captain's ordeal ended. He departed to pursue his business in Spain, first revealing to Chamberlain that he had gone into the box under a heavy load of anxiety from matters quite apart from the Commission. 'Once it came to fighting Russell, however', he said with characteristic bravado, 'all went well and I had him down round after round.'[86] In reality, he had contributed little to the case for *The Times*, since Russell, by bringing out the fact of his animosity to Parnell since 1886, had blunted the effect of his assertion that the facsimile letter, and others allegedly signed by Parnell, were genuine. His much-vaunted testimony concerning the events of 1882 had been largely irrelevant and may even have embarrassed Chamberlain by underlining the extent to which he had leaned on an emissary whose unreliability he had not fully fathomed until the ill-starred controversy with Parnell in July-August, 1888.

V

After O'Shea's departure the Commission fell back into its routine of laboriously pursuing any and every avenue which might prove the existence of Irish crime. No doubt the existence of such crime was proved in full measure, but as the tide of testimony mounted what most clearly emerged was that the crime was often the product of desperation and that here was a society which had come close to dissolution. This accumulated witness to the miseries of an unhappy country was too monotonous to attract more than a cursory attention from the public. It was not until 5 February 1889 that the court was again roused from somnolence. The occasion was the appearance in the witness-box of the man who called himself Henri Le Caron and who now proceeded, in his composed, almost pedantic, way to reveal how for many years he had been privy to the inmost secrets of the Clan na Gael and had systematically betrayed these secrets to his paymasters, the British government. Yet, though his personality made a profound impression upon the Commission, and although he certainly threw a lurid light upon the violent side of Irish-American nationalism, he did not materially advance the case against Parnell. True, his account of his interview in the House of Commons in April 1881, when, he alleged, Parnell told him 'he had long ceased to believe that anything but the force of arms would accomplish the redemption of Ireland', told severely against the Irish leader.* Yet even this was set off to some extent when Le Caron, under

*For the interview and its context, see above, pp. 155-7.

pressure from Russell, had to modify his initial statement that Parnell's American tour of 1880 had been organized by the extremists, admitting that this was in fact true only of his appearances in Chicago, Cincinnati and St Louis.[87]

Le Caron, having served his purpose, vanished from view, to die five years later, 'peacefully in his bed', as John Devoy sardonically remarked.[88] But the stir he had caused at the Commission had scarcely died down when at last, on 14 February 1889, on the fiftieth day of the sittings, the long-delayed investigation into *The Times*'s letters began.

The first to be called on the newspaper's behalf was Joseph Soames, who now revealed the conclusions which had been reached at Printing House Square about the letters. Briefly, these were that of the letters said to have been by Parnell, the body had actually been by his secretary, Henry Campbell, but the signatures were Parnell's own. It was apparently *The Times*'s intention at that point to introduce the handwriting expert, G. S. Inglis, who would have testified in this sense. Perhaps fortunately for his reputation, the judges ruled otherwise and it was decided to deal first with the provenance of the letters and with the question of how they came into *The Times*'s possession. Since it was the custom of the office that neither the proprietor nor the editor gave evidence in court cases, this led, of necessity, to the examination of the manager, J. C. Macdonald. He was left to Russell's junior, the rising young barrister, H. H. Asquith. It was an easy task, for Macdonald was everything a witness ought not to be – vague, inconsequential, unreliable, admitting without any attempt at concealment that he and his associates had believed the letters because they wanted to believe them, because, as Macdonald elegantly put it, they were the sort of letters he felt Mr Parnell was likely to write.[89]

Parnell, whose irregular attendance hitherto had so annoyed Sir Charles Russell, now followed the proceedings closely and with barely suppressed enjoyment. His previous absences had been partly due to recurrent ill-health, but, though apparently still suffering from rheumatism, he was punctual in court from the moment when Soames first began to explain why *The Times* had believed the letters to be genuine. And when on 19 February E. C. Houston stepped into the box, his interest became, if anything, keener. Houston began by explaining how he had procured the letters from Pigott while at the same time being careful *not* to ask where they came from. Admitting that up to December 1888 he had received various communications from Pigott which might have thrown some light on this crucial subject, he then said coolly that he had got rid of them. 'I wanted', he explained, 'to destroy all clue[s] to original sources.' Asked if he thought this fair to Parnell, Houston replied that he did not think Mr Parnell was entitled to any consideration. 'A curious exhibition of insolence and uneasiness – at which Mr Parnell smiled', noted one observer.[90] A moment or two later the same observer glanced towards Parnell when Houston was describing how Pigott had told him that the letters were in a certain black bag left behind him in Paris by Frank Byrne, but that he, Houston, had sedulously not enquired closely into the whereabouts or ownership of that black bag.* 'All this while Mr Parnell sat on the front bench. The collar of his dark brown great coat was drawn up to his ears. Mr Parnell was absorbed in watching Mr Houston. He gazed at him with an air of intense amusement.'[91]

VI

Through this accumulated testimony about the letters there ran a common thread, the name of Richard Pigott. By the time Russell had finished with Houston there was a general feeling, not just in court but in the world outside, that everything, everyone, was waiting for Pigott. Then, just before three o'clock on the afternoon of 20 February, at last he came. 'A short, stoutish, round-shouldered man is Pigott', wrote the correspondent of the *Daily News*, 'with a bald, shining head, bushy white whiskers and moustache, big, somewhat irresolute mouth, big, fleshy nose, and smallish eyes far apart.† "A benevolent-looking person" one spectator remarked. "Might be a church deacon", remarked another.'[92] Robbins of the *Birmingham Daily Post* saw him as 'a frockcoated, stoutish-built figure of fifty-four, white bearded, bald-headed, bland, smiling, and having the general appearance of a coarsely composed and rather cheapened Father Christmas'.[93] Webster took him as unobtrusively as possible through his evidence. The first stir came when he was asked if he had anything to do with the writing of the letters.

---

*The Commission was bedevilled by a plethora of black bags. It is important to distinguish between Pigott's probably imaginary black bag and Parnell's undoubtedly real one. The latter accompanied him regularly to the hearings and on being opened one day in his absence was found to contain nothing more treasonable than a spare pair of socks.

†It was not always thus. Twenty-five years earlier, at Dalkey on the coast south of Dublin, Pigott had come under the eagle eye of the young Bernard Shaw who remembered him as 'a spry-looking gentleman, with a single eye-glass' and known locally as 'the Major'. He was a fanatical swimmer and saved a man's life on one occasion. (*The Star*, 19 February 1889. I am indebted to Mr Ulick O'Connor for this information.)

Pigott changed colour, but replied calmly enough, 'Nothing whatever', adding gratuitously, 'it is quite untrue I forged them', an accusation that nobody had yet made publicly. Then followed his version of the interview with Parnell and Labouchere, and later with the solicitor, Lewis, on 24 October 1888 at Labouchere's house. As Pigott told it, of course, the purpose of the interview had been to persuade him to swear before the Commission that he had forged the letters, whereupon Labouchere would pay him £1000.[94]

The examination in chief lasted for the better part of two days and at lunch-time on the second day Pigott was still largely intact, though his version of the Labouchere interview was so grotesque as to arouse laughter in court. Everything therefore hinged upon his cross-examination by Sir Charles Russell. For a week beforehand Russell had been out of sorts – nervous, irritable, eating little and gloomily preoccupied. There was no doubt in his mind that Pigott was the forger, but the problem was how to get him to admit it, or else so to destroy his credibility as to strip all his defences away from him. It was a daunting task even for an advocate of Russell's calibre, and all the more daunting because he realized as much as anybody what tremendous issues hung upon the outcome.

He had two things to help him. One was the information from Egan in America which, as we saw earlier, had convinced Parnell and his friends that Pigott really was the culprit. The other was the fact that Archbishop Walsh had put in his hands certain letters (or copies of letters) which Pigott had written to the archbishop between March and May 1887. The first of the series, dated 4 March, informed Dr Walsh that Pigott was aware of certain proceedings which were being planned in order to destroy Parnell. He was referring, of course, to the impending series of articles on 'Parnellism and crime', but he went on to suggest to the archbishop that he knew how to defeat this dastardly design if His Grace would only put him in touch with the threatened parties. Pigott, in short, was playing each side against the other. Having been paid by Houston to produce material against Parnell, he was now preparing to sell his services to the victim. But the archbishop was not easily drawn. Pigott had to write twice more before he got an answer, which was a refusal in Dr Walsh's frostiest manner. Pigott persevered even after the publication of the facsimile letter on 18 April, but Walsh adamantly refused to have anything to do with him. The fact that Walsh returned at least some of his letters lulled Pigott into a false security – intensified by his belief that the correspondence came under the seal of the confessional.[95]

When he rose to cross-examine on the afternoon of 21 February, Russell was a changed man. All traces of nervous depression had disappeared and he greeted his wary adversary with elaborate courtesy. 'Mr Pigott', he began, 'would you be good enough, with My Lord's permission, to write some words on that sheet of paper for me?' A sheet was handed to Pigott who, visibly taken aback, agreed to sit down and write at Russell's dictation. He was asked to write 'livelihood', 'likelihood', then his own name, next 'proselytism' and finally ('I think I will not trouble you at present with any more', said Russell), 'Patrick Egan' and 'P. Egan', the name being pronounced by counsel with great emphasis. Then, apparently as an afterthought, Russell threw in one further word, 'hesitancy' – with a small 'h' he added, as if that were the vital point. When Pigott handed back his sheet of paper Russell knew that with that single manœuvre he had gained an important, perhaps a decisive, advantage, for Pigott had mis-spelt that last word, 'hesitency', as it was mis-spelt in the facsimile letter.[96]

A few minutes later, after some innocuous exchanges, Russell asked the witness in a sharper tone whether or not he had been aware that grave charges were to be made against Parnell in *The Times*. 'I was not aware of it until the publication actually commenced', said Pigott. 'Do you swear that?' asked Russell, looking straight at him. 'I do', replied Pigott, in an unusually aggressive tone. Then, in the pause which followed, Russell drew some papers from a shelf in front of him. Handing Pigott a letter, he asked him if it was his. Pigott admitted it was, and Russell then read it to the court. It was the letter of 4 March 1887 in which Pigott had told Archbishop Walsh of his awareness that there was a design on foot to destroy Parnell and his party. What then followed was one of the classic examples of the art of cross-examination in Victorian legal history. With short, sharp questions Russell drove Pigott deeper and deeper into the mire of confusion and self-contradiction. His statement that he did not know about the plot before the first article on 'Parnellism and crime' appeared was shown to be totally false and his attempt to deny that when writing to the archbishop he had in mind the incriminating letters ended in miserable confusion. For two hours he twisted and turned, the beads of perspiration standing out on his forehead and trickling down his face, but all to no avail.[97] By the end of his ordeal he was a broken man. Hauled back into court next day he was hounded afresh by the formidable Russell, who this time went back over his career to expose his record of blackmail and begging letters. The cross-examination had its ludicrous side, and even the judges on one occasion were reduced to helpless laughter. But a hunted human being is not a comic figure and in the eyes of some spectators at least pity was mixed with loathing. The wife of the English Liberal, Sydney Buxton, expressed this ambivalence admirably in her diary entry for those two days: 'It was the most exciting time I ever spent. In the end we came away astonished that a fellow-creature could be such a liar as Pigott. It was very funny, too; but I could not help thinking of Becky Sharp's "It's so easy to be virtuous on £5000 a year"; and to see that old man standing there, with everybody's hand against him, driven into a corner, after all his twists and turns, was somewhat pathetic.'[98]

When the court adjourned on Friday evening Russell had certainly reduced Pigott's reputation to tatters, but he had not yet succeeded in extracting from the unfortunate man an admission that he had himself forged *The Times* letters. It was assumed that when the Commission reassembled on Tuesday, 26 February, Russell would administer the *coup de grâce* without delay. But when on that morning Pigott was summoned there was no sign of him. After he stood down on Friday, Parnell, who had scrutinized him closely throughout, remarked: 'That man will not come into the box again.' Turning to his solicitor, he said: 'Mr Lewis, let that man be watched. If you do not keep your eye on him you will find that he will leave the country.'[99] Lewis, who made it clear that he thought it immaterial whether Pigott went or stayed, may or may not have obeyed his client's injunction. Whether the police took action to guard him, and if they did why they did not watch him more effectively, are questions equally obscure. But the story that gradually came out carried the saga of Pigott to a conclusion that had its own kind of *grand guignol* logic.

After an adjournment of twenty minutes on the Tuesday morning, Russell announced that Pigott had called, without invitation, on Labouchere at the latter's house in Grosvenor Gardens on the previous Saturday – the court having adjourned for the weekend – and had signed a full confession in the presence of a witness, the veteran journalist, George Augustus Sala. The confession was sent to Parnell's solicitor who forthwith returned it under Parnell's express instructions – a confession by private enterprise rather than in open court was, obviously, not what he wanted.[100] Later that same day Pigott sent for a Dublin solicitor, Shannon, who called on him then, and again on Sunday night, at his Fleet Street hotel. On the latter occasion Pigott made a statement, to which he swore an affidavit, in which he in effect revoked his confession, claiming that he had told Labouchere what he did because he was in fear of an immediate prosecution for perjury and in response to a promise that, provided he confessed to having forged all the letters, the prosecution would be stayed and £2000 bestowed on his children. He now maintained he had only forged some of the letters and that the rest, which he believed to be genuine, he had obtained from a man called Patrick Casey; one of the 'genuine' documents, he claimed, was the facsimile letter from which the whole strange history had originally derived. This affidavit was sworn to on Monday, 25 February and Pigott was apparently in Shannon's company up to about four o'clock that afternoon, after which he vanished without trace. It is possible, though nothing has emerged to prove this, that the affidavit destined for Shannon may have been merely one last device on Pigott's part to raise money from *The Times* to enable him to disappear. In fact he crossed to France that night, passing Davitt who was returning from Paris, having searched for but found no sign of him there.[101]

On 26 February the affidavit containing Pigott's semi-recantation was read to the Commission, but it did nothing to remove the indelible impression left by his previous cross-examination that he was an inveterate liar whose word could not be trusted. That same day he posted from Paris the confession he had made to Labouchere the previous Saturday before he had begun to blur the trail in his subsequent encounters with Shannon. This was a very different kind of document, so clear and detailed on the crucial points that it left little doubt in the minds of those who heard it read out. The essence of it was as follows:[102]

The circumstance connected with the obtaining of the letters, as I gave in evidence, are not true. No one save myself was concerned in the transaction. I told Houston that I had discovered the letters in Paris, but I grieve to have to confess that I simply myself fabricated them, using genuine letters of Messrs Parnell and Egan in copying certain words, phrases and general character of the handwriting. I traced some words and phrases by putting the genuine letter against the window, and placing on it the sheet of which copies have been read in court, and four or five letters of Mr Egan, which were also read in court. I destroyed these letters after using them. Some of the signatures I traced in this manner, and some I wrote. I then wrote to Houston telling him to come to Paris for the documents. I told him that they had been placed in a black bag with some old accounts, scraps of paper, and old newspapers. On his arrival I produced to him the letters, accounts, and scraps of paper. After a brief inspection he handed me a cheque on Cook for £500, the price that I told him I had agreed to pay for them. At the same time he gave me £105 in bank-notes as my own commission. The accounts put in were leaves torn from an old account book of my own, which contained details of the expenditure of Fenian money entrusted to me from time to time, which is mainly in the hand-writing of David Murphy, my cashier. The scraps I found in the bottom of an old writing-desk. I do not recollect whose writing they are.

The second batch of letters was also written by me. Mr Parnell's signature was imitated from that published in *The Times* facsimile letter. I do not now remember where I got the Egan letter from which I copied the signature.

A painful silence followed the reading of this confession. Then the Attorney-General rose and, on behalf of his clients, asked permission to withdraw from consideration by the Commission all question as to the genuineness of the letters. Next, Parnell, for the first time since the Commission had begun its hearings, appeared briefly in the witness-box formally to deny that it was his signature which appeared on any of the documents.

As for Pigott, the rest of his story is soon told. From France he travelled to Spain, arriving in Madrid on 28 February and taking a room at the Hotel Embajadores under the resplendent name of Roland Ponsonby. Some time in the course of that day he was observed in a café by the speculative eye of none other than Captain O'Shea.[103] Next day he visited a picture-gallery like any other tourist, but when he returned to his hotel in the evening the police were waiting for him. They had been alerted by the fact that he had sent a telegram to Shannon, care of Soames's London office, which, incidentally, lends support to the theory that his exploded affidavit had been primarily a means of raising the wind: 'Please ask Mr S to send me what you promised and write to Roland Ponsonby, Hotel Embajadores.' When he had retired to his room the police followed him upstairs. We may allow *The Times*, which had linked its fortunes so inextricably with his, to have the last word about what happened when he opened the door. 'He turned deathly pale, and for a moment seemed to lose his nerve completely. But he soon pulled himself together . . . At this moment the inspector entered the room and Pigott, muttering something about his luggage, stepped back a pace or two and opened the handbag which lay upon a chair. The inspector seemed to divine Pigott's object and sprang forward to seize him. It was too late. Pigott had a big revolver in his hand, placed the muzzle against his mouth, drew the trigger, and fell to the ground a horribly mutilated corpse.'[104]

CHAPTER 14

Apotheosis

'It may seem sentimental to say it – and especially when saying it respecting a man who can be the sternest of the stern, and among whose great gifts are an iron will and resolution – but sentimental or not, there was a touch of real pathos in the scene – Mr Parnell, with the signs of patient suffering still on his refined face, confronting – victoriously, indeed, but with an air of what remote indifference! – the men who laboured so long to blacken his name and ruin his career. Of feeling of triumph there was, in the pale countenance and calm gaze, not a trace.' (J. Macdonald, *The Daily News diary of the Parnell Commission* (27 February 1889), p. 109.)

'He really exhibited all the fruits of the spirit, love, peace, patience, gentleness, forbearance, long-suffering, meekness. His personality takes hold of one, the refined, delicate face, illuminating smile, fire-darting eyes, slight tall figure.' (Mary Gladstone, *Letters and diaries*, ed. Lucy Masterman (May 1889), pp. 408–9.)

I

In their different ways the diaries of Gladstone's daughter and of the professional journalist testify to the same effect – that the collapse and flight of Pigott had placed Parnell upon a pedestal far higher than any he had ever before occupied. This was perhaps a natural sequel, but it was also a dangerous one. The victory over Pigott was not only incomplete, he having escaped his final exposure in court, it was merely one round in a struggle which had still to be fought to a finish. *The Times*, in withdrawing the letters, had not abandoned the rest of its case and the imputation of a close connection with crime still hung over Parnell and his friends. And beyond the Special Commission lay the great world of politics where urgent decisions awaited the leader, decisions affecting the Plan of Campaign, decisions affecting the Liberal-nationalist alliance, decisions affecting the continuance of his own party as an effective political force. Moreover, all these decisions faced him at a moment when his health was precarious and when the probing search-lights of publicity threatened at any moment to penetrate the secret of his private life which also, at this very time, was hastening towards a crisis.

For these reasons it would be wrong to take the great wave of public sympathy which manifested itself in the spring of 1889 any more seriously than Parnell himself took it. Equally, it would be wrong to ignore it, for it helped to create in Britain an image of the Irish leader which, though not without some resemblance to the real man, was in certain important respects a distorted image. And this distortion was to play its part in the reaction which presently set in.

Meanwhile, all was sweetness and light. Parnell had immediate experience of this when he was followed down the Strand by a cheering crowd which accompanied him from the Law Courts to Bow Street, where he went to swear information against Pigott as a fugitive from justice.[1] But a more significant reception greeted him when on 1 March he appeared in the House of Commons for the first time after the Pigott fiasco. The debate on the Address was in progress and it was eleven o'clock at night when Parnell rose to speak. Before he could do so, Gladstone, by an apparently spontaneous act, led nearly the whole opposition (with the conspicuous exception of Hartington) in giving him a standing ovation, the Liberals and Irish alike cheering wildly and waving their hats. 'It was', noted Edward Hamilton primly, 'an unprecedented kind of ovation, which rather overstepped the bounds of decorum.'[2] Parnell, who was pale and perhaps more tense than those who did not know him well could have realized, confined himself to one of his brief, workmanlike interventions, as if nothing unusual had occurred. But according to his unreliable brother John, he sat down after it with pale face and twitching hands, saying to his neighbour, 'Why do you fellows stand up? It almost frightens me.'[3] The impression he made upon the government benches was scarcely less profound. 'It was', recalled Sir Edward Clarke, then Solicitor-General and soon to impinge more directly on Parnell's career, 'an incident which might have disturbed the balance of mind of a smaller man. I saw Mr Parnell erect among the whole standing crowd. He took no notice of it whatever. He had not asked them to get up. When they had finished standing up they sat down, and he took no notice either of their rising up or of their sitting down; and when they had resumed their places he proceeded to make a perfectly calm and quiet speech, in which he made not the slightest reference, direct or indirect, to the incident, extraordinary as it was, which had just happened.'[4]

In fact, though in the excitement few people could have realized it, he was seizing a golden opportunity in that speech to sound a note which was to be heard from him increasingly in the months ahead. It was unmistakably a note of conciliation:[5]

> It is legitimate and right [he said] that we, being the smaller country, should endeavour to conciliate you in every possible way, and yield to you, and agree to such safeguards as you think necessary and desirable for your own interests [cheers] . . . I am convinced that our people, knowing that England, Scotland and Wales have for the first time turned the ear of reason to the solution of this question, will steadily resist every incitement to disorder, to turbulence and to crime . . .

A week later he was at the Eighty Club to receive the homage of the Liberal party and especially to symbolize the Liberal-nationalist alliance by publicly and formally shaking hands with Lord Spencer, the Lord-Lieutenant at the time of the Phoenix Park murders. Once again there was a standing ovation and once again there was a characteristic display of indifference. 'He did not appear to be in the least moved by the warmth of his reception', said an onlooker. 'He could not have had a more sympathetic audience, but he seemed not to care whether he was in touch with us or not. The man has no heart, I thought. But he made a speech which I have never forgotten.'[6] It was a speech in which he put the alternatives for the future plainly before his hearers. There was, he said, only two ways to govern Ireland – either through self-rule or through coercion, and neither had been properly tried yet. But he looked to the Liberals for 'the recognition of our small claims, our small interests, our small rights to govern our own country, to manage it, to develop it, to build up our strength, to stop the wasting away of the resources of our national life, which surely you can spare and afford to us, poor Ireland, without loss or harm to yourselves.'[7]

The slight suggestion of the mendicant's whine which that speech most untypically carried is perhaps the measure of his almost desperate insistence at this period upon consolidating the Liberal alliance on the basis that the Irish claim, so far from being separatist, would cause the minimum disturbance to the relations between the two countries. He stressed this theme again a few days afterwards at a mass meeting in the St James's Hall to protest against government policy in Ireland. John Morley, who presided, took the wise precaution of calling for him well before the meeting. In the cab on the way to the Hall, Morley was intrigued to see Parnell carefully unwrapping a small box that contained a large white flower which he solemnly fastened into his button-hole – no words on politics or anything else being exchanged during this operation.[8] The public report of the proceedings described him as pale and composed, standing with his left hand in a sling – he had burned it in one of his everlasting chemical experiments – and impassively receiving an ovation of several minutes.[9] But Frederic Harrison, who sat near him, noticed a familiar symptom when he began to speak. 'He had one hand behind his back, which he kept closing and opening spasmodically all the time. It was curious to watch the signs of nervous excitement and tension which one saw looking from the back, while in front he stood like a soldier on duty, frigid, impassive, resolute – not a trace of nervousness or emotion.'[10] Yet although he appeared indifferent as always to his audience, the message of friendship for the Liberals in general, and for Gladstone in particular, came across with unmistakable clarity:[11]

> Ireland has now, since the introduction of Mr Gladstone's great measure in 1886, turned her back on the past of desperate and hopeless things. She is confident that in the ways of the Constitution lies her safeguard. Under the genius and guidance of that great devoted Englishman, a new hope has come into our hearts and our breasts today . . . We are now on the eve of a great popular upheaval and movement which will not subside until you have enabled your great leader to carry through the legislature of the empire a measure which will give to Ireland all legitimate control over her own future, her own interests, and her own welfare, without any shadow of harm or ill to your greater interests.

Small wonder that when he dined with the Gladstones a few weeks later they were 'much pleased with him'.[12]

But no one knew better than Parnell that his good standing would remain precarious so long as the Special Commission pursued its tortuous way. It was much debated at the time why Parnell did not instruct his counsel to withdraw after Pigott's collapse had demonstrated the falsity of the letters, the point above all others which Parnell himself was concerned to prove. According to Tim Healy, the advice on the Irish side was to pull out of the case there and then, but Parnell came under too much pressure in London to be able to do this.[13] Pressure in London seems to have meant primarily pressure from Russell, who had set his heart upon making the great speech which he did eventually deliver, but which he could not have done if the defence had not been heard.[14] But even if this was true, such a personal reason is unlikely to have weighed overmuch with Parnell. The determining factor surely was that even after the letters had been disposed of, the general charges of criminality and conspiracy remained; to have shied away from answering these would simply have meant that they would have been repeated *ad nauseam* whenever it suited Parnell's opponents to embarrass him by doing so. They had to be dealt with, and the sooner the better.

II

The most unfortunate consequence of the decision to continue was that Parnell himself had to take the stand. He proved to be a far from ideal witness. True, he made an impressive picture as he stood in the box – tall, pale, dignified, immaculate in a new frock coat which Katharine and his solicitor had conspired to trap him into.[15] But he, who normally never said a word more than was necessary, contrived to be both vague and diffuse under examination. If Sir Richard Webster had been a better informed and more intelligent man, Parnell's nine days of interrogation (from 30 April to 8 May) might have been an unmitigated disaster. As it was, the only major slip he made which was immediately detected was his famous reply when asked why on 7 January 1881 he had told the House of Commons that secret societies had ceased to exist in Ireland. 'I cannot exactly say without reading the context of my speech', he replied, 'what my view was in urging that argument, but it is possible that I was endeavouring to mislead the House on the occasion.' The Attorney-General, who was so obtuse that his attention had to be drawn to the opening by an urgent whisper from Sir Henry James, then charged at it in his best Heavy Dragoon manner. 'Did you or did you not', he asked, 'intend to mis-state the fact when you made that statement to the House?' – 'It is very possible that I did.' 'Deliberately?' – 'Deliberately, quite possible.' Yet the furore which resulted from this admission was little more than a storm in a teacup. Parnell, who had only made the damning admission at the end of a long and taxing day, next morning sought to retrieve the situation by saying that in the House he had been referring not to Fenianism but to the older type of agrarian combination or ribbon society. 'Of course', he said, 'I knew at the time that the great Fenian organization had branches all over Ireland, and in looking at the statement in the speech, a broad one that secret societies had ceased to exist, I supposed that I had referred to the cessation of the Fenian branches, as well as of the Ribbon Societies, which would have been manifestly a false statement.'[16]

This explanation, clumsy as it was, sufficed for most people and in the world of politics the episode made little lasting impression. It was indeed much less dangerous than some of the other things he either said or omitted to say. We saw earlier that about many of the critical episodes of his career, especially during the Land League period when he was balancing precariously between right and left, he displayed at the Commission a forgetfulness amounting almost to amnesia, though that his was a case of strictly controlled political amnesia there is little reason to doubt.* To anyone familiar with his past, his vagueness about John Devoy and the Clan na Gael, or about other Irish-Americans such as William Carroll and Alexander Sullivan, or about the 'new departure', or even about what happened to Pigott's newspapers after *United Ireland* had superseded them, was so comprehensive as to be highly suspect. The Attorney-General, lacking such familiarity, yet sensing intermittently that there was something wrong on which he could not put his finger, lost his temper repeatedly, but the testier he grew, the calmer and more icily polite his adversary became. The fact that Parnell quite obviously amused himself from time to time at Webster's expense certainly did not make what would always have been a difficult examination run any more smoothly. Two examples may suffice to show the extraordinary levity Parnell was capable of injecting into matters which were in themselves both serious and directly relevant to the charges being made against him.

The first arose out of his American tour in 1880. It was an important part of *The Times*'s case to show, if possible, that Parnell had been in such intimate relations with the extremists at that time that his programme had been arranged and supervised by the Clan na Gael. To buttress this case the Attorney-General introduced copious extracts from the *Irish World* which, he suggested, could bear no other interpretation. To this Parnell merely replied that various sections of the Irish-American community had been claiming the credit for his tour from that day to this. But when Webster challenged him to produce evidence that anyone save the Clan na Gael had ever claimed the credit for it Parnell answered, with a perfectly straight face, that he had brought home numerous newspaper cuttings which would have proved his point, 'but the mice got into my bureau and devoured many of them'.[17] Given the forlorn condition of Avondale during its master's frequent absences this was not perhaps quite so flippant as it seemed, but there was not even that excuse for the other exchange which to outsiders seemed to demonstrate his incorrigible frivolity. Here again the issue was a serious one. Parnell

*See above, pp. 111-2.

was genuinely anxious to convey the impression, doubtless accurate enough, that in his Land League days he had been careful not to enquire too closely into the antecedents of those who were active in the movement. Among the names thrown at him by the Attorney-General was that of John Ferguson of Glasgow, whom we saw earlier as a prominent member of the Home Rule Confederation of Great Britain.* Ferguson may or may not have been a Fenian – probably he was not – but he was certainly a militant nationalist and he moved in 'advanced' circles. Asked by Webster whether he knew Ferguson was a Fenian, Parnell replied that he did not, and then proceeded, in his most irritatingly diffuse manner, to add some entirely gratuitous information. 'Mr Ferguson', he said, 'was a member of the Council of the Home Rule League and also a very eloquent speaker.' To this the Attorney-General replied crossly: 'I was not asking you about his eloquence. I believe most of you Irishmen are very good speakers.' 'I am sorry to say', said Parnell politely, 'I am a prominent exception.' Whereupon the Attorney-General exploded with understandable exasperation. 'I have a difficult enough task. I ask you not to put things upon me which I am not asking about. I am not speaking about his eloquence . . .'[18]

It is impossible to read such passages, and they occur frequently in the three hundred or so pages of Parnell's evidence, without feeling that the Special Commission was in danger of degenerating from high tragedy into low farce. It could never become wholly farcical, of course, because the issues at stake remained as important as they had always been. But as the enquiry dragged on from month to month, and it became steadily more apparent that *The Times* was never going to be able to find the blood-and-thunder proofs of Parnellite complicity in crime which it so badly needed, the proceedings grew duller and duller. They were saved from banality only by three great set speeches – Sir Charles Russell's eight-day indictment of English rule in Ireland, Sir Henry James's twelve-day onslaught upon the violent propensities of Irish nationalism, and Michael Davitt's five-day defence of his entire career. The withdrawal of counsel for the defence on 12 July, after the court had refused to order E. C. Houston to produce the books of the Irish Loyal and Patriotic Union, meant that the remaining sessions were inevitably one-sided. Nevertheless, the judges continued to do their duty with the utmost conscientiousness and their report, when at last it appeared in February 1890, preserved a balance so exact as to allow each side to claim a victory.

*See above, pp. 55-6.

However, on what most people still regarded as the cardinal question – the letters printed by *The Times* or adduced as evidence on its behalf – the report declared *all* of them to be forgeries, absolutely acquitting Parnell of any charges based on them, and of all other personal charges. He and his fellow-respondents were likewise acquitted of treason. The judges found that they were not members of a conspiracy to bring about the complete independence of Ireland and that they did not directly incite persons to commit crime other than intimidation, i.e. boycotting. They found further that some of the respondents (including Parnell) did express genuine disapproval of crime and outrage. There was no foundation for the charge that Parnell was intimate with the Invincibles or that he recognized the Phoenix Park murders as their doing; neither did he pay any sum of money to Frank Byrne (who when secretary of the Land League of Great Britain had helped the Invincibles to procure their weapons) to escape from justice to France.

So far, from the Parnellite point of view, so good. But the report contained two other categories of verdict – 'not proven' and 'guilty'. It was not proven that the respondents paid other people to commit crimes; that they associated with notorious criminals or provided them with funds to escape from justice; that they knew the Clan na Gael controlled the Irish National League of America or that it collected funds for the parliamentary party; or that Parnell at the time of the Kilmainham negotiations knew that P. J. Sheridan and M. Boyton had been organizing outrage and wished to use them to put this process into reverse.

Finally, the respondents were found guilty of entering into a conspiracy to promote an agrarian agitation for the non-payment of rents. Certain of them (including Davitt, Dillon and William O'Brien) were guilty of having established or joined the Land League with the intention of using it to bring about the independence of Ireland as a separate nation. It was found further that the respondents disseminated the *Irish World* and other newspapers tending to incite to sedition and other crimes; also that they did not denounce the system of intimidation which led to crime and outrage, and that they defended persons charged with such offences and supported their families; that they made payments to compensate persons injured in the commission of crime; and that they invited and accepted the assistance of Patrick Ford of the *Irish World*, a known advocate of crime and of the use of dynamite. In addition, Michael Davitt was held to be guilty of certain specific charges, of which the chief were that he was a convicted Fenian, that he was intimately associated with American extremists, and that he was the principal architect in creating an alliance between the extremists and Parnell's parliamentary party.[19]

Clearly the Parnellites did not emerge unscathed from their ordeal and the British public was left in no doubt that in Ireland the line between lawful and unlawful agitation was so blurred as to be almost impossible to define. Those who wanted ammunition with which to attack the Irish parliamentary party would certainly find it in the Report, but it would be equally open to their opponents to claim that it was antiquated ammunition, containing mainly damp squibs. There was, after all, little that *The Times* or its lawyers had said about Parnell and his associates that had not previously been said by Gladstone and other eminently respectable politicians. Yet, although Parnell's reputation for political purity had been questionable for a long time, this had not prevented Liberals and Conservatives alike from negotiating with him whenever, from 1882 onwards, it had suited their respective books.

The fact was, as Parnell had always insisted, that the Pigott letters were the core of the case. Let that question once be decided in his favour and the remaining issues would sink into their proper perspective. *The Times* itself was so chastened by the Pigott disaster that it was happy to settle – for £5000 – the libel action Parnell eventually took against it, and although it maintained a bold front about the other charges, the *Official History* makes no bones about the shattering effect upon the newspaper of its defeat upon the central issue. In money terms alone the losses were catastrophic. The total cost of the proceedings for *The Times* was over £200,000, and indirectly also the economic consequences were grave; the price to be paid for devoting endless columns of newsprint to verbatim reports of the Commission's proceedings was that the general quality of the paper deteriorated just at the moment when the new cheap press was beginning to challenge its supremacy. For those in charge the outcome of the long struggle was no less catastrophic. Macdonald, who had carried the heaviest burden, fell ill and died in December 1889 without having seen the Commission's report. Buckle's prestige also suffered severely and the paper's reputation for infallibility was gone for ever.[20]

Moreover, between *The Times* and its governmental ally, the affair created a rift which was not easily mended. When the report was debated in the House of Commons, W. H. Smith joined in the general reprobation of Pigott's forgeries, but neglected, whether consciously or not is unclear, to make what *The Times* would have regarded as a proper distinction between the forger and the paper which had published his inventions. Writing that same day to Smith as Leader of the House, the editor, George Buckle, radiated a sense of injury. 'It was neither fair nor just', he wrote, 'to speak with equal "detestation" of the act of Pigott and *The Times*.' Smith apologized profusely a day or so later, but his use of the hoary fiction that he had been misreported was altogether unconvincing and a coolness between him and his old friend John Walter persisted for some time longer.[21] In the debate the government majority was sufficient to secure a simple 'acceptance' of the report, but it was an embarrassing occasion for ministers, made still more so by a violent onslaught from Lord Randolph Churchill.[22] Parnell was equally unmoved both by the debate and by the actual report. His comment on the latter to his friends was that 'really, between ourselves, I think it is just about what I would have said myself', and with that single phrase he dismissed it to a past which no longer had any relevance for him.

III

If it was no longer relevant, this was not just because of Parnell's own indifference, but because other matters had been clamouring for his attention even while the hunt for Pigott had been at its hottest. Of these, the Plan of Campaign was the most pressing. Since his speech virtually disowning it in May 1888 things had not gone well with the Plan. True, the Papal Rescript had missed its mark, but even without benefit of clergy Balfour's coercive regime had slowly and steadily been wearing down the resistance of the tenants and their leaders. Both Dillon and O'Brien had served terms in prison and during the year April 1888– April 1889 the number of branches of the Irish National League, on which they depended for their grass-roots organization, had fallen from 1031 to 975, the decrease being entirely accounted for by governmental suppressions. Worse even than this was the possibility of total financial breakdown, due primarily to the stark fact that the agitation had gone on longer and spread wider than had originally been intended. When Dillon was released from prison in mid-September 1888 after a sharp deterioration in his health, he came out to confront the daunting prospect of a fund-raising tour in Australia and New Zealand as a last desperate effort to keep the Plan in operation, but it was an open question whether his physique would stand the strain.[23]

When, therefore, he conferred with O'Brien before his departure, neither of them saw much hope on the horizon. It would take at least £25,000, they reckoned, to keep going for another year and even this might well be impossible if Parnell maintained his attitude of aloofness.[24]

But by Christmas, only six weeks later, with renewed evictions and a potato famine looming in the far west, a much speedier collapse threatened.[25] There was nothing for it but to throw themselves on Parnell's mercy and in mid-January 1889 Dillon, swallowing his pride, sent him a piteous appeal for funds. Increased evictions had involved increased expenditure, so that the organizers of the Plan were now in deficit and faced the imminent catastrophe of being unable to continue their regular payments. In short, they needed £5000 down and the assurance of a further £5000 not later than 1 March. For twelve long days no word at all came from Parnell. But at last Dillon got a reply which, though cold, gave him substantially what he wanted. Parnell intimated that when he received an expected remittance from Cecil Rhodes he hoped to be able to scrape together the £10,000 required.* 'But', he added sternly, 'I must remind you that I do not feel justified in selling any more bonds.'[26]

In March Dillon left for his tour and did not return until April 1890. During his absence the burden of conducting the agitation fell upon William O'Brien and Timothy Harrington, assisted by a rising young Parnellite MP, T. P. Gill. This trio had to grapple with Balfour's newest and most menacing tactic. Concentrating his forces for the defence of certain key estates, he secretly encouraged the formation of a syndicate of English and Irish landlords to come to the rescue of one of these properties – the Ponsonby estate – and administer it by a committee of which another landlord, A. H. Smith-Barry, was the driving force. This was a challenge which had to be met if the Plan was to survive. Early in July 1889 O'Brien, who was then between prison sentences, met Parnell and persuaded him to adopt the countermeasure which O'Brien himself regarded as essential. This, as was publicly announced a few days later, consisted in the formation of a Tenants Defence Association to protect the tenants against the landlords' combination. The new Association was declared to be 'the official act of the whole Irish party and will shortly be established at a convention'.[27]

But behind this confident assertion was a strange and troubled history. Writing to Dillon to describe his interview with Parnell, O'Brien explained that he had faced his leader with two alternatives. Either let him take full responsibility for calling off the agitation, in which case O'Brien would do his best to get reasonable terms for the tenants. Or else let him throw himself into the struggle by coming out

*For the circumstances of this remittance, see below, pp. 442-3.

openly in support of the Plan and personally inaugurating a national fund to raise £30,000.[28] The interview ended without Parnell committing himself to either course and a month later O'Brien went a second time to plead with him. The effect, as he described it to Dillon, was totally disastrous. 'Things have reached a crisis between Parnell and myself', he wrote. 'Having started the new Tenants' Defence League [sic] ,with the assurance that it would be used in defence of the Plan, he now flatly refuses to take any effective steps to put life into it. He first allows us to announce that he will throw himself into this fight and now says he cannot see his way to starting any new movement and will do nothing himself.' There then ensued a long, wrangling argument about the value of the agrarian agitation which only served to bring the two men closer to an open breach than they had ever been:

> I told him plainly that the moment I could communicate with you, we would have to consider whether we could any longer remain in so intolerable a position. He said with the most brutal frankness that we could not get out of it – that we had got ourselves into it, adding 'You forced me to say that'. I said, 'I am glad that I forced you to be frank, but I think you will find you are mistaken in supposing that you have us tied to the stake and that you can leave all the responsibility on our hands, while you take all the advantages and none of the labour . . .'

When they parted O'Brien had not succeeded in extracting from Parnell anything more than an offer to send Thomas Sexton as his representative to the Tipperary convention which was to launch the new Association. Though clearly tempted, as he said, to throw the whole business up in despair, O'Brien resolved, 'after the most horribly anxious deliberation', that he would 'retort Parnell's policy of silence upon him'. In other words, he would rely upon the expected money from Australia to make the movement independent of Parnell's aid, he would go himself to prison when the time came, would then delegate the supervision of the 'critical' estates to a few trusted helpers, and, by ignoring the new Association, would hope to coerce Parnell into taking some action after all. But he left his friend in no doubt that the wound had gone deep. 'If you were here, of course', he wrote wistfully, 'the difficulty would not have arisen for between us we could have struggled along, but alone *I cannot stand it any longer*, and it is full time to force him out of a cruel and infatuated policy of veiled hostility.'[29]

For once, things turned out pretty much as O'Brien had predicted. Parnell did *not* go to Tipperary to launch the new Association, but

O'Brien can scarcely have expected that he would. Instead, he persisted in sending Sexton and the Tenants Defence Association was duly launched on 15 October while O'Brien was serving the term in prison to which he had been sentenced the previous July. When he came out in December the fund for the relief of the evicted tenants was already well established and £61,000 had been raised within six months of its foundation. Not only that, the money had been collected at county conventions up and down the country presided over by nationalist MPs, so that, whatever the leader's reservations might be, in the eyes of the public his party were more deeply involved in the agitation than for several years past.[30]

This new development did indeed give a certain *élan* to the Plan, but almost immediately the essential precariousness of the tenants' position was once more demonstrated. Identifying Smith-Barry as the leader of the hated syndicate which had taken the Ponsonby estate in hand, his own tenants began to withhold their rents from him. He retaliated with evictions that included some shopkeepers in the town of Tipperary which stood on his land. In self-defence a number of the shopkeepers moved out of the town altogether and hastily constructed a market-centre of their own on a neighbouring estate. This, soon christened 'New Tipperary', caught O'Brien's imagination when he came out of prison at the end of the year and he at once committed himself to it with all the force of his impulsive personality. It proved a heavy mill-stone about the neck of the organizers of the Plan and may even have been the decisive mistake in their long-running war with the Chief Secretary. The result was that when Dillon returned in April 1890, full of fight and plunging immediately into a controversy with the Bishop of Limerick over the rights and wrongs of boycotting, he found a financial situation which, despite the considerable funds he and the Tenants Defence Association had collected, was once more critical. New Tipperary had swallowed up between £40,000 and £50,000 and since, in addition to that, the burden of maintaining from 800 to 1000 evicted families amounted to about £32,000 a year, it was clear that something drastic would have to be done.[31]

This involved yet another approach to Parnell and perhaps it is significant that this time the emissary was Dillon. The results, so far as they went, were satisfactory. Parnell agreed that a second levy should be launched in Ireland for the relief of the evicted tenants and he was prepared also to smooth the way for a fund-raising mission to America to be undertaken by prominent members of the party. Nevertheless, his own position remained tantalizingly obscure. The most notable illustration of this was his condemnation of the complex land purchase bill which Balfour introduced in April 1890. On the face of it, this was a massive new instalment of the policy Parnell had been advocating for years, the main intention being to provide £33 million of state-guaranteed loans to enable tenants to buy their holdings. Parnell attacked the bill – which, admittedly, was not popular even among the government's supporters – because, he said, it would place too heavy a strain on Irish funds, would affect only a quarter of the 600,000 tenants in the country, and was vitiated by the fact that it was transparently a device to enable a minority of the largest absentee landlords (about ten per cent of the total) to 'get out' of the country at a fat profit.[32] But these were criticisms of method rather than of purpose and it is probable that Parnell's opposition to a measure which, when raised and re-introduced next session under very different circumstances he warmly supported, was essentially a product of his Gladstonian alliance. Indeed, he was later to claim that his action in 1890 was taken at the request of the Liberals and though this was at once denied by John Morley, it is clear from a note the latter made of a conversation he had with Parnell in November 1890 (a conversation to which we must presently return) that the Irish leader's objections were objections of detail only. 'Generally his view was that we ought to make the most of the £33 million provided by the government bill.'[33]

His opposition in 1890 was not just a piece of personal eccentricity, since the bill was withdrawn partly as a result of prolonged Irish obstruction of that and other measures. But what made it sinister in the eyes of at least some of his colleagues was that he followed it with what seemed like a startling approach to Balfour for a peaceful settlement of the Plan of Campaign. The occasion he chose was the constabulary vote on the Irish estimates. At the outset of his short but electric speech he reiterated his original view of the Plan, though in a much more muted tone than those who had since tried to interest him in its operation might have been led to expect. Recalling his instruction to O'Brien at the beginning of the agitation to confine it to a limited number of estates, and the latter's objection that this would enable the landlords to concentrate their forces against those estates, he admitted that it might have been a mistake to overrule O'Brien, since it now seemed that his predictions were coming true. 'I may have been wrong in the position I took up', he said, 'but I thought it better that a small number of tenants should suffer or be sacrificed than that there should be the terrible evil of a general agrarian struggle.' Then, turning towards Balfour, he made a direct appeal to him to match his moderation by extending the benefits of the act of 1887 to the tenants of the Plan estates still in dispute and thus end the agitation by removing the cause:[34]

> I may say I have not discussed the suggestion I have made with any of my friends and may it not be supposed that my suggestion is any sign of weakness. The tenants will be protected and effectively protected to the end . . . I dare say my hon. friends would prefer to fight it out and are careless as to whether the suggestion I make is accepted. I have myself little doubt that my suggestion will have been made in vain, but I shall have the satisfaction of knowing that I have made it, and that the responsibility will not rest on me.

This remarkable olive branch was proffered to a House which received it with the profound silence of utter mystification. What could this strange initiative portend? 'Mr Gladstone', John Morley noted, 'laughed at the oddity of it all.' 'It is difficult enough for him to be absent and inaccessible, but if besides that, when he does appear – to plunge into unexplained politics, that is indeed too bad!'[35] One of the oddest features of the episode was that even Dillon was so confused by it that his first feeling was one of relief that Parnell, so it seemed to him, had at last assumed responsibility for the Plan. A few days' reflection convinced him that, on the contrary, 'it was a bad speech from the point of view of our mission to the States and also, though to a minor degree, of electioneering in this country. It will spread a kind of uneasy feeling among the Radicals that our opposition to Balfour and the Tory party is after all not so real.'[36]

The incident did more than spread an uneasy feeling among the Radicals. It provoked one of the most savage press attacks upon Parnell which he had had to face in the whole course of his career, the more vicious because it passed beyond criticism of his leadership to refer in the most offensive terms to the divorce suit which Captain O'Shea had at last filed in the previous December and which was at that moment pending.* The attack took the form of a report from Harold Frederic, the London correspondent of the *New York Times*, which was published in that paper on 15 July, copied from there into various Irish-American journals and eventually reproduced in the *Nation* at the beginning of August. To understand its inwardness two facts about Harold Frederic are relevant. The first is that he was a close friend of Tim Healy's, and the second is that, arising out of that friendship, he had already had one

---

*For the context of the divorce suit, see below, pp. 453–68.

brush with Parnell at the beginning of the year. Early in January, Frederic cabled information about the Galway 'mutiny' of 1886 to his paper, which was subsequently published in London and Dublin. According to one of the Parnellite MPs, a young and impecunious barrister named M. J. Kenny, Parnell was so irritated that he wrote to Frederic asking him what authority he had for the statement he had made. 'The result', Kenny informed a correspondent, 'has been a visit from Mr Frederic to Tim Healy in Dublin and a council of war in Great Charles Street [Healy's house] at which the men of Bantry assembled in their thousands and bound themselves like Cataline and his confederation in wine and blood to contest the supreme rule of Parnell and his friends.'[37] True, no more direct evidence linking Healy to Frederic's report in July has come to light, but the specific references it contained both to the Irish members and to the Radicals suggest that Frederic had an informant close to the centre of affairs, and since he was known to be on friendly terms with Healy, the possibility that 'Tiger Tim' was that informant cannot be ruled out. The following passages from the report speak for themselves:[38]

Just now this Irish question has taken an absorbingly interesting personal turn. Mr Parnell last night [11 July] calmly and with bold indifference kicked over all the work which his colleagues have done this session. It is impossible to describe the consternation and disgust with which the Irish members heard him unsay all that they had said, condemn the Plan of Campaign and coolly give away their whole case against Balfour by coolly inviting that gentleman to combine with him in remodelling the Land Purchase Bill.

Not a solitary Irish member had had the faintest inkling of his intention to take this course. He had not deigned to attend a single session since the Irish estimates came up, and ignored the fact that, during his absence, his colleagues had been subjected to unexampled insolence and truculent abuse from Mr Balfour. Last night the English Radicals were so furious at being thus hamstrung by the Irish leader when the ministry were trembling on the point of being put to rout, that Mr Labouchere could only with the greatest difficulty be restrained from a public denunciation of Mr Parnell.

It is now probable that on Monday some expression of his colleagues' proper indignation will be laid before Mr Parnell and it is even considered possible that he will retire at once from his post as leader, which latterly he has only used to insult and affront his colleagues. There has all along been the difficulty of seeing how he could maintain this post once the O'Shea case had come to trial, and last night a number of Irish members were disposed to fear that brooding upon this trouble had brought on the mental disturbance to which he is hereditarily predisposed. It is the only way in which they are able to account for his astonishing and contemptuous act of treachery to them.

This language, as was immediately and generally felt, went beyond all bounds and only succeeded in provoking a rally in Parnell's favour. The same issue of the *Nation* which printed the report contained also a letter signed by Thomas Sexton, John Dillon and William O'Brien, condemning Harold Frederic's dispatch as 'totally untrue'. 'We have taken pains', they wrote, 'to ascertain the feelings of our colleagues of the Irish parliamentary party and we are authorized to declare in their name as well as in our own, that the references to Mr Parnell in the *New York Times* are of a character too disgraceful to deserve notice; and that with respect to the alleged action of members of this party, the statements of the correspondent of the *New York Times* were read with indignation and disgust by our colleagues and ourselves and are absolutely without foundation.'[39]

The incident was ugly in itself, and uglier still, as we shall see presently, when taken in conjunction with certain other indications of friction within the party at this period, but Parnell characteristically gave no sign that he either cared or even noticed. So far as the *fons et origo* of the storm, the eternal land question, was concerned, a new turn of events quickly eclipsed the mystery of Parnell's parliamentary performance. The long-drawn-out conflict between Balfour and the leaders of the Plan of Campaign came at last to an exciting but totally unexpected climax. Knowing that Dillon and O'Brien were planning to go to the United States for their fund-raising tour, the Castle authorities stepped in to charge them with yet another offence, this time arising out of their involvement with New Tipperary. Following the usual practice, the two leaders remained at liberty on bail during the trial. But on 10 October they broke bail, with the agreement of their securities, eluded the vigilance of the police, and were smuggled out of Dalkey Harbour in a small yacht. Five days later they arrived in France, whence, after a few days' rest, they departed for America, soon to be joined there by the delegates deputed for this purpose by the parliamentary party.[40] In their absence much of the dynamism went out of the Plan of Campaign; indeed, their departure marked the virtual end of an agitation which was about to be overshadowed by the far more profound and searing struggle set in motion by the Parnell–O'Shea divorce suit.

IV

Parnell's aloofness from the Plan had remained constant through all its fluctuating fortunes and he never wavered in his two-fold objection to it. One was the practical consideration that the time was not ripe for an expanding commitment of time and money to a fight which seemed always to be against the odds. The other, in his mind probably more important, objection was that the agitation, from which some degree of outrage and violence was inseparable, threatened that alliance with the Liberals which, as he stressed repeatedly, had become since 1886 the fixed point of his policy. But for him that alliance meant something more than platitudinous rhetoric. It meant hammering out with his allies, in effect with Gladstone, the basis for agreement upon a specific Home Rule bill to be introduced when next the Liberals came to power, an event which the 'flowing tide' of by-election victories and the unimpressive showing of Salisbury's government seemed to bring closer almost month by month.

It was in March 1888 that Parnell and Gladstone first came seriously to grips with the fundamentals of Home Rule in the post-1886 situation. Preparing for the interview which they then had Gladstone noted down five points as guides for future action:[41]

1. To keep the admin. of the Coercion Act before the country and parlt. by speeches and statistics.

2. To remain detached in a condition to accept a settlement from the Tories.

3. What course shd. be taken if the Govt. offer measures good in themselves but insufficient for a settlement? Accept without prejudice?

4. Non-Irish legislation to be promoted.

5. Does the idea of the American Union offer a practical point of departure?

Two days later, on 10 March, Parnell called and the ensuing discussion revolved mainly round Gladstone's queries and suggestions. Only his account survives, but it is sufficiently precise in its record of Parnell's views for us to be reasonably confident that it expresses accurately what the Irish leader thought at that particular time – or rather, that it expresses as much as he judged it expedient to reveal of what he thought at that particular time. The references to his physical condition we have seen before,* but the document is such important evidence about the direction of Parnell's thought at this stage of his career that it is here reproduced in full:[42]

He looked not ill, but far from strong. He gave a favourable account of his health.

I pressed the first point [about publicizing the coercive record of the government] rather strongly. He did not appear to consider it much, but to give weight to it and he made a note on the subject.

The second I merely set out before him *pour acquit de conscience*.

He said he expected nothing from the Tories as long as they should feel that they could get on without concession.

On the third point, as indeed on all, he was extremely moderate and reasonable; and I was not entirely without an apprehension that the energies of his political pursuit were somewhat abated by his physical condition.

He thought the turning-point lay in a Dublin parliament. He did not see what could be given short of this that would be worth taking; whereas if this could be had, even with insufficient powers, it might be accepted. I understood him to mean might be accepted as a beginning.

I mentioned Sir E. Watkins's idea of provincial assemblies with a contingent power of election from themselves to constitute a body which should meet in Dublin for particular purposes. He thought it conceivable that this would resolve itself into a question of the mode of election.

He quite agreed as to No. 4.

Did not think the Irish people would be impatient even if Home Rule were not moved this year in the House of Commons.

Believed crime, properly so called, was declining.

My chief point with him was that [?contained] in No. 5. On this ground, that the opponents never so far as I know have condemned the American system as a possible basis of a plan of Home Rule and I have always held the hope that it might in case of need supply at least a phrase to cover them in point of consistency. I said I was aware of no difficulty unless it should be found to be in the capacity to touch contracts. On the practical working of which I had not been able to obtain sufficient information.

*See above, p. 382.

He thought this idea might be made a groundwork. Did not wholly repel even the idea of parliamentary intervention to stop extreme and violent proceedings in Dublin. I said a Const. would fix the lines of the respective provinces but [word illegible] parliamentary action.

Undoubtedly as a whole his tone was very conservative.

This picture of a languid and moderate Parnell, prepared even to toy with a federal solution which roused echoes of old Isaac Butt's universal panacea, may have been distorted by Gladstone's natural tendency to see only what he wanted to see, but unmistakable signs soon followed that the Irish leader was moving steadily closer to the English leader's conception of Home Rule. In May, as we saw earlier, Parnell in his Eighty Club speech not only in effect disowned the Plan of Campaign, but spoke of self-government in distinctly moderate terms. Next month a totally unexpected development presented the federal solution to him in a new and potentially attractive light. This happened almost by chance. In the autumn of 1887 one of the few Protestant members of the Irish parliamentary party, J. G. Swift MacNeill, met Cecil Rhodes on a voyage to South Africa. He discovered that Rhodes, while apparently sympathetic to the Home Rule cause, had been alienated by the original provision in the 1886 bill that the Irish members should be excluded from Westminster once a parliament had been established in Dublin. The fact that Parnell and his party had, initially at least, been prepared to accept this clause suggested to Rhodes that their ultimate aim was still complete separation from Britain. MacNeill protested that this was not true and was so convincing that a little later, when travelling with Rhodes in South Africa, he was gratified to hear from the latter that if he could give a pledge that the Irish members would be retained at Westminster under the next Home Rule bill, Rhodes would donate £10,000 to the funds of the Irish party.

MacNeill had no authority to give such a pledge, but he took Rhodes's proposition back with him in writing and duly reported to Parnell. Nothing happened until Rhodes's next visit to England. He arrived in April 1888 and then had several meetings with Parnell at which the conditions to be attached to the gift were further discussed. These meetings were followed by a formal exchange of letters in the course of which Parnell indicated that, as requested, he would press for the retention of the Irish members when the next Home Rule bill came to be discussed in detail.

The two men, naturally, approached the question with different aims in view. For Rhodes, a degree of Irish representation (he wanted a *reduced* number) might be a lever which could be used for the further-ance of his favourite design of making the British parliament a truly imperial legislature to which all the self-governing colonies would send members. For Parnell, who in 1886 had had an open mind on the sub-ject, though leaning towards exclusion because he believed that re-tention would afford a pretext for British interference in Irish affairs, continued representation at Westminster was now important for two reasons. First, because it was necessary to allay Liberal fears that exclusion would be the thin end of the wedge leading to eventual separation. Second, because if, as seemed possible, certain major Irish matters – such as the final settlement of the land question or the control of the police and the judiciary – were held over to be dealt with by the British parliament *after* Home Rule had been granted, it would be essential to have the full weight of the party present in the House of Commons to exert its customary pressure. Consequently, while his support for imperial federation was a trifle perfunctory, his support for the retention of the Irish members was as emphatic as Rhodes could have wished. Rhodes therefore proceeded to fulfil his part of the bargain, paying over within the next few weeks the sum of £5000, plus £1000 subscribed by John Morrogh, a business associate from Kimberley.[43] What happened to the balance of the £10,000 is obscure, but, as will appear, Parnell had by no means heard the last of the transaction.*

Clearly, the question of the future of Irish representation at West-minster had already by 1888 assumed a central significance in all dis-cussions of Home Rule and this was to grow greater rather than less as time went on. It did not really need Rhodes to demonstrate that it had an imperial as well as an Irish significance. Parnell went out of his way to stress this fact more than once, especially during 1889. But before we look at him in the unfamiliar guise of an 'imperial' politician, it is im-portant to realize that even in that year of his closest *rapprochement* with the Liberals, he could still strike a discordant note. Indeed, at the moment when, after the collapse of Pigott, he was being fêted and idolized on all sides, he summoned a meeting of the members of the leading nationalist town councils of Ireland (characteristically, he brought *them* to London instead of going himself to Dublin) which was at once an opportunity to express his real feelings about the Special Commission and also to reach that wider, and wilder, audience he could never quite leave out of his calculations. Predictably, what irked him most about the Commission was the indignity of having to undergo a

*See below, pp. 587-9.

minute investigation of his whole movement. 'I should have preferred', he said, 'to have gone to my grave with the stigma of these letters upon me – cowardly, mean and contemptible as they were – rather than submit my country and my countrymen to the humiliating ordeal that was forced upon us . . .' He and his friends had never admitted that the tribunal was a fair one, he declared, and he complained bitterly of the way that speeches made long ago had been 'twisted and tortured . . . into some construction not present to the mind of the speaker at the time they were delivered . . .' He continued:[44]

> We are told that it was our intention in this agitation of ours to subvert the authority of the Crown, and to organize an armed rebellion. Speaking for myself, I cannot recollect that I have ever – certainly not in public speech, but even in my own mind – contemplated the contingency of failure in our movement, and I certainly never have contemplated what our action would be if that movement failed.
>
> But I will say to you, gentlemen, tonight that if our constitutional movement were to fail . . . if it became evident that we could not by parliamentary action and continued representation at Westminster restore to Ireland the high privilege of self-government . . . I for one would not continue to remain for 24 hours longer in the House of Commons at Westminster [prolonged cheering] . . . But more than that, gentlemen, I believe the Irish constituencies would not consent to allow us to remain . . . the most advanced section of Irishmen, as well as the least advanced, have always thoroughly understood that the parliamentary policy was to be a trial and that we did not ourselves believe in the possibility of maintaining for all time, or for any lengthened period, an incorrupt and independent Irish representation at Westminster.

This, described at the time by the *Nation* as one of the most important speeches of Parnell's entire career, was also one of the most puzzling. How could a man so apparently committed to parliamentary action so lightheartedly turn his back upon it? Worse still, how could such a man take Cecil Rhodes's money on the understanding that Irish representation at Westminster would be permanent and in almost the next breath describe it as highly conditional and provisional? The gap between what since 1886 had come to be regarded as Parnell's norm and this echo from his period of *Sturm und Drang*, was so wide and seemed so bizarre that historians have found it no less difficult than contemporaries to explain. The most authoritative of them, Dr Cruise O'Brien, even goes so far as to see in it an elaborate manœuvre to prepare the way for a counter-attack in case the approaching personal crisis of his life should alienate his supporters.[45] This is surely excessively Machiavellian. It is true that Parnell was here adumbrating the theme to which he was to recur obsessively when the crisis finally arrived, but that was not until November 1890 and it is scarcely possible that he could, as far back as May 1889, have anticipated how things might ultimately turn out; on the contrary, right up to the crash, his expectation of how things *would* turn out was quite different from what actually happened.

There are at least two other explanations which are simpler and more consistent with Parnell's usual pattern of behaviour. One is that in this speech he was engaged in his favourite tactic of 'balancing'. It is worth recalling that his ordeal in the witness-box had ended only two weeks previously and that in the course of it he had attempted systematically to demolish every possible connection with extremism which had been alleged against him. Now that the ordeal was over, it was no more than common sense for him to seek to repair some of the damage which his grand renunciation might be expected to have done, especially in America. To do this by indulging in the old rhetoric which the new circumstances were unlikely ever to require him to translate into action, was a cheap and easy way out. The second explanation is that he said what he did because he believed it. At each of the critical phases of his career he had warned the party and the country about the corrupting and debilitating influences of the House of Commons upon Irish MPs, and nothing had happened since 1886 to change this situation; on the contrary, the eighteen months that elapsed between his speech and the challenge to his leadership which erupted at the end of 1890 were to reveal, as we shall see, more than one instance of how damaging those influences could be.

V

But for the present his main preoccupation continued to be with British audiences and with the overriding need to convince them that the Irish were neither savages nor separatists. Only two months after his disparaging remarks about constitutional agitation he chose the occasion when he was being given the freedom of Edinburgh to project the picture of a self-governing Ireland as a contented and participating member of the Empire. In the first of three speeches he made on that occasion he told a working-class audience that Ireland had never been rebellious except under the spur of 'bitter misgovernment'. 'I am glad to think', he said, 'that the old bad times have gone by . . . that England and Ireland will henceforward be united in the . . . strong and enduring bonds of friendship, mutual interest, and amity . . .' The following day he went out of his way to draw exactly the opposite conclusion about parliamentary pressure from that which he had tried to impress upon the Irish municipal worthies when he addressed them in London. Acknowledging that the inadequacy of the Irish performance at Westminster in earlier days had stimulated the growth of revolutionary nationalism, he declared that those days were gone. 'Nobody', he said, 'can pretend for a single instant . . . that constitutional action during the last ten years has not been most abundantly vindicated by its results and that Irishmen are not justified in looking to such constitutional means – and such constitutional means alone – for the future prosperity of their country and the success of their movement.'

So far so good. But at his final meeting, later in the evening of Saturday, 20 July, Parnell himself demonstrated that the corrupting effects of English political *mores* might not wholly have been confined to the rank and file of his party. Starting from the perfectly defensible proposition that public opinion in Ireland could not make itself felt so readily as, for example, in England or Scotland, he suggested that this was because the government relied on coercion to counter the effects of persuasion. He then made a strange admission:

> I have not spoken in Ireland for years and years, and I will tell you frankly the reason why: that I prefer to keep my head for better things than coming in contact with the butt-end of a policeman's musket. The Irish member who addresses his constituents does so with the knowledge beforehand that in all probability he will be brutally assaulted and left for dead. And these are risks which some are willing to take but which everybody is not willing to take. I confess that I am cowardly enough to have to place myself in the latter category.

No doubt he was making propaganda tongue in cheek, and these remarks were greeted with the laughter he invited, but they have a strange ring about them all the same. They exhibit in an extreme form that combination of effrontery and insensitivity which was characteristic of Parnell in a certain mood. Probably he never reflected on the gulf that separated this speech from his own behaviour in the days of the Land League; probably it never even entered his mind that an instructive contrast might be drawn between his airy apologia and what was then being risked and suffered in Ireland by such as Dillon and O'Brien. But if his British audience was too naïve to make that kind of damaging comparison, there were those in his own party who would not hesitate to do so if occasion served, and for Parnell to expose such a vulnerable flank was not wise at a moment when his leadership was more precarious than he realized.

At Edinburgh, naturally, Parnell was less concerned with Irish than with British reactions. Consequently, the burden of his speech was to drive home to his audience that a self-governing Ireland could not be a threat to Britain or to the empire. The balance of power between the two countries would not be disturbed, he said. On the contrary, Britain's position would be improved as she would then have moral as well as physical force on her side. 'What single means should we have beyond the constitution that we have not now to work your injury?' he asked. 'We should have none. But your strength would be greater to resist injustice for [he meant, "by"] weak and little Ireland against great and powerful Britain if we tried it. Your strength would be greater because you would have the moral power to put down rebellion before the world that you have not got [now] in Ireland.' The Irish people, he assured his hearers, had fundamentally changed 'their whole nature' since Gladstone had brought in his Home Rule bill and they were now willing 'to live with you in amity as fellow-citizens of a great Empire'. And he ended with a passage which intriguingly echoed Gladstone's remarks to him the previous year:[46]

> The principle which we contend for is a very simple one. It is the principle which has enabled your colonies to thrive and prosper and remain loyal to the Empire . . . It is a principle under which free America has consolidated and grown to the enormous extent which is the wonder and the admiration of the world . . . the principle of the happiness and prosperity of the greatest number, and the rule of the majority of a nation, and of the power of looking after those concerns, those small Irish concerns which you, the rich English nation, have been proved by experience to be utterly unable to attend to.

These were vague terms, of course – unmistakably conciliatory, but lacking coherent practicality. To achieve practicality a further consultation with Gladstone was essential. That this took so long to happen was not the Liberal leader's fault. During the summer of 1889 he waited patiently in the hope that Parnell might be tempted into paying a visit to Hawarden, and on 30 August wrote a polite note deprecating the delay which, he suggested delicately, might perhaps have been due to Parnell's wish to find out first whether the Tories would commit themselves to establishing an Irish university satisfactory to Roman Catholics;

if that did become a possibility it would be yet one more topic which they should discuss together.[47] Despite these blandishments, Parnell still held aloof and it was not until just before Christmas that he turned up at Hawarden. He arrived, however, in the odour of sanctity, having just made another speech (at Nottingham) which Gladstone's former secretary described in his diary as most moderate. 'But people are difficult to please', Hamilton added perceptively, 'for the more moderate he is, the more it is said that he is trying to humbug the British public.'[48]

This persistent prejudice made it all the more imperative that the meeting with Gladstone should produce positive results. This was Gladstone's view also, and to prepare the way for Parnell's visit he held an informal conference with some of his ex-colleagues at Hawarden in October. It was not an unmixed success. Although nearly everyone could agree that it was best not to tie their hands by premature decisions and disclosures about the contents of the next Home Rule bill, it rapidly became plain that a policy of wait and see was dictated as much by their own internal confusion as by rational political calculation. Much of the argument concerned the future of the Irish members – should they or should they not be returned at Westminster after Home Rule had been established?

Since 1886 most leading Liberals were, like Gladstone, thinking increasingly in terms of retention, though as to what kind of retention they were at sixes and sevens. At the informal conference Gladstone, Lord Ripon and John Morley were for retaining the Irish members on a reduced scale and Gladstone hankered after limiting their appearance at Westminster to debates on imperial questions only. But as Granville, who was also there, explained to the absent Spencer, Harcourt was firm that they should be diminished neither in number or in subjects. 'He believes that we shall want them for a Liberal majority. It is not clear that Parnell would consent to a diminished number, though he does not object to a total exclusion.'[49]

Granville's analysis, though wrong about Parnell, reveals clearly enough the disarray among the Liberals. This was not helped by the well-meaning Spencer, who was as Harcourt remarked, 'one of those children of light who has all the innocence of the dove, but little of the craft of the serpent'. Living up to this character, Spencer proceeded to make a speech at Stockton in which, while professedly avoiding any discussion of Home Rule details, he plumped for the retention of the Irish members, arguing that there seemed no middle course between total exclusion and total retention.[50]

The Stockton speech at once brought Harcourt on to the war-path. Complaining bitterly to Morley of Spencer's propensity to give the game away in advance, he insisted that merely to reduce the number of Irish MPs would be the worst possible expedient – impracticable, indefensible and probably impossible for Parnell to accept. If the object was to win a Liberal majority, he repeated, 'we can't afford to diminish the force of the Irish members'.[51] Two days later followed another broadside, chiding Morley for always thinking of what was due to Ireland. 'The fallacy', he acutely observed, 'lies in regarding our dealings with the Irish as a privilege of great price which we are called upon to surrender and for which we ought to have an equivalent. If you look at it from the point of view of a burden which we are glad to be rid of, why should there be any equivalent? The Irish won't interfere with us either more or less than they did before, and we are very glad not to be called upon to interfere with them.'[52]

Towards Gladstone he was necessarily more restrained. Having left the conference early, he had been dismayed to learn subsequently that opinion had seemed to move again towards retaining a diminished number of Irish members. This, he wrote, would not work in practice, since the fact that it would be for large imperial questions that the Irish would be retained would make it impossible to reduce their strength:[53]

> The proposal of course is supposed to get rid of the objection to Irish interference with British affairs, but though it may lessen the *amount* it does not really touch the *principle* of the objection. When parties are pretty equally divided fifty Irish votes may be as decisive as 100 . . . and when you have once conceded the objection to Irish interference you don't get rid of it any more than the young woman did of the baby by saying it's such a little one . . .

Harcourt's last word was that he personally could not defend retention in smaller numbers and he therefore pleaded passionately for 'reticence'. But Gladstone, agreeing in principle, left the door still open for further discussion, provided it was 'purely academic'. He aimed, he said, like Goethe, only for 'more light'. Warning Harcourt not to cut himself off from his colleagues, he personally reserved 'a rollicking liberty of choice'. 'I hope', he added archly, 'my epithet a little attracts your sympathy.'[54]

It did not. Harcourt, who knew his Gladstone, interpreted the letter to mean that the GOM would seek, as usual, to go as he pleased. 'He hugs the hope and belief', he told Morley, 'that ultimately he will carry his own plan of 1886 unaltered as to Irish MPs and all the rest. Don't he wish he may get it!'[55] Whether or not Gladstone would get it depended of course as much on Parnell as on the Liberal party and Gladstone prepared himself carefully for the long-awaited visit. From a memorandum he drew up a few hours before Parnell's arrival on 18 December, it is clear that he wanted to cover the ground as widely as possible – the topics he listed for discussion included the land question, the problem of contracts, the query as to whether the Home Rule bill should contain a clause expressly reserving the supremacy of the imperial parliament, the mode of delegation of powers, the making of judicial appointments and, in considerable detail, the issues of Irish representation at Westminster and of finance.[56]

Parnell did not arrive until five-thirty in the evening and was at once plunged by his eager host into two hours' discussion which the Irish leader then adjourned until next day, when they had two hours' more. Parnell seems to have made a favourable impression upon the household. Mary Gladstone sat next to him at dinner and talked with him about the Commission. She thought his voice low and weak, but his nose good and his eyes disturbing. 'He never shows emotion', she noted in her journal, 'has a cool, indifferent manner, in sharp contrast to the deep piercing gaze of his eyes, which look bang through, not at, yours. He looks more ill than any other I ever saw off a death bed, refined and gentlemanlike in looks, voice and ways, speaks with perfect calmness on burning points and quite frankly.'[57] Her father in his own way was no less impressed, and in his diary noted: 'He is certainly one of the very best people to deal with that I have ever known.'[58] And to his colleagues Gladstone reported as follows:[59]

Secret

After very long delay, of which I do not know the cause, Mr Parnell's promised visit came off last week. He appeared well and cheerful and proposed to accompany (without a gun) my younger sons who went out shooting.

Nothing could be more satisfactory than his conversation; full as I thought of good sense from beginning to end.

I had prepared carefully all the points that I could think of, or recall from the suggestions of others, as possible improvements (as to essence or as to prudential policy) in the Irish Government Bill or Land Bill.

I did not press him to positive conclusions, but learned pretty well the leaning of his mind; and ascertained that, so far as I could judge, nothing like a crotchet, or an irrational demand, from his side, was likely to interfere with the proper freedom of our deliberations when the proper time comes for practical steps . . .

I may say, however, that we were quite agreed in thinking the real difficulty lies in determining the particular form in which an Irish representation may have to be retained at Westminster. We conversed at large on the different modes. He has no absolute or foregone conclusion.

He emphatically agreed in the wisdom and necessity of reserving our judgement on this matter until a crisis is at hand.

Will those of my late colleagues who may see this paper kindly note the fact by their initials.

It is evident that Gladstone felt that the discussions had gone well even if, perhaps because, the conclusions actually reached had been so indefinite. His conviction that he had a genuine meeting of minds with Parnell was to be of great importance in the days to come. Equally important, again in the light of future events, was the fact that Parnell went direct from Hawarden to Liverpool and there expressed, publicly and privately, his extreme satisfaction with the outcome of his visit. To a public meeting he spoke in the most glowing terms of the Liberal leader and called upon the English people to help in winning 'the great battle I trust we are on the eve of entering upon'.[60] His Liverpool host, the prominent Liberal, E. Evans, wrote later to Gladstone, after Parnell had put out a quite different version of the Hawarden interview, that when he had stayed with him he had shown himself 'very much impressed with his visit to you, and your cordiality, but more than all with the thoroughness of your proposals in regard to Ireland which went really further than he could have expected from any great English statesman and that they meant a most satisfactory solution'.[61]

A 'solution' the Hawarden interview most certainly did not provide. But it had been significant in two other, scarcely less crucial, ways. On the one hand, it had demonstrated conclusively that one of the weaknesses of the hurried bill of 1886 – the lack of co-ordinated discussion and planning – was in a fair way to being overcome and that Gladstone and Parnell had reached the point where constructive dialogue could take place between them. On the other hand, that Parnell should be received as an honoured guest at Hawarden, and thus admitted to the inmost citadel of Liberalism, seemed to all observers the culminating point of his apotheosis, the attainment of the zenith towards which his star had climbed so steadily since Pigott's disgrace and death.

Yet the moment of triumph, though real, could hardly have been more ephemeral. It was on 19 December that Parnell left Hawarden for Liverpool. Exactly five days later, on Christmas Eve, the cloud which had hung over him for so long finally burst. On that day Captain O'Shea filed a petition for divorce from his wife, citing his former leader as the co-respondent.[62]

CHAPTER 15

The Crash

'He and she undefended, and he has lived this life of lies all these years. A heart-breaking revelation. "Blot out his name".' (Mary Gladstone, *Letters and diaries* (November 1890), p. 413.)

I

That O'Shea should at long last have braced himself to take the plunge can scarcely have surprised either the guilty parties themselves or anyone who knew anything about the situation which had been building up for so many years. But why he should have chosen the particular moment he did, baffled many people at the time and has ever since remained a matter of controversy. There are two possible explanations, one political, the other personal. The political explanation is that the divorce suit was simply another attempt to vilify Parnell by the same enemies who had failed to bring him down by the Pigott forgeries. Parnell himself was partly responsible for giving currency to this interpretation, though how far he actually believed it is open to doubt; he could certainly not have believed it to the exclusion of the alternative, personal, explanation to be considered in a moment.

His public reaction, given to a reporter from the *Freeman's Journal* directly after the suit had been filed, was remarkably explicit. He had, he said, reliable information that O'Shea had been incited by E. C. Houston, 'the hirer of Pigott', in the interests of *The Times*, in the hope of diminishing the damages Parnell was likely to secure in his libel action against that newspaper. *The Times*, Parnell insisted, 'having failed to assassinate his character by means of forged letters, now attempts the same end by other means'. Accepting this theory, the *Freeman* came out strongly against O'Shea and his supposed accomplices, even going so far as to mention Chamberlain specifically. 'If this', the editorial observed darkly, 'is to be the party game of the future, some proud names and great personages will yet be lowered.'[1]

No conclusive evidence has ever been produced to implicate either *The Times* or Houston in the affair, though there are enough oddities lying around the fringes of the case to awaken at least some suspicion. It is known, for example, that early in 1889 Houston and O'Shea were in correspondence on matters connected with the Special Commission.[2] Although there is nothing to indicate that this correspondence carried over into the divorce proceedings, the two names were again linked in a letter written on 15 October 1890 by an Irishwoman living in London. She was Miss Esther Johnston, who had kept a hotel in Dublin between 1880 and 1882 and claimed to know many of the Irish political figures of the day. She attended the sittings of the Commission assiduously and wrote several times to *The Times* offering whatever assistance she could give. Actually, she had nothing to give save gossip and her letters, to others as well as to Macdonald of *The Times*, show her to have been not only a romantic nationalist but also a highly volatile one who in successive letters could range from extravagant praise of Parnell to equally extravagant abuse. Still, she apparently moved in circles where the comings and goings of prominent people connected with Ireland were minutely scrutinized, hence the letter of 15 October to an Irish friend, telling him that 'Houston has been in Paris and elsewhere – probably "squaring matters for the ex-Hussar". There's no lack of money and Wontner has all the information that was and is in the archives of the past or present government.'[3]

This, of course, was no more than hearsay, but the mention of the name of Wontner leads on to yet another peculiarity of the case. Wontner was O'Shea's solicitor. He was an eminently worthy person, but O'Shea had only arrived on his doorstep by an extremely circuitous route. He was O'Shea's third choice, or rather was chosen for him by his counsel Sir Edward Clarke, when the latter found to his horror who the two previous candidates had been. The first was none other than Joseph Soames, the solicitor for *The Times*. Soames was not noted for his perspicacity, but even he could see the impropriety of his acting for O'Shea while the Special Commission was still sitting, and he passed his dangerous client on to someone else. That someone else was a young man of only ten months' standing in his profession. But worse, far worse, than his inexperience was the fact that his father, Mr Justice Day, happened to be one of the three judges then presiding over the Commission. Small wonder that Clarke exerted himself so strenuously to steer O'Shea into the safe anchorage of Mr Wontner's impeccable respectability.[4]

Yet although this overlapping between the Special Commission and the divorce proceedings is certainly suggestive, it falls far short of proving Parnell's thesis. No evidence in support of that thesis is to be found in the archives of *The Times*, but that is hardly surprising. The only tenuous documentary link that appears to have survived comes rather from the papers of W. H. Smith. To him, a few days before O'Shea filed his petition, the editor, George Buckle, wrote that he had been advised by Lord Salisbury to seek an interview with Smith. 'I should much like a talk with you', Buckle added, 'in reference to this horrid scandal.'[5] Even here the 'horrid scandal' is not identified by name, but since in that delectable field the Parnell-O'Shea affair had no competitors at the time, it is not improbable that the minister and the editor whose fortunes had been so intertwined during the Special Commission should have wished to consult together about what possible benefit might be extracted from the impending blow against Parnell.

But consultation, if it took place, does not amount to collaboration, and since it is by no means clear what bearing the divorce suit could have upon the libel case, Parnell's newspaper comment must remain suspect. The gloss put upon it by the *Freeman's Journal*, that among O'Shea's accomplices was Joseph Chamberlain, cannot, however, be so easily dismissed. Indeed, Parnell's chief apologist, Henry Harrison, went so far in after years as to state quite categorically that the divorce was used by what he calls 'the Chamberlain–O'Shea combination' as a deliberate device to retrieve the disaster of the Special Commission.[6] The most 'direct' evidence he adduced in support of this assertion was a recollection written down many years after the event by Alfred Robbins of the *Birmingham Daily Post*. Robbins's recollection was that soon after parliament had risen in August 1889, 'I was asked by one on the inside of the Liberal Unionist "machine" whether Parnell would be politically ruined by a divorce, the then recent Dilke case being given as a precedent, and Captain O'Shea, it was added, being willing to take proceedings'. Robbins, though finding the idea deeply repugnant, contented himself with pointing out the risk inherent in attacking Parnell so soon after the Pigott forgeries. He doubted whether the Unionist managers, 'who were indicated to be wavering', would find that any such action would pay dividends.[7] Robbins did not reveal the name of his interrogator, but though the approach sounds rather too crude to have emanated directly from Chamberlain, little happened in the Birmingham caucus of which he was unaware, and he is unlikely to have entirely overlooked the fact that O'Shea, while he had outlived his usefulness as a go-between, might still serve an ulterior purpose as an aggrieved husband.

Moreover, Chamberlain was not dependent on third parties for news of O'Shea's affairs. On the contrary, in October 1889, the Captain wrote him, at considerable length, 'an explanation of some personal matters'. These included not only the beginnings of the dispute over the will of his wife's Aunt Ben – who had finally died in May 1889, leaving the whole of her large fortune and estate to her niece – but also some details about the 'perfidy' with which Katharine and Parnell had behaved towards him.[8] Enclosed with this letter was a copy of the famous *Pall Mall Gazette* paragraph of 24 May 1886 on 'Mr Parnell's suburban retreat'.* Upon this, O'Shea's comment to Chamberlain was that it was not until 13 June 1887 that he discovered that the *Pall Mall Gazette* paragraph had been accurate, and that he had then sent his wife a message through their son Gerard that he would take proceedings against her if she did not give a pledge of better behaviour – which pledge she gave in the form of a letter to Gerard which O'Shea reproduced as follows for Chamberlain's benefit:[9]

> My dear Gerardie,
>
> I now write to confirm my telegram to you in which I said I was willing to meet the wishes you expressed in regard to Mr Parnell.
>
> I am most anxious everything should be made as pleasant as possible for you and that nobody should come here who is in any way obnoxious to you, and I therefore readily agree that there shall be no further communication direct or indirect with him.
>
> > Ever, my darling Gerardie,
> > Your loving Mother.

To this deluge of domestic infelicity, Chamberlain returned a guarded, not to say a prim, reply. He was sorry, he said, to hear of O'Shea's anxieties. 'I have never listened to scandalous reports affecting my friends and in your case I have heard nothing, and knew nothing, beyond what you have told me.' But he added: 'I am not sure that the boldest course is not always the wisest.'[10] There then ensued a pause, partially filled, it would seem, by an ill-judged and vain attempt on the part of the Captain to win Cardinal Manning to his side, and to obtain his approval for a divorce.[11]

The pause did not last long. In December, after his triumphant visit to Hawarden, Parnell made his way to Brighton where Katharine was apparently maintaining two different establishments. Thither also went Captain O'Shea and his son. The latter, calling unexpectedly at one of his mother's houses, found there possessions belonging to Parnell, some of which he threw out of the window in a rage. What happened next was described to Chamberlain by O'Shea in a telegram, followed by a letter,

*See above, pp. 335, 338–9.

both of which reached their recipient, then in Egypt, several days after the event. 'There was a dreadful scene', wrote O'Shea, 'and on our return to London we went to the lawyers and settled that an action should be immediately instituted.'[12] Chamberlain's response gave little away, except perhaps that he could be as cool in the shadow of the Pyramids as on his native heath at Highbury. 'You know', he wrote, 'that I have never presumed to refer to your private affairs, in regard to which every man must judge for himself; but now that you have taken the decisive step, I may be allowed to say that it seems to me to have been forced upon you, and that any further hesitation would have given rise to an accusation of complacency under an injury which no honourable man can patiently endure.'[13]

This letter, and Chamberlain's earlier letter of 14 October, were alike dismissed by Henry Harrison as 'show letters', designed to protect Chamberlain's position in case his correspondence with O'Shea ever came to be published. Harrison called them show letters because he was convinced that Chamberlain, through his involvement, first with the Kilmainham 'treaty', and then with the 'central board' negotiations, had known since 1882 of the triangular relationship between Parnell and the O'Sheas.[14] It is likely enough that Chamberlain did know of the relationship, but that does not prove that the letters were show letters, much less that the divorce was either instigated or stage-managed by Chamberlain. It is true that in December 1889, when writing to Balfour to acquaint him with his decision to move for a divorce, O'Shea described Chamberlain as 'acquainted with the facts'.[15] But there is nothing to say that 'the facts', such as they were, had been known to Chamberlain before O'Shea communicated them to him in October 1889 or that this knowledge laid Chamberlain open to the charge of complicity, any more than did the further circumstance, which was unknown to Harrison, that in February 1891, after the divorce had gone through, Chamberlain lent O'Shea £400 to tide him over one of his periodic bouts of insolvency.[16] For even if Chamberlain *had* been well aware of the situation for years, he was not on such intimate terms with O'Shea as to be quite sure how much the injured husband really knew, or how long he had known it. Few people enjoy having to tell a cuckold of his condition and when O'Shea eventually informed Chamberlain that he had nerved himself to strike, Chamberlain was unlikely to write back saying that he was only astonished the Captain had not struck long ago.

But if, for the sake of argument, we admit that Harrison was right and these were show letters, they still do not come near to proving the case that the divorce suit was an essentially political device to restore the fortunes of the government or to strengthen the forces of Unionism and with them Chamberlain's own position. No solid evidence, it is necessary to insist in the face of Harrison's eloquent pertinacity, has ever emerged to demonstrate the existence of such a conspiracy. For while it is true that O'Shea's action had immense political consequences, it is no less true that he himself had more than adequate personal reasons for taking it, irrespective of any other prompting he may or may not have received.[17]

II

What were those personal reasons? They were mainly, if not wholly, variations on one predictable theme – money. When Henry Harrison discussed the matter with Katharine the year after Parnell's death she stressed to him what we have seen already, that Captain O'Shea had generally been short of funds and that apart from the fact that his rooms at Albert Mansions were paid for by her aunt, he had also received other financial assistance periodically from the same source. O'Shea himself told much the same story to Chamberlain in 1892. His income from 1880 to 1889, he reckoned, had averaged £2500 p.a., 'irrespective of any present from Mrs Wood who allowed my former wife about £4000 a year; but often, and especially in 1882, I was in want of money . . . and I certainly pressed my former wife to keep her aunt up to her promises'.[18]

Beyond these crumbs from the rich woman's table lay very great expectations – that Katharine would inherit all her aunt's property provided that aunt, whose moral code was strict, did not discover that her favourite niece, though admittedly neglected by her husband, had for years been living in adultery under the roof she herself had paid for. Since Aunt Ben was already 88 when the Parnell–O'Shea relationship became 'regularized' in 1881, it was reasonable to suppose that natural causes would ensure that the *ménage à trois* need only be briefly maintained. The fact that she shattered all prognostications by living until 19 May 1889 meant that this dangerous situation had to last far longer than originally expected.[19] Yet if the risks were vast, so also was the potential prize. In November 1888 O'Shea opened his mind on the subject to his usual confidant, Joseph Chamberlain:[20]

As I am going away I had better tell you that the anxiety I felt was occasioned by the fact that Mrs O'Shea is under a written engagement not to communicate directly or indirectly with Mr Parnell, and the latter under a written order not to do so with Mrs O'Shea.

I daresay a great many people have some notion of the state of affairs, but I am most anxious for my children's sake that nothing about it should be actually published, because a very large fortune for them may depend upon it not coming into print.

I believe Mrs Wood of Eltham is worth £200,000 or more, all left to them, and . . . Mrs O'Shea's relations would use any weapon to change her will.

Years ago I begged that affairs should be so arranged that *in no case* could I myself inherit any of this money. It is on their account that I can safely say to you that the anxiety was in no way personal.

Chamberlain's reply was tactful, but revealing. 'I have felt that I could not say a word to you on the subject until you spoke to me', he wrote, thus conveying the clear impression that he knew which way the wind was blowing.[21] If he had not done so already, then O'Shea's letter must surely have enlightened him, which in turn somewhat strengthens the argument that Chamberlain's elaborately careful letters to O'Shea in the critical year of 1889 were designed to secure his own position by suggesting that he knew less than he really did. But however much or little he admitted to knowing, it is doubtful if he was at any time taken in by the Captain's projection of himself as a paragon of disinterested virtue. Certainly, after Aunt Ben's death six months later, O'Shea's protestations became notably less impersonal. In her last will she had left her entire fortune, apart from a few minor legacies, to Katharine in such a way that it could not be made the basis of any claim by her husband nor be brought within the scope of her marriage-settlement.[22] Since the bequest consisted, as O'Shea did not fail to tell Chamberlain, of £145,000 in Consols and some land in Gloucestershire, it was not surprising that O'Shea should have joined forces with Katharine's brothers and sisters to contest the will. Indeed, the Woods themselves had attempted to have the old lady committed as insane so as to have the will set aside while she was still alive. They were foiled, mainly because Gladstone's physician, Sir Andrew Clark, was called in to establish her mental health. His services were provided after not only Katharine, but Parnell as well, had written to Gladstone requesting this assistance. That Parnell should have stooped to ask a personal, as distinct from a political, favour from an English statesman for the first and only time in his life – and this favour of all favours – is an indication of how complete his infatuation had now become.[23] After

Mrs Wood's death, of course, it was an obvious tactic to resume the struggle and to claim that Katharine had abused her favoured position to secure the whole legacy for herself by exercising undue influence over her aged and incapable aunt.

But this turn of events involved much more than Captain O'Shea's frustrated cupidity. However the probate case might be decided, the fact that it now loomed on the horizon meant that Aunt Ben's money was out of reach for an indefinite period (in fact for three years), and this in turn meant that his original pecuniary motive for withholding divorce proceedings was no longer valid. Indeed, the wheel had turned full circle, for the divorce might now actually be made to serve the purpose it had formerly obstructed – that is, the diversion of a portion of Aunt Ben's wealth towards the O'Shea side of the family. For if it could be shown in court that Katharine had been deceiving her aunt over a long period of years, this might help to discredit her standing in a way most beneficial to the aggrieved parties who were contesting the will. It is reasonable, therefore, to regard the death of Aunt Ben and the ensuing controversy over the disposal of her estate as the proximate causes of O'Shea's decision to move in the matter of the divorce and to see the 'hideous scene' at Brighton, when Gerard threw Parnell's belongings out of the window, as being in effect the fuse that detonated a mine already well prepared.

For O'Shea to join in the family assault on the will was, admittedly, not without risks, since, if the action was successful, the estate would be fragmented among so many claimants that the expectations of each would be substantially diminished. Yet even here there was a possibility that the situation could be turned to his advantage. If the divorce suit really was likely to have a serious bearing on the probate case, then O'Shea clearly had something to sell – his willingness to withdraw the suit if an adequate *quid pro quo* could be arranged. Or rather, not merely to withdraw the suit but – again for a sufficient consideration – to offer no defence against counter-charges of adultery on his part or, alternatively, of having condoned and connived at Parnell's relationship with his wife. Which set of accusations he would be expected to stomach depended on whether Parnell and Katharine still wanted the divorce to go through (but with her divorcing Willie, and not the other way round) or whether they would be content merely to block her husband's original suit by proving his connivance.

The months between the filing of the suit in December 1889 and its actual trial in November 1890 were filled with complex negotiations on these vexed questions about which little information has survived. But enough remains to indicate that on the issue of whether or not to go for an outright divorce Parnell and Katharine may have been at least partially at variance. For him, the overriding consideration, to which he clung passionately through the endless twists and turns of the affair, was that her marriage with O'Shea should at all costs be ended so that he could claim her as his wife before the whole world. Her views seem to have been more complex. Elucidation of them is not helped by the fact that she quarrelled with her solicitor, George Lewis, and dealt with her counsel, Frank (later Sir Frank) Lockwood, in her own amateurish fashion. Lewis gained the impression that she wanted to force the divorce through, but he is hardly a trustworthy guide since he found her, on his own admission, 'a very charming lady, but an impossible one'.[24] Her real feeling apparently was that the case should have been fought. It could have been fought either by proving O'Shea's adultery or by proving his connivance. In the first instance, the effect that Parnell aimed at would have been satisfactorily achieved. In the second instance, if connivance had been proved, the case would have collapsed and O'Shea would have stood confessed as a man who for motives of political and financial gain had acquiesced over many years in his own humiliation. Katharine herself told Henry Harrison when it was all over that she was anxious there should be no divorce since she feared the harm it would do to Parnell's career, and in old age she recorded in her book that Sir Frank Lockwood had begged her to get Parnell to allow him to contest the case, presumably with a view to establishing O'Shea's frailty and thus causing his action to fail.[25] But this would have been both naïve and useless. A collapsed divorce would not leave the situation *in statu quo*. It might indeed demonstrate that O'Shea was a conniving husband, but it would also demonstrate that Parnell had been an adulterer for a large part of his public life and this would be almost as damaging as an actual divorce, for he would still stand convicted of having broken that most imperative of all Victorian commandments, 'Thou shalt not be found out'.

Parnell was therefore surely right from his standpoint in insisting that there should be a divorce, especially since the possibility remained that matters might be so arranged that Katharine would divorce Willie rather than he her. She claimed later, in conversation with Harrison, that proof of some seventeen infidelities by the Captain had been assembled for use against him. This may or may not have been true, but if it was only partially true it makes all the more incomprehensible the fact that when the counter-charges were produced in the preliminaries to the hearing, the privilege of being supposed to have been the object of O'Shea's illicit intentions was reserved exclusively for Katharine's own sister, Anna Steele. O'Shea's astonishment, reporting the news to Chamberlain in August 1890, though excessively self-righteous, is vehement enough to carry some conviction. The counter-charges, he wrote, 'are absolutely unfounded, the principal one being that in 1881 I committed adultery with one of her [Katharine's] sisters.* During the intervening nine years she has not hinted such a thing either to myself or to any member of the family. You can imagine the indignation of her brothers and sisters. Low as she had sunk with him before, I confess I was astounded when I heard of the depths to which Parnell has now dragged her.'[26] But this invention, if it was an invention, seems not to have been Parnell's. It may rather have sprung – as Mrs Steele herself asserted in court – from the fact that the sisters had quarrelled over Aunt Ben's will and that no one thereafter could dissuade the headstrong Katharine from besmirching Anna as part of a wider battle.[27]

Still, there remained a hope that Captain O'Shea, virtuous protestations notwithstanding, might be persuaded to confess to adultery with some party, if not with his sister-in-law. Indeed, in the letter to Chamberlain just quoted he hints as much. 'I am being subjected to every kind of injury and persecution; slander, gross extortion, attempts to corrupt witnesses of mine, unremitting shadowings. My solicitors withal are constantly plied with suggestions for compromise. "No difficulty as to terms" . . .'[28] What kind of terms? On this point, though differing as to detail, O'Shea and his wife are in unusual agreement that what was involved was a lump sum to be paid to the Captain on condition that instead of he divorcing her, she should divorce him. To Henry Harrison she said, little more than a year later, that £20,000 would have purchased his consent, and O'Shea informed his own counsel, Sir Edward Clarke, that he had been offered precisely that sum to drop the suit. It tells us a good deal about Sir Edward's opinion of his client that he believed up to the very last moment that O'Shea would not appear in court.[29] Apparently, he had some reason for so thinking. When the trial had taken place and O'Shea had begun to survey the ravaged landscape, he confided, in his familiar vein of self-pity, to Chamberlain: 'Nobody except myself knows what a fight it was or the influences, religious, social and pecuniary, that were brought to

*The date may be significant. It was in 1881 that Anna Steele was said to have helped to avoid a duel taking place between Parnell and O'Shea; it was also the year when O'Shea, flinging out of the house at Eltham in a rage, walked to Anna's house in London, arriving there at four o'clock in the morning, an hour not calculated to buttress her reputation for respectability (see above, p. 152).

bear in the hope of "squaring" me. The last offer was made to me through my son the evening before the trial and was equivalent to over £60,000.'[30]

The conclusion Chamberlain was presumably intended to draw from this was that his irreproachable correspondent had steadfastly refused to participate in such a vile bargain to frustrate the course of justice. Mrs O'Shea, however, told a different story. Her version was that with the supply of ready cash cut off by her aunt's death and with the will in jeopardy she was short of money and a dubious prospect for a loan. It was not her husband's high-minded rejection of the money, she assured Harrison, but her own inability to raise it, that prevented the deal from going through.[31]

Since no money changed hands it is impossible to establish the truth as between these two assertions. Had the money been available, O'Shea might still have refused it, either because he preferred to wrap the last shreds of his dignity round him, or because it was plain to him – had even, perhaps, been made plain to him by others – that the political potentialities of the divorce were so great that at all costs he must persist with his suit. But much more important than his motives and actions is the fact that Parnell's own belief that O'Shea could and would be 'squared' prompted him to give repeated assurances to anyone who dared to beard him on the subject that all would come right in the end.

Without that belief, his utterances between December 1889 and November 1890 make no sense whatever. They were not numerous, but they were quite explicit. To Michael Davitt, in a personal interview which seems to have taken place about February 1890, he said that he would emerge from the case 'without a stain on his name or reputation'.[32] He wrote in similar terms to William O'Brien and to T. P. Gill. To O'Brien, whose influence upon Irish opinion would be crucial, Parnell used these words: 'If this case is ever fully gone into, a matter which is exceedingly doubtful, you may rest assured that it will be shown that the dishonour and discredit have not been upon my side.' And that one at least of his correspondents understood clearly what he meant is suggested by a remark which T. P. Gill made to Wilfrid Scawen Blunt several years later. 'Parnell had a complete case in defence against O'Shea', Gill told him, 'O'Shea having connived throughout and profited in a money way.'[33] A trusting faith in the leader, and a readiness to accept his public statement that this was merely another phase in the conspiracy against him, seem at this point to have been widespread among the members of the party. Many of them

would probably have endorsed the almost offhand dismissal of the
affair which Dr Kenny dispatched to Dillon who, perhaps fortunately
for himself, was still absent on his Australian tour when the news first
broke:[34]

> Now I don't know whether there is any truth in the allegation and
> personally I don't care, except in the sense that I should be truly
> sorry poor P. should be in a position in which he must suffer more or
> less mental annoyance . . . I believe he is much more sensitive than he
> gets credit for, but this in my opinion is our plain duty, that come
> what will we are bound to stand to him as one man and show that no
> amount of obloquy will displace him from his position as our leader.
> It is quite plain that . . . the matter has been timed by that vile hound,
> O'Shea, who, if it is at all true, sold her as a matter of sale or barter,
> so as to serve the enemy who are up to some new game to revenge
> themselves for the defeat over the forgeries.*

III

Parnell's fate would ultimately depend at least as much upon English
reactions as upon Irish. At the outset these were decidedly mixed.
Edward Hamilton, for example, took a man of the world's pragmatic
view. 'Her intimacy with Parnell', he noted in his diary, 'has been a
notorious and recognized fact almost ever since he became a political
personage; and it is somewhat remarkable, not to say awkward for
Captain O'Shea, that he should only file a petition at this late hour. The
obvious inference is that, so long as Parnell was a friend in need to
O'Shea, the gallant Captain winked at the relations between his wife and
Parnell; and that it was only after the friendship between the two men
terminated and supplies consequently stopped, that O'Shea woke to the
fact that there was something wrong in his domestic circle.'[35] When
news reached him a few weeks later of Davitt's interview with Parnell,
Hamilton's scepticism was undiminished. 'Parnell, I am informed on

---

*It is worth noting that Parnell's secretary, Henry Campbell, when successfully
defending himself in June 1891 against the charge, made by the *Cork Herald*,
that he had lent himself to the business of hiring houses for the immoral
purposes of his leader, let fall in evidence that he had seen the brief which had
been drawn up for the defence in the divorce case, and that if it had been
utilized it would have blown O'Shea's case 'to atoms'. Naturally, he did not
disclose the details of this explosive document (*Nation*, 20 and 27 June 1891).
Parnell's comment on Campbell's libel action is in *Nation*, 4 July 1891; see also
F. S. L. Lyons, *The fall of Parnell*, p. 293, n.3.

good authority', he recorded, 'has assured Davitt that he is innocent of the charge of adultery with Mrs O'Shea, that nothing will be proved against him, and that Davitt may safely proclaim his innocence in Ireland. Parnell may be as good as his word; or else O'Shea may have been squared.'[36]

The fact that Hamilton should have taken Parnell's assurance to Davitt as meaning that he was innocent of the charge of adultery – which was precisely what he had *not* said – is itself an indication of how confusing even well-informed onlookers found this whole mysterious business. About the same time another inveterate diarist, Reginald Brett, met the journalist, W. T. Stead, who had also been talking to Katharine's cast-off solicitor, George Lewis. Stead was exceedingly dubious about the outcome of the suit and, as the editor who had published the *Pall Mall Gazette* paragraph of 1886 about 'Mr Parnell's suburban retreat', he had every reason to be dubious.[37] It was in this mood that he wrote to Archbishop Walsh at the end of January, exploring the available choices with his usual heavy-handed candour.

Since, he wrote, it was no longer possible to hope that Parnell could establish the innocence of his intimacy with Mrs O'Shea, what was the next best thing? Ideally it would be 'for P. to cease conjugal relations with Mrs O'Shea, say *peccavi* and publicly confess his sin'. But this, Stead admitted, was 'not attainable'. Therefore he fell back on his second-best solution, which was that he should not defend the action and marry Mrs O'Shea. 'I have reason to believe', he added, 'that this course is favoured by at least one of the parties to the suit.' Recollecting belatedly that he was addressing a Roman Catholic archbishop, he conceded the objection 'based on the interdict of the remarriage of divorcees', but, he concluded bluntly, 'what better solution is possible?'[38]

This, admittedly, was written before the Parnell–Davitt interview, and Brett in his note of a visit to Harcourt in January well conveys the confusion which prevailed in Liberal–nationalist circles until that interview had taken place. 'He [Harcourt] thinks Parnell is done for', noted Brett. 'Morley thinks he will be all right in Ireland but damaged in England. Stead thinks he will be all right in England, but damaged in Ireland. Davitt thinks he will be ruined in Ireland. Parnell thinks he will be all right all round.'[39]

Then, in early February, came Parnell's assurance to Davitt, the ambiguity of which seems to have escaped both Davitt himself and those to whom he imparted the good news. The immediate effect was to relieve the tension and Stead, especially, was so much impressed by what he evidently regarded as a guarantee of innocence that for once he had no gratuitous advice to offer. 'I subsequently heard from Davitt', he told Archbishop Walsh, 'that Mr Parnell is quite certain that he is going to come off with flying colours and that the whole thing is to break down and that of course was another reason for not committing ourselves.'[40]

Matters remained in this hopeful condition until the trial came on in November. Parnell, whenever he was approached, continued up to the last moment to use the same sort of language as he had used at the beginning of the year – naturally, given his assumption that O'Shea could be 'squared' according to the exigencies of the case. Particular significance, therefore, attached to the interview he had with John Morley on 10 November, just five days before the hearings began. Morley, like many others, had been disquieted by the ugly rumours which had continued to circulate throughout the year and on the day Parnell came to see him had written to Harcourt that he had heard that Sir Edward Clarke, O'Shea's counsel, had assembled 'some terribly odious material'.[41] Morley's purpose in meeting Parnell was partly to report to Gladstone as to whether or not the ugly rumours were true, and partly to sound out the Irish leader about political co-operation in the immediate future, assuming there was to be a future.[42]

They began, as we saw earlier, by discussing Balfour's land bill.* Next, as Morley recorded, 'we had some curious talk about the future'. Parnell seemed moderately favourable to the idea that Spencer might again be Lord-Lieutenant in the next Liberal administration, but he reacted sharply to Morley's daring suggestion that he, Parnell, should be Chief Secretary. It was quite out of the question, he said, that he or any member of his party should join a government, and he took it for granted that Morley would pick up the threads where he had left them in 1886. Morley then raised with him the possibility of finding a seat for one of the two Irish law officers in the next Liberal administration and Parnell replied that he would do his best to find a seat when the general election came, but not before. This innocuous exchange was to undergo a strange transformation before many weeks had passed.

In general, Morley found his guest more relaxed and more prepared to talk about himself and his colleagues than he had ever known him. 'More than usually cordial and gracious', he agreed to stay to dinner. But he hugged the fire closely and, when the waiter came into the room, turned his face away 'as if by a mechanical impulse'. He talked benignly

---

*For this aspect of their conversation, see above, p. 436.

about the members of his party, with the marked exception of one whose name Morley tactfully left blank, but who was almost certainly Healy. He was as hostile to the Plan of Campaign as ever, because it engendered violence, but about the actual administration of Ireland by Dublin Castle he was astonishingly vague. 'By the way', he said, 'who is the Under-Secretary? I forget.' In this context they touched on two matters which had come up in his Hawarden conversation with Gladstone – the police and the future of Irish representation at Westminster. As to the former, he did not seem to object to an idea broached, he said, by Mr Gladstone, that control of the RIC should be vested for a period in the Governor-General. 'But he let fall, as if speaking to the fire, the sinister observation, "Of course, if you once give us a legislative assembly, details like this of the constabulary we can put to right after".' On the question of the Irish members he thought the only way out of the dilemma was to reduce them to around 30. Morley, surprised, reminded him that he had once said he would never repeat Grattan's mistake of disbanding his Volunteers. To which Parnell merely replied that if the country was prepared to accept reduction as helping towards a solution, he would make no difficulty. The Irish, he added, were not a bad people to govern, but Ireland was a very good place to live out of.

Just before this, and taking advantage of his unwonted geniality, Morley had asked him the question he had been itching to ask all evening. His account of what followed is worth quoting at length:

At the end of dinner I said to him, 'There's one point on which I have no right to speak to you – and if you don't like it, you can say so. But it is important we should know whether certain legal proceedings are likely to end in your disappearance from the lead for a time.' He smiled all over his face, playing with his fork.

'My disappearance? Oh no. No chance of it. Nothing in the least leading to disappearance, so far as I am concerned, will come out of the legal proceedings. The other side don't know what a broken-kneed horse they are riding.' 'I'm delighted to hear that', I said, 'for I, for my part, regard you as vital to the whole business.' 'Well', he said, 'the Irish people are very slow to give a man their confidence, and they are still more slow to withdraw it.' I inferred from his talk of the broken-kneed horse that he meant there would be no adverse decree.

The effect of this conversation, duly reported to Hawarden, was greatly to reassure Gladstone. Only a few days earlier he had written to a colleague: 'I fear a thundercloud is about to burst over Parnell's head and I suppose it will end the career of a man in many respects invaluable.' Now it seemed from Morley's news that all was going to come right in the end.[43] But neither Gladstone nor Morley could know that the latter's optimistic report would have a life of no more than forty-eight hours.

IV

The appalling contrast between what Parnell told Morley at Brighton and what was unfolded in the divorce court on 15 and 17 November was to have a dire impact upon Liberal opinion and upon the attitudes of the Liberal leaders in the days that followed. But before we can begin to assess the effect of the 'revelations' at the trial, it is necessary to make a point of quite a different kind. This is that, despite the air of calm superiority with which Parnell impressed Morley, his position in his own country and even in his own party had begun during 1890 to exhibit ominous symptoms of deterioration.

The evidence for this is scattered and diverse, but it all points in the same direction – that his day-to-day contact with his followers, and therefore his control over them, had dwindled almost to vanishing-point. Whether this was due primarily to his preoccupation with the divorce, or to his continuing poor health, or to a combination of both, it is impossible to say with certainty, but what is clear is that the signs of mismanagement – worse still, of no management – were multiplying and were not going unnoticed. We have already seen that his eccentric and unheralded intervention in the debate on the Irish estimates in July 1890 had provoked a violent, and probably 'inspired', attack by Harold Frederic in the *New York Times*. That attack, through its very crudity, had provoked a reaction in Parnell's favour, but such a reaction was much harder to discern in the three other troubling and troublesome incidents which occurred in the summer and autumn of that tense year.

The series began with a stinging public rebuke to the Irish party by the Archbishop of Dublin for their alleged failure to seize the opportunity of a snap vote to defeat the government. On 19 June, with many members at Ascot races, the Tory majority on a critical division fell to four and would have been wiped out altogether if eighteen Irish members, including Parnell, who was ill, had not been absent from their places. To make matters worse, not only had there been no party whip for the occasion, but some undisciplined members had over-indulged in supplementary questions, so that the Tory whips were given time in which to lay their hands on returning celebrants from Ascot and rush them through the lobby. The affair might have been dismissed as the ordinary incident of parliamentary warfare which it in fact was if the archbishop had not weighed in with his reprimand, pointing out not only that it was obvious that a crucial vote was imminent on the night in question, but also that the government's majority had been shaky for days past, on all of which days, he alleged, Irish members had unwarrantably deserted their parliamentary posts. 'For my part', he wrote, 'I feel bound to lose not a moment in stating that if a satisfactory explanation is not forthcoming for what occurred, I do not care who the absentees may be, I shall find it hard to place any further trust in the action of the present Irish parliamentary party.'[44]

Although Dr Walsh's remarks were not specifically directed at Parnell, the obvious inference was that he, as chairman, bore the primary responsibility for this unsatisfactory state of affairs. Parnell, characteristically, gave no sign whatever that he was even aware of the existence of the letter and it fell to others to remonstrate with the archbishop. The nationalist press rallied strongly round the party and from the old Land Leaguer, A. J. Kettle, Dr Walsh received a novel interpretation of the party's laxness. Kettle maintained that it was purposeful, not purposeless, and explained that when he had met Parnell at Liverpool immediately after his visit to Hawarden, the leader had declared that rather than see the Liberals come back to power with a small majority which would enable the House of Lords to delay or destroy the next Home Rule bill, he would prefer to wait, if necessary, for another two years until Irish propaganda could take effect in England. The implication was that snap defeats of the government were no part of Parnell's (or of Gladstone's) policy and Kettle ended with something like a counter-reprimand to the archbishop:[45]

> You, My Lord, and Mr Parnell have such important parts to play in the present crisis of Ireland's history, it is so important to keep our forces as compact as possible, and I know him to be such a singular personage that I thought it might be of some use to put this view of the present phase of the fight before you ... I believe it to be authentic, and I feel that Your Lordship's opinion that 'Mr Parnell generally knows his own business best' will be again verified in this matter.

This ingenious theory may or may not have been correct, though it did accord closely with what both Liberals and nationalists seemed to be doing in practice. But if it was the agreed strategy of the allies to let the Tories stew in their own juice, it was not a strategy which could be shouted from the roof-tops without risking serious loss of morale among their supporters. Nor was it so shouted. Parnell himself made apparently no reference to it whatever and Gladstone did not mention it even in the confidential report on the Hawarden interview he sent to his colleagues. It is doubtful, therefore, if Kettle's theory weighed much with Archbishop Walsh, who preferred to judge men by their actual performance. And indeed, Parnell's own performance was so minimal – he voted in 50 out of 250 divisions during the 1890 session – as to suggest that for him absenteeism was less an act of policy, more a way of life.[46]

That he and his friends should thus have fallen foul of Archbishop Walsh was the more unfortunate since the second untoward incident of that stressful year nearly brought the party into direct confrontation with the entire hierarchy – would have done so, in fact, had not the archbishop this time come to their rescue. The trouble arose from a bitter quarrel between John Dillon and Dr Edward O'Dwyer, the Bishop of Limerick. Dr O'Dwyer, who was regarded by many as a 'Castle' bishop, was not popular with his colleagues, but when they saw him assailed on the public platform by a layman, and attacked without restraint in a newspaper, *United Ireland*, controlled by another layman, every instinct of offended dignity and of political solidarity dictated that they should close ranks behind their brother prelate.

The quarrel was directly related to the Plan of Campaign. During 1890 some deeply resented evictions had occurred within the bishop's diocese, but he, with peculiar insensitivity, chose that moment to renew his previous condemnations of boycotting and to prohibit the Plan in the area covered by his jurisdiction. Dillon thereupon denounced the bishop's decree as 'one of the most infamous, cowardly, dastardly letters ever penned by ecclesiastical hand'. Dr O'Dwyer replied in kind, but was unable to prevent Dillon flouting his authority by holding a mass-meeting – in effect a defence of boycotting – in the cathedral city of Limerick.[47]

To some of the bishops this defiance of Dr O'Dwyer represented a deliberate attempt by the overweening Irish party to assert themselves in contempt of the natural leaders of the country. The point was uncompromisingly made by Dr Gillooly, the conservative and outspoken Bishop of Elphin, in a letter written to Archbishop Walsh when Dillon's descent on Limerick was imminent. Reporting the view of various of his colleagues, he said that they all agreed that the meeting should either be prevented or else publicly condemned by the episcopal body. 'We regard it', Dr Gillooly declared, 'as the first act of a system of outrage and intimidation against the clergy who may dare to differ in opinion or action from the parliamentary party or self-constituted leaders thereof.' If this were not resisted 'incalculable evils' would result. Among these would be the strengthening of O'Dwyer's influence at Rome (the assumption was that nobody wanted that), the open condemnation of the political leaders by the Holy See, and their general ostracism by the clergy of Ireland and other countries. 'No bishop or priest can without self-compromise maintain friendly and confidential relations with such proud, misguided men or submit to their tyrannical dictation . . .'[48]

His views were echoed by an even more influential cleric, Michael Logue, who in 1887 had been translated from Raphoe to the archbishopric of Armagh. Logue's grievance was the old one – the indifferent, he thought contemptuous, attitude of the party when the estimates for the much-hated Queen's Colleges came up. 'My impression is', he wrote to Walsh, 'that they have fallen into the position of a mere tail to the Radical party in England; and any question that would displease that party they will not touch.' And he added bitterly:[49]

> They have climbed to their present influential positions on the shoulders of Irish priests and Irish bishops. It was the priests who worked up the registers for them, the priests who fought the elections, yes and it was the priests who contributed the sinews of war . . . They now think they are secure enough to kick away the ladder by which they mounted.
>
> I fear we are only in the beginning of the trouble. These gentlemen have now got the priests into their hands, and in a little while they will be able to attack the bishops, priests and the Pope himself with impunity.

It is against this background of growing distrust and disgust that the action of the bishops that autumn has to be seen. After a general meeting in October they issued a Pastoral Address to their clergy and to the laity which reiterated their warning of two years previously 'against the use of any hasty or irreverent language with reference to the Sovereign Pontiff, or to any of the Sacred Congregations through which he usually issues his Decrees to the faithful'.[50] In addition, Archbishop Logue was deputed to write to Parnell calling his attention to two matters about which resolutions had been passed and concerning which the bishops' disapproval would have been 'long since notified to their flocks', but for their anxiety to preserve nationalist unity and their expectation that there would have been spontaneous improvement without their interference:[51]

The matters to which the bishops presently request your attention are:

1. The independent action of individual members of the party in originating and sustaining movements involving the gravest consequences, political, social and moral, without the sanction of the party as such.

Manifestly this sanction should in all acts of importance be sought and obtained before priests and people are invited to give their co-operation.

The bishops feel that the time has come to declare that they cannot in future sanction the co-operation of their clergy in proceedings taken under individual responsibility.

2. The want of supervision, even in matters of gravest importance, over *United Ireland*. This paper is regarded as the organ of the national party, and for that reason the clergy who co-operate actively with the party, are, by many, held responsible for its editorial comments, even its vituperative attacks on individuals.

Although this reprimand was at bottom a direct attack on the Plan of Campaign, it is clear that Parnell's own failure to control his subordinates was simultaneously being rebuked. Later, when the party had split asunder, the rumour circulated that the bishops had also contemplated protesting against the election of Protestant members to the parliamentary ranks. Archbishop Walsh was able to assure Dillon that this was not so, but he made a comment which was revealing enough:[52]

I may add – but this is IN THE VERY STRICTEST CONFIDENCE, ONLY FOR YOU TWO [Dillon and O'Brien] that in the draft letter as proposed to us for consideration, there was a paragraph complaining that the original programme had been departed from in reference to the selection of members, and a request that the system of selection in conventions *on the lines laid down in the programme of 1885* should be maintained.*

Walsh himself had intervened to prevent this – mainly on the ground that it would be said that the bishops were objecting to some of the

*It is relevant to note that in the election of 1886 after the rejection of the Home Rule Bill, Parnell had, as a deliberate policy, tried to fill several seats with Protestant nationalists. (Parnell to Thomas Shillington (a Portadown businessman), 25 June 1886. I am indebted to Shillington's grandson, Mr James Shillington, for this reference.) Parnell wanted Thomas Shillington to take Captain O'Shea's place in Galway; not surprisingly, Shillington refused.

selections that had been made, 'which of course we did not'. But that did not prevent Dr Gillooly from returning to the charge a few days later. He was all for sending to Rome a copy of the letter to Parnell as finally agreed, and felt strongly that each bishop should stand ready to implement the declaration against the clergy co-operating in any public movement 'being undertaken on the individual responsibility of one or more members of the parliamentary party'. 'What does Your Grace think', he added, 'of conveying in due time to Mr Parnell that this resolution would include the selection of MPs by himself?'[53]

What His Grace thought is not recorded, though almost certainly he would have recoiled from any such crude frontal attack. What Parnell thought is not recorded either, since he never bothered to reply to the bishops' letter. By the time he received it, indeed, he was already deeply involved in the last of the three episodes which placed a strain upon his leadership in those months before the divorce suit threw everything else into the shade. This too was linked with the Plan of Campaign. It had been decided to hold a meeting of the parliamentary party in Dublin at the beginning of October to clarify the existing situation and to settle future policy. The natural assumption was that at such a critical conference Parnell himself would take the chair. Yet, when the time came, and despite his explicit promise to be there, he summoned his long-suffering vice-chairman, Justin McCarthy, to take his place. Of course, as McCarthy told his lady novelist friend, Mrs Praed, this had happened scores of times before. 'But just now the whole country . . . is waiting to hear what Parnell will say – and I shall have to get up and try to reconcile my own party to the fact that he is not going to say anything and to give the world no information as to why he is not there. My dear colleague, there are occasions when one's loyalty is tried and this is one of them.'[54]

Nevertheless, he went to Dublin as directed. The meeting passed off better than he had dared to hope. The allegiance of the party was apparently unshaken, and McCarthy was even able to declare without open ridicule that 'our great leader . . . is in entire and active co-operation with us in everything we do'. Resolutions were passed calling for the reinstatement of the evicted tenants, demanding the suspension of further evictions on the famine-threatened western seaboard, reprobating the government's vain attempt to prevent the departure of Dillon and O'Brien on their fund-raising mission to America, and commissioning T. P. O'Connor, T. D. Sullivan, Timothy Harrington and T. P. Gill to join them on their tour.[55]

All this was encouraging, but McCarthy returned from Dublin still revolving the question that had plagued him from the outset – why had Parnell kept away from the meeting? 'I know nothing as yet', he told Mrs Praed. 'It may be ill-health kept concealed – it may be some understanding with Hawarden – I do not know, but I am sure there must be some good reason – only, of course, the results are unfortunate, for the enemy are making enormous capital out of his absence from such a meeting – at such a time.'[56] The police were also pondering Parnell's non-appearance and they had evolved a theory which may have been close to the truth. In a secret report to the under-secretary, an officer of the G (detective) division of the Dublin Metropolitan Police, Superintendent William Reddy, relying, he said, upon an informant 'very closely connected with one of the MPs present at the convention', stated that Parnell would have attended had he not learnt that Dillon and O'Brien were planning to leave for America during the Tipperary trial and that this manœuvre was likely to be discussed at the meeting. Disapproving of the whole idea, the leader had stayed away. 'My informant states', added Reddy, 'that Mr Parnell is very much annoyed at the action of Dillon and O'Brien, and has declared to some members that he is unable to control either, especially William O'Brien.'[57]

This, no doubt, was only hearsay, but it was at least an interesting coincidence that it should have been on 9 October, only three days after the Dublin meeting, that Dillon and O'Brien broke bail and made their dramatic voyage to France.* If the superintendent's informant was correct, then that escapade, added to the other indications of stress we have been considering, points towards serious and unresolved differences between the leader and his principal lieutenants, differences mostly arising out of the all too familiar problem of how to run an agrarian agitation and a parliamentary movement in tandem. Yet, if the problem was all too familiar, Parnell's reaction to this latest phase of it could hardly have been more disturbing. It was essentially a negative reaction, almost the reaction of one who hoped that if he ignored the situation long enough, it would quietly go away. For this sublime indifference to the affairs of the party he was supposed to be leading there are several possible explanations. One was his continuing and mysterious ill-health which, though kept rigorously in the background, was most probably a continuance of his kidney disease. A second, beyond question, was his preoccupation with Katharine O'Shea, intensified as this was bound to be by the changed circumstances of 1890 and the interlocking divorce and probate suits. A third, less easy to identify, but

*See above, p. 439.

possibly the most important of all, may have been the feeling, to which his Hawarden visit can only have contributed, that a satisfactory settlement was so imminent that he could afford to ignore the trivial internal squabbles of his own party. Since such a settlement depended upon the Liberals, it was understandable that he should wish to pursue a policy which paid more attention to the needs of the alliance than to the actual situation at home. On this reasoning, the immediate objective of the party should therefore be less to topple the Tory government than to convince the British electorate that Home Rule was a sensible and moderate solution to the Irish question which would be a source of strength, not of weakness, to the empire. This necessarily implied a strong preference for sober platform oratory over irresponsible agrarian fireworks and that in turn reinforced his already deep antipathy to the Plan of Campaign and his firm intention never to become involved in it himself.

Yet, though this may have been a long-sighted view, it exacted a short-term penalty. Whether or not he actually admitted in so many words that he could not control Dillon and O'Brien is less important than the fact that in practice he had manifestly failed to do so. This had two important consequences. One was that it raised serious doubts about his ability to conduct business with the same authority as he had done in the past. The other was that his political inactivity accustomed the people to look to his lieutenants for the day-to-day leadership which the exigencies of the land question demanded. His increasing isolation from his natural power-base, the Irish constituencies, combined with his apparent lack of a forward policy in 1889–90, was raising up at home an 'alternative government'. That Parnell should have failed to realize this is not surprising. His personal prestige had been so great for so long that it was hard for him to believe that it was not only a limited but a wasting asset. It remained as true in 1890 as it had been when *The Times* attacked him in 1887 that any pressure from an external source was more likely – unless the circumstances were altogether exceptional – to unite the party around him than to split it into warring sections. Outwardly, then, the leader whom Morley interviewed in Brighton was neither a stricken nor a hunted man. He seemed, on the contrary, to be master of his own fate and arbiter of that of Ireland. How tragic that illusion, how precarious Parnell's position, how real the internal divisions of his party, events were now to demonstrate with shattering force.

V

The key, obviously, lay in the divorce proceedings. John Morley, discussing the impending trial with Dillon in September, had gathered from him that the country would close ranks behind Parnell provided 'there was no disclosure of nauseous details'.[58] Unhappily, the actual course taken by the trial made it virtually certain that 'nauseous details' would be disclosed without either the respondent or the co-respondent being able to rebut them or to give them the gloss which might have transformed them in the eyes of many. Because Parnell wanted to marry Katharine, and because it proved impossible to bully or bribe O'Shea either into dropping the case or allowing himself to be divorced by his wife, the trial had to go on in the form in which he had originally set it in motion. Since Parnell refused even to employ counsel, and Katharine's adviser, Frank Lockwood, held only a watching brief, Sir Edward Clarke had the field to himself. As his client had been made the target of damaging counter-charges, he was able to bring him into the witness-box and extract from him a tale of long-deceived innocence impressive enough to convince those who knew nothing either of the Captain or of his way of life. Worse still, Sir Edward was able to call supporting evidence which, in the absence of hostile questioning and of the interpretation which the other parties in the case would have put upon it, could scarcely have seemed more damning. Nothing, naturally, was said about O'Shea's possible connivance in a situation which had lasted so long as to make his gullibility almost incredible. Instead, there gradually unfolded a squalid tale of false names assumed by Parnell, of the renting of houses under these false names and of other ignoble shifts; such as his alleged resort to the notorious fire-escape at Medina Terrace.* This last allegation rested, as we know, on shaky foundations and could quite possibly have been destroyed in cross-examination. But since there was no cross-examination it was allowed to stand, and was to be used against Parnell with devastating effect in the months to come.[59]

In these circumstances the result was a foregone conclusion. Captain O'Shea got his decree *nisi* with the custody of all the children under the age of sixteen; the costs were to be paid by the co-respondent and by the respondent if it were to be found that she had a separate estate. Parnell, then, had the result he had wanted all along, but with one consequence which made him, in Lockwood's ominous phrase, 'so wild and peculiar

---

*For the fire-escape episode, see above, pp. 240-1.

in his manner as to show signs of madness'.[60] This was the loss of the two children, born in 1883 and 1884, who were unmistakably his. Even before the trial he had frantically sought advice as to whether there was any European country to which he could take them and their mother, and where he could keep them safely despite the order of an English court.[61] But it was not possible and this shadow hung over him and Katharine to the day of his death. Only in 1892, as part of the probate settlement, and under pressure from Katharine's doctors, did O'Shea agree to surrender the custody of the younger children (of the elder, Norah O'Shea had stayed with her mother and Gerard and Carmen with the Captain) but for the father of those younger children it was then too late.[62]

CHAPTER 16

Confrontation

'What price your friend Parnell now, eh? You wicked old man!!!'
(Anonymous postcard to Mr Gladstone, posted at Chester,
19 November 1890.)

I

Although Parnell had consistently regarded the divorce as his own affair, that it would have immense political consequences if events did not take the course he had so confidently predicted was something on which both his friends and his enemies had been reckoning ever since Captain O'Shea first filed his suit. Just what those consequences would be, however, was still utterly unknown when the verdict was given on 18 November. They would depend partly on Parnell himself, but also upon a whole complex of other forces – upon the Irish party, the Irish church and the Irish people, and no less upon the Liberal party, especially the non-conformist element within that party. From the collision and inter-mingling of these forces was to spring a confused and ultimately tragic situation, but it took time before this emerged, or before men could get their bearings in what rapidly turned before their eyes into a crisis of vast proportions.

The man who stood at the centre of the whirlwind seemed as out-wardly composed after the divorce as he had been before it. The papers which carried the first instalment of the proceedings at the trial carried also Parnell's customary letter to the members of his party summoning them to assemble on 25 November for their eve-of-session meeting, without the faintest suggestion that he might not be there to lead them.[1] The *Freeman's Journal* firmly took the line that it was the political future which mattered and that the vital decision about that future, whether Parnell was to remain at the head of the movement or not, was an Irish, not a British, one. On that point the *Freeman* was quite ex-plicit. There could be no 'swapping or changing of leaders'. 'We would not if we could. We could not if we would.'[2] The *Nation*, sometimes in the past more critical of Parnell, was likewise emphatic that it was the duty of every Irishman 'to rally to and confirm the leadership of Mr Parnell', while recording 'a feeling of sorrow at the sin of one whom the nation honoured, and of bitter disappointment that the high ideal to which the Irish people have always longed to see their public men conform is no longer the measure of its political leader's character'. But that the political leader would continue in that role there was no doubt:[3]

> Yes, Mr Parnell will still lead. We recognize his past services; we know he can serve us still in spite of this fall, which we all deplore, which we all condemn. We are mindful, too, that in standing out from his own class and taking his stand by the poor and down-trodden of his countrymen, he shut himself out from the pleasures and companionships of his old life. He forfeited them for the people; and he thus exposed himself to the plotters by whom he has fallen and increased their chances. We do not forget either that he has been attacked chiefly because of the work he has done for Ireland.

The muddled thinking of this paragraph well conveys the confusion into which the unexpected outcome of the divorce case had plunged most honest Irishmen. Here, jumbled up together, were loyalty, gratitude, shame and indignation, while the writer simultaneously sought to blame Parnell for his moral lapse, to reaffirm his leadership, and to explain the affair on the grounds – not flattering to either of the two lovers – that Parnell had only taken to the like of Mrs O'Shea because his devotion to Ireland had cut him off from 'the pleasures and companionships of his old life'.

But if the *Nation* blew with a somewhat uncertain trumpet, this was not true of Parnell's parliamentary colleagues. A meeting of the Central Branch of the Irish National League was quickly assembled in Dublin on 18 November. John Redmond presided and most of those who spoke were to reveal themselves presently as staunch Parnellites. At the time, though, there was no such thing as 'Parnellite' or 'anti-Parnellite' and the meeting emphatically endorsed Redmond's pledge of loyalty. 'I think it desirable', he said, 'that our friends in England should not be deceived in this matter, and should clearly understand that Mr Parnell today, just as yesterday, or the day before, commands the unswerving allegiance of the Irish race.'[4]

This meeting, which may to some extent have been a contrived affair, was soon dwarfed by a much larger and more important gathering at the Leinster Hall, Dublin, two days later. Although originally designed as a means of whipping up renewed financial support for the evicted tenants, it was attended by many members of the party and, naturally, it was dominated by the question of the leadership. Justin McCarthy, as vice-chairman, proposed a resolution of support for his chief and took the occasion to observe that so far as the divorce court revelations were concerned, appearances might be found to have been deceptive. Privately, it appears that he was despondent about the future and doubted if the party could survive the shock without some of the latent antagonisms within it coming to the surface, but his public resolution swept both the moral issue and his own anxieties aside, declaring that 'in all political matters Mr Parnell possesses the confidence of the Irish nation'; the meeting, his resolution further asserted, 'rejoices at the determination of the Irish parliamentary party to stand by their leader'.[5]

This resolution was passed unanimously for two main reasons. The first was the initial reaction to the crisis of the powerful fund-raising delegation which had just begun its operations in America. The role which the delegates were now called upon to play was both difficult and crucially important. It was difficult because, the storm having broken so soon after their arrival, their mission on behalf of the evicted tenants was eclipsed, while they themselves were besieged in their hotels by reporters eager for their views and deluged with letters from Irish-Americans, some vehemently for Parnell, others as vehemently against him. Their role was important chiefly because the leaders of the delegation, Dillon and O'Brien, were the two men who had virtually headed the movement during Parnell's long absence from the firing-line and their verdict was bound to carry great weight in Ireland. The verdict seemed to be, in the beginning unquestionably was, favourable to Parnell. Of the six members of the group only one, T. D. Sullivan, came out firmly against him on the ground that his moral offence precluded his continuance in the leadership. But Sullivan was perhaps a less influential figure than he once had been. His family paper, the *Nation*, had suffered from the competition of *United Ireland* and his own financial situation had seriously deteriorated.[6] The end result had been that in April 1890 he had had to sell the *Nation*.[7] No doubt it was his ardent Catholic background which mainly prompted him to repudiate Parnell (though other good Catholics felt no such compulsion) but the fact that he was both uncle and father-in-law to Tim Healy can scarcely have been irrelevant to his decision.

Initially, the delegation took its tone from John Dillon who had already committed himself, while the divorce trial was in mid-course, to the proposition that Parnell's retirement was impossible in the existing condition of affairs.[8] This was, perhaps, less than enthusiastic, but when the widely scattered delegates converged on Buffalo, they found a cable from John Redmond and Dr Kenny pressing for their overt support of Parnell. With little time to reflect and with even less firm news from home, all of them save Sullivan – that is, Dillon, O'Brien, T. P. O'Connor, T. Harrington and T. P. Gill – hastily concluded that a cable of confidence in their leader was what the occasion demanded. It was this cable which was read out at the Leinster Hall meeting with tremendous effect.[9]

There was a curious irony that it should have been Sullivan who refused to sign the cable, because the other factor which helped to sway the Leinster Hall meeting was the remarkable intervention of his relation, Tim Healy. In the weeks before the trial Healy had been seriously ill with typhoid and he had barely recovered when the crisis broke. Nevertheless, the short speech he managed to deliver at the meeting created an immediate sensation. Not merely did he second McCarthy's resolution of support for Parnell, he denounced as 'criminal' any move to surrender their leader at the first breath of criticism and ended his remarks with a warning to his audience which was to haunt him for many months – 'not to speak to the man at the wheel'. Since these sentiments had hardly been reflected in Healy's own conduct during and since the Galway election, it may seem strange that he should have come out so strongly for Parnell at this early stage. There are two possible explanations and one reservation about what he actually said. Of the two explanations, one is personal and the other political. On the personal level, those who judged Healy only by his irascible temper and his rasping tongue had missed an important aspect of his character, which was that he was a highly volatile human being who could respond generously or savagely according to circumstances. An intensely emotional occasion, as was the Leinster Hall meeting, was likely enough to bring out the chivalrous side of his nature. But, and this is the political explanation for his conduct, it seems that at that early stage he was prepared, like many others, to believe that an expression of loyalty to Parnell would make it *more* rather than *less* likely that he would retire. And here the reservation in his speech was important. Putting the hypothetical question – was the party guilty of servility in thus registering its support for Parnell, he fiercely answered: 'Servile to Mr Parnell! Who is servile to him? I am no man's man but Ireland's; and if I stand here tonight, as I gladly do, to second this resolution, I do so, not for the sake of Parnell as an individual, but for the sake of Ireland as a nation.' He then added a plain warning which indicated how conditional his promise of support really was:[10]

Let me however say this – that while we owe a duty to Mr Parnell, Mr Parnell owes a duty to us. We have stood by Mr Parnell: Mr Parnell must stand by us. He, too, as we have to consider our position, let him consider his, and as we are acting with sole thought to the interests of Ireland, so we may fairly demand that in every act and determination and resolution of his, he shall act with equal singleness of purpose.

So far, amid the chorus of support, and leaving aside Sullivan's negative but silent verdict, there had only been one Irish voice of importance raised against the leader. This was the voice of Michael Davitt, publicly expressed through the newspaper he was struggling to run at that time, the *Labour World*, and privately in what he said and wrote to those whose influence could be brought to bear on Parnell to enforce his retirement. Davitt, as we know, had been one of the first to receive Parnell's assurance that he would come stainless out of the divorce proceedings, though what Parnell really meant by this Davitt had scarcely been in a position to understand. When the case came on, seeming to disclose everything he had feared, or worse, he jumped at once to the conclusion that he had been deliberately deceived and his anger knew no bounds. This was ominous because his contacts with British radicalism, and especially with the leaders of working-class opinion, enabled him to grasp, more quickly perhaps than any other Irishman, the likely effect of the divorce upon the Liberal alliance. Yet even so, Davitt did not call for more than Parnell's temporary retirement. Writing to Archbishop Walsh before the outcome of the Leinster Hall meeting was known, Davitt explained that in that day's *Labour World* he was going to ask Parnell to note the tone of the British Home Rule press and to 'efface himself' for a few months. 'Now *why* cannot Parnell retire, for this session? Is he going to force himself and his paramour upon Ireland at the expense of Home Rule? . . . If he appears next Tuesday at the opening of parliament as the *newly elected* leader of the Irish people, goodbye for this generation to Home Rule, and God help Ireland.'[11]

That Davitt should turn at once to the archbishop was significant, but Walsh's reply was strikingly low-keyed. The case, he agreed, was deplorable and the crisis the worst that had yet arisen. Instead of grave deliberation, a particular course had been urged upon the country so vehemently (he was writing after the Leinster Hall meeting) that all who took a different view had either to stay silent or else risk causing a split in the ranks. 'We stand clear of the responsibility that has been so rashly undertaken by others. But I cannot think that the proceeding is

very encouraging to those who had grown hopeful of seeing built up a
united Irish nation.' As for himself, he said, he saw nothing for it but
'to stand by'. 'Of course, if I have to do that, I will do it simply *by
abstention* for the future.'[12]

Archbishop Walsh could hardly have seemed more dismissive if he
had called for a bowl of water and washed his hands in public. But, as so
often with him, appearance was not the true reality. The day before
Davitt wrote to him he had already been pressed by Dr Kenny, who
sought approval for what had been done so far and hoped also to secure
the archbishop's backing for the line to be adopted at the Leinster Hall
meeting the following day.[13] Dr Walsh, having both spoken and written
to Kenny on 19 November, made it clear that he would not attend that
meeting, emphasized the necessity to look after the evicted tenants, and
pointedly refrained from saying anything whatever about Parnell.[14]

A little later, just before Kenny was due to leave for the crucial eve-
of-session meeting of the party in London on 25 November, Archbishop Walsh saw him again, the Leinster Hall declaration of support
for Parnell having been passed in the interval. This time Dr Walsh
urged that Parnell should be pressed to retire, reiterating that the party
should concentrate on the desperate needs of the evicted tenants.
Kenny was not impressed. Later that day he wrote blandly assuming
that the archbishop still saw things as he did. 'It is a great comfort', he
wrote, 'to have Your Grace's support at such a time. I cross over tomorrow night for [the] party meeting, for no matter what course he
himself may determine to adopt for a time, we are determined to elect
him as chairman unanimously.'[15] This, so absolutely what the archbishop did not want to happen, provoked him next day to write Kenny
a letter, intended apparently to be shown to Parnell, in which once more
he urged that the party should strive to preserve its fragile unity by
making the evicted tenants the common ground on which they could
all hold together. This letter, which an exchange of telegrams between
the two men on 26 November established as not having been shown to
Parnell up to that date, ended with an unmistakable warning that the
leader should go:[16]

Anything beyond this, it is, I am satisfied, hopeless to look for unless
the leader by a bold manly act now adds one more to the many claims
he has established upon the country. The question now really is this,
whether we are to have things go on unchanged, or to have Home
Rule in our time. Both cannot be combined.

All that has been done by the members up to this is excellent. It puts an end for ever to the stories of disunion. But *above all*, it makes it easy for him now to do the right thing . . .

It is clear from these exchanges that the archbishop was exerting the utmost self-control. Having possibly the best political sense, as well as the keenest intellect, among all the Irish bishops, he realized from the start, as almost no other ecclesiastic did, how dangerous an open intervention by the church would be in a situation so fraught with emotion as this one had already become. He therefore turned a deaf ear – for the time being at least – to the admonitions which poured in upon him from all sides. Cardinal Manning, for example, saw the problem in terms remarkably simple for so subtle a mind. On 19 November he wrote twice to Walsh. On the first occasion he pledged his own silence, and urged that Parnell be replaced by a committee of the party. But in his second letter he recorded that the judgement of 'the most vital friends of Ireland' was that if the leadership remained unchanged 'the bishops, priests and people of Ireland will be seriously affected in the judgement of all English friends or the chief of them'. He was sure, also, he said of 'the judgement and feeling of Rome'. 'Apart from all this', he added revealingly, 'if ten years ago the bishops and priests had spoken and acted together, the movement would not have fallen into the hands of laymen. There is now both in Ireland and in Rome the opportunity of your regaining the lead and direction.'[17]

Dr Walsh, significantly, did not reply to these letters, but he passed the second of them to the Archbishop of Cashel, whose views most nearly coincided with his own. Dr Croke's reply was that while he did not agree with Manning that Parnell's retention of the leadership would mean ruin, it would do serious damage. Moreover, in view of the Leinster Hall meeting, the possibility of intervention was greatly reduced. 'Had silence been observed up to this, something might have been done to facilitate, or to bring about, a reasonable compromise, such as abstention from the House of Parnell for a month or so, or for all the present session. But now, really, I fear things must be allowed to take the direction given them by the Irish members – come what may. I see no practical way out of the difficulty. Davitt, though substantially right, was as usual precipitate.' At the same time, Croke made it clear that his own view of Parnell had fundamentally altered and that the crisis might yet be made the occasion for reasserting ecclesiastical authority over the party:[18]

I have flung him away from me for ever. His bust, which for some time has held a prominent place in my hall, I kicked out yesterday.

And as for the 'Party' generally, I go with you entirely in thinking that they make small, or no account of the bishops and priests now, as independent agents, and only value them as money gatherers and useful auxiliaries in the agitation. This I have noticed for a considerable time past; and I believe we shall have to let them see and feel, unmistakably, that without us, they would be simply nowhere and nobodies.

If this was the mood of the Archbishop of Cashel, the friend and protector of Dillon and O'Brien, the man regarded in many quarters – not least in Rome – as the most militantly nationalistic of all the Irish bishops, it was not surprising that the rank-and-file reaction should have been even stronger. At the outset, it is true, a hope still lingered that the whole nightmare might magically be dissolved as the nightmare of the Special Commission had been. Dr Woodlock, the Bishop of Ardagh, for example, had originally been convinced that the divorce would be as much a trumped-up affair as the Pigott letters, but when the sequel showed him wrong, his disillusionment flowed over. 'For my part', he wrote to Dr Walsh, 'I cannot but look forward with dismay to our interests, religious as well as civil, being placed under the guidance of a convicted adulterer. A man false to God and to friendship cannot be expected to be true to his country – and especially that country being Catholic Ireland.'[19] Dr Gillooly, the Bishop of Elphin, within two days of the divorce trial ending was clamouring for a special meeting of the Standing Committee. 'Our silence', he wrote to Dr Walsh, 'will be sure to be interpreted and quoted by the party leaders as an approval of the policy they have adopted. And should Parnell marry the adulteress, as is not unlikely, can we still condone the outrage to Catholic doctrine and morality by our silence?'[20] Nevertheless, Archbishop Walsh's view, which was to wait and see what happened at the party meeting, prevailed and that meeting duly took place on 25 November without any public pressure having been applied by the Irish hierarchy and with only Dr Walsh's letter to Dr Kenny of 24 November – which Kenny did not show to Parnell until at least a day after the meeting – as a private expression of their feelings and wishes.

II

But other kinds of pressure had already begun to be applied. The moment the divorce trial ended it became a main topic of newspaper comment in England. Parnell's traditional enemies in the Conservative press naturally had a field-day and *The Times* especially leaped in to pay off old scores and to try to drive its familiar wedge between the Irish and the Liberals.[21] What the Liberals themselves had to say was of course far more important than the thunders of Printing House Square. At first their newspapers spoke with a divided voice. Their chief organ, the *Daily News*, found itself, indeed, without a voice at all and remained silent for the whole of the first crucial week. *The Star* and the weekly *Speaker* initially took the view that the decision as to whether or not Parnell should continue to lead was primarily an Irish one, and in *Truth* Labouchere urged him to go on as if nothing had happened. In the provinces, the *Manchester Guardian* was against him being hounded out of public life, but the *Leeds Mercury* and the *Sheffield Independent* – both much read by nonconformists – came out strongly for his retirement.[22]

It was, however, the *Pall Mall Gazette* which was hottest on Parnell's trail. It was no longer edited by W. T. Stead, but the 'moral purity' stamp he had given it was firmly maintained by his successor, E. T. Cook, who at once struck the note to be heard so often in the months to come. Parnell's clear duty, he said, was to resign. 'Can any sane man believe that the Home Rule cause will benefit during the next six months by the hero of the many aliases being retained as one of the twin commanders-in-chief, or that the fire-escape will be the golden bridge to conduct the waverers back to the Liberal party?'[23]

Stead himself, as was to be expected from his previous involvement in the case, erupted violently. Already by 19 November he had seen Davitt, Cardinal Manning, the Baptist minister, Dr John Clifford, Reginald Brett and Lady Ripon. That same day he reported his findings to Gladstone and served notice that unless Parnell resigned the leadership he, Stead, would go 'most unwillingly' on the warpath against 'having this convicted liar and thorough-paced scoundrel foisted upon us by virtue of our Home Rule alliance'. 'This is not an affair of adultery', he continued, 'it is an affair of confidence and no one henceforth can ever have confidence in Mr Parnell.'[24] The same message went to Archbishop Walsh. 'The way in which he [Parnell] has deceived Davitt', Stead wrote, 'convinces me that he is capable of anything in the way of deception.' 'He has betrayed us', he repeated two days later, 'and trust can never be placed in him again.'[25]

The implication of this mounting pressure was that the Liberal leaders would shortly have to decide whether to intervene and if so, how. Once again, Stead was free with his advice. Writing to Gladstone on 20 November and enclosing a proof of an article attacking Parnell which he proposed to publish in the *Daily Chronicle* next day, he sounded an alarm bell which was to become a veritable tocsin in the days ahead. 'I know my Nonconformists well', he wrote, 'and no power on earth will induce them to follow that man to the poll, or you either, if you are arm in arm with him.'[26] In fact, the nonconformists had already begun to speak out on their own account. On 18 November a Baptist minister from Chatham, the Reverend T. Hancocks, wrote urging Gladstone that the cause and the man must be separated. 'Home Rule with Mr Parnell at the head of the Irish party is clearly impossible.'[27] And the next day a more eminent Baptist, Dr Clifford, published in *The Star* the letter which, perhaps above any other single utterance, served as a rallying-call to the free churchmen:[28]

> If the members of the Irish parliamentary party do not wish to alienate the sympathy of the radicals of England and Wales, and indefinitely postpone the victory of a policy based on justice and right, they must insist on Mr Parnell's immediate retirement. *He must go.* British politics are not what they were. The conscience of the nation is aroused. Men legally convicted of immorality will not be permitted to lead in the legislation [sic] of the kingdom.

Had the nonconformist reaction stopped there it would have confronted both Gladstone and the Irish party with a grave enough dilemma. But it did not stop there. On the contrary, in the person of the Methodist, Hugh Price Hughes, it injected into the controversy a note of hysterical racialism which may well have been one of the factors influencing the Leinster Hall meeting in Dublin to range itself as firmly behind Parnell as it did. Writing in the *Methodist Times*, Price Hughes took it for granted that Parnell must go, but he then added this extraordinary passage:[29]

> We do not hesitate to say that if the Irish race deliberately select as their recognized representative an adulterer of Mr Parnell's type they are as incapable of self-government as their bitterest enemies have asserted. So obscene a race as in those circumstances they would prove themselves to be would obviously be unfit for anything except a military despotism.

By Sunday, 23 November, when pulpits all over the country were pressed into service for the campaign, it was clear that every one of the free churches had come out strongly against Parnell. Two pronouncements on that day of rest attracted particular attention. The first was the famous 'one-minute sermon' of the Congregationalist, Dr Joseph

Parker, in which he denounced the 'madmen' who were urging Parnell to retain the leadership. Home Rule, he said, had never been a purely political question. 'We have talked of "justice" and "a union of hearts", but all this becomes infamous trash if the leaders obliterate moral distinctions.'[30] The other pronouncement, even more celebrated, was the address given by Hugh Price Hughes to a crowded audience at St James's Hall. Declaring vehemently that 'it would be an infamous thing for any Englishman to compel his chaste and virtuous Queen to receive as her first Irish prime minister an adulterer of this type', he prophesied woe for the Liberal party and the Irish cause for a generation if Parnell did not retire:[31]

> We love Ireland. We passionately desire her well-being, but our first obedience and our highest devotion must be to God. We have sacrificed much for Ireland. She is entitled to many sacrifices at our hands. But there is one thing we will never sacrifice, and that is our religion. We stand immovably on this eternal rock: what is morally wrong can never be politically right; and we are certain that any politician who is the acknowledged enemy of God and social purity can, under no circumstances, be the true friend and rightful leader of men.

Price Hughes ended his address with a triple appeal – to Parnell to retire; to Cardinal Manning to use his supposed influence with the Irish bishops; and to Gladstone to save the party and the cause from ruin. The first of these appeals fell, predictably, on deaf ears – indeed, it is quite on the cards that Parnell never heard of it. The second had already been anticipated by Manning, though as yet with no results. The third merely added to the torrent of letters and advice which Gladstone, still ensconced at Hawarden, received by every post. Among these were urgent demands for action from Cardinal Manning, from numerous nonconformist ministers and from important nonconformist laymen. Of these perhaps the most influential was 'the mustard man', J. J. Colman, who spoke no doubt for many nonconformist electors when he impressed upon Gladstone that 'if the Irish party generally takes the attitude many of them do, of insisting on his continuing as their leader', the effect would be that the electors would refuse to trust the Irish nation to Parnell and would regard those who upheld him as 'no more worthy of support than he is'.[32]

These pressures undoubtedly had a cumulative effect upon the Liberal leader. At the outset Gladstone's instinctive feeling had been that the divorce case would be fatal. He had been reassured by Morley's favourable account of his Brighton interview with the Irish leader, but he had hardly digested that before the divorce court 'revelations' had apparently cancelled it out. 'What could he mean by his language to you?' he asked Morley, adding with curious simplicity: 'The Pope has now clearly got a commandment under which to pull him up. It surely cannot have been always thus; for he represented his diocese in the church synod.'[33] But Morley still, at this stage, thought Parnell's chances of survival good. 'I am pretty sure', he replied, 'that the Irish will stomach it, tho' no priest will be able to go on to a platform with him for a long time to come. I daresay, the hateful thing will pretty quickly recede into the background, but what a perversion of character must have been worked by all that mean hiding, lying and the rest of it.'[34]

Speculation was an idle luxury. What was needed was action, since the annual meeting of the National Liberal Federation was due to be held at Sheffield on 19 and 20 November. Gladstone's first notion, to say nothing and do nothing, was not easily sustained, especially when Morley, who had with Harcourt to attend the Sheffield meeting, asked for guidance.[35] To him therefore Gladstone next day made the first of his oracular, though still private, pronouncements:[36]

I feel

1. That the Irish have abstractedly a right to decide the question;
2. that on account of Parnell's enormous services – he has done for Home Rule something like what Cobden did for Free Trade, set the argument on its legs – they are in a position of immense difficulty;
3. that we the Liberal party as a whole, and especially we its leaders, have for the moment nothing to say to it, that we must be passive, must wait and watch. But I again and again say to myself the words I have already quoted, say them, I mean, in the interior and silent forum. 'It'll na dee.'

Armed with this delphic utterance, Morley and Harcourt went off to Sheffield. Morley's normal tendency towards pessimism quickly reasserted itself. 'We are', he had written Harcourt before they joined forces, 'in about as bad a fix as Ministers were on the explosion of Pigott. Only the effects of the blow will be more lasting – as Pigott had at least the good sense to take himself off from this sublunary stage . . . Dillon told me when I was last in Ireland that the Irish would stand firm, unless any secrets of the alcove came out. No alcove without a fire-escape – I wonder whether the Irish will think this too strong a secret for the simple piety of their land.'[37] At Sheffield both were non-committal to the point of anaesthesia, but from the meeting a perceptible and predictable view emerged. One of the rank-and-file Liberals present there described it to Gladstone with bleak clarity. 'There are', he wrote, 'differences of opinion as to whether Mr Parnell's withdrawal should be permanent or temporary, and if temporary, for how long, and there are differences of opinion on the moral aspects of the case and some other points. But alike from members of parliament, candidates, chairmen of Liberal Associations, and political agents, there is an all but unanimous concensus [sic] of opinion that the practical result of his appearance at the present time as leader will have a disastrous effect on the by-elections in Great Britain.'[38]

Morley and Harcourt told the same tale. What impressed the former most was that it was 'not only the devout world' that was against Parnell, 'the secular caucus man was quite as strong'. 'The breach of moral law', he noted in his diary, '. . . was not all. It was accompanied by small incidents that lent themselves to ridicule and a sense of squalor. How could candidate or voter fight elections under a banner so peculiarly tainted?'[39] 'Some declare', he reported to Gladstone, 'that they would rather vote for a Tory, than for Home Rule under Parnell. Most, however, take the more moderate line that his installation as leader now would be a piece of bravado, and that he must at any rate subject himself to a period of quarantine.'[40] Harcourt, as usual, was more emphatic. The expression of opinion at Sheffield, he wrote, did not just represent 'screamers' like Stead, but was *'absolutely unanimous and extremely strong'* that for Parnell to remain as leader would mean the end of the Liberal–nationalist alliance. 'You know that the Nonconformists are the backbone of our party, and their judgement on this matter is unhesitating and decisive.' Since there was little hope that Parnell would voluntarily retire, it was essential that Gladstone himself should speak out on the subject without delay. 'Whether it means a severance from the Irish party I know not, but any other course will certainly involve the alienation of the greater and better portion of the Liberal party of Great Britain – which after all is that which we have mainly to consider.'[41]

This had the desired effect. 'My own opinion', Gladstone wrote to Arnold Morley, 'has been the same from the first, and I conceive that the time for action has now come.'[42] He decided therefore to move at once from Hawarden to London, and asked Arnold Morley to assemble Harcourt and John Morley to meet him when he arrived on Monday, 24 November. To Harcourt he suggested that Justin McCarthy be asked 'whether I am to expect any communication from Mr Parnell on the subject of the present situation'. He might be reminded of Parnell's offer of resignation immediately after the Phoenix Park murders, with the obvious implication that a similar approach would be welcome on this occasion. (It appears that in the privacy of his family circle Gladstone was expecting Parnell to resign not merely the leadership but his seat as well.)[43] If nothing came from the Irish leader, McCarthy should be informed that 'the last week had been spent in observing the evidences rife in every quarter of a profound movement of the public mind in Great Britain . . .' Then followed a declaration which, while carefully avoiding any judgement of the merits of the case, defined Gladstone's own position:[44]

> The effect of that observation corroborated by counsel with my friends, is to convince me that the continuance of Mr Parnell in the leadership of the Irish party at the present moment would be, notwithstanding his splendid services to his country, so to act upon British sentiment as to produce the gravest mischief to the cause of Ireland; to place those who represent the party in a position of irremediable difficulty; and to make the further maintenance of my own leadership for the purposes of that cause little better than a nullity.

So far from being persuaded by these ominous hints, Parnell was not even available to receive them. At the moment when the whole of British politics seemed to revolve round his future, he had withdrawn once more into impenetrable domesticity with Mrs O'Shea. John Morley, who had tried to trace his movements during the week after the divorce, was able to get no closer than a series of second-hand and unreliable accounts of what appeared to be the Irish leader's fluctuating mood. It was rumoured that whereas on the Wednesday (19 November, two days after the trial ended), he had been at his most inflexible, on the Friday he was more alive to the consequences of obduracy, not the least of which might be a snap election, a Tory victory, and the final eclipse of Gladstone's usefulness to the cause.[45] But that was all. He vanished from sight and nothing more was heard of him or from him.

However, on Sunday, 23 November – the day before Gladstone's arrival in London – Justin McCarthy received a visit from that bird of ill omen, Henry Labouchere. Labouchere said he had been sent by Morley and Harcourt. They thought Parnell should retire – would a letter from Gladstone have the desired effect? McCarthy was as vague as usual – had no idea where his leader was to be found, could offer only the address of the club to which Parnell's secretary, Henry Campbell, belonged. It seems, though, that he did express the view that the Irish party could not take the initiative in throwing over their chairman – if the initiative came from *him*, of course, 'that would be quite a different thing'.[46] The same night Morley tracked down Campbell and the latter undertook to deliver a message from Morley to the effect that he would 'almost certainly' have a communication to make to Parnell on Tuesday morning; the understanding was that Morley was to be informed by eleven o'clock on that day where he and Parnell should meet.[47]

III

Events now began to move rapidly. Next day, 24 November, Gladstone arrived in London to stay with Stuart Rendel in Carlton Gardens. He was in a state of barely suppressed excitement when Rendel met him at Euston with his carriage, for, as Rendel later recalled, 'No sooner was he in it than Mr Gladstone broke out, striking my knee with his hand. Parnell was now impossible! The party would not stand it! Overwhelming evidence had reached him! Parnell must go!'[48] Arrived at Carlton Gardens, he at once plunged into conference with Lord Granville, Harcourt and the two Morleys. Harcourt was for giving Parnell short shrift. He should be told to go *tout court* and Gladstone should tell him plainly that it was Parnell's immorality that had made him impossible. Gladstone strongly demurred. 'What', he cried, 'because a man is what is called leader of a party, does that constitute him a judge and accuser of faith and morals? I will not accept it. It would make life impossible.'[49]

At this point Justin McCarthy, who had been summoned to Carlton Gardens at Gladstone's behest, was announced. Gladstone went upstairs to speak to him alone and Morley's understanding was that the communication McCarthy would be asked to make to Parnell would be on the lines of Gladstone's letter to Harcourt already quoted.[50] But matters now began to go seriously wrong. McCarthy was greatly taken aback by what Gladstone had to tell him, so taken aback that he did not fully understand its import, as his account of the interview, written that same night, reveals:[51]

> He [Gladstone] spoke with chivalrous consideration of Parnell's 'splendid and unrivalled services to Ireland', but told me very sadly that his remaining in the leadership now means the loss of the next elections and the putting off of home rule until the time when he [Gladstone] will no longer be able to bear a hand in the great struggle to which he has devoted the later years of his life. He spoke with

intense feeling and earnestness. He said he would not write this to Parnell himself, because it might seem harsh and dictatorial and might hurt Irish feeling: but he authorized me to convey his views to Parnell when I see him. This will not be until tomorrow . . . I have written to Parnell asking him to decide nothing as to himself until he sees me in the house, and have sent the letter to the house on the off-chance of his going or sending there early tomorrow . . . I am much perturbed . . . all depends upon tomorrow.

When the shattered McCarthy had gone away Gladstone rejoined the group in the library downstairs and reported that while McCarthy (true to form) did not know where Parnell was, he hoped to see him next day and had undertaken to show him a short, pithy letter which Gladstone was to prepare. John Morley, describing this episode, gives the impression that when he and the other visitors left the house, Gladstone had already drafted the letter.[52] Perhaps he did so and perhaps, as he later assured Parnell's biographer, it was subsequently revised and completed, but a few days after the event, in a memorandum setting out how he had dealt with the situation, he carefully distinguished between what he *said* to McCarthy and what, in a letter to which we must turn in a moment, he *wrote* to John Morley. He wrote to Morley, he said, 'as a stronger measure than that taken through Mr McCarthy, because it was more full, and because, *as it was in writing* [my italics], it admitted of the ulterior step of immediate publication.'[53] It would therefore seem, despite the long and involved controversy which soon developed over this episode, that Gladstone, in his dealings with McCarthy, relied upon the spoken rather than the written word.* If so, it was an unwise decision, for whenever the latter subsequently tried to recall what had happened, he seemed always to get it wrong. In November 1891, for example, when the affair was beginning to pass into history, he wrote to the press maintaining that he had passed on to Parnell what Gladstone had told him – that Parnell's retention of the leadership would mean the loss of the election – but immediately proceeded to spoil the effect of this impressive evidence by confessing that he had not understood that Gladstone contemplated retiring from the Liberal leadership if Parnell remained at the head of *his* party.[54] And a few years later, when tempers had cooled and recollections dimmed, he went so far as to tell Barry

*On no less than three occasions in the ensuing months Parnell asserted that McCarthy *had* got a letter from Gladstone, but each time the vice-chairman managed to avoid saying definitely whether he had or not. (F. S. L. Lyons, *The fall of Parnell*, p. 87.)

O'Brien not only that Gladstone had not asked for Parnell's resignation – which, in the sense that he had not done so directly, may have been true – but that he had not asked him, McCarthy, to convey anything to Parnell, which was manifestly wrong.[55]

The controversy is important chiefly because it helps to establish the unreliability of McCarthy as an intermediary between the Liberals and his chief. But the Liberals wisely did not depend upon him as their sole channel. Before the meeting at Carlton Gardens broke up it was decided that Gladstone should write a letter to John Morley (if Gladstone did not continue his intended letter to McCarthy, this decision probably explains why), and that Morley should show it to Parnell when, as he expected, he met the Irish leader next morning. When they assembled again a few hours later for an eve-of-session dinner, Gladstone handed Morley his draft letter. Morley saw immediately that Gladstone had omitted the all-essential point – that if Parnell remained at the head of the Irish party, then Gladstone's leadership of the Liberals would become 'almost a nullity'. Gladstone, though afterwards admitting that he thought this was to have been a postscript ('what a postscript to be sure!' is Morley's comment) agreed then and there to insert the all-important passage into the body of the letter which in its final form closely resembled the letter Gladstone had written Harcourt on 23 November.* This was very much a personal transaction between Gladstone and Morley and nobody else in the room saw it or was consulted about it save Harcourt, who thought it should have been addressed directly to Parnell, thus completely missing the point of Gladstone's subtlety in *refraining* from seeming to point his pistol straight at his ally's head. Interestingly enough, in that whole gathering of ex-ministers the only man who doubted the rightness of putting the screw on Parnell was the man who had perhaps suffered most from him in bygone days, Earl Spencer.[56] The essence of this historic letter was as follows:[57]

While clinging to the hope of a communication from Mr Parnell, to whomsoever addressed, I thought it necessary, viewing the arrangements for the commencement of the session tomorrow, to acquaint Mr McCarthy with the conclusion at which, after using all the means of observation and reflection in my power, I had myself arrived. It was that notwithstanding the splendid services rendered by Mr Parnell to his country, his continuance at the present moment in the

*See above, p. 491.

leadership would be productive of consequences disastrous in the highest degree to the cause of Ireland. I think I may be warranted in asking you so far to expand the conclusion I have given above, as to add that the continuance I speak of would not only place many hearty and effective friends of the Irish cause in a position of great embarrassment, but would render my retention of the leadership of the liberal party, based as it has been mainly upon the prosecution of the Irish cause, almost a nullity. This explanation of my views I begged Mr McCarthy to regard as confidential, and not intended for his colleagues generally, if he found that Mr Parnell contemplated spontaneous action; but I also begged that he would make known to the Irish party, at their meeting tomorrow afternoon, that such was my conclusion, if he should find that Mr Parnell had not in contemplation any step of the nature indicated. I now write to you, in case Mr McCarthy should be unable to communicate with Mr Parnell, as I understand you may possibly have an opening tomorrow through another channel. Should you have such an opening, I beg you to make known to Mr Parnell the conclusion itself, which I have stated in the earlier part of this letter . . .

Everything now depended upon one or both of Gladstone's emissaries making contact with Parnell on Tuesday, 25 November, before the meeting of the Irish parliamentary party. The day began badly when at about 11.45 a.m. Morley received a telegram from Henry Campbell saying he had been unable to find his chief. Morley at once jumped to the conclusion that Parnell was deliberately keeping out of reach and that this meant there was going to be a fight. In that assumption he was probably correct. There is no firm foundation for Tim Healy's statement that Henry Campbell had boasted to one of his colleagues that he had prevented Morley from conveying Gladstone's letter to Parnell; given the latter's talent for inaccessibility, he hardly needed Campbell's help.[58] Still further from the truth was another rumour current at the time – that Mrs O'Shea had got hold of and destroyed the communication before Parnell could see it. This could not have happened, since the letter never reached Brighton, being in Morley's possession all the time.[59]

But it was still possible for Parnell to be intercepted before the meeting of the Irish party began. No specific time of assembly had been announced, but so far from the hour being 'accelerated' (as Morley wrongly asserted later), the proceedings did not begin until 2.45 p.m., three-quarters of an hour later than usual.[60] While members gathered upstairs for their meeting, McCarthy waited for Parnell below. When the latter at last arrived, he was as calm and cool as ever. Asked by Alfred Robbins what was likely to happen, he merely said, 'Wait for the meeting'.[61] According to Stuart Rendel, who had it from McCarthy himself 'shortly afterwards', McCarthy, knowing Parnell's habit of collecting his mail at the House of Commons Post Office, lay in wait for his quarry there. At the last moment in walked Parnell, took his bundle of letters and rapidly walked out again through the lobby and the galleries and up the staircase to the committee-room, opening letters as he went. McCarthy trotted beside him all the way, trying, and apparently failing, to capture his attention.[62]

There remains, however, an element of confusion about this encounter, arising principally from McCarthy's incorrigible vagueness. From a note which John Morley made in his diary under this day's date, it appears that he, Morley, having failed to make contact with Parnell, went to Carlton Gardens after lunch, where he found Gladstone 'eager and agitated', having just heard from Arnold Morley that McCarthy had been to him (Arnold Morley) a little after two o'clock to report that Parnell 'meant to stand to his guns'. If this is correct, and being closer in time to the events it describes, it has a better chance of being correct than McCarthy's later account to Rendel, then it is probable that McCarthy was rather longer in Parnell's company than he subsequently admitted. But if *that* is correct, then his failure to convey Gladstone's message to Parnell, and his own conduct once the meeting had begun, can perhaps best be explained in terms of an abject failure of nerve. At all events, it seems clear that Parnell entered the room as the meeting was about to begin without having received any communication, direct or indirect, from Gladstone other than McCarthy's hurried, and possibly garbled, report.[63] Thus, it was open to him to claim later, as he did not hesitate to do, that if Gladstone had conveyed to him 'by hint, whisper or innuendo' that his leadership was undesirable, he would have sought the advice of his colleagues.[64]

What happened next is briefly described in the party minutes. The chair was taken initially by the Chief Whip, Richard Power, and as soon as the meeting began, Thomas Sexton moved and Colonel Nolan seconded, that Parnell be re-elected chairman for the coming session. This was passed with acclamation and Parnell, having reassumed the chair, thanked the party for its confidence in him and then spoke briefly about the divorce court proceedings. To anyone familiar with the O'Shea *ménage* his few elliptical remarks would have made excellent sense, but to his unenlightened audience they can only have increased the mystery surrounding the whole affair. Here is the official report of his speech:[65]

> He asked his friends and colleagues to keep their lips sealed as his were on this subject until the time came when he could speak freely on the topic. When that time came they would find their confidence in him was not misplaced. He would not further allude to the matter beyond once more asking them to keep their lips closed in reference to that topic.

The very sparseness of this account is suspect. Not even Parnell could have been so sublimely indifferent to the movement of opinion as to ignore the intense pressures under which the members of his party had been since the divorce. True, Ireland seemed to have spoken for the chief, and the bishops had not publicly condemned him, but the outpourings of the Liberal and nonconformist press must have shown them that to re-elect Parnell would precipitate a crisis. That very morning the Liberal *Daily News* had carried the warning that Parnell 'ought to know that for thousands of his English supporters there are higher considerations than party politics, and that neither for him nor for any man will they condone a distinct violation of the moral law'. 'Having made careful enquiries from the best sources of information, we are enabled to tell Mr Parnell that if he continues to lead the Irish party, Home Rule cannot be carried.'[66] For the party to re-elect its leader in the face of such admonitions was an act of faith and loyalty which demanded an equivalent return.

It seems in fact that he did say rather more than was recorded in the minutes and also that the meeting did not run quite as smoothly as the official account indicated. Later that day, Donal Sullivan, the brother of T. D. Sullivan, wrote an account of the proceedings to his nephew, Tim Healy, who was still not well enough to leave Dublin. Sullivan said that after the motion to re-elect Parnell had been put to the meeting, Jeremiah Jordan (a northern Protestant and, ironically enough, Captain O'Shea's successor as a member for Clare) appealed to Parnell to retire, if only for one month. 'He did his work creditably and *most feelingly*. It was received in silence.' Sullivan's account continues:[67]

> Then Parnell rose amidst cheers and cheers again . . . He made a *long speech*, delivered coldly, calmly and bloodlessly. His strongest points were (1) That his lips were sealed – for some time. He asked his colleagues to seal theirs! (2) He *never* called O'Shea his friend! (3) He never drank a glass of wine at O'Shea's expense, nor accepted any

hospitality from him. O'Shea never paid a sixpence for any compliment ever paid to him. (4) He asked his 'friends around' to continue their confidence in him till the 'fight he and his dead friend, Joseph Biggar* commenced, was won'. (5) When they began it – only the two of them – they had to fight and did fight, not alone with the Tories, but the Whigs, the Liberals and the Radicals. (6) Was he today with 85 trusted friends at his back to surrender? NO – the position of esteem and confidence which his countrymen placed him in he would not surrender for any section or party, and so he would remain to assist them and to guide them to their *final* victory.

Since Sullivan was a professional journalist and made notes while Parnell was speaking, this is as accurate a record as we are likely to get. It is a further indication of its reliability that although it comes from a source decidedly hostile to Parnell, it was not questioned even by that enthusiastic Parnellite, Henry Harrison, who was present; indeed, Harrison himself confirmed that Parnell had described O'Shea as his 'bitter and unrelenting enemy'.[68] Two things further emerge from Sullivan's account, one positive, the other negative. The first is that many of those present (including Sullivan himself), while listening to a tirade designed to prove what they all knew anyway – that Parnell and O'Shea had not exactly been bosom friends – believed that Parnell would end his speech by gracefully resigning. 'We all expected it', wrote Sullivan, and while that was certainly an exaggeration, a number of members did genuinely believe that despite, or rather *because of*, the English attacks made on him in the past week, their duty was to re-elect him so as to make it easier for him to resign. In this belief it is possible, as Sullivan later suggested, that some of them were sustained by a statement in that morning's *Standard*, and said to have been inspired by J. M. Tuohy, the much respected London correspondent of the *Freeman's Journal*, that Parnell would retire if elected.[69] But the assumption that if they did their duty by electing him, Parnell would do his by resigning, reflected more credit on their hearts than on their heads and indicated how little they really knew their man.

The second, and negative, fact which Sullivan's account reveals is that McCarthy remained silent throughout and this although the whole purport of his interview with Gladstone the previous day had been to avert what the hapless vice-chairman now saw coming to pass under his very eyes. After the damage was done McCarthy told his friends that

*Joseph Biggar had died in February 1890.

he had informed Parnell beforehand that there was a communication from Gladstone, and had himself therefore assumed that Parnell would retire after re-election.[70] But this was an assumption he had no right to make and it seems that he failed dismally in his duty by not ensuring that the party was in possession of all the available information before coming to its crucial decision.

The outcome was that the meeting, having re-elected Parnell, broke up without having heard any official word of the Liberal point of view. But there remained Gladstone's letter to Morley, which had still to be laid before Parnell. Morley came upon him just after the Irish meeting had broken up (it had only lasted for about an hour) and Parnell greeted him, Morley noted in his diary, 'with much cordiality'. His account continues:[71]

'I am very sorry,' he said, 'that I could not make an appointment, but the truth is I did not get your message until I came down to the House, and then it was too late.' I asked him to come round with me to Mr Gladstone's room. As we went along the corridor he informed me in a casual way that the party had again elected him chairman. When we reached the sunless little room, I told him I was sorry to hear the election was over, for I had a communication to make to him which might, as I hoped, still make a difference. I then read out to him Gladstone's letter. As he listened, I knew the look on his face quite well enough to see that he was obdurate.

The conversation that followed was brief and unhelpful. Parnell brushed the whole affair aside as a storm in a teacup. Morley replied that 'he might know Ireland, but he did not half know England'. The storm was a real storm and it would not pass if he did not withdraw for a time; after all, Morley added waspishly, Parnell had virtually been absent from the leadership for two years already. But Parnell was immovable:[72]

He answered, in his slow dry way, that he must look to the future; that he had made up his mind to stick to the House of Commons and to his present position in his party, until he was convinced, and he would not soon be convinced, that it was impossible to obtain Home Rule from a British parliament; that if he gave up the leadership for a time, he should never return to it; that if he once let go, it was all over. There was the usual iteration on both sides, in a conversation of the kind, but this is the substance of what passed. His manner throughout was perfectly cool and quiet, and his unresonant voice was unshaken.

He was paler than usual, and now and then a wintry smile passed over his face. I saw that nothing would be gained by further parley, so I rose and he somewhat slowly did the same. 'Of course', he said, as I held the door open for him to leave, 'Mr Gladstone will have to attack me. I shall expect that. He will have a right to do that.' So we parted.

I waited for Mr Gladstone, who arrived in a few minutes . . . I told him shortly what had passed. He stood at the table, dumb for some instants, looking at me as if he could not believe what I had said. Then he burst out that we must at once publish his letter to me; at once, that very afternoon. I said, ''Tis too late now.' 'Oh, no', said he, 'the *Pall Mall* will bring it out in a special edition.' 'Well, but', I persisted, 'we ought really to consider it a little.' Reluctantly he yielded, and we went into the House. Harcourt presently joined us on the bench, and we told him the news. It was by and by decided that the letter should be immediately published. Mr Gladstone thought that I should at once inform Mr Parnell of this. There he was at that moment, pleasant and smiling, in his usual place on the Irish bench. I went into our lobby, and sent somebody to bring him out . . . I told him that it was thought right, under the new circumstances, to send the letter to the press. 'Yes', he said amicably, as if it were no particular concern of his, 'I think Mr Gladstone will be quite right to do that; it will put him straight with his party.'

From this vital decision, rather than from the initial action of the Irish party in re-electing Parnell, came the real impetus to disaster. Gladstone's action, though a natural one for a leader who wished to preserve his own position, and understandable in the light of the severe pressure upon him during the previous week to speak out, had two dire effects. First, it faced the Irish party, and Irishmen in general, with a choice between Parnell and Home Rule – in effect a choice between the Liberal alliance and the man who since 1886 had made that alliance the cornerstone of his policy. And second, because the letter had been published, it was no longer possible to exert a discreet and diplomatic pressure behind the scenes. Everything thereafter would have to be acted out in the full glare of publicity. Gladstone's action was extraordinarily precipitate and his justification for this in a note made three days later, seems totally inadequate. He explained that he had previously (24 November) asked McCarthy to acquaint the Irish leader with his views, 'and I begged that my message to Mr Parnell might be made known to the Irish party, in the absence of a spontaneous retirement'. Then had come the meeting on Tuesday afternoon. 'When we found that Mr

McCarthy's representation had had no effect, that the Irish party had not been informed, and that Mr Morley's making known the material parts of my letter was likewise without result, it at once was decided to publish the letter; just too late for the *Pall Mall Gazette*, it was given for publication to the morning papers, and during the evening it became known in the lobbies of the House.'[73]

This disposes of Healy's claim that Gladstone was under the impression that his letter *had* been read to the party when he decided to publish it.[74] Had this been so, his hasty reaction would have been comprehensible, but since he specifically stated that 'the Irish party was not consulted', he deprived his own precipitancy of even that excuse. It seems, incidentally, that he moved with such speed that the letter did reach a late edition of the *Pall Mall Gazette* after all, which was where most of the Irish members learned of it for the first time.[75] By thus publishing the document Gladstone no doubt placated the nonconformists and secured his own position, but by denying to his Irish allies the right to decide *in private* what weight to attach to it he placed them in a cruel dilemma. On the one hand, if Home Rule was the *raison d'être* of their party, and if Gladstone alone could deliver that, the case was strong for sacrificing Parnell. On the other hand, to sacrifice him after the public *fiat* of the Liberal leader would be to appear before their countrymen in an abject light. Either way, national pride was sure to be deeply involved, with incalculable consequences for the future relations of the two countries.

IV

The immediate impact upon the Irish party was, naturally, shattering. Some were for reassembling that night and an informal meeting did take place, but as Parnell ignored it no action resulted. However, over thirty signatures were collected for a requisition demanding a proper meeting next day at two o'clock. On that occasion John Barry moved 'that a full meeting of the party be held on Friday to give Mr Parnell an opportunity of reconsidering his position'. After this had been seconded, Parnell rose to speak. He was brief but adamant. The party had re-elected him and it was for the party to take the responsibility if it wished to reverse its verdict. Numerous speeches followed on predictable lines. The Liberal alliance was essential to Home Rule and to the evicted tenants, said some. Liberal dictation was intolerable, said others. After an inconclusive debate it was decided to adjourn until the following Monday, 1 December; in the interval an agreed cable would be sent to the delegates in America to elicit their views. It had not been an easy meeting, for it had disclosed the fissures that already threatened to crack the party into fragments. Outwardly, Parnell had seemed as much in command as ever; so much so that, as Sexton remarked, if any intelligent foreigner had entered the room he would have imagined it was the party who were being tried for adultery with Parnell as the judge.[76] But he was too perceptive not to sense that the opposition was becoming formidable and that night at Brighton, Katharine later recalled, he took her into his arms saying, 'I think we shall have to fight, Queenie. Can you bear it? I'm afraid it's going to be tough work.'[77]

The fact that the adjournment lasted for five days had an important bearing on the rapid transformation that now set in. Men had to decide where they stood and on each side the reinforcements began to gather. For Parnell's supporters the *Freeman's Journal* already pointed the way. Ireland, it proclaimed, had 'with one voice' declared that Parnell should continue to lead her and she must not sacrifice him at the behest of Gladstone, whose letter had 'violated the principle of independent opposition – the hinge on which the Irish party turns'.[78] But the opposition was powerfully strengthened by T. M. Healy, who came over from Dublin on 27 November and, learning that Parnell was contemplating a manifesto 'to crush both ourselves and the Gladstonians', pressed for a party meeting to condemn the issue of any declaration intended to overawe or influence the party's debate on the coming Monday. Such a meeting was actually held on 28 November, but since Parnell stayed away it could achieve nothing and therefore, as the minutes record, 'fell through'.[79] Parnell himself was already at work upon his counterstroke, the manifesto which Healy's meeting had been expressly designed to foil.

He had begun to prepare it directly he had got back to Brighton from the meeting on Wednesday, 26 November, when it had first become plain to him that he had a fight on his hands. From the moment he sat down to write it, Katharine noticed, he was totally absorbed. While he worked she wondered what she should do. Should she urge him to come away and leave all the turmoil behind him? That he would do this if she wished it, she had no doubt. 'But then I knew that he would not forget that he would come at my bidding, but that his desertion of Ireland would lie at his heart; that if he was to be happy he must fight to the end . . . even if it killed him I must let him fight . . . it was himself – the great self that I loved, and that I would not spoil even through my love, though it might bring the end in death.'[80]

CHAPTER 17

Breaking-Point

'As well ask famishing wretches on a raft at sea to bear themselves with calmness and act with forbearance, when they see certain relief disappear, through their own differences as to the conduct of their captain.' (Unpublished 'Autobiography' of Alfred Webb, MP, p. 463.)

I

Before Parnell launched his thunderbolt Justin McCarthy made a last effort to avert the gathering storm. On Thursday, 27 November, he persuaded his chief to hold back the manifesto until he, McCarthy, had had another interview with Gladstone. What passed between them was never made public, but from a note Gladstone made at the time, it appears that they touched on the details of the next Home Rule bill, with special reference to the future of the Irish members at Westminster. 'My disposition', Gladstone wrote, 'is to settle it in such a particular shape as shall best conduce to the effectual and satisfactory settlement of the general question; and I should allow no predilection of my own as to details to interfere with this broad principle.'[1]

This was Gladstone at his most delphic and even McCarthy doubted whether it would make much difference to Parnell.[2] In reality, it made none and when on Friday night the vice-chairman was summoned to hear his leader read out the document to a few, mainly 'Parnellite', members of the party before sending it to the press, he realized that an outright clash could no longer be avoided.[3] The manifesto – 'To the People of Ireland' – fell into four main sections. The first was a strong attack on Gladstone for attempting to influence the Irish party in their choice of leader and a no less strong indictment of those members who had already shown signs of yielding to this pressure. 'The independence and integrity of a section of the Irish party having apparently been sapped and destroyed by the wire-pulling of the English Liberal party', the manifesto ominously began, 'it has become necessary for me as the leader of the Irish nation to take counsel with you . . .'* Gladstone's letter to Morley, Parnell argued, amounted to a claim that the Liberal party should have a virtual veto over the choice of an Irish leader. The threat that unless the veto were conceded Home Rule would be postponed, 'repeated so insolently on many English public platforms and in numerous British newspapers', compelled him, he said, to release certain information which would enable his readers truly to assess the loss with which they were menaced 'unless you consent to throw me to the English wolves now howling for my destruction'.

There was nothing new in this emphasis on the need for the Irish party to preserve its independence. Parnell had said fundamentally the same thing at every stage of his career. But he had seldom said it so abrasively and never in circumstances where his own abrasiveness was so certain to be turned back upon him by indignant English readers. Unhappily, there was worse to come. In the second section of the manifesto he gave what purported to be details of the Home Rule settlement that the Liberals proposed to bring in if they won the next election; allegedly, these were presented in the form in which Gladstone had imparted them to Parnell at Hawarden the previous December. The four principal points which the manifesto singled out may be summarized as follows:

1. Parnell claimed that Gladstone and the Liberals were determined to retain the Irish members at Westminster, but to reduce their numbers from 103 to 32.
2. Gladstone was next represented as having said that he would try to persuade the Liberals to attempt to solve the land question on the same lines as in 1886, but that he would put no pressure on them to do so.
3. Control of the Irish constabulary, Parnell asserted, was to remain under imperial authority for an indefinite period, though the funds for maintaining, paying and equipping this semi-military police would be compulsorily provided from Irish sources.
4. Finally, he alleged, Gladstone had suggested that the right of appointing the judiciary (from supreme court judges down to resident magistrates) should be retained in the hands of the imperial authority for ten or twelve years.

These points were all highly controversial. The third and fourth, for example, were particularly sensitive matters in Ireland where both the

---

*The full text, reproduced from *F.J.* 29 November 1890, is in F. S. L. Lyons, *The fall of Parnell*, pp. 320–6.

police and the judiciary were popularly regarded as instruments of
British rule; in Britain, by contrast, they were seen as bulwarks of law
and order and a necessary protection for Irish Unionists when Home
Rule began to operate. As for the land question, it was not only, next to
Home Rule, the major issue between the two countries, but it was also
a highly contentious issue inside the Liberal party, which had by no
means reconciled itself to a large purchase scheme as an integral part of
an Irish settlement. Finally, the question whether or not to retain the
Irish members was one on which Gladstone and his colleagues were still
undecided. But, said Parnell in the manifesto, so long as the land, the
police and the judiciary were outside Irish control, it would be essential
to retain *full* Irish representation at Westminster where these important
matters would be decided. At Hawarden, and in order to conciliate
English opinion, he had agreed, or so he said, to the withholding from
the Irish parliament of full control over the police and the judiciary,
while protesting against the failure to provide 'any suitable prospect of
land settlement'. Despite this, he had been told that, pending the
general election, 'silence should be absolutely preserved with regard to
any points of difference on the question of the retention of the Irish
members'.

Much controversy was to envelope this rendering of the Hawarden
interview. Scarcely less controversial, though of relatively minor
significance, were Parnell's two last sections. In the first of these he
attempted to fasten on the Liberals, and especially on John Morley, the
responsibility for his, Parnell's, attack on Balfour's land bill the previous
session. This seemed merely a gratuitous attack on Morley, but in
reality it was a tactical manœuvre, enabling Parnell to switch sides and
support the measure which was about to be reintroduced. The bill, after
all, did offer real advantages to the tenants, and it would be convenient,
to say the least, if in the weeks ahead he were to be able to identify
himself with a reform which made available some £33 millions of public
money for loans in aid of purchase, while his opponents were still
toeing the Liberal line of sterile negation.

Morley was also Parnell's target in his closing paragraphs which gave
an account of the Brighton interview very different from that which
Morley had already passed on to Gladstone. What had been a casual
discussion about the Chief Secretaryship and the possibility of finding a
seat for an Irish law officer at the next election, now blossomed out as 'a
remarkable proposal', not merely that Parnell himself or one of his
colleagues should become Chief Secretary, but also that it would be
desirable to fill one of the Irish law offices by 'a legal member of my

party'. This ingenious formulation allowed Parnell both to point a finger at Healy (obviously recognizable as the 'legal member'), and also to demonstrate the principle of independent opposition in action. 'I told him', he wrote, 'amazed as I was at the proposal, that I could not agree to forfeit in any way the independence of the party or of any of its members.' Not content with thus maligning Morley, Parnell also sought to turn the tables on him in regard to the evicted tenants. In their Brighton talk, as Morley had noted, Parnell's view had been that if the Tories lost the election, the landlords would surrender at discretion and the problem would solve itself – a view which Morley himself had thought far too optimistic.[4] But in the manifesto Morley was made to say that when the Liberals came back to office it would be impossible for them to do anything for the evicted tenants by direct action, and that it would be outside the power of an Irish parliament to help them either. The purpose of this allegation was probably less to make a liar of Morley than to help Parnell to combat the argument, already audible in some quarters, that the evicted tenants would suffer unless the Liberals came in, which they might not do if Parnell were not sacrificed. On the contrary, Parnell now asserted, the evicted tenants must look to him for succour, since they could expect nothing from the Liberals; he omitted to mention, naturally, that they had had little enough from him by way of succour during the four preceding years.

As a final flourish, he restated once more a familiar theme. The Irish party, he claimed, had been independent of all other parties during the entire period of his leadership and the winning of Home Rule would depend upon their remaining independent in the future. Independence, he insisted, was far more vital than victory here and now. 'I believe that the Irish people throughout the world would agree with me that postponement would be preferable to a compromise of our national rights by the acceptance of a measure which would not realize the aspirations of our race.'

So ended this extraordinary document – perhaps the longest he ever wrote and certainly the strangest. Because it had the immediate effect of intensifying the opposition to him in both Britain and Ireland, the manifesto has generally been seen by historians as one of Parnell's gravest miscalculations. No doubt, if the yardstick to be used is the grouping of forces on either side of the great divide, there is much to be said for this view and incontestably it swung against him some who in other circumstances might have remained sympathetic. It was, as nearly everyone agreed, highly unlikely that either Gladstone or Morley had actually said what they were represented to have said. But even supposing the manifesto to have been an exact record of every-thing that had occurred at the Brighton and Hawarden interviews, it was still open to serious objection on several grounds. First, these com-munications with the Liberal leaders had been confidential, and to break that confidentiality in such a peculiarly gross way was to forfeit all claims to future trust. Second, if the terms offered were as Parnell stated them in the manifesto, they were totally inadequate and should not have been entertained for a moment by a responsible Irish leader. Third, so far from rejecting what Gladstone had allegedly said at Hawarden, Parnell had gone out of his way at Liverpool immediately afterwards to express his entire satisfaction both publicly and privately. He therefore stood convicted, if not of falsehood, at least of extreme disingenuousness, either in his remarks at Liverpool or in his manifesto, or possibly in both. And finally, whether the Liberal proposals (if proposals they were) were good or bad, why did he keep them to himself and not share them with his colleagues?

All these criticisms, and more, were to be made many times over in the debate which the Irish party resumed on 1 December in Committee Room Fifteen. The answers Parnell then gave – that because the talks were confidential he could not discuss them with his colleagues, that the proposals were not final, that he wanted to allow Gladstone time to mature them further – were not convincing and they certainly did not mollify his opponents. But for him this was largely irrelevant. Equally irrelevant was the widely-held opinion that his patience and judgement had broken under the strain of the divorce trial and of the English bombardment which had followed it, and that he was hitting out wildly in all directions regardless of consequences.[5]

The truth is that this image of a Samson Agonistes pulling the temple down on top of him, however close he may have come to it at a later stage of the conflict, does not fit with the Parnell who wrote the manifesto. It was a most carefully pondered document, every word of which was pregnant with meaning. But what meaning, and to produce what effect? The most striking fact about the manifesto is that, with breathtaking effrontery, it said not a single word about the divorce suit. The reason for this is plain. He desperately needed a diversionary tactic and Gladstone's letter to Morley gave him his opportunity. Typically, once he saw the opening he exploited it with great skill. On the one hand, he proceeded to use the letter to link the Liberal inter-ference with his own well-worn insistence on the need to preserve the independence of the Irish party. On the other, by introducing into the manifesto precisely those themes most calculated to confuse the

Liberals, he sought simultaneously to throw his opponents into disarray and to warn his countrymen against placing too much reliance on the promises of English politicians, however friendly they might seem.

Against this reasoning two objections could be, and were, raised. First, if the Liberals were so unreliable, why had Parnell himself preached the virtues of alliance with them almost every time he had opened his mouth in public during the past two years? Second, given that the alliance needed to be rethought, and given that independence needed to be reasserted, why was it necessary to use the language he did and so make it virtually certain that the Liberals would never treat with him again?

The answers to these questions can only be hypothetical, but answers suggest themselves nevertheless. It would seem that despite his calm reception of the news of Gladstone's letter to Morley and his outward indifference to the fact of its publication, he had quickly grasped how drastically it was likely to affect the Liberal-nationalist alliance. When this development was seen in the context of the great upsurge of non-conformist opinion, there were ample grounds for believing that the alliance had already broken in his hands. If the Liberals insisted on his retirement as the price of their continued championship of Home Rule, then the choice before him was stark. Either he obeyed the injunction to retire, leaving behind him a party which might or might not prove equal to the tough bargaining which lay ahead, or else he stayed where he was and resumed his freedom of action. The manifesto made it clear that he was opting for the latter course, but it was a course which pre-supposed that the policy of balance, of freedom, of independent opposition, was as available in 1890 as it had been in 1885. He was to spend the remainder of his life attempting to build on this assumption, but, paradoxically, the manifesto itself made it certain that in doing so he would have to fight against fearful odds – not merely against out-raged Liberals, but against powerful forces in Ireland, including the church and some of the most responsible and respected of his own for-mer colleagues.

In retrospect, all this seems so obvious that we may well wonder why a politician so astute as Parnell had not anticipated it before issuing his manifesto. The answer may well be that he did anticipate it and that he may actually have welcomed the storm it raised as a means of purging and disciplining the party while at the same time clearing the decks of the Liberal encumbrance. After all, 1890 had not been a happy year in the history of the parliamentary movement. The signs of internecine rivalry, the complaints from outside about the lack of supervision, had become too plain to be overlooked. Parnell did not go out of his way to create the crisis (even the precipitating factor, the divorce suit, had not turned out as he had expected) and doubtless he would have preferred to go on as if nothing had happened. But once the crisis came it gave him the chance to appeal over the heads of his disgruntled colleagues to a public opinion at home which might yet react in his favour. True, such an appeal was a fearful gamble for a man so out of touch with Ireland as he had become in recent years. But we have to remember that when he issued the manifesto there had been no overt, and very little private, opposition to his continuance in the leadership. Such evidence as there was – the support of the *Freeman's Journal*, the enthusiasm at the Central Branch and Leinster Hall meetings, the favourable resolutions that were beginning to come in from various bodies up and down the country – pointed strongly in his favour. This constituted a powerful inducement to put the issue to the test and transfer the struggle from London to Ireland, from a party mesmerized by Liberal 'wire-pullers' to a country still deemed to be loyal to the 'chief', whose people might yet respond atavistically to a summons designed to reawaken all their deep instinctive fears about the corrupting effect of British politics upon their own parliamentarians.

There was, finally, one further motive behind the manifesto which only gradually became apparent but which may have been already in Parnell's mind when Justin McCarthy visited him on 27 November. The distorted accounts he gave in the manifesto of the Hawarden and Brighton interviews were superficially shocking, no doubt, but at a deeper level they offered a basis for manœuvre which it might be possible to exploit. For if the Liberals insisted adamantly that Parnell must go, then he might be able to insist in his turn upon their conceding guarantees about Home Rule which would set at rest the doubts he had raised in the manifesto concerning Liberal reliability on certain sensitive areas of the projected settlement. This could be made to serve either of two purposes. On the one hand, if Parnell had to retire but only withdrew after winning his guarantees, he would go equipped with a powerful card of re-entry whenever he wished it, since he could then claim to be the architect of the next Home Rule bill. On the other hand, if the Liberals insisted on his disappearance *without* conceding the guarantees, then Irishmen at home and abroad might begin to wonder if the charges of Liberal dictation were not perhaps substantially correct. And if they once started to think in those terms, they might easily come to think also that Parnell and not Gladstone was the man to whom they should cleave.

II

The first intimations that the manifesto might begin to operate in precisely this way came on the day it was published, when McCarthy wrote urgently to Gladstone seeking another interview, this time for Sunday, 30 November. Parnell explained at the party meeting of 1 December that he himself had asked McCarthy to undertake the mission on the understanding that if it were successful he would retire. It appears, from a report made to Archbishop Walsh by the wealthy businessman, William Martin Murphy, that the mission was discussed at an informal meeting of 24 Irish MPs on the evening of Saturday, the day the manifesto appeared. Those present then heard for the first time what Murphy called 'a most insidious proposition', to the effect that Parnell would retire if Gladstone were to give written guarantees that the next Home Rule bill would provide for the settlement of the land question, and also for the control of the police to be in the hands of the Irish parliament.[6] Thus early did the concept of a bargain make its appearance.

Gladstone, meanwhile, had reacted publicly to the manifesto much as might have been expected. It was, he told Rendel, 'an astounding document', in which Parnell had 'utterly mis-stated' every one of the four modifications of Home Rule said to have been proposed by him, Gladstone, at Hawarden.[7] By lunchtime he had drafted his reply for the journalists who converged on Carlton Gardens. 'He looked', recorded one of them, 'very brisk and overflowing with a kind of battle glee.'[8] Morley and Harcourt read the letter of refutation before it went off and the latter could not refrain from remarking complacently, 'I told you so, I told you so.'[9] Gladstone's repudiation of Parnell's version of the Hawarden interview was crushingly explicit in detail and no less damning in its general conclusion – that 'to publish even a true account of it is to break the seal of confidence which alone renders political co-operation possible'.[10] Morley was equally emphatic in his denials and in private was flabbergasted by Parnell's conduct which, he told Lord Spencer, 'reveals an infamy of character which I had never expected'.[11] Harcourt, by contrast, was delighted to have done with Parnell, and if it meant the postponement of Home Rule, that, clearly, would not break his heart either. 'I feel some satisfaction', he wrote to his wife, 'in remembering that I have never shaken hands with him.'[12] 'We may have better men to deal with hereafter', he told Spencer, 'we cannot have worse . . . what will be the future of the nationalist party is dark enough, but it is plain that we have saved the Liberal party, which was the paramount consideration.'[13]

The omens were therefore not propitious when McCarthy called at Carlton Gardens for his promised interview with Gladstone at 2.30 p.m. on 30 November. From Gladstone's record it is evident that the Parnell manifesto was already beginning to take effect. McCarthy, it appeared, had been instructed to ask if Gladstone, Harcourt and Morley would give him a written statement that in the event of the return of the Liberal party to power they would introduce a Home Rule bill which would include as 'vital' provisions that the control of the police be given to an Irish executive responsible to an Irish parliament and that such a parliament should have power to deal with the land question if this had not already been disposed of by the imperial parliament. 'My answer', noted Gladstone, 'was . . . that I could deal in relation to the Home Rule question only with the Irish parliamentary party through its leader or those whom it had authorized to approach me, whereas Mr P. had renounced this party and going from it had [? exercised] a right of appeal to the Irish nation.' Harcourt, he added, coming in during the interview, had replied in the same sense.[14]

This was, as it were, a dress rehearsal for a manœuvre which was to be repeated more than once in the critical days ahead. Clearly, although Parnell's Irish critics did not accept everything he had said in his manifesto, they were sufficiently affected by it to seek to persuade the Liberals into giving precise assurances about the points in the coming Home Rule bill on which Parnell had cast most doubt. But precise assurances were what Gladstone and his ex-colleagues most wanted to avoid, and this for two reasons. First, they could not give them on matters which still divided them internally; nor, anyway, would they have wished to expose so much of their hand in advance. Second, to give assurances of any kind while Parnell was still the head of the Irish party would be in effect to recognize his leadership and thus to run dangerously counter to the urgent demand from their own supporters that Parnell must go.

The effect of this rebuff to McCarthy was to throw back upon the Irish members the responsibility of themselves deciding the leadership issue before looking to the Liberals for a resumption of the dialogue about Home Rule. It was already apparent that, quite apart from Gladstone's pressure, the forces pushing the party towards such a decision were increasing day by day. Two of these were of particular importance. One was the delegation in America. It will be remembered that the initial impulse of all but T. D. Sullivan had been to throw their weight behind Parnell. But the news which had reached them since the meeting of the Irish party on 25 November had begun to swing them – with the single exception of Timothy Harrington – round to Sullivan's way of thinking, though not necessarily for the same reasons. The publication of Gladstone's letter to Morley first brought home to them the deeper political implications of the crisis and by the time they had converged on Cincinnati to await Parnell's manifesto, it was evident that it would have to be a very persuasive document indeed to retain their loyalty to the leader. Even before it was published, the whole delegation, minus Harrington, cabled Parnell urging him to retire in favour of McCarthy, and Harrington too thought privately that a voluntary retirement from the chair 'would on the whole be the best way out of the difficulty'.[15] The manifesto, however, was the decisive factor. All save Harrington united in condemning it immediately in a cable home which made it clear that the document had convinced them that Parnell's continued leadership was impossible. They then travelled to Chicago and from there launched a counter-manifesto of their own. The five who signed it committed themselves to what seemed a totally uncompromising opposition to the leader. 'Mr Parnell', they wrote, 'has entered upon a rash and fatal path, upon which every consideration of Ireland's safety, as well as of our personal honour, forbids us absolutely to follow him.'[16]

The adhesion of the principal members of the delegation to the growing opposition to Parnell was one ominous portent. No less ominous was a second – that in Ireland the bishops were at last beginning to move. From the moment of Parnell's re-election and the publication of Gladstone's letter to Morley, Archbishop Walsh had had a hard job to hold them in and prevent a ham-handed intervention which could only have done harm. The Bishop of Ardagh, never a man for political refinements, was a case in point. 'Is it not the duty of us bishops', he burst out on the day after the fateful party meeting, 'to speak for our people, and to tell the *Freeman* and our MPs that God's commandments must be respected and that *He* cannot be ignored? What a Grand Old Man Gladstone is! and are we to allow him and a lot of nondescript [Dr Woodlock's version of nonconformist] Ministers to proclaim the laws of Christian morality, while we are *canes muti non valantes latrare*?'[17]

The bishop wanted an immediate meeting of the Standing Committee of the hierarchy, but although Walsh was able to dissuade him, there were indications that some prelates were preparing to take things into their own hands. Dr Gillooly, for example, wrote to his colleague Dr Woodlock and to Archbishop Walsh on the same day, suggesting that individual bishops should contact the MPs best known to them. 'I think it would be well', he wrote, 'to communicate our views to some of our MPs *before* Monday next, in order to influence the decision of that day, as we have the best possible right to do.'[18] Dr McCormack, the mild Bishop of Galway, was moved to describe the conduct of the Irish party as 'most intolerable'. 'It is a disastrous business that England should be forcing her view on morality in favourable contrast with Irish representatives.'[19] And from the Bishop of Clogher came an almost despairing cry for action. 'The crisis is an awful one and a meeting of the bishops, at least of the Standing Committee, is called for.'[20]

But the archbishop was by no means so aloof as he seemed. On 26 November, after the party had re-elected Parnell, W. M. Murphy telegraphed that the situation was 'most serious'. Gladstone's message to McCarthy had not been conveyed to the party the previous day, he said, and the party had re-elected Parnell in ignorance of this vital fact. Murphy thought Parnell intended to hold on – 'no one here strong enough to avert catastrophe'. This produced a reply from Walsh which, though still guarded, lent itself to the kind of interpretation Murphy was seeking. 'Dr Kenny knows my view by private letter. It is unchangeable. Manifestly members hold no mandate from the country to wreck the national movement. Take time. There never was a cause more clearly requiring calm and full deliberation.'[21] Later that evening, after the requisitioned meeting had met and agreed to an adjournment until 1 December, Murphy wrote a fuller account of what was happening. The feeling, he reported, was 'overwhelmingly' in favour of Parnell's retirement. 'The most passionate appeals were made to him by his oldest followers, but he set his teeth and declared that he would not stir unless the party voted him out of the leadership.'[22]

For Walsh, this was a signal to move. Up to then, as he told Cardinal Manning, he had refrained in the hope that the Irish members would manage the business themselves. Even as late as 26 November he had still felt that it would be better 'if we can discharge our duty by speaking with them in quiet conference, without being forced to speak to the world outside'. But, after he had received Murphy's letter written that same day, he felt that time was ripe to summon the Episcopal Standing Committee, though, with his usual sagacity, he arranged that it should meet on 3 December, *after* the party had resumed its deliberations on Monday. 'This', he pointed out to Manning, 'will exercise a strong influence on Monday's proceedings, and in a form no politicians can object to.'[23] Meanwhile, on 29 November he broke silence with an 'arranged' letter to the editor of the *Irish Catholic*. Again, it was the acme of caution. He refused, he said, to state his opinion as an individual bishop until he had consulted his brethren. He noted that the Irish party would meet on 1 December to decide their course of action and though he confessed to an illogical hope that the affair might turn out as had 'certain events of not very remote occurrence' (he meant the Pigott forgeries), his reference to the party meeting contained a hint which nobody could ignore:[24]

> It is easy to conceive that the decision then come to by our parliamentary representatives may have the effect of opening up a new phase of the Irish national movement and that the situation resulting from the decision may be one that will put upon the bishops of Ireland . . . a very grave duty – the duty of considering whether, or how far, it will be in our power to continue in future to place in the Irish parliamentary party that confidence, as a body, we felt justified in placing in it in the past.

Simultaneously with this there appeared Parnell's manifesto. Its effect upon the bishops was much what its effect had been upon the delegates in America. 'Why not a word of defence?' wrote the Archbishop of Tuam. 'It is evidently meant to wreck Gladstone & Co., and break faith with them all . . . Home Rule with such men, what would it be but crippling the Irish Church and relegating the priests to the sacristies as long as they would be allowed to use them? Great harm I anticipate will come of the breaking up of the party which I regard as inevitable, be the result of Monday what it may. Plenty of secret societies and to spare.'[25] But by the time this lament had reached him, Dr Walsh had combined with Archbishop Croke to exercise a more direct influence on the situation. On 29 November Croke telegraphed to Justin McCarthy urging that Parnell should still be pressed to retire 'quietly and with good grace' from the leadership, but prophesying every kind of woe if he did not.[26] Next day, Archbishop Walsh released this telegram to the press and himself at last spoke out in no uncertain terms. 'If the Irish leader', he said, 'would not or could not, give a public assurance that his honour was unsullied, the party that takes him or retains him as its leader can no longer count on the support of the bishops of Ireland.'[27] At the same time he wrote to Healy and telegraphed Murphy. To the former, whom he authorized to make any use of his letter short of publishing it, he said: 'The leadership, I take it, is practically vacant. If there was any doubt, or room for doubt, on that point up to this, there will, I trust, be none tomorrow.'[28] And to Murphy, who had telegraphed that the letter to the *Irish Catholic* was being construed in some quarters as too favourable to Parnell, because of its veiled reference to the Pigott forgeries, Walsh replied: 'We have been slow to act trusting party will act manfully. Our deliberate silence and reserve are being dishonestly misrepresented. Cashel's telegram goes to *Freeman* for publication tomorrow. This will make further misrepresentation in any quarter impossible.'[29]

The archbishop had thus negotiated both ecclesiastical and secular shoals with remarkable skill. He had not only avoided the danger of a potentially damaging intrusion into a delicate political situation, but had done so without unduly ruffling the sensibilities either of Rome or of his fellow-bishops. His calculated delay had allowed the party to regroup for the assault upon Parnell, while his eventual declaration came just in time to make it perfectly clear how the Irish hierarchy expected members to do their duty on 1 December. His dexterity would not save him, of course, from facile accusations of ecclesiastical intervention. But such accusations were unduly naïve, for they overlooked the simple fact that in such a case ecclesiastical intervention there was sooner or later bound to be. What Dr Walsh's navigation had ensured was that in all the fierce controversies which were soon to erupt it would be possible to demonstrate that by their early inaction the bishops had practised deliberate restraint and that the legend upon which W. B. Yeats later seized when he wrote that 'the bishops and the party that tragic story made', assigned to the hierarchy just the kind of role which the Archbishop of Dublin had been at particular pains to avoid.[30]

III

At last the forces were massed for the great battle which began on 1 December in Committee Room Fifteen. The events of the previous week had shown plainly enough that the party was deeply divided on the crucial issue of Parnell's leadership, but nobody could tell how the balance of numbers would fall out. It was obvious that a powerful and influential group dedicated to Parnell's removal had emerged in the week following his re-election to the chair; but although that group had been greatly strengthened by the decision of the American delegates to go against Parnell, and by the last-minute intervention of Archbishops Walsh and Croke, it was far from certain that these reinforcements would secure a majority for deposition. That Parnell's following was fanatically devoted to him was common knowledge, but just how large that following would be was impossible to predict. True, he was backed by the *Freeman's Journal* – *United Ireland* looked to William O'Brien for guidance – and the resolutions forwarded to Dublin from the branches of the Irish National League seemed to indicate widespread support for him in the country. It may have been the case, as Tim Healy alleged – though the Parnellites denied it – that some of these branches were being 'worked' in the Parnellite interest, but the plain fact was that until the quarrel was transferred to Ireland there was no saying which side would come out on top.[31]

The most that can be ventured, then, about this deeply confused situation was that on 1 December the weight of influence and debating power within the party was against Parnell, whereas at home the tide appeared to be flowing strongly in his favour. In Committee Room Fifteen Parnell had therefore to strive for two main objectives. First, he had to divert the discussion away from a direct attack on his leadership, or at least delay it, preferably by trying a new variant of the manœuvre blocked by Gladstone the previous day – that is to say, making the manifesto the basis for negotiation about the future Home Rule settlement. Second, when the leadership question forced its way inexorably to the surface, then he and his supporters must labour the theme of independent opposition *versus* Liberal dictation. Thus, if guarantees could not be obtained from Gladstone, and if a majority of those present voted to depose him, he would still be in a good position to appeal to the country against the party.

The task of the anti-Parnellites, as they may now be called, was in some respects more difficult. They had, obviously, to concentrate their efforts on the leadership question, but it was not easy for them to exploit it in all its aspects. It was scarcely open to them to use the divorce court 'revelations' as an argument against Parnell – this, admittedly, did not inhibit Tim Healy, though he was almost alone in so doing – because too many of them had pledged support to the leader *after* Captain O'Shea had done his worst. This meant that they had to fall back upon Gladstone's letter to John Morley, but that was not an ideal position either, since to dismiss Parnell on that account would expose them to the charge of surrendering to Liberal dictation and Irish feeling had already been so exacerbated by nonconformist strictures that there was a serious danger of an anti-English reaction setting in. All that remained was to place the future of Home Rule in the balance against loyalty to the leader – the cause against the man. This was to be the staple of the anti-Parnellite speeches, but even it was a two-edged weapon, since if Home Rule really was the paramount issue, then Parnell's contention, that the large questions he had raised in the manifesto should be satisfactorily settled before his services were dispensed with, became difficult to resist. But a protracted debate would be perilous, partly because it would allow time for Parnellite manipulation of opinion at home, but still more because the longer the dispute dragged on, the greater would be the temptation for the Tories to call a snap election, with all the dangers to Home Rule which that involved.

The stage on which these opposing passions and ambitions were to clash for the next six days was a spacious oak-panelled room looking out upon the Thames from an upper floor of the House of Commons. It was dominated by a large horseshoe-shaped table. Parnell sat in the centre with Justin McCarthy on his right and Henry Campbell on his left. Opponents and supporters of the leader were interspersed around this table and at smaller tables in other parts of the room, but a tendency to 'group' according to faction was evident from the beginning.

The only reporters allowed into the room were the team of five produced by the *Freeman's Journal* under the direction of J. M. Tuohy, the London correspondent of the paper. It was alleged by some that their reporting was biased in Parnell's favour, but this was not the view of the party as a whole, which simply inserted into the minute-book the *verbatim* printed reports from the *Freeman's Journal* as the only official record of what happened between 1 December and 6 December. Other newspapers, including the Liberal *Daily News* and even the implacably anti-Parnellite *Times*, were content to base their accounts on the shorthand notes dictated by the *Freeman's* team to the hungry journalists perpetually on watch outside the door of Committee Room Fifteen.[32]

At the outset a remarkably high proportion of the party – 73 out of 86 – was present. Six were absent in America, five were ill, one was in prison and one seat was vacant – otherwise, all were there. It was quickly obvious that Parnell, though he claimed to be following the standing orders of the House of Commons, was prepared to use his position as chairman quite ruthlessly. He began by trying, vainly, to maintain that when the party had been adjourned on the previous Wednesday (26 November) to 'Friday', this meant Friday, 5 December, and not, as was obvious from the context, 28 November. Next, when accepting amendments to this adjournment motion, he ruled out of order one which called for his chairmanship of the party to be terminated, and accepted instead one from his own supporter, Colonel Nolan, to the effect that the question of the chairmanship be postponed until members had had an opportunity of consulting their constituents.

Yet, despite this early evidence that Parnell would fight tooth and nail to defend his position, the debate, during the first two days at least, was conducted with dignity and ability. The episode has been described many times and here it is only necessary to dwell upon those incidents which directly affected Parnell's own future.[33] The burden of the initial attack was carried mainly by Sexton, who called for the chairman's retirement, 'for the time being at least', on the ground that the Liberal alliance being essential to Home Rule, the maintenance of the alliance demanded his withdrawal. He was supported by T. M. Healy, who with his fatal gift for wounding invective, injected the first traces of bad temper into the discussion. Admittedly, he was still far from well, but his long-standing hostility had been sharpened by a belief that after his arrival in London, Parnell had deliberately cut him.[34] Yet, abrasive or not, he was a man of weight with power to influence waverers. After opposing the idea of an adjournment to Dublin, he addressed himself to the damaging proposition that in sacrificing Parnell the party would be yielding to English clamour. In accepting the original bill of 1886, he argued, the party had also yielded to similar pressures, for that bill too had been unsatisfactory in that it had not given the Irish parliament control of either police or judiciary, and had even at one time envisaged the exclusion of the entire Irish membership from Westminster. Yet, though in 1886 they had all, including Parnell, accepted the bill as adequate, Parnell now complained of Gladstone's similar treatment of these same themes at Hawarden, even though directly after his visit there he had gone straight to Liverpool and expressed his complete faith in Gladstone and what he had to offer. 'If', Healy added vituperatively, 'the Hawarden interview be the capital matter on which Mr Parnell bases himself in his manifesto, why, I say, were these false words uttered at Liverpool? Either Mr Parnell at Liverpool was false, or else his manifesto was false.'

This, for a moment, shattered Parnell's regal calm. 'I will not stand an accusation of falsehood from Timothy Healy', he said angrily, 'and I call upon him to withdraw.' This Healy did at once, turning instead to explain how his own attitude had changed between the Leinster Hall meeting and the present occasion. The brute fact was that Parnell could no longer deliver what he had promised, because the favourable situation he had created in 1886 had been destroyed by his own action in 1890. Why, asked Healy rhetorically, did he, Healy, defer now to English opinion? Why had they all likewise deferred in 1886? The answer he gave is a classic statement of the achievement of the constitutional movement under Parnell's leadership:

We were willing to do so because we were led by Charles Stewart Parnell, and he was able so to abate the passion and the recollection of wrong and of centuries of suffering on the part of Ireland as to insure this acceptance, almost without exception, by every body of representatives of the Irish nation. Ireland possesses neither armies nor fleets. Having neither armies nor fleets we are bound to rely upon constitutional and parliamentary methods. There is no hope, there was no hope, for Ireland until Mr Parnell succeeded in obtaining from Mr Gladstone the promise of a Home Rule settlement. He did it in consultation with English opinion, abating many of our demands, forgetting much of our wrongs and sufferings, and when we to-day calculate from the expression of English opinion that, not in units or in tens of thousands, but millions, the voters of the liberal party have declared . . . that the . . . mischief which will result to Ireland by his continuance in the leadership must be fatal to the hopes of our country, I found myself upon the hard necessities of the case, and while I would rather, if I could, prevent this cataclysm in the party . . . I say that the necessities of Ireland are paramount.

Healy was followed by Parnell himself. Hitherto the case for supporting him had been ably put by the young John Redmond. It was, inevitably, a case resting on the thesis that the independence of the party was more precious than the Liberal alliance, even if this involved the postponement of Home Rule. Still, there were awkward questions to be answered, which only Parnell could deal with. Of these the most crucial was the one Healy had already posed – why did Parnell take one position about his conversations with Gladstone after he had left Hawarden and a quite different position in his manifesto? As he approached this vital point, Parnell's self-possession temporarily deserted him and he laboured visibly to keep his temper under control, remarking bitterly that the man to whom he had given his chance in life was now his severest critic. 'That Mr Healy should be here today to destroy me is due to myself', he said. But Healy was not the only one. What of those others who had supported him at the Leinster Hall and had now gone against him? 'Why did you encourage me to stand forward and maintain my leadership in the face of the world if you were not going to stand by me?' And turning unmistakably towards John Barry, he summoned a piercing memory from the past when he ground out an almost unintelligible allusion to 'the leader killer who sharpens his poniard to stab me as he stabbed the old lion, Isaac Butt, in the days gone by'.*

As for the Hawarden conversations, he had not reported them to the

*For Barry's part in the fall of Butt, see above, p. 67.

party, he claimed, because they were strictly confidential and because he regarded Gladstone's ideas as still evolving. It was not, perhaps, a very convincing explanation, inviting as it did the criticism that he had no business to bind himself to such a vow of secrecy, or, having bound himself, to speak afterwards in such unnecessarily fulsome terms as he had done at Liverpool. It was also open to the objection that if Gladstone was still in process of making up his mind at Hawarden why was he represented in the manifesto as having expressed himself in such conclusive language? The answer to that was already becoming apparent. In the opening speech of this first session Redmond had observed that 'where we are asked to sell our own leader to preserve an alliance, it seems to me that we are bound to enquire into what we are getting for the price we are paying'. Upon this, Parnell had interjected: 'Don't sell me for nothing. If you get my value you may change me tomorrow.' In his own speech he now reverted to the weekend manœuvre by which he had sought to obtain, through Justin McCarthy, guarantees from the Liberal leaders on the vexed questions of the police and land reform. As we saw, he had been thwarted by the refusal of Gladstone and Harcourt to give any such undertakings. But, so far from abandoning his tactics, Parnell contrived in his closing remarks not only to advert to them again, but in doing so to strike a note of genuine pathos. 'If I am to leave you tonight, I should like to leave you in security. I should like – and it is not an unfair thing for me to ask – that I should come within sight of the promised land.'[35]

These were the key exchanges in a debate which continued for eleven hours before being adjourned to the following day. Some signs of friction, due mainly to exhaustion, had already begun to appear, and Healy spoke for many when that night he wrote to Archbishop Walsh, 'In all my life, I never spent so awful a time and I am harassed in body and soul.'[36] To his wife he admitted that Parnell's conduct in the chair had been dignified. 'Even in his reply to me, considering what I had said, there was nothing to complain of.'[37] The second day, however, was distinctly more tense, partly because many members were eager to end the discussion quickly whatever the cost, but still more because the divorce proceedings, almost entirely avoided on the first day, now began to edge into the discussions. There was, unavoidably, much wearisome reiteration of the same threadbare arguments and it was not until darkness had fallen, and the room dimly lit by candles and lamps scattered about the tables, that Captain Nolan's amendment to remove their deliberations to Ireland was defeated by 44 votes to 29. The result was received in silence and the members, deeply conscious of their disunity, and no less deeply uncertain about the future, adjourned once more, to meet again on Wednesday, 3 December.[38]

IV

When they reassembled they spent the first hour and a half in secret session with Parnell absent from the chair. At this session one of his supporters, J. J. Clancy, put forward yet another variant of the scheme suggested to Gladstone and Harcourt the previous Sunday. This, which was formally an amendment to Barry's motion to adjourn, proposed that in view of the difference of opinion between Gladstone and Parnell as to the accuracy of the latter's version of the Hawarden interview, the party whips be instructed to obtain from Gladstone, Harcourt and John Morley their views in regard to the 'two vital points' relating to the settlement of the land question and the control of the constabulary.[39]

It may seem incredible that after what had happened at the weekend the party could have been led to debate this proposition seriously, let alone accept it. But members had before them Parnell's assurance, solemnly conveyed to them by Clancy, that if satisfactory guarantees could be gained on the 'two vital points', he would retire from the chair. Moreover, the fact that this time it would be the whips who would be approaching the Liberal leaders, invested the scheme with a degree of formality which some found alluring. Whether the Liberals would find it equally alluring was dubious. They had already made it perfectly clear that they would not deal with the party while Parnell remained its chairman and there was no reason to suppose that they would deviate from that position.

From the Irish standpoint there was a great deal to be said for attempting this new approach, for the gains which could result from it – the voluntary retirement of Parnell and the simultaneous improvement of the Home Rule terms – were so immense that desperate men could hardly be blamed for clutching at it eagerly. Yet it was far from certain that Parnell could be classed among them. In his absence, Sexton had greeted Clancy's amendment with the reasonable comment that it was so grave and weighty that the party should adjourn to consider it. Parnell himself arrived at this point and when he had taken the chair Sexton renewed his request for an adjournment, but then asked him two highly pertinent questions. First, who was to pronounce on the adequacy of the Liberal assurances – would Parnell be content to abide by a majority vote of the party? Second, if the assurances were given and found ad equate by the majority, would Parnell then voluntarily retire? Healy, emotionally volatile as ever, interjected vehemently that if Parnell could satisfy the party on these two points, he would be the first to call him back as leader of the Irish race 'at the very earliest moment possible, consonant with the liberties of this country'. All Parnell seems to have said in reply was that he too needed time for consideration. And so it was agreed to adjourn until Thursday.

Thursday found him once more inflexible. It was rumoured that this was Mrs O'Shea's doing, but there is no evidence to connect her with his change of mood. On the contrary, her impulse was to take him away from the fight – an impulse restrained only by a more powerful intuition that for him to desist at her pleading would be ruinous for both of them. It is more probable that his pride and his tenacity, perhaps temporarily weakened by the pressures of the previous days, had reasserted themselves and that he was now prepared to resume the offensive.[40] 'My position', he said proudly, 'has been granted to me, not because I am the mere leader of a parliamentary party, but because I am the leader of the Irish nation . . . And you, gentlemen, know, and I know, that there is no man living, if I am gone, who could succeed in reconciling the feelings of the Irish people to the provisions of the Hawarden proposals.' He then read out a resolution which he asked them to pass:[41]

> That, in the opinion of the Irish parliamentary party, no home rule will be satisfactory or acceptable to the Irish people which will not confer the immediate control of the Irish police on the executive responsible to the Irish parliament; and secondly, which does not confer upon the Irish parliament full power to deal with the land question.

If the party agreed to this resolution, and if the Liberal assurances proved satisfactory, he would resign from the chairmanship. He then suggested a mechanism whereby three delegates from his supporters and three from his opponents should be chosen to seek an interview with Gladstone, Harcourt and Morley to find whether their views accorded with those of the Irish party on the points at issue, and whether they would agree to embody those views as vital clauses in the next Home Rule bill.

This was an attempt, at once blatant and subtle, to turn the flank of his critics. It was blatant because, by giving equal representation to both sides it coolly ignored the vote of Tuesday evening, and also because it substituted concrete demands for the exploration of views envisaged by Clancy's amendment. It was subtle because the demands now to be made upon the Liberals were Parnell's own demands. If they were conceded he might indeed have to resign the chair, but he would march out with the honours of war. And who could doubt that such a withdrawal would be merely *reculer pour mieux sauter*? Alternatively, if the Liberals refused his demands, he would still remain as 'leader of the Irish nation', well placed to rally his fellow-countrymen against 'Liberal dictation'.

Yet there was a flaw in this reasoning. He had no rational grounds for supposing that the majority which had out-voted him on Tuesday would be ready to fall into line behind him on Thursday. On the contrary, there were excellent grounds for supposing the opposite, for at last the Standing Committee of the Irish bishops had met (on Wednesday, 3 December) and their resounding denunciation of Parnell appeared in the papers on the day he launched his new manœuvre. This 'unqualified pronouncement', as Archbishop Walsh called it in a private telegram to McCarthy, was based, the bishops said, not on political grounds, 'but simply and solely on the facts and circumstances revealed in the London Divorce Court'. 'Surely', they asked, 'Catholic Ireland, so eminently conspicuous for its virtue and the purity of its social life, will not accept as its leader a man thus dishonoured, and wholly unworthy of Christian confidence?' Nevertheless, the bishops, though taking this high pastoral line, were not unmindful of political consequences, among which they enumerated – if Parnell remained leader – 'inevitable defeat at the approaching general elections, and, as a result, Home Rule indefinitely postponed, coercion perpetuated, the hands of the evictor strengthened, and the tenants already evicted left without the shadow of a hope of being ever restored to their homes.'[42]

But no one knew better than Archbishop Walsh that the hierarchical thunders would not in themselves be decisive. He did not believe, he told Manning despondently, that the disruption of the party could be avoided, and though he tried to buoy up the confidence of W. M. Murphy, and through him of the opposition to Parnell, he confided to the cardinal his disgust at the feebleness of that opposition. 'They will be led on', he wrote on 5 December, 'from point to point, their position gradually becoming weaker and weaker, and their majority probably dwindling away, at each successive demonstration of their miserable inability to hold their own.'[43]

In Committee Room Fifteen the opposition to Parnell was certainly strengthened by the public evidence of episcopal support. But even without it, Parnell's new tactic would have provoked his critics beyond endurance and the debate which followed his two propositions was the most bad-tempered that had yet occurred. It was marked by another major clash with Healy, who charged Parnell with refusing to submit himself to the judgement of the party and challenged him to accept a plain majority ruling as to whether the Liberal assurances were satisfactory or not. Parnell replied that he would stand or fall by his own proposal. 'Then you will fall, Mr Parnell', said Healy, amid ironical Parnellite cries of 'Crucify him' and 'Away with him', which in turn drew angry accusations of blasphemy from their opponents. Healy, continuing, tried to show yet again that Parnell had been enthusiastic about the Liberal attitude to Home Rule as recently as the previous June, but he grew visibly more irritable as he went on. What, he demanded, broke the Liberal alliance? Colonel Nolan and Dr Fitzgerald with one voice said it had been broken by Gladstone's letter to Morley. No, rejoined Healy savagely, it had perished 'in the stench of the divorce-court'. And turning towards Parnell he likened him to a Frankenstein who, having created the party, was able and determined to destroy it. 'If you, sir', he said, 'should go down, you are only one man gone. Heads of greater leaders have been stricken on the block before now for Ireland '[Not by their own friends, not by their own allies' from Colonel Nolan] and the Irish cause remained. The Irish people can put us down, but the Irish cause will remain always.'[44]

This phase of the debate ended in a defeat for Parnell, who agreed not to press his proposals to a vote. Clancy's amendment therefore held the field and a committee was appointed (including both Parnell and Healy) to take the necessary steps to obtain the views of Gladstone, Harcourt and Morley on the future position regarding the land and the police. This committee was evenly divided between the two sections, as was the delegation it chose from among its members to visit the Liberal leaders. The members selected for this difficult mission were Sexton, Healy, John Redmond and Edmund Leamy.

It was a forlorn hope from the start. Harcourt and Morley refused to meet the delegation at all and Gladstone himself declined to consider the matter 'with a selection of my friends and former colleagues which has been made neither by me, nor by the Liberal party of this country'. Harcourt urged strongly that Gladstone should keep his hands absolutely free. 'It is a very dangerous thing to approach an expiring cat', he had warned his chief at the beginning of that eventful week, and all that had happened since had confirmed him in his profound conviction that Parnell must be got rid of as quickly as possible.[45] On 4 December when the signs all pointed to Parnell's manœuvre being adopted, he wrote agitatedly to Gladstone:

The deputation is his creation and the deputies his creatures. It is a mistake to suppose that there are *two parties* in the business now.

Healy, Sexton and Parnell are at this moment hob-nobbing over their whisky downstairs. They are not waiting for you to make peace for them. They have signed it already and at your expense. It is all what they call on the racecourse a 'put up job', and they are supping together like actors who have been murdering one another on the stage for the amusement of the public. There is no reality, no sincerity in their professed antagonism to Parnell's leadership. They have tried their strength, been beaten and surrendered at discretion.

The only thing to be done, he suggested, was to refuse to treat with the delegates and to give them no possible handle for misrepresentation. 'Anything which could bear the semblance of parleying with Parnell or the captives of Parnell will be fatal to the Liberal party. Your great authority depends upon the belief that you have withstood him to the face and that you will continue to withstand him.'[46]

It is unlikely that Gladstone took quite such a crude view of the situation as Harcourt. Not only was his judgement sounder, his experience vaster, and his sympathies wider, but he also had other sources of information. Healy had been talking to a prominent Liberal, James Stansfeld, and Stansfeld reported back persuasively to Carlton Gardens. 'He says the press is wrong; that we don't understand the situation; that Parnell is "cornered" and not they.' Gladstone would be asked to receive a deputation from the Irish party, *not* from Parnell, and they would want Gladstone to say two things only – that the land question should either be dealt with by the imperial parliament or delegated to the Irish parliament, and that the Home Rule Bill should specify the date on which the RIC would pass under Irish control.[47] In the event, Gladstone received the delegation by himself and Sexton read him out the points on which the party wished to be reassured. Gladstone then riposted by reading in his turn a statement which barred any conference with Irish members 'when it was sought for the declared purpose of determining a question of recollection as to the Hawarden conversation'. Asked if discussions might proceed, were this barrier removed, Gladstone replied that in that case he would regard the matter as if the barrier had not existed; as the delegation left the room he added that he would not have much difficulty in speaking about the police.[48]

After further consultations on the Irish side it was decided to call a private session of the party for that afternoon – Friday, 5 December. At this meeting Clancy's amendment was rescinded and another substituted for it. The latter omitted the offending reference to the Hawarden conversations and simply empowered the same four delegates to seek a further conference with Gladstone to ascertain the Liberal intentions with regard to certain details connected with the settlement of the Irish land question and the control of the Irish police.[49] The whips then wrote to Gladstone requesting another interview. But the climate had grown markedly colder. Gladstone's memorandum of his original meeting notes that it was 'not liked by Harcourt, Morley and [H.E.] Childers' and in the interval between that encounter and the second approach he had again come under pressure from his own friends.[50] These included most of the ex-ministers who, apparently, were unanimous that no pledges should be given.[51] Rather than endure another painful session, therefore, Gladstone wrote to the Irish whips refusing to enter into any further discussion about Liberal intentions until the Irish party had settled the problem of the leadership.[52]

It seems that Gladstone would have preferred to communicate his personal opinions on the land and police questions to the Irish emissaries, but that, after having 'rather resisted', he was over-borne by Harcourt and Morley.[53] Given their implacable hostility to Parnell, their anxieties about the whole manœuvre, and no doubt also their reluctance to have their hands tied in advance by Gladstone on important aspects of Home Rule, this was understandable. But in retrospect we may regret that they were quite so adamant in their refusal to help the Irish party out of a difficulty which was infinitely more serious than Harcourt for one was prepared to admit. Even if a further conference had merely established that Gladstone could not commit himself sufficiently to satisfy the Irish, at least he would have been seen to have made an effort to do so. If, beyond this, he had actually been able to give the assurances the Irish were seeking then Parnell's bluff, if bluff it was, would have been called in a way he would have found impossible to evade. Either he would have had to admit that the assurances *were* satisfactory and carry out his part of the bargain by resigning, or else he would have been driven back upon a factious opposition which might easily have lost him his more moderate supporters.[54]

The reality was far otherwise. Both sections of the Irish party had to recognize the fact that Gladstone's refusal brought them back inexorably to the question of the leadership. Late on Friday night, after the negotiations had failed, Healy and Sexton went to Parnell and urged him to bow to the necessities of the case. He replied that he would take that night to consider. Next morning, when they saw him again he told them that his responsibility to Ireland would not allow him to retire

They warned him that no further obstruction would be tolerated and that, if need be, the majority would withdraw.[55] Before they left, there occurred an incident which Healy remembered all his life:[56]

> As we went towards the door, he drew me towards one of the pillars in the hall, saying 'Healy, let us shake hands for, it may be, the last time. I am told you believed yesterday that I had a revolver in my pocket and was about to use it. I assure you that this was not so. I should not dream of bringing a weapon into any meeting of my countrymen, especially where excitement was likely to be kindled.' I replied, 'Thank you, Parnell.' We shook hands and so parted for ever.

The end was indeed near. When the party reassembled on Saturday one of the Protestant members, William Abraham, as previously arranged by Parnell's opponents, rose to propose the motion he had tried to put at the beginning of the week, that Parnell's chairmanship be terminated. Almost simultaneously a Parnellite, John O'Connor, stood up to move a resolution calling the attention of the Irish people to the fact that Gladstone had refused to state his views on Home Rule until the party had first removed Parnell from the chairmanship. Parnell called on O'Connor to speak and pandemonium at once broke out. Abraham insisted on trying to read his motion, but as he could not be heard, passed the paper on which it was written to Justin McCarthy. William Martin Murphy, writing to Archbishop Walsh at 4.30 that afternoon, only a few moments after this episode, described Parnell's reaction:[57]

> A dreadful scene followed in which he snatched a paper out of Justin McCarthy's hand and dashed it to the ground.[58] At length Sexton got him to undertake, after John O'Connor's resolution expressing dissatisfaction with Gladstone's answer had been seconded, that Abraham will be called on. He will personally move Parnell's deposition as an amendment and if he refuses to receive it we shall leave in a body and constitute ourselves, being a majority of the entire party, as a meeting and pass our resolutions. If he does receive it we shall insist on a vote being taken – if that is refused we shall leave in the same manner.

Murphy had not overstated the case. Parnell had been so beside himself with rage that even his supporters had thought he was about to strike the inoffensive McCarthy and Redmond and Leamy rushed forward to prevent this. The meeting seemed about to dissolve in uproar amid which the implacable John Barry could be heard calling Parnell 'a dirty trickster'. Gradually the clamour died down as men looked shame-facedly at each other. O'Connor was then allowed to continue with his speech and during it Parnell apologized to McCarthy who responded with his usual good nature.[59]

The calm did not last long. When John O'Connor asserted that if the party rejected Parnell it would in effect be placing itself under Glad-stone's leadership, his namesake, the anti-Parnellite, Arthur O'Connor, retorted that Gladstone was not a member of the Irish party. The *Freeman's Journal* 'official' account continues:[60]

> *Mr J. Redmond:* 'The master of the party' (cheers and counter cheers).
>
> *Mr T. M. Healy:* 'Who is to be the mistress of the party?' (cries of 'shame', noise, several members calling out re-marks which could not be distinguished in the uproar).
>
> *Mr W. Redmond:* 'They must be very badly off, when they go to arguments like that.'
>
> *A voice:* 'It is true.'

At this, Parnell rose once more in fury and now it seemed as if he really would become violent. Healy's friends gathered round him and Arthur O'Connor called out placatingly, 'I appeal to my friend the chairman.' To this Parnell replied with inexpressible bitterness, 'Better appeal to your own friends. Better appeal to that cowardly little scoundrel there, who dares in an assembly of Irishmen to insult a woman.'[61] 'I made no reply', Healy commented to his wife, 'being contented with the thrust which will stick as long as his cry about Gladstone's "dictation" con-tinues.'[62]

With this exchange the point of no return was finally reached. The meeting continued for a little longer, but it was only a question of when and how the end would come. After O'Connor's resolution had been seconded, Abraham asked leave to move his original resolution as an amendment to O'Connor's motion. Predictably, Parnell replied that it could not possibly be considered an amendment and ruled it out of order. This produced another, though lesser, clash between Healy and himself and after a couple of desultory speeches from Arthur O'Connor and Edmund Leamy, Justin McCarthy at last grasped the nettle. 'I see no further use', he said, 'in carrying on a discussion which must be barren of all but reproach, ill-temper, controversy and indignity, and I will suggest that all who think with me at this grave crisis should withdraw with me from this room.'[63] He then departed with 44 of his colleagues. So accurate had been the anti-Parnellite calculations that W. M. Murphy had estimated to Archbishop Walsh before the meeting began that the number of those who would secede would be 44. The fact that it was one more than this was due to the last-minute decision of Justin Huntly McCarthy to go with his father rather than stay with Parnell for whom he had previously voted.

This occurred shortly after five o'clock in the darkness of the December afternoon.[64] Contrary to some contemporary accounts, the parting was not acrimonious and there is no reason to disbelieve Healy's account of it. 'Many of us shook hands with those from whom we were separating. It was a friendly break-off and dignity was preserved throughout.'[65] Reporting to Archbishop Walsh that things had turned out as he had anticipated, Murphy added a prescient forecast. 'Parnell', he wrote, 'will "cut up" very badly, I feel sure, will hold on to the funds and otherwise endeavour to destroy the Irish cause to revenge his defeat; for he knows full well he can no longer serve it.'[66] Parnell did indeed 'cut up rough'. Gathering his followers round him, he moved the adjournment of the meeting and in so doing spoke out to the Irish public which had still to pronounce the final verdict. And the last words he uttered in Committee Room Fifteen were as defiant an exposition of the doctrine of the necessity for an independent party as any he had ever made:[67]

I wish to say in putting this resolution that the men who have deserted from our party this evening have deserted on the eve of the day when we were about to return to our own country and that these men, while clamouring for a decision, clamoured for that decision because they dreaded the lightning of public opinion in Ireland . . . Gentlemen, we have won today. Although our ranks are reduced in numbers, I hold this chair still . . . They left this room because their position here was no longer tenable. They saw they had arrayed against them that great force without which none of them would ever have come here. And recognizing that, they stand today in the most contemptible of all positions – the position of men who, having taken pledges to be true to their party, to be true to their leaders, to be true to their country, have been false to all these pledges.

CHAPTER 18

A Time of Rending

'The proceedings of this week have opened to our view a new chapter of human character and the experience of life.

It is like a demoniacal possession when the evil spirit will not depart without rending the body in which it has resided.'
(Gladstone to Cardinal Manning, 4 December 1890.)

I

Although the damage done in Committee Room Fifteen was so grave that the party split could not be healed for ten whole years thereafter, this was mercifully hidden from the two sides when they parted company on that December evening. The issue, as both knew, had to be fought to a finish in Ireland and no one could be sure how it would turn out. Each faction was early in the field, and while the party were still locked in debate Parnellites and anti-Parnellites had already begun to organize at home. On 1 December a number of Parnell's supporters met at the National Club, 1 Rutland (now Parnell) Square – the effective headquarters of Dublin Parnellism – and passed a resolution calling for the establishment of a committee 'to uphold Mr Parnell as a leader of the Irish people'. Two days later the first Parnell Leadership Committee was formed and other similar bodies quickly appeared elsewhere; within six months over eighty had been set up and though some of these had probably no more than a nominal membership, their geographical distribution was wide enough to indicate that Parnellism was far from being an isolated Dublin phenomenon.[1]

Almost simultaneously, the anti-Parnellites launched their own organization – the so-called 'National Committee' which, however, only got properly under way when the party members returned to Ireland after their ordeal in Committee Room Fifteen had ended. But even before they left London they had begun the almost unthinkable operation of creating a party without Parnell. On withdrawing from the final session on 6 December, the 45 gathered in another room, passed a resolution declaring that Parnell's chairmanship was terminated, and elected Justin McCarthy in his place. Later that evening they met informally and appointed another committee to launch a new Irish daily newspaper to combat the *Freeman's Journal*, which remained ferociously loyal to Parnell. Its principal member was T. M. Healy, who in the coming months was virtually to discontinue his lucrative career at the bar and give his whole time to running the paper and writing a considerable part of it.

At the same time, the first moves were made to raise funds – a desperately urgent matter, since 28 of the 45 seceding members were dependent on being paid a salary from the party treasure-chest, £200 a year for each needy individual when the money was available, much less when, as now, it was almost non-existent.* It was also decided to dispatch emissaries to France, to prevent Parnell from laying hands on the 'Paris fund', amounting to between £40,000 and £50,000. Finally, at a further meeting on 8 December, the anti-Parnellites elected a party committee, in effect their governing body, and also instructed Justin McCarthy to issue an address to the Irish people. This, when it appeared two days later, laid the blame for the crisis firmly on Parnell for not retiring after his re-election on 25 November, and insisted that his subsequent manifesto had made him politically impossible.[2]

All this was merely the prelude to the transfer of the struggle to Ireland, a transfer aptly symbolized by the fact that Parnell and Healy left London by the same train on the evening of 9 December. Perhaps it was also symbolic that in Dublin next morning Parnell received a rapturous welcome, while Tim Healy was assaulted in the streets.[3] Parnell's immediate purpose was to establish his authority in the capital beyond any shadow of a doubt. That done, he proposed to visit his constituents in Cork, and go from there to Kilkenny where a by-election was to provide the first trial of strength between the two sides. He was not long in Ireland before a startled country learned that it had a very different Parnell to deal with from the cold, aloof, invisible 'Chief' of other days.

His first target was *United Ireland*, which he still regarded as his own mouthpiece. In William O'Brien's absence, the paper was being run by

---

*Fourteen of the Parnellites were likewise dependent on salaries, but their position was less precarious since, as we shall see presently, Parnell was better placed financially than his opponents.

†There were in existence two 'Paris funds', the 'general' which comprised the much diminished balance of the Land League funds and the 'special' which had been accumulated since 1886; it was the latter which was the main object of dispute since it accounted for nearly all of the revenue mentioned above.

his deputy Matthew Bodkin. At the outset, he had adopted what was then the orthodox pro-Parnellite position, but a week later he had begun to waver. Then had followed Parnell's manifesto and the repudiation of it, and him, by the delegates in America. The unfortunate Bodkin was at once assailed by both sides. On 2 December he received two telegrams. One was from Parnell demanding that the leading article in the next issue be submitted to him before publication. The other was from O'Brien with instructions that if the party voted for Parnell in Committee Room Fifteen he should hand the paper over to Parnell's nominees, but that if the vote went against Parnell he should support the views expressed by the delegates in America and let no one else interfere. For Bodkin, the vote against Colonel Nolan's amendment on 2 December was the signal he needed and on 6 December he came out strongly on the anti-Parnellite side.[4]

When Parnell arrived in Dublin he went straight to the offices of *United Ireland*, accompanied by a few of his supporters and by the large, excitable crowd which dogged his footsteps whenever he moved about the city. Bodkin, returning after breakfast, found him in possession. Parnell dismissed him on the spot. Bodkin tried to argue that he had no right to do so and refused to leave the room when ordered, but when a mob poured into the office he surrendered at discretion. One of the Parnellites present laconically described the scene: 'I went up to Matty Bodkin. "Matty", says I, "will you walk out or would you like to be thrown out" and Matty walked out.'[5]

But this was merely a preliminary skirmish. Parnell's main objective was to use a mass meeting of his supporters at the Rotunda that night as a means of speaking directly to his countrymen for the first time since the beginning of the crisis. Just before the meeting, in an interview with the London correspondent of the New York *World*, he ruthlessly, or recklessly, widened the gap between himself and his opponents. Repeating the argument he had used in Committee Room Fifteen, that he had kept silent about the Hawarden conversations in the hope that better terms might be obtained thereafter, he was then asked why he had revealed the details in his manifesto. To this he replied: 'Because Mr Gladstone's letter meant the breaking-off of negotiations with me. He appealed to the Irish party as my judge, and consequently as my successor. It was, therefore, necessary for me, doubtful as I was of the stability of the party and its capacity for negotiation, to impart my knowledge to Ireland.' This set the pattern for Parnell's strategy which was, characteristically, to take the offensive whenever possible. It was based on the assumption – incorrect, but widely shared – that a general election was imminent and that this would be the final arbiter of the quarrel. Until then, it would be war to the knife.[6]

There remained one further possibility – that members of the American delegation might mediate in the dispute. They had waited helplessly, and with fluctuating feelings, while the debates in London swayed this way and that. O'Brien, impulsive as always, was bitterly disillusioned and vehement, though, as Harrington noted, less against Parnell than against his supporters. Dillon, calmer and more resolute, was divided between a determination never to serve under Parnell again and a professional admiration for his political expertise.[7] When the party was persuaded to accept the Clancy amendment on 4 December and to seek guarantees from the Liberals, Dillon was sure that Parnell had won. 'It seems to me now', he recorded in his diary, 'that the only way out of the imbroglio is that Parnell should resume the lead, and all members of the party who can reconcile it to their conscience and honour to follow him should fall into line again.'[8] Even when Gladstone had checked this manœuvre, Dillon was still convinced that Parnell not only had outwitted, but would continue to outwit, his enemies. 'Every fresh development', he wrote, 'only increases my admiration for the infinite political skill of Parnell, his power of planning a campaign, of *seeing* what ideas will take hold of the minds of the people, of diverting discussion from the real points in controversy . . .'[9]

At this point telegrams flowed in from both sections of the party. On 6 December Justin McCarthy cabled for authority to add their names to the anti-Parnellite address he had just been charged with drawing up.[10] Significantly, they refused to give it.[11] Then, on 8 December cables began to arrive from Parnell. One was for Harrington, telling him to return to Ireland at once. The other was for William O'Brien and contained the remarkable news that Parnell would be willing to meet him for discussions.[12] Next day, further cables came from John Redmond and Dr Kenny, urging the delegates, and particularly O'Brien, to come to France for consultation.[13] (The choice of France was dictated by the fact that if Dillon and O'Brien landed anywhere in the United Kingdom they would be arrested immediately to serve the sentences from which they had escaped in September.) This suggestion may not have been known to Parnell, but his own cable and a statement in the *Freeman's Journal* on 10 December that O'Brien was preparing to go to France to meet him, indicate clearly enough that the idea of a conference between them was in the offing even at that early stage.[14]

Yet he allowed none of this to appear in public. On the contrary, when asked if the return of Dillon and O'Brien would be of assistance, he replied loftily that it was too late. 'Mr Gladstone's obstinacy on the one hand, and the ignorance and inexperience of so many members of the party on the other, had produced the catastrophe.' 'Messrs Dillon and O'Brien, instead of taking up the position of mediators, took sides against me from the first, and so lost the opportunity of successful intervention.'[15] This, besides not being strictly true, did not look promising for the prospects of future negotiation. But, as so often with Parnell, the inconsistency between his public and his secret utterances was more apparent than real. To open a private line of communication to the American delegates was an obvious tactic, but one that only needed to be used in extremity. If things went right in Ireland then his position would be so strong that his enemies would either be silenced or driven to sue for terms. But if things went wrong – if, for instance, the fight at Kilkenny was lost – then it might become highly desirable to bring the American delegates back into play and take up with them the threads which had been severed so decisively in Committee Room Fifteen.

Meanwhile there was Dublin to be conquered. As he marched in torch-lit procession through the streets to the Rotunda she yielded herself a willing, almost a languorous, victim. Here is how the young poet, Katharine Tynan, who was present, described the scene:[16]

It was nearly 8.30 when we heard the bands coming; then the windows were lit up by the lurid glare of thousands of torches in the street outside. There was a distant roaring like the sea. The great gathering within waited silently with expectation. Then the cheering began, and we craned our necks and looked on eagerly, and there was the tall, slender, distinguished figure of the Irish leader making its way across the platform. I don't think any words could do justice to his reception. The house rose at him; everywhere around there was a sea of passionate faces, loving, admiring, almost worshipping that silent, pale man. The cheering broke out again and again; there was no quelling it. Mr Parnell bowed from side to side, sweeping the assemblage with his eagle glance. The people were fairly mad with excitement . . .

I said to Dr Kenny, who was standing by me, 'He is the only quiet man here.' 'Outwardly', said the keen medical man, emphatically. Looking again, one saw the dilated nostrils, the flashing eye, the passionate face: the leader was simply drinking in thirstily this immense love, which must have been more heartening than one can say after that bitter time in the English capital. Mr Parnell looked frail enough in body – perhaps the black frock-coat, buttoned so tightly across his chest, gave him that look of attenuation; but he also looked full of indomitable spirit and fire.

Although it may have been true, as Archbishop Walsh surmised, that the Rotunda audience was hand-picked, there was no denying either its size or its frenzied enthusiasm for 'the Chief'.[17] Nor could it be denied that he seized his opportunity with both hands. Using Gladstone's letter to Morley as his text, he preached the sermon he was to preach repeatedly during the coming months – that while independent opposition was the key to parliamentary politics, parliamentary politics themselves might not in the end be enough. At each previous crisis of his career, this well-worn doctrine had been paraded almost as though it were the ark of the covenant, but never before had circumstances given it such significance. With the Liberal alliance apparently dissolved and the Irish party itself in pieces, what he had to say about the fragility of the constitutional movement acquired a new and frightening relevance:[18]

I have not misled you. I have never said that this constitutional movement must succeed. I have never promised you absolute success, but I have promised you this, that if you trust me, I will do all that mortal man can do to perform it. What is the position? We stand at the parting of the ways ... It is an issue which means the life or death of the constitutional movement ... if Ireland cannot win upon this line within the constitution, she can win upon no other line within the constitution, and if our constitutional movement of today is broken, sundered, separated, discredited and forgotten, England will be face to face with that imperishable force which tonight gives me vitality and power, and without which we are broken reeds ... And if Ireland leaves this path upon which I have led her ... I will not for my part say that I will not accompany her further.

Almost at once he had an opportunity to demonstrate the doctrine in action. While he was speaking at the Rotunda, some bold anti-Parnellites reoccupied the office of *United Ireland*. Learning of this at breakfast next morning, Parnell resolved to retrieve the situation before leaving for Cork. Jumping into a carriage, he drove headlong towards the newspaper's premises where an expectant crowd had already gathered. Parnell dashed through them as if they did not exist, and arrived at the office, checked his horse so abruptly that it fell flat in the street. He sprang out, rushed up the steps and hammered on the door. All was silent within. There was a brief pause while he held a muttered conference with his followers. Then a pickaxe and a crowbar were brought. Someone mentioned the possibility of storming the fortress through the basement. In a flash Parnell made as if to vault the railings and drop into the area. His friends held him back and his voice rang out clearly: 'Go yourselves, if you will not let me.' Go they did, but while they forced an entrance below, Parnell seized the crowbar and smashed in the main door. He and those around him charged into the hall and immediately collided with the other storming party rushing up from below. Then, having sorted themselves out, the invaders surged upstairs only to find an almost empty office. The occupying force had prudently withdrawn through a back door and a small rearguard was easily overpowered. What happened next was described by a fascinated bystander:[19]

> One of the windows on the second storey was removed and Parnell suddenly appeared in the aperture. He had conquered. The enthusiasm which greeted him cannot be described. His face was ghastly pale, save only that on either cheek a hectic crimson spot was glowing. His hat was off now, his hair dishevelled, the dust of conflict begrimed his well-brushed coat. The people were spellbound, almost terrified, as they gazed on him. For myself, I felt a thrill of dread, as if I looked at a tiger in the frenzy of its rage. Then he spoke and the tone of his voice was even more terrible than his look. He was brief, rapid, decisive, and the closing words of his speech still ring in my ear: 'I rely on Dublin. Dublin is true. What Dublin says today Ireland will say tomorrow.'*

II

But would Ireland follow Dublin? The issue had to be put to the test without delay. From the capture of *United Ireland* he went straight to King's Bridge station where he boarded the train for Cork. That evening he arrived in his constituency to be met by huge, excited crowds similar to those which had accompanied him everywhere in Dublin. At once he plunged into a frantic succession of meetings and

---

*United Ireland, thus recaptured, remained in Parnell's possession. For three days – 13, 15 and 16 December – the indefatigable Bodkin brought out a substitute called '*Suppressed*' *United Ireland*. When Parnell secured an injunction to prevent him using the name *United Ireland*, Bodkin altered the title to *Insuppressible* and continued to publish it under great difficulties until 24 January 1891 when it ceased to appear in circumstances described below.

speeches, all designed to drive home the message he had proclaimed incessantly since his return to Ireland – that he had always anticipated that Gladstone and Ireland might once more be in conflict and that therefore the country must stand firm on the line of independent opposition. It was noticeable, though, that in Cork he began to develop a second theme which was soon to become familiar – that the basis for the national support he was seeking would be the working-class whose interests he pledged himself to support. It seemed that in his revulsion from the parliamentary party he was swinging away from the business-men and the lawyers, so many of whom had repudiated his authority, and turning instinctively towards the dumb multitudes with whose concerns, if the truth be told, he had not greatly occupied himself for many years past.[20]

Yet, for all this exhilarating action, which probably represented for him an essential psychological release, there was a physical price to be paid. Most descriptions of him refer to his fatigue and evident frailty. In London on 8 December, just before he set off for his whirlwind visit to Ireland, he sent for the journalist Barry O'Brien, to talk to him about the Kilkenny election. Before the split there had been an agreed candidate, the eccentric ex-colonial governor, Sir John Pope-Hennessy, who had sat in parliament as an Irish Tory many years before and who may have served Trollope as one of the models for Phineas Finn.[21] 'He [Parnell] looked tired, ill, distressed', noted O'Brien. 'He seemed to me to be absolutely without energy. He leant back on the seat and appeared to be quite absent-minded.' Speaking in a low voice 'and as if suffering physical pain', he asked O'Brien to be his candidate if Pope-Hennessy declared – as next day he did – for the anti-Parnellite side. O'Brien objected that a man with enough money to fight the election was what was really needed and this ruled him out. Yielding to that argument, Parnell instead persuaded a wealthy supporter, Vincent Scully, to stand. But O'Brien agreed to act as a reserve and thus became a fascinated eye-witness of the campaign.[22]

It hardly seemed as if Parnell would have the strength to get there, let alone fight the election. At Cork his old friend, M. J. Horgan, sat near him in the Victoria Hotel. 'He looked', he said afterwards, 'like a hunted hind; his hair was dishevelled, his beard unkempt, his eyes were wild and restless. The room was full of people. He sat down to a chop; but he only made a pretence at eating.' Eventually Horgan took him home to bed. There, he swallowed two raw eggs in rapid succession and went off to sleep. Yet at seven o'clock next morning, he was sitting up in bed with a glass of hot water in his hands, full of impracticable plans for dealing with the Plan of Campaign.[23]

From Cork Parnell went straight to Kilkenny, whither some of his leading opponents had already preceded him. The anti-Parnellite strategy was planned by Tim Healy and Michael Davitt, who divided the constituency into districts, assigning several members of their party to each district. The Parnellites worked to a similar plan and Healy may not have been far out in estimating the number of MPs who poured into the constituency at about seventy.[24] Since the entire campaign was confined to ten days – between 12 December and 22 December – both sides made an all-out effort. But the weather conditions were so bad and the strain so intense, that the barriers of restraint soon crumbled, tempers were lost, unforgivable things were said, and argument eventually degenerated into actual violence.

Parnell arrived on 12 December and made his headquarters at the Victoria Hotel in Kilkenny town. There Barry O'Brien found him next evening stretched out upon some chairs to catch an hour's sleep in front of the fire. He looked like a dying man. 'He's been very ill', said the faithful J. J. O'Kelly, and indeed the whole upper floor of the hotel had the atmosphere of a sick-room.[25] However, O'Kelly bullied him into bed and by next morning his remarkable physical and mental resilience had reasserted itself. He turned Barry O'Brien into an honorary private secretary and asked him to open his letters, keeping those he thought important (as well as all telegrams) but destroying the rest – this being, of course, the principle upon which he had conducted his correspondence for years past. Freed from these administrative encumbrances he flung himself heart and soul into the election, travelling all over the constituency in rain and cold, speaking at innumerable meetings and hammering away endlessly at the necessity for 'independent opposition', and more ominously, hinting at the alternative which lay behind if that did not prove sufficient.

Not surprisingly, Parnell's cause once more began to attract the attention of the Fenians. To Michael Davitt, who had long since made his grand renunciation of revolutionary politics, this was the most sinister and tragic development which the crisis had yet produced. The mere notion that armed rebellion might be substituted for constitutional agitation now filled him with anguish. It would, he said, be 'criminal folly for him [Parnell] or any other man to ask the young men of Ireland to face the overwhelming might of England in the field. Mr Parnell himself would be the last man to lead the way in this policy of madness and desperation . . .'[26]

Even if Parnell did not propose to go to such extremes – and though he talked much about what he *might* do in certain circumstances, he said little about what he actually *would* do – the Fenians were undoubtedly behind him. At the height of the struggle there appeared in his name (though apparently without his permission, perhaps even without his knowledge) an 'appeal to the hillside men'. They had been best defined a couple of years earlier by, of all people, Captain O'Shea, when he described the 'old nationalists' as 'the men who thought the day might come when they could fight their country's battle on the hill-side against the British forces . . .'[27] At Kilkenny John Redmond echoed this definition when he said that Parnell's fight was the same fight that had been carried on for centuries. 'It was the same old fight that in the old dark days was fought by the brave Irishmen on the hill-sides, which was fought by other weapons in the days of the Land League.'[28] The 'appeal' itself certainly minced no words:[29]

> Will you give him up to the Saxon wolves who howl for his destruction? Or will you rally round him as your fathers rallied round the men of '98, and shout with a thousand voices, 'No surrender!' 'Hurrah for Charles Stewart Parnell, the leader of an independent Irish party, and down with the faction which would make the Irish people the servants of a foreign power!'

Parnell, admittedly, was careful to repudiate the document and in a key speech at Kilkenny he explicitly denied having any intention to hurl the young men of Ireland against the armed might of England. So long, he said, as he could lead an independent party in the English parliament there was still hope of winning legislative independence by constitutional means. 'But . . . when I can no longer hope to obtain our constitution by constitutional means, I will in a moment so declare it to the people of Ireland, and returning at the head of my party, I will take counsel with you as to the next step.' This, he claimed, was essentially what he had said at Cork ten years earlier when he had first emerged as leader.* 'If the young men of Ireland have trusted in me it is because they know that I am not a mere parliamentarian; that I can be trusted to keep my word to them to go as far as a brave and honest heart can go on this parliamentary alliance . . . and that when and if I find it useless and unavailing to persevere further, they can depend upon me to tell them so.'[30]

True, in this speech he did not specify what not being 'a mere parliamentarian' actually meant. True, he did not commit himself, in

---

*For his position in 1880, see above, p. 130.. In fact he had been much more explicit in 1885. See above, pp. 260-1.

the event of the constitutional movement breaking down, to anything more blood-curdling than coming among the people 'to take counsel' with them. True, he had said much the same thing before, and more recently than 1880.* But circumstances alter cases and in the hectic atmosphere of the split, the men of Kilkenny, like the men of Dublin and the men of Cork, could be forgiven for feeling that he had moved decisively away from constitutional politics.

Although in cold blood Parnell's doctrine was desolate enough – for it meant abandoning virtually every political vantage-point that had been won in the last ten years – in the high fever of the election it was potentially more alluring than the cautious moderation which was the only line left open to his opponents. Their infinitely more difficult task was to demonstrate to an inflamed electorate that although they all, save Davitt, had rallied to their leader after the divorce court verdict, Gladstone's intervention and Parnell's manifesto had so changed the situation that they had had to jettison the man to save the cause. But behind this well-worn argument lay a bitterness that had its roots in resentment at the attitude of casual mastery which Parnell had for so long taken towards his colleagues. 'Were they', as Davitt asked, 'prepared to sacrifice Home Rule for one man's ambition and allow an insolent dictator to destroy the hopes built up in the last twelve years?'[31]

Unhappily, it was easy, once the quality of Parnell's leadership had been called in question, to descend from argument to abuse. And with the divorce court 'revelations' plain for all to read, it was obvious where the main arsenal of abuse would be found. With increasing frequency the name of Katharine O'Shea began to creep into the speeches of Parnell's opponents and Healy, particularly, used this weapon repeatedly, even reverting to the Galway election of 1886 to tell his audience that 'he knew, and Mr Biggar knew, the true facts in connection with the Eltham intrigue . . . they knew he [Parnell] was prostituting a seat in parliament to the interests of his own private intrigues'.[32] More crudely still, he observed two days later that Parnell had put O'Shea into Galway 'as the price of his wife'.[33]

This would have been deplorable at any time but at that moment it was doubly so, for a reason Healy could not have known. By a strange chance Parnell was just then engaged in a highly secret exchange with Archbishop Walsh on the subject of his relationship with Katharine O'Shea. The evidence is incomplete, but enough has survived to

*For example, during the 1885 election and after the Pigott fiasco in 1889; see above, pp. 260-1, 443-4.

indicate that the archbishop, who had clung tenaciously to the hope that Parnell would be able to offer a satisfactory explanation, sent him a message through the editor of the *Freeman's Journal*, intimating that if Parnell cared to make a confidential statement to him, Dr Walsh would be glad to hear it.[34] Parnell, of course, could not respond without endangering the decree *nisi*, but he was moved to write a letter to the archbishop which if it did nothing else, showed at what a different level the whole controversy might have been conducted in other circumstances. 'I highly appreciate', he wrote, 'the feeling which induced Your Grace to accept the suggestion that I should speak to you fully and confidentially upon a certain subject.' He had explained to the editor, he said, that while 'most anxious' to do anything in his power, it was not possible for him to speak freely 'at present' even to the archbishop. 'I do not however wish Your Grace to suppose that this reticence need be permanent as after a brief period I hope to be in a position to speak confidentially.' 'I will always remember', he concluded almost wistfully, 'the kindness which has induced Your Grace to consent to receiving any confidential communication from me upon this subject.'[35]

The reticence of which Parnell spoke was necessitated by the fact that six months had to elapse before the decree *nisi* could be made absolute. If, during that period, any hint of O'Shea's connivance in the relations of his wife with Parnell had been made public, then the marriage on which Parnell had set his heart would have been in jeopardy. The contrast between the archbishop's tact and the crudity of Parnell's parliamentary opponents may well have made the latter's gibes still more difficult to bear, provoking him to retaliate with a concentrated venom which betrayed the strain he was under. He, the calm, unruffled leader, so long accustomed to keeping his party at a distance, now sank to gutter abuse which would have seemed childish had it not also been tragic. Thus, in rapid succession, he allowed himself to refer to Dr Tanner MP as 'a cock-sparrow', Davitt as 'a jackdaw' and Justin McCarthy as 'a nice old gent for a tea-party'.[36]

It was not wise to include Davitt in this menagerie. In some ways the most formidable of all Parnell's opponents he at once struck back with the accusation most calculated to touch his adversary on the raw. 'False to friends and false to country', he wrote in an article designed for English consumption, but reproduced in the *Freeman's Journal*, 'he now stands revealed as a tyrant the most unscrupulous that ever rode roughshod over the hopes and sentiments of a nation . . . Well may it be asked: "Is Mr Parnell mad?" That there are evidences of insanity in his actions no one can doubt. But surely all who follow him are not tainted with madness? Surely the Irish race will not allow this man to wreck their hopes?'[37] It was a question Davitt was not alone in asking. To Gladstone and his friends, looking on appalled and fascinated at the hell let loose in Ireland, the same thought had occurred. Parnell must be 'off his head' wrote Granville to Spencer.[38] Cardinal Manning told Gladstone that his belief that Parnell was of unsound mind was 'still more confirmed', while the appeal to the hillside men (which he assumed was Parnell's own work) was 'the last scintillation'.[39] Gladstone himself was reminded, so he told John Morley, of the internecine fury of the Jewish factions in Jerusalem while Titus and his legions were marching on the city; he did not specify who, if not himself, qualified for the role of Titus on this occasion.[40]

From verbal savagery it was a short step to physical violence. North Kilkenny was an intimidating constituency at the best of times, containing not only a large population of rugged farmers, but also the miners of Castlecomer, while in Kilkenny city itself a volatile mob swirled constantly around the headquarters of the rival factions. Given the circumstances it was only too likely that argument by blackthorn would usurp the place of reason, but when the violence did occur it was curiously symbolic that the two leading figures – Parnell and Davitt – should both have been its victims almost simultaneously. This happened largely because both men chose to speak at the same places on the same day (16 December). Two ugly incidents occurred in rapid succession. First, at Ballinakill, a confused scuffle broke out between the two sides during which the one-armed Davitt received a heavy blow from a stick. Then a little later, in Castlecomer, Parnell so infuriated the audience by his personal attacks on Davitt that as he drove away from the meeting the brake upon which he was sitting was showered with mud and stones and slaked lime. He was hit in one eye over which, for some days thereafter, he wore a bandage. It was typical of the bitterness which the election had generated that a dispute broke out immediately as to whether Parnell had been struck by lime or merely by flour. Parnell himself was naturally anxious to reassure Katharine, but his telegram making light of the matter was intercepted and published to prove that there was nothing wrong with him. Henry Harrison, who was at Parnell's side when the incident happened, assured the present writer – some sixty years afterwards but in the most vivid terms – that lime did enter Parnell's eye which was for a time considerably inflamed.[41]

Yet, in the end, the casual violence of unruly roughs was a marginal factor. The real struggle was between the magic of Parnell's name, linked as that increasingly was with a shadowy Fenianism, and the forces of Catholic nationalism headed by the priests. That the role of the priests was significant, probably decisive, was the view of many contemporaries, pre-eminent among whom was the local Bishop of Ossory, Dr Abraham Brownrigg. Even before the campaign began, he assured Archbishop Walsh that there was no place in Ireland where Parnell could have fought which was so unfavourable to him. 'Happily', he wrote, 'in every single instance but one in the diocese the local branches of the [Irish National] League are presided over by the priests, so that we may regard them as reflecting the views of the clergy.'[42] Three days later, with the election in full swing, he reported that his priests assured him of victory, though he was cautious enough to add that since Irish voters were so untrustworthy it was impossible to be sure:

> I may say that the whole city of Kilkenny turned out last night to receive Parnell. Amongst them some of those who always professed greatest friendship for me. The *ladies* (so called) were the most demonstrative of all. The lowest dregs of the people, the Fenian element, and the working-classes are all to a man with Parnell. Money flows and has been flowing in golden streams in Kilkenny for the past fortnight and it was only yesterday that this became known to us . . . in a word, everything bad or corrupt has come to the surface in favour of Parnell.

This was not perhaps a very subtle analysis, but believing it implicitly himself, the bishop was spurred to further effort. 'All that mortal man can do', he promised, 'shall be done by me and my priests and by all whom I can, in any way, influence.' Nor did Dr Brownrigg disdain more spiritual aids. 'It would do no harm', he added, 'if prayers could be got for Ireland, especially in our convents, at this terrible crisis.'[43]

But the struggle on the ground took an altogether more brutal form. So brutal indeed that the bishop began, as Dr Croke reported to Dublin, to be 'very nervous' and 'very doubtful' about the outcome.[44] 'The battle has been a dreadful one', Dr Brownrigg wrote. 'No doubt but the first choice of the people would be Parnell. We had to dislodge him from their prejudices, which with weak, ignorant and unreflecting people is no easy task.' But the clergy (all anti-Parnellite save a mere handful) were leaving no stone unturned. 'Today they are off canvassing in all directions.'[45] On voting day, he wrote soon after, the priests from the different parishes 'will head their men and march to the polling-place'. With shocked surprise he recorded that rumours were circulating that if Parnell's candidate were unsuccessful, a petition would be lodged to

unseat his opponent on the ground of undue clerical influence. However, he wrote cheerfully, 'they have not a shred of hope. For beyond
the natural and legitimate influence, none other was used.'[46] By 22
December he thought the worst was over. Even in the city support for
Parnell seemed to be ebbing 'and his followers are like spaniels at the
feet of the priests, watching for a token of forgiveness'.[47] On Christmas
Eve he was able to register a resounding success, the credit for which he
attributed unhesitatingly to his clergy. 'All worked night and day and
strained every energy to win and it is to them that is really due the
victory that crowns our banners.'[48]

Parnell would certainly have agreed with him. He had throughout
been fully aware of the extent of clerical pressure and of its likely effect
upon the result. At one stage, enraged by the news that priests were preparing to act as personation agents in the polling-booths – that is, to be
present when illiterates declared to the returning-officer how they wished
to vote – he contemplated a protest to the sheriff and fell violently out
of humour with his supporters when they tried to make him see that the
practice, however undesirable, was perfectly legal. He only desisted
when Barry O'Brien pointed out that to send his protest to the sheriff
would in effect be 'drawing the sword on the whole order instead of
objecting to the action of any individual priest. "O'Connell could afford
to do this; you can't. If the priests are to be fought, they must be fought
by Catholics, not by Protestants." "Ah, now", he said, "you have said
something which is quite true . . ." "Shall I tear this?" I said, holding
up the protest. "Yes", he answered with his old pleasant and winning
smile.'[49] In the result, the clergy did so act and Tim Harrington, who
had arrived back from America just in time for the *dénouement*, wrote
angrily to William O'Brien that Kilkenny was 'the saddest sight I ever
witnessed in Ireland'. 'In every polling-booth in the division a priest sat
at the table as a personation agent. The people were instructed to declare they could not read and the voters came in bodies with the priests
[? at] their heads declaring they were Catholics and would vote with
their clergy.'[50]

III

With such forces operating against Parnell there could be little doubt as
to the result, though right up to the end the excitement remained fierce.
It was even rumoured that the Fenians were planning an attack on the
ballot-boxes as these were brought in from the outlying, and strongly
anti-Parnellite, district of Castlecomer. It was said that the plot was

betrayed to Davitt who promptly notified the sheriff. Certainly, extreme precautions were taken, and Healy, who accompanied the precious boxes through a night of pouring rain, has left a vivid account of how startled he was to see rifle barrels gleaming amid the hedgerows in the reflected light of the carriage lamps, until he realized that they belonged to the RIC.[51] Once the Castlecomer votes were safely harvested victory was certain and when the result was announced (Pope-Hennessy 2527 votes, Scully 1362 votes) the margin of 1165 was almost precisely what Healy himself had prophesied a few days earlier.[52]

This came as no surprise to Parnell. On the eve of polling day he came back to his hotel, stripped off his coat, hat and scarf, removed his boots and socks, warmed his feet and remained in deep silence for twenty minutes. Then turning with a smile to Barry O'Brien, he said: 'They are making calculations in the other room of our majority. I think they will be surprised when the poll is declared tomorrow. We have been well beaten. But it is only the first battle of the campaign. I will contest every election in the country. I will fight while I live.'[53] After the result was announced this was the burden of his message to the world at large. He would fight, he said, in every constituency as occasion offered, and when it seemed to him hopeless to expect legislative independence from Britain by means within the constitution, he would call upon his colleagues 'to shake the dust off our feet upon the palace at Westminster' and return to Ireland to take counsel with the people. But he ended on a characteristically ambiguous note:[54]

> I renew to you men of Kilkenny the pledge which I made to the citizens of Cork in 1880 . . . I will never allow my name and my authority to be used to tempt the people of Ireland into any hopeless struggle, either constitutional or otherwise, and when constitutional struggle, if it ever does (I don't say it ever will) becomes useless and unavailing, at that moment I will declare my belief to you and I will take your advice and be guided by your judgement.

The qualifications here are obvious in retrospect, but at the time, naturally, his actions spoke louder than his words, and even among his words it was the most uncompromising which rang out the loudest. Disregarding his efforts to keep his options open, men fastened instead upon what seemed to them the most potent fact of the situation. This was that when Parnell stepped down, or was cast down, from his pedestal he revealed himself as a human being, vulnerable and a prey to passion, like anyone else. And like anyone else, his judgement was not only fallible, but seen to be fallible. The deliberate breach of faith with Gladstone, the breaking off of the Liberal alliance, the aspersions hurled at his former colleagues, the violence of his behaviour in Dublin, the invective poured upon his opponents at Kilkenny – all these suggested hidden depths which made men shudder and fear for his reason.

Yet, despite Davitt's savage questioning of his sanity, there was no real cause to believe that he was mad. On the contrary, his political instincts were as keen as ever and the next few weeks were to show that his genius for tactical manœuvre was still immense. It is easy, indeed, to understand that his enemies should have jumped to the conclusion that he had lost his wits, partly because his family history planted a doubt in many people's minds, and still more because the almost demonic energy he had displayed in the weeks since the divorce suit had ended was so much at variance with the mysterious aloofness which had come to be accepted as his normal pattern of behaviour. But they failed to allow sufficiently for two salient features of his personality. The first was his pride, which had been deeply wounded both by the attacks upon Katharine and by the fact that a majority of his own party had repudiated him. The second was that at bottom he remained as always a man of action. The calm he had habitually maintained in politics had been a tense, precarious calm, and in Committee Room Fifteen he had been like a coiled spring. Dublin and Kilkenny allowed that spring to release itself in action, but the action, though extreme, was not unbalanced – on the contrary, it was the natural response of a born fighter to a situation where deeds at last took welcome precedence over debate.

Nevertheless, even if his tactics and attitudes could be explained in rational terms, there was no avoiding the central fact which Kilkenny had demonstrated beyond a doubt; that the whole trend of his policy, which was in effect to resume the freedom of manœuvre he had voluntarily surrendered in 1886, was a breathtaking *volte face*, based on a fundamental assumption that was no longer true. Ireland simply did not have, *within the constitutional framework*, the freedom of choice she had had before Gladstone had declared for Home Rule and the Tories had declared against it. The inescapable logic of 1886 was that the only possible hope for Home Rule in any foreseeable future lay in the Liberal alliance; it might be a strong hope or a feeble hope, but it remained the only hope. Therefore, to disrupt the pattern Parnell himself had been at such pains to establish in the previous five years could mean at best indefinite postponement, at worst the ruin, of the constitutional movement he had almost single-handedly created.

There were those, of course, for whom the postponement of Home Rule was a minor matter and the ruin of the constitutional movement a positive gain. It was in the logic of Parnell's new situation – or rather of his attempt to recreate an old situation – that the men who had hoped for great things from him at the start of his career should gather round him again now that it had reached its decisive crisis. From the moment the party split in two Fenian support for Parnell had become increasingly articulate. For obvious reasons, the degree of backing actually supplied by a secret society like the Irish Republican Brotherhood is impossible to quantify, but the unanimity of leading individuals in ranging themselves on his side is too striking to be ignored. Early in December two of the most famous names of the previous generation, James Stephens and John O'Leary, declared in his favour. Although both were old men, long out of active politics, they were symbols of a tradition which had never accepted the suppression of revolutionary action by parliamentary debate.[55] Nor were they alone. In England there were plain indications that Fenian influence, such as it was, would be exerted on his behalf, and in America the most formidable Irish extremist on either side of the Atlantic, John Devoy, left no one in any doubt where his sympathies lay.[56] The appeal to the hillside men in Kilkenny, and their apparent response to it, seemed therefore to confirm what moderate men had already begun to think and say, that the moment he cut loose from constitutional politics, Parnell would find himself in thrall to the Fenians.

This was not only a dubious reinforcement, but also a reinforcement which had rallied to Parnell's banner without really understanding what the battle was about. For, although he was fighting with his back to the wall, it was scarcely conceivable that he would commit himself to the revolutionary movement any more wholeheartedly in 1890 than he had done in 1878 or 1879. On the contrary, the reservations, implicit or explicit, in the major speeches he had made since his return to Ireland, suggested strongly that the most he was prepared to do was to lay before the people what the future *might* be like if the parliamentary party were to base itself upon subservience to the Liberals. But whether he could stand upon this middle ground between militancy and moderation remained extremely doubtful. For if the Kilkenny election indicated anything, it indicated that when he put to the voters his policy of the middle ground – that is, the resumption of independent opposition, leading on in certain circumstances to abstention from Westminster – the voters were moved by powerful pressures to reject it. No doubt the influence of the church was prominent, even paramount, in bringing about this rejection, but it would be naïve to deny that the defeat of Parnell's candidate at Kilkenny was partly also a product of the unwillingness of many ordinary and deeply confused people to abandon overnight the belief which Parnell himself had instilled into them, that if Home Rule was to come in their lifetime it could come only from the alliance with the Liberal party forged in and after 1886.

Yet Kilkenny, as Parnell said, was only the first battle in the campaign. It had been for him a bruising, damaging defeat, but he allowed no trace of this to appear in his outward demeanour. Returning to Dublin, he was cheered to the echo by the vast crowd assembled at King's Bridge to meet him. From the station he was escorted with bands and banners and flaming torches to the Parnell Leadership Committee rooms in Rutland Square. Once again he added to the fast-growing legend of the new Parnell. As he stood up in the waggonette to acknowledge the cheers, he was an awesome sight – his hair and beard ruffled in the wind, a bandage still covering his injured eye. When the procession passed the Bank of Ireland in College Green, which had originally housed Grattan's parliament, he spoke no word, but flung out his arm and pointed to the building. Did he inwardly recall a similar moment, and a similar gesture, in the vastly different circumstances of 1881? We cannot tell. But the element of parody was hidden from the crowd, which responded with a deep roar of applause.[57] For them, the gesture symbolized both his policy and his resolve. Nothing, it seemed, had been changed by Kilkenny.

CHAPTER 19

Last Chance

'Now I am wholly convinced that an understanding with him is *our* only salvation also, if the country is to be held together . . . Let *nothing* tempt us to join in any howl for his destruction. If we smash his men, we will be smashed ourselves.' (William O'Brien to John Dillon, 13 December 1890.)

I

In reality a great deal had been changed by Kilkenny. Parnell himself might still be indomitable, but there could be no disguising either that there *had* been a defeat, or that this, strongly identified as it was by both sides with clerical intervention on the grand scale, pointed a moral from which many would draw inescapable conclusions.

It is against this background that the next episode in the struggle – the so-called 'Boulogne negotiations' – has to be seen. We saw earlier that Parnell had expressed his readiness to meet William O'Brien and that O'Brien was prepared to go to France for that purpose. But Parnell's double assault on *United Ireland* had not improved the prospects for a successful conference and Bodkin's almost incoherent cable to O'Brien was hardly calculated to ease the latter's mind:[1]

> Resolute manifesto from you, Dillon, sorely needed. Parnell playing with you. Strikes foul blow while you hold your hands. Retook offices mid-night. Today Parnell himself broke in with crowbars assisted by O'Connor, Kenny, Leamy, Redmond and mob, police standing by. Old employees expelled. Rumours actively circulated that you, Dillon, coming round to Parnell. *Freeman, Telegraph* blackguard, rousing mob. Country with us. Vigour and promptness win. *Suppressed United Ireland* appearing today . . . Cable supporting paper.

But O'Brien proved a disappointment to his deputy, who was working like a slave to produce any kind of paper at all and expected full support from America. True, the anti-Parnellite delegates in the States did issue a manifesto which stressed the importance of the Liberal alliance and asserted that the winning of the next general election would be impossible if Parnell continued as leader.[2] But of the leader himself they spoke with careful moderation, and it is clear from what survives of their private conversations that the news from Ireland had made them both more hopeless and more conciliatory. O'Brien especially, whom Harrington visited just before leaving for Ireland, asked that it should be explained to Parnell how they deprecated the attacks on him and hated finding themselves on the same side as Healy, Davitt and the priests. Harrington took away the strong impression that they were 'most ready' to discuss peace proposals, but that no terms would be admissible which did not include Parnell's temporary retirement from the chairmanship.[3]

Neither O'Brien nor Dillon was therefore receptive when Bodkin's warlike communications began to arrive from Dublin. He, naturally, was concerned to vindicate himself and to make the absent delegates realize the intensity of the crisis at home. On 17 December, when he had got his substitute paper into print by superhuman efforts, he wrote to explain that if he had not gone strongly against Parnell, 'in a week's time Parnellism would have swept the country like a whirlwind'. Recognizing that O'Brien's moderate stance might give him considerable leverage as a peace-maker, Bodkin still insisted that if it had been universally adopted 'the violence of the other side would have swept the country before your arrival'.[4] But Bodkin was beating the air. On 11 December, O'Brien, T. P. O'Connor and T. P. Gill met in New York to discuss what terms O'Brien might offer if and when he met Parnell in France. They were remarkably generous terms, indicating not only what immense importance the delegates attached to re-establishing the unity of the party, but also how out of touch they were with the raw asperities of the struggle as it was developing in Ireland. Almost every point they jotted down for O'Brien's guidance represented a concession to Parnell.

He was indeed to be asked to retire, but it was to be suggested to him that this would probably be only temporary, that his influence would continue to be dominant and that his return to the leadership would be welcomed under certain, unspecified conditions. They even apparently considered allowing him to nominate his successor for the coming year, but though they abandoned this they were prepared to admit that McCarthy's election had been informal and, if Parnell wished it, to submit his name for re-election by the whole party. It seems that they also contemplated some public declaration by the party explaining the mitigating circumstances which had influenced Parnell's action during the crisis. More remarkable still, they aimed to persuade Archbishops Croke and Walsh to withdraw their denunciations of him.

In practical terms, they were prepared to allow Parnell to remain president of the Irish National League, and to be joint treasurer of the party's funds with two others elected by the party. If he objected to the committee which had been elected after the split, it could either be 'thrown overboard' or he could nominate an equal number of his supporters to serve on it. Most important of all, when the time came to negotiate with the Liberals their proposals for the next Home Rule bill, Parnell was to have the right to share with the then chairman of the Irish party in all such discussions.[5]

These proposals were breathtaking in their bland readiness to over-rule virtually every step taken by the majority with whom Dillon and O'Brien had hitherto publicly aligned themselves. They demanded so much from everyone except Parnell – and from him only temporary retirement from the chairmanship – that it is hard to imagine how any, let alone all, of the conditions could have been satisfactorily fulfilled. Naturally, the peace-makers took this likelihood into account and in their discussion on 11 December they decided that they themselves were only prepared to work with the party if both Parnell and his opponents agreed to reasonable terms – their own, or some comparable equivalent. If Parnell rejected the compromise this would inevitably incline them more towards his opponents, but upon them also they were prepared to impose conditions. The chief of these were that the American tour should go on; that the party would agree to take responsibility for the evicted tenants; that there should be a reasonable prospect of the party establishing their own fund for the future; and that the *Freeman's Journal*'s support for Parnell be ended either voluntarily or by the force of competition.[6]

All these hypothetical propositions had to be tested against a constantly changing situation. O'Brien, accompanied by T. P. Gill, left for France on 13 December and was thus out of action for most of the period covered by the Kilkenny election. It devolved, therefore, upon Dillon to state the 'American' view, since only he and O'Connor now remained in New York. He had a difficult task. On the one hand, because he and O'Brien were privately agreed that the one hope for the future was to negotiate a compromise with Parnell, he could not take too extreme an anti-Parnellite line. On the other it was highly desirable that Parnell should be beaten at Kilkenny, as this alone was likely to put him in the proper frame of mind to discuss rational peace terms. In the event, and responding no doubt to his instinctive revulsion against Parnell's tactics, Dillon spoke out strongly, probably more strongly than O'Brien would have approved. Charging Parnell with having plunged the country into conflict for purely personal ends, he condemned him trenchantly for having used 'language and base accusations, revolting to every free man, which, unless altered, show that he is unfit to be the leader of a nation aspiring to be free'.[7] A few days later he and T. P. O'Connor issued an appeal to the electors to vote for Sir John Pope-Hennessy as an essential step towards unity.[8]

But as North Kilkenny took its virulent course Dillon recoiled no less from the methods being used by Parnell's opponents. 'Healy is maddening', he wrote to O'Brien, 'and I expect Davitt will be as bad. And it infuriates me to read of Parnell being hounded down by the priests.'[9] His annoyance was increased by the news he received from home. His cousin, Valentine Dillon, a Parnellite, wrote that while several of Parnell's closest friends – he mentioned J. J. Clancy, Dr Kenny and John Redmond – would welcome an honourable compromise which dealt tenderly with their leader, the very vehemence with which he was being attacked made this almost impossible.[10] There came also a long and affectionate letter from Dr Kenny, describing what he called the 'thirst' to destroy Parnell exhibited by some members of the party at their first meeting after the publication of Gladstone's letter – long before Parnell's provocative manifesto which was now claimed as the main justification for attacking him.[11] Not surprisingly, Dillon, tortured by dyspepsia and tormented with doubt, relapsed into his habitual but perceptive pessimism. The spectre particularly haunting him was the one which events were even then transforming into a visible reality – that Parnell, beaten at Kilkenny, would fight on come wrack, come ruin. He sent a despondent letter to O'Brien which analysed with bleak clarity the consequences that might then follow:[12]

I believe that with private encouragement from him the Fenian party would rapidly become once more formidable, and that a parliamentary party relying on the bishops and priests for support, and having Parnell and the extremists on its flanks, would soon become utterly contemptible, and would be either at the mercy of the Liberals, or would be obliged to break with Gladstone . . . and thereby fully justify Parnell's action and put themselves in a position from which *no* amount of explanation would ever extricate them.

I believe that in this event the election would be hopelessly lost. And it is quite possible that when the Liberals saw that the election could not be won with Home Rule they might then throw over Home

Rule at the last moment. And this again would fully justify Parnell in the eyes of the multitude.

For Dillon the logical conclusion was that the only hope of winning the election on a Home Rule basis was that Parnell should retire and appeal 'to the Irish race' to give the party every possible support. Since there was little prospect of this happening, all his instincts drove him towards despair. But O'Brien, whose temperament responded to the prospect of action, grew steadily more optimistic as his ship drew nearer France. Basing himself on the simple thesis that the more roughly Parnell had been handled at Kilkenny the more amenable to reason he might become, the happy warrior stepped ashore at Boulogne on a bitterly cold Christmas morning with all the glad confidence of a god from the machine.

II

Unhappily, this was not how others saw him. Long before he had landed the rumour that he was bent on peace-making caused a flurry in the anti-Parnellite camp. 'We cannot compromise with Parnell', the Archbishop of Cashel trumpeted to the Archbishop of Dublin. 'He is dead and buried so far as leadership in Ireland is concerned.'[13] And to O'Brien Dr Croke wrote begging him not to treat with a leader who was already beaten:[14]

> Parnell has hopelessly fallen. The bishops and priests and all good men are determinedly *against* him, and his future leadership, under any conditions, is absolutely impossible so far as they are concerned.
>
> How then can you touch him? What good can he do? See how he has acted towards Gladstone and our English allies. Do not recede a bit from the attitude of declared hostility to him. He will be beaten at Kilkenny on Monday. He will, therefore, be prepared for a compromise. If victorious he would not think of it.

This was perhaps not so effective a warning as the archbishop hoped, since O'Brien's hopes of a negotiated settlement had all along depended on precisely what Dr Croke feared most, that defeat at Kilkenny would predispose Parnell for compromise. At the same time, O'Brien was shocked to learn from his Parnellite friends that the bitterness of the election had 'widened the breach horribly' and that the manifesto John Dillon and T. P. O'Connor had addressed to the Kilkenny electors had affected Parnell so adversely that it took severe pressure to get him to agree to come to France at all.[15] Even then, reported Harrington, he apparently made an ominous distinction between O'Brien and Dillon. 'He has told his followers all along that he would [rely?] to the fullest upon your sincerity, but he never could be got to make a similar declaration with regard to John.'[16]

Still, the fact remained that Parnell *was* prepared to come. O'Brien was therefore able to begin clearing the ground by conferring with the anti-Parnellites who came out by tender to greet him. They included Justin McCarthy and Thomas Sexton, who were not unfriendly, though everyone else, as O'Brien recorded afterwards, 'spoke swords and daggers'.[17] O'Brien's preliminary soundings were satisfactory in so far as they indicated a willingness to make concessions which might ease Parnell's path towards a voluntary retirement, but he evidently sensed that he was skating on thin ice, for seemingly he said nothing about inducing the two archbishops to retract their denunciations, nor about Parnell having a voice in subsequent Home Rule discussions with the Liberals, nor about his retirement being only temporary. Even as it was, McCarthy, who privately doubted O'Brien's ability to stand up to Parnell, strove to impress upon his euphoric friend that Parnell was extremely unlikely to agree to any compromise but that this mattered little since the struggle was practically over.[18]

Nevertheless, O'Brien persisted with his arrangements to meet Parnell. On 30 December the latter arrived at Boulogne surrounded by an entourage which included the Redmond brothers. According to an (undated) account which John Redmond later gave Barry O'Brien, the contrast between the two men could hardly have been more striking. O'Brien was gushing, emotional, eager to plunge into business at once. But Parnell saluted his former lieutenant as casually as if they had only parted the previous day and insisted on having something to eat before the conference began. To O'Brien, Parnell had 'the pathetic air of a cedar struck by lightning', but to his own followers it seemed that he was in one of his flintier moods. 'When luncheon was over', Redmond's account continues, 'Parnell said: "Now William, we will talk." We then adjourned to another room. Parnell remained silent, reserved, cold. He did not in any way encourage O'Brien to talk. He looked around at the rest of us, as much as to say, "Well, what the devil do you want?" The rest of us soon withdrew, leaving Parnell and O'Brien together.'[19]

Their conversation was thus conducted in strict secrecy and it was only after Parnell's death that varying accounts began to appear, from which it is possible to reconstruct most of what occurred.* Parnell began

---

*See my detailed analysis in *The fall of Parnell*, pp. 197–202.

by launching into a tirade against the conduct of the majority since the beginning of the crisis. O'Brien could not get a word in edgeways and emerged 'flabbergasted', telling John Redmond that though he had proposals to put forward it was useless to do so unless Parnell changed his tone. There followed an uneasy pause, but during a break for an evening meal Gill outlined the New York scheme to Redmond, who passed it on to Parnell.[20] Gill was summoned to the presence to explain himself further and O'Brien was persuaded back into the conference. According to Gill's account, Parnell and O'Brien then discussed most of the topics originally covered by the trio in New York, including some of those not mentioned by O'Brien to Sexton and McCarthy.[21]

Unfortunately, this account breaks off in mid-sentence and at a crucial point. After listing the topics discussed, it ends thus: 'The conversation proceeded on these lines when Mr Parnell said – ' For what Mr Parnell said we have to rely on O'Brien's recollections, but it was something so shattering that he was unlikely to forget it. It was that the only conditions upon which Parnell could agree to retire would be that O'Brien should succeed him as chairman of the party and should also decline the chairmanship of the new company to launch the *National Press* as a competitor to the *Freeman's Journal* which the anti-Parnellites wanted him to undertake. O'Brien's first impulse was to laugh. But when Parnell persisted, his second impulse was to propose, to his old leader's evident embarrassment, that the succession should go instead to John Dillon. A long inconsequential discussion followed, which ended with O'Brien not absolutely rejecting Parnell's suggestion, but stipulating that he must have time to consult Dillon before making his decision.

Next day Parnell left for England, taking with him – perhaps intentionally, perhaps absent-mindedly – the only copy of the terms actually proposed, a fact which was to cause O'Brien much trouble later on. The document was eventually published by Timothy Harrington during the controversies which followed Parnell's death and the terms it embodied were described by T. P. Gill (who seems to have been the person who actually wrote them down) as 'in the main identical' with those agreed between Dillon, O'Brien and O'Connor in New York.[22] Since this document is the only authoritative statement of what was actually decided upon at Boulogne it is worth reproducing in full:[23]

1. Meeting of the whole party; acknowledgement of informality of McCarthy's election and re-election of McCarthy as chairman by agreement of whole party.
2. All possible personal satisfaction in shape of public declaration of

party expressing gratitude, and enumerating circumstances of misunderstanding tending to account for conflict.

3. All possible efforts to be made to secure from Gladstone acknowledgement of mistake of precipitate publication of his letter and admission that he had not taken sufficient account of national sentiment in Ireland and of Parnell's position.

4. Possible retraction, in some shape, of bishops' manifesto by Dr Croke or Dr Walsh.

5. Vote of party only to affect chairmanship of party; P. to continue president of the National League; and, if desirable, prominent men of both sections to accompany him to a meeting, under his presidency, of the central branch in Dublin.

6. In case committee appointed by party, Parnell to have nomination of half thereof.

7. Any special recognition of Parnell that he can suggest that would secure his influence in all negotiations touching the home rule bill or other Irish legislation.

8. In case of agreement on these lines, O'Brien to decline chairmanship of new newspaper company, and any rival committee to National League to be discouraged.

For Parnell this agreement opened up a dazzling prospect, provided the other parties agreed to play the parts assigned to them. If they did, then he would have emerged with the substance of his power intact. But if, as was much more likely, the agreement failed to materialize because the Liberals preferred not to become Parnell's scapegoats, then he would be able to proclaim that they were so set upon destroying him that they refused an offer of peace which came not from him alone but from the most influential of his opponents inside his own party. This might not cut much ice in England, but it could be a most valuable weapon in Ireland if it served to detach O'Brien, and possibly also Dillon, from the ranks of his enemies.

A great deal, therefore, hung upon Dillon's answer. Dillon, not unnaturally, was lost in bafflement, mingled with that reluctant admiration which the spectacle of Parnell at full stretch could always evoke in him. 'Men say here that Parnell is mad', he noted in his diary, 'but it seems to me that his astuteness is absolutely infinite . . . The moment I read the cable [which O'Brien had sent him on 31 December, outlining Parnell's suggestion] I felt that P. had executed a master-stroke and all my reflection since has only deepened this conviction – and increased my alarm and uneasiness.'[24] However, after consulting with T. P.

O'Connor, he replied assuring O'Brien of their warmest co-operation, but also warning him not to commit himself absolutely until he had tested the reaction of the majority section and until he could be sure that he was not putting Justin McCarthy in an impossible position. O'Brien thereupon hastened to renew contact with Parnell, asking only that he be allowed to take McCarthy and Sexton into his confidence.[25] But quick as he was, Parnell was quicker still and in a long letter written from London on New Year's Day took the initiative clean out of O'Brien's hands.

The burden of his unusually long epistle was that on reflection he did not feel that the proposals offered sufficient solid ground for a settlement and would not allow him to retire 'with any consistency or regard for my responsibility'. He therefore proposed to substitute what he called a much simpler plan, but one ominously resembling the device he had used in his attempt to turn Gladstone's flank during the debates in Committee Room Fifteen. The essence of it was that O'Brien should ask Justin McCarthy to seek an interview with Gladstone to obtain from him a memorandum expressing the intentions of himself and his colleagues on the matters raised by the delegation from the Irish party which had met him on 5 December. Should Gladstone furnish such a memorandum, then McCarthy was to be required to transfer it to O'Brien and if, after consultation, O'Brien and Parnell together deemed it satisfactory, then Parnell would retire forthwith from the chairmanship of the party. The memorandum, he added, was not to be disclosed to any other person until the introduction of the next Home Rule bill and not even then unless the bill failed to meet the terms agreed; if, however, the bill *was* adequate, Parnell claimed the right to publish the memorandum after the measure had become law.[26]

Yet, although this was in effect the old bargain, it was in one important respect subtly different. Since Parnell had last pressed this demand upon the Liberals McCarthy had been elected chairman by the majority of the Irish party. Gladstone had declared on the previous occasion that he would not negotiate until the leadership issue had been settled. Now that McCarthy was a duly elected leader there need no longer be any bar to Gladstone conferring with him. And this new scheme had the additional attraction that it quietly abandoned all those laudatory resolutions and confessions of guilt with which the New York plan had been festooned. But beneath this alluring simplicity a rather more sinister design could be discerned. McCarthy, it seemed, would be no more than an elderly and impotent Mercury. His errand would be discharged when he handed the Liberal guarantees to O'Brien and Parnell, and the latter clearly still reserved to himself an effective voice in the final decision as to whether or not the guarantees were satisfactory. Further, the proviso that if the guarantees were not embodied in the Home Rule bill, or even if they were, he could publish them in his own vindication, gave Parnell a strong card of re-entry. Either he would make a graceful exit, having exhibited his diplomatic genius to the end, but without indicating whether his retirement was to be temporary or permanent; or else the delicate chain of consequences would snap somewhere under the strain and he could continue the fight, fortified by being able to point to yet one more illustration of how his patriotic and self-sacrificing gestures were constantly being foiled by the wicked Liberals and/or his mean-spirited Irish opponents.

Whether Parnell really expected this manœuvre to succeed cannot be said for certain. He imparted his inmost thoughts to nobody, but the probability is that while he may genuinely have felt that some good might come of it, he was also fully alive to the various ways in which the situation might be exploited if the need arose. At all events, he had put the ball firmly back in O'Brien's court and ensured that the next move must come from Boulogne. O'Brien was uneasy, as well he might be. Also, he was bewildered, for Parnell had omitted, no doubt deliberately, to make it clear whether, if all went well and he did retire, McCarthy or O'Brien was to succeed him. He therefore cabled Harrington, Parnell's principal deputy in these discussions, saying he would accept the new conditions if McCarthy was to be chairman. Back came the uncompromising response – it must be O'Brien and no one else. O'Brien, wilting in this cold wind, replied that when they met again he would propose an alternative solution which might suit all parties and avert the 'appalling prospect' of a breakdown.[27]

The fact was that the unfortunate peace-maker was being caught between the hammer and the anvil. During these exchanges he had moved to Paris to stay with his wife's family and there Tim Healy descended upon him to persuade him into helping to launch the *National Press* and generally to bring home to him the apprehensions he was arousing by these continued flirtations with Parnell. But their arguments rebounded from his invincible optimism and Healy found it impossible to penetrate his defences. 'We cannot look for help from him in a struggle', he told Archbishop Walsh, 'altho' he insists on helping us to prevent one, in spite of our declaration that his supposed help will be purely mischievous to those who are prepared to fight. He declares emphatically, however, against P's leadership, and if platonic views on the point are helpful, no doubt they will be forthcoming intersprinkled and begemmed with tears.'[28] And to his wife he commented bitterly: 'Apparently, everything that we have done has been ill done, and nothing has been done that ought to have been done, and William and Gill are the only men to put matters right. Anything more hopeless it is impossible to conceive.'[29]

But O'Brien bore Healy's onslaught, as Healy himself confessed, 'with a gentle egoism beyond reproof', and went ahead with his plans for a second meeting with Parnell. Parnell had already begun that exhausting routine of weekly visits to Ireland which was to hasten his death.[30] That winter was one of the coldest of the century, with heavy snowfalls in many places, and this added to the hardships of the peripatetic existence Parnell was leading. However, the cumulative strain had not yet begun to tell on him seriously, the eye injury he had received at Kilkenny had healed, and during the two days he spent in France – 6 and 7 January – he seemed in control of himself and of the situation. According to John Redmond and Harrington, who accompanied him, the discussion centred first on O'Brien's alternative solution, which turned out to be the suggestion that if he was to be the new chairman, then it should be he, not McCarthy, who should make the pilgrimage to Hawarden. Redmond later described the short shrift this received. 'I saw him [Parnell] alone first and we had a short private talk about O'Brien's new plan. He said nothing, but looked at me with an amused, and amusing, smile. I could not help feeling what a pair of children O'Brien and I were in the hands of this man. The meaning of the smile was as plain as words. It meant: "Well, really you are excellent fellows, right good fellows, but 'pon my soul a damned pair of fools; sending William O'Brien to Hawarden to negotiate with Mr Gladstone! Delightful."'[31]

However, O'Brien did not give up easily and at once produced yet another set of proposals. The first was that John Dillon, not himself, should be chairman. The second was that he, O'Brien, should be free to confide to Sexton and McCarthy all that had happened so far. And the third was that McCarthy should join with Parnell and O'Brien in judging the adequacy of the Liberal guarantees. It was now Parnell's turn to recoil. The prospect of Dillon as chairman clearly repelled him and in the end he had almost to be 'bullied' by his friends into accepting the suggestion. According to Harrington, they had to work nearly as hard to prevent him imposing a counter-condition which would surely have been fatal – that guarantees should be secured from Harcourt as well as from Gladstone.[32] But the eventual outcome was more favourable than any of those present, with the possible exception of Parnell himself, could have dared to hope. With his own hand he drafted 'Heads of Agreement' embodying their 'settlement' and from this document it is plain that, apart from accepting Dillon as chairman, he had his way in all matters of substance.

The plan of action was that McCarthy was to obtain from Gladstone a memorandum stating whether the Liberals intended to reserve the land question for settlement by the imperial parliament (and if so how it was to be dealt with) or to relinquish it to the Irish parliament for settlement; whether they intended to insert into the next Home Rule bill a provision limiting imperial authority over the Irish constabulary to a specific period, e.g. five years; and whether they would agree that the 'solution of these questions . . . upon the lines agreed upon shall be regarded as vital'. If such a memorandum were secured, McCarthy was to transfer it to William O'Brien and Parnell. They having found it satisfactory, the whole party should be called together and a resolution proposed acknowledging the 'informality' of McCarthy's election to the chair. After this was passed, Parnell would resign from the chairmanship and McCarthy from the vice-chairmanship. Dillon would then be elected chairman. Finally, it was agreed that the terms of the memorandum should not be disclosed to anyone save those named in the Heads of Agreement until after the introduction of the Home Rule bill and then only if it failed to conform to the terms of the memorandum. If the bill proved satisfactory, Parnell should be allowed to publish the memorandum after the Home Rule legislation was on the statute-book.[33]

III

It was all highly precarious, of course, and depended for its success on various individuals behaving as the negotiators had decreed that they should behave. Not the least unpredictable of these was John Dillon, who was dumbfounded to receive at 7.30 on the evening of 6 January a cable from O'Brien propounding the new conditions, based as these were upon Dillon agreeing to be drafted into the chair. Dillon immediately suspected a trap and cabled back a firm refusal, though adding that he himself would come to France and that O'Brien must do nothing further until he arrived. In his diary he recorded that the offer was 'on terms such as I would rather earn an honest living by blacking shoes than accept'.[34] However, his underlying belief that only through unity could Home Rule, and indeed the parliamentary party itself, be saved was so intense that for the time being he stifled his better judgement and sailed for France on 10 January.

Even this cold comfort was eagerly snapped up by O'Brien, who now radiated confidence that he had at last found a solution. The basis of this confidence was his conviction that Parnell was still such a vital force in Irish politics that, if not effectively placated, he would continue to tear the movement and the country apart while he lived. His support, so O'Brien told Archbishop Croke, would be substantial, especially if this latest chance of agreement were squandered. 'We have', he added pointedly, 'a dozen excellent front-bench men, but there is no other Parnell.'[35] To those who had been in the midst of the struggle, and who saw no end to it short of Parnell's complete elimination, O'Brien's readiness to traffic with him was both offensive and deeply disturbing. Archbishop Croke, for one, remained entirely unconvinced, suspecting, not without reason, that O'Brien had succumbed yet again to the familiar Parnellite glamour. His anxieties cannot have been diminished when both Parnell and Harrington made provocative speeches at Limerick on 10 and 11 January.[36] Parnell himself seemed as intransigent as ever. In a rare reference to the divorce, he maintained that the issue at stake had always been political, never moral. If it had been moral, he said, the bishops would have spoken at the outset – when they did intervene it was too late. Next day he turned his attention to the Liberals and delivered what was in effect an extended version of his manifesto. On all the disputed points – land, police, judges, the retention of the Irish members at Westminster – he remorselessly rubbed salt in old wounds, careless, apparently, of the effect this might have on the impending negotiations.[37]

That was not the only difficulty looming ahead. On 9 January, McCarthy and Sexton arrived at Boulogne, to be instructed by O'Brien about the latest developments, including the humiliating task to be imposed upon McCarthy of fetching from Gladstone the Liberal guarantees which would be his own marching orders. O'Brien was sufficiently satisfied with this conference to cable to Parnell that he assumed there would now be no difficulty about giving McCarthy a voice in deciding as to whether or not the Liberal guarantees were satisfactory – an assumption entirely at variance with the Heads of Agreement recorded at Boulogne. Back from Limerick came the inexorable reply that Parnell must insist upon exact adherence to the terms agreed in France. McCarthy on his side now began to have second thoughts. On 12 January he cabled to say that he could not resign without the consent of those who had elected him, and he assured Tim Healy that apart from Parnell's acceptance of Dillon as chairman, the situation remained unaltered. 'We simply say that we can do nothing without the knowledge and consent of the party – which we maintain to be *the* party.'[38]

This was particularly ominous, because the attacks upon Parnell emanating from Healy and his friends were all the while becoming more and more unrestrained. On the same weekend that Parnell had been speaking at Limerick, Healy had been waging his own kind of war at Nenagh. On Saturday he dismissed the Boulogne negotiations as merely an attempt by Parnell to play the game of Committee Room Fifteen all over again, and on Sunday he drew the crudest of distinctions between the two negotiators. 'When Mr Parnell was on the fire-escape at Eltham, William O'Brien was on the plank bed at Tullamore [prison].' O'Brien himself came under fire from the Parnellites for allowing *Insuppressible* to be published under his name, and this at a time when it demanded Parnell's 'irrevocable retirement', speaking of the leader as having gone to Boulogne 'to entreat the intercession of William O'Brien for terms of surrender'.[39] But O'Brien was unwilling to abandon *Insuppressible* too precipitately, for it could be a useful bargaining-counter in certain circumstances, and from the editor he had a stream of mitigating letters. Bodkin was constantly being reproached, he said, not for his violence, but for his moderation. 'There is no disguising the fact that a very bitter feeling exists about the conference and the delay. This so far as I can ascertain [is] unanimous amongst the priests, bishops and opponents of Parnell in the party. Even [from] the men most devoted to you I get letters and resolutions in the no conference strain. Archbishop Croke is I understand strongest on this point.'[40]

There remained a further unknown factor in O'Brien's complex equation – the reaction of the Liberal leaders to a renewal of the plea for guarantees which Gladstone had rejected twice already. The omens were not propitious. While the Irish factions were locked in combat at Kilkenny, an English by-election at Bassetlaw had resulted in an increased Unionist majority. Inevitably, this reinforced the Liberal demand that their allies *must* get rid of Parnell without delay.[41] To Gladstone himself that single by-election portended the rolling of the stone down the hill again all the way back to 1886. 'For me that is notice to quit. Another five years agitation at my age would be impossible – ludicrous.'[42] Harcourt, however, contemplated the crash with, he wrote ironically to Morley, 'such stoicism as I can'. Characteristically, he complained that what he most objected to in Parnell's appeal to the Irish people was its denial of '*all mutuality*'. 'His demand is that Ireland alone shall prescribe the terms of H.R. *I have no hesitation in saying that on such conditions I am as much opposed to H.R. as anyone in the Unionist camp.*'[43] 'What I have to say about Home Rule', he explained to Morley early in January, 'may be packed up in a very small parcel as thus: I believe the present system of government in Ireland to be a bad one. I was very willingly a party to an attempt to create a better. The Irish people and their leaders have proved themselves incapable and unworthy. *Voilà tout.*'[44]

Morley demurred as best he could, but the letters which passed between the various Liberal leaders in those dark days of the New Year indicated that Harcourt's line was likely to be the popular one. Arnold Morley, Lord Ripon, Gladstone himself, began to cast about for alternative planks to their platform and although Arnold Morley was able to report from the constituencies a hundred letters of support for Home Rule to every one demanding its abandonment, it was clear that the crisis had shaken the morale of those responsible for deciding policy. It was fortunate indeed for O'Brien and his emissary, T. P. Gill, that John Morley at least remained a committed Home Ruler. Gill saw him on 12 January and explained the *mise en scène* to him in detail. He thought Morley sympathetic but might have been unpleasantly surprised had he known that, in forwarding the Irish proposals to Gladstone, Morley described them as 'painful in some ways . . . childish in others'. Publicly, however, he kept faith, demonstrating his Home Rule loyalties in a speech at Newcastle, two days after Parnell's escapade at Limerick, which did much to convince O'Brien, and above all Dillon, that there was yet a chance of reconstructing the alliance.[45]

But Gladstone's reaction to the proposals was what counted most. And Gladstone was distinctly cool, still insisting that the Irish really must make up their minds who was their leader before he could agree to negotiate; that he could not easily sign a document binding colleagues; and that the land question would have to be left open until Balfour's purchase bill then before parliament had assumed its final form. All this was duly passed on to Gill when on 16 January he paid a second visit to Morley. Gill countered by reminding Morley that Gladstone would have no official knowledge that McCarthy was about to abdicate when he gave him the required guarantees and that he could therefore deal with him as leader. Morley was susceptible to this argument, mainly perhaps because he was so nervous about the possible consequences of the Liberals refusing to treat. 'If no assurances can be given', he warned Gladstone, 'and the Boulogne device falls through, then I anticipate that Dillon and O'Brien will throw all up; will go to prison and will come out to find the whole movement in pretty complete collapse, or else Parnell practically master of a demoralized party.'[46]

Whatever effect these admonitions had on Gladstone, they had none at all on Harcourt. Boiling with indignation at Parnell's Limerick speeches, he rushed into print with a letter developing trenchantly the concept of 'mutuality' he had already explained to Morley. 'If separation and hostility to Great Britain and not an honourable and cordial alliance is aimed at . . . then I have no hesitation in saying that Home Rule has no chance and ought to have no chance.'[47] This was written *before* he learnt of the Boulogne proposals. When, next day, Morley broke the news to him, he was torn between anger and irony at a scheme 'worthy of the Beggar's Opera'. 'I for one', he told Morley, 'will be no party to buying off this Gaul of Eltham with pledges.'[48]

Gladstone did his best to smooth down his irate colleague and lead him gently towards the possibility of negotiation. He shared most of Harcourt's views, he said. He disliked secret agreements. 'I would sooner deal with a convicted swindler than with Parnell.' He 'distrusted entirely the O'Brien proceedings', and he could not conceive how there could be confidential conversations on Irish land until they knew the fate of the government's legislation. On the other hand, he shrank from assisting at the death of Home Rule. 'I look at Ireland', he continued, 'through the majority of the constitutional representatives of the country favourable to Home Rule. They have deposed Parnell. I will not, and I think ought not to, suppose it possible that the country will disown its parliamentary party . . . I think Healy and his friends have the strongest claims, political and moral, on both our consideration and our support.'[49] In the end Harcourt, realizing belatedly that his vehemence was isolating him from his colleagues, gradually moderated his tone. He was helped by a remarkable by-election at West Hartlepool, where the Liberal candidate professing an unashamed attachment to Home Rule, converted a Liberal Unionist majority of 1000 into a Liberal majority of 300. This, as even Harcourt admitted, 'spread a holy calm' among Gladstone's ex-colleagues and once satisfied that the negotiations were not to be secret Sir William withdrew, for the moment at least, his hitherto immovable opposition.[50]

IV

Meanwhile, the pause necessitated by the fact that Dillon was on the high seas was drawing to an end. He arrived at Le Havre on 18 January, and O'Brien and Gill, who met him, were agreeably surprised by his frame of mind. He had discarded his usual pessimism and had allowed himself to believe, if only temporarily, that the strange enterprise into which he had been persuaded might just possibly succeed. Positively, he was impressed by the disinterested conduct of McCarthy and Sexton, by Morley's staunchness towards Home Rule, and by O'Brien's conviction that Parnell, and still more some of his key men, were genuinely anxious for peace. Negatively, he was influenced by what he later described as 'the outrageous attitude assumed by Healy's faction . . . and by the bishops. And the scandalous attempts made by Healy and others to misrepresent W. O'B and to thwart his attempts to make peace.'[51]

So began three hectic weeks of coming and going, designed to persuade the Liberals to commit themselves to pledges which would satisfy Parnell but which would, ostensibly, be given not to him, but to McCarthy. These delicate manœuvres had always to be conducted under Parnell's shadow and it was plain from his speeches in Ireland that he had no intention of softening his tone to facilitate an agreement. Thus, at Athlone, the day after Dillon's arrival in France, he dropped one of his periodic and ambiguous hints that Home Rule might not be the end of the road, and the following week at Waterford he took up uncompromising positions on each of the subjects under discussion with the Liberals at that time. The police were to be under Irish control, he said, the land question was to be settled by an Irish parliament and he was adamant against what he called the 'English veto'. 'We will have no English veto. An English veto, whether on the appointment of your leader or on the laws that you shall make, would break down and destroy the parliament before it had been two years in existence.'[52] Sentiments of this kind, expressed in such language, amply explain the anxiety of the negotiators to keep Parnell off-stage until the final phase was reached; they explain also why speed was of the essence, since they could never be sure that he might not suddenly disrupt all their careful plans.

Because the negotiations were mostly carried on by word of mouth, we know little of their inner history. It seems clear, though, from the few letters which were exchanged between Gladstone and his colleagues that they were all well aware that Parnell was being consulted by the negotiators in France, but that despite this knowledge they did not stand inflexibly on their original condition that the leadership issue should be disposed of before the guarantees were given. This was largely due to the influence of John Morley. 'We know nothing as to future manœuvres', he told Spencer. 'But what is certain is that if Mr G. does not give assurances as to land and police, we shall lose Dillon and O'Brien. The assurances constitute the only instrument by which they baffle Parnell. I don't believe that P. means to withdraw, but the battle against him will be hopeless unless we have Dillon with us.'[53] The formula eventually adopted was frankly face-saving. Guarantees would be given to McCarthy as 'leader of the Irish party' and beyond that the Liberal leaders would be discreet enough not to look.[54] Since Gill was able to report to Morley on 28 January that Parnell was prepared to accept, instead of a private undertaking, a public letter or statement by Gladstone which would be, outwardly at least, 'entirely independent of the Boulogne negotiation', the obstacles to agreement seemed to be fast disappearing. In fact, on that same day, Gladstone brought together in his room at the House of Commons his principal colleagues – Spencer, Ripon, Harcourt and John Morley – where they finally settled the terms to be transmitted to O'Brien in France. The land question, they agreed, 'must . . . either be settled by the imperial parliament simultaneously with the establishment of home rule, or within a limited period, thereafter to be specified in the home rule bill; or the power to deal with it must be committed to the Irish legislature'. As for the existing 'semi-military police', they estimated that it could be replaced by a civil force by the Irish government within five years or less. 'During that interval', they proposed, 'the present armed police under the control of the Lord-Lieutenant would undergo a rapid reduction or transformation (subject, of course, to a strict observance of all engagements made by the imperial government with the Royal Irish Constabulary), and would, on the completion of the arrangement for a civil force, finally disappear.'[55]

It was explained to the Irish intermediaries that Gladstone and his colleagues would regard it as their duty to include these in the next Home Rule bill as 'essential provisions'. O'Brien and Dillon found them highly satisfactory and cabled to Parnell that he should come and inspect them without delay.[56] 'If P. comes over tonight', O'Brien telegraphed to Harrington on 30 January, 'I think it perfectly possible the whole thing will be finished by Tuesday – Dillon's election and all. All depends now on good faith. Heaven grant for his sake and for all our sakes there may be no further hitch. It is the last barrier between us and destruction.'[57]

On all sides the clouds looked to be lifting. Archbishop Walsh, who was admitted into the secret in mid-January, had so far come round to the view that the negotiations were vital that towards the end of the month he took the unusual step of writing a confidential letter to Gladstone offering – apparently by putting forward the proposals as his own and getting Gladstone to endorse them – to ease the path of compromise.[58] Such an obvious manœuvre to cut the ground from under

Parnell's feet would have had disastrous consequences if adopted. The mind boggles at the capital Parnell would have made out of the spectacle of the Liberals and the church in combination, but at least the suggestion showed that if the archbishop's wits were momentarily astray, his heart was in the right place. This was not to be taken as a sign of any weakening towards Parnell. On the contrary, writing to Dillon two days earlier to reassure him about the relations between the hierarchy and the party, he ended on this stern note:[59]

> No matter what arrangement the party may come to, the opposition to him will go on, and . . . I am keeping well within the mark when I say that there are fully one-half of the seats now safely held by nationalists in which neither he, nor anyone supposed to be . . . in favour of him as leader, will have the smallest chance of success at the general election. The only way to save the election, and to save the cause, is to *get rid of him at once*. Whether he is willing to go or not should not make a particle of difference in the case.

Getting rid of him at once would obviously be much easier if the way were smoothed for him to go quietly, as was the hope of the negotiators in France. Even Tim Healy, though still suspicious of Parnell's *bona fides*, could see a silver lining now that the assurances had been given. 'If he show bad faith', he told the archbishop, 'I understand his followers or some of them will come over to us under a Dillon leadership and of course if they or any responsible section of them quit him and Dillon and O'Brien issue a strong manifesto he is dished.'[60] As for O'Brien, he too had crossed a kind of Rubicon, for the previous week he had finally withdrawn his support from *Insuppressible*, which collapsed on 24 January, not long before its editor did likewise from physical exhaustion.[61]

Everything, naturally, depended on Parnell. The first prognostications were hopeful. On 28 January, just before the Liberals had completed their deliberations, Gill visited him and found him 'entirely reasonable', though it is evident from Gill's report to O'Brien that he, Gill, was playing a dangerous game, since he had concealed from Parnell all knowledge of his interviews with John Morley.[62] But Parnell's moods in those anxious days were transient and unpredictable. Part of this no doubt reflected the prolonged strain imposed by the uncertainty of his own position, but part of it must surely have been a product of cumulative fatigue. Thus, before going to France, he travelled from Brighton to Ennis, in the extreme south-west of Ireland, where, incidentally, he spoke loftily of the coming Home Rule parliament as one which would be 'sovereign in Ireland', a phrase which was certainly not in the Liberals' vocabulary. He left Ennis on Sunday evening, travelled all that night and all the next day, crossed to France to confer with O'Brien, and was in his place in the House of Commons by 7 o'clock on Tuesday night. To Alfred Robbins, who met him then, he seemed 'miserably haggard and worn'.[63] 'I never saw him look or heard him sound so tired.'

It was hardly surprising, therefore, that when he arrived at Calais on the evening of 2 February Parnell gave every sign of being worn out. He was much irritated by newspaper reports that the whole business had already been settled behind his back and O'Brien had hard work to calm him down sufficiently to consider the guarantees with himself and Dillon. What happened next was variously described by Timothy Harrington and by O'Brien (who produced three different versions during the next twenty years, all reflecting his political affiliations at the dates they were written). These accounts do not coincide in all particulars, but they agree that the first shock came when Parnell and Dillon were discussing the funds which would be at Dillon's disposal to pay parliamentary salaries when he became chairman. Dillon, apparently, wanted enough money from the Paris fund to enable him to keep the salaries going for the next three years. According to Harrington, whose account was not contradicted when he published it in November 1891, 'I have it both from Mr Parnell and Mr Dillon that the latter gentleman declined to take the chair if this was not done'.[64] O'Brien's version – that is, the highly-coloured one he published in his memoirs – has it that Parnell suggested that the money should be lodged in both their names, which Dillon interpreted as meaning that the first time he was in need of money Parnell could cut off his supplies and render him impotent. 'Parnell rose to his feet, white with passion. "Dillon", he said, with that power of his to produce the effect of ice and of fire at the same moment, "Dillon, that is not the kind of expression I had a right to expect from you after the way I have behaved to you".'[65]

This, it must be said, is the O'Brien of 1910, who had become deeply estranged from Dillon, and we must balance him by the O'Brien of 1895, who was then Dillon's most intimate friend and who went out of his way to exonerate him from any blame for what had happened.[66] Nevertheless, there is other testimony to show that money *was* at the root of what John Redmond called 'the very bad effect' which the interview had produced upon Parnell. Tim Harrington, writing to O'Brien a few days afterwards, observed: 'I think John said something to him about the funds in Paris which wounded him terribly . . .'[67]

And this seemed to be confirmed by a letter O'Brien had from T. P. Gill who, as principal go-between, was in a better position than most to know the truth. 'P. seemed to feel very much what passed between him and D. about the money.'[68]

Yet, while O'Brien was probably right in emphasizing the unfortunate consequences of this exchange, he was not justified in saying that after it they resumed their discussion 'with the unreality of doctors prescribing for a patient who had already expired under our eyes'.[69] On the contrary, while the episode demonstrated both Parnell's nervous irritability and the difficulty he and Dillon always had in personal relations, the negotiations did not founder then and there. Parnell certainly appeared ready to take the assurances seriously and even Healy was impressed. 'It seems', he wrote to Archbishop Walsh a few days later, 'as if P. were thinking of giving in. He has raised a point on the assurances as to the police, which I don't think is insuperable and I imagine public declarations from the Liberals may be looked for about Monday.'[70]

Alas, by the time that letter was written, the fair prospect it announced had already begun to darken. When Parnell got back to London he wrote to Gill that he had failed to notice that the clause dealing with the land question had made no provision for the retention of the full number of Irish MPs at Westminster in the event of the imperial parliament reserving that question for the proposed 'limited period'. It would never do, he said, to reduce the number of members while either the land or the police remained under imperial control, and it would be absolutely necessary to insert a provision to that effect.[71] Next day Gill saw him and noted down, not merely this requirement, but also a further demand that when the Royal Irish Constabulary was abolished this was 'to be brought about *legislatively by an essential provision of the Home Rule bill*', the intention being to guard against the possibility that a future British government might refuse to carry out this disbandment if it were simply left to the executive action of the Lord-Lieutenant. This was an unlikely eventuality and Parnell's amendment was probably unnecessarily fussy, but at least it reflected his habitual attention to detail and it certainly did not indicate any intention to break off the negotiations.

Nor did Gill believe that this was his intention. Writing to O'Brien next day, he reported that he himself, Sexton and McCarthy had all thought the request about the retention of Irish members reasonable. But he added ominously that Morley, who was distinctly 'raspy' and difficult to convince, had warned him that the Liberal leaders, having drawn up their assurances and been led to understand that they were satisfactory, would be disinclined 'to alter a comma'.[72] We have only Parnell's version of what occurred when Gill reported to him, but apparently he contrived to give Parnell the impression that the Liberal leaders had laid it down as a condition of continuing the negotiations that their assurances were not to be submitted to him, but to O'Brien alone, and that the latter would have to bind himself to accept them before they could be published. This, Parnell wrote to Gill on 5 February, put him in 'a humiliating and disgraceful position', which neither his own self-respect nor that of the Irish people would allow him to occupy for a moment. Nor was this all. He went on to say that within the past twenty-four hours 'information of a most startling character' had reached him, though from what source he did not reveal. It was that the full number of Irish members would be retained at Westminster *permanently*; this he found 'ominous and alarming'.[73]

Astounded by this communication, Gill wrote at once that it was vital for him to see Parnell, the first part of whose remarks was founded on a misunderstanding he could remove.[74] After further fruitless exchanges Parnell brushed him aside and opened his batteries upon O'Brien in France.[75] There, up to 6 February, even Dillon had been basking in unwonted optimism. Next day, however, came a cable from Gill that the Liberals had indeed refused 'to alter a comma' of their guarantees and that Parnell was now in his turn intractable. That night (7 February) the crestfallen envoy arrived in person bringing with him Parnell's devastating letter of 5 February – 'a most treacherous document' Dillon immediately called it. From the moment they read that letter Dillon and O'Brien were convinced that the negotiations were doomed; they can only have been confirmed in this opinion when Gill told them that just before he left London he had heard from Parnell's supporters that he had called them to a meeting at which he had been in the worst possible temper. O'Brien's reaction, in a letter to Redmond, was to say that the story of new conditions being imposed by the Liberals was 'absolute rubbish – not a shadow of foundation for it', but that he supposed it was no longer any use to prolong the agony. He wrote also, more temperately, to Parnell, on 8 and 9 February assuring him that nothing had happened to change the terms agreed on at Calais and thus leaving open the possibility of one last combined effort to reach a solution.

But Parnell was inflexible. In a letter dated 10 February, though apparently not sent and only published after his death, he reiterated his belief that the Liberal guarantees were only to be shown to O'Brien and that O'Brien would be required to pronounce judgement on them 'apart from me'. If this was a misunderstanding, he said, no one had yet been able to clear it up. And even if it could be cleared up, the recently promulgated pastorals of several Irish bishops condemning him in the strongest terms, represented yet another serious obstacle to peace. 'They create great doubts in my mind', he said, 'as to whether the peace we are struggling for is at all possible, and as to whether we are not compelled to raise even greater and larger issues than those yet raised in this struggle.'[76] One reason why his letter was not sent may have been because Gill, meeting him on that same date (10 February) had at last been able to persuade him that the 'misunderstanding' between them was simply a misunderstanding, and nothing more sinister. But this made no difference to the outcome, for Gill had also to tell him that the Liberals had refused to make any changes in their offer. This coincided with what John Redmond had already written to Parnell the previous evening. 'I have some good reason', Redmond said, 'for believing that the Liberals won't agree to amend the memo in *any* respect even as to the constabulary and that therefore, if you so choose, you will be able to break off on that ground – which I'm sure you see would be an infinitely safer ground than the "new condition" which O'Brien never heard of and didn't agree to.'[77] Accordingly, late on the night of 10 February Parnell sent a cable to O'Brien and Dillon which virtually ended the negotiations. 'On learning amendments will not be accepted', it ran, 'I must adhere to my position at Calais. Misunderstanding with Gill fully cleared up. Writing fully.'[78] Next day came two letters from him, one public and putting the blame for the breakdown – which he now regarded as final – on the rigidity of the Liberals, the other private and full of friendliness for O'Brien, who, with Dillon, next day crossed to Folkestone, where they were at once arrested and taken to Scotland Yard *en route* for the six months' sentence awaiting them in Galway jail.[79]

V

So ended the last chance Parnell and his opponents were to have for a negotiated settlement which might have preserved the unity of the party, ended the strife in Ireland, left the Liberal alliance intact, and prepared the way for the next Home Rule campaign. The failure of the 'Boulogne negotiations' was a bitter blow to those on both sides who had looked to them for salvation. Yet, even though they missed their main objectives, they were not, as John Morley later described them, 'idle from the start'.[80] Some positive gains were salvaged from the general ruin. The

Liberals, after all, had been brought to give substantial assurances on two major issues and the fact that these were immediately published made it difficult, if not impossible, for them to go back upon their pledges in the future.[81] Moreover, meetings between McCarthy and Parnell during the negotiations had liberated £8000 from the Paris fund for the evicted tenants.[82]

Still, these gains fell far short of the high hopes O'Brien had cherished so passionately, and although many on the anti-Parnellite side heaved a sigh of relief when the negotiations were over, there was much speculation at the time, and has been ever since, as to why Parnell finally rejected an agreement which seemed so favourable to him. Did he really take the negotiations seriously, or were they merely part of a larger, more inscrutable, strategy? His biographer, Barry O'Brien, who saw him frequently at this time, propagated the theory that his aim was partly to divide his Irish opponents and partly to drive a wedge between them and their Liberal allies.[83] In the first of these objectives – whether he intended it or not – he undoubtedly had some success. Both Dillon and O'Brien risked prestige and popularity during the prolonged discussions and Healy, for one, regarded their activities with intense suspicion, believing apparently that O'Brien would best have liked to take the leadership himself 'as a warming-pan for Parnell'.[84] But Healy's distrust of the negotiators was more than balanced by their detestation of him, and it was significant that their final statement before withdrawing to prison took the form of a denunciation of the methods used against Parnell and an assertion that peace might have been secured but for the irreconcilables on *both* sides.[85] When their friends flocked to see them at Scotland Yard after their arrest, the impression they carried away was that while Dillon would not serve again under Parnell at any price, O'Brien still kept an open mind. It was at any rate clear that both men regarded him as a continuing force in politics and there was nothing to show that when they came out of prison they would necessarily side with his opponents.[86] To that extent, a wedge had been driven between Dillon and O'Brien on the one hand, and the victors of Kilkenny on the other, though it hardly needed the elaborate Boulogne negotiations to have brought this about.

As for the second alleged objective, to splinter the Liberal-nationalist alliance, that might indeed have happened if the Liberals had been as unyielding in February 1891 as they were in December 1890. But once they had braced themselves to give the required assurances, and once O'Brien had accepted these as broadly satisfactory, no rift between the majority of the Irish party and their English friends was likely to develop. And even though Parnell did induce O'Brien to forward his amendments to the Liberals, any resentment the latter may have felt on this score was directed not against the Irish party, but against its discredited leader.

The crucial question remains – did Parnell really mean the negotiations to fail? Two considerations suggest that he did not. The first is the evidence of some of his own closest followers – for example, John Redmond, J. J. Clancy and Valentine Dillon – who all believed that he genuinely intended a settlement.[87] So too did William O'Brien, T. P. Gill, John Dillon (for a while) and (even more briefly) T. M. Healy.[88] Gill and Dillon in later years came to believe that Parnell had several times been on the verge of compromise but that Mrs O'Shea had each time stiffened his resistance.[89] There is not the slightest evidence that this was so; indeed, the assumption ignores the fact that Katharine's attraction for Parnell was precisely that she gave him domesticity, not politics. But that two of the principal negotiators should have felt that the blame lay elsewhere at least suggests that they did not think it rested wholly, or perhaps even primarily, with Parnell.

The second point which goes against the theory of a deliberate breakup is simply that the terms offered Parnell were so favourable that every consideration of political strategy would have compelled him to take them seriously. All he was being asked was to retire from the chairmanship of the party and it was not even clear at the end whether this was to be temporary or permanent. Retirement from the party did not touch his presidency of the Irish National League and though the imagination reels at what might have resulted from this kind of dualism, the fact that it was apparently contemplated as part of the bargain made that bargain, from Parnell's standpoint, additionally attractive.

If then the terms were so generous and if Parnell took them seriously, why did the break occur? Part of the explanation is surely to be found in the attitude of the Liberals. When Parnell suggested his amendments, their instinct was to assume that this was further trickery on his part and therefore to be ignored without compunction. Thus, while the issue was still in the balance, Morley, whom the Irish justly regarded as sympathetic to their cause, could write of Dillon and O'Brien in these terms to Lord Spencer. 'They (no doubt at the instigation of Parnell who was over there on Sunday*) pressed for small changes. Mr G. – most wisely – stuck to it that we would not alter a comma.' But, Morley added,

---

*Morley was in error here. Parnell arrived at Calais late on Monday, 2 February, and left the following day.

Gladstone had been tempted to urge McCarthy not to resign the leadership, only that he, Morley, had reminded him that the leadership was the business of the Irish, not the Liberals.[90] On Morley's own admission, then, it appears that not only did the Liberals refuse to consider what he himself described as 'small changes' but Gladstone, despite all that had passed in and since Committee Room Fifteen, was still hankering after interfering with the leadership and thus laying himself open to the precise charge Parnell had been trying to pin on him since the outbreak of the crisis.

It can be said in extenuation that the Liberal leaders had suffered much at Parnell's hands – breach of faith, misrepresentation, personal vilification. And it was also true that they had their own public opinion to consider, watchful, suspicious and utterly opposed to any dealings with the Irish leader. All the same, if they cared about Home Rule – some, no doubt, cared decidedly less than others – it seems remarkable that having come so far, they could not bring themselves to go that little bit further. It would have cost them nothing to consider the amendments; had they found them reasonable and agreed to accept them, they would then have called Parnell's bluff and laid firmly upon him the burden of success or failure. As it was, their stern refusal to 'alter a comma' made it certain that the struggle would go on, that Parnell would have further fuel to add to the flames, and that the future of Home Rule would be more than ever endangered.

Yet if the Liberals were insensitive and lacking in judgement, so also was Parnell. The reason is not far to seek. The Boulogne negotiations can only be properly understood in the context of the life he was leading at that time. His health, as we know, was already precarious and the incessant travelling and speaking in that severe winter had taken a heavy toll. The strain was as much psychological as physical. Fighting with his back to the wall, his private life dragged in the mud, his personal ascendancy shattered beyond recovery, he was almost mortally wounded in his most vulnerable part – his fierce, unbending pride. Inevitably, he was irritated, indecisive, and hypersensitive to anything that seemed to touch his honour. His interview with Dillon at Calais, his 'misunderstanding' with Gill, his anger at newspaper paragraphs and at the bishops' pastoral letters, his stormy conference with his own followers – all these suggest a man near the end of his tether. And if to the Liberals his amendments to their guarantees were the last straw, to Parnell their abrupt rejection of those amendments was the final insult.

His own after-view of the negotiations tended to be inconsistent. On one occasion he confided to Barry O'Brien that he hoped some good might come of them, but another time, when Barry O'Brien told him people were saying he was talking peace when he meant war, he replied smiling: 'Oh, indeed, do they? Well you know, if you want peace you must be ready for war.'[91] Perhaps this very inconsistency expressed some profound uncertainty about the future. We shall never know the whole truth, but the most convincing explanation may simply be that he was pulled different ways by conflicting currents at different times – that in one mood he genuinely wanted a settlement, that in another he dreaded lest retirement *would* be permanent, whatever might be said or left unsaid, and that all the while the instinctive tactician in him may have rejoiced at the opportunity to sow discord among his enemies. But however obscure his motives, the consequences of his actions were starkly clear. This had been the last real chance of reconciliation. It was a fight to the death that lay ahead.

CHAPTER 20

La Commedia è Finita

An age is the reversal of an age:
When strangers murdered Emmet, Fitzgerald, Tone,
We lived like men that watch a painted stage.
What matter for the scene, the scene once gone:
It had not touched our lives. But popular rage,
Hysterica passio dragged this quarry down.
None shared our guilt; nor did we play a part
Upon a painted stage when we devoured his heart.

(W. B. Yeats, 'Parnell's Funeral'.)

I

The negotiations in France had hardly ended before Parnell resumed and intensified the pattern of life he had adopted from the moment of the defeat at Kilkenny. It seemed almost as if the peace-talks with O'Brien had been a kind of suspension of time when everything was held in abeyance until the outcome was known. Thereafter both sides re-engaged with all their force in a struggle of which the issue was still dubious and obscure.

In the beginning Parnell had certain definite advantages. His base in Dublin was strong and he had already used it to tighten his grip on the Irish National League, whose headquarters were in the capital. Other towns, notably Waterford and Kilkenny, were faithful to him and in Cork he had undoubtedly a large following, though the bishop reported to Dr Walsh early in the campaign that feeling ran high in both camps. 'The Fenians and vintners' were, he thought, Parnell's principal supporters.[1] But a week later he had to extend this list. 'An extraordinary fact', he wrote, 'is that many women, even devotees, have gone mad in his favour and I was horrified to find a convent of nuns infected with the fury which became known to the children.' 'It may be', he added ruefully, 'that a liking for such people is a weakness of women's character.'[2] The administrator of the diocese, Canon O'Mahony, was made of sterner stuff. 'We are now acting on the principle', he wrote, 'that the county, which is sound, can be utilized to keep the city straight. Through the priests in the country and county towns we are contriving to *quietly* withdraw customers from those who secretly organized the rabble to hiss and hoot at the clergy . . . These aggressive fellows are amenable to no other influence.'[3]

It is impossible to say how many ordinary citizens were amenable to this ingenious adaptation of the boycott, but Parnell could afford to disdain local pressures so long as he controlled the major national newspapers, and with both the *Freeman's Journal* and *United Ireland* still behind him as the battle entered its new phase, he could count on ample publicity for his every move. His plan was simple. Weekend after weekend he would travel from Brighton to Dublin and thence to speak in all parts of the country – a one-man crusade in almost perpetual motion. It was, quite literally, a killing regime and friends and enemies alike noted the change that came over him. Healy saw him occasionally at close quarters in the House of Commons and wrote of him that, though sometimes cast-iron as of old, at other moments he was 'awfully haggard', and at the end of June was so white that even he felt sorry for him.[4] Justin McCarthy, who met him more frequently than most on business connected with the evicted tenants, also thought him 'pale and haggard'. Afterwards, when all was over, he described how Parnell would come to him late at night and sit long in friendly discussion. One occasion he remembered with particular vividness:[5]

> It came to be three in the morning before he rose to go . . . and he then told me that he was going to drive to the Euston Hotel, get a short sleep there, and start for Ireland by the train leaving Euston station shortly after seven o'clock that morning. I remonstrated with him for sitting up so late under such conditions, and expressed to him my strong fear that the incessant travelling and speech-making . . . must do some permanent injury to his health. He seemed for the moment quite like his old self. He smiled the once familiar sweet smile, grasped my hand and assured me that, on the contrary, he felt convinced that, in his present condition of mind, the travelling and the speech-making were really doing him good.

Perhaps his over-wrought nerves did find some relief in action, but as the summer wore on it was evident that the deterioration in his physique was matched by the deterioration in what he had to say and how he said it. His speeches became drearily repetitive, coarser in tone, increasingly filled with tedious personal invective. He had few themes and even fewer variations. It was noticed especially how often he traversed the stale history of the Boulogne negotiations, castigating the Liberals, not only for the 'inadequacy' of their guarantees, but for their continued 'dictation' to the Irish party. From this he soon moved almost somnam-bulistically back into the past to resume his ancient quarrels with Glad-stone. 'He taught the Tories', he said at Wicklow in a speech typical of many, 'how to pass a Crimes Act, he suppressed public meetings in Ireland . . . he prohibited organization, the forces under his control shot down the people and bayoneted women and children. All these things were tried by Mr Gladstone and the Liberal party before they adopted the policy of conciliation and concession to the Irish national de-mands . . .'[6] Such reckless preaching of what was at bottom no more than a gospel of hate may have earned him the applause of the ground-lings but it simply alienated those who still hoped for an eventual return to constructive politics. And since such a return presupposed the necessity of some kind of understanding with the Liberals, Parnell's savage attacks on Gladstone made him more than ever impossible as a future leader. Moderates could draw only one conclusion from speeches such as the extraordinary outburst Parnell made at Bermondsey only a couple of weeks after the speech just quoted: 'Supposing Mr Gladstone comes into power at the next election he will not give Ireland her legitimate freedom. Supposing this dispute had never arisen Mr Glad-stone, upon coming into power, would not have given Ireland her legitimate freedom.'[7]

From the theme of independent opposition he passed easily and frequently to a resurrection of his old King Charles's head, the weakness of parliamentary action, and the alternative which might have to be put in its place. Thus, on one occasion when addressing an audience in Navan as 'men of royal Meath', he could add wildly that someone in the future 'may have the privilege of addressing you as men of republican Meath'.[8] On another occasion he could not resist the old cliché which had figured in his speeches at intervals ever since the start of his career – that he would not repeat Grattan's mistake of disbanding the Volunteers, 'until such a measure of legislative independence has been granted to Ireland as will enable her to take care of her own future . . .'[9] Parnell, it is true, did not have any Volunteers to disband, but his remarks gained a certain significance from the fact that he was addressing a gathering of Gaelic clubs, which even then were becoming a nursery of a newer and more intransigent nationalism. What he really had in mind, however, as he told a friend, was not military action, which was impracticable, but a campaign of civil disobedience – in fact, something not unlike the policy Sinn Fein was to put into operation a quarter of a century later.[10]

To this litany of vituperation and recrimination there were two exceptions, though each exposed him to different kinds of criticism. The first was his decision to support Balfour's Land Bill which passed into law during the session of 1891. As we saw earlier, it provided £33 million in the form of credits to enable tenants to purchase their holdings; it also made a positive contribution towards solving the problem of the endemic poverty of the west of Ireland by setting up the Congested Districts Board which, among other activities, endeavoured to promote cottage industries as an alternative, or supplement, to agriculture. Balfour's measure was far from a final solution, but it did mark a considerable step towards the elimination of landlordism and Parnell, who repeatedly claimed that his (half-hearted) opposition of the previous session had been in deference to Liberal wishes, now seized on it eagerly. His own attitude towards English reforms had always been consistent and he had no difficulty in defending it after the split. At Irishtown, for example, in April 1891, he rejected absolutely the notion 'that if you were any better off you would become less determined nationalists, and less anxious to obtain Home Rule'.[11] 'My views are', he said later in the year, 'to accept anything good that we can get from any English party, but at the same time not to surrender our independence to any English party.'[12]

Here, admittedly, he was begging a large question, whether or not it was possible to 'kill Home Rule with kindness'. But it hardly lay in the mouths of his Irish opponents to criticize him on this score, since their own ambivalent attitude to land purchase seemed more related to placating their Liberal allies than to the merits of the question. Indeed, the debates, especially in committee, were often less about the welfare of the tenants than about the disunity of the politicians. Balfour, who found his legislation going through on oiled castors, watched the two factions with a mixture of cynical amusement and professional admiration. After one such encounter – inevitably, between Parnell and Healy – he wrote to his under-secretary that Parnell's speech was, in its way, 'a masterpiece'. 'The concentrated and over-mastering power of Parnell's personality as he retorted with crushing effect upon Healy made it a most extraordinary scene to witness.'[13]

The second of Parnell's ventures into what appeared to be more constructive politics was his courtship of the working-class in both England and Ireland. He opened his attack with a speech at Clerkenwell, in London, which struck most contemporaries as no more than a crude attempt to drive a wedge between the Liberals and Labour. Parnell appeared on this occasion in the guise of an advanced radical who looked forward to shorter hours for miners and others, to the setting up of boards of conciliation in industry, and to a measure of state control over large monopolies such as the railway companies.[14] The moral of his speech was that since he was now a free agent – he meant, not tied to the Liberals – he could become the workers' friend he had always wanted to be, and, speaking in Dublin ten days later, he went out of his way to express his regret for having in 1888, under Liberal pressure, thrown the Irish vote against Keir Hardie at the Mid-Lanark election. For this, it is fair to add, Keir Hardie bore him no grudge, and after Parnell's death wrote of him as 'the one man in politics for whom I was ever able to feel a genuine respect'.[15]

The meeting at Dublin had a wider significance, since it gave Parnell his first opportunity to develop his new-found radicalism before a large conference of trade unionists. The conference was presided over by Fred Allen (at that time prominent in the IRB) and it had on its agenda an imposing programme of reform, which included manhood suffrage ('one man one vote') for all elections from parliament to poor-law boards; payment of members and of all election expenses; a universal eight-hour day; nationalization of the land; the reduction of food taxes; state control of railways and inland transport; extension of the factory acts; and increased building of labourers' dwellings at decreased rents. To nearly all of this Parnell gave his 'general and practical agreement', though he hedged on the eight-hour day and on land nationalization. The eight-hour day, he thought, would be practicable only if established by international convention, since no country could be expected to put itself at a possible disadvantage with its competitors. As for land nationalization (shades of Davitt!), all he would say was that he agreed with the principle – though not with what he called 'the crude theories hitherto put forward' – but he remained extremely vague about what he meant by the term. It was all bound up with the removal of food taxes, he said mysteriously, and begged his audience not to press him further for the time being.[16]

Not unnaturally, these protestations struck his critics as humbug, a desperate casting about for fresh allies, any allies on any terms, for a losing cause. It was, said *The Times* severely, 'an undisguised and impudent bid for the support of the labour vote in Great Britain'.[17] Davitt, who had legitimate reason to feel aggrieved at this incursion into his own domain, observed acidly that Parnell's declaration would have had an electric effect if delivered *before* the split. Coming when

and as it did, it was merely a despicable attempt to woo the workers –
and what was worse, to woo them with a programme lifted from his own
Labour World.[18] Parnell, of course, paid no attention to these strictures
and three months later was to be found advocating further limitation of
the hours of work in mines and unhealthy trades, always provided
that this was achieved internationally. 'The future', he proclaimed
dramatically, 'is undoubtedly with the working-classes.'[19] But the
prevailing impression remained that this startling revelation had been
vouchsafed to him too late to serve any but the crudest of propaganda
purposes.

II

'Too late' is indeed the epitaph for all these speeches. There runs
through them a note of urgency, of desperation, as if Parnell had
realized that time, which had been on his side while the Boulogne
negotiations lasted, had begun to ebb away from him. In the early
stages of the struggle his two immense assets – virtual control of the
press and absolute control of the Irish National League – had put his
opponents at a serious disadvantage. They had met many difficulties in
their attempts to create a rival newspaper and a rival organization.
However, both came into being at the beginning of March and although
the organization, the Irish National Federation, was slow to take root,
the *National Press* swung into action at once, rapidly becoming a
major agency in prosecuting and exacerbating the quarrel.[20]

From the anti-Parnellite standpoint it was not a moment too soon,
for almost immediately after the paper first appeared on 7 March, the
death of P. A. Macdonald, the sitting member for North Sligo, created
the first opportunity since Kilkenny for testing opinion at the polls.
Macdonald had followed the majority in repudiating Parnell and to take
his place the anti-Parnellites nominated a strong candidate, the Sligo
merchant and alderman, Bernard Collery. Parnell's candidate was the
Dublin solicitor, Valentine Dillon, who had backed him consistently
since the split. Both candidates were in large measure pawns, for the
contest quickly resolved itself into another round of the everlasting duel
between Parnell and the majority leaders, each side putting out its
whole strength to win a crucial victory.

As at Kilkenny the result turned largely on the extent to which
clerical influence was exerted against the Parnellite candidate. But in
North Sligo there were complications which had not existed in the
earlier battle. Although the writ for the election was moved by Thomas

Sexton, under urgent pressure from the local bishop, Dr Lawrence Gillooly, Bishop of Elphin, it quickly appeared that neither he, nor his brethren of Ardagh, Achonry and Killala, whose dioceses all over-lapped with North Sligo, could count upon the massive loyalty of their clergy as Dr Brownrigg had been able to do in Kilkenny. Even the bishops were not wholly at one, for Dr Lyster, Bishop of Achonry, reported to Gillooly that Dr Conway, Bishop of Killala, was showing signs of wanting to hold aloof. 'His priests approved of this policy', wrote Dr Lyster, 'and so, many of them wish to be neutral in this electoral contest. He cannot and will not force them to actively oppose Parnell: the grounds he assigns being he could not press them to oppose their own people.' The best Dr Conway would do was to promise to write to his priests cautioning them against supporting Parnell. 'He accompanied me to the train', wrote the disappointed Bishop of Achonry, 'and we had to pass through Parnell's meeting. As we worked our way through the crowd ringing cheers were given for Dr Conway; it is quite clear the rank and file believe that he is with them.' 'His sickness has left traces on his Lordship', was Dr Lyster's semi-charitable conclusion, 'he is hazy and stupid; and my belief is – he is not fully aware of what is going on.'[21]

Hazy and stupid the bishop might have been, but not so his political priests. As the election proceeded so many of them turned out to be Parnellites that the outcome was seriously in doubt. There was a real possibility that if the electors of the Killala diocese sided with Parnell, and if they were supported by the Tory voters in the constituency, estimated at about a thousand, his candidate might win. Parnell himself was buoyant and wrote enthusiastically to Katharine about the mag-nificent reception he had had in his headquarters at Ballina. 'The whole country for twenty-five miles from here to the town of Sligo is solid for us', he said, 'the priests being in our favour with one exception, and the seceders being unable to hold a meeting anywhere.'[22] Understandably, this did not make him any more conciliatory and during the contest he threw out yet more personal insults which would be remembered long after the shouting had died away. Of these, perhaps the most offensive was his remark that he would gladly yield his leadership whenever a real alternative appeared, but that none of 'the seceders' came within range of qualifying:[23]

Can you make any one of them a leader? Who would unite with him any section of the country or any section of his colleagues? Can you select the foul-mouthed Timothy Healy? Can you trust in uncertain and wobbling Tom Sexton? And can you follow hysterical Davitt who never belongs to any one party for twenty-four hours together?

Davitt was a target because once again the main burden of the campaign fell upon him. Tim Healy, who would normally have led the opposition to Parnell, was out of action, since he had rashly ventured into Cork and promptly been injured by a Parnellite mob.[24] However, his brother Maurice was in the thick of the fray and from him presumably came the information which Tim Healy passed on to Archbishop Walsh. The worst district, he said, was Tireragh, where the anti-Parnellites were actually stoned out of the parish, but Ballina was nearly as bad. 'When they went into the houses to canvass and argue with the voters, the very women took up stools and spade handles and tried to assault them, the moment they announced their mission.' Healy, who had complacently accepted priestly aid at Kilkenny, now registered pious horror when it threatened to go the other way. 'To lend a sanction to violence and to encourage it by altar denunciations, after all that has passed about Parnell, argues an amazing spirit, which undoubtedly is most formidable at election times.'[25]

With the constituency so deeply divided, the balance of power rested effectively with the Unionist vote. Arthur Balfour took the situation seriously enough to write to the local Unionist association himself, though his advice was too delphic to be of much use to those who had to make decisions on the ground. There was nothing, he thought, to choose between the 'respective demerits' of the candidates and if he were a Unionist voter he would either abstain or vote for the candidate whose return would 'do least benefit to the party of separation'.[26] In fact, the Sligo Tories for the most part abstained and in so doing almost certainly decided the fate of the election. When the result was announced on 3 April Collery had a majority of 768 votes – 3261 against 2493 – and it was the shrewd opinion of the Under-Secretary, Ridgeway, that if the Unionist vote had gone solidly for Parnell he would not only have won the election but would probably have been irresistible thereafter.[27] Certainly, T. M. Healy was under no illusions that a disaster had narrowly been averted. In the letter to Archbishop Walsh already cited, he wrote:[28]

Out of 120 illiterates in one booth 6 only voted for Collery and those did so I am told with terror depicted on their faces, and we have similar reports from all the Tireragh booths. The wonder is that we won, which we owe entirely to Sligo town. The whole affair has given our men an awful shake, and has enormously encouraged Parnell. He can overawe or seduce the unthinking element easily enough, Heaven knows, without the priests helping him to raise the mobs against us.

Healy's accusations about undue influence being exerted upon illiterate voters were echoed by the other side, but that each could point to instances of clerical intimidation only reinforces the thesis that North Sligo repeated the pattern of North Kilkenny, though more complexly. For if both elections were effectively decided by priestly influence, the significant feature of North Sligo was that such influence was exerted *for* Parnell as well as *against* him. This in turn illustrates a fact about the struggle which is too often overlooked – that although the bishops were in general firmly against Parnell, it by no means followed automatically that parish priests and curates would take the same line. In many cases, no doubt, it could confidently be assumed that they would. But, as North Sligo proved, where a district had strong Fenian associations, the local clergy, sprung from the people and often sharing as well as moulding their views, could respond as readily as their flocks to the Parnellite emphasis upon the frailty of the parliamentary movement and the need to reassert the doctrine of independent opposition. To this extent, North Sligo might well inspire Healy with alarm and Parnell with confidence. Yet the very closeness of the verdict meant that neither side could regard it as conclusive. It was William O'Brien, listening to the distant clash of arms from behind the walls of Galway jail, who summed up most clearly the possibilities inherent in the situation. 'Any bad beating for P. in Sligo will make the others so cockahoop that there will be no standing them.' On the other hand, if Parnell won, 'he would be quite entitled to say the country was with him, and I for one should not say him nay'.[29]

All the same, even if North Sligo did not offer a reliable guide to the state of opinion in the country as a whole, for Parnell, with time running out, and needing more urgently than ever to win some victory at the polls before the general election to which he pinned his hopes, the result was a serious, perhaps decisive, set-back. It meant that he had to fight the battle for public opinion in a climate that was becoming more and not less hostile. Sadly, but inevitably in the circumstances, the battle came to turn increasingly upon the central issue of the political role of the church. Just as Dillon had protested during the Plan of Campaign against ecclesiastical intervention, so now the Parnellites struggled fiercely to restate the distinction between faith and morals, which they recognized as a proper sphere of episcopal authority, and politics, in which laymen had the right to make up their own minds. The case was put by John Redmond with bleak clarity. 'I am entitled', he said early in 1891, 'when the bishops, in a political question, advocate a course which my intelligence and my conscience tell me is a wrong one, to perfect freedom to dissent from them, and to recall how, time and time again in the history of our country, the prelates took action which has long since been proved to be short-sighted and unpatriotic.' Parnell's leadership, he insisted, was 'a purely political question', and if the bishops were able to make their power paramount upon such an issue, 'they will thereby have created the most formidable obstacle to the granting of Home Rule by the English people that the wit of man could devise'.[30]

At any time it would have been difficult to distinguish between 'proper' and 'improper' expressions of ecclesiastical opinion, but Parnell's case, where the sin of adultery had, after all, been publicly admitted, ceased to be a matter of private conscience once he had indicated his determination to remain 'the leader of the Irish race'. He could not be accepted as leader, said Archbishop Croke in reply to a series of pre-arranged questions put to him by the *National Press*, not precisely because he had committed a grievous offence against the moral law, but because, having shown no sign of repentance, he should not be 'set up on a pinnacle by a Christian people to be respected and consulted as a leader should be'. 'In other words you cannot support Mr Parnell's leadership without giving public scandal, condoning his offence . . . and thus disturbing the landmarks of social morality.'[31]

Parnell, it seemed, was impossible because he was both eminent and obdurate. Did this necessarily bring him within the jurisdiction of the bishops? The Parnellites said not, but, asked Dr Croke, who was to decide whether any specific issue fell into the category of faith and morals, or into the category of politics? Surely, he said, for Catholics the final decision must rest with the church, speaking through the bishops. Otherwise, what would be the point of endowing them with a plenary jurisdiction over faith and morals 'if individual members of the fold can . . . render that jurisdiction nugatory by stating that they cannot accept the ruling of the bishops in a particular case, inasmuch as it involved only secular issues'.[32]

Here the archbishop exposed the essential weakness of the Parnellite position. As good Catholics they freely admitted the primacy of the bishops in matters concerning faith and morals, but the moment they excluded Parnell's leadership from that sphere, they arrogated to themselves a right of selection which, if conceded by the hierarchy, could have led to proliferating independent judgements on any number of topics. This the church could not, and did not, allow, but although there were distinct traces of anti-clericalism in some Parnellite speeches at this period it is significant that this did not develop on a large scale. That it failed to do so may partly have been due to the circumspectness which Archbishop Walsh had enjoined upon his episcopal brethren at the outset. Yet it was surely no less due to the realization by most Irishmen that Parnell's trangression had been both moral *and* political. The bishops might pronounce him unfit for the leadership because of his adultery, and this pronouncement might indeed have political consequences, but there were also perfectly good grounds for opposing him which had nothing to do with his supposed moral lapse. It was one thing to overlook his relations with Mrs O'Shea, but quite another thing to overlook his relations with Gladstone after the latter had made it clear that his continuance at the head of the Irish party jeopardized, not merely the Liberal-nationalist alliance, but Home Rule itself. It was this threat, rather than the bishops' condemnation, which stripped Parnell of his support in the country and which, by reducing the Parnellites to a small minority of the Irish representation, helped to avoid a collision between the church and the laity.

III

Unhappily, the circumstances of the time made it virtually certain that the debate about the role of the church could not be confined to the abstract, and it was ironical that it should have been Dr Croke who provided the occasion for the angriest controversy that the crisis had yet thrown up. Perhaps it was inevitable that the quarrel should have been about money, since money was so crucial to the campaign. All through these months McCarthy struggled ineffectually to persuade Parnell that others should be associated with them in administering the Paris fund, which was urgently needed for the relief of the evicted tenants. To every such appeal Parnell merely replied that he could not share his responsibility with anyone save McCarthy and the dispute seemed likely to continue indefinitely.[33]

But money was a source of irritation apart altogether from the fate of the evicted tenants, mainly because Parnell's possession of it – and he appeared to have plenty – contrasted so sharply with the acute shortage felt by his opponents, especially those of them who depended on party funds for the payment of their parliamentary salaries. Indeed, had it not been for the help given to the majority section by a few of their wealthier colleagues, it is hard to see how they could have carried on. This, however, was a strictly limited resource and by the end of February McCarthy was reporting to Archbishop Walsh that it was already exhausted.[34]

It is against this background that Archbishop Croke's action has to be seen. Towards the end of May he made a speech at Kilteely in which he asked how it was that Parnell was able to go by special train through Ireland every week 'to knock the bottom out of the priests'. He then instanced various revenues which had never been fully accounted for – the 'Parnell tribute' of 1883, the Defence Fund relating to the Special Commission, half of the £10,000 given by Cecil Rhodes, and a cheque for £1000 presented by Rhodes's friend, John Morrogh, at about the same time. And how much, asked the archbishop, was there in the Paris fund? 'I do not', he exclaimed, 'for a moment wish to insinuate that there was any embezzlement going on or any misapplication of the funds, but I simply express my opinion that a public audit of all financial transactions is absolutely necessary.'[35]

This was a challenge which Parnell could not ignore and next day he dealt with it, somewhat off-handedly, in a speech at Wicklow. The Parnell tribute, he said, had been a personal gift to him and he did not have to account to anyone for it; it seems, in fact, to have been swallowed up by the debts incurred on his estate.[36] The balance of the Defence Fund (he did not specify how much) he held in his own hands and would use for public purposes whenever he judged fit. The contribution of £1000 from John Morrogh had been made before Morrogh became an MP and Parnell did not offer any explanation as to what had happened to it. The Paris fund, which he reckoned at £43–44,000, was controlled by joint treasurers and withdrawals from it went either to the Irish National League, to the National League of Great Britain, or to the parliamentary party. On the question of audit, the books of the two Leagues were annually inspected by an accountant, and it was the business of the party's treasurer, J. F. X. O'Brien, to arrange for a proper audit of its accounts.[37]

There remained one intriguing item – the gift which Cecil Rhodes had made to Parnell in 1888. The amount of this gift is usually understood to have been £10,000. Of this, half passed through the books of the parliamentary party in the form of a single payment of £5000.[38] Part of the remainder Parnell claimed in his Wicklow speech to have given to William O'Brien (for the evicted tenants), and the balance, he said, remained in his possession. But the actual position may have been more complicated than this. It would appear that in March 1891 Rhodes and Parnell were in contact with each other twice, each time on the subject of money. At the beginning of that month, reacting angrily to Parnell's Navan speech about the prospect of 'royal Meath' eventually becoming 'republican Meath', Rhodes wrote accusing him of having gone back on their agreement to work together for imperial federation and asking that his donation be handed over to charity.* Parnell, it seems, returned a soft answer, regretting the republican reference and pointing to other passages in the same speech which cancelled it out.[39] Rhodes, apparently mollified, not only left the balance of his original gift with the Irish leader, but, on meeting him in London later in the month, is said to have offered him a second £10,000 in the presence of a witness. The witness was the young Edmund Dwyer Gray, son of the lately dead proprietor of the *Freeman's Journal*. Gray only published his recollections of the Parnell–Rhodes interview in 1926 – they appeared anonymously in an obscure Tasmanian newspaper – but he was quite emphatic both that the offer was made and that Parnell refused either to accept it or to let the fact of the offer be made public. In taking this stand, he was probably actuated by the tactical consideration that it would have been difficult to justify his monopoly of a second donation when the party was deeply divided on the leadership question and still more difficult when, largely because of that division, the evicted tenants were *in extremis*. Moreover, since he and his followers were once more attracting Fenian support, a too publicized connection with the imperialist Rhodes would have done him no good at all. Rhodes's own motive almost certainly related to his continuing obsession with imperial federation. The Navan speech had indicated that Parnell's loyalty to that cause was suspect. Rhodes, while accepting the Parnellite gloss upon the speech, may still have felt that the cash nexus would be a surer bond in future. Being accustomed to buy whatever he wanted, it would have made sense to him to buy Parnell with a further donation, on condition that he reaffirmed his acceptance of the central principle of Rhodes's scheme, which was the retention of some Irish members at Westminster as the nucleus of the federal parliament he dreamed of. Since Parnell's Irish opponents were by definition committed to the Liberal alliance, and therefore 'sounder' on retention, the offer of a further £10,000 to Parnell alone suggests that for Rhodes the backing of this powerful, if unpredictable, horse was a desirable way of hedging his bets in the imperial federation stakes.[40]

None of this was public knowledge when Dr Croke asked his em-

---

*For the agreement with Rhodes in 1888 and the Navan speech, see above, pp. 442–3 and 578 respectively.

barrassing questions about Parnell's financial resources. All that he and others had to go on was Parnell's casual reply in his Wicklow speech. At once it was made brutally clear that this was not going to be good enough. From the inevitable Tim Healy came an immediate and deadly riposte. On the day the report of the Wicklow speech appeared, he published in the *National Press* an article entitled 'Stop, Thief', accusing Parnell of having shirked the whole question of an audit over a long period. 'Why? Because for years *he has been stealing the money entrusted to his charge.*'[41] He then went on to contradict Parnell's account of how the gift from Rhodes had been handled and roundly asserted that Parnell had lodged the cheque from Morrogh into his own account. Next day came a second, even fiercer attack. The *National Press*, said Healy, had been expecting a writ for libel, but none had appeared. 'We called Mr Parnell a thief. We repeat that epithet.' 'This charge', he wrote, 'if he fails to face it has come to stay . . . We will force him to face it, or amidst the contempt of his own supporters "lash the rascal naked through the world".'[42]

These two articles represent the ultimate point of savagery reached in the entire struggle. Parnell, typically, disdained to notice them beyond a reference in his speech at Inchicore a few days later to the effect that he would prepare a balance-sheet to explain the disputed items and would submit it to William O'Brien when he came out of jail.[43] 'The position of nominee-auditor for an accused thief', the *National Press* no less typically commented, 'is not one to be coveted, and after the experience of Mr Parnell in Boulogne, it is hardly likely to be accepted.'[44] In fact, no such balance-sheet, or record of it, has come to light and as John Dillon intervened to prevent further accusations, the matter was allowed to drop.[45] But it had served its twin purposes of further embittering the quarrel and throwing Parnell on to the defensive. For though he affected to make light of it, the charge had placed him in an ugly dilemma. If he did *not* bring a libel action, this would encourage the suspicion that he did not because he dare not, and would also leave Healy free to resurrect his charges whenever he pleased. But if he brought an action, and even if he won it, he would still have had to submit the inner workings and the financial resources of his movement to a microscopic scrutiny which would have revealed altogether too much about the strengths and weaknesses of his position. Though either way he stood to lose, it is probable that the factor which weighed most with him was psychological, not prudential. Never in his life had he stooped to justify himself to Timothy Healy and it was not likely that he would begin now, after all that had passed between them since the beginning of the crisis.

IV

From these sordid depths it is a relief to turn briefly to the event for which all Parnell's tribulations had been, in a sense, the preparation. 'On June 25th', wrote Katharine long afterwards, 'I was awakened at daybreak by my lover's tapping at my door and calling to me: "Get up, get up, it is time to be married".' Then followed an hour of hectic excitement to get everyone out of the house before the newspapermen, who had got wind of what was afoot, invaded them. Katharine's old nurse, and her maid Phyllis, who were to be the witnesses, were packed off by train to the register office at Steyning where the wedding was to take place. Parnell himself supervised the harnessing of his horse, Dictator, to the phaeton which took them so fast to their destination that they covered the nine miles from Brighton before the train arrived. Parnell was in an ebullient, excited mood. For once, he even noticed what she was wearing – 'your things become you always' was the most extreme compliment she could usually extract from him – and he fastened white roses at her breast with his own hands. While they waited for their witnesses in the tiny office his high spirits soared still further. 'My King', she recollected, 'looked at us both in the small mirror on the wall of the little room, and, adjusting his white rose in his frock-coat, said joyously, "It is not every woman who makes so good a marriage as you are making, Queenie, is it? and to such a handsome fellow too!" blowing kisses to me in the glass. Then the two maids arrived, and the little ceremony that was to legalize our union of many years was quickly over.'[46]

Back at Walsingham Terrace they had to run the gauntlet of the pressmen who, however, gave way at Parnell's imperious command: 'Stand back; let Mrs Parnell pass.' It was a wedding-breakfast *à deux*, and one without a wedding-cake, 'because he said he would not be able to bear seeing me eat *our* wedding-cake without him and, as I knew, the very sight of a rich cake made him ill'. After that came the reporters who resorted to every device to force or bribe an entrance. One of them got as far as the hall and Phyllis, out of habit, asked if Mrs O'Shea would see him. '*Who* is Mrs O'Shea?' thundered Parnell and went off to deal with the journalists himself.[47] After they had gone he changed into an old coat, smoked quietly in an easy chair and watched her steadily until she grew nervous and insisted that they go out. They wandered across the then open fields to Aldrington where Parnell watched workmen making bricks, trying his hand at one or two himself. Afterwards they walked towards the sea and sat there talking of the future, when Ireland would have settled down and Parnell could abdicate, after which they could go to a better climate for his health's sake. They talked, too, of the summer visits they would make to Avondale, of the golden time when he would never have to leave her. 'And we talked of Ireland, for Parnell loved her, and what he loved I would not hate or thrust out from his thoughts, even on this day that God had made.' Her account continues:[48]

> Yet, as we sat together, silent now, even though we spoke together still with the happiness that knows no words, a storm came over the sea. It had been very hot all day, and a thunderstorm was inevitable, but as we sheltered under the breakwater, I wished that this one day might have been without a storm.
>
> Reading my thoughts, he said: 'The storms and thundering will never hurt us now, Queenie, my wife, for there is nothing in the wide world that can be greater than our love: there is nothing in all the world but you and I.' And I was comforted because I did not remember death.

V

But the storm over the sea in Ireland did not die down and their honeymoon lasted only that single summer's day. Even before they were married the preliminary moves had already been made in the third and last of the electoral battles Parnell was to fight in the constituencies. This was in Carlow, where a vacancy had just been caused by the death of that old warrior the O'Gorman Mahon, who eleven years earlier had played so large a part in bringing Katharine and Parnell together, but who, though absent from Committee Room Fifteen through illness, had subsequently declared against his former chief and friend. To take his place the anti-Parnellites had nominated a local merchant from Carlow town, John Hammond. Against him a Parnellite convention chose to run another figure from Parnell's past, Andrew Kettle, the Land Leaguer of other days. Kettle was a loyal supporter and a hard fighter, so it was ominous that even he should only have agreed to stand with the utmost reluctance and on condition that his election expenses were paid.[49]

Into this conflict Parnell flung himself with the same febrile energy as before. It was a noisy rather than a violent election (though there was persistent stone-throwing) and clerical influence, while certainly in evidence, was not the controversial issue it had been at either Kilkenny or Sligo. Part of the reason may well have been the feeling, insidious but strong, that this time Parnell was beaten before he had started. Carlow was a modestly affluent, mainly rural constituency, stretching out in all directions from the prosperous county town of the same name. This was not Fenian territory and neither priests nor laymen were galvanized into any dramatic clashes in response to Parnell's by now stereotyped appeals. Even the considerable Unionist element in the constituency did not run according to form. So far from voting for Parnell's candidate, or remaining neutral as in Sligo, some Unionists seem actually to have voted for John Hammond because of his high standing in the district.[50]

There were other more fundamental explanations for the Parnellite defeat. One may well have been simple *ennui*, a reaction on the part of an over-satiated public against the traumatic scenes of the previous months. Another was the fact that, for reasons to be examined in a moment, the *Freeman's Journal* was at last beginning to waver. A third was the decision of the bishops to speak out collectively once more against Parnell. On 25 June, Parnell's wedding-day, the hierarchy marked the occasion by passing a resolution recording 'the solemn expression of our judgement, as pastors of the Irish people, that Mr Parnell, by his public misconduct, has utterly disqualified himself to be their leader'. Apart from Parnell's own actions, the resolution continued, the open hostility of his agents and newspapers to ecclesiastical authority supplied further proof that he was 'wholly unworthy' of the confidence of Catholics. 'We therefore feel bound on this occasion to call on our people to repudiate his leadership.'[51]

The resolution was almost, but not quite, unanimous. The Bishop of Limerick did not sign, though he later 'heartily concurred' and the Bishop of Kerry, Dr Coffey, confirmed his reputation as the hierarchy's leading political eccentric by telling Archbishop Walsh that 'I believe Dillon, O'Brien and Healy and their following are more dangerous to the church and future of this country than Parnell'.[52] But the Carlow electors evidently thought otherwise, for they gave Hammond the verdict by 3755 votes to Kettle's 1539. This was indeed, as the Under-Secretary reported to Balfour, 'a crusher for Parnell' and the first indication that a general election might bring him not the victory he anticipated, but a decisive defeat.[53]

Parnell himself remained unmoved. Though his friends were beginning to be seriously worried about his health, marriage clearly agreed with him. Now, if briefly, he came as near to bonhomie, even on occasion to buffoonery, as he ever got in his whole career. During the Carlow election, for example, he disconcerted one of his principal supporters, Patrick O'Brien, who was in the middle of a speech, by urging him *sotto voce* to break into a popular ballad. 'Of course I refused', said O'Brien afterwards, 'but he kept poking me in the ribs all the time, saying "Sing it" . . . The whole thing seemed to have amused him immensely.'[54] Nor did his euphoria waver in face of the Carlow defeat, for Balfour's cousin, Lord Edward Cecil, crossing from Dublin on the same boat with him found him 'in the highest possible good humour and good spirits'.[55] So far was he from being dejected that within a fortnight he had summoned to Dublin a convention of the Irish National League to restore his followers' wilting morale. It was noticeable, though, that of the 1600 who were named as attending, four counties (Dublin, Meath, Wicklow and Kildare) accounted for more than fifty per cent, while Dublin city and county together supplied more than a third of the total.[56] The proceedings no doubt conveyed to the faithful that the leader's determination to fight on was as inflexible as ever, but nothing could disguise the fact, which the convention itself may actually have advertised, that support was ebbing and the future darkly uncertain.

VI

Increasingly, one has the impression of a man drawing upon his last reserves of energy and courage to put the best face on a situation which has begun to slip out of his control. If it had begun to slip before Carlow, the pace was certainly accelerated after that election. The most significant indication of this was the changing attitude of the *Freeman's Journal*, where the influence of the young Edmund Dwyer Gray and his mother – between them they owned 12,000 out of a total of 25,000 shares – was bound to be important. Gray had at first accepted the paper's Parnellite stance. But after the Sligo election he began to contemplate a *volte face*, though his uncertainty persisted some time longer. His statement to John Morley – that he would not make up his mind until Dillon and O'Brien emerged from prison – reflected a deep confusion of mind, for, as Morley commented to Gladstone, 'what possible good can come to Dillon and his aims from giving Parnell the *Freeman's* support for three months longer?'[57] Nevertheless, a decision was becoming urgent, partly because the paper was losing money heavily through its support for Parnell, and partly because there was a danger that if it persisted in that course it might incur papal condemnation. To avert this fate Gray made a personal appeal to the Pope, but did not get much comfort, being told to place himself under the guidance of Archbishop Walsh, who, of course, was certain to impel him inexorably towards Parnell's opponents.[58]

Yet, despite these pressures, Gray remained faithful to his determination not to commit himself until Dillon and O'Brien came out of Galway jail. Many others in both camps waited with equal anxiety for the pronouncement which the two leaders were expected to make on their release. While still in prison they endlessly debated the matter in letters smuggled from cell to cell. The one thing clearly emerging from this fragmentary correspondence was that they were adamant against any kind of agreement or fusion with Parnell, though they did have hopes of detaching some of his more moderate supporters, notably John Redmond, by advocating a policy of general reconciliation. At the same time they were acutely aware of how difficult it would be to mount such a policy while Healy was still on the warpath. Dillon therefore impressed upon a reluctant O'Brien the importance of making their gesture of reconciliation after they had joined the majority, where they would be well placed to deal with any attack by Healy. 'I would take up the challenge immediately and I am confident that we could beat him with slaughter. A fight of that nature might be the very occasion for getting over a lot of P's men.'[59]

In deciding to join the majority the two friends were swayed primarily by the deep obligation they felt towards the evicted tenants. They were also influenced by the Carlow election and by the news that Gray was ready to evacuate the *Freeman's Journal* from the sinking Parnellite ship. Accordingly, when they were released on 30 July, Dillon and O'Brien adhered strictly to the programme they had mapped out. Both made elaborately moderate speeches, but both went out of their way to emphasize that their break with Parnell was absolute and irrevocable.

The most immediate consequence was that Gray finally deserted Parnell, though, characteristically, he also clutched at Parnell's marriage to justify his ratting. This, as he explained unctuously to Archbishop Walsh, would provide 'a good *Catholic* reason for abandoning him', and the day after the release of Dillon and O'Brien, the *Freeman* duly carried an article declaring that the marriage had 'rendered it impossible that he should ever be recognized by the hierarchy as the leader of the Catholic people of Ireland'.[60] The archbishop, though well able to assess Gray's argument at its true worth, could not resist improving on it himself, pointing out a few days later that in the eyes of the church marriage with a divorced woman was no real marriage and that Parnell's offence was deepened rather than mitigated by the ceremony.[61]

Parnell seemed indifferent to this massing of fresh forces against him. He spoke at Thurles the Sunday after the two men came out of prison, but though he referred to O'Brien affectionately, it was ominous that he simultaneously accused Dillon of indiscipline. Since he also chose to make one of his periodic references to the limits of constitutional action, it was obvious that he had no intention of bidding for their support, or even their neutrality. Dillon and O'Brien neither expected nor wished that he would. On the contrary, the more inflexible he was, the more they might hope to draw the moderate Parnellites away from him. But this turned out to be a delusion. Given the implacability of Parnell on the one side and of Healy on the other, it was virtually impossible that any major shift of allegiance could have been negotiated and no shift in fact occurred.[61a]

By thus throwing in their lot with the anti-Parnellites Dillon and O'Brien probably tilted the balance decisively against Parnell. Their choice, once made, was irrevocable and was not to be changed even by external pressures such as those which John Devoy now tried to exert. Towards the end of October he sent from America certain proposals for ending the conflict. He suggested that both sections should agree to a joint meeting of the entire parliamentary party whereat Parnell and McCarthy should resign from the chairmanship of their respective sections; that Parnell should resign the chairmanship of the reunited party, while remaining a member of it; and that Dillon should then be elected chairman. Devoy further proposed that Parnell be asked to go on a fund-raising tour among the Irish overseas and that the party should pledge itself to accept no bill which did not include an executive responsible to an Irish parliament, and confer the right to appoint the judiciary and the magistracy, as well as control over police, land and public works. No member of the party should take office until such a Home Rule bill became law. To these ingenious but unreal proposals Dillon simply replied that something similar had been offered to Parnell at Boulogne. His rejection of terms then and his continuing determination to ignore the claims of unity and discipline had made it impossible for O'Brien and Dillon to enter again upon that path. Since Parnell remained obdurate they were bound to fight him. 'Against such a programme as this we have no choice. We must fight against it or give up all claim to the name of the Irish nationalist party. It is with the Irish party a struggle for existence. For parley with such a policy would be the basest cowardice.'[62]

VII

But it mattered little what Devoy said, or what Dillon said, or what O'Brien said, or what Healy said. All ultimately turned upon Parnell. And Parnell showed no sign of surrender. As summer merged into autumn he continued to drive himself as remorselessly as ever and the stream of Irish meetings flowed on, weekend after weekend, as he tried to prepare for the general election which he still believed would be his great opportunity to regain all the ground lost since November. To Barry O'Brien this seemed such a dangerous illusion that he tried to cushion Parnell against the possibility of defeat. 'It will take you ten years to pull the country together', O'Brien said to him once:[63]

'No', he rejoined very quietly. 'I will do it in five years – that is what I calculate.'

'Well, Gladstone will be dead by then', I said. 'The whole question to me is, you and Mr Gladstone. If you both go, Home Rule will go with you for this generation.'

'But I will not go', he answered angrily. 'I am a young man and I will not go.' And there was a fierce flash in his eyes which was not pleasant to look at.

On at least one other occasion Barry O'Brien, who had the knack of saying unpleasant truths to 'the chief' without rousing his ire, spoke with Parnell about the future. It was their final encounter and O'Brien remembered it as a vivid illustration both of Parnell's obstinacy and of his curious indifference to his surroundings. O'Brien was seeing him off at Euston and the train was about to start, when Parnell said to him casually, 'I should like to know what you think will be the result of the general election'. O'Brien answered: 'I should think that you will come back with about five followers, and I should not be surprised if you came back absolutely alone.' 'Well', Parnell replied impassively, 'if I do come back absolutely alone, one thing is certain, I shall then represent a party whose independence will not be sapped.' At this point the train began to move slowly away. Parnell walked forward unhurriedly and an anxious porter threw open the door of one carriage after another for him. He rejected each until he came to one where his supporter, J. L. Carew, was sitting. By this time the train had stopped altogether. He decided to travel with Carew, got in, and the train started again. The last sight Barry O'Brien had of him was at the open window, waving goodbye, a smile on his pale, sad face.[64]

It was this same stubborn tenacity which enabled him to brush aside every reverse as if it had not happened. Even the loss of the *Freeman's Journal*, which began to take effect towards the end of September, only had the effect of galvanizing him into launching a new paper, to be called the *Irish Daily Independent*. The plans for this had not been completed by the time of his death, but in the preliminary stages he showed all his old energy and flair.[65] Yet dark questions hung over all this frenetic activity. How long could he keep it up before his fragile health finally collapsed? And when the collapse came would it be purely physical, or perhaps mental as well? Those who saw him at close quarters during those late summer and early autumn months noted his strange fluctuations of mood, and how, especially, his old dislike of being on his own for any length of time came back upon him so strongly. Patrick O'Brien, one of those moderates whom Dillon and William O'Brien had hoped to win over, afterwards recalled that on one occasion at this time Parnell had insisted on going to the theatre in Dublin with him, something he had not done, he said in his precise way, for twenty-four years, forgetting, perhaps, that evening in the box he had spent with Katharine after his first dinner-party with her. Patrick O'Brien took him, as luck would have it, to the opera, which one would have imagined to be torture for the unmusical Parnell. But the music was the least part of the performance to him; it was the atmosphere, the light, the warmth, the company he craved. So immersed was he in this novel experience that he was totally unaware that far more eyes were fixed on him than on the stage. At the end, such a crowd had gathered that he had to be smuggled out by a side door and even then, after a late supper, he kept O'Brien walking to and fro between Morrison's Hotel and the National Club. 'I do not like to be alone', he said.[66]

Yet others found him mellower and more genial than of old. Pierce Mahony, who entertained him in Kerry shortly before the end, recalled him as 'a very pleasant man in a house', provided the house was warm. He was, however, as superstitious as always and caused one of his host's sons to leave the dinner-table because they were thirteen. But this troubled him and soon he had the boy brought back to sit, not at the table, but beside him, where he talked politics to him as gravely as if the lad were grown up. 'He used to talk more during the split than ever before', Mahony noticed.[67]

This was also the impression formed by his sister Emily Dickinson who was living in Ireland and saw a good deal of him during those months. She went with him to the last but one of his meetings, at Cabinteely near Dublin, and observed, as others also did, how the old superstitions clung to him. They had driven in a closed carriage to the meeting when the crowd pressing in upon them broke one of the windows. 'He did not say anything', she recalled, 'but I could see by his face that the breaking of the glass disturbed him. We always thought it unlucky to break glass.' It was a wet autumn and he spoke that day with his head uncovered in the rain. Later, he took Emily and her daughter Delia to dinner at the Royal Marine Hotel in Kingstown. He sat in his wet clothes, but drank champagne and seemed in the best of spirits. Afterwards he walked with them to the station, lecturing his niece on astronomy as they went. 'Putting us . . . in the carriage of a train for Bray, he kissed us both as the train started', Emily remembered. 'He himself was bound for Dublin for the night, whence he was to leave for England in the morning. I never saw him again.'[68]

The routine was slowly wearing him down and increasingly those about him were conscious of his pallor, his tendency to feel cold however warm the weather, and his failing strength. The incessant journeys to Ireland made physical demands he could no longer meet and about now he is said to have written to his mother (though the letter may be her invention), that he was 'weary of these troubles, weary unto death . . . With health and the assistance of my friends I am confident of the result.'[69] But health he would never have again, and the journalist, Michael Macdonagh, watching him at Listowel on 13 September, was shocked by how pale and worn he seemed in the sunlight, as he addressed a small crowd in the market-square. Yet his words were as defiant as ever:[70]

If I were dead and gone tomorrow the men who are fighting against English influence in Irish public life would fight on still. They would still be independent nationalists. They would still believe in the future of Ireland as a nation. And they would still protest that it was not by taking orders from an English minister that Ireland's future could be saved, protected or secured.

It was only two weeks after this that he made his final speech in Ireland. Whether because of exposure to the rain at Cabinteely the previous Sunday, or because he was at last cracking under the accumulated strains of the past eleven months, he was quite evidently ill before he left Brighton – so ill that Katharine begged him to see Sir Henry Thompson, the specialist they had consulted in 1886 when Parnell's kidney disease had first attacked him. He refused, saying he was only tired and would not waste his brief intervals of rest in visits to doctors. But for once Katharine argued with him, urging him to give up the struggle and come away with her for a long rest. He watched her while she spoke, then, after a long pause, said: 'I am in your hands Queenie and you shall do with me what you will; but you promised.' 'You mean', she replied, 'I promised I would never make you less than – ' 'Less than your king', he interrupted, 'and if I give in now I shall be less than that. I would rather die than give in now – give in to the howling of the English mob. But if you say it, I will do it . . .' This, at least, is how she remembered the scene in after years and though, as so often in her memoir of their love-story, the language is stylized, the urgency of her account carries its own conviction. Well it may, for it would have been strange indeed if the question of renunciation had not at some time come between them. But when he put it to her in those terms she knew she could not press him further, that he would have to fight on to the end.[71]

He went off to Dublin cheerfully enough. But he was far from well by the time he got there and sent at once for Dr Kenny. Kenny advised him not to carry out his engagement to speak at the remote village of Creggs on the borders of Galway and Roscommon. Parnell brushed him aside. He had promised and he would not disappoint his audience. No one dared to stop him and he set out on the tedious journey, sharing a rail-way carriage with reporters from the *Freeman's Journal*. He talked cheerfully, if not perhaps tactfully, of his new paper, but admitted that he was feeling very ill. He carried his arm in a sling and it was evident that the rheumatism which had attacked him at intervals during the year was gaining ground. By evil chance the day was as wet as the Sunday before had been at Cabinteely. Nevertheless, he rejected the umbrella which had been offered to him and spoke bareheaded. To make matters worse, the small bag in which Katharine had packed a change of clothing for him was mislaid and for several hours afterwards he had to sit in damp clothes. He began so hesitantly that his words could be taken down in longhand. He excused himself, saying that his doctor had forbidden him to come. 'However, I do not think that any material harm will come to me from this meeting. If I was to allow the suggestion of such a thought we should have our enemies throwing up their hats and announcing I was buried before I was dead.' His speech, like all the others of recent weeks, breathed defiance, as if his fierce spirit were blazing up for the last time before being extinguished for ever. The message he gave to the crowd, and bequeathed to posterity, was the same one he had given Barry O'Brien at Euston station – that the fight must go on, regardless of the odds:[72]

We shall continue this fight. We fight not for faction but for freedom. If there ever was a fight which men would have desired to avoid, it would have been the fight which my friends throughout Ireland are now waging and waging so bravely. I honour them for their courage and I will not leave them until they get a better leader. I regret that you should have to submit to this persecution. I know that you look to Ireland's future as a nation if we can gain it. We may not be able to gain it, but if not it will be left for those who come after us to win; but we will do our best.

He slept that night at a local hotel and one of the journalists who had covered the meeting remembered vividly one last example of 'the Chief's' superstition. 'I was descending the stairs as he was coming up with a candlestick in his hand, going to bed. He had got up five or six steps when he saw me. He immediately went back, and remained at the bottom till I came down, and then wished me goodnight.'[73] He travelled back to Dublin with the same reporter, who recalled later that, though he was obviously in great pain, he talked all the way and would not let his companion sleep. 'You can take a Turkish bath when you arrive in Dublin', Parnell said, 'and that will make you all right.'[74] Arrived in the city he went to Dr Kenny's house and stayed there for the next three days, attending to the business of the new paper. All that time he looked unwell, ate little, suffered acute pain in his left hand and arm. On Wednesday night, waving aside as usual Dr Kenny's medical advice, that he was not fit to travel, he took the boat to England. 'I shall come back on Saturday week', he said.[75]

Reaching London in the early hours of Thursday morning, he used himself the favourite remedy he had recommended to the reporter and took a Turkish bath before catching the train to Brighton. There, his wife was waiting for him and she saw at a glance how ill he was. The weather was warm, but he was so chilled that he needed a blazing fire. After a meal and a rest he made to go into the next room, but his legs would not carry him. Now deeply alarmed, Katharine, not without difficulty, helped him upstairs to bed.

He never came down again alive. That night he was wakeful and restless. Katharine did the best she could for him, massaging his shoulders and arms with another of his favourite remedies, firwood oil, and wrapping the damaged arm in wool. According to her account, he talked a good deal of the Irish country folk, of the dampness of their cabins, of the prevalence of rheumatism (the association of ideas is obvious) and of the need to do something for them. 'But there is always so much in between', he said. By morning his astonishing resilience seemed to have asserted itself yet again and, though still in bed, he ate a good breakfast, smoked a cigar and busied himself with notes for a speech. All the same, on the next day, Saturday, 3 October, he was sufficiently anxious to write to Sir Henry Thompson, describing his symptoms. Before the specialist could reply, Parnell's condition deteriorated so sharply that he yielded to Katharine's pressure and agreed to see a local physician, Dr Benjamin Jowers, junior, who was able to ease his pain a little.

That night he did not sleep and this worried him greatly, for one of his superstitions was that if he did not sleep for two consecutive nights he would die. The distraught Katharine begged to be allowed to telegraph to Sir Henry Thompson, but Parnell grew so feverish at the thought that she had to desist. During the morning Thompson himself sent a wire, recommending another local doctor. Dr Jowers had made a favourable impression on his patient and no change was made. Nevertheless, the pain and the fever continued to grow. During Monday Parnell became delirious, felt oppressed by some unseen power, tried to struggle out of bed to fight it. Then his mind cleared again and he and Katharine spoke, as so often before, of that 'sunny land' where they would go when he was better. 'We will be so happy, Queenie', he said, 'there are so many things happier than politics.' On the Monday night, as on the Sunday, he did not sleep, and on Tuesday he was flushed, with a high fever. Most of the day he dozed gently, smiling if she touched him, but otherwise inert. Towards nightfall, sitting by his bed, Katharine heard him mutter, 'the Conservative party'. What happened next only she could describe, because only she was present:[76]

> Late in the evening he suddenly opened his eyes and said: 'Kiss me, sweet Wifie, and I will try to sleep a little.' I lay down by his side, and kissed the burning lips he pressed to mine for the last time. The fire of them, fierce beyond any I had ever felt, startled me, and as I slipped my hand from under his head he gave a little sigh and became unconscious. The doctor came at once, but no remedies prevailed against this sudden failure of the heart's action, and my husband died without regaining consciousness, before his last kiss was cold on my lips.

It was shortly before midnight on Tuesday, 6 October, that Parnell breathed his last. The doctor who attended him later certified that the cause of death was rheumatic fever, though he added a rider that Parnell's heart was weak in any event.* But Sir Henry Thompson,

*I have referred the medical evidence, scanty though it is, to the Dean of the

writing to Katharine on 7 October and deliberately avoiding medical terminology, probably came as near as anyone to summing up the fundamental cause of Parnell's sudden and rapid decline. 'I doubt', he said, 'whether anything would have saved him when passing through London. A blow had been struck – not so heavy – apparently a light one; but his worn-out constitution, of late fearfully overtaxed by a spirit too strong for its bodily tenement, had no power to resist . . . Hence what would in a fairly robust state of health have been only a temporary conflict with a mild attack of inflammation, developed into a severe form, overwhelming the vital force . . . and rendering all medical aid powerless. I don't believe that any medicine, any treatment, could have enabled his weakened condition to resist successfully. He wanted no medicine to combat the complaint. He wanted physical force, increased vitality to keep the attack at bay.'[77]

The end, when it came, was as he would have wanted it. That intensely private man, doomed to live nearly all his life in the glare of the public eye, died in his wife's arms, murmuring her name, with no one else present. Soon a 'last speech' was fabricated for him by the faithful, and his dying words were said to have been, 'Let my love be given to my colleagues and to the Irish people'.[78] But Parnell was never one for cheap histrionics of that kind. When his widow indignantly repudiated the legend and insisted that the murmured endearment was what he really said, both her sincerity and the fact that the words themselves, like so many of their intimacies, trembled on the edge of bathos, compel the belief that she spoke the truth.

At the time of death Parnell's body temperature was so high that no

---

Medical Faculty in Trinity College, Dublin, Professor J. S. McCormick. He would distinguish between the chronic illness from which Parnell suffered from 1887 onwards and the illness which killed him. The latter he diagnoses as most likely to have been lobar pneumonia. The damaged left arm was probably rheumatic, but Professor McCormick feels that there is insufficient evidence to permit a diagnosis of either rheumatic heart disease or, *pace* Dr Jowers, rheumatic fever. Of the longer-term possibilities mentioned by contemporaries – cancer and kidney disease – cancer might conceivably have arisen some time after 1887, through a benign gastric ulcer becoming malignant. This, if true, could explain Parnell's wasted appearance and would suggest that the pain in his arm might have been a secondary growth. But the positive evidence of kidney disease (see pp. 361–2, 367 above) would still appear to outweigh the speculation about cancer. If the fatal and the long-term illnesses have a common link, Professor McCormick, while emphasizing that no more than guess-work is possible, inclines to the view that Parnell's death was due to lobar pneumonia complicating kidney failure of unknown cause.

death-mask could be made and the body itself had to be placed in a lead casket without delay. This made the oaken outer coffin heavy to move and gave rise almost at once to the wild rumour that it contained only rocks and that Parnell himself was not really dead and buried after all. The legend of the lost leader was to live on for many years and even John Dillon, not a man given to hallucinations, believed he saw and heard him once at a performance of *Götterdämmerung*, in Munich of all unlikely places.[79] In reality, at least two of his colleagues, Dr J. G. Fitzgerald and Henry Harrison, saw their leader's body before it was closed for ever from human gaze. Harrison, like most people, had only learnt of his chief's death from the evening papers on 7 October, and he, with some other Parnellites, and with the dead man's sister, Emily, had gone at once to Brighton. Upon their insistence Katharine overcame her natural repugnance to a public funeral in Dublin and on Saturday, 10 October the cortège set out from Brighton.[80]

The dead Parnell returned to Ireland on Sunday, 11 October, the day on which he had promised to address his next meeting. A far greater crowd greeted his body as it was carried through the streets than had ever attended the great man even in his prime. He was laid in his grave at Glasnevin where, later, his resting-place was marked by a great boulder of Wicklow granite, on it the single word PARNELL. At Brighton, his widow was left alone with her memories which, on the day he left her for the last time, travelled back irresistibly to their first encounter. Before the lid was lowered on the coffin, Harrison saw her place on Parnell's breast a withered flower. It was all that remained of the rose she had dropped in front of him that day in Palace Yard at Westminster, when he had stepped out from the House of Commons into her life and the world lay all before them.

VIII

What remains of the story may be quickly told. Most of those who had been directly involved in the tragedy fell back into the darkness when Parnell's flame had burnt itself out. Katharine herself was the saddest case of all. She was seriously ill for many weeks after his death and perhaps never fully recovered either her physical or her mental health. Her plight was complicated by the quarrel over her aunt's will which came to a head six months later, when she was confronted by a phalanx of O'Sheas and Woods bent upon contesting her right to be the sole heiress of Aunt Ben's fortune. At one time it almost seemed as if the battles of the Special Commission and the divorce court were to be fought out again under the rules of probate. The Attorney-General and Sir Henry James, who had appeared previously for *The Times*, and Sir Edward Clarke, who had represented Captain O'Shea in the divorce court, headed the counsel for Katharine's opponents, while Sir Charles Russell, who had defended Parnell at the Commission, now conducted the case for his widow. But the issues were too large and too dubious for either party to risk a head-on collision and in the end Mrs Parnell, under pressure from Russell, reluctantly accepted a compromise. One half of the estate – estimated in total at £144,000 and thus considerably less than the £200,000 of Captain O'Shea's luxuriant imagination – was to go to Willie and Katharine and their children, while the other half was to be divided amongst the remaining litigants. Effectively, and after various deductions, this meant that the Captain and his former wife each received the life-interest on £25,000 plus a cash payment of £6000 for her and £3000 for him. When their life-interests had expired the capital sums were to be divided between all the children, but the fact that the shares allotted to Gerard, Norah and Carmen were markedly larger than those allotted to Clare and Katie was a further indication, to those who possessed the key, that the two latter were differently treated because they were Parnell's children and not O'Shea's.[81]

Misfortune continued to dog Katharine to the end. Some years after the settlement she once again changed solicitors and early in the new century she lost much of her money at the hands of a speculating embezzler. What little was saved from the wreck was invested in the Grand Trunk Railway of Canada which ceased paying dividends before the First World War. And as if that were not enough, Parnell's dearest wish, that Avondale should pass to her and to their children, was frustrated by their joint ignorance of the law. He had made a will to that effect before their marriage, but was unaware that it had to be re-validated after they had become man and wife. Consequently, when death took him unawares, the house and the Wicklow estate passed to his brother John, who, ignoring Henry Harrison's plain hints as to Parnell's intentions, came home from America to take up his inheritance. It was a melancholy inheritance. John found that his brother had left debts of over £50,000 and he was not the man to move mountains of that kind.[82] Instead, after denuding the woods of any timber that would fetch a price, he was obliged to part with the house, which he eventually sold to a Dublin butcher for £8000. From him it passed into government hands and is now, under the auspices of the Irish Forestry Commission, maintained with loving care. It is not quite the museum which John Redmond had once hoped to make of it, but it retains enough of its original character to be powerfully evocative to any visitor sensitive to atmosphere. One small fragment was salvaged from the estate in a way which might perhaps have pleased Parnell. The shooting lodge at Aughavanagh was bought by Redmond, who used it as a country house for many years. For him, as for his leader, the remote peace of Wicklow offered an essential refuge from the stresses of Irish politics.

Nearly seven years after Charles died Avondale witnessed one further sudden death to add to the many which figured in the family history. His mother had returned from Bordenstown to end her days in the house which once she had regarded as a prison. She still retained much of her old vitality and her anti-English sentiments, though perhaps a little dated, were no less vigorous than before. But she was now 82 and increasingly frail. The morning after a dinner-party given, with typical bravado, as a gesture in the teeth of near bankruptcy, she sat by the fire in her bedroom. Suddenly, no one quite knows how, the flames touched her garments and in a few seconds she was a blazing torch. The fire was put out by Emily and her daughter Delia, but the burns were too severe and after some hours of agony the old lady died where so many of her children had been born.[83]

Katharine never visited Ireland. Instead, she moved restlessly from one rented house to another, tended by her daughter Norah who sacrificed her whole existence to that task. It cannot have been easy, especially since the daughter could not bring herself to regard the author of what she felt to be her mother's ruin with more than what she herself called 'inimical tolerance'. But Katharine never shook off the sorrow of her loss. Norah, writing to Henry Harrison when her mother was dying, used words which lift the veil a little on the long aftermath of the tragedy. 'She never has stopped mourning Parnell and I, knowing the misery of her heart and soul, have spent my life in keeping her from the follies of so many human ways of "forgetting for a little while" when I could; and when I couldn't in nursing her back to health and sanity.'[84] That letter was written on 1 February 1921. Four days later, shortly after her seventy-sixth birthday, Katharine Parnell died, having endured a widowhood of nearly thirty years, made bearable only by the belief, as Norah expressed it, that 'Parnell comes to her at night, when things are worst and draws her "out of the dark waves"'. Norah herself, the mainspring of her life removed, sought to make a new career in nursing, but contracted lupus and died in 1923; she was buried in her mother's grave at Littlehampton in Sussex.[85]

Little of significance is known about either her sister Carmen or her brother Gerard. Carmen married a doctor practising in Hove, Arthur Herbert Buck, by whom she had three children. Dr Buck divorced her in 1914 on the grounds of her adultery with one Edward Lucas, who later inherited a baronetcy. Although she married Lucas, Carmen seems not to have been happy and there is a persistent family legend that she became an alcoholic; she died in 1921, the same year as her mother.[86] Gerard emerged briefly from obscurity in 1913–14, when he made his seemingly decisive intervention to ensure that his mother's memoir of her love-affair with Parnell should protect the memory of his father. Later, we hear of Gerard O'Shea serving in the First World War, developing an interest in horses, and in the mid-1930s protesting – not without reason – about an American play on the life of Parnell; but this, apparently, did not prevent him from acting as a highly paid adviser for the extraordinary film based on the play in which Clark Gable played the part of Parnell and Myrna Loy was a beautiful but totally unconvincing Katharine.[87] After that, Gerard vanishes from view. As for the egregious Captain himself, though not as flush as he had hoped – reality never had measured up to his expectations – he was sufficiently provided for to be able to live out his life in comfortable retirement. Ineffably thick-skinned to the last, he chose to live it out at Brighton (more strictly, Hove), where he died on 22 April 1905, at the age of sixty-five.

Parnell's hope of perpetuating his blood through his daughters perished like all his other hopes. The younger of his two surviving daughters, Katie, remains a shadowy figure and almost nothing is known about her. It seems likely, however, that she married an army officer, Captain Louis D'Oyley Horsford Moule, who served mostly abroad; apparently they had one still-born child. By the mid-thirties, Mrs Moule was in reduced circumstances; her declining years were spent in an asylum and she died in 1947.* Her elder sister, Clare, who

---

*In her recent book about Katharine O'Shea, *The uncrowned queen of Ireland*, Joyce Marlow, on the basis of a difference of Christian names in this Katie's birth and marriage certificates, speculates that she may actually have been an illegitimate daughter of Captain O'Shea's, born in Spain. But the evidence for this is scanty and is outweighed by the fact that Father John Maunsell, the son by a second marriage of the man who married Parnell's other daughter, Clare (see above), and the chief repository of the family history, unhesitatingly accepted the Moule marriage as genuine (Father John Maunsell to Sir Shane Leslie, 25 January 1956). See also Dr Bertram Maunsell to D. R. Gwynn, 22 September 1936 (J. F. Horgan Papers, NLI MS 18, 268) and a letter from Sir Shane Leslie to the *Irish Times*, 4 January 1967.

strongly resembled their father, married a doctor, Bertram Maunsell, and died in 1909 while giving birth to a son. This son, Assheton Clare Bowyer-Lane Maunsell, who inherited his mother's likeness to Parnell, became an officer in the British Army and died of enteric fever in India in July 1934. The line of direct descent from Parnell therefore ends in a cemetery at Lahore.

CHAPTER 21

Myth and Reality

'Parnell's part in these things never ceases to fill me with amazement – even though I knew him and appraised him as a demigod – such vision, such simplicity, such concentrated passion.' (Henry Harrison to W. B. Yeats, 23 July 1936, presenting the poet with a copy of *Parnell vindicated*.)

> The Bishops and the Party
> That tragic story made,
> A husband that had sold his wife
> And after that betrayed;
> But stories that live longest
> Are sung above the glass,
> And Parnell loved his country,
> And Parnell loved his lass.

(W. B. Yeats, 'Come gather round me Parnellites', from *Last Poems*, 1936–39.)

What, at the end of the journey, can we say by way of summing up? How are we to assess that strange personality, that career of brilliant light and deepest shade, that enigma which baffled contemporaries and has baffled posterity ever since? We can perhaps do it best by attempting to separate the myth from the reality. Given the circumstances of Parnell's fall, his own repeated emphasis upon the limits of parliamentary action, and the fact that the Fenians clustered about his end as about his beginning, it was probably inevitable that he should have become the symbol, not of the limited independence he had actually sought, but of the independence which would only be satisfied by freedom interpreted in the widest and most absolute terms. It was not for nothing that the hurlers of the Gaelic Athletic Association (whom the police readily identified with republicanism) marched at his funeral, not for nothing that Arthur Griffith found in him the precursor of the Sinn Fein policy of self-reliance, not for nothing that both Pearse and Connolly annexed him for their diverse but overlapping pantheons.

This mythologizing was itself a part of the transformation of Irish life and thought which took place in the twenty years after Parnell's death. The process, indeed, had already begun while he was still in mid-career, for the formation of the Gaelic Athletic Association in 1884 had signalled that a different nationalism – paradoxically, both older and newer than the nationalism of the eighties – was beginning to emerge. It was a nationalism which looked backward with nostalgia to an ancient Irish civilization with its own language, literature and history, and looked forward in anticipation to the time when the way would be prepared for the re-creation of that civilization by a revolution abolishing not only English sovereignty, but also the more subtle thraldom of English cultural domination. The crucial moment in this revolution came two years after Parnell died, when a group of dedicated men created the Gaelic League to revive the Irish language and to foster a literature in that language. Though it was not apparent then or for two decades after, this initiative was a decisive turning-point in the double movement of repudiation and regeneration which now slowly began to gather way.

Two developments combined to accelerate its progress in the early years of the new century. The first was the fact that the poison of the Parnell split paralysed the parliamentarians for the whole decade of the nineties, so that although the party was reunited in 1900 under Parnell's chief heir, John Redmond, and with Parnell's chief traducer, Tim Healy, reduced to isolated opposition, the self-inflicted wounds of 1890–1 never completely healed. The party and its machine continued to control the constituencies, but they never recaptured the mind, still less the imagination, of the generation which grew up in the shadow of Parnell's fall. Success in pursuing the Home Rule for which Parnell had been sacrificed might perhaps have lifted that shadow. But though this seemed near for a brief moment between 1912 and 1914, the failure of Asquith's government to overcome either the fierce Tory opposition or the armed mobilization of the Ulster Unionists against the prospect of a Dublin parliament, exposed pitilessly the inadequacies of the much-vaunted and long-cherished Liberal alliance. As Home Rule faded into invisibility so the older tradition of armed resistance moved once more to the foreground, to flame into open insurrection at Easter, 1916. For young men nurtured on contempt for 'the party', the Irish Republican Brotherhood not only offered more hope of fulfilment, but also was recognizably the spiritual heir of the 'hillside men' who had gathered round Parnell in his last fight.

Here we meet a seeming paradox. During his lifetime Parnell, though in later years he tended to subordinate everything else to the struggle for Home Rule, had never believed that such material progress as could be won on the way to that final goal, would corrode the people's will to liberty. On the contrary, he had maintained that the starving man could never be a good nationalist. In the years after his death fewer Irishmen starved than for many decades before it, and many of the politico-economic objectives he had set himself came within sight of being realized. With the Local Government Act of 1898 the tentative proposals by which Chamberlain had set such store in the eighties were easily surpassed. With the creation of the Department of Agriculture and Technical Instruction in the following year the way was cleared for that fostering of Irish industry which Parnell had had so much at heart. With the Wyndham Act of 1903 the conditions for the creation of a peasant proprietary *en masse* were at last established.

As a consequence of these reforms the country appeared to be settling down into somnolent and satisfied prosperity. For many people, no doubt, this was a consummation devoutly to be wished. Yet, and here was the seeming paradox, the urge to independence obstinately refused to be killed by kindness.

What happened was something familiar enough in history. The revolution, when it came, did not come from a population made desperate by oppression and deprivation. Neither did it come from a population grown sleek under a benevolently paternalistic government. It came rather from a minority – mainly, though not exclusively, composed of intellectuals – whose determination to make their protest in arms was inspired in part precisely by the fear that nationalism might after all be blunted by even the modest affluence which Ireland was experiencing just before, and in the early stages of, the First World War. To such a minority the absolute of an independent republic was far more seductive than the relativities of limited self-government and graduated land-purchase which were the essence of what the parliamentarians had to offer. Can we wonder, then, that in a climate of gathering extremism, the myth of the 'extreme' Parnell should have become so firmly rooted in the imagination of the time, or that Pearse should summon his 'pale and angry ghost' to stand beside Tone and Davis and Lalor and Mitchel.[1]

That the myth should have become rooted so quickly and so deeply was due mainly to the second transforming development of those post-Parnellite years, the complex cultural phenomenon sometimes called, with dangerous simplicity, the Irish literary movement. The Parnell tragedy fitted marvellously well with a tradition which went far back into the underground life of Ireland. It has been called a Messianic tradition because, as is common among peoples long held in subjection, it looked for deliverance to the coming of a Messiah or leader. Parnell had seemed to be that leader, but the leader had been sacrificed. Yet, the idea of sacrifice too was implicit in the myth, for from sacrifice came the resurrection from which the true leader might spring. As a modern writer, Herbert Howarth, has well said, Parnell, both in his style and in his fate, had personified the legend. 'His aloofness, his very despotism, had made men ready to worship him. His followers invested him with the status of a prophet. Those who hated him most after the divorce proceedings hated him most because they could not bear their prophet to be less than immaculate. The Irish committed the crucial act of killing their prophet, and the guilt, the desire to purify the guilt, the belief that his sacrifice sanctified, the belief that sacrifice assures rebirth, gave them irresistible vigour in the next generation.'[2]

But if, as Mr Howarth suggests, the literary movement thus inflamed, albeit half-consciously, the politically militant movement, there was also a sense in which that literary movement used the Parnell crisis for a second purpose no less necessary to an evolving nationalism – the purpose of self-criticism, or indeed self-flagellation. Two examples will suffice. When Yeats was receiving his Nobel Prize, the lecture he delivered on that occasion started from the point that the modern literature of Ireland had begun when Parnell fell from power in 1891. 'A disillusioned and embittered Ireland turned from parliamentary politics; an event was conceived; and the race began, as I think, to be troubled by that event's long gestation.'[3] For Yeats himself through most of his life Parnell remained an evocative symbol, a symbol which could be put to many uses, but which he related again and again to the theme of nobility overcome by baseness.[4] Equally, James Joyce, though from a very different standpoint, used the fall of Parnell repeatedly as a means of expressing his disgust at, and revulsion from, the Irish paralysis and the sources – priestly power, moral cowardice, social hypocrisy – which in his view fed that paralysis.

In all of this, it is necessary to insist, there was little enough resemblance to the real Parnell. Or rather, myth and symbol fastened only upon one facet of his character, one aspect of his career, to produce a portrait which, while recognizable, was manifestly distorted. It was distorted, partly because it mistook the nature of the man, partly because it mistook the character of his achievement. Any attempt to identify him with a particular stereotype will always fail for the simple reason that there was not one Parnell, but at least four different Parnells. There was, first, the country gentleman with his rough tweeds, his love of horses and dogs and shooting, his keen eye to his estate, his automatic assumption that the natural function of a Parnell of Avondale was to govern. Then there was that much more complex individual, the political genius who achieved his dominance by a tactical skill which was apparently instinctive, and also by a style of leadership which for much of his career impressed all who met him – Irish farmers and parliamentarians, Fenians at home and overseas, English politicians of whatever shade – with his extraordinary ability to control men and events and bend them to his steely will.

That this triumph of the will was only bought at the price of extreme psychological tension, few even of those who knew him best were allowed to divine. Among those few were some who would have found this tightly coiled spring all the harder to understand because they knew also a third, and quite other, Parnell. This was the engaging companion, happy to relax with those who talked better, or at least more volubly, than he could on everything under the sun (except his own subject of the applied sciences), exerting apparently effortless charm upon both men and women with his deprecating smile, his light, rather hesitant, voice, his regal manners and his striking good looks. *That* Parnell was not only less rigid than the public Parnell, he was also a great deal more human – casual about his clothes and appearance, fussy about his health, incurably unpunctual, inordinately lazy about his correspondence, and apparently hag-ridden by his superstitions. These personal foibles – and especially his dread of the colour green, of the number thirteen, of death in any shape or form – had a necessary part to play in softening the too bleak image of the aloof, indifferent dictator, and those who were closest to him tended to regard them as engaging human weaknesses which, if anything, increased his magnetic attraction. Perhaps, though, they were over-indulgent, not reckoning that these irrational fears belonged to the dark side of an intensely complicated personality.

The dark side was exhibited to the full only intermittently by the fourth Parnell, the man of passion, driven by demonic pride and self-will to prodigies of concentrated energy. There were traces of him in his earliest beginnings – in the tyrant of the Avondale nursery, in the boorish and sullen schoolboy, in the pugnacious undergraduate, in the assertive new recruit to Isaac Butt's fumbling Home Rulers. After he had reached the front rank this particular Parnell was generally suppressed by the calculating politician, but he was never entirely vanquished. The tiny handful who could claim some intimacy with him soon learned to recognize the portents of the coming storm in a sudden heightening of his normal pallor, in the glare of those strange eyes –

'Red Indian's eyes' T. P. O'Connor called them – and in that ability of his to convey, as William O'Brien well described it, the impression of ice and fire at the same moment.

It would be easy, but wrong, to lay at the door of Katharine O'Shea the gradual predominance of the passionate Parnell over all the other Parnells. It would be wrong because it would be to ignore the fact that though passion certainly lay at the root of his infatuation with her, tender domesticity was much more the key-note of their love-affair. That is not to say, of course, that there were not intermittent flashes from the depths. This was evident, for example, in the letters he wrote her from Kilmainham. It was evident in his fierce attachment to their children. It was evident again in that incident she recorded in after years when, apparently not long before the divorce, they were both standing at the end of the Chain Pier in Brighton during a storm and he suddenly picked her up and held her over the boiling sea, saying, 'Oh, my wife, my wife, I believe I'll jump in with you and we shall be free for ever.'[5] But it was not until after the divorce, when it became clear that his determination to prise her loose from Captain O'Shea would clash with his equal determination to go on leading his party in the teeth of Irish Catholics and English nonconformists, that the flame became an all-consuming inferno. Even then it is impossible to be sure how much of the final destructive urge was devotion to Katharine and how much injured pride at his own rejection by his followers. All we can say is that devotion and pride together provided the dynamism for that last frenzied campaign.

It was that campaign, of course, which gave birth to the legend of the prophet sacrificed by his people. Yet, to dwell exclusively upon those ultimate months is to misinterpret Parnell's tragedy by overlooking the extent to which he contributed to that tragedy himself. To endure for nearly ten years the triangular relationship upon which he had embarked in 1880–1 was to invite a humiliation, and to risk a catastrophe, which no responsible leader could be justified in incurring. To have prolonged the danger for so long as he did was especially condemnable when the reason behind it was Katharine's anxiety to lay hands on the whole of her aunt's legacy. To hazard his leadership and his cause for a pecuniary motive of such a kind exposes Parnell to the charge to which there is no convincing answer, that he had subordinated his judgement to that of his mistress and in so doing had recklessly jeopardized the important national interests committed to his charge.

Even after the crisis had come upon him, Parnell's own actions helped to prepare the way for his downfall. We do not have to minimize the

various parts played in bringing about that downfall by English and
Irish opinion, by Liberal leaders and Irish bishops, to recognize that at
certain crucial moments – when he issued his manifesto and when he
threw away the advantages which the Boulogne negotiations so nearly
gave him – he was in a measure digging his own grave. We have here to
distinguish between his tactics, which were frequently as brilliant as
they had ever been, and his strategy, which was manifestly based on
false premises. He seemed to assume that the twin cries of 'Liberal
dictation' and 'independent opposition' would rally the country to him.
So they might have done if his own manœuvres had not at one and the
same time united so many formidable enemies against him and surrendered so much of what otherwise might have been a strong defensive
position. What Parnell appeared to be proposing was the rupture of the
Liberal alliance and the indefinite postponement of Home Rule. To
compensate for this uninviting prospect he offered only the presumed
magic of his name. He failed, until it was too late, to realize that the
magic had not only perished, to use Healy's deadly phrase, 'in the
stench of the divorce court', but had begun to be tarnished long before
Captain O'Shea had filed his suit, in the days when the lieutenants had
been left to their own devices and the commander, shattered in his
health and mesmerized by his infatuation, had all but withdrawn from
the fray.

The fact that in the final paroxysm Parnell and his 'faithful few'
seemed bent upon turning the clock back to the days of the land war and
fashioning a new alliance between an 'independent' parliamentary party
and the Fenians, powerfully reinforced the later tendency to mytholo-
gize him as the forerunner of a more extreme nationalism. Yet this, too,
was an illusion. Not only was Parnell careful, even in his last phase, to
avoid any clear commitment to the 'hillside men' and to go on pinning
his hopes to the next general election, but his whole career belied the
wishful thinking of the militants who claimed him for their own. It is
certainly true that in his early days he looked as carefully at the Fenians
as the Fenians looked at him. It is possible that the 'last link' speech at
Cincinnati, or something like what was attributed to him on that occasion, may have approximated to the ideal which he, as a fiery young
neophyte, may for a space have regarded as his ultimate objective. But
if he was, as Pearse called him, a 'separatist by instinct', then we can only
say that he was a separatist whose unsentimental political education soon
brought him to a much harsher and more limited appreciation of political
realities.

The nearest he ever came to heading a genuine revolution was between 1879 and 1881, when the land war seemed to threaten a collapse of the social fabric. But that experience appears to have been decisive in determining the future thrust of his policy. The extreme difficulty of controlling an agrarian agitation when hunger was rampant and passions rose high, together with the horrendous prospect of chaos which he looked out upon from behind the bars of Kilmainham, convinced him that the way forward lay only through constructive parliamentary pressure. Hence the 'treaty' of April 1882, which was in effect a massive retreat from agrarian agitation; hence the emphasis upon building up a new party between then and the election of 1885; hence the repudiation of the Plan of Campaign; hence, above all, the overwhelming emphasis on 'the union of hearts' from the introduction of the Home Rule bill until the onset of the final crisis.

To most Irishmen at the time, and to nearly all historians since, this uncompromising emphasis on constitutional action seemed to be justified by results, and Parnell's reputation as a national leader to rest ultimately upon his parliamentary record. There is truth in that judgement, though it is not the whole truth. In the realm of positive achievement his principal successes were – the Land Act of 1881; the creation of a 'third force' in the House of Commons by the forging of a disciplined, pledge-bound parliamentary party; the inclusion of Ireland in the Reform Act of 1884 without loss of numerical representation in terms of parliamentary seats; the development, through the Irish National League, of constituency organization – the system of county conventions – which habituated the people to some of the forms of democratic self-government; the bringing of Home Rule on to the centre of the stage at Westminster; and the involvement of the Liberal party in the cause of Ireland.

This is a glittering list of trophies, yet not all that glitters here is pure gold. Some of Parnell's achievements were not his alone, some came about almost fortuitously, some promised more than they actually performed. Thus, the Land Act of 1881 was due primarily to the conviction being forced upon Gladstone that without it a social convulsion in Ireland could not be averted. What carried that conviction most clearly to his mind was the Land League, and the father of the Land League was Michael Davitt. His role and Parnell's were no doubt complementary, but without Davitt the League would never have been launched and would never have become the effective instrument it was. Again, the 1884 Reform Act, and the concessions made to Ireland therein, were a product of the British, not the Irish, political situation. So too, indeed, was Gladstone's commitment (for what that was worth).

to Home Rule in 1885-6; and this commitment, it was already evident by 1890, was by no means equally shared by all the Liberals who had remained loyal to him and supposedly also to the nationalist alliance. As for the vaunted experience of democratic politics which the county conventions were presumed to have given the Irish electorate, though this was probably real enough up to a point, its extent and depth were limited by the fact that Parnell retained in his own hands effective control of nominations for elections to the 85 Irish seats normally held by the parliamentary party. And we have to remember that since, after 1886, he allowed the day-to-day conduct of the other aspects of the movement to slip out of his hands, if participation at a humble level did have an educative effect on local patriots, the credit for it belongs to those who carried the burden in his absence.

Another way of putting this is to say that Parnell was neither a creative thinker nor a radical innovator. All the ideas to which at different times he lent the force of his personality – the 'new departure', 'the land for the people', the concept of independent opposition, the vulnerability of an Irish parliamentary party at Westminster, Home Rule itself, had been originated by other men. Furthermore, his notions about the ultimate form an Irish settlement might take tended to be less evolutionary than circular. Indeed, his speeches in 1889 even suggest that if the divorce suit had not released the avalanche, it was well within the bounds of possibility that he might have ended by accepting from Gladstone a federal solution not very far from that propounded by the ageing Butt and excoriated by the youthful Parnell.

To say this is not to minimize his achievement – it is rather to define it more precisely by emphasizing, in a way the Parnell myth conspicuously fails to do, that the greatness of the achievement lay in Parnell's ability to realize his potential despite the limitations inherent in his own character and in the Irish context within which he had to work. The essence of what he did can be summed up in a single sentence. *He gave his people back their self-respect.* He did this in the first instance, with Davitt and the other Land Leaguers, by rallying an inert and submissive peasantry to a belief that by organized and disciplined protest they could win a better life for themselves and their children. He did it further, and still more strikingly, by demonstrating on the floor of the House of Commons, long before he had 'the 86 of 86' at his back, that even a small Irish party could disrupt the business of the greatest legislature in the world and, by a combination of skill and tenacity, could deal on equal terms with – eventually, hold the balance between – the two major English parties.

These were certainly extraordinary feats, made more extraordinary both by the dramatic incidents which accompanied each turn of the story and by the nature of the genius who accomplished them, so far removed from the people he led, so superbly confident that they were his to lead. But if it was Parnell's initial obstructionism in the House of Commons which laid the foundation of his reputation and made him the obvious leader for a mass-movement at home, then it was his leadership of that movement, combined with his majestic disdain for English political men and English political institutions, that elevated him to the position of commanding power he held between 1880 and 1882. Yet the very brevity of the span implied by those two dates suggests some of the major constraints upon that power. The Kilmainham 'treaty', which in effect terminated his double role, was a decisive turning-point for him in two distinct ways. First, as already suggested, it marked his recognition that the land war, being so difficult to control, held too many dangers for a constitutional politician. In 1882, no doubt, circumstances made it comparatively easy to damp down the agitation, but because the endemic problem of the land remained unsolved, it was inevitable that when economic pressures reasserted themselves, a new phase of unrest would ensue. By abdicating the leadership of this new phase, the Plan of Campaign, Parnell substantially weakened his base, not merely in Ireland, but also in Britain where thenceforth he lacked the leverage which the leadership of a popular movement at home had previously given him.

In Britain, indeed, Kilmainham had weakened his base much earlier than the Plan of Campaign, though in a subtle and subterranean way. Ostensibly, and here was his second turning-point, the new course he adopted after 1882 took him towards a constructive role in the British political system. But this in turn made him much more a prisoner of the system than he had ever been before. In one sense this had obvious advantages, since it allowed him to assume, gradually, the same sort of balancing position at Westminster which he had so successfully exploited in Ireland at the outset of his career. But there was a heavy price to be paid. For the mere fact of increased involvement, coupled with the necessity, as it seemed, to foster the Liberal alliance after Gladstone had declared for Home Rule, reduced his room for manœuvre with the disastrous consequences that became plain in 1890.

Despite the rumours and explorations of an understanding with the Tories in 1885, the Liberal alliance turned out to be all that was available, and if Parnell wanted to introduce the concept of Home Rule into practical politics, he had little choice but to seize upon the alliance and make it the key element in his strategy. But this was in some important respects the least favourable outcome of the complex situation which in the mid-eighties he had seemed to dominate. It was the least favourable because the Liberals, even if the Irish issue had not split them as it did in 1886, were neither well placed to pass a Home Rule bill through parliament where the Tory-controlled House of Lords still had an unlimited power of veto, nor were they what many in Ireland would have regarded as the 'natural' party for the Parnellites to seek as allies. In two spheres of fundamental importance to most Irishmen – the land and education – the party of Salisbury in the mid-eighties showed a much more acceptable face than the party of Gladstone. Tories rather than Liberals embraced land purchase without squeamishness, and Tories, much more than Liberals, understood the significance of the denominational principle in education from the university downwards. From an Irish standpoint it was therefore a tragedy that, the two great English parties having divided over Home Rule in the way they did, it should have fallen to the Tories to administer Ireland during the outburst of agrarian agitation which followed the rejection of Gladstone's bill and the return of economic depression. Salisbury's prescription of 'resolute government' was a sad falling-off from the constructive, though not necessarily compatible, ideas of Carnarvon and Lord Randolph Churchill. Yet even so, the same ministers who fought the Plan of Campaign and carried the 'perpetual' Coercion Act of 1887, passed also the major Land Act of 1891 and made a respectable effort towards solving the university question as well.

Not the least part of the tragedy was that the Home Rule quarrel itself should have become inextricably entangled with the already deep-seated religious fears and animosities in Ireland. When viewed through British eyes Irish self-government presented itself primarily as an imperial question which could be, and was, phrased in two quite different ways. Would a parliament in Dublin be an entering wedge for a totally independent Ireland whose very existence would constitute a threat to the security and integrity of the Empire? And, in any event, were the Irish fit for the kind of self-government which so far had been confined to the larger, predominantly British, colonies? To the first of these questions Tories, and a good many Liberal Unionists, returned a resounding affirmative. The answer to the second question, though more *sotto voce*, was no less affirmative. Recent research has demonstrated all too clearly the amount of anti-Irish feeling which existed in nineteenth-century Britain, especially from the Fenian outbreaks of the 1860s onwards.[6] This was connected with the evidence of Irish poverty and degradation which the great cities of Britain daily exhibited, though it may also have been a reflection of what, in some quarters, it has become fashionable to describe as Victorian racism. Whatever its origins, it was certainly fed by the land war, by the Phoenix Park murders, by Maamtrasna, and by all the other instances of brutality and seeming barbarism which the newspapers recorded in lavish detail. Parnell, himself despising the English, probably never grasped how deeply the English despised the Irish, even though, with hindsight, we can see that his own assault upon the inmost citadel of law and order, the House of Commons, may well have had upon the educated classes an effect not dissimilar to the effect the Invincibles had upon the public at large.

One aspect of anti-Irish feeling, and a most important one, was the antipathy the more extreme English Protestants felt towards Irish Catholics, who were regarded as being, almost by definition, priestridden and therefore incapable of developing and maintaining free institutions. To those who felt like that, it was an obvious tactic to ally with Irish, and more specifically with Ulster, Protestantism in its most intractable form; for though Lord Randolph Churchill, even when playing 'the Orange card', may inwardly have felt that his new colleagues were still at bottom 'those foul Ulster Tories' he complained of in his private correspondence, adversity makes strange bedfellows. And for the Conservative party as a whole co-operation with the Ulster Unionists to thwart Home Rule became from 1886 onwards an almost instinctive reaction to the threat posed by the Liberal-nationalist alliance.

That the conflict over Home Rule should so quickly have taken on sectarian overtones was for Parnell a double misfortune. It was a misfortune because he largely shared Lord Randolph Churchill's unflattering opinion of Ulster Protestantism and never came remotely within reach of developing a constructive approach to the potentially lethal problem it presented, either during the debates on the Home Rule bill or on any of the other recorded occasions when he discussed, publicly or privately, how to deal with the north in the context of a self-governing Ireland.

It was still more a misfortune because, as a southern Protestant himself, he desperately needed to persuade his Catholic fellow-countrymen that Home Rule, among its other virtues, would be a healing and a reconciling influence in Irish society. He needed this so desperately because, although his personal ascendancy over the Catholic masses was undoubtedly great, his attitude, and that of his party, towards the Irish hierarchy, was decidedly ambiguous. In his earliest days he had been suspect to many bishops not only because he was a Protestant, but because he kept dubious company (Charles Bradlaugh, Victor Hugo, Henri Rochefort), and because the land agitation contributed to the growth of violence and of actual crime, with a corresponding decline, in some areas at least, of the authority which ecclesiastics might expect to wield over their flocks. It was true, no doubt, that the more ardently 'nationalist' clergy identified themselves, even at archiepiscopal level, with the agitation, but, as has recently been argued, they may often have done so out of a feeling that the land war was, at any rate in part, a crusade against the eviction of Catholic tenants by Protestant landlords. Even as late as 1888 Archbishop Walsh could remark to Cardinal Manning 'that the seventeenth century has not passed away, that the people were still struggling for their religion and their land, and that the permanency of the one depended to no little extent on the possession of the latter'.[7]

It was not so easy to take this view after 1888 when the Plan of Campaign earned the condemnation of the Pope. From the moment the Papal Rescript appeared the hierarchy drew back. More than that, when Parnell's lieutenants, Dillon and William O'Brien, began to prosecute their public quarrel with the conservative Dr O'Dwyer of Limerick, this moved his fellow-bishops, even that impressive selection of them who disliked him heartily, to rally to his defence. For Parnell this involved a strange irony. In England he received plaudits for denouncing the Plan of Campaign. But in Ireland, outside the narrow circle of those who directed the agitation and had felt the full weight of his displeasure, his denunciation roused little echo. He was still 'the Chief' and, as such, responsible. Therefore, episcopal bile was discharged as much in his direction as in that of his lieutenants and, as we saw earlier, the months preceding the divorce suit revealed increasing signs of tension between the party and the church. This was not in itself particularly surprising. The party, after all, represented an alternative source of authority from which, should Home Rule materialize, would presumably come the government of Ireland. The church was bound to regard a secular agency of this kind with jealousy and suspicion, the more so because the exigencies of parliamentary politics between 1886 and 1890 seemed to be turning the Irish members into what Archbishop Logue described as 'a mere tail to the Radical party in England'. And when some of the leading Parnellites combined with their apparently slavish adherence to the Liberal alliance an excessive degree of independence in pursuing the land agitation, it was hardly surprising that the resentment of the hierarchy should have culminated in the angry salvo directed at Parnell in October 1890.

The fact that the divorce crisis followed hard on the heels of this episode was, as one bishop observed, 'providential'.[8] Indeed, it was providential in more than one way. Not merely had Parnell revealed himself for what he was – or for what he appeared to be – *before* Home Rule had been granted and the nation trusted to his care, but he had also offered the church an unprecedented opportunity for reasserting its leadership on impeccably moral grounds. Of course, the fact that the crisis was political in essence carried with it grave dangers of a reaction against clerical interference, and nothing so much revealed the sagacity of Archbishop Walsh as the way in which he restrained his more impetuous brethren from an over-hasty interference which would have provoked precisely such a reaction. It was too much to hope that anticlericalism could be avoided altogether and the bitterness of Parnell's supporters ensured that it would not be. But that this was limited to a minority, and a small minority at that, was due not merely to Archbishop Walsh's circumspection. It was due as much and probably more, to Parnell's own insistence on fighting his battle on a ground that was unacceptable to most of his compatriots. To narrow the issue to a stark choice between the leader and the cause was to ask too much of a people who had been habituated by the leader to believe that the cause was almost won. That the cup should be dashed from their lips through the frailty of a man whose long dereliction of duty was now, on the one-sided evidence of the divorce court, assumed to have been primarily due to his obsession with his mistress, was more than Irish opinion was prepared to tolerate.

Yet, in the end, one has to insist that the violence of the final conflict, and the inevitable tendency of Parnell's opponents to argue that on both moral and political grounds, he was unfit for leadership, together miss the real point – that his unfitness had begun to manifest itself long before the O'Shea affair had exploded in the public view. That this unfitness was intimately connected with his love for Katharine seems indisputable. We have seen from very early on in their relationship that Eltham had a magnetic attraction for him and how prone he was to cut short his Irish engagements to return where his compass always pointed. However, though his pattern of life became increasingly 'marital' after 1882, and still more so after 1886, this was far from being a case of 'all for love and the world well lost'. Right to the last scene of the drama Parnell showed every sign of wanting to have both his love and his world. He won his love, but what he and others failed to realize was that his world had already begun to slip away from him.

It did so for two reasons. The first was purely physical. Despite the dearth of technical medical evidence, we know enough about Parnell's condition from the autumn of 1886 onwards to realize how precarious his hold on life actually was. Kidney disease, a suspect heart, the ominous advance of rheumatism – these were a formidable burden to a man who for much of his career had impressed his contemporaries as fragile beyond the ordinary. When we reflect that few members of his family had lived to a serene old age, we may well doubt whether he would have been equal to the long uphill struggle which would still have stretched ahead of him had he never heard of Katharine O'Shea.

And here we approach the second reason why his world was slipping away from him even before the crisis of 1890. This was, quite simply, that it was a world which was probably unattainable at that time by any means, and certainly unattainable by the means he chose to pursue. The bland assumption apparently shared between 1886 and 1890 by Gladstone and Parnell and their respective followers that all would come right on the night – that they would win a comfortable victory at the next general election and Home Rule would then pass majestically into law – had no basis in reality. True, the communications that passed between the two leaders in the post-1886 period were at least an improvement on the almost total lack of consultation which had preceded the *débâcle* of the first Home Rule bill, but the surviving evidence of the ground they covered suggests that they had still done little more than skirt the foothills of the Himalayan range of problems that remained to be surmounted. And although the guarantees on land and police which emerged from the Boulogne negotiations did mark a definite advance, it was ominous that the Liberals found it so difficult to make up their minds on the relatively straightforward issue of whether or not the Irish members should be retained at Westminster. That they should make such heavy weather of this did not inspire much confidence as to their capacity, perhaps even their will, to deal with the larger questions such as the veto power of the House of Lords, the resistance of Protestant Ulstermen to Home Rule, or even, supposing those massive obstacles to have been overcome, the distribution of power between the two countries under whatever form of devolution they ultimately decided to adopt.

All the signs are that Parnell realized at least some of the difficulties inherent in a Home Rule settlement sooner than most of his contemporaries, whether Irish or British. Paradoxically, the difficulties he seems to have envisaged most clearly were those relating to England, and there is little in the whole range of his speeches to indicate that he had thought very deeply about what kind of Ireland would emerge under the native government which, it was generally assumed, he himself would form. His views on the land question, as we know, outraged Michael Davitt, but though Parnell's conservatism in this area probably corresponded closely to the conservatism of the tenant-farmers he was pledged to help, what strikes one most about his opinions on other vital topics is not so much that they were conservative as that they were banal or even non-existent. About the crucial relationship between church and state, for example, and especially about the vexed question of education, his observations were so perfunctory as to be almost negligible. Worse still, he seems never to have asked himself what he meant by the 'Irish nation' or 'the Irish race' which he claimed to lead, and the idea that Ireland might possibly contain two nations, not one, apparently never entered his head.

In mitigation, it may be argued that his concentration on the English aspect of the Irish question merely meant that he had got his priorities right. The problems of a self-governing Ireland could only be properly faced when a self-governing Ireland actually existed, and since this could not happen without English consent, that was the point at which all possible pressure had to be brought to bear. The whole drive of Parnell's policy – tentatively between 1882 and 1885, emphatically from 1886 onwards – was therefore to conciliate English opinion by demonstrating that Home Rule, so far from being the gateway to separation, meant a different kind of partnership in which the two countries would be linked by friendship, not force.

By adopting this placatory tone Parnell was obviously taking a great risk. How great a risk can be judged from his progressive abandonment of the two resources which had made him so powerful between 1879 and 1882. First, by turning his back on the land agitation he isolated himself from the mass support in Ireland without which a parliamentary leader at Westminster was, if not impotent, at any rate extremely vulnerable. Second, by adopting the Liberal alliance as the key to his strategy he jettisoned the principle of 'independent opposition' which he had so consistently claimed to be indispensable to the proper functioning of an Irish party in the House of Commons. The danger that this might lose him support at home, and among the Irish-Americans, was partly, though not wholly, averted by the occasional 'extreme' speeches of the old, balancing kind which he still continued to make from time to time, and partly also by *The Times* attack upon him which united nationalists of all shades in his support during the years 1887 to 1890, when he was making his most sustained bid to mollify English opinion. Nevertheless, his ostentatious shunning of the Plan of Campaign, and his long, unexplained absences both from Ireland and from the meetings of his own party created a power vacuum which others were beginning to fill. Not the least important feature of that all-important year, 1890, was the way in which events demonstrated well *before* the divorce court 'revelations' that the filling of the vacuum had already had direct and serious effects upon Parnell's authority as a leader.

The irony of this situation was that while Parnell was thus losing ground in Ireland his advances in England were much too slight to offer an adequate compensation. True, the Liberal alliance appeared to flourish and the 'flowing tide' seemed to be flowing irresistibly towards Home Rule. But all this was highly conditional. Not only were the Liberals themselves deeply confused about what sort of settlement they intended for Ireland, but English opinion remained sceptical about the genuineness of Parnell's conversion from agitation to conciliation. The very things which helped him to survive in Ireland militated against him in Britain. The accusations of *The Times* were believed by many Englishmen because they wanted to believe them and the report of the Special Commission, though it cleared Parnell of the graver charges levelled at him, left enough mud sticking to his name to counteract considerably the pro-Parnellite hysteria momentarily evoked by the exposure of the Pigott forgeries. And the fact that the Plan of Campaign still continued to throw up instances of agrarian crime and intimidation made it easy for simple minds, which could scarcely be expected to understand the extent of Parnell's dissociation from the Plan, to regard this as merely a new phase of the old land war and to connect the leader with the agitation as if nothing had changed since 1880. Although this was an absurdity, and known to be so by responsible people, to the man in the street who read even the less sensational newspapers, Parnell's occasional 'balancing' speeches conveyed only the information that whatever he might say about peace, war was what he really wanted.

When, therefore, the divorce suit precipitated the final crisis, Parnell was so placed that he could scarcely avoid making the worst of both worlds. In Ireland his furious attempt to reassert his leadership, though it came near to success initially and was not decisively defeated until the North Sligo election in March–April 1891, foundered not simply on the moral and political issues raised by the split, but also on the inescapable fact that his long semi-abdication had brought into being an 'alternative government' which proved itself capable of doing without him. In England, on the other hand, the violence of his onslaught on the Liberals, his seeming appeals to 'the hillside men', and his dogmatic re-assertion of the principle of independent opposition, all combined to destroy overnight the image of the constructive, conciliatory statesman he had laboured to build during the previous four years. This made it all too easy for those who, from motives both honourable and devious, wanted to eliminate him from the great game of politics, to do so in the comforting belief that he was still at heart the irreconcilable enemy of England and that it was a mercy of providence he had been found out before a self-governing Ireland had been committed to his charge.

Such a *dénouement* was exactly calculated to bring out in Parnell those qualities, with their mingled strength and weakness, which were most deeply ingrained in his character. Thus, throughout the eleven-month nightmare which ensued before death ended the dance, he displayed for the last time all the courage, the pride, the tenacity, the ruthlessness, the obstinacy, the resilience, the concentrated passion which, though muted in the latter half of his career, had in his prime made him an almost elemental force in British and Irish affairs. But after Boulogne there was no way out for him except to wage an incessant struggle of which the fatal outcome became steadily clearer as month succeeded month and blow followed blow. With Macbeth, he could say at the end:

> They have tied me to a stake; I cannot fly
> But, bear-like, I must fight the course.

And so doing, he died.

Notes

CHAPTER 1: THE MEETING OF THE WATERS

1 T. P. O'Connor, *Life of Charles Stewart Parnell* (London, 1891, hereafter cited as *Parnell*), p. 11, records Parnell as saying he thought he was born in Brighton, but his mother's evidence points conclusively to Avondale (R. M. MacWade, *The uncrowned king: the life and services of the Hon. Charles Stewart Parnell* (Edgewood Publishing Co., USA, 1891, chap. 4, hereafter cited as *The uncrowned king*). The parish register of the Church of Ireland, Rathdrum, shows that Parnell was baptized there on 9 August 1846.

2 *DNB* (1959–60 reprint), article by G. A. Aitken.

3 S. Johnson, *Lives of the poets*, ed. G. Birkbeck Hill (Oxford, 1905), ii, 54.

4 O. Goldsmith, *Works*, ed. P. Cunningham (London, 1854), iv, 131.

5 Sir J. Barrington, *Historical memoirs of Ireland* (London, 1833), i, 119–20.

6 *Irish Parliamentary Debates* xii, 180–1 (1792); xiii, 320–2 (1793).

7 *Journals and correspondence of William, Lord Auckland*, ed. by his son (London, 1862), iv, 77–8.

8 G. C. Bolton, *The passing of the Irish Act of Union* (London, 1966), pp. 106–7; R. F. Foster, *Charles Stewart Parnell: the man and his family* (Sussex, 1976), pp. 4–11.

9 C. Ross, ed., *Correspondence of Charles, first Marquis Cornwallis* (London, 1859), iii, 323.

10 For Henry Parnell, see *DNB*, article by G. F. R. Baker.

11 *The life of Frances Cobbe*, by herself (2 vols, London, 1894), i, 191.

12 For the second Lord Congleton, see *DNB*, article by G. F. R. Barker; for C. S. Parnell and the Brethren, see *The Times*, 28 June 1886 and T. P. O'Connor, *Parnell*, pp. 170–1.

13 For William Parnell's career, see R. B. O'Brien, *The life of Charles Stewart Parnell* (London, 3rd ed., 1899, henceforth cited as R. B. O'Brien), i, 16–17; also *DNB*, article by Charles Goodwin.

14 R. B. O'Brien, i, 19.

15 ibid., i, 20–8; see also the article by R. W. Irwin in *Dictionary of American Biography* (New York, 1935–6).

16 T. Sherlock, *The life of Charles Stewart Parnell* (Boston, 1881), pp. 27–9, 187–200; R. MacWade, *The uncrowned king*, chap. 2; see also the article by C. K. Bolton in the *Dictionary of American Biography*.

17 R. MacWade, op. cit., pp. 37–45; J. H. Parnell, *Charles Stewart Parnell:*

a memoir (London, 1916, hereafter cited as *Charles Stewart Parnell*), pp. 302–3.

18 Emily Dickinson, *A patriot's mistake* (London, 1905), p. 8. This book is such a tissue of inaccuracies and imagined fantasies that it has been dismissed by some as 'a patriot's sister's mistake'. But it can be made to yield some insight into what it was like to grow up at Avondale.

19 St John Ervine, *Parnell* (London, 1925), pp. 36–47.

20 J. H. Parnell, *Charles Stewart Parnell*, p. 72.

21 ibid., p. 38.

22 *The Times*, 28 June 1886.

23 J. H. Parnell, *Charles Stewart Parnell*, pp. 27–8.

24 T. P. O'Connor, *Parnell*, pp. 17–18.

25 Material supplied by Mr John Williamson; see also his article in the *Derby Evening Telegraph*, 5 June 1973.

26 J. H. Parnell, op. cit., p. 29; *Derby Evening Telegraph*, 5 June 1973.

27 ibid., pp. 43–4.

28 ibid., p. 44.
   Middlesex County Times, 17 October 1891; *Local Historian* (Greater Ealing Local History Society, No. 3) (1961), pp. 40–4.

29 He told a student audience at the Catholic University that he was 'one of those unfortunate beings . . . who only acquired a knowledge of Irish history at a very late period' (speech of 13 December 1877, printed in the *Nation*, 14 September 1889).

30 Justin McCarthy, *Reminiscences* (London, 1899), ii, 100.

31 J. H. Parnell, *Charles Stewart Parnell*, pp. 49–50.

32 R. B. O'Brien, i, 38–9.

33 J. H. Parnell, op. cit., pp. 49–50.

34 For his career at Cambridge see G. M. [artin], 'A Parnell centenary', in *Magdalene College Magazine and Record* (New Series, No. 14, 1969–70), aud the same author's 'Parnell at Cambridge: the education of an Irish nationalist', in *IHS*, xix, No. 73 (March 1974), 72–82.

35 R. B. O'Brien, i, 41.

36 Emily Dickinson, *A patriot's mistake*, pp. 49–59; H. Harrison, *Parnell vindicated: the lifting of the veil* (London, 1931, hereafter cited as *Parnell vindicated*), pp. 430–6. The story finds credence in St John Ervine, *Parnell*, pp. 69–72 (written before Harrison's exposé) and more recently in Jules Abels, *The Parnell tragedy* (London, 1966), pp. 21–2.

37 See the *Cambridge Independent Press* and the *Cambridge Chronicle*, both of 22 May 1869.

38 M. Davitt, *The fall of feudalism in Ireland* (London and New York, 1904), p. 107.

39 Evidence of P. C. Carter, *Cambridge Independent Press*, 22 May 1869.

40 *Cambridge Chronicle*, 22 May 1869.

41 J. H. Parnell, *Charles Stewart Parnell*, pp. 71–2.

42 Justin McCarthy, *Reminiscences*, ii, 109. McCarthy wrongly attributes the

incident to Avondale.

43 J. H. Parnell, op. cit., p. 70.
44 *Special Commission Act, 1888; reprint of the shorthand notes of the speeches, proceedings and evidence taken before the commissioners appointed under the above-named Act* (hereafter cited as *Spec. Comm. Proc.*), vii, 1.
45 J. H. Parnell, op. cit., p. 71.
46 For these incidents, see T. P. O'Connor, *Parnell*, pp. 25–7.
47 R. B. O'Brien, i, 52–3.
48 ibid., i, 54–5.
49 J. H. Parnell, *Charles Stewart Parnell*, p. 102.
50 ibid., p. 107.

CHAPTER 2: APPRENTICESHIP

1 For Butt's career see L. J. McCaffrey, 'Irish federalism in the 1870s: a study in conservative nationalism', in *Transactions of the American Philosophical Society* (Philadelphia), new series, vol. 1, ii, part 6 (1962) and D. A. Thornley, *Isaac Butt and Home Rule* (London, 1964) especially chaps. 1 to 3.
2 D. Thornley, *Isaac Butt and Home Rule*, pp. 164–5.
3 *Spec. Comm. Proc.*, vii, 1–2.
4 T. Sherlock, *The life of Charles Stewart Parnell*, p. 66; T. P. O'Connor, *Parnell*, p. 33; R. B. O'Brien, i, 57.
5 R. B. O'Brien, i, 56–7.
6 J. H. Parnell, *Charles Stewart Parnell*, p. 131.
7 ibid., p. 121. R. B. O'Brien, i, 70, states that John accompanied his brother to the interview with Gray, but this is contradicted by John's own memoir which, on a personal detail of this kind, is probably to be preferred.
8 J. H. Parnell, op. cit., pp. 122–4, 133–7; R. B. O'Brien, i, 70–2.
9 T. Sherlock, *The life of Charles Stewart Parnell*, p. 73.
10 R. B. O'Brien, i, 75.
11 A. M. Sullivan, *New Ireland* (London, 16th ed., n.d.), p. 409.
12 Reproduced in the *Nation*, 23 August 1879.
13 Parnell to Lord Howth, 14 March 1874 (NLI MS 5934).
14 T. Sherlock, *The life of Charles Stewart Parnell*, pp. 75–6.
15 D. A. Thornley, *Isaac Butt and Home Rule*, p. 213.
16 ibid., chap. 6.
17 R. B. O'Brien, i, 77.
18 F. S. L. Lyons, *John Dillon: a biography* (London, 1968, hereafter cited as *John Dillon*), pp. 16–17.
19 Father R. Galvin to J. Hickey, 23 March 1875 (C. G. Doran Papers).
20 William Dillon to W. H. Madden, 27 March [185] (C. G. Doran Papers).

21 W. O'Brien and D. Ryan (ed.), *Devoy's Post-bag 1871–1928* (Dublin, 1948, hereafter cited as *DPB*), i, 299.

22 W. H. Madden to Charles Doran, 28 March 1875 (C. G. Doran Papers).

23 D. A. Thornley, *Isaac Butt and Home Rule*, pp. 248–50.

24 J. H. Parnell, *Charles Stewart Parnell*, pp. 139-40.

25 Parnell to Father George Taafe, 26 January 1876 (NLI MS 5934); Parnell to Father Michael Tormey, 5 August 1878 (NLI MS 15,735).

26 *Drogheda Argus*, 17 April 1875.

27 R. B. O'Brien, i, 93.

28 Hansard, H. C. deb., 3s, ccxxiii, cols. 1643–5 (26 April 1875).

29 T. P. O'Connor, *Parnell*, pp. 213–14.

30 Justin McCarthy, *Reminiscences*, ii, chap. 19; W. O'Brien, *The Parnell of real life* (London, 1926), chap. 4.

31 J. McCarthy, op. cit., i, 104.

32 *Nation*, 3 July 1875; *Irish Times*, 23 October 1875.

33 *Nation*, 22 January 1876.

34 Hansard, H. C. deb., 3s, ccxxix, cols. 113–14 (9 February 1876).

35 Hansard, H. C. deb., 3s, ccxxix, cols. 1046–8 (22 May 1876).

36 Hansard, H. C. deb., 3s, ccxxx, cols. 803, 808 (30 June 1876).

37 R. B. O'Brien, i, 97–8.

38 *Nation*, 19 August 1876.

39 Chief Secretary's Office (hereafter cited as CSO), Registered Papers, 463/1877.

40 *Nation*, 27 August 1876.

41 J. H. Parnell, *Charles Stewart Parnell*, pp. 146-8.

42 The correspondence relating to the incident is in *Nation*, 11 November 1876.

43 T. Sherlock, *The life of Charles Stewart Parnell*, p. 98; R. B. O'Brien, i, 100.

44 R. B. O'Brien, i, 102.

45 *Nation*, 25 November 1876.

46 D. A. Thornley, *Isaac Butt and Home Rule*, p. 300.

47 D. A. Thornley, 'The Irish Home Rule party and parliamentary obstruction, 1874–87', in *Irish Historical Studies*, xii, No. 45 (March 1960).

48 R. B. O'Brien, i, 110–11.

49 Hansard, H. C. deb., 3s, ccxxxiii, cols. 1042–50 (12–13 April 1877).

50 Parnell to Butt, 13 April 1877 (D. A. Thornley, *Isaac Butt and Home Rule*, p. 318).

51 Butt to Parnell, 13 April 1877 (NLI MS, 8705).

52 *FJ*, 17 April 1877.

53 *Nation*, 2 June 1877.

54 *Nation*, 2 June 1877.

55 *Nation*, 21 July 1877.

56 *Nation*, 30 June 1877.

57 *Nation*, 21 July 1877.
58 Hansard, H. C. deb., 3s, ccxxxv, cols. 1797–1833.
59 D. A. Thornley, *Isaac Butt and Home Rule*, p. 313.
60 *Nation*, 4 August 1877.
61 *Nation*, 4 August 1877.
62 *Nation*, 11 August 1877.
63 *Nation*, 11 August 1877.
64 *Nation*, 25 August 1877.
65 R. B. O'Brien, i, 145.
66 *FJ*, 28 and 29 August 1877; *Irish Times*, 28 and 29 August 1877; *Nation*, 1 and 8 September 1877.
67 *Nation*, 8 September 1877.
68 *FJ*, 7 September 1877.
69 *Nation*, 13 October 1877.
70 *Nation*, 19 January 1878.
71 *Nation*, 15 December 1877.

CHAPTER 3: RISING HIGH

1 Parnell to John Dillon, 20 April 1877 (DP).
2 Parnell to John Dillon, 25 July, 6, 9 and 21 August 1877 (DP).
3 F. S. L. Lyons, *John Dillon*, p. 22.
4 J. J. O'Kelly to John Devoy, 5 August 1877 (*DPB* i, 267–8).
5 J. J. O'Kelly to John Devoy, 21 August 1877 (ibid., i, 269–70).
6 For the rise of the Clan, see T. N. Brown, *Irish-American nationalism* (Philadelphia and New York, 1966), especially chap. 4.
7 William Carroll to John Devoy, 27 September 1877 (*DPB*, i, 273–5).
8 *Nation*, 19 and 26 January 1878.
9 M. Davitt, *The fall of feudalism in Ireland*, pp. 110–11.
10 William Carroll to John Devoy, 24 July 1906 (*DPB*, i, 298).
11 John Devoy, *Recollections of an Irish rebel* (New York, 1928), p. 283; T. W. Moody and L. ó Broin, 'The IRB Supreme Council, 1868–78', in *IHS*, ix, No. 75 (March 1975), 286–332.
12 R. B. O'Brien, i, 159–60; F. H. O'Donnell, *History of the Irish parliamentary party* (London, 1910), i, 271–5.
13 *Spec. Comm. Proc.*, vii, 104–5.
14 D. A. Thornley, *Isaac Butt and Home Rule*, pp. 350–4.
15 ibid., p. 215.
16 Parnell to John Dillon, 28 June 1878 (DP).
17 Parnell to John Dillon, 13 July 1878 (DP).
18 D. A. Thornley, op. cit., p. 363.
19 M. Davitt, *The fall of feudalism*, p. 113.
20 ibid., pp. 111–13.
21 *Irish World*, 21 September 1878; R. B. O'Brien, i, 166–7.

22 J. Devoy, *The land of Eire* (New York, 1882), p. 42.

23 *Irish World*, 26 October 1878; *DPB*, i, 362.

24 *Nation*, 26 October 1878.

25 *FJ*, 11 November 1878; *Nation*, 16 November 1878; Davitt, *Fall of feudalism*, pp. 125–6 where the telegram is wrongly dated; *DPB*, i, 370, where clause 4 is incorrectly stated.

26 *Spec. Comm. Proc.*, vii, 88, 92; R. B. O'Brien, i, 168–9; *DPB*, i, 370.

27 New York *Herald*, 27 October 1878.

28 John Devoy, 'Davitt's career', part vi in *Gaelic American*, 14 July 1906.

29 *FJ*, 27 December 1878. The letter had been discussed with leading Irish-American Fenians before his departure. Though it bore the date, 11 December, Devoy revised it during the voyage to Europe.

30 John Devoy, 'Davitt's career', part x in *Gaelic American*.

31 *Irish Freedom*, October–December 1914; John Devoy, *Recollections* p. 314; *DPB*, i, 402–3.

32 B. Solow, *The land question and the Irish economy, 1870–1903* (Cambridge, Mass., 1971), chap. 3.

33 ibid., chaps. 4 and 5 for the changing economic situation.

34 *Nation*, 9 November 1878, speech at Ballinasloe, 3 November.

35 *Nation*, 23 November 1878, speech at Tralee, 16 November.

36 *Nation*, 16 November 1878.

37 *FJ*, 2 December 1878.

38 *Nation*, 7 December 1878.

39 During December 1878 there was a progressive hardening of tone in the *Nation*, the *Freeman's Journal* and the *Cork Examiner*.

40 *FJ*, 5 February 1879.

41 *FJ*, 5 February 1879; *Nation*, 8 February 1879.

42 *Nation*, 15 February 1879.

43 John Devoy, 'Davitt's career', part xiv, *Gaelic American; Spec. Comm. Proc.*, vii, 10, 88, 95–6; M. Davitt, *Fall of feudalism*, pp. 176–7.

44 *Connaught Telegraph*, 21 April 1879; *Nation*, 3 May 1879; M. Davitt, *Fall of feudalism*, chap. 12.

45 *Spec. Comm. Proc.*, vii, 10, 95; M. Davitt, *Fall of feudalism*, pp. 151–2.

46 He had been advertised to speak since about the end of April, but confirmed his intention to be present a day or so before 1 June. See Archbishop McHale's letter to the editor of the *Freeman's Journal*, dated 5 June and published two days later: also Parnell's own speech at Westport (*FJ*, 9 June 1879).

47 For this information I am indebted to Professor T. W. Moody.

48 John Devoy, 'Davitt's career', in *Gaelic American*, part xv.

49 John Devoy, 'Parnell and the Fenians', in *Chicago Journal*, 24 March 1899.

50 M. Davitt, *Fall of feudalism*, pp. 176–7.

51 *Spec. Comm. Proc.*, vii, 94–6, 104–5.

52 ibid., vii, 10, 95.

53 ibid., vii, 107.

54 *FJ*, 9 June 1879.

55 M. Davitt, *Fall of feudalism*, p. 154.

56 F. H. O'Donnell, *History of the Irish parliamentary party*, i, 331–2.

57 Parnell to Maurice Lenihan, 5 August 1879 (NLI MS 5934).

58 *UI*, 8 December 1883.

59 *Nation*, 9 and 16 August 1879; R. B. O'Brien, i, 191–2; T. M. Healy to Maurice Healy, 7 August 1879 (*Letters and leaders of my day* (Dublin, 1929), hereafter cited as *Letters and leaders*), i, 72.

60 *Nation*, 27 September 1879.

61 *Nation*, 4 and 11 October 1879.

62 *Nation*, 18 October 1879.

63 *Saunders' Irish Daily News*, 13 October 1879.

64 *FJ*, 13 October 1889.

65 *Nation*, 18 October 1879.

66 *FJ*, 18 August 1879.

67 M. Davitt, *Fall of feudalism*, pp. 163–4.

68 *Spec. Comm. Proc.*, vii, 227.

69 M. Davitt, *Fall of feudalism*, pp. 170–3.

70 ibid., p. 173.

71 *Spec. Comm. Proc.*, vii, 27.

72 *Nation*, 1 November 1879.

73 *Nation*, 15 and 22 November 1879, speeches at Manchester and Roscommon.

74 *Nation*, 22 November 1879; M. Davitt, *Fall of feudalism*, p. 178.

75 *Nation*, 22 November 1879.

76 *FJ*, 19 November 1879.

77 *Nation*, 13 December 1879, speech at Castlerea.

78 *FJ*, 22 November 1879.

79 *Nation*, 29 November 1879; F. S. L. Lyons, *John Dillon*, p. 32.

80 *FJ*, 24 November 1879.

81 *Nation*, 18 October 1879, speech at Belfast, 15 October.

82 *Nation*, 6 December 1879, speeches at Liverpool and Birkenhead, 29 and 30 November.

83 *Nation*, 8 November 1879, citing the *London Echo*.

84 M. Davitt, *Fall of feudalism*, pp. 175–6.

85 *Spec. Comm. Proc.*, vii, 11–12.

86 William O'Brien, *Recollections* (London, 1905), p. 239 *n*.

87 *Spec. Comm. Proc.*, vii, 13–14.

88 T. M. Healy to his brother Maurice, 4 December 1879 (T. M. Healy, *Letters and leaders*, i, 78).

89 Various estimates have been given, but these are Parnell's own figures; they are more precise than most others and they include sums which arrived after his return home, thus representing a grand total rather than an interim one (*Spec. Comm. Proc.*, vii, 26–7).

90 N. D. Palmer, *The Irish Land League crisis* (New Haven, 1940), p. 149.

91 *Nation*, 14 February 1880, speech at Cleveland, 24 January.

92 Davitt to Devoy, 6 February 1880 (*DPB*, i, 482–3).

93 C. S. Parnell, 'The Irish land question', in *North American Review* cxxx (April 1880); for Fanny's authorship see T. M. Healy to his brother, 20 March 1880 (*Letters and leaders*, i, 87).

94 The Congress speech is printed in M. Davitt, *Fall of feudalism*, pp. 198–203.

95 *DPB*, i, 479–80.

96 William Carroll to Devoy, 6 February 1880 (*DPB*, i, 484).

97 Carroll to Devoy, 12 and 13 March, 29 and 30 April 1880 (*DPB*, i, 499–500; 504–8; 520–4).

98 For these speeches, see R. B. O'Brien, i, 201–3.

99 For these exchanges and for the newspaper references, see *Spec. Comm. Proc.*, vii, 22–3, 110–11, 117. I am indebted to Professor Emmet Larkin of Chicago University for information about the Cincinnati newspapers.

100 R. B. O'Brien, i, 203–4.

101 *Nation*, 31 January 1880.

102 Healy to his brother Maurice, 20 March 1880 (*Letters and leaders*, i, 85–8).

103 ibid., i, 83.

104 R. B. O'Brien, i, 206.

CHAPTER 4: CRISIS

1 *Nation*, 27 March 1880; T. M. Healy, *Letters and leaders*, i, 89.

2 *Nation*, 27 March 1880.

3 R. B. O'Brien, i, 214–19.

4 W. J. Walsh to Archbishop McCabe, 10 January 1880 (Dublin Diocesan Archives, hereafter cited as DDA).

5 James Donnelly, Bishop of Clogher to Archbishop McCabe, 17 February 1880 (DDA); Michael Logue, Bishop of Raphoe, to Archbishop McCabe, 18 April 1880 (DDA).

6 Archbishop McCabe to Dr Lucas, 17 February 1880 (DDA).

7 Dr Warren, Bishop of Wexford to Archbishop McCabe, 25 March 1880 (DDA).

8 For example, R. B. O'Brien, i, 213–14; St John Ervine, *Parnell*, p. 138; Joan Haslip, *Parnell* (London, 1932), p. 120.

9 T. M. Healy, *Letters and leaders*, i, 91.

10 *Nation*, 3 April 1880.

11 T. P. O'Connor, *Parnell*, p. 78.

12 *Nation*, 3 April 1880; *Spec. Comm. Proc.*, vii, 28.

13 Father D. Kane to Archbishop McCabe, 1 April 1880 (DDA).

14 *Nation*, 3 April 1880.

15 *Nation*, 10 April and 29 May 1880.

16 C. Cruise O'Brien, *Parnell and his party* (Oxford, 1961), chap. 1.

17 For his career, see his *Memoirs of an old parliamentarian*, 2 vols (London, 1929); Hamilton Fyfe, *T. P. O'Connor* (London, 1934). There is no study of Thomas Sexton, but see the article by Joseph Hone in *DNB*, *1930–1940*.

18 *FJ*, 22 May 1880.

19 F. H. O'Donnell, *History of the Irish parliamentary party*, i, 464; H. Fyfe, *T. P. O'Connor*, p. 102.

20 T. P. O'Connor, *Parnell*, pp. 90–2.

21 *Nation*, 3 July 1880, where there is a suggestion that O'Donnell himself was seriously unbalanced at this time.

22 W. L. Arnstein, *The Bradlaugh case* (Oxford, 1965), pp. 203–10.

23 *Nation*, 22 May 1880; T. P. O'Connor, *Parnell*, pp. 79–83.

24 T. P. O'Connor, *Parnell*, p. 82.

25 W. S. Blunt, *The land war in Ireland* (London, 1912), pp. 28–9.

26 *DNB*, second supplement, 1912, article by S. Fryer; K. O'Shea, *Charles Stewart Parnell: his love-story and political life* (London, 1914, hereafter cited as 'K. O'Shea'), i, 25–8, 54-5.

27 K. O'Shea, i, chap. 13.

28 K. O'Shea, i, 108–23; H. Harrison, *Parnell vindicated* (London, 1931), pp. 118–29.

29 K. O'Shea, i, 134.

30 ibid., i, 135–6.

31 ibid., i, 138–9.

32 Parnell to Mrs O'Shea, 9 and 11 September 1880 (ibid., i, 141–2).

33 ibid., i, 143–5.

34 ibid., i, 149, 153.

35 *Nation*, 8 May 1880; M. Davitt, *Fall of feudalism*, pp. 240–4.

36 *Spec. Comm. Proc.*, vii, 114–15, 219; J. Macdonald, *The Daily News diary of the Special Commission* (London, 1890), p. 225.

37 C. Cruise O'Brien, *Parnell and his party*, pp. 36–45.

38 R. B. O'Brien, i, 233–4.

39 Hansard, H. C. deb., 3s, cclv, col. 786 (10 August 1880).

40 *FJ*, 17 August 1880.

41 G. Errington to Archbishop McCabe, 12 August 1880 (DDA).

42 *Nation*, 4 September 1880.

43 *Nation*, 28 August 1880, speech of James Redpath at Leenane, 16 August; *Nation*, 11 September 1880, speech of John Dillon in Dublin, 5 September; *Police Reports* for speech of J. W. Walsh in county Leitrim, 5 September 1880.

44 *Nation*, 10 July 1880. Devoy's letter, written originally to the *Freeman's Journal*, was dated 18 June 1880.

45 Dr L. Gillooly, Bishop of Elphin, to Archbishop McCabe, 10 June 1880 (DDA); see also E. Larkin, *The Roman Catholic Church and the creation*

of the modern Irish state, 1878–1886 (Philadelphia and Dublin, 1975), pp. 24–53.

46 Dr P. Duggan, Bishop of Clonfert, to Archbishop McCabe, 27 October 1880 (DDA).

47 Speech at New Ross, 26 September 1880 (*Police Reports*).

48 *Nation*, 2 October 1880. This was a meeting of the League executive, held on 28 September; it was said to have been the first Parnell had attended since returning to Ireland for the recess.

49 T. P. O'Connor, *Parnell*, pp. 102–3.

50 Speech at Galway, 24 October 1880 (*Police Reports*).

51 Speeches at Tipperary and Athlone, 31 October and 7 November 1880 (*Police Reports*).

52 Joyce Marlow, *Captain Boycott and the Irish* (London, 1973), *passim*.

53 J. L. Hammond, *Gladstone and the Irish nation* (London, 1964 impression), p. 193; B. Solow, *The land question and the Irish economy, 1870–1903* (Cambridge, Mass., 1971), pp. 55–6. See also *Return by provinces and counties . . . of cases of evictions in each of the years 1849 to 1886 inclusive and of agrarian and general crime*, reprinted in *Spec. Comm. Proc.*, vii, 177.

54 T. Wemyss Reid, *The Life of the Rt. Hon. William Edward Forster* (London, 1889), pp. 458–9.

55 *Nation*, 1 January 1881; *FJ*, 18 October 1882; C. Cruise O'Brien, *Parnell and his party*, p. 56, *n.* 1.

CHAPTER 5: IN THE EYE OF THE STORM

1 T. P. O'Connor, *Parnell*, pp. 104–7; M. M. O'Hara, *Chief and Tribune: Parnell and Davitt*, p. 146.

2 Cited in *Nation*, 24 July 1880.

3 *Nation*, 20 November 1880, based on an undated report in the London *Standard*.

4 *Nation*, 4 December 1880, reprinted from the *World*.

5 Return by provinces and counties . . . of cases of evictions in each of the years 1849 to 1886 inclusive and of agrarian and general crime, cited in *Spec. Comm. Proc.*, vii, 177; see also T. P. O'Connor, *The Parnell movement* (London, 1886), pp. 401–2; B. Solow, *The Land Question and the Irish Economy, 1870–1903*, pp. 55–6.

6 *Nation*, 1 January 1881.

7 Davitt to Devoy, 16 December 1880 (*DPB*, ii, 23).

8 According to Davitt's own memoirs the arrest actually occurred on 4 February, but this seems an error of recollection (*Fall of feudalism*, p. 302).

9 Hansard, H. C. deb., 3s, cclviii, cols. 69–72, for the interventions by Dillon and Parnell.

10 Hansard, H. C. Debates, 3g, cclvii, cols. 902–14 (17 January 1881).

11 A. J. Kettle, *The material for victory*, ed. Lawrence J. Kettle (Dublin, 1958), pp. 39–42; Davitt, *Fall of feudalism*, p. 302, ascribes a less positive role to Parnell but agrees substantially with Kettle as to what was decided.

12 *Nation*, 12 February 1881.

13 *Nation*, 13 February 1881.

14 *FJ*, 5 February 1881.

15 C. Cruise O'Brien, *Parnell and his party*, p. 61.

16 William O'Brien, *The Parnell of real life* (London, 1926), pp. 38–9.

17 M. Davitt, *Fall of feudalism*, p. 304; F. S. L. Lyons, *John Dillon*, p. 46.

18 T. M. Healy, *Letters and leaders*, i, 109; private information supplied to present writer by members of John Dillon's family.

19 T. M. Healy, *Letters and leaders*, i, 109.

20 T. P. O'Connor, *Parnell*, p. 133.

21 M. Davitt, *Fall of feudalism*, p. 306.

22 K. O'Shea, i, 178–80; ii, 165.

23 ibid., i, 157–8, 161, 169–70.

24 ibid., i, 149–52, 157–8, 161, 169–70, 171–2.

25 ibid., i, 189.

26 H. Harrison, *Parnell vindicated*, pp. 124–5, 125–6, 288–9.

27 For O'Shea's testimony, see *The Times*, 17 November 1890. The remaining evidence is in K. O'Shea, i, 187–91, and H. Harrison, *Parnell vindicated*, pp. 288–9.

28 A. J. Kettle, *The material for victory*, p. 45.

29 M. Davitt, *Fall of feudalism*, pp. 307–8.

30 *FJ*, 25 February 1881; *Nation*, 26 February and 5 March 1881.

31 W. Lomasney to Devoy, 18 February 1881 (*DPB*, ii, 40).

32 *Nation*, 5 March 1881; Hansard, H. C. deb., 3s, cclix, cols. 336 et seq. for the speeches of Dillon and Parnell; *Spec. Comm. Proc.*, vii, 336–47; M. Davitt, *Fall of feudalism*, p. 128 *n*; *DPB*, ii, 41–5.

33 Le Caron's evidence is in *Spec. Comm. Proc.*, iv, 489–633; v, 1–65. See also his book, *Twenty-five years in the secret service* (London, 6th ed., 1892), pp. 172–87, and R. A. Anderson, *Sidelights on the Home Rule movement* (London, 1906), chap. 15.

34 *Spec. Comm. Proc.*, vii, 40.

35 ibid., vii, 41.

36 ibid., vii, 291.

37 B. Solow, *The land question and the Irish economy*, pp. 156–7.

38 ibid., p. 155. Chapter 6 of this work contains a penetrating criticism of the Act in detail.

39 *Nation*, 16 April 1881.

40 *Nation*, 23 April 1881.

41 *FJ*, 13 April 1881.

42 *Nation*, 30 April 1881.

43 *Nation*, 14 May 1881.

44 A. M. Sullivan, to J. R. Richardson, 31 December 1881 (PRONI, D 1006/3/1/13).

45 Patrick Egan to Thomas Brennan, 22 May 1881 (NLI MS 8577 (i)). See also his public letter in *Nation*, 4 June 1881.

46 For this negotiation see J. L. Hammond, *Gladstone and the Irish nation* (London, 1964 reprint), pp. 221–3; also Joseph Chamberlain, *A political memoir*, 1880–92, ed., C. H. D. Howard (London, 1953, hereafter cited as J. Chamberlain, *Political memoir*), pp. 30–4.

47 Hansard, H. C. deb., 3s, cclxiv, cols. 385–90; R. B. O'Brien, i, 297–8.

48 W. O'Brien, *Recollections*, pp. 300–2.

49 *Spec. Comm. Proc.*, vii, 161–6, 204–14.

50 W. O'Brien, 'Diary', 17 November 1878 (*Recollections*, p. 198).

51 W. O'Brien, *Recollections*, pp. 304–5.

52 C. Cruise O'Brien, *Parnell and his party*, pp. 68–70.

53 *Nation*, 6 August 1881.

54 *FJ*, 30 August 1881.

55 *Nation*, 24 September 1881.

56 N. D. Palmer, *The Irish land league crisis*, p. 281.

57 *Nation*, 1 October 1881.

58 T. Wemyss Reid, *Life of the Rt. Hon. W. E. Forster*, p. 506.

59 W. E. Forster to Gladstone, 2 October 1881 (ibid., pp. 507–8).

60 *Nation*, 8 October 1881; W. O'Brien, *Recollections*, p. 338.

61 W. O'Brien, *Recollections*, p. 337.

62 *Daily News*, 8 October 1881; *Nation*, 15 October 1881.

63 For a description, see D. W. R. Bahlman (ed.) *The diary of Sir Edward Walter Hamilton*, 1880–85 (Oxford, 1972), i, 174; hereafter cited as E. W. Hamilton, *Diary* (Bahlman).

64 *FJ*, 10 October 1881.

65 R. B. O'Brien, i, 311–12.

66 Parnell to Katharine O'Shea, 11 October 1881 (K. O'Shea, i, 202). She claims that on 12 October she got wind of the cabinet decision and exchanged telegrams with him on the subject that day (ibid., i, 203–4).

67 T. Wemyss Reid, op. cit., pp. 514–15.

68 *FJ*, 14 October 1881.

69 CSO, Registered Papers, 1882/21/040 (SPOI).

70 *FJ*, 14 October 1881.

CHAPTER 6: KILMAINHAM

1 *The Times*, 14 October 1881.

2 F. S. L. Lyons, *John Dillon*, p. 56.

3 Parnell to Dillon, 'Thursday' [13 October 1881] (DP); F. S. L. Lyons, op. cit., p. 57.

4 *FJ*, 15 October 1881.

5 Parnell to Dillon, 14 October 1881 (photostat copy), cited in F. S. L. Lyons, *John Dillon*, p. 58.

6 W. O'Brien, *Recollections*, pp. 353–6.

7 ibid., p. 365.

8 K. O'Shea, i, 209.

9 R. B. O'Brien, i, 319–20.

10 *Spec. Comm. Proc.*, vii, 43.

11 M. Davitt, *Fall of feudalism*, pp. 335–7.

12 A. J. Kettle, *The material for victory*, p. 56; F. S. L. Lyons, *John Dillon*, p. 60.

13 M. Davitt, *Fall of feudalism*, p. 338.

14 A. J. Kettle, *The material for victory*, pp. 56–7.

15 T. Harrington to Parnell, 12 October 1881 (NLI MS 8578).

16 Parnell to Katharine O'Shea, 21 October 1881 (K. O'Shea, i, 212–13).

17 K. O'Shea, i, 207.

18 *The Times*, 17 November 1890, evidence of Captain O'Shea. O'Shea did not mention the birth of Claude Sophie in 1882, and his counsel only did so in passing, but he did claim two further children born in 1883 and 1884 as his, though, as we shall see presently, they were unquestionably Parnell's.

19 *The Times*, 10 September 1913 and K. O'Shea, i, xii–xiii. For a discussion of the 'O'Shea influence' in the writing of the book, see Henry Harrison, *Parnell vindicated*, chap. 15.

20 K. O'Shea, i, 207.

21 ibid., i, 244.

22 W. H. O'Shea to Chamberlain, 25 April 1882 (JC 8/8/1/1).

23 K. O'Shea, i, 247–8.

24 Parnell to Katharine O'Shea, 21 November 1881 (K. O'Shea, i, 220-21).

25 *FJ*, 20 October 1881; *Nation*, 22 October 1881; W. O'Brien, *Recollections*, pp. 371–2.

26 R. B. O'Brien, i, 329–30.

27 *Nation*, 5 and 19 February 1881; M. Davitt, *Fall of feudalism*, pp. 299–300; T. W. Moody, 'Anna Parnell and the Land League', a paper read at the conference on Irish studies held at New York, 20 March 1965 (*Hermathena*, No. cxvii (Summer, 1974) pp. 5–17).

28 Cited by C. J. Woods, 'The politics of Cardinal McCabe, Archbishop of Dublin, 1879–85', in *Dublin Historical Record*, xxvi, No. 3 (June 1973).

29 *FJ*, 17 March 1881; Archbishop Croke to Archbishop McCabe, 8 April 1881 (DDA); M. Davitt, *Fall of feudalism*, pp. 314–15; E. Larkin, *The Roman Catholic Church and the creation of the modern Irish state, 1878–1886*, pp. 98–107.

30 W. O'Brien, *Recollections*, p. 409.

31 CSO, Registered Papers, 38700/81 (SPOI).

32 CSO, Registered Papers, 38903/81 (SPOI).

33 W. O'Brien, *The Parnell of real life*, p. 35.

34 *FJ*, 14 October 1881.

35 W. O'Brien, *Recollections*, pp. 401–2.

36 CSO, Registered Papers, 1716/82. The Governor also complained of the clemency shown by Forster to William O'Brien, who was allowed out of prison from time to time to visit his dying mother.

37 *Nation*, 22 October and 17 December 1881, and 2 January 1886; W. O'Brien, *Recollections*, pp. 395–404; K. O'Shea, i, chap. 23. See also the account by an English visitor, W. H. Duignan, to Parnell and others on 12 November 1881 and reported by Duignan to Chamberlain two days later (C. H. D. Howard, 'The man on a tricycle: W. H. Duignan and Ireland, 1881–85', in *IHS*, xiv, No. 55 (March 1965)).

38 W. O'Brien, *Recollections*, pp. 399–400.

39 ibid., pp. 398–9; K. O'Shea, i, 221.

40 T. M. Healy, *Letters and leaders*, i, 152–3.

41 CSO, Registered Papers 1882/21 040, unsigned report in Dr J. E. Kenny's hand, dated 30 October 1881 and sent to Dr J. Carte, prison doctor, 2 November 1881 (SPOI).

42 ibid., reported by Dr J. Carte, 6 November 1881.

43 CSO, Registered Papers, 40461/81, extracts from Dr Kenny's journal, 15 and 17 November 1881 (SPOI).

44 Parnell to Katharine O'Shea, 21 October 1881 (K. O'Shea, i, 212–13).

45 Parnell to Katharine O'Shea, 5 November 1881 (ibid., i, 217).

46 Parnell to Katharine O'Shea, 7 December 1881 (ibid., i, 223).

47 *FJ*, 9 December 1881; *Nation*, 17 December 1881.

48 Parnell to Katharine O'Shea, 9 and 14 December 1881 (K. O'Shea, i, 224–5).

49 Parnell to Katharine O'Shea, 14 February 1882 (ibid., i, 235–6).

50 Parnell to Katharine O'Shea, 16, 23 and 27 March and 5 April 1882 (ibid., i, 239–40, 243).

51 *Nation*, 17 December 1881.

52 W. O'Brien, *Recollections*, p. 394.

53 *FJ*, 21 November 1881.

54 Parnell to Katharine O'Shea, 9 December 1881 (K. O'Shea, i, 224).

55 F. S. L. Lyons, *John Dillon*, pp. 61–2.

56 Parnell to Katharine O'Shea, 12 November 1881 (K. O'Shea, i, 218–19).

57 Parnell to Katharine O'Shea, 3 and 9 December 1881 (ibid., i, 222, 224).

58 Parnell to Katharine O'Shea, 13 October 1881 (ibid., i, 207).

59 Parnell to Katharine O'Shea, 19 October and 5 November 1881 and 16 March 1882 (ibid., i, 211–12, 217, 238).

60 Parnell to Katharine O'Shea, 12 November 1881 (ibid., i, 219).

61 Parnell to Katharine O'Shea, 14 December 1881 (ibid., i, 225).

62 Parnell to Katharine O'Shea, 16 December 1881 (ibid., i, 226).

63 Parnell to Katharine O'Shea, 11 January 1882 (ibid., i, 230).

64 Parnell to Katharine O'Shea, 28 January 1882 (ibid., i, 233).

65 Parnell to Katharine O'Shea, 14 February [1882] (ibid., i, 235–6).

66 CSO, Registered Papers, 28 March 1882, 14860/82 (SPOI).

67 Parnell to Katharine O'Shea, 5 April 1882 (ibid., i, 242).

68 Parnell to Katharine O'Shea, 7 April 1882 (ibid., i, 243–4); *Nation*, 15 April 1882.

69 *Spec. Comm. Proc.*, vii, 43–4.

70 *Spec. Comm. Proc.*, i, 344.

71 ibid., i, 344.

72 W. H. O'Shea to Gladstone, 13 April 1882 (Joseph Chamberlain, *Political memoir*, pp. 30–4).

73 A. B. Cooke and John Vincent, 'Herbert Gladstone, Forster and Ireland 1881–2', in *IHS*, xviii, No. 68 (September 1971), 521–48; and *IHS*, xviii, No. 69 (March 1972), 74–89. See especially the latter issue, p. 77, *n*. 3.

74 O'Shea to Chamberlain, 15 April 1882 (J. Chamberlain, *Political memoir*, pp. 29–30).

75 J. L. Garvin, *Joseph Chamberlain* (London, 1932), i, 351 (hereafter cited as J. L. Garvin).

76 Chamberlain to O'Shea, 17 April 1882 (J. Chamberlain, *Political memoir*, 34–5).

77 ibid., pp. 35–6.

78 Chamberlain to Gladstone, 18 April 1882 (J. L. Garvin, i, 352).

79 Forster to Gladstone, 7 April 1882 (T. Wemyss Reid, *Life of the Rt. Hon. W. E. Forster*, pp. 549–51).

80 *Pall Mall Gazette*, 3 April 1882; Forster to Gladstone, 4 April 1882 (T. Wemyss Reid, op. cit., p. 547).

81 Forster to Gladstone, 18 April 1882 (T. Wemyss Reid, op. cit., pp. 54–6).

82 Forster to Gladstone, 25 October 1880, cited by R. Hawkins, 'Gladstone, Forster and the release of Parnell, 1882–8', in *IHS*, xvi, No. 64 (September 1969), 417–45.

83 Forster to Gladstone, 10 October 1881 (R. Hawkins, loc. cit., p. 437).

84 T. Wemyss Reid, op. cit., pp. 556–7.

85 ibid., pp. 549–51; E. W. Hamilton, *Diary*, 12 April 1882 (Bahlman, i, 249–50).

86 E. W. Hamilton, *Diary*, 16 April 1882 (Bahlman, i, 253).

87 A. B. Cooke and John Vincent, 'Herbert Gladstone, Forster and Ireland, 1881–2', in *IHS*, xviii, No. 69 (March 1972), 77–8, 87–9.

88 J. Chamberlain, *Political memoir*, pp. 38–9.

89 Parnell to Katharine O'Shea, 13 April 1882 (K. O'Shea, i, 245).

90 Parnell to Katharine O'Shea, 15 and 16 April 1882 (ibid., i, 246).

91 Parnell to Emily Dickinson, 17 April 1882 (NLI MS 15,735); R. B. O'Brien, i, 324.

92 *Spec. Comm. Proc.*, i, 345–6.

93 K. O'Shea, i, 247.

94 Parnell to Katharine O'Shea, 25 April 1882 (K. O'Shea, i, 253).

95 Parnell to Justin McCarthy, 25 April 1882 (R. B. O'Brien, i, 341–2).

96 J. Chamberlain, *Political memoir*, pp. 39–41.

97 ibid., pp. 41–4.

98 ibid., p. 44; A. B. Cooke and John Vincent, *IHS*, xviii, No. 69 (March 1972), 80 and note. See also Hansard, H. C. deb., 3s, cclxviii, cols. 1488–97 (26 April 1882).

99 T. Wemyss Reid, *Life of the Rt. Hon. W. E. Forster*, pp. 558–9; R. Hawkins, *IHS*, xvi, No. 64 (September 1969), 443.

100 J. Chamberlain, *Political memoir*, pp. 45–7.

101 ibid., p. 48; T. Wemyss Reid, op. cit., p. 559; J. L. Garvin, i, 356.

102 T. Wemyss Reid, op. cit., p. 561, account dictated by Forster to his wife, immediately after his meeting with O'Shea.

103 W. E. Gladstone, 'Memorandum of conversation with W. H. O'Shea', 5 May 1882 (BM, Add. MS 44766, ff. 71–2).

104 *Spec. Comm. Proc.*, i, 347–8.

105 M. Davitt, *Fall of feudalism*, p. 353; F. S. L. Lyons, *John Dillon*, p. 65.

106 *Spec. Comm. Proc.*, vii, 46.

107 J. Chamberlain, *Political memoir*, pp. 49–50.

108 Cited in J. L. Hammond, *Gladstone and the Irish nation*, p. 275.

109 Parnell to Katharine O'Shea, 30 April 1882 (K. O'Shea, i, 255).

110 Forster to Gladstone, 29 April 1882 (T. Wemyss Reid, op. cit., pp. 559–60).

111 ibid., pp. 560–1.

112 Gladstone to W. E. Forster, 30 April 1882 (cited in J. L. Hammond, p. 279).

113 Gladstone to Lord Granville, 30 April 1882 (Agatha Ramm (ed.) *The political correspondence of Mr Gladstone and Lord Granville* (Oxford, 1962), hereafter cited as 'A. Ramm').

114 E. W. Hamilton, *Diary*, 4 May 1882 (Bahlman, i, 261–2).

115 T. Wemyss Reid, *Life of the Rt. Hon. W. E. Forster*, pp. 563–4.

116 W. E. Gladstone, 'Mr Forster and Ireland', in *Nineteenth Century* (September 1888); this was a review of T. Wemyss Reid's biography of Forster. But reporting to the Queen as early as 10 May 1882, Gladstone was already arguing that Parnell's release was 'a simple question of legal right'. For a valuable discussion of the issues raised in the controversy, see R. Hawkins, 'Gladstone, Forster and the release of Parnell, 1882–8', in *IHS*, xvi, No. 64 (September 1969), 417–45.

117 R. Hawkins, loc. cit., p. 442.

118 *The Times*, 21 September 1888.

119 Gladstone to Earl Cowper, 2 May 1882 (J. L. Hammond, *Gladstone and the Irish nation*, pp. 278–9).

120 Hansard, H. C. deb., 3s, cclxviii, 1965–70.

121 *FJ*, 4 May 1882.

122 R. B. O'Brien, i, 349–50. O'Brien does not identify O'Kelly by name, but the newspapers make it clear it was he who accompanied Parnell to Avondale.

123 E. W. Hamilton, *Diary*, 5 May 1882 (Bahlman, i, 264).

124 R. B. O'Brien, i, 352–3.

125 *Spec. Comm. Proc.*, i, 352–3.

126 W. H. O'Shea to J. Chamberlain, 2 May [1882] (JC/8/8/1/2).

127 W. E. Gladstone, 'Memorandum of conversation with W. H. O'Shea', 5 May 1882 (BM, Add. MS 44766, ff. 71–2); F. S. L. Lyons, *John Dillon*, p. 65.

128 Gladstone to Earl Spencer, 6 May 1882 (SP).

129 M. Davitt, *Fall of feudalism*, pp. 355–7.

130 A. B. Cooke and J. R. Vincent, 'Lord Spencer on the Phoenix Park murders', in *IHS*, xviii, No. 72 (September 1973), 583–91.

131 R. B. O'Brien, i, 355. The best account of the crime is T. Corfe, *The Phoenix Park murders* (London, 1968), pp. 183–96.

CHAPTER 7: THE NEW COURSE

1 M. Davitt, *Fall of feudalism*, p. 357.

2 K. O'Shea, i, 262–3.

3 *Spec. Comm. Proc.*, i, 353–4; John Morley, *The life of William Ewart Gladstone* (London, 1911 ed.), iii, 57 (hereafter cited as J. Morley, *Gladstone*). This contemporary account suggests that Gladstone's recollections in old age were at fault when he told Barry O'Brien that Parnell had merely asked him what effect he thought the murders would have on English opinion in relation to his, Parnell's, leadership. Gladstone's memory was that he had sent back word that Parnell's retirement would do more harm than good (R. B. O'Brien, i, 357).

4 For the text and authorship of the manifesto, see *UI*, 13 May 1882; *Spec. Comm. Proc.*, i, 353–4; vii, 49. Also M. Davitt, *Fall of feudalism*, p. 359 and H. Harrison, *Parnell vindicated*, pp. 322–3, 326.

5 Justin McCarthy and R. M. Praed, *Our book of memories* (London, 1912), pp. 95–8.

6 J. Chamberlain, *Political memoir*, pp. 62–3.

7 *Spec. Comm. Proc.*, i, 353–4; vii, 49.

8 J. McCarthy and R. Praed, op. cit., pp. 95–8.

9 Hansard, 3s, cclxix, cols. 462–72 (11 May 1882).

10 Hansard, 3s, cclxix, cols. 106–18 (4 May 1882).

11 *The Times*, 8 May 1882.

12 *Spec. Comm. Proc.*, i, 351.

13 *UI*, 27 May 1882.

14 T. M. Healy, *Letters and leaders*, i, 162.

15 Cited in A. B. Cooke and John Vincent, 'Herbert Gladstone, Forster and Ireland, 1881–2', in *IHS*, xviii, No. 69 (March 1972), p. 86.

16 H. Labouchere to J. Chamberlain, 16 May 1882 (A. L. Thorold, *The life of Henry Labouchere*) (London, 1913), p. 161.

17 CSO, Registered Papers, 33858/82, especially the reports by Superintendent Mallon of 22 April and 4 May 1882.

18 *The Times*, 25 May 1882.

19 W. E. Gladstone to Earl Spencer, 24 May 1882 (SP).

20 W. H. O'Shea to J. Chamberlain, 25 May 1882 (JC/8/8/1/5).

21 *The Times*, 26 May 1882.

22 J. Chamberlain, *Political memoir*, pp. 65–6.

23 Sir W. Harcourt to Earl Spencer, 17 May 1882 (SP).

24 Sir W. Harcourt to Earl Spencer, 22 May 1882 (SP).

25 Sir Charles Dilke, 'Diary' (BM, Add. MS 43, 924, ff. 81–7); and 'Memoir' (BM, Add. MS 43, 936, ff. 110–11); S. Gwynn and G. Tuckwell, *Life of Sir Charles Dilke* (London, 1917), i, 445.

26 *The Times*, 18 May 1882.

27 Earl Granville to W. E. Gladstone, 24 May [1882] (BM, Add. MS 44, 174, f. 127).

28 W. S. Blunt, *My diaries*, ii, 280–1, entry for 25 October 1909.

29 Sir W. Harcourt, 'Memorandum for cabinet', 22 May 1882 (HP).

30 Sir W. Harcourt to Earl Spencer, 25 May 1882, copy (HP).

31 J. Chamberlain to Earl Spencer, 20 May 1882, copy (JC/8/9/3/7).

32 Earl Spencer to J. Chamberlain, 21 May 1882 (JC/8/9/3/8).

33 J. Chamberlain to Earl Spencer, 26 May 1882, copy (JC/8/9/3/11).

34 H. Labouchere to J. Chamberlain, 16 May 1882 (A. L. Thorold, *The life of Henry Labouchere*, p. 161).

35 H. Labouchere to J. Chamberlain, 22 May 1882 (ibid., pp. 162–3).

36 H. Labouchere to J. Chamberlain, 3 June 1882 (ibid., pp. 163–5).

37 Sir W. Harcourt to Earl Spencer, 29 May and 8 June 1882, copies (HP).

38 H. Labouchere to J. Chamberlain, 8 June 1882 (A. L. Thorold, op. cit., p. 165).

39 W. E. Gladstone to J. Chamberlain, 8 June 1882 (J. Chamberlain, *Political memoir*, pp. 67–9).

40 E. W. Hamilton, *Diary*, 20 June 1882 (Bahlman, i, 289).

41 Earl Granville to Earl Spencer, 11 June 1882 (SP).

42 Sir W. Harcourt to Earl Spencer, 12 June 1882, copy (HP); J. Chamberlain, *Political memoir*, p. 69.

43 E. W. Hamilton, *Diary*, 20 June 1882 (Bahlman, i, 289).

44 W. H. O'Shea to J. Chamberlain, 23 June [1882] (JC/8/8/1/7).

45 J. Chamberlain to W. H. O'Shea, 28 June 1882 (JC/8/8/1/10).

46 W. E. Gladstone to Katharine O'Shea, 23 May 1882 (J. L. Hammond, *Gladstone and the Irish nation*, p. 296).

47 Viscount Gladstone, *After thirty years* (London, 1928), pp. 295–305.

48 K. O'Shea, i, 269–75; ii, chap. 1.

49 A. G. Gardiner, *The life of Sir William Harcourt* (London, 1923), i, 447–88; J. L. Hammond, *Gladstone and the Irish nation*, pp. 298–300.

50 Sir W. Harcourt to W. E. Gladstone, 9 July 1882, copy (HP); Gardiner, *Harcourt*, i, 451–2.

51 J. L. Hammond, *Gladstone and the Irish nation*, p. 304.

52 H. Le Caron, *Twenty-five years in the secret service*, pp. 262–4; *DPB*, ii, 232–3.

53 C. Cruise O'Brien, *Parnell and his party*, p. 135, *n.* 4.

54 *FJ*, 18 October 1882; M. Davitt, *Fall of feudalism*, p. 373.

55 W. E. Gladstone to Earl Spencer, 29 August 1882 (SP).

56 Parnell to John Dillon, 9 August 1882 (DP).

57 *Spec. Comm. Proc.*, vii, 50–1.

58 Parnell to John Dillon, 11 August 1882 (DP).

59 *New York World*, 21 July 1882.

60 *FJ*, 25 September 1911; T. W. Moody, 'Anna Parnell and the Land League', in *Hermathena*, No. cxvii, Summer 1974, p. 9.

61 Parnell to Katharine O'Shea, 20 August 1882 (K. O'Shea, ii, 51).

62 W. E. Gladstone to Earl Spencer, 29 August 1882 (SP).

63 *UI*, 29 July 1882.

64 F. S. L. Lyons, *John Dillon*, pp. 67–8.

65 *UI*, 12 and 26 August 1882.

66 M. Davitt, *Fall of feudalism*, pp. 370–1.

67 F. S. L. Lyons, *John Dillon*, pp. 68–70.

68 C. E. H. Vincent to Sir William Harcourt, 11 May 1882 (HP).

69 *UI*, 27 May 1882.

70 *UI*, 10 June 1882.

71 *UI*, 17 June 1882.

72 William O'Brien, *Recollections*, p. 445.

73 *UI*, 24 June 1882.

74 *UI*, 8 July 1882.

75 *UI*, 8 July 1882.

76 T. N. Brown, *Irish-American nationalism*, pp. 129–30.

77 F. S. L. Lyons, *John Dillon*, p. 69.

78 W. O'Brien, *Recollections*, p. 458; M. Davitt, *Fall of feudalism*, p. 371.

79 T. M. Healy, *Letters and leaders*, i, 169–70.

80 *FJ*, 18 October 1882.

81 M. Davitt, *Fall of feudalism*, pp. 377–8.

CHAPTER 8: GATHERING PACE

1 Parnell to Katharine O'Shea, 10 and 14 October 1882 (K. O'Shea, ii, 52).

2 Sir Edward Clarke, *The story of my life* (London, 1918), pp. 286, 291.

3 H. Harrison, *Parnell vindicated*, pp. 215–16.

4 *The Times*, 17 November 1890; K. O'Shea, ii, 66–8.

5 *The Times*, 17 November 1890.

6 H. Harrison, op. cit., pp. 296–303.

7 *The Times*, 17 November 1890.

8 *The Times*, 17 November 1890.

9 T. P. O'Connor, *Parnell*, pp. 144–5.

10 Parnell to Katharine O'Shea, 'Tuesday', but from internal evidence belonging to July 1883 (K. O'Shea, ii, 64–5).

11 Hansard, H. C. deb., 3s, cclxxvi, cols. 607–33 (22 February 1883).

12 K. O'Shea, ii, 60.

13 Hansard, H. C. deb., 3s, cclxxvi, cols. 716–25 (23 February 1883); F. H. O'Donnell, *History of the Irish parliamentary party*, ii, 147–8.

14 *UI*, 16 December 1882; R. F. Foster, *Charles Stewart Parnell, the man and his family*, p. 190.

15 *UI*, 23 December 1882; *Nation*, 31 January 1885.

16 Unpublished article by Dom M. Tierney, 'Dr Croke, Rome and the Parnell Testimonial Fund, January to June 1883', p. 6. I am much indebted to Dom Tierney for his kindness in letting me have a copy of the typescript of his article. See also C. J. Woods, 'Ireland and Anglo-Papal relations', in *IHS*, xviii, No. 69 (March 1972), 29–60.

17 *Nation*, 3 March 1883; *UI*, 10 March 1883.

18 *UI*, 10 March 1883.

19 M. Tierney, loc. cit., p. 2.

20 ibid., pp. 4–6.

21 ibid., pp. 10–14; C. J. Woods, loc. cit.; E. Larkin, *The Roman Catholic Church and the creation of the modern Irish state*, pp. 183–94.

22 *UI*, 15 December 1883; *Nation*, 31 January 1885. The precise figure was £37,883–15–10.

23 R. B. O'Brien, i, 11.

24 *UI*, 15 December 1883.

25 T. M. Healy, *Letters and leaders*, i, 194.

26 *DPB*, ii, 180.

27 *Nation*, 5 May 1883.

28 E. G. Jenkinson, 'Memorandum', 26 January 1885 (HP); the convention is described in graphic detail in H. Le Caron, *Twenty-five years in the secret service*, pp. 213–16.

29 *Spec. Comm. Proc.*, vi, 326; C. Cruise O'Brien, *Parnell and his party*, pp. 133–6.

30 T. N. Brown, *Irish-American nationalism*, p. 170.

31 ibid., pp. 170–1.

32 *UI*, 30 June 1883; T. M. Healy, *Letters and leaders*, i, 390–2; F. J. Higginbottom, *The vivid life: a journalist's career* (London, 1934), pp. 151–2.

33 *UI*, 1 September 1883.

34 *Nation*, 23 February 1884.

35 *Nation*, 1 March 1884.

36 *Nation*, 2 August 1884.

37 *Nation*, 6 December 1884.

38 *UI*, 10 February 1883.

39 *UI*, 7 April 1883. Four counties, including Queen's, had launched funds by January 1884 (*Nation*, 26 January 1884).

40 *UI*, 19 May 1883.

41 *Nation*, 17 January 1885.

42 Parnell to Archbishop Croke, 18 December 1884 (Croke Papers, NLI microfilm, p. 6011).

43 *Nation*, 10 January 1885.

44 W. L. Arnstein, *The Bradlaugh case*, chap. 19.

45 Dr W. J. Walsh to Cardinal McCabe, 12 February 1884 (DDA).

46 H. Bellingham to Cardinal McCabe, 30 May 1884 (DDA).

47 F. H. O'Donnell to Cardinal McCabe, 4 August [1884] (DDA).

48 Dr A. Higgins to Cardinal McCabe, 26 March [?1884] (DDA).

49 Parnell to the Bishops of Ardagh and Clonmacnoise (Dr Woodlock) and Raphoe (Dr Michael Logue), 31 October 1884 (DDA); see also *Nation*, 4 October 1884, which gives the date of the bishops' meeting as 30 September.

50 *Nation*, 4 October 1884.

51 *Nation*, 14 February 1885.

52 P. J. Walsh, *William J. Walsh: Archbishop of Dublin* (Dublin, 1928), chap. 7. See also C. J. Woods, loc. cit., pp. 57–8; E. Larkin, *The Roman Catholic Church and the creation of the modern Irish state*, pp. 253–301.

53 C. Cruise O'Brien, *Parnell and his party*, pp. 126–9.

54 ibid., pp. 142–3.

55 *UI*, 23 December 1882, speech at Cork on 17 December.

56 *Nation*, 19 April 1884, speech at Cork on 15 April.

57 *UI*, 23 December 1882.

58 *UI*, 31 March 1883.

59 *Nation*, 17 January 1885.

60 *Nation*, 24 January 1885, speech at Cork on 21 January. For the significance of this speech in the evolution of his thought, see F. S. L. Lyons, 'The political ideas of Parnell', in *The Historical Journal*, xvi, 4 (1973), 749–75.

61 R. B. O'Brien, ii, 40.

62 The lecture is in the *Nation*, 31 January 1885.

63 *UI*, 15 December 1883; *Nation*, 29 March 1884.

64 *UI*, 23 December 1882, speech at Cork on 17 December.

65 *Nation*, 22 March 1884, speech in London on St Patrick's night.

66 Sir W. Harcourt to Earl Spencer, 29 January 1883, copy (HP). For cabinet attitudes to Irish local government see Sir E. Hamilton, *Diary*, 24 January 1883 (Bahlman, ii, 392–3); also A. Ramm, (ed.) *The political correspondence of Mr Gladstone and Lord Granville, 1876–1886* (Oxford, 1962), ii, 9–13 (hereafter cited as A. Ramm).

67 Parnell to W. H. Smith, 26 August 1883 (Hambleden Papers, PS 8/60–61).

68 W. H. Smith to Parnell, 19 September 1883 (ibid.).

69 Parnell to W. H. Smith, 20 September and 29 October 1883 (ibid.).

70 *Nation*, 24 May and 7 June 1884.

71 F. S. L. Lyons, 'The economic ideas of Parnell', in M. Roberts (ed.), *Historical Studies* (London, 1959), ii, 68.

72 Cited in A. Jones, *The politics of reform, 1884* (Cambridge, 1972), p. 83.

73 *UI*, 21 October 1882.

74 *Nation*, 31 January 1885.

75 *UI*, 15 December 1883.

76 *Nation*, 29 March 1884.

77 E. W. Hamilton, *Diary*, 16 January 1884 (Bahlman, ii, 545); E. W. Hamilton to W. E. Gladstone, 17 January 1884 (BM, Add. MS 44, 190, f. 6).

78 E. W. Hamilton, *Diary*, 23 January 1884 (Bahlman, ii, 54).

79 W. E. Gladstone to G. O. Trevelyan, 23 October 1883, cited in A. Jones, op. cit., p. 21.

80 *UI*, 26 August and 23 December 1882; *Nation*, 19 April 1884.

81 For these arguments see A. Jones, op. cit., pp. 21–3.

82 C. J. Kickham to P. J. Quinn, 27 May 1882 (NLI MS 5930).

83 A. Jones, op. cit., pp. 85–6.

84 J. L. Hammond, *Gladstone and the Irish question*, p. 313.

85 J. Chamberlain to W. H. O'Shea, 2 and 15 August 1883 (JC/8/8/1/16, 18).

86 Parnell to J. Chamberlain, 10 April 1884 (JC/8/6/32/1).

87 C. Cruise O'Brien, *Parnell and his party*, p. 90.

88 C. H. D. Howard (ed.), 'Documents relating to the Irish "central board" scheme, 1884–5', in *IHS*, viii, No. 31 (March 1953), 237–63 (hereafter cited as C. H. D. Howard, 'Documents'); C. H. D. Howard, 'Joseph Chamberlain, Parnell and the Irish "central board" scheme, 1884–5', in *IHS*, viii, No. 32 (September 1953), 324–61 (hereafter cited as C. H. D. Howard, 'Central board scheme').

89 C. H. D. Howard, 'Documents', p. 240; 'Central board scheme', p. 328.

90 C. H. D. Howard, 'Documents', pp. 240–2; 'Central board scheme', p. 333.

91 Printed subsequently in *The Times*, 13 August 1888.

92 Parnell to W. H. O'Shea, 13 January 1885 (C. H. D. Howard 'Documents', p. 245).

93 Parnell to W. H. O'Shea, 5 January 1885 (ibid., p. 242).

94 W. H. O'Shea to Parnell, 6 January 1885 and Parnell to W. H. O'Shea, 13 January 1885 (ibid., pp. 243, 245–6).

95 Parnell to W. H. O'Shea, 13 January 1885 (ibid., pp. 245–6).

96 J. Chamberlain, *Political memoir*, pp. 138–9.

97 C. H. D. Howard, 'Central board scheme', p. 336.

98 J. Chamberlain, *Political memoir*, p. 141.

99 W. H. O'Shea to Parnell, 19 January 1885 (C. H. D. Howard, 'Documents', pp. 246–8).

100 C. H. D. Howard, 'Central board scheme', p. 337.

101 ibid., pp. 339–41.

102 S. Gwynn and G. Tuckwell, *The life of the Rt. Hon. Sir Charles W. Dilke*, ii, 129. See also E. Larkin, *The Roman Catholic Church and the creation of the modern Irish state*, pp. 278–83.

103 C. H. D. Howard, 'Documents', pp. 255–7.

104 Cardinal Manning to J. Chamberlain, 4 May 1885 (ibid., p. 262).

105 Cardinal Manning to J. Chamberlain, 23 June 1886 (C. H. D. Howard, 'Central board scheme', p. 346).

106 O'Shea's diary, 28 April 1885 (C. H. D. Howard, 'Documents', p. 259).

107 O'Shea's diary, 29–30 April 1885 (ibid., pp. 259–60).

108 O'Shea's note of interview with Parnell, 30 April 1885 (ibid., p. 261).

109 S. Gwynn and G. Tuckwell, op. cit., ii, 132.

110 ibid., ii, 132; J. Chamberlain, *Political memoir*, p. 149.

111 For a discussion of Chamberlain's possible aims, see A. B. Cooke and John Vincent, *The governing passion* (The Harvester Press, Brighton, 1974), pp. 32–5.

112 J. Chamberlain, *Political memoir*, p. 150.

CHAPTER 9: TOWARDS THE FULCRUM

1 E. W. Hamilton, *Diary*, 24 February 1885 (Bahlman, ii, 800).

2 E. W. Hamilton, *Diary*, 27 February 1885 (ibid., ii, 802).

3 E. W. Hamilton, *Diary*, 28 February 1885 (Bahlman, ii, 803).

4 R. Winn to Lord Salisbury, 28 February 1885, enclosing a memorandum of his interview with Parnell held on 27 February (Salisbury Papers).

5 E. W. Hamilton, *Diary*, 3 and 7 March 1885 (ibid., ii, 805–8). For other Liberal suspicions of a Tory-Parnellite pact, see A. B. Cooke and John Vincent, *The governing passion*, pp. 68–9, and sources there quoted.

6 *Nation*, 21 March 1885.

7 R. B. O'Brien, ii, 42; J. J. Horgan, *Parnell to Pearse*, p. 30.

8 *Nation*, 18 April 1885.

9 *Nation*, 21 March 1885.

10 C. Cruise O'Brien, *Parnell and his party*, p. 134.

11 W. S. Churchill, *Lord Randolph Churchill* (London, 1906), i, 391, 395; S. Gwynn and G. Tuckwell, *Life of Sir Charles W. Dilke*, ii, 133.

12 *The Times*, 21 May 1885.

13 J. Morley, *Gladstone*, iii, 152.

14 A. B. Cooke and John Vincent, op. cit., pp. 249–52.

15 Cited in J. L. Hammond, *Gladstone and the Irish nation*, p. 373, *n*. 1.

16 A. B. Cooke and J. Vincent, op. cit., p. 252.

17 R. Winn to Salisbury, 20 June 1885 (Salisbury Papers); also A. B. Cooke and John Vincent (ed.), 'Ireland and party politics, 1885–7; an unpublished Conservative memoir', in *IHS*, xvi, No. 62 (September 1968), 157, *n*. 6.

18 A. A. Hardinge, *The life of Henry Howard Molyneux Herbert, fourth Earl of Carnarvon, 1831–1890* (London, 1925, hereafter cited as *Life of Carnarvon*), iii, 151; J. L. Hammond, op. cit., pp. 376–7.

19 A. B. Cooke and J. Vincent, *The governing passion*, pp. 71–3.

20 Carnarvon to Salisbury (copy), 1 July 1885 (PRO 30, 6/53); A. B. Cooke and J. Vincent, 'Ireland and party politics, 1885–7', in *IHS*, xvi, No. 62 (September 1968), 157–8.

21 A. B. Cooke and J. Vincent, *The governing passion*, p. 271.

22 Justin McCarthy, *Reminiscences*, ii, 111–12; S. H. Jeyes and F. D. How, *The life of Sir Howard Vincent* (London, 1912), chap. 10.

23 Justin McCarthy and R. M. Praed, *Our book of memories* (London, 1913), p. 12.

24 Lady C. Cecil, *Life of Robert, Marquis of Salisbury* (London, 1921–31), iii, 154–5.

25 Hansard, H. C. deb., 3s, ccxcix, cols. 1064–83 (17 July 1885); *Nation*, 25 July 1885. For the background, see A. B. Cooke and J. Vincent, *The governing passion*, pp. 276–9.

26 *Nation*, 15 August 1885.

27 Sir A. Hardinge, *Life of Carnarvon*, iii, 178–81.

28 Carnarvon to Salisbury, 23 June 1886 (Hardinge, op. cit., iii, 178) and 20 March 1890 (Salisbury Papers). Carnarvon's recollection was that three ministers knew of the interview.

29 Sir A. Hardinge, *Life of Carnarvon*, iii, 178–81; L. P. Curtis, *Coercion and conciliation in Ireland*, pp. 49–52, 115.

30 J. McCarthy, *Reminiscences*, ii, 112–13; R. B. O'Brien, ii, 52.

31 Hansard, H. C. deb., 3s, cccvi, cols. 1181, 1199, 1200 (7 June 1886); L. P. Curtis, jr., *Coercion and conciliation in Ireland, 1880–92* (Princeton, 1963), p. 114.

32 Hansard, H. L. deb., 3s, cccvi, cols. 1256–60 (10 June 1886).

33 *The Times*, 12 June 1886; R. B. O'Brien, ii, 55–7.

34 *The Times*, 13 and 14 June 1886, for the continuing correspondence.

35 A. B. Cooke and J. Vincent, *The governing passion*, p. 282.

36 C. Cruise O'Brien, *Parnell and his party*, pp. 99–100.

37 Sir A. Hardinge, *Life of Carnarvon*, iii, 161.

38 J. L. Garvin, ii, 11.

39 W. H. O'Shea to Chamberlain, 28 and 29 June (J. L. Garvin, ii, 19–20).

40 J. Chamberlain, *Political memoir*, p. 157.

41 S. Gwynn and G. Tuckwell, *Life of Sir Charles Dilke*, ii, 152 *n*; C. Cruise O'Brien, *Parnell and his party*, p. 101, *n*. 4.

42 W. S. Blunt, *The land war in Ireland*, p. 12; A. B. Cooke and J. Vincent, *The governing passion*, pp. 74–6.

43 W. E. Gladstone to Earl Spencer, 6 July 1885 (SP); *The Times*, 13 August 1888; J. Chamberlain, *Political memoir*, pp. 140–1.

44 W. E. Gladstone to Lord R. Grosvenor, 6 July 1885 (BM, Add. MS 44, 316, f. 5).

45 Lord R. Grosvenor to Mrs K. O'Shea, 14 July 1885 (ibid., f. 14).

46 *The Times*, 15 July 1885.

47 Mrs K. O'Shea to Lord R. Grosvenor, 15 July [1885] (BM, Add. MS 44, 316, ff. 18–19).

48 Lord R. Grosvenor to W. E. Gladstone, 23 and 28 July 1885 (ibid., ff. 20, 21).

49 Mrs K. O'Shea to W. E. Gladstone, 5 August 1886 (BM, Add. MS 56, 446, no folio number). This letter was not available to J. L. Hammond, when he described the negotiations in *Gladstone and the Irish nation*, p. 421.

50 W. E. Gladstone to Mrs K. O'Shea, 8 August 1885 (J. L. Hammond, *Gladstone and the Irish nation*, p. 421).

51 J. McCarthy and R. M. Praed, *Our book of memories*, p. 15.

52 *Nation*, 25 July 1885, speech in London on 22 July.

53 R. B. O'Brien, ii, 45.

54 A. L. Thorold, *The life of Henry Labouchere*, pp. 230–2.

55 *Nation*, 25 July 1885.

56 *Nation*, 29 August 1885.

57 W. H. O'Shea to J. Chamberlain, 3 September 1885 (JC 8/8/1/56).

58 *The Times*, 31 August and 9 September 1885, for speeches by Hartington at Waterfoot on 30 August and by Chamberlain at Warrington on 8 September.

59 W. H. O'Shea to J. Chamberlain, 3 September 1885 (JC 8/8/1/56).

60 *Nation*, 5 September 1885.

61 W. E. Gladstone to Earl Granville, 9 September 1885 (A. Ramm, ii, 392–3).

62 *The Times*, 18 September 1885.

63 *FJ*, 21 August 1885.

64 *The Times*, 9 September 1885.

64a For the controversy, contemporary and subsequent, aroused by the protectionist issue, see C. Cruise O'Brien, *Parnell and his party*, pp. 109–13.

65 *Nation*, 10 October 1885, speech at Wicklow on 5 October.

66 W. E. Gladstone to Earl Granville, 10 October 1885 (A. Ramm, ii, 408).

67 *Nation*, 17 October 1885, speech at Kildare on 10 October; W. E. Gladstone to Earl Granville, 22 October 1885 (A. Ramm, ii, 421).

68 A. B. Cooke and J. Vincent (ed.), 'Ireland and party politics, 1885–7', in *IHS*, xvi, No. 62 (September 1968), 163.

69 Earl of Carnarvon to Sir M. Hicks Beach, 23 September 1885 (PRO 30, 6/53); A. B. Cooke and J. Vincent, *The governing passion*, pp. 286–7.

70 *The Times*, 8 October 1885.

71 R. B. O'Brien, ii, 101–6.

72 M. Davitt to H. Labouchere, 9 October 1885 (A. L. Thorold, *The life of Henry Labouchere*, p. 234).

73 T. M. Healy to H. Labouchere, 15 October 1885 (ibid., pp. 235–6).

74 J. L. Hammond, *Gladstone and the Irish nation*, pp. 422–3.

74a ibid., pp. 423–5.

75 *Nation*, 7 November 1885.

76 *Nation*, 14 November 1885, speech at Wexford on 5 November.

77 ibid., Salisbury's speech at Guildhall, 9 November.

78 ibid., Gladstone's speech at Edinburgh, 9 November.

79 ibid., Parnell's speech at Liverpool, 10 November.

80 *The Times*, 18 November 1885.

81 *Nation*, 28 November 1885.

82 J. L. Hammond, op. cit., p. 426.

83 Parnell to T. P. O'Connor, 16 November 1885 (NLI MS 15, 735).

84 *Nation*, 28 November 1885, speech at Liverpool, 22 November.

85 T. M. Healy, *Letters and leaders*, i, 213.

86 T. P. O'Connor, *Memoirs of an old parliamentarian*, ii, 9.

87 M. Davitt to H. Labouchere, 9 October 1885 (A. L. Thorold, *The life of Henry Labouchere*, p. 234).

88 *The Tablet*, 24 October 1885.

89 C. H. D. Howard, 'The Parnell manifesto of 21 November 1885 and the Schools Question', in *EHR*, 1 x 11 (January 1947).

90 V. A. McClelland, *Cardinal Manning, his public life and influence*, 1865–92, pp. 187–90; M. Hurst, *Parnell and Irish nationalism* (London, 1968), pp. 104–7.

91 C. Cruise O'Brien, *Parnell and his party*, pp. 115–18.

92 W. H. O'Shea to J. Chamberlain, 28 June [1885] (JC 8/8/1/47).

93 J. L. Hammond, *Gladstone and the Irish nation*, pp. 425–6.

94 W. O'Brien, *Evening memories*, pp. 91–2; M. Davitt, *Fall of feudalism*, p. 481.

95 A. L. Thorold, op. cit., p. 231.

96 ibid., pp. 235–6.

97 M. Davitt, *Fall of feudalism*, p. 481.

98 J. Morley, *Gladstone*, iii, 184; J. L. Garvin, ii, 189.

99 *Nation*, 19 December 1885.

100 *Nation*, 12 December 1885.
101 *Nation*, 12 December 1885.
102 *Nation*, 5 December 1885.
103 T. M. Healy, *Letters and leaders*, i, 230–1.
104 ibid., i, 190–1, 231; T. P. O'Connor, *Memoirs of an old parliamentarian*, ii, 17–19.
105 A. J. Kettle, *The materials for victory*, pp. 67–8.
106 *Nation*, 5 December 1885.
107 *Irish Times*, 4 December 1885.
108 *Nation*, 12 December 1885.
109 K. O'Shea, ii, 26–9.
110 Viscount Gladstone, *After thirty years*, pp. 396–8.
111 ibid., chap. 7.
112 J. McCarthy, *Reminiscences*, ii, 113; also Carnarvon's memorandum of this conversation, cited in A. B. Cooke and J. Vincent, *The governing passion*, pp. 291–2.
113 T. M. Healy, *Letters and leaders*, i, 236.
114 J. McCarthy and R. M. Praed, *Our book of memories*, p. 28 ('December', 1888).
115 A. B. Cooke and J. Vincent, *The governing passion*, p. 296.
116 Parnell to Healy, 17 December 1885 (*Letters and leaders*, i, 237).
117 J. Chamberlain to Parnell, 22 January 1886 (J. L. Garvin, ii, 167).
118 A. L. Thorold, *The life of Henry Labouchere*, p. 250.
119 ibid., p. 251.

CHAPTER 10: THE GALWAY 'MUTINY'

1 *Nation*, 9 February 1884.
2 *Nation*, 21 June 1884.
3 K. O'Shea, ii, 200.
4 *Spec. Comm. Proc.*, i, 361–2, evidence of Captain O'Shea.
5 ibid., ii, 85.
6 W. H. O'Shea to Katharine O'Shea, undated letter [1885] (ibid., ii, 205).
7 W. H. O'Shea to Katharine O'Shea, 17 March 1885 (ibid., ii, 206).
8 W. H. O'Shea to Katharine O'Shea, 4 May 1885 and undated letter probably belonging to late June or early July (ibid., ii, 205–6, 209). The latter communication is placed out of sequence in Mrs O'Shea's book and was misdated by Henry Harrison (*Parnell vindicated*, pp. 356–7) as March 1885. This is wrong, because it contains an aggrieved reference to the attack made by *United Ireland* on the proposed visit to Ireland of Chamberlain and Dilke. Since this appeared on 27 June, the letter must have been written after that date.
9 H. Harrison, *Parnell vindicated*, p. 358.

10 W. H. O'Shea to Katharine O'Shea, 'Tuesday' [late June 1885] (K. O'Shea, ii, 212–13).

11 W. H. O'Shea to J. Chamberlain, 3 September 1885 (JC 8/8/1/56).

12 W. H. O'Shea to J. Chamberlain, 5 September 1885 (JC 8/8/1/58).

13 T. P. O'Connor, *Parnell*, pp. 158–9.

14 Parnell to Katharine O'Shea, 23 October 1885 and W. H. O'Shea to Katharine O'Shea, 19 November 1885 (K. O'Shea, ii, 85–6, 101).

15 Katharine O'Shea to Lord R. Grosvenor, 23 October 1885 (BM, Add. MS 44, 316, ff. 63–7).

16 W. E. Gladstone to Lord R. Grosvenor, 24 October 1885 (ibid., f. 69).

17 W. H. O'Shea to Lord R. Grosvenor, 25 October 1885 (ibid., ff. 70–1).

18 W. H. O'Shea to J. Chamberlain, n.d. [25 October 1885] (JC 8/8/1/61).

19 W. H. O'Shea to J. Chamberlain, 28 October 1885 (JC 8/8/1/62).

20 Lord R. Grosvenor to W. E. Gladstone, 26 October 1885; W. E. Gladstone to Lord R. Grosvenor, 28 October 1885 (BM, Add. MS 44, 316, ff. 72–3, 75–6).

21 Lord R. Grosvenor to W. E. Gladstone, 28 October 1885 (ibid., ff. 77–8).

22 S. Walker to Lord R. Grosvenor, 29 and 21 October 1885 and 1 November 1885 (ibid., ff. 80–1, 82–3, 84–5).

23 W. H. O'Shea to Lord R. Grosvenor, n.d. [end of October 1885?] (ibid., f. 79).

24 K. O'Shea, ii, 87.

25 W. H. O'Shea to Katharine O'Shea, 2 November 1885 (K. O'Shea, ii, 90).

26 Lord R. Grosvenor to W. E. Gladstone, 26 October 1885 (BM, Add. MS 44, 316, ff. 72–3).

27 W. H. O'Shea to J. Chamberlain, 8 November 1885 (JC 8/8/1/64).

28 W. E. Gladstone to Lord R. Grosvenor, 18 November 1885 (BM, Add. MS 44, 316, ff. 111–13).

29 K. O'Shea, ii, 96–7.

30 *Nation*, 28 November 1885.

31 K. O'Shea, ii, 98–9.

32 E. R. Russell to W. E. Gladstone, 22 November 1890 (BM, Add. MS 56, 446).

33 K. O'Shea, ii, 99–100.

34 W. H. O'Shea to Katharine O'Shea, 22 December 1885 (K. O'Shea, ii, 214).

35 K. O'Shea, ii, 105.

36 ibid., ii, 234; J. L. Garvin, ii, 382.

37 J. Chamberlain to E. D. Gray, 18 December 1885 and Parnell to E. D. Gray, 24 December 1885 (T. W. Moody (ed.), 'Parnell and the Galway election of 1886', in *IHS*, ix, No. 35 (March 1955), 331–3; hereafter cited as T. W. Moody, 'The Galway election').

38 E. D. Gray to Parnell, 26 December 1885 (ibid., 333–5).

39 K. O'Shea, ii, 107; T. P. O'Connor, *Parnell*, p. 160 and *Memoirs*, ii, 94.

40 T. P. O'Connor, *Memoirs*, ii, 94.

41 T. M. Healy, *Letters and leaders*, i, 239.

42 ibid., i, 243–4, where the date is wrongly given as 8 February.

43 *FJ*, 29 December 1890.

44 T. M. Healy, *Letters and leaders*, i, 240.

45 T. P. O'Connor, *Parnell*, p. 166.

46 T. W. Moody, 'The Galway election', pp. 335–7. Biggar's letter is mistakenly dated 5 February, on which day he was still in London.

47 As Chamberlain had quickly discovered (J. Chamberlain, *Political memoir*, p. 154).

48 H. Harrison, *Parnell vindicated*, p. 362.

49 R. B. O'Brien, ii, 123–4.

50 T. M. Healy, *Letters and leaders*, ii, 242.

51 T. W. Moody, 'The Galway election', pp. 324–5.

52 T. P. O'Connor, *Memoirs*, ii, 101.

53 ibid., ii, 104.

54 T. W. Moody, 'The Galway election', pp. 325–6.

55 T. M. Healy, *Letters and leaders*, i, 241–2.

56 T. W. Moody, 'The Galway election', p. 337 *n*; C. Cruise O'Brien, *Parnell and his party*, p. 177.

57 F. S. L. Lyons, *John Dillon*, pp. 77–8.

58 T. W. Moody, 'The Galway election', p. 327.

59 T. M. Healy, *Letters and leaders*, i, 242.

60 T. M. Healy to W. O'Brien, 7 February 1886 (W. O'Brien Papers, Cork collection, Box AA).

61 K. O'Shea, ii, 228–33.

62 T. W. Moody, 'The Galway election', p. 326.

63 T. M. Healy, *Letters and leaders*, i, 241.

64 *FJ*, 8 February 1886.

65 C. Cruise O'Brien, *Parnell and his party*, pp. 179–80.

66 *FJ*, 9 February 1886.

67 *FJ*, 9 February 1886. For Archbishop Walsh's view, see T. W. Moody, 'The Galway election', p. 337.

68 *Nation*, 13 February 1886; C. Cruise O'Brien, op. cit., pp. 178 *n* 1, 180, *n* 3.

69 T. M. Healy to W. O'Brien, 8 February 1886 (W. O'Brien Papers, Cork collection, Box AA).

70 T. P. O'Connor, *Parnell*, pp. 170–1; *Memoirs*, ii, 98. The recollection of the journalist, Thomas Marlowe, which O'Connor prints in his *Memoirs*, ii, 103–5, that Parnell arrived on 10 February is incorrect.

71 *Galway Express*, 13 February 1886.

72 T. P. O'Connor, *Parnell*, pp. 173–4.

73 T. P. O'Connor, *Memoirs*, ii, 100.

74 T. P. O'Connor, *Parnell*, p. 175, and *Memoirs*, ii, 105.

75 C. Cruise O'Brien, *Parnell and his party*, pp. 181–2.

76 R. B. O'Brien, ii, 127.

77 T. P. O'Connor, *Parnell*, p. 175.

78 C. Cruise O'Brien, *Parnell and his party*, p. 182.

79 *FJ*, 10 February 1886; T. W. Moody, 'The Galway election', p. 326, *n. 22*.

80 *Galway Express*, 13 February 1886; C. Cruise O'Brien, *Parnell and his party*, p. 182.

81 *FJ*, 13–18 May 1886; K. O'Shea, ii, 230–1.

82 *Galway Express*, 13 February 1886.

83 Cited in C. Cruise O'Brien, op. cit., p. 183, *n. 2*.

84 W. S. Blunt, 'Diary', 12 February 1886 (*The land war in Ireland*, pp. 28–9).

85 F. H. O'Donnell, *History of the Irish parliamentary party*, ii, 167.

86 *Spec. Comm. Proc.*, i, 343.

87 *The Times*, 18 November 1890.

88 *The Times*, 17 November 1890.

89 *Spec. Comm. Proc.*, i, 367.

90 *FJ*, 30 December 1889.

91 W. S. Blunt, 'Diary', 25 February 1886 (*The land war in Ireland*, p. 33).

92 *Pall Mall Gazette*, 24 May 1886.

93 *The Times*, 17 November 1890.

94 For the letter and the hypothesis, see H. Harrison, *Parnell vindicated*, pp. 267–81.

95 Katharine O'Shea to W. E. Gladstone, 16 April [1886] (BM, Add. MS 56, 446); Gladstone's note on the back of this letter is dated 16 April 1886.

96 See the transcripts, in shorthand and longhand, of fragments of what appear to be a letter from him of 23 April (possibly a misreading of August) 1886 and one from her dated 25 August 1886. The provenance of these letters is not known, but the transcripts are in the first of two bound volumes of F. J. Tuohy letters in the National Library, Dublin (NLI MS 8882). Other letters of a similar type are printed in the divorce proceedings reported by *The Times*, 17 November 1890.

97 *The Times*, 17 November 1890.

98 *Pall Mall Gazette*, 18 December 1886; *Review of Reviews* (November 1890), ii, 599–601.

99 Katharine O'Shea to W. H. O'Shea, copy of part of letter dated 25 August 1886 (NLI MS 8882).

CHAPTER 11: THE VIEW FROM PISGAH

1 Archbishop W. J. Walsh to W. E. Gladstone, 17 February 1886 (BM, Add. MS 56, 446); E. Larkin, *The Roman Catholic Church and the modern Irish state*, pp. 362–4.

2 *FJ*, 17 February 1886, speech in Dublin.

3 W. E. Gladstone to Mrs K. O'Shea, 29 January 1886, secret, copy (BM, Add. MS 56, 446).

4 Mrs K. O'Shea to W. E. Gladstone, 25 March 1886, secret (BM, Add. MS 56, 446).

5 J. McCarthy and R. M. Praed, *Our book of memories*, p. 33.

6 T. M. Healy, *Letters and leaders of my day*, 1, 234.

7 ibid., 1, 254; T. P. O'Connor, *Parnell*, p. 182 and *Memoirs*, ii, 31; W. O'Brien, *Evening memories*, p. 111; M. Davitt, *Fall of feudalism*, pp. 489–90.

8 J. Morley, *Gladstone*, iii, 231.

9 W. O'Brien, *Evening memories*, pp. 108–9.

10 J. McCarthy and R. M. Praed, *Our book of memories*, p. 35.

11 T. M. Healy, *Letters and leaders*, i, 251; M. Davitt, *Fall of feudalism*, pp. 490–1.

12 J. Morley, *Gladstone*, iii, 241, *n*. 3.

13 W. O'Brien, *Evening memories*, pp. 109–10.

14 J. Morley, *Gladstone*, iii, 231.

15 'Minutes of the Irish parliamentary party', 8 April 1886 (cited in C. Cruise O'Brien, *Parnell and his party*, p. 186).

16 Hansard, H. C. deb., 3s, ccciv, cols. 1124-34 (8 April 1886).

17 *The Times*, 14 May 1886.

18 A. B. Cooke and J. Vincent, *The governing passion*, pp. 407–8.

19 J. L. Hammond, *Gladstone and the Irish nation*, pp. 526–7.

20 A. L. Thorold, *The life of Henry Labouchere*, p. 301; W. O'Brien, *Evening memories*, p. 122.

21 J. Morley, *Gladstone*, iii, 252.

22 ibid., iii, 252.

23 W. O'Brien, *Evening memories*, p. 125.

24 J. Morley, *Gladstone*, iii, 255.

25 Hansard, H. C. deb., 3s, cccvi, cols. 1168-84.

26 P. O'Farrell, *Ireland's English question* (New York, 1971), p. 189. For a detailed exposition of this viewpoint, see chap. 10 of Professor O'Farrell's stimulating book.

27 *The Times*, 26 June 1886, speech at Portsmouth.

28 *The Times*, 28 June 1886, speech at Plymouth.

29 T. N. Brown, *Irish-American nationalism*, p. 111.

30 W. O'Brien, *Evening memories*, p. 145.

31 T. N. Brown, op. cit., p. 162.

CHAPTER 12: IN THE SHADOWS

1 *Report of the royal commission on the Land Law (Ireland) Act of 1881 and the Purchase of Land (Ireland) Act, 1885* [C.4969], HC 1887, xxvi, 9, para. 19.

2 C. Cruise O'Brien, *Parnell and his party*, pp. 197–8.

3 W. S. Blunt, *The land war in Ireland*, pp. 96, 137.

4 C. Cruise O'Brien, op. cit., p. 199.

5 J. Morley, *Gladstone*, iii, 279; J. McCarthy and R. M. Praed, *Our book of memories*, pp. 44–8.

6 *Irish Times*, 25 August 1886.

7 L. P. Curtis, *Coercion and conciliation in Ireland*, pp. 138–42.

8 W. E. Gladstone to Sir W. Harcourt, 7 and 10 September 1886 (HP).

9 *The Times*, 9 September 1886.

10 *UI*, 23 October 1886. A precedent of a kind had been set in the same area in January 1886, but it was premature and proved abortive (F. S. L. Lyons, 'John Dillon and the Plan of Campaign', in *IHS*, xiv, No. 56 (September 1965), p. 316, *n*. 9).

11 *UI*, 23 October 1886.

12 *Irish Times*, 4 September 1886.

13 T. M. Healy, *Letters and leaders*, i, 266–7. 'Bill' and 'Timmy' were of course William O'Brien and Healy himself.

14 R. B. O'Brien, ii, 160–1; K. O'Shea, ii, 114–16.

15 J. McCarthy and R. M. Praed, *Our book of memories*, pp. 101–8.

16 W. O'Brien, *Evening memories*, p. 187.

17 A. Robbins, *Parnell: the last five years*, pp. 197–8.

18 T. M. Healy, op. cit., 1, 266; M. Davitt, *Fall of feudalism*, pp. 517 et. seq.

19 R. B. O'Brien, ii, 171–2.

20 W. O'Brien, *Evening memories*, pp. 156–7.

21 *UI*, 2 October 1886.

22 *FJ*, 6 December 1886.

23 J. Morley, *Gladstone*, iii, 280.

24 W. O'Brien, *Evening memories*, pp. 177–8.

25 ibid., pp. 176–83.

26 J. Morley, *Gladstone*, iii, 281; F. S. L. Lyons, *John Dillon*, p. 87.

27 J. Morley, *Gladstone*, iii, 280.

28 J. Macdonald, *The Daily News Diary of the Parnell Commission* (London, 1890), pp. 145–50.

29 *The History of The Times, 1884–1912* (London, 1947), pp. 43–7.

30 ibid., p. 48.

31 *The Times*, 21 December 1886.

32 *The History of The Times, 1884–1912*, p. 48.

33 ibid., p. 48.
34 John Walter to J. C. Macdonald, 28 January 1887 (PHSP).
35 J. C. Macdonald to W. H. Smith, 27 January 1887, photostat copy (PHSP).
36 Henry Matthews to 'My dear Sir' (if not Macdonald, then probably either John Walter or George Buckle), 14 February and 12 April 1887 (PHSP).
37 *The Times*, 7 March 1887.
38 *The Times*, 8 February 1887.
39 *Nation*, 12 February 1887.
40 *Nation*, 5 March 1887.
41 *Nation*, 21 May 1887.
42 *Nation*, 11 June 1887.
43 *The Times*, 18 April 1887.
44 Statement by John Walter, undated, probably 1889 (PHSP).
45 *The History of The Times*, pp. 44, 46–8.
46 K. O'Shea, ii, 129–31.
47 R. B. O'Brien, ii, 198–9.
48 A. Robbins, *Parnell: the last five years*, p. 44.
49 J. McCarthy and R. M. Praed, *Our book of memories*, pp. 93–5.
50 Hansard, H. C. deb., 3s, cccxxviii, cols. 1225–32 (18 April 1887).
51 J. Morley, *Gladstone*, iii, 297.
52 J. McCarthy and R. M. Praed, *Our book of memories*, pp. 102–3.
53 *The Times*, 21 April 1887.
54 A. Robbins, *Parnell: the last five years*, p. 46.
55 J. McCarthy and R. Praed, *Our book of memories*, pp. 107–8.
56 A. Robbins, op. cit., p. 49.
57 L. P. Curtis, *Coercion and conciliation in Ireland*, chaps. 10–12.
58 F. S. L. Lyons, *John Dillon*, pp. 88–9.
59 C. Cruise O'Brien, *Parnell and his party*, pp. 208–9.
60 J. McCarthy and R. M. Praed, *Our book of memories*, pp. 115–16, 117.
61 *FJ*, 21 July 1887.
62 *FJ*, 14 September 1887.
63 J. McCarthy and R. M. Praed, op. cit., pp. 132–3.
64 *Nation*, 10 September 1887.
65 M. Moser (detective) to Joseph Soames, 22 November 1887 (PHSP), *The Times*, 26 November 1887; K. O'Shea, ii, 125.
66 *Nation*, 7, 14 and 21 January 1888.
67 *FJ*, 14 February 1888.
68 W. E. Gladstone, 'Memorandum of meeting with C. S. Parnell', 10 March 1888 (BM, Add. MS 44, 773, ff. 49–50).
69 J. McCarthy, *Reminiscences*, ii, 108–9.
70 For these events, see P. J. Walsh, *William J. Walsh, Archbishop of Dublin* (Dublin and Cork, 1928), chap. 13; P. J. Joyce, *John Healy, Archbishop of Tuam* (Dublin, 1931), chap. 5; C. Cruise O'Brien, *Parnell*

and his party, pp. 213–16; L. P. Curtis, *Coercion and conciliation in Ireland*, pp. 270–7.

71 L. P. Curtis, op. cit., pp. 270–2.

72 *FJ*, 27 and 30 April 1888.

73 C. Cruise O'Brien, *Parnell and his party*, pp. 213–25; F. S. L. Lyons, 'John Dillon and the Plan of Campaign', in *IHS*, xiv, No. 56 (September 1965), 326–9.

74 *FJ*, 8 May 1888.

75 C. Cruise O'Brien, op. cit., pp. 218–20.

76 *FJ*, 9 May 1888.

77 F. S. L. Lyons, *John Dillon*, p. 250.

78 Signed 'John Dillon, Wednesday night, 9 May 1888' (cited in C. Cruise O'Brien, *Parnell and his party*, p. 220 and *n*. 2).

79 *FJ*, 18 May 1888.

80 Archbishop Walsh, admittedly a shrewder tactician than most, took this line as early as July 1888 in a circular to his clergy accompanying a further, and milder, letter from Rome (P. J. Walsh, *William J. Walsh*, p. 367).

81 Sir J. West Ridgeway to A. J. Balfour, 10 May 1888 (BM, Add. MS 49, 808, f. 129).

82 John Dillon to T. C. Harrington, 12 December 1887 (DP).

83 *The Times*, 3, 4, 5 and 6 July 1888.

84 F. H. O'Donnell, *History of the Irish parliamentary party*, ii, 243–4, 258.

CHAPTER 13: IRELAND IN THE STRAND

1 J. Morley, *Gladstone*, iii, 299.

2 Hansard, H. C. deb., 3s, cccxxxviii, cols. 575–81 (6 July 1888).

3 J. Morley, *Gladstone*, iii, 298.

4 Sir W. Harcourt to John Morley, 6 July 1888 (HP, box II/B.1–4).

5 J. Morley, *Gladstone*, iii, 299.

6 J. McCarthy and R. Praed, *Our book of memories*, pp. 157–8.

7 Hansard, H. C. deb., 3s, cccxxxviii, cols. 712–13 (9 July 1888).

8 ibid., cols. 1101–2 (12 July 1888).

9 ibid., cols. 1495–1501 (17 July 1888).

10 For the considerations underlying the government's anxiety to avoid a select committee, see F. S. L. Lyons, 'Parnellism and crime, 1887–1890' in *Transactions of the Royal Historical Society*, 5th series, Vol. 24, 1974, 123–40.

11 Sir E. Clarke, *The story of my life*, p. 274.

12 J. L. Garvin, ii, 386.

13 ibid., ii, 387.

14 For the motivation of what he calls the Chamberlain-O'Shea combination, see H. Harrison, *Parnell, Joseph Chamberlain and Mr Garvin* (London, 1938), chap. 10. The omission from the official *History of The Times* of any reference to Chamberlain led Mr Harrison to draw attention to this and other deficiencies in the account there given as a result of which *The Times* eventually made honourable amends (*The History of the Times, 1921–1948* (London, 1952), pp. 1145–8); also H. Harrison, *Parnell, Joseph Chamberlain and The Times* (Dublin and Belfast, 1953).

15 W. S. Churchill, *Lord Randolph Churchill*, pp. 757–60. For other contemporary reactions, see L. P. Curtis, *Coercion and conciliation in Ireland*, pp. 280–1.

16 Hansard, H. C. deb., 3s, cccxxviii, cols. 1408–13 (16 July 1888).

17 ibid., cols. 1495–1501 (16 July 1888).

18 Hansard, H. C. deb., 3s, cccxxix, cols. 241–5 (23 July 1888).

19 ibid., cols. 245–56 (23 July 1888).

20 ibid., cols. 1012–15 (31 July 1888).

21 J. L. Garvin, ii, 387.

22 Hansard, H. C. deb., 3s, cccxxix, cols. 350–64 (23 July 1888).

23 *The Times*, 31 July 1888.

24 Sir Henry Lucy, *A diary of the Salisbury parliament 1886–92* (London, 1892), pp. 97–101; J. L. Garvin, ii, 388.

25 Hansard, H. C. deb., 3s, cccxxix, cols. 961–72; *The Times*, 1 August 1888.

26 For an example of Chamberlain's attitude towards cabinet secrecy, see H. Harrison, *Parnell, Joseph Chamberlain and Mr Garvin*, p. 51.

27 Note of visit from Captain O'Shea, 1 August 1888 (JC 8/8/1/92).

28 J. L. Garvin, ii, 391.

29 *The Times*, 2 August 1888.

30 H. Harrison, op. cit., p. 179.

31 *The Times*, 6 August 1888; the letter itself was dated 5 August.

32 *The Times*, 7 August 1888.

33 J. Chamberlain to J. Morley, copy, 21 January 1885 (C. H. D. Howard (ed.), 'Documents relating to the Irish "central board" scheme, 1884–5', in *IHS*, viii, No. 31 (March 1953), 249–51).

34 J. L. Garvin, ii, 391–2.

35 W. H. O'Shea to J. Chamberlain, 10 August 1888 (JC 8/8/1/96).

36 J. L. Garvin, ii, 392.

37 J. Chamberlain to W. H. O'Shea, copy, 11 August 1888 (JC 8/8/1/98).

38 *The Times*, 13 August 1888 (letter dated 11 August). Henry Harrison makes much play with this letter in his account of the episode, but this should be treated with caution since the version he gives in his text does not accord with the version, purporting to be complete, which he prints in an appendix (*Parnell, Joseph Chamberlain and Mr Garvin*, pp. 183, 246–8).

39 Hansard, H. C. deb., 3s, cccxxix, cols. 369–70 (23 July 1888).

40 Sir W. Harcourt to John Morley, 15 July 1888 (HP, box II B/1–4); Sir W. Harcourt to W. E. Gladstone, 18 [July] 1888 (BM, Add. MS 44, 201, ff. 210–11).

41 John Morley to W. E. Gladstone, 10 August 1888 (BM, Add. MS 44, 255, ff. 252–5).

42 W. E. Gladstone to John Morley, copy, 11 August 1888 (ibid., ff. 256–9).

43 John Morley to W. E. Gladstone, 24 August 1888 (ibid., ff. 264–5).

44 *Report of the Special Commission, 1888*, pp. 3–4, 123; for the charges, see T. W. Moody, '*The Times* versus Parnell and Co., 1887–90' in T. W. Moody (ed.), *Historical Studies* (London, 1968), vi, 147–82.

45 For his career, see R. B. O'Brien, *Lord Russell of Killowen* (London, 1904).

46 M. Davitt, *Fall of feudalism*, p. 547.

47 ibid., pp. 596–8.

48 Hansard, H. C. deb., 3s, cccxxviii, cols. 575–6 (6 July 1888).

49 F. H. O'Donnell, *History of the Irish parliamentary party*, ii, 226–7. During the debate on the second reading of the Special Commission Bill, Webster referred to the advice given to O'Donnell's counsel by two eminent lawyers, both Liberal MPs, and without saying that Russell was one of them he observed pointedly that Russell had sat silent whenever the point came up in the House (Hansard, H. C. deb., 3s, cccxxix, cols. 426–7 (24 July 1888)).

50 T. M. Healy, *Letters and leaders*, i, 287–94.

51 Sir R. Webster to W. H. Smith, n.d. [August 1888], cited in L. P. Curtis, *Coercion and conciliation in Ireland*, p. 281; Sir Edward Clarke, *The story of my life*, pp. 274–5.

52 L. P. Curtis, op. cit., p. 282.

53 Sir R. Webster to Lord Salisbury, 7 September 1888 (Salisbury Papers).

54 Viscount Alverstone (Sir Richard Webster), *Recollections of bar and bench*, pp. 144–5; Sir E. Clarke, *The story of my life*, pp. 274–5.

55 Lord Salisbury to A. J. Balfour, 20 September 1888 (Salisbury Papers).

56 A. J. Balfour to Lord Salisbury, 17 August 1888 (Salisbury Papers).

57 Salisbury to A. J. Balfour, 22 August 1888 (BM, Add. MS 49, 689, ff. 29–30).

58 R. A. Anderson, *The lighter side of my official life* (London, 1910), pp. 31–2, 111, 283–6; he disclosed his authorship in an article in *Blackwood's Magazine*, April 1910. For a discussion of his role, see L. ó Broin, *The prime informer* (London, 1971), chap. 10. The connection between Anderson and Le Caron can be followed in H. Le Caron, *Twenty-five years in the secret service*, pp. 60 et seq. and R. A. Anderson, *Sidelights on the Home Rule movement* (London, 1906), chap. 15.

59 L. P. Curtis, op. cit., p. 285.

60 Sir R. Webster to W. H. Smith, 6 January 1889 (Hambleden Papers).

61 These various forms of assistance are well summarized in T. W. Moody, '*The Times* versus Parnell and Co.', pp. 159–65. Much (though by no means all) of this evidence of government involvement depends upon the documents collected by Joyce, of which only copies of some remain, and on a memorandum written by him in 1910 when he was a disappointed and embittered man (NLI MS 11, 119); these materials form the subject of L. ó Broin's able study, *The prime informer*. But see also A. J. Balfour to Henry Matthews, 4 March 1889 (J. S. Sandars Papers) for Balfour's anxiety that officials in England, especially Anderson, should co-operate fully with Joyce.

62 *Spec. Comm. Proc.*, v, 254–332; J. Macdonald, *The Daily News diary of the Parnell Commission*, p. 141.

63 Sir J. West Ridgeway to A. J. Balfour, 9 and 15 November 1888 (L. P. Curtis, op. cit., p. 285).

64 P. Egan to M. Davitt, 26 August 1888 (M. Davitt, *Fall of feudalism*, p. 535).

65 ibid., p. 535; also A. L. Thorold, *The life of Henry Labouchere*, p. 346.

66 R. B. O'Brien, ii, 211–12.

67 A. L. Thorold, op. cit., pp. 341–2. Even about the offer of £5000 from *The Times* Pigott seems to have lied. According to the evidence of Joseph Soames, Pigott asked for £5000 from Houston, not from *The Times*, on the ground that if he did go into the witness-box, he could never again live in Ireland (J. Macdonald, *Daily News diary of the Parnell Commission*, p. 142).

68 *The History of The Times, 1884–1912*, p. 65.

69 M. Davitt, *Fall of feudalism*, p. 583.

70 ibid., p. 582.

71 J. Macdonald, op. cit., p. 142.

72 *Spec. Comm. Proc.*, ii, 9.

73 *Spec. Comm. Proc.*, v, 475–8; vi, 8–14.

74 A. L. Thorold, op. cit., pp. 344–6.

75 E. W. Hamilton, 'Diary', 14 December 1888 (BM, Add. MS 48, 650).

76 A. Robbins, *Parnell: the last five years*, p. 65.

77 ibid., pp. 76–7.

78 *Dublin Daily Express*, 2 November 1888.

79 *Spec. Comm. Proc.*, i, 357–8.

80 W. H. O'Shea to J. Chamberlain [23 August 1888] (JC 8/8/1/102). The letter is undated, but the postmark is 23 August and the text refers to the dinner of 22 August as having been 'last night'.

81 *Spec. Comm. Proc.*, i, 358, 360–1.

82 W. H. O'Shea to J. Chamberlain, 27 August [1888] (JC 8/8/1/106).

83 A. Robbins, op. cit., p. 71.

84 *Spec. Comm. Proc.*, i, 367.

85 ibid., i, 354, 379–80.

86 W. H. O'Shea to J. Chamberlain, 1 November 1888 (JC 8/8/1/114).

87 J. Macdonald, *The Daily News diary of the Parnell Commission*, pp. 132–3.

88 *Chicago Sunday Times*, 8 April 1895; see also J. Sweeney, *At Scotland Yard* (London, 1904), pp. 150–1.

89 J. Macdonald, *The Daily News diary of the Parnell Commission*, p. 143; *The History of The Times, 1884–1912*, pp. 69–71.

90 J. Macdonald, op. cit., p. 146.

91 ibid., pp. 147–8.

92 ibid., p. 150.

93 A. Robbins, *Parnell: the last five years*, p. 84.

94 *Spec. Comm. Proc.*, v, 479–83.

95 P. J. Walsh, *William J. Walsh, Archbishop of Dublin*, pp. 393–9.

96 R. B. O'Brien, *Lord Russell of Killowen*, pp. 228–9.

97 ibid., pp. 232–7 and 237–40 for a vivid account of how Russell demolished Pigott.

98 Cited in R. B. O'Brien, *Parnell*, ii, 218.

99 ibid., ii, 213.

100 A. L. Thorold, *The life of Henry Labouchere*, pp. 361–3.

101 M. Davitt, *Fall of feudalism*, pp. 584–5.

102 A. L. Thorold, op. cit., p. 358.

103 W. H. O'Shea to J. Chamberlain, 9 March 1889 (J. L. Garvin, ii, 395).

104 *The Times*, 2 and 4 March 1889.

CHAPTER 14: APOTHEOSIS

1 M. Davitt, *Fall of feudalism*, pp. 586–7.

2 E. W. Hamilton, 'Diary', 2 February [misdated for March] 1889 (BM, Add. MS 48, 650).

3 J. H. Parnell, *Charles Stewart Parnell*, p. 228.

4 A. Robbins, *Parnell: the last five years*, p. 103.

5 Hansard, H. C. deb., 3s, ccciii, cols. 301–6; *The Times*, 2 March 1889.

6 R. B. O'Brien, ii, 229.

7 *The Times*, 9 March 1889; *Nation*, 16 March 1889.

8 R. B. O'Brien, ii, 178.

9 *Nation*, 23 March 1889.

10 R. B. O'Brien, ii, 178.

11 *Nation*, 23 March 1889.

12 E. W. Hamilton, 'Diary', 9 April 1889 (BM, Add. MS 48, 650).

13 T. M. Healy, *Letters and leaders*, i, 305.

14 A. Robbins, op. cit., p. 108; R. B. O'Brien, *Lord Russell of Killowen*, pp. 243–4.

15 K. O'Shea, ii, 134–5.

16 *Spec. Comm. Proc.*, vii, 245–7, 258; A. Robbins, op. cit., pp. 110–11.

17 ibid., vii, 127–8.

18 ibid., vii, 141.

19 *Report of the Special Commission, 1888* (London, 1890), *passim.*

20 *The History of The Times, 1884–1912*, pp. 88–9.

21 G. Buckle to W. H. Smith, 14 February 1890 and W. H. Smith to John Walter, copy, 17 February 1890 (Hambleden Papers, PS 15/8 and PS 15/9).

22 F. S. L. Lyons, 'Parnellism and crime, 1887–90', in *Transactions of the Royal Historical Society*, 5th series, vol. xxiv (1974), 123–40.

23 For the deteriorating situation between May and December 1888, see F. S. L. Lyons, 'John Dillon and the Plan of Campaign', in *IHS*, xiv, No. 56 (September 1965), 329–33.

24 J. Dillon, 'Diary', 5 November 1888 (DP).

25 ibid., 23, 24 and 27 December 1888 (DP).

26 J. Dillon to Parnell, 14 January 1889; Parnell to J. Dillon, 26 January 1889 (DP).

27 *UI*, 13 July 1888; W. O'Brien, *Evening memories*, pp. 423–4.

28 W. O'Brien to J. Dillon, 14 July 1889 (DP).

29 W. O'Brien to J. Dillon, 14 August 1889 (DP).

30 F. S. L. Lyons, 'John Dillon and the Plan of Campaign', p. 338.

31 ibid., p. 342.

32 Hansard, H. C. deb., 3s, cccxliii, cols. 980, 983, 996, 1002, 1006–7, 1307, 1311; see also his critique in the *North American Review*, ccciii, 665–70 (1890).

33 *FJ*, 29 November 1890; *The Times*, 1 December 1890; J. Morley, *Recollections*, i, 251–2.

34 Hansard, H. C. deb., 3s, cccxlvi, cols. 316–20 (11 July 1890).

35 J. Morley, *Recollections*, i, 245.

36 John Dillon, 'Diary', 10 [wrongly dated for 11] and 16 July 1890.

37 M. J. Kenny to Capt. J. J. Dunne [the letter is unsigned but other signed letters in the same hand identify it as Kenny's], 24 January 1890 (NLI MS 10, 946).

38 *Nation*, 2 August 1890.

39 ibid.

40 F. S. L. Lyons, *John Dillon*, pp. 110–12.

41 W. E. Gladstone, 'Notes for interview with Parnell', 8 March 1888 (BM, Add. MS 44, 773, f. 48).

42 W. E. Gladstone, 'Memorandum of meeting with Parnell' [10 March 1888] BM, Add. MS 44, 773, ff. 49–50).

43 The exchange of letters is in *The Times*, 9 July 1888; see also R. B. O'Brien, ii, 187–9. For the background to the episode, see G. P. Taylor, 'Cecil Rhodes and the second Home Rule Bill', in *The Historical Journal*, xiv, No. 4 (1971), 771–81.

44 *Nation*, 1 June 1889, speech in London, 23 May.

45 C. Cruise O'Brien, *Parnell and his party*, p. 234, *n.* 1.
46 The three Edinburgh speeches are all in the *Nation*, 27 July 1889.
47 W. E. Gladstone to Parnell, copy, 30 August 1889 (BM, Add. MS 44, 507, ff. 203–4).
48 E. W. Hamilton, 'Diary', 18 December 1889; *Nation*, 21 December 1889.
49 Earl Granville to Earl Spencer, 22 October 1889 (SP).
50 *The Times*, 25 October 1889; Sir W. Harcourt to John Morley, 27 October 1889 (A. G. Gardiner, *Harcourt*, ii, 148–9).
51 Sir W. Harcourt to John Morley, 27 October 1889 (HP).
52 Sir W. Harcourt to John Morley, 29 October 1889 (HP).
53 Sir W. Harcourt to W. E. Gladstone, 27 October 1889, copy (HP).
54 W. E. Gladstone to Sir W. Harcourt, 29 October 1889 (HP).
55 A. G. Gardiner, *Harcourt*, ii, 150.
56 Printed in J. L. Hammond, *Gladstone and the Irish nation*, pp. 619–21.
57 Mary Gladstone, *Letters and diaries*, p. 411.
58 J. L. Hammond, *Gladstone and the Irish nation*, p. 605.
59 W. E. Gladstone, 'Memorandum on Parnell's visit to Hawarden', 23 December 1889 (BM, Add. MS 44, 773, ff. 170–1).
60 *The Times*, 20 December 1889.
61 E. Evans to W. E. Gladstone, 28 (misdated for 29) November 1890 (BM, Add. MS 44, 511, f. 199).
62 *The Times*, 27 December 1889.

CHAPTER 15: THE CRASH

1 *FJ*, 30 December 1889; *Nation*, 4 January 1890.
2 E. C. Houston to W. H. O'Shea, 6 March [1889] (JC 8/8/1/122).
3 Miss E. H. Johnston to Capt. J. J. Dunne, 15 October 1890 (NLI MS 10, 946).
4 Sir E. Clarke, *The story of my life*, pp. 284–5; A. Robbins, *Parnell: the last five years*, pp. 135–7.
5 G. E. Buckle to W. H. Smith, 10 December 1889 (Hambleden Papers, PS 14/48–136).
6 H. Harrison, *Parnell, Joseph Chamberlain and Mr Garvin*, pp. 201–24.
7 A. Robbins, *Parnell: the last five years*, pp. 132–3.
8 W. H. O'Shea to J. Chamberlain, 13 October 1889 (JC 8/8/1/127).
9 Memorandum and letters enclosed by O'Shea with the letter to Chamberlain cited in the preceding footnote (JC 8/8/1/128).
10 J. Chamberlain to W. H. O'Shea, 14 October 1889 (JC 8/8/1/129).
11 K. O'Shea, ii, 221–7; Sir E. Clarke, *The story of my life*, pp. 283–4; Blanche E. C. Dugdale, *Arthur James Balfour* (London, 1936), i, 182–3.
12 W. H. O'Shea to J. Chamberlain, 30 December 1889 (JC 8/8/1/130); J. L. Garvin, ii, 400–1).

13 J. L. Garvin, ii, 401.

14 H. Harrison, *Parnell, Joseph Chamberlain and Mr Garvin*, pp. 205–7.

15 Blanche E. C. Dugdale, op. cit., i, 182–3.

16 C. H. D. Howard (ed.), 'Joseph Chamberlain, W. H. O'Shea and Parnell, 1884, 1891–2', in *IHS*, xiii, No. 49 (March 1962), 33–8.

17 F. S. L. Lyons, *The fall of Parnell*, p. 67.

18 W. H. O'Shea to J. Chamberlain, 30 March 1892 (JC 8/8/1/166; J. L. Garvin, ii, 399, *n.* 2).

19 *The Times*, 21 May 1889.

20 W. H. O'Shea to J. Chamberlain, 3 November 1888 (J. L. Garvin, ii, 397–8).

21 J. Chamberlain to W. H. O'Shea, 5 December 1888 (J. L. Garvin, ii, 398).

22 H. Harrison, *Parnell vindicated*, p. 187.

23 W. H. O'Shea to J. Chamberlain, 13 October 1889 (JC 8/8/1/127); C. S. Parnell to W. E. Gladstone (BM, Add. MS 44, 503, ff. 157–8); Joyce Marlow, *The uncrowned queen of Ireland* (London, 1975), pp. 192–5.

24 Viscount Esher, *Journals and letters*, ed. M. V. Brett (London, 1934), i, 142; H. Harrison, *Parnell vindicated*, p. 108.

25 K. O'Shea, ii, 158; H. Harrison, *Parnell vindicated*, p. 129.

26 W. H. O'Shea to J. Chamberlain, 3 August 1890 (JC 8/8/1/144).

27 H. Harrison, *Parnell vindicated*, pp. 108, 146–9.

28 See above, *n.* 26; cited in J. L. Garvin, ii, 402.

29 Sir E. Clarke, *The story of my life*, pp. 289–90; H. Harrison, *Parnell vindicated*, pp. 128–9.

30 W. H. O'Shea to J. Chamberlain, 15 December 1890 (JC 8/8/1/152).

31 H. Harrison, *Parnell vindicated*, pp. 150–1.

32 M. Davitt, *Fall of feudalism*, p. 637.

33 Parnell to T. P. Gill, 31 December 1889, signed but not written by Parnell (Gill Papers); W. S. Blunt, *My diaries*, i, 218–19; W. O'Brien, *Evening memories*, p. 466.

34 J. E. Kenny to J. Dillon, 1 January 1890 (F. S. L. Lyons, *John Dillon*, p. 114).

35 Sir E. W. Hamilton, 'Diary', 1 January 1890 (BM, Add. MS 48652).

36 ibid., 14 February 1890.

37 Viscount Esher, *Journals and letters*, i, 142 (23 January 1890).

38 W. T. Stead to Archbishop Walsh, 24 January 1890 (DDA).

39 Viscount Esher, *Journals and letters*, i, 142 (31 January 1890).

40 W. T. Stead to Archbishop Walsh, 15 February 1890 (DDA).

41 A. G. Gardiner, *Harcourt*, ii, 82.

42 The interview is described in considerable detail, on the basis of a note written by John Morley the following morning, in his *Recollections*, i, 251–6.

43 Morley to W. E. Gladstone, 13 November 1890 (BM, Add. MS 44,

256, ff. 63–5); J. Morley, *Gladstone*, iii, 323.

44 *FJ*, 20 June 1890; *Nation*, 28 June 1890.

45 A. J. Kettle to Archbishop Walsh, 20 June 1890 (DDA).

46 *Nation*, 20 December 1890.

47 F. S. L. Lyons, 'John Dillon and the Plan of Campaign' in *IHS*, xiv, No. 56 (September 1965), 339–41.

48 Dr L. Gillooly to Archbishop Walsh, 16 August 1890 (DDA).

49 Archbishop Logue to Archbishop Walsh, 31 July 1890 (DDA).

50 'Pastoral Address of the Archbishops and Bishops of Ireland', 16 October 1890.

51 Archbishop Logue to Parnell, 15 October 1890, copy in Archbishop Walsh's hand (DDA).

52 Archbishop Walsh to John Dillon, 26 January 1891 (DP); there is a copy in Archbishop Walsh's papers in the Dublin Diocesan Archives.

53 Dr L. Gillooly to Archbishop Walsh, 19 October 1890 (DDA).

54 J. McCarthy and R. M. Praed, *Our book of memories*, p. 251.

55 *Nation*, 14 October 1890, reporting the meeting of 6 October.

56 J. McCarthy and R. M. Praed, op. cit., p. 252.

57 Report of Supt. W. Reddy, 15 October 1890 (CSO, Registered Papers, Green File, No. 99).

58 J. Morley to W. E. Gladstone, 17 November 1890 (BM, Add. MS 44, 256, ff. 72–3).

59 The trial is reported in detail in *The Times*, 17 and 18 November 1890.

60 Lord Askwith, *Lord James of Hereford* (London, 1930), p. 220.

61 Sir E. Clarke, *The story of my life*, pp. 290–1.

62 H. Harrison, *Parnell vindicated*, pp. 109–10.

CHAPTER 16: CONFRONTATION

1 *FJ*, 17 November 1890.

2 *FJ*, 18 November 1890.

3 *Nation*, 22 November 1890.

4 *Nation*, 22 November 1890.

5 *FJ*, 21 November 1890; J. McCarthy and R. M. Praed, *Our book of memories*, p. 256.

6 T. D. Sullivan to Archbishop Walsh, 18 February 1889 (DDA).

7 *Nation*, 26 April 1890.

8 *FJ*, 17 November 1890.

9 W. O'Brien, *An olive branch in Ireland* (London, 1910), pp. 11–14, hereafter cited as *Olive branch*.

10 *FJ*, 21 November 1890.

11 M. Davitt to Archbishop Walsh, 20 November 1890 (DDA); *Labour World*, 20 November 1890.

12 Archbishop Walsh to M. Davitt, 21 November 1890 (DDA).

13 Dr J. E. Kenny to Archbishop Walsh, 19 November 1890 (DDA).

14 Archbishop Walsh to Dr J. E. Kenny, copy, 19 November 1890 (DDA).

15 Dr J. E. Kenny to Archbishop Walsh, 23 November 1890 (DDA).

16 Archbishop Walsh to Dr J. E. Kenny, 24 November 1890 (DDA); P. J. Walsh, *William J. Walsh*, p. 410.

17 P. J. Walsh, *William J. Walsh*, pp. 408–9.

18 Archbishop Croke to Archbishop Walsh, 22 November [1890] (DDA).

19 Dr B. Woodlock to Archbishop Walsh, 25 November 1890 (DDA).

20 Dr L. Gillooly to Archbishop Walsh, 19 November 1890 (DDA).

21 *The Times*, 18 November 1890. See also Trowbridge H. Ford, 'Dicey's Conversion to Unionism' in *IHS*, xviii, No. 72 (September 1973), 555–82.

22 J. F. Glaser, 'Parnell's fall and the nonconformist conscience', in *IHS*, xii, No. 46 (September 1960), 121–3.

23 *Pall Mall Gazette*, 18 November 1890.

24 W. T. Stead to W. E. Gladstone, 19 November 1890 (BM, Add. MS 56, 466, unfoliated).

25 W. T. Stead to Archbishop Walsh, 18 and 20 November 1890 (DDA).

26 W. T. Stead to W. E. Gladstone, 20 November 1890 (BM, Add. MS 56, 446).

27 T. Hancocks to W. E. Gladstone, 18 November 1890 (ibid.).

28 *The Star*, 19 November 1890.

29 *Methodist Times*, 20 November 1890.

30 *Daily News*, 24 November 1890.

31 Cited in J. F. Glaser, loc. cit., 128.

32 ibid., 125.

33 J. Morley, *Gladstone*, iii, 323.

34 J. Morley to W. E. Gladstone, 17 November 1890 (BM, Add. MS 44, 256, ff. 72–3).

35 W. E. Gladstone to J. Morley, 18 November 1890 (J. Morley, *Gladstone*, iii, 324); J. Morley to W. E. Gladstone, 18 November 1890 (BM, Add. MS 44, 256, f. 74).

36 W. E. Gladstone to J. Morley, 19 November 1890 (BM, Add. MS 44, 256, ff. 79–80).

37 J. Morley to Sir W. Harcourt, 18 November 1890 (HP).

38 H. J. Wilson to W. E. Gladstone, copy, 22 November 1890 (BM, Add. MS 56, 446). The well-known nonconformist, P. J. Bunting, wrote next day to the same effect, adding that Davitt had told him that Gladstone was the best person to bring pressure on Parnell to retire (BM, Add. MS 56, 446).

39 J. Morley, *Recollections*, i, 256–7.

40 J. Morley to W. E. Gladstone, 22 November 1890 (BM, Add. MS 44, 256, ff. 82–3).

41 Sir W. Harcourt to W. E. Gladstone, 22 November 1890 (A. G. Gardiner, *Harcourt*, ii, 83–4).

42 W. E. Gladstone to A. Morley, 23 November 1890 (J. Morley, *Gladstone*, iii, 326).

43 Mary Gladstone, *Letters and diaries*, p. 413 (22 November 1890).

44 W. E. Gladstone to Sir W. Harcourt, 23 November 1890 (A. G. Gardiner, *Harcourt*, ii, 84–5).

45 J. Morley, *Gladstone*, iii, 329.

46 J. McCarthy and R. M. Praed, *Our book of memories*, pp. 256–7.

47 J. Morley, *Gladstone*, iii, 330; and *Recollections*, i, 259.

48 F. E. Hamer (ed.), *The personal papers of Lord Rendel*, p. 26.

49 J. Morley, *Recollections*, i, 259–60.

50 ibid., i, 260; Lord E. Fitzmaurice, *Life of the second Earl Granville* (1st ed., London, 1905), p. 499.

51 J. McCarthy and R. M. Praed, *Our book of memories*, p. 258.

52 J. Morley, *Recollections*, i, 260.

53 J. Morley, *Gladstone*, iii, 334; R. B. O'Brien, ii, 366–7, interview with Gladstone in January 1897.

54 *Pall Mall Gazette*, 9 November 1891.

55 R. B. O'Brien, ii, 247. O'Brien does not give the date of this account, or say whether it was oral or written.

56 J. Morley, *Gladstone*, iii, 328–9 and *Recollections*, i, 260–1.

57 J. Morley, *Gladstone*, iii, 329.

58 T. M. Healy, *Letters and leaders*, i, 322.

59 A. Robbins, *Parnell: the last five years*, p. 159.

60 *FJ*, 26 November 1890 and 18 and 19 August 1891.

61 A. Robbins, op. cit., p. 159.

62 F. E. Hamer (ed.), *The personal papers of Lord Rendel*, p. 28.

63 ibid., p. 28; J. Morley, *Recollections*, i, 262.

64 T. M. Healy, *Letters and leaders*, i, 322. Healy alleges, though without proof, that two days previously Parnell had rejected an appeal from a well-disposed member of the party to consult with his friends.

65 'Minutes of the Irish parliamentary party', 25 November 1890. These were formerly in the Dillon Papers, but they have disappeared since I first used them some fifteen years ago.

66 *Daily News*, 25 November 1890.

67 D. Sullivan to T. M. Healy, 25 November 1890 (T. M. Healy, op. cit., i, 322–3).

68 H. Harrison, *Parnell vindicated*, p. 10.

69 *National Press*, 21 November 1891.

70 T. M. Healy, *Letters and leaders*, i, 323.

71 J. Morley, *Gladstone*, iii, 331.

72 ibid., iii, 331–2.

73 ibid., iii, 334.

74 T. M. Healy, *Letters and leaders*, i, 323.

75 A. Robbins, *Parnell: the last five years*, p. 160.

76 Viscount Esher, *Journals and letters*, i, 146; T. M. Healy, op. cit., i, 326.

77 K. O'Shea, ii, 161.
78 *FJ*, 26 November 1890.
79 F. S. L. Lyons, *The fall of Parnell*, pp. 96–7.
80 K. O'Shea, ii, 162–3.

CHAPTER 17: BREAKING-POINT

1 Note in Gladstone's hand for use of Justin McCarthy, 28 November 1890 (BM, Add. MS 56, 446).
2 *Pall Mall Gazette*, 14 January 1891; *FJ*, 16 January 1891; J. McCarthy and R. M. Praed, *Our book of memories*, p. 261.
3 R. B. O'Brien, ii, 257. There were in addition a few others present who later took sides against Parnell (D. Sullivan, 'The Story of Room Fifteen', in *National Press*, 24 November 1891).
4 J. Morley, *Recollections*, i, 253.
5 *Daily News*, 29 November 1890.
6 J. McCarthy to W. E. Gladstone, 29 November 1890 (BM, Add. MS 56, 446); W. M. Murphy to Archbishop Walsh, 30 November 1890 (DDA); *FJ*, 2 December 1890.
7 F. E. Hamer (ed.), *The personal papers of Lord Rendel*, pp. 75–6; A. Robbins, *Parnell: the last five years*, pp. 165–6.
8 J. Saxon Mills, *Sir Edward Cook* (London, 1921), pp. 110–11.
9 F. E. Hamer, op. cit., p. 76.
10 Gladstone's and Morley's refutations are in *The Times*, 1 December 1890.
11 J. Morley to Earl Spencer, 1 December 1890 (SP); *The Times*, 1 December 1890.
12 A. G. Gardiner, *Harcourt*, ii, 87.
13 Sir W. Harcourt to Earl Spencer, 1 December 1890 (SP).
14 W. E. Gladstone, 'Memorandum of conversation with Justin McCarthy', 30 November 1890 (BM, Add. MS 56, 446).
15 Copy of cable to Parnell, 28 November 1890 (Gill Papers); T. Harrington, 'Diary', 28 and 29 November 1890 (NLI MS 2195).
16 For these developments, see F. S. L. Lyons, *The fall of Parnell*, pp. 111–14.
17 Dr B. Woodlock to Archbishop Walsh, 26 November 1890 (DDA).
18 Dr L. Gillooly to Dr B. Woodlock, 28 November 1890 (DDA); Dr L. Gillooly to Archbishop Walsh, 28 November 1890 (DDA).
19 Dr F. J. McCormack to Archbishop Walsh, 28 November 1890 (DDA).
20 Dr James Donnelly to Archbishop Walsh, 28 November 1890 (DDA).
21 P. J. Walsh, *William J. Walsh*, p. 412.
22 W. M. Murphy to Archbishop Walsh, 26 November 1890 (DDA); P. J. Walsh, op. cit., pp. 412–13.
23 Archbishop Walsh to Cardinal Manning, 26 and 28 November 1890,

cited in E. Larkin, 'The Roman Catholic hierarchy and the fall of Parnell', in *Victorian Studies*, iv, No. 1 (June 1961), p. 325.

24 P. J. Walsh, *William J. Walsh*, pp. 413–14.

25 Dr J. MacEvilly to Archbishop Walsh, 29 November 1890 (DDA).

26 Archbishop Croke to Justin McCarthy, 29 November 1890 (DDA).

27 *FJ*, 1 December 1890.

28 P. J. Walsh, *William J. Walsh*, p. 416.

29 W. M. Murphy to Archbishop Walsh, 29 November 1890 and Archbishop Walsh to W. M. Murphy, 30 November 1890 (DDA).

50 E. Larkin, loc. cit., pp. 328–30.

31 T. M. Healy to his wife, 2 December 1890 (*Letters and leaders*, i, 332); *FJ*, 5 December 1890.

32 F. S. L. Lyons, *The fall of Parnell*, pp. 119–20.

33 ibid., chap. 5 for a fuller analysis of the debates.

34 T. M. Healy, *Letters and leaders*, i, 324.

35 The first day's debates are in *FJ*, 2 December 1890.

36 T. M. Healy to Archbishop Walsh, 1 December 1890 (DDA).

37 T. M. Healy to his wife, 1 December 1890 (*Letters and leaders*, i, 331).

38 For the second day's debates, see *FJ*, 3 December 1890.

39 *FJ*, 5 December 1890.

40 Donal Sullivan in *National Press*, 28 November 1891; K. O'Shea, ii, 175; T. M. Healy, *Letters and leaders*, i, 333.

41 *FJ*, 5 December 1890.

42 P. J. Walsh, *William J. Walsh*, pp. 418–20.

43 Archbishop Walsh to Cardinal Manning, 4 and 6 December 1890, and to W. M. Murphy, 5 December 1890 (cited in E. Larkin, loc. cit., pp. 331–2).

44 *FJ*, 5 December 1890.

45 Sir W. Harcourt to W. E. Gladstone, 30 November 1890 (A. G. Gardiner, *Harcourt*, ii, 87–8).

46 Sir W. Harcourt to W. E. Gladstone, 4 December 1890 (BM, Add. MS 56, 449).

47 J. Stansfeld to W. E. Gladstone, 4 December 1890 (BM, Add. MS 56, 449).

48 W. E. Gladstone, 'Memorandum of proceedings during visit of Irish deputation, 5 December 1890'. (BM, Add. MS 56, 449); *FJ*, 8 December 1890. In his memorandum Gladstone noted: 'Police of Ireland should be placed under Irish authority at the earliest moment which considerations of practical convenience permit.'

49 *FJ*, 8 December 1890.

50 W. E. Gladstone, 'Memorandum of Proceedings . . . 5 December 1890' (BM, Add. MS 56, 449).

51 'Notes dictated by Sir W. V. H. Harcourt to his son L. Harcourt on Divorce Crisis, 1890', undated but written apparently soon after the event (HP); *FJ*, 8 December 1890.

52 *FJ*, 8 December 1890.

53 Sir W. Harcourt, 'Notes' as in *n.* 52 above.

54 T. M. Healy to his wife, 5 December 1890 (*Letters and leaders*, i, 334–5). Healy thought Redmond and Leamy would have left Parnell if he had tried to 'fox'.

55 J. Morley, *Gladstone*, iii, 339.

56 T. M. Healy, *Letters and leaders*, i, 336.

57 W. M. Murphy to Archbishop Walsh, 6 December 1890 (DDA).

58 The paper is preserved in the National Library in Dublin (NLI MS 4572).

59 D. Sullivan, 'The Story of Room Fifteen' in *National Press*, 2 December 1891; J. Morley, *Gladstone*, iii, 451; T. M. Healy, *Letters and leaders*, i, 336.

60 *FJ*, 8 December 1890.

61 *FJ*, 8 December 1890; M. Macdonagh, *The Home Rule movement*, pp. 220–1.

62 T. M. Healy to his wife, 6 December 1890 (*Letters and leaders*, i, 336).

63 *FJ*, 8 December 1890.

64 The official account (which I followed in *The fall of Parnell*) is, I am now convinced, wrong in placing the time at 4.30, while T. M. Healy errs in the other direction by placing it at six o'clock. Alfred Webb, writing some thirteen to fourteen years after the event, timed it at 5.13, but the most exact contemporary evidence is that of W. M. Murphy, whose telegram to Dr Walsh – 'Have just withdrawn in a body' – is timed 5.24 p.m. (DDA).

65 T. M. Healy, *Letters and leaders*, i, 336.

66 W. M. Murphy to Archbishop Walsh, 6 p.m., 6 December 1890 (DDA).

67 *FJ*, 8 December 1890.

CHAPTER 18: A TIME OF RENDING

1 There is a list of 88 leadership committees, excluding Dublin, in *FJ*, 24 July 1891.

2 For these developments see F. S. L. Lyons, *The fall of Parnell*, pp. 150–4.

3 *FJ*, 11 December 1890; T. M. Healy, *Letters and leaders*, i, 340.

4 F. S. L. Lyons, op. cit., pp. 154–6.

5 R. B. O'Brien, ii, 291; Katharine Tynan, *Twenty-five years: reminiscences* (London, 1913), p. 325.

6 *FJ*, 11 December 1890.

7 T. Harrington, 'Diary', 2 December 1890 (NLI MS 2195).

8 J. Dillon, 'Diary', 4 December 1890 (DP); T. Harrington, 'Diary', 4 December 1890 (NLI MS 2195).

9 J. Dillon, 'Diary', 6 December 1890 (DP).

10 J. McCarthy to Dillon and O'Brien, 6 December 1890 (Gill Papers).

11 *The Times*, 8 December 1890; *FJ*, 9 and 10 December 1890.

12 Parnell to W. O'Brien, 8 December 1890 (Gill Papers); T. Harrington, 'Diary', 8 and 9 December 1890 (NLI MS 2195).

13 John Redmond to T. P. Gill, 8 December 1890; John Redmond and Dr J. Kenny to William O'Brien, 9 December 1890 (Gill Papers).

14 *FJ*, 10 December 1890; *The Times*, 10 December 1890.

15 *FJ*, 11 December 1890.

16 R. B. O'Brien, ii, 291–2.

17 Archbishop Walsh to Cardinal Manning, 14 December 1890, cited by E. Larkin, 'Mounting the counter-attack: the Roman Catholic hierarchy and the destruction of Parnellism', in *The Review of Politics*, xxv, No. 2 (April 1963), 157–82.

18 *FJ*, 11 December 1890.

19 R. B. O'Brien, ii, 296.

20 *UI*, 13 December 1890; C. Cruise O'Brien, *Parnell and his party*, pp. 327–8.

21 *The Times*, 18 October 1891; *DNB*, article by C. A. Harris; introduction by John Sutherland to the Penguin edition of *Phineas Finn*, where the claims of Gladstone's adviser on Irish land, Chichester Samuel Fortescue, are preferred.

22 R. B. O'Brien, ii, 289–90.

23 ibid., ii, 297–8.

24 T. M. Healy, *Letters and leaders*, i, 341.

25 R. B. O'Brien, ii, 300.

26 *FJ*, 22 December 1890.

27 *Spec. Comm. Proc.*, i, 371.

28 *Daily News*, 20 December 1890.

29 *Daily News*, 18 December 1890.

30 *FJ*, 22 December 1890; *UI*, 27 December 1890.

31 *Insuppressible*, 17 December 1890.

32 *FJ*, 13 December 1890.

33 *Kilkenny Journal*, 17 December 1890; *The Times*, 15 December 1890 has 'as the price of his wife's shame'.

34 Archbishop Walsh to Dr E. J. Byrne, 17 December 1890 (DDA).

35 Parnell to Archbishop Walsh, 18 December 1890 (DDA).

36 *FJ*, 17 and 22 December 1890.

37 *FJ*, 19 December 1890.

38 Earl Granville to Earl Spencer, 20 December 1890 (SP).

39 Cardinal Manning to W. E. Gladstone, 21 December 1890 (BM, Add. MS 44, 250, f. 36).

40 J. Morley, *Gladstone*, iii, 341.

41 For the incident, see *FJ*, 17 December 1890; *Daily News*, 17 December 1890; *Insuppressible*, 31 December 1890; T. M. Healy, *Letters and leaders*, i, 345–6; K. O'Shea, ii, 181–2.

42 Dr A. Brownrigg to Archbishop Walsh, 10 December 1890 (DDA).

43 Dr A. Brownrigg to Archbishop Walsh, 13 December 1890 (DDA).

44 Archbishop Croke to Archbishop Walsh, 19 December 1890 (DDA).

45 Dr A. Brownrigg to Archbishop Walsh, 19 December 1890 (DDA).

46 Dr A. Brownrigg to Archbishop Walsh, 20 December 1890 (DDA).

47 Dr A. Brownrigg to Archbishop Walsh, 22 December 1890 (DDA).

48 Dr A. Brownrigg to Archbishop Walsh, 24 December 1890 (DDA).

49 R. B. O'Brien, ii, 306-7.

50 T. Harrington to W. O'Brien, 27 December 1890 (Gill Papers); evidence to the same effect reached John Devoy indirectly from J. J. O'Kelly about this time (*DPB*, ii, 317-18).

51 Dr A. Brownrigg to Archbishop Walsh, 26 December 1890 (DDA); T. M. Healy, *Letters and leaders*, i, 346.

52 T. M. Healy to his wife, 18 December 1890 (*Letters and leaders*, i, 345).

53 R. B. O'Brien, ii, 307.

54 *FJ*, 24 and 25 December 1890.

55 *FJ*, 3 December 1890; Katharine Tynan, op. cit., p. 344.

56 M. Ryan, *Fenian memories* (Dublin, 1945 pp. 148-56); *DPB*, ii, 316-17.

57 *FJ*, 24 and 25 December 1890; M. Macdonagh, *The Home Rule movement*, pp. 226-7.

CHAPTER 19: LAST CHANCE

1 M. Bodkin to W. O'Brien (Gill Papers).

2 *FJ*, 12 December 1890.

3 J. Dillon, 'Diary', 10 December 1890 (DP); T. Harrington, 'Diary', 12 December 1890 (NLI MS 2195).

4 M. Bodkin to W. O'Brien, 17 December 1890 (W. O'Brien Papers, Cork collection, box AC).

5 F. S. L. Lyons, *The fall of Parnell*, pp. 183-5.

6 ibid., pp. 186-7.

7 *FJ*, 16 December 1890.

8 *Insuppressible*, 22 December 1890.

9 J. Dillon to W. O'Brien, 13 December 1890 (Gill Papers).

10 V. B. Dillon to J. Dillon, 13 December 1890 (DP).

11 J. E. Kenny to J. Dillon, 13 December 1890 (DP).

12 J. Dillon to W. O'Brien, 18 December 1890 (Gill Papers).

13 Archbishop Croke to Archbishop Walsh, 16 December [1890] (DDA).

14 Archbishop Croke to W. O'Brien, 19 December 1890 (Gill Papers).

15 V. B. Dillon to W. O'Brien, 28 December 1890 (Gill Papers).

16 T. Harrington to W. O'Brien, 27 December 1890 (Gill Papers).

17 W. O'Brien, *Olive branch*, pp. 20-2.

18 'Note of interview at Boulogne, Christmas Day, 1890, between Messrs Justin McCarthy, MP, Sexton, MP, Condon, MP, on one part and Messrs William O'Brien, MP, and Gill, MP, on the other' (Gill Papers); Justin McCarthy to Mrs Praed, 26 December 1890 (J. McCarthy and R. M. Praed, *Our book of memories*, p. 272).

19 R. B. O'Brien, ii, 310–11; W. O'Brien, *Olive branch*, p. 25.

20 Redmond's narrative places this after lunch, O'Brien's before it. T. P. Gill, in a memorandum made at the time on the writing paper of the Hotel du Louvre, where the conference was held, says it took place 'before dinner'. In *The fall of Parnell* I accepted O'Brien's version, but on reflection I feel that Gill's account, which is more neutral, is probably also more accurate; it is strengthened by the clear evidence that Parnell insisted on having lunch before conferring.

21 'Memorandum of Mr John Redmond, MP's and Mr T. P. Gill, MP's conversations at Boulogne on 30 and 31 December 1890' (Gill Papers).

22 T. P. Gill to W. O'Brien, 10 November 1891 (Gill Papers); *FJ*, 14 November 1891.

23 *FJ*, 12 November 1891.

24 J. Dillon, 'Diary', 31 December 1890 (DP).

25 F. S. L. Lyons, *The fall of Parnell*, pp. 202–4.

26 *FJ*, 11 and 12 November 1891.

27 F. S. L. Lyons, op. cit., pp. 205–7.

28 T. M. Healy to Archbishop Walsh, 5 January 1891 (DDA).

29 T. M. Healy to his wife, 5 January 1891 (*Letters and leaders*, i, 347).

30 *Evening Telegraph*, 5 January 1891.

31 R. B. O'Brien, ii, 316.

32 W. O'Brien to Archbishop Croke, 12 January 1891 (*Evening memories*, pp. 479–80); *FJ*, 12 November 1891.

33 *FJ*, 4 and 12 November 1891; W. O'Brien, *Olive branch*, pp. 35–6.

34 J. Dillon to W. O'Brien, cable, 9.45 p.m., 6 January 1891, copy (DP); J. Dillon, 'Diary', 6 January 1891 (DP).

35 W. O'Brien to Archbishop Croke, 12 January 1891 (*Evening memories*, pp. 479–80).

36 E. Larkin, 'Mounting the counter-attack', pp. 169–70.

37 *FJ*, 12 January 1891.

38 J. McCarthy to T. M. Healy, 12 January 1891 (*Letters and leaders*, i, 350).

39 For these exchanges, see F. S. L. Lyons, *The fall of Parnell*, pp. 220–2.

40 M. Bodkin to W. O'Brien, 12 and 14 January 1891 [misdated 1890] (W. O'Brien Papers, Cork collection, box AD).

41 *Daily News*, 17 December 1890.

42 J. Morley, *Gladstone*, iii, 340.

43 A. G. Gardiner, *Harcourt*, ii, 91.

44 Sir W. Harcourt to J. Morley, 3 and 4 January 1891 (HP); Gardiner, ii, 92.

45 F. S. L. Lyons, *The fall of Parnell*, pp. 223–5.
46 J. Morley to Sir W. Harcourt, 16 January 1891 (A. G. Gardiner, *Harcourt*, ii, 96); J. Morley to W. E. Gladstone, 16 January 1891 (BM, Add. MS 44, 256, ff. 120–1).
47 *FJ*, 16 January 1891.
48 F. S. L. Lyons, op. cit., pp. 226–7.
49 W. E. Gladstone to Sir W. Harcourt, 19 January 1891 (HP).
50 F. S. L. Lyons, op. cit., pp. 228–9.
51 ibid., p. 230.
52 W. O'Brien to Parnell, telegram 21 January 1891 and J. Redmond and T. Harrington to Parnell, telegram 24 January 1891 (NLI MS 8581/2); *Evening Telegraph*, 22 and 26 January 1891.
53 J. Morley to Earl Spencer, 27 January 1891 (SP); for the Liberal position generally, see F. S. L. Lyons, *The fall of Parnell*, pp. 233–4.
54 W. E. Gladstone to J. Dillon, 21 January 1891; W. E. Gladstone to J. McCarthy, 21 January 1891; draft note by W. E. Gladstone, apparently for his use in conversation with McCarthy, 31 January 1891 (all the foregoing in BM, Add. MS 56, 449).
55 'Minutes of the Irish parliamentary party', 12 February 1891 (DP). These take the form of a newspaper cutting (I have not been able to trace the original of the document handed to McCarthy for transmission to France, but some of the phrases are foreshadowed in a group of undated memoranda, mostly in Gladstone's own hand, in BM, Add. MS 56, 449).
56 *FJ*, 12 November 1891; R. B. O'Brien, ii, 318.
57 W. O'Brien to T. Harrington, 30 January 1891 (NLI MS 8581).
58 Cited in E. Larkin, 'Mounting the counter-attack', pp. 171–2; W. E. Gladstone to Archbishop Walsh, 29 January 1891 (DDA).
59 Archbishop Walsh to J. Dillon, 26 January 1891 (DP); copy in DDA.
60 T. M. Healy to Archbishop Walsh, 31 January 1891 (DDA).
61 M. Bodkin to T. P. Gill, 17 January 1891; *Insuppressible*, 24 January 1891; W. O'Brien, *Olive branch*, pp. 38–9; M. Bodkin, *Recollections of an Irish judge* (London, 1914), pp. 175–7.
62 T. P. Gill to W. O'Brien, 28 January [1891] (W. O'Brien Papers, Cork collection, box AD).
63 *Evening Telegraph*, 2 and 4 February 1891; A. Robbins, *Parnell: the last five years*, pp. 183–4.
64 *FJ*, 12 November 1891.
65 W. O'Brien, *Olive branch*, pp. 47–8.
66 For this incident see F. S. L. Lyons, *John Dillon*, pp. 132–3.
67 *FJ*, 4 November 1891; W. O'Brien, *Olive branch*, pp. 44–5.
68 T. P. Gill to W. O'Brien, 4 February 1891 (W. O'Brien Papers, Cork collection, box AD).
69 W. O'Brien, *Olive branch*, p. 48.
70 T. M. Healy to Archbishop Walsh, 4 February 1891 (DDA).

71 Parnell to T. P. Gill, 3 February 1891 (Gill Papers).

72 T. P. Gill to W. O'Brien, 4 February 1891 (W. O'Brien Papers, Cork collection, box AD).

73 Parnell to T. P. Gill, 5 February 1891 (*FJ*, 4 and 12 November 1891; R. B. O'Brien, ii, 319–22).

74 T. P. Gill to Parnell, 'Thursday night', 5 February 1891, copy (NLI MS 8581); *FJ*, 12 November 1891.

75 For these exchanges see F. S. L. Lyons, *The fall of Parnell*, p. 240 and notes.

76 ibid., pp. 242-3.

77 J. E. Redmond to Parnell, copy, 'Monday night' [9 February 1891] (NLI MS 8581); F. S. L. Lyons, op. cit., p. 243.

78 Parnell to W. O'Brien, 10 February 1891 (Gill Papers); *FJ*, 4 November 1891.

79 Parnell to W. O'Brien, 11 February 1891, copy but signed by Parnell (Gill Papers; also copy in NLI, MS 85812); T. P. Gill to J. E. Redmond, 27 November 1891 *FJ*, 4 and 12 November 1891; W. O'Brien, *Olive branch*, p. 53.

80 J. Morley, *Recollections*, i, 263.

81 *FJ*, 13 February 1891.

82 For the disposition of this money, see F. S. L. Lyons, op. cit., p. 251, *n.* 3.

83 R. B. O'Brien, ii, 326–8.

84 T. M. Healy to his brother Maurice, 23 February 1891 (*Letters and leaders*, i, 355).

85 *FJ*, 12 February 1891.

86 F. S. L. Lyons, *The fall of Parnell*, p. 252 and sources there cited.

87 J. Redmond to W. O'Brien, 5 February 1891 (Gill Papers); J. J. Clancy to W. O'Brien, 4 and 5 February 1891 (Gill Papers); V. B. Dillon to W. O'Brien, 6 February 1891 (Gill Papers).

88 T. M. Healy to Archbishop Walsh, 4 February 1891 (DDA); J. Dillon, 'Diary', 6 and 12 February 1891.

89 W. S. Blunt, *My diaries* (London, 2nd ed., 1921), i, 218–19, conversation with T. P. Gill, 7 March 1896; ii, 381, conversation with J. Dillon, 10 March 1912.

90 J. Morley to Earl Spencer, 8 February 1891 (SP).

91 R. B. O'Brien, ii, 328–9.

CHAPTER 20: LA COMMEDIA È FINITA

1 Dr T. O'Callaghan to Archbishop Walsh, 14 December 1890 (DDA).

2 Dr T. O'Callaghan to Archbishop Walsh, 20 December 1890 (DDA).

3 Canon D. O'Mahony to Archbishop Walsh, 30 December 18   (DDA).

4 T. M. Healy, *Letters and leaders*, ii, 361, 362.

5 J. McCarthy, *Reminiscences*, ii, 115–16.

6 *FJ*, 1 June 1891, speech at Wicklow.

7 *FJ*, 18 June 1891.

8 *FJ*, 2 March 1891.

9 *FJ*, 25 February 1891.

10 J. J. Horgan, *Parnell to Pearse*, p. 48.

11 *FJ*, 20 April 1891.

12 *FJ*, 4 July 1891, speech at Carlow.

13 A. J. Balfour to Sir J. W. Ridgeway, 18 April 1891, cited in L. P. Curtis, 'Government policy and the Irish party crisis, 1890–92', in *IHS*, xiii, No. 52 (September 1963), 305; Parnell's speech is in Hansard, H. C. deb., 3s, ccclii, cols. 840–4 (April 17).

14 *FJ*, 5 March 1891.

15 E. Hughes, (ed.), *Keir Hardie's speeches and writings, 1888–1915* (Glasgow, 3rd ed., 1928), p. 38.

16 F. S. L. Lyons, 'The economic ideas of Parnell', pp. 73–4; see above p. 648, *n*. 71.

17 *The Times*, 15 March 1891.

18 *National Press*, 18 March 1891.

19 *FJ*, 8 June 1891, speech at Inchicore, Dublin.

20 F. S. L. Lyons, *The fall of Parnell*, pp. 260–1.

21 Dr J. Lyster to Dr L. Gillooly, 23 March 1891, cited in E. Larkin, 'Launching the counter-attack: part II of the Roman Catholic hierarchy and the destruction of Parnellism', in *The Review of Politics*, xxviii, No. 3 (July 1966), pp. 362–3.

22 K. O'Shea, ii, 260–1.

23 *FJ*, 30 March 1891.

24 *National Press*, 30 March 1891.

25 T. M. Healy to Archbishop Walsh, 4 April 1891 [misdated 1890] (DDA).

26 L. P. Curtis, loc. cit., p. 303.

27 ibid., p. 304.

28 T. M. Healy to Archbishop Walsh, 4 April 1891 (DDA).

29 W. O'Brien to T. P. Gill, 'Wednesday' [18 March 1891] (Gill Papers).

30 *FJ*, 25 February 1891.

31 *National Press*, 9 March 1891, cited in F. S. L. Lyons, *The fall of Parnell*, p. 269.

32 ibid., p. 269.

33 F. S. L. Lyons, op. cit., p. 271, *n*. 1.

34 J. McCarthy to Archbishop Walsh, 27 February 1891 (DDA); F. S. L. Lyons, *The fall of Parnell*, Appendix II, especially pp. 328–30.

35 *National Press*, 30 May 1891.

36 J. H. Parnell, *Charles Stewart Parnell*, p. 286.

37 *FJ*, 1 June 1891.

38 F. S. L. Lyons, op. cit., p. 273, *n.* 3.

39 G. P. Taylor, 'Cecil Rhodes and the second Home Rule Bill', in *The Historical Journal*, xiv, 4 (1971), 377.

40 I am indebted to Mr Richard Davis for showing me his article, 'C. S. Parnell, Cecil Rhodes, Edmund Dwyer-Gray and imperial federation', in *Papers and proceedings of the Tasmanian Historical Research Association*, Vol. 21, No. 3 (September 1974), pp. 125–32. Gray, who had been on a trip to Australia when his father died, returned there after the Parnell split and made his career in Tasmanian journalism and politics until his death in 1945. The hyphenated version of his name 'Dwyer-Gray' is a Tasmanian exotic, not found in the Irish sources.

41 *National Press*, 1 June 1891. For the authorship of the article, which was an unsigned editorial, see F. S. L. Lyons, op. cit., p. 272 and *n.* 4.

42 *National Press*, 2 June 1891.

43 *FJ*, 8 June 1891.

44 *National Press*, 8 June 1891.

45 M. Bodkin to J. Dillon, 19 and 21 August 1891 (DP).

46 K. O'Shea, ii, 250–3.

47 ibid., ii, 253–4.

48 ibid., ii, 256–7.

49 *FJ*, 29 June 1891; A. J. Kettle, *Material for victory*, pp. 95–6.

50 L. P. Curtis, 'Government policy and the Irish party crisis, 1890–92', 306.

51 'Resolution of the General Meeting of Bishops', 25 June 1891 (*National Press*, 2 July 1891).

52 Dr J. Coffey to Archbishop Walsh, 1 July 1891 (DDA); *National Press*, 16 July 1891.

53 L. P. Curtis, loc. cit., 306.

54 R. B. O'Brien, ii, 331, *n.* 1.

55 L. P. Curtis, loc. cit. 306–7.

56 *FJ*, 24 July 1891; *National Press*, 25 July 1891.

57 J. Morley to W. E. Gladstone, 23 May 1891 (BM, Add. MS 44, 256, ff. 141–2).

58 E. Larkin, 'Launching the counter-attack', pp. 367–71; F. S. L. Lyons, op. cit., pp. 279–80.

59 For these exchanges see F. S. L. Lyons, op. cit., pp. 281–9.

60 E. D. Gray to Archbishop Walsh, undated but probably 30 July 1891 (DDA); *FJ*, 31 July 1891.

61 *National Press*, 6 August 1891.

61a F. S. L. Lyons, op. cit., pp. 295–8.

62 ibid., pp. 300–2.

63 R. B. O'Brien, ii, 340.

64 ibid., ii, 347.

65 F. S. L. Lyons, op. cit., p. 303.

66 R. B. O'Brien, ii, 341–4.

67 ibid., ii, 344–5.

68 ibid., ii, 347–8; E. Dickinson, *A patriot's mistake*, pp. 181–3.

69 K. O'Shea, ii, 176; R. Foster, op. cit., p. 239.

70 *FJ*, 14 September 1891; M. Macdonagh, *The Home Rule movement*, pp. 238–9.

71 K. O'Shea, ii, 263–4.

72 *FJ*, 28 September 1891.

73 R. B. O'Brien, ii, 350.

74 ibid., ii, 350.

75 *FJ*, 2 October 1891; R. B. O'Brien, ii, 351; M. Macdonagh, *The Home Rule movement*, p. 240, has 'Sunday week'.

76 K. O'Shea, ii, 275.

77 ibid., ii, 272–3.

78 *FJ*, 9 October 1891.

79 J. Dillon, 'Diary', 27 September 1894 (DP).

80 H. Harrison, *Parnell vindicated*, pp. 92–9.

81 For the probate case and its aftermath, see H. Harrison, op. cit., pp. 199–214.

82 J. H. Parnell, *Charles Stewart Parnell*, p. 288.

83 Emily Dickinson, *A patriot's mistake*, chap. 16.

84 H. Harrison, *Parnell vindicated*, pp. 215–16.

85 Father John Maunsell to Sir Shane Leslie, 30 January 1956 (Parnell Papers in Kilmainham Jail Historical Museum); T. P. O'Connor, *Memoirs of an old parliamentarian*, ii, 327.

86 Father John Maunsell to Sir Shane Leslie, 25 January 1956 (Parnell Papers in Kilmainham Jail Historical Museum); Joyce Marlow, *The uncrowned queen of Ireland*, pp. 301–2.

87 Joyce Marlow, op. cit., p. 302.

CHAPTER 21: MYTH AND REALITY

1 P. Pearse, *Political writings and speeches* (Dublin, n.d.), p. 244.

2 H. Howarth, *The Irish writers, 1880–1940* (London, 1958), pp. 4–5.

3 W. B. Yeats, *Autobiographies* (London, 1955), p. 559.

4 This is true not only of the ballad 'Come gather round me Parnellites', cited at the head of this chapter, but also of 'Parnell's funeral' (1935), 'To a friend whose work has come to nothing' (1914), and even of the undistinguished verses, 'Mourn – and then onward', which he wrote for Parnell's funeral and published in *United Ireland*.

5 K. O'Shea, ii, 153–4.

6 See, for example, two books by L. P. Curtis, jr., *Anglo-Saxons and Celts* (Bridgeport, Conn., 1968), and *Apes and angels* (Washington, 1971).

7 Cited in P. O'Farrell, *Ireland's English question* (London, 1971), p. 176.

8 ibid., p. 200.

Bibliographical Note

The manuscript and printed sources for this biography are set out fully in the footnotes and I have not thought it necessary to duplicate them here. However, since there are no Parnell Papers as such, and since original material relating to him is widely diffused, it seems desirable to list the principal collections which have proved useful.

1. Collections of Private Papers

A. J. Balfour Papers (British Museum)
F. S. Burke Papers (National Library of Ireland)
Isaac Butt Papers (National Library of Ireland)
Sir Henry Campbell-Bannerman Papers (British Museum)
Fourth Earl of Carnarvon Papers (Public Record Office, London)
Joseph Chamberlain Papers (Birmingham University)
Lord Randolph Churchill Papers (Churchill College, Cambridge)
Archbishop T. W. Croke Papers (microfilm copies in National Library of Ireland)
Michael Davitt Papers (private possession)
Eighth Duke of Devonshire Papers (Chatsworth)
John Devoy Papers (National Library of Ireland)
Sir Charles Dilke Papers (British Museum)
John Dillon Papers (Trinity College, Dublin)
C. J. Doran Papers (private possession)
T. P. Gill Papers (National Library of Ireland)
Herbert Gladstone Papers (British Museum)
W. E. Gladstone Papers (British Museum)
Second Earl Granville Papers (Public Record Office, London)
Sir William Harcourt Papers (Bodleian Library, Oxford)
T. C. Harrington Papers (National Library of Ireland and private possession)
J. J. Horgan Papers (microfilm copies in the National Library of Ireland)
M. J. Horgan Papers (National Library of Ireland)
Cardinal E. McCabe Papers (Dublin Diocesan Archives)
M. Macdonagh Papers (National Library of Ireland)
J. F. X. O'Brien Papers (National Library of Ireland)
William O'Brien Papers (National Library of Ireland, and University College, Cork)
W. H. O'Shea Papers (National Library of Ireland)

Anna Parnell Papers (National Library of Ireland)

C. S. Parnell (Miscellaneous letters in the National Library of Ireland)

C. S. Parnell (Miscellaneous letters in the Kilmainham Jail Historical Museum)

Printing House Square Papers (*Times* Archives, New Printing House Square)

P. J. Quinn Papers (National Library of Ireland)

John Redmond Papers (National Library of Ireland)

J. R. Richardson Papers (Public Record Office, Northern Ireland)

First Marquess of Ripon Papers (British Museum)

Third Marquess of Salisbury Papers (Christ Church, Oxford)

J. S. Sandars Papers (Bodleian Library, Oxford)

Fifth Earl Spencer Papers (Althorp Park)

W. T. Stead Papers (private possession)

T. D. Sullivan Papers (National Library of Ireland)

J. F. Tuohy papers (National Library of Ireland)

Archbishop W. J. Walsh Papers (Dublin Diocesan Archives)

Alfred Webb Papers (private possession)

W. B. Yeats Papers (private possession)

2. State Papers

Cabinet Papers, 1880–6 (Public Record Office, London)

Chief Secretary's Office, Registered Papers (State Paper Office, Dublin)

Crime Branch, Special Papers (State Paper Office, Dublin)

Index

Croke, Dr Thomas William [*contd.*]
Gray and Parnell, 94; and 1881 Land Bill, 159-60; denounces 'no-rent' manifesto, 177; supports Ladies' Land League, 179; activities, 245, 256; and Parnell Testimonial Fund, 246, 587-8; relations with Parnell, 252; fears extreme nationalists, 272; favours local government proposals, 272; supports Plan of Campaign, 383, 386; in Parnell leadership crisis, 484-5, 514-15, 551, 553-5, 556, 561-2, 585; and Kilkenny by-election, 543; on Parnell's finances, 587-8

Daly, James, of Castlebar, 100, 122
Daly, John, of Limerick, 47-8, 79
Davitt, Michael, on Parnell at Cambridge, 33; imprisonment, 53, 71, 78; release, 73; meets Parnell, 73; Fenianism, 78-9; and Devoy's proposals, 81, 85, 91; and Land League, 87, 91, 95-8, 100-1, 129-30, 615-16; and 1879 land agitation meeting, 88-9, 92; and Irish-American alliance, 89-91; relations with Parnell, 105, 207; on Parnell's land policy, 99, 130, 623; re-arrest, 100, 145-7, 149, 153, 199; on Parnell's U.S. visit, 109; welcomes Parnell from U.S.A., 116; on Parnell and Land League, 129; condemns agrarian crime, 139; anti-coercion tactics, 145-7, 149, 153; and Parnell and Mrs O'Shea, 150; 'no-rent' policy, 173-4; and Ladies' Land League, 178; prison release, 205-6, 230; and Phoenix Park murders, 208-9, 231-2; conflict with Parnell, 215, 226, 228-30, 233-4, 262; Harcourt attacks, 225; and Land League funds, 227; at Avondale conference, 230; change in political ideas (land nationalization), 230-4, 258, 580; visits U.S.A., 233-4; on Parnell's acceptance of

coercion, 235; and Irish National League, 235; Parnellite opposition to, 269; O'Shea on, 294; and 1885 election tactics, 303-4; attends 1886 Chicago convention, 355-6; conflict with Parnell over land question, 357-8, 362; and Special Commission, 404, 406, 429-30; on Russell, 405; and Pigott letters, 410-11, 421; and Parnell in O'Shea divorce, 463-6, 482; presses for Parnell's retirement, 482, 484, 486, 540; and Kilkenny by-election, 538, 542, 545, 552; Parnell abuses, 541, 583; on Parnell's 'madness', 541-2, 546; opposes Parnell, 550
Day, Mr Justice, 454
Deasy, John, 250, 322, 355
Democratic League of Great Britain and Ireland, 124
Dempsey, Anthony, 101, 102
Devoy, John, cited, 70; letters from O'Kelly, on Parnell, 71; career, 72-3; and Carroll, 74; 'new departure' in Fenian policy, 79-82, 85, 88-90, 98, 110, 113, 148; and U.S. Irish support, 80, 155, 356; and land reform agitation, 89; Parnell denies meeting, at Special Commission, 90-1, 428; and Parnell's U.S. fund-raising trip, 107, 109; and Parnell's sisters, 114; and American Land League, 114; and land agitation, 135-6; opposes coercion, 145, 154; letter from Lomasney on Parnell, 154; extremism, 154-5; and Fenians, 156, 547; quarrel with Sullivan, 247; on Le Caron, 416; supports Parnell, 547, 595-6
Dickinson, Capt. Arthur Monroe, 26, 43
Dickinson, Delia, 26, 598, 605
Dickinson, Emily (née Parnell), cited, 24, 32, 34; marriage, 26, 43; childhood, 27; and Henry Thomson's death, 196; on Parnell's prison release, 204; annuity, 244; on Parnell's superstitiousness, 597; on